Y0-ATL-548

Materialien zur Kunde

des

älteren Englischen Dramas

Materialien zur Kunde des älteren Englischen Dramas

UNTER MITWIRKUNG DER HERREN

F. S. Boas-London, A. Brandl-Berlin, R. Brotanek-Wien, F. I. Carpenter-Chicago, Ch. Crawford-London, G. B. Churchill-Amherst, W. Creizenach-Krakau, E. Eckhardt-Freiburg i. B., A. Feuillerat-Rennes, R. Fischer-Innsbruck, W. W. Greg-London, F. Holthausen-Kiel, J. Hoops-Heidelberg, W. Keller-Jena, R. B. Mc Kerrow-London, G. L. Kittredge-Cambridge, Mass., E. Koeppel-Strassburg, J. Le Gay Brereton-Sidney, H. Logeman-Gent, J. M. Manly-Chicago, G. Sarrazin-Breslau, †L. Proescholdt-Friedrichsdorf, A. Schröer-Cöln, G. C. Moore Smith-Sheffield, G. Gregory Smith-Belfast, A. E. H. Swaen-Groningen, A. H. Thorndike-Evanston, Ill., A. Wagner-Halle a. S.

BEGRUENDET UND HERAUSGEGEBEN

VON

W. Bang

o. ö. Professor der Englischen Philologie an der Universität Louvain

---

EINUNDZWANZIGSTER BAND

LOUVAIN
A. UYSTPRUYST

1908

Reprinted with the permission of the original publishers
KRAUS REPRINT LTD.
Vaduz
1963

DOCUMENTS

RELATING TO THE

OFFICE OF THE REVELS

IN THE TIME OF

QUEEN ELIZABETH

EDITED, WITH NOTES AND INDEXES

BY

Albert Feuillerat

LOUVAIN
A. UYSTPRUYST
1908

KRAUS REPRINT
Nendeln/Liechtenstein
1968

Reprinted with the permission of the original publisher
by
KRAUS REPRINT
A Division of
KRAUS-THOMSON ORGANIZATION LIMITED
Nendeln/Liechtenstein
1968

Printed in Germany
Lessingdruckerei in Wiesbaden

TO

PROFESSOR W. BANG

THE LEARNED AND DISINTERESTED EDITOR

OF THE « MATERIALIEN »

I DEDICATE THIS VOLUME

AS A TOKEN OF MY

SINCERE FRIENDSHIP

TABLE OF CONTENTS

APPENDIX.

PREFACE

This volume is but the first of a series which will be the fulfilment of a wish I have long cherished: to bring together, as in a sort of *Corpus*, all the documents relating to the history of the English Court drama, as well such as have been already printed as those which still remain unpublished in public or private archives. A second volume relating to the Revels in the time of Edward VI and Mary, chiefly from the Loseley MSS., is ready; and Prof. Bang, the energetic Editor of the *Materialien*, is anxious to print it as soon as possible. A third volume on the Court Festivities in Henry VIII's time is in preparation, and will be followed later on by a fourth on the Revels in the days of the Stuarts. If I succeed in bringing this ambitious undertaking to an end, I trust I shall have rendered some service to the historians of the English stage.

It may seem somewhat odd that, with this program in view, I should begin with the Revels of Elizabeth's time, and thus be obliged, in my future publications, to go backwards. My simple reason is, that I had to collect these later documents before the others for literary researches of my own, and that my keeping them by me would have delayed the execution of my design for a considerable time. Besides, they cover the most important period in the history of the Court drama, and most of them have been published by Cunningham, or used by Collier. Both of these editors are discredited, though constantly, if reluctantly, quoted for want of more reliable sources. It was most urgent, therefore, that somebody should dispel the mist of suspicion which has for long paralyzed the efforts of many scholars, when it has not led them into dangerous pitfalls.

This has been the more important — and, perhaps, the more useful — part of my work in the present volume (1); for Collier and Cunningham were indefatigable searchers, and they have not left much for their successors to discover. The kindness of Mr. W. More Molyneux, however, enables me to lay before the public for the first time a valuable Revels Book and a still more valuable Inventory of the Office of the Revels. I present also a certain number of Exchequer documents, which had not yet been searched systematically, and which form the first nearly unbroken record of the expenses of the Revels. Lastly, my notes contain a batch of extracts from, or references to, other documents in the Record Office which I have not printed in the body of my book, either because they were not interesting enough, or because they would have been a useless repetition. I hope I have thus gathered into one volume all the remaining documents on the subject for the reign of Elizabeth.

It was my intention to write an Introduction to this volume, in which I should have given, as it were, the marrow of the documents. But while correcting the proofs, I realized better their importance in the history of stage scenery in England; and finally, as my enquiries on the subject grew to

(1) I am glad to say that in the part of Cunningham's *Revels* included in this volume (I leave the 1605 and 1612 Books out of the question at present) I have found no forgery; on the contrary, it is but just to say that his publication is most accurate, and that I have counted no more than five or six serious misreadings. Unfortunately, I cannot say the same of Collier, as my notes will show.

cumbersome proportions, I decided not to swell too greatly the size of a book already too bulky, but to treat the question elsewhere with all the amplitude it deserves.

There remains to say a few words on the method adopted in this publication. I have endeavoured to reproduce the documents, not exactly in facsimile, but as nearly as it is possible to imitate written documents with printers' type. The spelling and the punctuation have been religiously preserved. In the case of certain letters, I have even tried to distinguish between true capitals (printed in my book as such) and mere initial forms (printed as minuscules); but this, I recognise, is mere loss of time, and I shall never do it again, so long as I have to deal with XVIth century, and even XVth century documents. For typographical reasons, I have omitted the « probantur's », « examinatur's » and other notes with which the Auditors have sometimes lavishly covered the pages of the originals (1). But whenever such annotations have the smallest tittle of interest they have been recorded in the notes. All contractions (those still in use excepted) have been expanded, and are indicated by italics. When the documents are in two or more hands, the handwritings other than that of the document have been set in different type, and are preceded by an asterisk (*). When it was doubtful whether what looked like an addition was or was not in a different hand, I have printed it in the same type as the rest of the document, but I have used an asterisk to distinguish it. These are somewhat complicated rules, and, to be sure, they have caused me much trouble, sometimes necessitating five and even six « proofs » (2); but this complication may be of use to those who are familiar with old documents, and like to imagine what the original may have been. I hope there are not many inconsistencies in the application of those rules, but I shall not be astonished if a few contradictions have been unavoidable in a work of this length, in which I have had to deal with at least seventy different scribes. At any rate, true paleographers, if they come across any irregularities, will, I am sure, excuse me.

I have several obligations to acknowledge. To Mr W. More Molyneux, the enlightened possessor of a splendid collection, the Editor of the *Materialien* and myself return our most heartfelt thanks for permitting us to include some of his literary treasures in this volume, and to him, historians of the drama will soon be indebted for the publication, so long wished for, of the Loseley MSS. Dr F. J. Furnivall, as disinterested as a man as he is great as a scholar, has added to the many obligations I have to him by revising the manuscript of my notes. To Mr R. A. Roberts whose courtesy is unexampled, to Mr E. Salisbury, of the Record Office, and generally to the officials of this Institution, to Mr J. A. Herbert, of the British Museum, whose patience is inexhaustible, I am much indebted for valuable help and the facilities they have given me. To M. A. Macé, Professor of Latin Paleography at the University of Rennes, I owe also many a suggestion. To my friend Prof. W. Bang I apologize for spoiling his holidays last year, by my incessant pouring-in of proofs; in fact, he has had as large a share in the printing of the book as myself. Finally, I thank my wife — last but not least — who has been to me the most patient and the most intelligent of secretaries. Without her help in searching and transcribing, this book would never have seen the light, and therefore, if it prove useful to scholars, the greater thanks are due to her. She has also compiled the Index of Proper Names.

A. F.

(1) I have made one or two exceptions to this rule when such annotations were particularly interesting for the history of the drama.

(2) I may perhaps mention that I have corrected all the documents by the originals at least three times.

A Chronological List of Plays, Masques &c. mentioned in this volume. (1559-1589)

YEAR	DAY OF PERFORMANCE	TITLE OF THE PLAY OR MASQUE	PLACE OF PERFORMANCE	COMPANY OF ACTORS	REFERENCES
1558/9	January 16	A Maske	? Westminster		**88**.17 & **89.8**
	January 22	A Maske	? Westminster		**88**.24 & **89.8**
	Shrove Sunday	A Maske of swartrutters	? Westminster		**94**.20 & **95.**25
	Shrove Tuesday	[A Maske of] ffysshermen and fysshwyves	? Westminster		**94**.28 & d°
		[A Maske of] Market wives	? Westminster		**28**.15 & d°
1559	May	A Maske of Astronomers	Westminster		**97**.4
	September ?	A Maske of Shypmenn and maydes of the cuntrye	Horsley		**105**.4-5
	New Year's Eve	A Maske	Whitehall		**110**.20
1559/60	New Year's Day	A Maske of Barbarians	d°		**20**.7 & **110.20**
	Twelfth Night	A Maske of Patriarkes	d°		**80**.4 & d°
		A Maske of Italyen wemen	d°		**82**.20 ; **85**.26 & **110**.20. Cf. **19.20**
	Shrovetide	Two Maskes of men	d°		**110**.34-37
	Shrove Tuesday	One Maske of wemen	d°		**110**.34-37 & **34**.30
	?	A Play		Children of the Chapel	**34**.40 & *n*
1563	Christmas &	Three Plays	Windsor		**116**.3-4
1563/4	Candlemas				
1564	June	Thre Masks and other devisses	Richmond		**116**.23-4
	Christmas	A Maske			**116**.39
		A Showe			
		A Play (Edwardes tragedy)		Children of the Chapel	d° & **116**.36
1564/5	January	Plays		Grammar School of Westminster & Children of Paul's	**117**.1-2
	February	A play maid by Sir percivall hartts Sones			**117**.8
		A Maske of huntars & diuers devisses			**117**.9
	Shrovetide	Showes. Diana. Pallas		Gentlemen of Gray's Inn	**117**.17
		Foure masks	(Two of them not used)		**117**.14

YEAR	DAY OF PERFORMANCE	TITLE OF THE PLAY OR MASQUE	PLACE OF PERFORMANCE	COMPANY OF ACTORS	REFERENCES
1567 &		A Play: as playne as Canne be			
1567-8		— The paynfull plillgrimage			
		— Iacke and Iyll			
	Christmas	— Sixe fooles			
	&	— Witte and will			**119**.13 &c.
	Shrovetide	— Prodigallitie			
		— Orestes			
		A Tragedie of the kinge of Scottes			
		Sixe Maskes	(Two of them not shown)		
1568	Christmas	Playes			
	&	Tragidies			**124**.8
1568/9	Shrovetide	Maskes			
1569	Christmas	Playes			
	&	Tragedyes			**125**.8
1569/70	Shrovetide	Maskes			
1570	Christmas	Comodies			
	&	Tragedies			**126**.8
1570/1	Shrovetide	Maskes and Showes			
1571	St John's Day	Lady Barbara		Sir Robert Lane's	**145**.1
	Innocents' Day	Effiginia a Tragedye		Children of Paul's	**145**.3
1571/2	New Year's Day	Aiax and Vlisses		Children of Windsor	**145**.5
	Twelfth Day	Narcisses		Children of the Chapel	**145**.7
	Shrove Sunday	Cloridon and Radiamanta		Sir Robert Lane's	**145**.9
	Shrove Tuesday	Paris and Vienna		Children of Westminster	**145**.11
	?	vi Maskes			**146**.18
1572	June	One Maske	Whitehall		**153**.6
		A Play	Hampton Court	Children of Paul's	**180**.22. Cf. **171**.6 & **174**.19
		A Play	d°	Earl of Lincoln's	**176**.2 & *n* d°
	Christmas	A Play	d°	Earl of Leicester's	**180**. 8 d°
		A Play	d°	Earl of Leicester's	**180**.15 d°
		A Play	d°	Children of Windsor	**174**.24 & *n*; **180**.4 d°
1572/3	[New Year's Day]	A Maske (perhaps the Maske of Ianvs mentioned below)	d°		**180**.29 d°
	[Twelfth Day]	A Play	d°	Children of Eton	**174**.15 & *n*; 27; **180**.39 Cf. **171**.6
	[Shrove Tuesday]	A Play	Greenwich	Merchant Taylors'	**174**.22 & *n*; 33. Cf. **171**.6
	?	Maske of Ianvs	?		**175**.30
	?	A dubble Mask	?		**180**.36
1573	November or Dec.	A Mask	Greenwich		**191**.4
	St Stephen's Day	Predor: & Lucia	Whitehall	Earl of Leicester's	**193**.12
	St John's Day	Alkmeon	d°	Children of Paul's	**193**.15
		A Maske of Lanceknightes	d°		**193**.28

YEAR	DAY OF PERFORMANCE	TITLE OF THE PLAY OR MASQUE	PLACE OF PERFORMANCE	COMPANY OF ACTORS	REFERENCES
	Innocents' Day	Mamillia	Whitehall	Earl of Leicester's	**193**.17
1573/4	New Year's Day	Truth, ffaythfullnesse, & Mercye	d°	Children of Westminster	**193**.19
		AMaske of fforesters or hunters	d°		**193**.32
	January 3	Herpetulus the blew knighte & perobia	d°	Lord Clinton's	**193**.22
	Twelfth Day	Quintus ffabius	d°	Children of Windsor	**193**.25
		A Maske of Sages	d°		**193**.36
	Candlemas	Timoclia at the sege of Thebes by Alexander	Hampton Court	Merchant Taylors'	**206**.4
		A Maske of vi Vertues	(not shown)		**206**.6
	Shrove Monday	Philemon & philecia	Hampton Court	Earl of Leicester's	**213**.11
	Shrove Tuesday	Percius & Anthomiris	d°	Merchant Taylors'	**213**.13
		A Maske of Warriers	d°		**213**.15
		A Maske of Ladyes	d°		**213**.17
1574	*c.* July	Pastyme	Windsor	Italian players	**225**.15-6 & **227**.35
	July	d° [A pastoral]	Reading	d°	d° & **227**.37*n*
	[St Stephen's Day]	A Play	Hampton Court	Earl of Leicester's boys	**237**.21-2 ; **239**.3 ; 25 *n*
	[St John's Day]	? Pretestus	d°	Lord Clinton's	d°; **238**.42-4&*n*
1574/5	[New Year's Day]	Panecia	d°	Earl of Leicester's men	d° **238**.29 ; **239**.25 & *n*
	[January 2]	? Two Plays	d°	Lord Clinton's	d° **238**.47
	[Twelfth Day]	A Play	d°	Children of Windsor	d° **238**.7 & *n*
	[Candlemas]	A Play	d°	Children of Paul's	**241**.20; 26 & *n*
	[Shrove Sunday]	A Play	Richmond	Children of the Chapel	**241**.34 & *n*; 36
	? Christmas	The Pedlers Mask	? Hampton Court		**238**.34
	? Christmas	The history of Phedrastus & Phigon and Lucia	? Hampton Court	Lord Chamberlain's	**238**.21 & *n*
1576	St Stephen's Day	The Paynters daughter	Hampton Court	Earl of Warwick's	**256**.13
	St John's Day	Toolie	d°	Lord Howard's	**256**.15
	December 30	The historie of the Collyer	d°	Earl of Leicester's	**256**.17
1576/7	New Year's Day	The historie of Error	d°	Children of Paul's	**256**.19
	Twelfth Day	The historye of Mutius Sceuola	d°	Children of Windsor and the Chapel	**256**.21
	Candlemas	The historye of the Cenofalles	d°	Lord Chamberlain's	**256**.23
	Shrove Sunday	The Historie of the Solitarie knight	Whitehall	Lord Howard's	**270**.14
	Shrove Monday	The Irisshe Knyght	d°	Earl of Warwick's	**270**.16
	Shrove Tuesday	The historye of Titus and Gisippus	d°	Children of Paul's	**270**.18
		A longe Maske	d°		**270**.20
	?	A Play of Cutwell	?	?	**277**.12 & *n*
1578	St Stephen's Day	An Inventyon or playe of the three Systers of Mantua	Richmond	Earl of Warwick's	**286**.11
	St John's Day	The historie of.....	d°	Children of the Chapel	**286**.15

YEAR	DAY OF PERFORMANCE	TITLE OF THE PLAY OR MASQUE	PLACE OF PERFORMANCE	COMPANY OF ACTORS	REFERENCES
	Innocents' Day	An history of the creweltie of A Stepmother	Richmond	Lord Chamberlain's	**286**.19
1578/9	January 4 (but see note to **286**.23)	A Morrall of the marryage of Mynde and Measure	d°	Children of Paul's	**286**.22
		A pastorell or historie of A Greeke maide	d°	Earl of Leicester's	**286**.25
	Twelfth Day	The historie of the Rape of the second Helene	d°	[Lord Chamberlain's]	**286**.28
	January 11	A Maske of Amasones	d°		**286**.30; **287**.6 & **299**.12-16
		A Maske of knightes	d°		**287**.11&**299**.12-16
	Candlemas	The history of.....	(not shown)	Earl of Warwick's	**303**.11
	Shrove Sunday	The history of the Knight in the Burnyng Rock	Whitehall	Earl of Warwick's	**303**.16
	Shrove Monday	The history of Loyaltie and bewtie	d°	Children of the Chapel	**303**.19
	Shrove Tuesday	The history of murderous mychaell	d°	Lord Chamberlain's	**303**.23
		A mores maske	(not shown)		**308**.26
1579	St Stephen's Day	A history of the Duke of Millayn and the Marques of Mantua	Whitehall	Lord Chamberlain's	**320**.19
	St John's Day	A history of Alucius	d°	Children of the Chapel	**320**.25
	Innocents' Day	A historye of......	(not shown)	Earl of Leicester's	**320**.31
1579/80	New Year's Day	A history of the foure sonnes of ffabyous	Whitehall	Earl of Warwick's	**320**.36
	Sunday aft. Jan. 1	The history of Cipio Africanus	d°	Children of Paul's	**321**.1
	Twelfth Day	The history of......	d°	Earl of Leicester's	**321**.7
	Candlemas	The history of Portio and demorantes	d°	Lord Chamberlain's	**321**.13
	Shrove Sunday	The history of the Soldan and the Duke of......	d°	Earl of Derby's	**321**.18
	Shrove Tuesday	The history of Serpedon	d°	Lord Chamberlain's	**321**.23
1580	St Stephen's Day	A Comodie called delighte	Whitehall	Earl of Leicester's	**336**.9
	St John's Day	A storie of......	[d°]	Lord Chamberlain's	**336**.12
1580/1	New Year's Day	A storie of......	d°	Earl of Derby's	**336**.14
	Twelfth Day	A storie of Pompey	[? White] hall	Children of Paul's	**336**.17
	Jan. 6, Jan. 22	A Challendge at the Tilte	d°		**336**.20
	Candlemas	A storie of......	?	Lord Chamberlain's	**336**.24
	Shrove Sunday	A Storie of	?	Children of the Chapel	**336**.27
	Shrove Tuesday	A Storie of......	[? White] hall	Earl of Leicester's	**336**.31
	March	Maskes	(? not shown)		**340**.3 & **341**.[illegible]
	? d°	A challendge & a tryumphe	?		**341**.4-5
1581 & 1581/2	Christmas & Shrovetide	v Playes twoe Maskes & one fightinge at Barriers with diuerse Devises			T II. 5

YEAR	DAY OF PERFORMANCE	TITLE OF THE PLAY OR MASQUE	PLACE OF PERFORMANCE	COMPANY OF ACTORS	REFERENCES
1582	St Stephen's Day	A Comodie or Morrall devised on A game of the Cardes	Windsor	Children of the Chapel	**349**.12
	St John's Day	A Comodie of Bewtie and Huswyfery	d°	Lord Hunsdon's	**349**.18
	Sunday bef. Jan. 1	A Historie of Loue and ffortune	d°	Earl of Derby's	**349**.23
1582/3	New Year's Day	Sundrey feates of Tumbling and Activitie	[d°]	Lord Strange's	**349**.28
	January 5	A maske of Ladies	d°		**349**.32
	Twelfth Day	A historie of fferrar	d°	Lord Chamberlain's	**350**.1
	Shrove Sunday	A historie of Telomo	Richmond	Earl of Leicester's	**350**.6
	Shrove Tuesday	A historie of Ariodante and Geneuora	[d°]	Merchant Taylors'	**350**.11
	?	A Maske of Sixe Seamen	(not shown)		**350**.17
1583 / 1583/4	Christmas & Shrovetide	vi histories, one Comedie one Maske and other devises			**T** III. 5
1584	St Stephen's Day	A pastorall of phillyda & Choryn	Greenwich	Queen's	**365**.12
	St John's Day	The history of Agamemnon & Vlisses	d°	Earl of Oxford's boys	**365**.18
1584/5	New Year's Day	Dyuers feates of Actyuytie	d°	Symons & his fellows	**365**.21
	Sunday aft. Jan. 1	The history of felix & philiomena	d°	Queen's	**365**.26
	Twelfth Day	An Inuention called ffiue playes in one	d°	Queen's	**365**.30
	Shrove Sunday	An Inuention of three playes in one	(not shown)	Queen's	**365**.35
	Shrove Tuesday	An Antick playe & a comodye	Somerset Place	Queen's	**365**.39
1587 / 1587/8	Christmas & Shrovetide	vii playes besides feattes of Activitie and other shewes	Greenwich	Queen's / Children of Paul's / Gentlemen of Gray's Inn	**378**.13-6
1588 / 1588/9	Christmas / New Year's tide / Twelfth-tide	ffyve playes besides sondry feates of actyvity tumbling & Matachives	Richmond	Queen's / Children of Paul's / Lord Admiral's	**388**.24-30
	Shrovetide	twoe plaies besides sondry feates of actyvity tumbling & Matachives	Whitehall		
1589	September	A maske sent into Scotland			**392**

PART I

THE OFFICE & OFFICERS

I

Of the first Institution of the Revels with a Draught of certain Rules to be Observed for the better Management of the Office.

British Museum. Lansdowne MSS. 83. art. 59.

In what state the office of the Revelles is reported to haue bene in.

The Office of the Revelles as it shoulde seeme by reporte hath in tymes past bene in that order That the Prince beinge disposed to pastyme would at one tyme appoynte one persone, at sometyme an other, suche as for creditte pleasaunte witte and habilitye in learnynge he thought meete to be the M*aster* of the Revelles for that tyme, to sett fourthe suche devises as might be most agreable to the Princes expectacion/ The workes beinge fynyshed It is thought that the Princes Tayler havinge the oversight of the workemanshippe brought in the Bill of charg*es* and was payed for it wherevpon is gathered that Iohn Houlte yeoman of the Revelles vsed to saye Concerninge allowaunce of charges in the office of the Revelles it hath bene but a Taylers Bill.

The Reuelles Tentes and Toyles made an Office.

It is alledged by some that afterwardes The Revelles togethers with the Tent*es* and Toylles was made an office and certen of the king*es* householde servaunt*es* appoynted by patent to have care thereof Off whiche office there was a Seriaunt yeoman groomes &c some of theym by the Kinge speciallye appoynted as it shoulde seeme for that they hadde l*ett*res patent*es* of the same office where co*m*monlye others of their callinge in office in the Courte have their offices without patent, And some thinke that the Revelles was kept and wrought within the Princes owne pallace :

The first Master of that office by patent.

After the deathe of Travers Seriaunt of the said office Sir Thomas Carden Knight beinge of the king*es* Maiesties pryvie Chamber beinge skilfull and delightinge in matters of devise, preferred to that office, did mislyke to be tearmed a Seriaunt because of his better countenaunce of roome and place beinge of the King*es* Maiesties privye Chamber And so became he by patent the first M*aster* of the Revelles.

The first Clerke Comptroller by patent.

Afterwardes Sir Thomas Carden havinge by all likelihoode mistrust of loose and negligent dealing*es* by Inferio*ur* officers or others in that office and because hym selfe coulde not be alwayes there p*re*sent to oversee the charge of the office procured at the king*es* handes That there shoulde be also a Clerke Comptroller of the said office who beinge the Princes sworne man and caryinge that name might with some countenaunce or aucthoritye stande hym in good steede for the better governement and direccion of the said office, and for the amendement of the loose dealing*es* both to his owne ease and the Princes good service/ whiche Clerke Comptroller was Iohn Barnard who was the first Clerke Comptroller of the said office for the Revelles and Tent*es* by patent.

It might seeme that in tymes past the same office beinge kept in the King*es* house The Clerke Comptrollers of the King*es* houshold or one of theym hadde eye vpon the Princes charges in that behalfe whiche might enduce a President for the establishement of a Clerke Comptroller in the said office.

The first Clerke by Patent.

Sir Thomas Carden after that beinge driven as it should seeme from tyme to tyme to have his bookes of accompte made vp by the Clerke of the King*es* woork*es* as the office might be vsed when it was kepte in the Princ*es* Courte thought it expedient by reason of greate charge and expences daylie growinge by reason of the same office To have some necessarye person who beinge the Princes sworne servaunte and havinge office and wages or fee by Patent therefore might regester and enter the | charges anye waye growen by reason of the said office from tyme to tyme fo 158 r. who also might be a good witnes of the vpright service both of the masters and others dealing*es* in the said office and to make vppe and perfitt the bookes reconyng*es* and accompt*es* of the said office with more readye vnderstandinge by reason of attendaunce then the Clerke of the work*es* beinge a straunger thervnto coulde doe, procured Thomas Philippes to be Clerke of the said office who was the first Clerke by Patent of the said office

The deuision of the Offices

The Quenes maiestye that nowe [is] devided the said Office into diverse offices vide*licet*.

The Revelles to Sir Thomas Benger knight.

The Tent*es* to Mr Henrye Sakeford of her Maiesties privie Chamber.

The Toyles to Mr Tamworth of her Maiesties privie Chamber.

The offices bi deathe to be vnyted agayne into one.

Yf the offices of the Tent*es* and Toyles might in tyme be vnyted agayne into the said office of the Revelles The Prince might therebye have an office of better accompte The officers might also be the better enhabled to do her Maiestye good service and her highnes charges might somewhat be dyminished.

The habilitye of the officers of the Revelles for their trust and skill might sufficientlye serve for execucion of anye of the other offices.

The woorkemen servinge in the Revelles may very aptly serve in the other offices.

The prouision maye be made by one Co*mm*ission for all.

The Storehouses of theym all be presentlye in one place.

The Clerke Comptroller and the Clerke of the Revelles have hitherto bene and yet are officers both for the Revelles and tent*es*.

Syr Thomas Carden as I am enformed hadde the dealing*es* of all three offices at once.

Howe the office might be taken in

It maye be thought that if the officers weare discharged That the Quenes Maiestye might be served by [some] one person to take charge thereof after a rate for lesse then her Maiestye is nowe charged with This muche I knowe That the officers whiche be presentlye in the said office doe spende in the convenyent service of the prince whiche of necessitye cannot be avoyded havinge consideracion what is meete and due to the Princes service more then is allowed by the Prince in fee or wages for the execucion of the said office/ I suppose that anye one that will enter into that service for tyme of Continuaunce after a rate will rather seeke to gayne by it then loose by it And then will the office be more chargeable to the Prince then nowe it is I see not howe any man takinge it by an annuall rate canne performe it but either the Prince must be overcharged or the partye muche hyndered and in daunger of vndoynge vnles he be of very greate wealthe/ Bycause the charge of that office will alwayes growe accordinge to the Princes pleasure/ if the party be overcharged releife wilbe sought and obtayned at the Princes handes (and by that meanes the more easelye to be adventured) to be taken in hande/yf the Prince shalbe overcharged by the rate so muche the more wilbe the parties gayne, if the partye shall gayne any thinge thereby It is more then the officers presentlye desire to doe.

ferme after a rate is very vncertaine.

The next waye after a rate that canne be devised is for the Prince to appoynte an ordynarye howe manye maskes howe manye playes everye maske of what value everye playe of what charge wherein the nomber is to be considered | and the richenes of the stuffe Devises and shewes cannot well be put in nomber or valued for the charge that shalbelonge therevnto/ yf there shalbe an ordynarye charge, and an extraordynarye as it must needes, because Princes are alwayes to have thinges accordinge to their pleasure Then is it not of certentye for anye man to gesse the annuall charge/ ffor the banquetinge houses the charges will growe accordinge to the Princes pleasure in the nomber of theym in the length bredth fasshion and forme of theym and in the costlye or sleight deckinge or trymynge of theym The charges thereof as I thinke cannot be well gessed and therefore not be vndertaken by annuall rate but either the Prince ouercharged or the partye as aforesaid in hazarde of vndoinge.

fo 158 v.

No rate can well be made of thoffice.

ffor the nomber of officers that be presentlye or for the Princes charge in that behalfe It maye be sayed and trulye sayed That they and their servauntes if everye one hadde more then they have weare not to manye to looke to all the workemen both for the hast of the preparacion and safegard of the stuffe whiche some of the woorkemen and manye there is readye to spoyle filche or steale without good oversight/ No officer carefull of the office but shall of necessitye spende more then his fee and wages cometh vnto and be driven to attende and watche both daye and night Noe service more troblesome for the tyme of the woorkes then the service of the Revelles both for the bodye and the mynde The fee and wages whiche anye one of the officers hath will not in my symple opynyon suffice to maynteyne any man beinge of meane and symple estate accompted the Princes officer (havinge nothinge els to take to) albeit he were a sole man without charge of wife or children.

The nomber of officers breedes not the charge to the Prynce.

The Eyringes necessarie.

It may be thought that the charges maye growe to muche for the Eyring*es* It is very convenyent the stuffe be layed abroade and eayred and that the officers in tyme of Eayringe be present to see to the safetye of it and to gather vpon the layinge of it abroade certen devises from tyme to tyme howe thing*es* translated or amended maye serve afterwardes to good purpose where otherwise it is not possible for the officers to carye in memorye the forme of thing*es* they be so manye and of suche diversitye whiche manye tymes maye serve aswell to purpose as if the Quenes Maiestye shoulde be at charge to make newe/ A tyme of eyring*es* maye be certenlye appoynted and howe manye dayes everye Eyringe shall laste.

One officer more to be added to the office.

ffor the better execucion of the office of the Revelles in my simple opinion yf one officer more weare added to the office the Prince might be the better served and the office better ordered whereof I most humblye crave to vtter my meaninge.

The Maister ot the office.

ffirst I woulde wishe for the Princes hono*ur* That some one of Countenaunce and of creditt with the Prince might beare the name of M*aster* Suche as the Quenes Maiestye thought meetest to receyve her highnes pleasure from tyme to tyme attendaunt in the Courte and to delyver the same over by speache or platt to one suche as followeth. videl*ice*t.

A Seriaunt of the office.

A Seriaunte of the Revelles learned and skilfull howe to execute the devise receyved or to invente a newe meete and necessarye with the allowaunce of the M*aster* whiche S*er*iaunte is thoroughly to followe the devise in the office of the Revelles from the begynnynge to the latter ende ffor if a platte be never so well devised yf it be not aswell followed it will never come to his perfeccion whiche said Seriaunt after the devise of the M*aster* is to bende hym selfe wholye to devise and to see everye man to woorke accordinge to his devise whiche will occupye hym sufficientlye and thoroughlye and this will muche ease the M*aster* who cannot alwayes wayte vpon the Queenes pleasure and vpon the devise and all the workemen/ fortherevnto may belonge devise vpon devise The Seriaunt besides is with the M*aster* and the reast of the officers to be at the rehersall of playes, he is to conceyve the Masters opynyon to correcte and chaunge the matter after the Masters mynde to see wrought and sett fourthe anye devise that belongeth therevnto that ought to be followed for matter of learninge and devise The rest of the officers for the provision of the stuffe and for makinge of the garment*es* and other thing*es* accordingelye | **f° 159 r.**

A Privitie to be amongest the officers.

The Maister and Seriaunte are bothe to calle and conferre with the Clerke Comptroller Clerke and yeoman of the office howe their devise maye be ordered to the leste charge of the Prince with the helpe of suche stuffe as the office is furnyshed alreadye with all And that the devise growe not more chargeable then well satisfyinge the Princes expectacion of necessitye it ought.

The Clerke Comptrollers office.

The Clerke Comptroller is to be contynuallye attendaunte in the office of the Revelles in the tyme of service who in dede shoulde have the speciall charge of husbandinge of the stuffe or prouision of the office and of Checke and rate for the Prynces co*m*moditye but to prouide no stuffe of anye greate charge to the Prince nor deliver the like to be occupyed without warraunte from the M*aster* or Seriaunte The Clerke Comptroller to kepe with the Clerke of the same office a Iornall booke of the charg*es* of the office, both their Iornall bookes to be extant at all tymes of the woorkes in the office to the ende the M*aster* and Seriaunt maye be alwayes privye therevnto The Clerke Comptroller to make noe prouision of anye matter of weight in charge to the Prince without the consent of the M*aster* and Seriaunte and the privitye of the rest of the officers for the Price.

The Clerkes office.

The Clerke is to note all the partes of the service from tyme to tyme to kepe perfect bookes to enter all the woorkemans names to call theym mornynge and eveninge and other tymes of the daye by name to note their absence to make the Clerke Comptroller privie to their default*es* whereby he maye checke theym of their wages accordinge to their desert*es* The Clerke is also to make vppe and perfitt all reconyng*es* considered of by the officers besides the keapinge his Iornall booke whiche Clerke maye be a good witnes of the good or ill service of the Prince and a meete man by reason of entringe of the charg*es* to discerne whither the Prince be abused in the service or noe.

The Masters Superioritye

The Master of the office alwayes to have aucthoritye to call to accompte any the said officers for anye thinge apperteyninge to the Princ*es* service

Question of ordynaunces.

It maye be also thought that the M*aster* of an office, is to have the onelye care and governement of the same accordinge to his discresion without further order to be prescribed then suche as he shall appoynte/ And it maye be thought also vnmete and inconvenyent that inferio*ur* officers shoulde seeke to procure anye other ordynaunc*es* or articles besides But forasmuche as a platte forme of certen ordy-naunc*es* touchinge the said office hathe bene before my tyme delyvered over to some of the Quenes Maiesties most honorable privye Counsell The whiche or the copye whereof remayneth with some of theym as I am enformed at this present I make bolde to bringe to remembraunce some parte of those ordynaunc*es* hereafter followinge and to adde therevnto some more articles and ordynaunc*es* to be con-sidered of/ whiche ratified and allowed by the Quenes Maiesties Counsell woulde I suppose stande the office in verye good steede, for the Princes better service/ And touchinge the cause that doth me to be of that mynde whereof others weare before me I desire that two poynt*es* next followinge maye speciallye be noted.

One pointe concerninge the Masters aucthoritie whether ordinaunces be requisite or no.

The one whether the Quenes Maiestie or her highnes privy Counsell shall please to allowe That the M*aster* of the said office shall have suche absolute power and aucthoritye as that the vnder officers shall onelye doe that whiche he co*m*maund-eth and that the M*aster* onelye shall make prouision rate price of wares and stuffe rate wages give allowaunce of all manner of thing*es* accordinge to his discresion onelye And that his hande setto the booke for all allowaunc*es* and charges whatsoever shalbe sufficient warraunte to the inferi*our* officers to subscribe their handes to the booke whereby the Prince is to be charged and to make payment for the same accordingely yf this maye be vnderstande to the inferi*our* officers to be the Princes pleasure and that some warraunt might be hadde in that behalfe Then shall they be assured that perforrninge their diligence accordinge to the Masters appoyntement they shalbe free from the Princ*es* blame and besides not accomptable to the Prince but onely to the M*aster* of the said office The M*aster* onelye to have prayse or blame for the well or yll execucion of the office and he onelye to aunswere for all thing*es* done in the said office In this poynte the Inferi*our* officers shall neede no other ordynaunc*es* then suche as the M*aster* shall prescribe. | f° 159 v.

But this perhapps maye followe that if the M*aster* shalbe blamed for thing*es* not done accordinge to the Princ*es* expectation that he will partelye excuse hym selfe and alledge that he cannot so well rule the inferi*our* officers beinge the Princ*es* sworne servaunt*es* as he coulde his owne/ So maye the M*aster* put the blame from hym selfe to theym Albeit they wilbe more carefull to obeye those his com-maundement*es* whiche apperteyne unto the Princes service as dutye bindeth theym to doe then his owne servaunt*es* woulde be Surelye this waye without verye good choyce of a speciall good M*aster* The Prynce maye be worse served Then if the M*aster* onelye shoulde take the charge throughlie to performe it by hym selfe and his owne servaunt*es*/ ffor when blame maye be shifted of by one meane or other There wilbe the lesse foresight howe to avoide it Thus muche of the first poynte.

A Seconde pointe concernynge ordinaunces.

The other poynte/ yf there shalbe a M*aster* of the said office that will vse anye indirect dealing*es* whereby the Prynce may be ill served And that the Quenes Maiestie doth make accompte that the inferi*our* officers shoulde helpe it or complayne for remedye It is not for Inferi*our* officers to repugne the M*aste*r his doing*es* hym selfe beinge in place Albeit there be never so greate cause but shalbe ruled over as shall please the M*aste*r vnles some good ordynaunc*es* remayninge of recorde in the same office discribinge perticulerlye everye mans charge for most necessarye dealing*es* weare to leade order therein And the same ordynaunc*es* ratified and allowed either by aucthoritye of the Prince or some of her maiestyes most honorable Pryvie Counsell at all tymes to be extant in the said office ffor when matters of greate charge are to be executed with greate spede Inferi*ours* with sup*eriours* are not to dispute or to vse controversye concerninge their aucthoritye given to theym by patent especiallye with a M*aster* of an office Therefore desired that theise ordynaunc*es* and Articles hereafter followinge maye be considered of and standinge with the Princes pleasure or the pleasure of the Counsell to be co*m*maunded to be penned and perfited by some suche as theye shall thinke meete and ratified and allowed.

Ordinaunces concernynge the Reuelles.

Articles and ordynaunces concernyng the office of the Revelles aswell for the due execucion of all workes laboures and attendaunc*es* and other busynes to be done exercised and practized within the same office as for the Prouision receipt induccion employment bestowinge safekepinge and true aunsweringe of all suche store garment*es* vestures tooles instrument*es* and other utensells and employment*es* of the same for the good and due vsage thereof to the most hono*ur* profitte and good service of the Quenes Maiestie by her highnes with the aduise of her most honorable Pryvye Counsell the daye of Anno d*omi*ni in the fiftenth yere of her most gracious Reigne appoynted established and stractlye co*m*maunded to be observed p*er*formed fulfilled and kepte of the officers woorkemen attendaunt*es* and all others chargeable and that have to doe within that office in all poynt*es* accordinge to certen articles and Instruccions herevnder lymyted videl*icet*.

Meetinge of officers togithers.

ffirst against Hollantide Christmas Candelmas and Shrovetide and all other tymes appoynted for preparacion of any thinge to be done within the office or for the accomplishement of any appoyntement from the Prince or by speciall warraunte or order from the Lorde Chamberleyne the vice Chamberleyne or others in that behalfe aucthorised or assigned The M*aster* and Officers aforesaid shall repayer to the office and there togithers pervse the remayne of the whole stuffe and other store lefte at the last vewe ffor consideracion what is best and meetest to make that whiche is there alreadye to stretche to serve to the turne requyred with lest spoyle and charges And what monye is to be demaunded in Prest aswell for payment daylie to be yssued as for husbandrye of empcions to be hadd at lesse price for readye monye then canne be gotten of trust or otherwise as shalbe most expedient for the Quenes Maiesties better service :

whiche Platt devised to be drawen and sett fourthe in payntinge by some connynge Artificer in that Arte and to be considered of by all the officers And the best devise that canne be to serve the Prince accordinge to the devisors inuencion with lest charge to the Prince as aforesaid may be used as shall seeme meete to the
fo 160 r. M*aster* of the said office. |

The trust of the office.

The trust concernynge the Princes charges in that office woulde be co*m*mytted to some carefull and diligent persons suche as will more regarde the Princes profitt then their owne paynes more the Princes savinge then their owne co*m*moditye more the pleasinge of the Prince then the displeasure of wastfull persons and that of a greate nomber whiche have bene are and wilbe contynuallye gapinge after spoyle in the same office Those servitours must be contynuallye attendaunt within the said office and have aucthoritye to rate prices to rate wages to place and displace anye workeman misdemeanynge hym selfe not beinge an officer appoynted by patent.

The cheife busines of the office.

The cheife busynes of the office resteth speciallye in three poynt*es* In makinge of garment*es* In makinge of hedpece*s* and in payntinge.

The conninge of the office.

The connynge of the office resteth in skill of devise, in understandinge of historyes, in iudgement of comedies, tragedyes and shewes, in sight of p*er*spective and architecture some smacke of geometrye and other thing*es* wherefore the best helpe for thofficers is to make good choyce of cunynge artificers severally accordinge to their best qualitie, and for one man to allowe of an other mans invencion as it is worthie especiallye to vnderstande the Princ*es* vayne and to order it so that every man may learne somewhat the more what service meaneth and as everye officer maye be made the more able to serve/ ffor whiche service there woulde be an order made as nere as maye be what shoulde be every mans charge within the office accordinge to his skill and habilitye &c.

Howe workemen shall be appoynted.

At the beginnynge of the woorkes the Clerke Comptroller and yeoman are to agree howe manye woorkemen shalbe appoynted to woorke and their names to be entred ymediatelye into the Clerk*es* booke and their wages agreed vpon and rated by the Clerke Comptroller otherwise comynge to woorke without that order The Clerke Comptroller to discharge the Prince of charges for theym.

Howe many howers workemen shall worke.

Everie of those woorkemen to woorke for their dayes wages tenne howres and for their night wages sixe houres.

The entrie and checke of their names.

And for the better execucion of these woorkes The Clerke of the said office shall keepe entrye of their contynuaunce at worke & delyver over a Coppye of their names to thende the Clerke Comptroller maye checke their default*es*.

for prest monye.

As it weare necessarye that monye shoulde be allowed in prest for the better service of the said office because readye monye will muche further to the abatement of a greate parte of charge that otherwise woulde be more burdenous to the Prince by givinge creditte to the office Soe is it meete to appoynte to whom the ymprest shalbe delyvered by whom it may most conuenyentlye be layed fourthe that a iuste ymployment thereof may be aunswered.

Concerninge stuffe brought into the office

And lykewise for the receipte of stuffe from the Quenes Maiesties greate warderobe or other places of store there woulde be order to whom the stuffe brought into the office and entred into the Iornall book*es* it shalbe delyvered in custodye, and in what sorte it shalbe delyvered out that a iust employment may be made thereof and entred into the Iornall book*es*.

for empcions in the office.

for empcyons of stuffe wantinge besides the warderobe store there woulde be order taken by whose warraunte everye thinge accordinge to the Qualitie thereof it maye be prouided into whose custodye and by what order to be redelyvered so as as iust employment maye be aunswered agayne thereof.

for receyvinge things by measure and weight

All stuffe brought into thoffice the measure weight qualitie or quantitye to be considered of by some one to be appoynted in the receipte and so to be deliu*er*ed by like weight measure &c. and the purpose shewed by the delyverer or demaunder and entred perticulerly into the Iornall book*es* In whiche cheifely and most co*m*monlye are to be noted theis parcells followinge most vsuallye occupied. | f° 160 v.

Stuffe cheifelie occupied in the Revelles.

warderobe stuffe vizardes heare Lawne ffringe lace Buttons Buckerams thredd silke wood coles light*es* collours for paynters besides manye other thing*es* thousand*es* that cannot be rehersed presentlye

Howe wardrobe stuffe may be ordered.

ffor the warderobe stuffe because it is a matter of greate charge to the Prince I have thought good partelye to declare myne opynion howe it maye be best ordered in receipte and in employment.

A speciall order concernynge wardrobe stuffe.

I take it, the warderobe stuffe especiallye for anye masse of stuffe woulde be delivered openlye in the office in the presence of the officers and the same stuffe receyved measured out and entred into the Iornall book*es* yt would then be put in chest*es* or presse as shall seeme most convenyent vnder the severall lock*es* and keys of the M*aster* Clerke Comptroller and Clerke when it shalbe taken out the purpose therefore declared and entred into the Iornall bookes and likewise what cut out and what remayninge.

The employment of warderobe stuffe.

There woulde also be a speciall order that the yeoman shall cutte out noe garment but by the appoyntement of the M*aster* or Clerke Comptroller and in the presence of theym or one of theym and the Clerke to thende it maye be entred into the Iornall book*es* what cutt out and what remayninge yf the yeoman shall refuse so to doe, or be absent in tyme of necessitye of the Princes service Then that the officers maye have libertye to call some other workeman in his place to cutt out and make suche garment*es* as shalbe requysite and needefull by reason of his absence or defaulte Otherwise shall the officers be subiecte to the wilfulnes of the yeoman in tyme of spede and the yeoman maye also co*m*mitte that wast whiche the officers cannot helpe.

The yeomans fees woulde be certeyne.

An order of emploiment of fringe lace &c.

ffor frynge lace and Buckerams &c. they maye remayne in presse or Chest*es* vnder the lock*es* and keys of the Clerke Comptroller and Clerke to be delyu*er*ed over in their presence by their servaunt*es* to suche as shall neede it alwayes entringe the same into the Iornall book*es* the cause wherefore &c. and in like sorte other stuffe of diverse kindes.

for woode and coles.

for woode coles light*es* &c. The Clerke Comptroller to take suche order as with the allowaunce of the M*aster* shalbe thought meete.

for painters and coloures.

for the Paynters prouision of colours to be made by the officers/ And one of their servaunt*es* to be contynuallye attendaunt vpon theym, so that as litle wast as maye be [be] vsed the rest of the Coloures to be reserved and to put in a place of store The paynters names and their servaunt*es* to be entred the tyme of their service and their wages, Some one speciall officer to have co*m*maundement over theym and Co*m*mission to rate their wages and to punyshe theym for their absence or negligence, otherwise the Prince is like most co*m*monlye to be ill served of those kinde of men bothe for absence wages wast and loyteringe whiche breadeth the Prince many tymes muche more charge then neadeth.

Translacion of garmentes

Anye garment translated vpon the newe translacion woulde ymediatelye be brought and showed vnto the Clerke Comptroller and Clerke that the same maye be entred into the Iornall book*es* in the same sorte as it is in his first forme to be discharged, and in the newe forme to be charged, in the Indenture of Inuentorye remayninge with the yeoman.

Concernynge newe garmen*tes* made in the office.

Anye suyte of garment*es* newe made vpon the fynyshinge of the same and anye other other garment newe made woulde be entred into the Iornall bookes vpon the fynyshinge of theym to thende they maye be afterwardes entred into the Indenture of Inuentorye This woulde be done before the tyme they be occupied in the Prince service to thende it maye be knowen what is lackinge if anye disorder happen in the tyme of service as many tymes it dothe.

An order for Properties.

And likewise all propertyes and other thing*es* newe made and fynyshed whatsoever to be likewise entred and so co*m*mitted over to the yeoman to take charge thereof till the service be done. | fo 161 r.

Parte of the Yeomans charge.

The seruice done and all thing*es* shewed It woulde be the yeomans charge to see all thing*es* safelye brought into the office The whiche of hym selfe if he cannot doe then officers then to aide hym in that behalfe.

Meetinge of officers after service done.

The officers all togithers if they canne or the most parte of theym within three dayes after the service done to meete at the office and see the estate of every thinge as it remayneth and cause everye thinge to be fayer layed vppe and entred into the Indenture of Inventorye and so delyvered over in charge to the yeoman safelye to be kepte.

Consideracion of the Iornall Bookes.

Item at that tyme woulde the Iornall book*es* be considered of and the remayne of stuffe seene and noted and the officers hand*es* sett to the Iornall book*es* in allowinge or disalowinge and order taken for the p*er*fitinge vppe of theym into some breife order whereto daye woulde be given as they see cause.

Daie giuen to Creditours to bringe in their Billes.

At that tyme also woulde order be given .what daye the Creditours shall bringe in their bills at their perill if any bill be not readye at that tyme whiche woulde be a verye shorte daye then that they tarye till the next accompte ffor that the Clerke is to make vppe his bookes after the Bills brought in.

The Prince not to be charged but bi the testimonye of the officers.

In that breife booke it woulde be ordered that the Clerke enter no bill or other matter to charge the Prince or the office vnles the handes of the officers or suche of theym as shalbe appoynted shalbe subscribed therevnto.

A ligearde booke for the office.

And lykewise a greate Ligearde booke woulde be kepte in the office wherein that observacion would likewise be kepte by the Clerke.

Debenters for the Creditours.

At the bringinge of the breife booke woulde all deb*tes* to everye p*er*son be debentered vnder the handes of the M*aster* or Clerke Comptroller So that it may be knowen to everye Credito*ur* what he is to trust to.

A cunnynge painter to put in recorde all shewes maskes etc.

At that syttinge woulde order be given to a connynge paynter to enter into a fayer large ligeard booke in the manner of L[y]mnynge the maskes and showes sett fourthe in that last service to thende varyetye may be vsed from tyme to tyme.

A quarter daie to be kepte for meetinge of the officers.

It were goode that once everye quarter The officers did appoynte as it weare a quarter daye of meetinge both to consider of the state of the office and of thing*es* meete and necessarye to be thought of concernynge the same.

Item an Yerelie meetinge for the consideracion of the Inuentorie.

Item once euery yere at a daye certen they all togithers to meete and to consider of the stuffe and to conferre the Inventorye with the same.

That the QuenesMaiesties stuffe be not lent forthe

Item concernynge the lendinge furthe of the Queenes Maiesties stuffe in the office of the Revelles The stuffe once made and put in Inventorye resteth onelye in the yeomans charge who hath the kepinge of it by Patent and therefore the rest of the officers not to be charged for any misdemeanour concerninge the same Nevertheles suche order may be taken therefore as shall seeme meete and convenyent.

Officers fees to be considered of.

The officers of the Revelles (as other officers servinge the Queenes Maiestie in other offices) have hadd their fees whiche have bene knowen to be certen for the whiche some order maye be taken and noe hinderaunce to the Prince and yet some suche benefitte to the officers as therebye they maye be encoraged to serve the more paynefullye & somewhat the more be enabled to serve and yet reape no more benefit then shall countervayle their charges spente in the Princes service where otherwise if pore men shalbe preferred to theis offices the Quenes Maiestie maye be worse served

A commission verie necessarie for the office.

ffor the better execucion of the said office There woulde be a Commission for the same office whiche wantinge the Queenes Maiestye cannot be so well served as otherwise her highnes may be and yet noe Iniurye offred vnto the Subiectes vnles they shall muche abuse theym selves in refusinge to doe conuenient service for the Prince it needeth not be vsed whiche if they shall refuse to doe It weare meete to have suche Commission as might enforce theym and also punyshe theym and any other notorious malefactours concerninge the same office.

Thys Platte of orders and state of the office is the first and surest meane whereby the Quenes Maiestie may be most truly, aptelie and honorablie serued, if it may be throwghlie obserued in all poyntes /

The seconde is that the Maister of the office be appointed and choisen suche, as be neither gallant, prodigall, nedye, nor gredye, for if any of theis, suerlie he will never be fullie lyhable to this order, but make waiste, sucke the Quene, or pynche the poore, or all thre, And that he also be of suche learning wytt and experience as hable of hym self to make and devise suche shewes and devises as may best fitt and furnisshe the tyme place and state with leaste burden, and to frame all other speciall appointementes to the best shewe with leaste chardge and most spede/

The thirde meane viz. to eaze or spare the greatest Disburcementes of money which riseth by emption and provision of the costliest and most sumptiest parte of theis affaires is that oute of the privye or speciall wardrops of her Maiesties seuerall houses or the tower or greate wardrop of suche store as hath layen longe and decaied or now growen vnmete for the first purpose or to serve the present vse any lenger may be deliuered over to be ymploied to the best and ferthest stretche of this turne (as was in Sir Thomas Cardens tyme as well oute of the hole pece as in hanginges and garmentes and other sorte) but not any other thing which is not alredy there of olde store to come from thence by any new provision but by the officers to be chosen most metest for fitnes to serve and eaze of chardge and taken and bought at the first hande for redy money /

The fourth is that redy money may be vpon reasonable request deliuered for the chepest prouision of necessaries and other Emptions in suche tyme as they may be best had by the officers appointement of them which can best skill of it / And preparacion to be made of that is knowen mete to be put in a redynes to be before hande better done by them which are most meete and for more reasonable hier in hope of present payment then can be had or done vpon the soden (which asketh doble waiges for watche and hynderaunce of their advauntage in tyme of worke and gayne and greater price for seking when and where is scante and no choise nor certeyntie of payment but feare of longe forbering their money) which shall never be well done by any straunger to the office, nor withoute redy money /

And this advice taking place, I dare take vpon me, that her Maiestie, shall haue more done, and bettre by a thirde parte for lesse chardge by a thirde parte then hetherto I haue knowen, and will yelde a iust and trewe accompte both of stuffe and money / If it please her highnes to bestowe the Mastership of the office vpon me (as I trust myne experience by acquayntaunce with those thaffaires and contynuall dealing therein by the space of xxvij or xxviij yeres deserveth being also the auncient of the office by at the leaste xxiiij of those yeres otherwise I wolde be lothe hereafter to deale nor medle with it nor in it further then apperteyneth to the clerke whose waiges and allowaunces is so small as I gyve it holy to be discharged of the toyle and attendaunce, I haue hetherto withoute recompence to my greate chardge and hynderaunce, borne the burden of the Master and taken the care and paynes of that, others haue had the thanks and rewarde for, which I trust her Maiestie will not put me to, withoute the fee alowaunce and estimacion longing to it/ nor if her highnes vouchesafe not to bestowe it vpon me to let me passe withoute recompence for that is done and paste /

If the ffee and allowaunce be thought to muche, then let what her Maiestie and honerable counsaile shall thincke mete for any man that shall supplie that burden and place to haue towardes his chardges be appointed of certeyntie and I will take that, and serve for as litle as any man that meanes to Deale truly so I be not to greate a loser by it/

The Costes of any thing to be done oute of this office can not be aymed at any neare estymate withoute fore knowledge what is required and loked for as howe many maskes, and whether riche or slite, what plaies banketing houses and other shewes of pastyme / and those whether statelie or meane may suffice to be ordinarelie appointed for her highnes recreacion which growing to some certeyn pitche the chardge may be roved at / Or her highnes resolving vpon some certeyn yerelie somme of money which she will not passe, the Master and officers may frame to stretche the same to her highnes most honour and liking, and yet finding her contentacion served with lesse then that is appointed deale accordinglie and be aunswerable the remayn vpon accompte /

f° 157. [Endorsed :] ordres for ye Revells

III

An Inventory of the Stuff of the Revells taken in 1560.

Loseley MSS.

Revell*es*

The Charge Imploymente and remayne aswell of all the Stuff and Store *with*in that Office ffounde and lefte chargeable and meete to serve agayne by a Survey the xxvjth daye of Marche. 1555. In the ffirste and Second yeares of the Reignes of the late kinge Philippe and queene Marie, taken by S*ir* Iohn Gage knighte then Lorde Chamberleyne, and Sir Robert Rochester, and Sir ffraunces Inglefeld knightes, then of the said queenes Privie Counsaill and Comyssioners emonges others speciallie appointed and aucthorised to viewe and take the Accompte State and remayne of that Office, as of all suche p*er*cell*es* of Stuff and Store as vpon warraunt*es* either ffrom the said late queene Marie or Elizabeth the quenes Maiestie that nowe is hathe ben*e* deliu*er*ed oute of theire greate Warderoopes into this Office ffrom the said xxvjth of Marche vntill the   of   . 1560. in the Second yeare of the Raigne of o*ur* seid Sou*er*aigne Ladie Elizabethe by the grace of god quene of England ffraunce and Ireland defend*our* of the ffaithe &c. Hard viewed p*er*vsed examyned taken and allowed by the Righte Honorable

fo 1 r.

Mennes Maskes

	Charge	Implоymente	Remayne
Maryners. viij.	**viij** Ierkins of purple clothe of golde barred over *with* gardes of clothe of grene Silver. Sleves of the same & hood*es* of blewe clothe of gold edged aboute *with* redd Silke lace.	All the blewe and purple clothe of gold of this Maske translated into vj hungarians garment*es with* longe sleves and ageyne translated iiij of them into wemens kirtels of Dianas Nymphes, and thother twoo to p*er*forme the winges and collors of the patriarkes maske	n*i*l. sole but in the Maskes of the patriarkes and Nymphes to be charged as percell of the same.
	viij paire of Sloppes parted, the one legge of the said blewe clothe of golde and the other of greene Clothe of Silver.	the greene clothe of Silver translated into lyninge of the Almaynes sloppes and agayne cut in peces to payne ffissher mens sloppes & bodies and agayne translated in to A Maske of Marryners and againe translated into Torchebearers for a maske of Turkes	n*i*l. for the same beinge so often shewen and translated was forworne and not seruiceable nor chargeable but dampned for ffees.
Venecian Senators Patrons of galleys. **viij.**	**viij** longe streighte gownes of Clothe of Tissewe gold & Silver raysed playne.	translated into viij Almayne Ierkins *with* greate wide sleves and plackerd*es* and agayne translated into vj garment*es* of A womans maske.	n*i*l. but in A Maske of Weemen that Served on Twelf nighte. 1559. A° S*ecun*do regine Elizabeth as p*er*cell of the same.
	Longe hanginge sleves on y*e* same *with* collo*urs* of Clothe of Tissewe gold and redd velvett. Vnder sleves of the same	translated into hed peces & vndersleves for Turkes and ageyne from thence in to Shoes and nowe	not Serviceable nor chargeable.

f° 1 v.

* T. Blagrave
* Iohn holt*es* marke †
* Rychard Leys

	Charge	Implyoymente	Remayne
Turkes. Magistrates. **vj.**	**vj** longe streighte turkye gownes of redd cloth of gold *with* Roses and Scalloppe shells stripped downe and garded *with* a brode gard of Redd Dornixe embrodered vpon *with* clothe of gold and Siluer threed and edged *with* blacke silke lace. Longe Sleves of the same Vnder Sleves of clothe of gold figured *with* white red and greene vellvett. Capes of the same figured clothe of gold.	translated into a Maske of Astronomers and againe into A Maske of Barbarians and so Shewen on Newyeares daye at Nighte. 1559. anno S*ecun*do Regine Elizabeth and yeate remayninge.	n*i*l. sole but in the said Maske of Barbariens and the same so often translated and shewen forwo*r*ne and knowen as no more seruiceable nor chargeable
Greekes. Woorthyes **vj.**	**vj** longe garment*es* the vpper bodies and vpper baces of white clothe of silu*er* stayned *with* colo*urs* and on the backes & brest*es* the names of hercules Iason percius Pirothus Achilles & Theseus writen The middle baces & vpper shorte Sleves of white clothe of Silu*er* and redd satten p*ar*tie paned and stayned withe collo*urs*. The nether baces of the same white clothe of silu*er* stayned withe colo*urs*. vnder sleves of the same white clothe of Silu*er* vnstayned	translated into A maske of Conquerers and againe the beste of that taken oute and translated in to A Maske of Moores and the Residue remaynes in peces not Serviceable to any vse, and of that which therof was then serviceable nowe remaynes.	n*i*l but in the said Maske of Moores as p*er*cell of the same, w*hi*ch allso beinge often vsed & shewen is so fforwo*r*ne and knowen as no more seruiceable nor chargeable.

* T Blagrave
* Iohn holtes marke †
* Rychard Leys

fo 2 r.

	Charge	Imploymente	Remayne.
Albomas. Warryers. **vj.**	**vj** straighte gownes of clothe of golde blew velvet *with* Roses of gold raysed Longe streighte pendaunte Sleves of the same	translated into a maske of Irishemen and againe in to A Maske of ffisshermen & againe into Marryn*ers* and after into players garment*es* and so often shewen and forworne as therof	n*i*l lefte seruiceable nor chargeable but taken for ffees.
	Vnder sleves of clothe of silver purple velvett Capes of the same clothe of Silu*er* lyned w*ith* blewe Clothe of Silver.	the same was translated in to Irisshe cappes cutte and all to be ffrenged and since often vsed by players and nowe	not chargeable
Turkes. Archers. **vj.**	**vj** Turkye gownes of Crymesen rewed with golde threed	translated in to buskyns.	not Seruiceable nor Chargeable.
	Longe Sleves paned of redd Satten and gardes of Clothe of gold embrodered vpon Orrenge colored Satten cutte oute of the hanginges	the same being forworne to moche knowen and not seruiceable to any vse were taken for ffees. and	
	Vndersleves of Damaske Bawdekyn white and redd partie paned taken oute of the hanginges The Collers turned downe *with* Orenge colo*ur* clothe of Silver	translated into Sloppes ffor children to playe in and so vsed knowen and forworne to noughte as nowe any more.	

* T Blagrave
* Iohn holt*es* marke †
* Rychard Leys

f° 2 v.

	Charge	Imploymente	Remayne.
Irisshe keyrens. **vj.**	**vj** vpper garmentes with baces of Crymesen Clothe of golde frenged w*ith* greene Silke. vj shert*es* of yellowe sarcenett frenged w*ith* white and grene Caddace ffrenge.	translated into Allmaynes for Torchebearers to the Rutters and so forworne to moche knowen and vsed as nowe any more	not Seruiceable nor chargeable.

* T Blagrave
* Iohn holt*es* marke †
* Rychard Leys

f° 3 r.

Maskes of **woomen.**

	Charge	Implyomente	Remayne
Huntresses viij.	**viij** vpper garmentes of redd Tinsell and Purple Clothe of Silver the bodies of small Scalloppe Shell*es* and the brest*es* and collors in Ruffes and lyned and pulled oute w*ith* white Sarcenett shorte dooble baces of red clothe of Sillver. **viij** neither bodyes and Sleves of blacke and Tawnye tynsell ruffed garded w*ith* broode gardes of redd clothe of golde embrodered vpon redd Satten Silu*er* threed	the same being often translated disguised & vsed so forworne & to moche knowen as nowe any more	not Seruiceable nor chargeable

* T. Blagrave
* Iohn holt*es* marke †
* Rychard Leys

f°3v.

	Charge	Imploymente	Remayne
Venusses or Amorouse Ladies vj.	**vj** vpper bodies withe baces of redd clothe of gold ruffed and turned in garded w*ith* a broode garde of clothe of gold embrodred vpon Crymesen Satten taken oute of the Hanginges The fforestockes of the Sleves of the same garde ruffed in panes pulled oute w*ith* white Sarcenett. Thunder Sleves and nethe partes of partie panes of white Clothe of Silver purple velvett pinked rewe w*ith* Silver threed*es* yellowe clothe of gold cutte compasse wise garded w*ith* clothe of golde chevered w*ith* blacke velvett	The same beinge often translated transformed and disguised are so forworne and to moche knowen as nowe any more	not Seruiceable. nor Chargeable.

* T. Blagrave
* Iohn holt*es* marke †
* Rychard Leys

f°4r.

In the tyme of Sir **ThomasCarden** knighte then *Master* of the Revell*es* vpon sondry warrauntes videlicet by	**Stuff** receyued oute of the greate or Standinge **warderoppe** into the Revell*es* by warrauntes. ffrom the Charge	Imploymente	Remayne
	velvett red **xxv** yardes velvett Carnacion Ten yardes. More of the same velvet .v. yardes 40.	Imployed into viij paire of Sloppes for Allmaynes .3. into the lyninge of viij paire of Sleves and viij plackard*es* of of the same Maske and the welting and Iagginge therof 10/ wherof the hosen were translated into torchbearers to the Swarte Rutters and againe the ffissher men and there reste. And the lyninges were translated into nether baces of the wemen on Twelf nighte .1559. Anno S*ecun*do Reg*in*e Elizabeth and so reste	n*i*l but in the garment*es* w*ith*in mencioned as p*ar*cell of the same.
	Clothe of Silu*er* w*ith* workes iiij yardes.	Imployed into vj Bagges for Pallmers	n*i*l for they were all taken awey by the Straungers and lord*es* that masked in the same.
	purple gold Sarcenet ix yard*es* di. di. q*uar*ter	Imployed into gerdells of the same Pallmers	
The late queene Marye directed to s*ir* Edwarde Walgrave knight then *Master* of the Wardroppe.	**Sarcenet** yellowe .xxvj. yard*es* di. di. q*uar*ter.	Imployed into x of the Irisshe mens Shertes whiche were torchebearers to Allmaynes and pallmers, And after that agayne translated into lyninge pullinges oute tuftes tyringes and other garnisshinge as nowe therof	n*i*l Seruiceable nor chargeable
	Sarsenet Redd. xlix yard*es* di.	Imployed into the furniture of iiij drom*m*es and fifes & twoo bagge pipes for the maske of Allmaynes pallmers and Irisshmen .36. w*hi*ch they had to theire owne vse by composic*i*on and into girdles garters tuftes & tyringes for the same Maske .12. so that nowe therof	n*i*l Seruiceable nor Chargeable

* T Blagrave
* Iohn holt*es* marke †
* Rychard Leys

f° 5 r.

Charge.	Imploymente.	Remayne
Sarsenet white xxxiij yard*es* di. di. quarter.	Imployed and spente in pulling*es* oute tuftynges tyringes gyrdles garters and garnisshinge of head peces of the said Maske of Allmaynes Pallmers and Irisshe men being in suche ffraction as therof	n*i*l Seruiceable nor chargeable
velvet white xxxix. yardes. **velvet** white lukes. ix yard*es* q*uar*ter	Imployed into two white ffriers .16. w*h*ich were againe translated into Morisshe ffryers and two more added to them .16. w*ith* iiij^{or} Scaplers .10. and iiij hoodes .6. allso newe made to them. All w*h*ich were againe translated and imployed to the p*er*formaunce of the Nusquams and so r*e*st*e*th*e*	n*i*l Sole but in the garment*es* within said charged as p*ar*cell of the same.
velvet yellowe xxix yardes. **velvet** yellow xj yard*es* iij q*uar*ters.	Imployed into two yellowe ffryers w*ith* Scaplers & hoodes .20. In paninge of two Sumpners cotes .10. In paninge of the sleves hood*es* and Scaplers of twooe russett ffryers and twoo grene ffriers 10/ the Sumpners cotes translated againe into apparell of drome and fife the ffriers cotes altered into cassock*es* of Acteons torchebearers the Scaplers and hoodes into longe sleves and head peces of the same torchebearers and so r*e*st*e*th*e*	
velvet russet xiiij yard*es* iij q*uar*ters.	Imployed whoolie into Twooe Longe garmentes of Russet ffryers and so	
velvet blacke iij yardes. **velvet** blacke xxij yard*es*. **vellet** blacke vij yard*es* q*uar*ter di.	Imployed wholie into legges ffeete Armes and hand*es* for a maske of Moores wherof the lord*es* that masked toke awey parte & the reste was cut into high shoes for the cloynes maske and so therof nowe	n*i*l Seruiceable nor chargeable
velvet redd x yardes iij q*uar*ters di. **velvet** red or Crymmesen. v yard*es* di.	Imployed in p*er*formans of vj grete paire of Allmayne sleves and againe translated into torchebearers for the Marryners Maske and often vsed by players and so knowen and worne as nowe therof.	

* T. Blagrave

* Iohn holt*es* marke †

* ...... Leys. f° 5 v.

Charge.	Imploymente.	Remayne.
Satten purple vj yardes. di. q*ua*rter. **Satten** purple xxiij yard*es* q*ua*rter di. **Satten** purple xxxiiij yard*es* q*ua*rter.	Imployed into iiij large garment*es* for two Cardenall*es*. 40. and two hatt*es* and twoo hoodes to them .6. and in paninge of the Scaplers hoodes and sleves of two ffriers and two Monkes and for the whole hodes of the twoo Monkes .17. The same ffoure garment*es* and ij hoodes againe were translated into iiijor garment*es* of the torche bearers to the Nymphes And the Scaplers sleves and hoodes paned translated into two paire of longe Sleves of the torche bearers to Acteons Maske and so therof.	
Satten. Crymmesen. xxv yardes iij q*ua*rters di. **Satten**. Crymmesen xij yardes iij q*ua*rters. **Satten** crymmesen xlj yardes di. q*ua*rter **Satten** crymmesen lvij yard*es* iij q*ua*rters di. **Satten** crymmesen xix yardes.	Imployed into vj large garment*es* for twoo Cardinalls and two bishoppes .60. of whiche vj garment*es* iiijor di. were translated in to viij clownes garment*es* and hattes and other .j di. in the gardinge of vj compassed garment*es* for women and so therof. In to Ierkins and half Sleves of Thextronomers. 20 w*hi*ch were againe translated into barbariens and so therof. Into gardinge of the neither bace & false sleves of vj Moores garment*es*. 8. Into viij head peces of the Moorisshe ffriers w*ith* longe pendaunt*es* .24. the pendant*es* againe translated to gard the Sleves of ye said compassed garment*es*.	nil but in the w*ith*in said Garmentes charged as p*er*cell of the same
	Into vj nighte cappes & toppes of turkes headd*es* peces. 6. In to gardinge of viij white ffriers to the mores .8. into wrethes of Scaplers and buskins of turkes and moores .4. In to garnisshinge of vj hungariens garme*n*t*es* .6. In to greate Cardinalls hattes and hoodes .4. In to panes of two peire of Sleves and ij paire of sloppes for drom and fife to the ffissher men w*hi*ch they had for theire ffee. 8. and in to paning of the said two Sumpners cotes w*hi*ch were againe translated into Ierkins & sloppes for the drom and fife to Acteons Maske whiche they had for theire ffee 8	not Chargeable.

* T Blagrave
* Iohn holt*es* marke †
* Rychard Leys

f. 6 r.

	Charge.	Imploymente.	Remayne.
Late Quene **Mary** directed to S*ir* Edward Wallgrave knighte then M*aster* of the Warderobe	**Satten** Incarnate iiij yardes. di.	Imployed in to depe hoodes and scaplers of iiij ffryers and againe translated in to panes of vnder Sleves of torche bearers to the Nusquams and so therof	n*i*l but in the garment*es* w*ith*in said as p*ar*cell of the same.
	Satten yellowe xxv yard*es* iij q*ua*rters di. **Satten** yellowe iiij yard*es* di. quarter.	Imployed in to paninge of two longe garment*es* for two vergers .7. w*hi*ch were agayne translated in to garment*es* for drom and fife. In fflamynge of viij Cassockes and viij paire of Sloppes for torche bearers to the Extronomers maske .12. w*hi*ch were removed and sett againe vpon cassockes of the torche bearers to the Cloynes. Into wrethes of Scaplers and buskins and hed peces of turkes and mores. 4. In lyninge of eares of the hed peces of the Moorisshe ffriers. 1. and in garding of the Mores Maskes. 6. of all whiche	n*i*l but in the garment*es* w*ith*in said and that not chargeable
	Satten greene xix yard*es* di quarter.	Imployed to pane Scaplers and hoodes for the ffryers. 10. which were Againe translated in to panes of longe pendante Sleves for Acteons torche bearers and cappes fro drom and fife/ Into ffore sleves of twooe Cotes of grasiers .2. whiche were againe translated in to Clownes sleves/ In to vj Scaplers for Moores .2. w*hi*ch were translated to turne vp the hand*es* of the patriarke.	n*i*l but in the garment*es* w*ith*in said charged as p*ar*cell of the same
		In to panes of the twooe Sump*n*aers Cotes. 5. whiche were translated againe in to garment*es* for Drom and fife	not chargeable.

* T Blagrave

* Iohn holt*es* marke †

* Rychard Leys

f° 6v.

Charge.	Imploymente.	Remayne.
Satten Russett xxj yard*es* **Satten** russett xx^{ti} yard*es* di.	Imployed into greate longe ffrockes w*ith* Sleves for priestes .16. Into iiij^{or} priest*es* Cappes and into twoe greate gownes large and wide with hoodes and Sleves whiche were loste the nighte they served .25. and therfore	nil Chargeable.
Damaske Crymmesen xj yardes quarter/ **Damaske** Caffa crymsen ix yardes quarter. **Damaske** Crymsen xx yard*es*.	Imployed into ffrockes and priestes gownes w*ith* wide Sleves translated twise agayne in to torche bearers and vsed by players and to them geven by Composic*i*on .24. and into clokes and Sloppes for torchebearers .16. w*hi*ch was altered agayne for players and to them geven by the M*aste*r by composicion and so therof	
	Imployed in to twoo white Englisshe ffriers whiche were translated in to ij Moorishe ffriers and in to iiij morisshe ffryers then newe made to them. 60. All whiche w*ith* more added to them were againe translated in to torche bearers to the Barbarians and therof	nil but in the garment*es* Charged as parcell of the same.
Damaske white xviij yard*es* di/ **Damaske** white iiij^{xx} iij yard*es*	In to Sleves and garnisshinge of the vergers .10. whiche were agayne translated to garment*es* of Drom and fife and taken for theire ffees and so therof. Into vj hedpeces for the torche bearers to the Barbaryans .6./ In to panynge of the said twoo Sompners cootes w*ith* plites .7. After that translated againe in to clokes for Drom and ffife. In to fflaminge of vj paire of vnder Sleves of the torche bearers to the barbaryans. and in to Iagges and Snippes for defacinge of torche bearers twise shewen .10.	nil Chargeable.

* T Blagrave

* Iohn holt*es* marke †

fo 7 r. * Richard Leys

Charge.	Imploymente.	Remayne
Damaske greene .lij yard*es* di. **Damaske** greene xviij yardes.	Imployed into viij Cassock*es* for torche bearers to thextronomers .48 agayne translated in to viij paire of hoosen & vij paire of Sleves for the cloynes maske	nil but in the garmentes as p*ar*cell of the same
	Into panynge of the said two vergers garmentes .13. againe translated in to drom and fife. Into Scaplers and garnisshinge of head peces and turninges vp .9.	nil Chargeable
Damaske blacke xxiij yard*es* quarter. di.	Imployed whoolye in to twoo greate gownes w*ith* Ruff Sleves for Grasiers or Ientlemen of the contrey and so therof	nil but in the garmentes.
Damaske yellowe. xij yard*es*	Imployed all whoolie into vj greate Scaplers of mynstrells to the ffisshe wives and Market wives on Shroff Tuisdaye nighte	nil but in the garmentes
Taffita blacke xxxv yard*es* di. quarter.	Imployed whoolie in to iiij^{or} greate Large garmentes for twoo Monckes with Cooles.	nil but in the garmentes
Sarcenet redd xxij yardes iij quarters. **Sarcenet** redd xlviij yard*es*	Imployed in to viij paire of Sloppes for Torche bearers to the Extronomers 24. whiche was againe translated and w*ith* more put in to the Clownes	nil but in ye garment*es* and that not seruiceable
	In lyninge of visers pullinges oute tuftinges tveng*es* girdles garters and garnisshinges spente at the Coronacion of the queene that nowe is .46.	nil Chargeable.
Sarcenet white xx^{ti} yardes	Imployed whollie into iiij Rochett*es* for popes and Cardinall*es* and After spente in gerdles tyenges.	
Sarcenet Tawnye liiij yard*es*	Imployed in lyninge of the two priest*es* gownes, lyninge of vysers cou*er*ing of neck*es* girdels tyeng*es* lyning*es* of hed peces and ffurnissbinge of Drome and ffifes.	

* T Blagrave
* Iohn holt*es* marke †
* Rychard Leys

f° 7 v.

Charge.	Imploymente.	Remayne
Sarcenet yel-lowe. xlvj yardes quarter di.	Imployed in to the lyninges of.viij. paire of Sloppes for torche bearers and Drom and ffife to the Rutters Maske. 24.	n*i*l but in the garmentes.
Sarcenet yel-lowe xxx yard*es*	Into the lyninge and tyeng of xx[ti] head peces of wicker for wemen 25. and in to gerdles tyeng*es* coveringe of neckes and garnishinge. 27.	n*i*l Chargeable.
Sarcenet rus-sett. lv. yard*es*	Imployed in to the lyninge of all the panes and vestures of the Swarte Rutters Maske	
Sarcenet Blacke. lix. yardes.	Imployed in to vj paire of Sloppes for Moores.12.	n*i*l but in the garmentes
	In to twooe Tippett*es*.6. and twooe Cooles. 10. for blacke ffryers whiche were spente agayne in to lyninges and in to girdles coveringe of neck*es* lyninges of head peces and other garnisshinge. 30.	not Chargeable

* T Blagrave
* Iohn holt*es* marke †
* Rychard Leys

f° 8 r.

	Charge.	Implovmente.	Remayne.
In the tyme of Sir **Thomas Benger** knighte nowe M*aster* of the Revell*es*	**Grene** clothe of gold w*ith* workes xxix yard*es* di. q*ua*rter **Grene** clothe of gold w*ith* workes j yard q*uarter* iij nayles	Imployed whoolie into the gownes of A Maske of Patriarkes shewen on Twelff nighte whiche allso toke five yard*es* iij quarters and one nayle more of like stuff boughte for the p*er*formaunce therof and so therof.	n*i*l but in the garment*es* *with*in said charged as p*ar*cell of the same.
	Purple Clothe of Silu*er* tissued the backe side tynsell ix yardes iij q*uar*ters	Imployed whoolie in a gowne and kirtell for Diana and therof.	
	Purple Clothe of gold w*ith* workes xix y*ar*d*es* di.	Imployed in to twoo garment*es* for twoo Nymphes of Dyana .10/ In turninge downe and p*er*forminge of Stertops and garnisshinge of head peces. wherof .6.	n*i*l chargeable.
		In the Stuff not imployed to any vse.	iij yardes. di.
	karnacion Clothe of Siluer withe workes xj yard*es* di. q*ua*rter.	Imployed whoolie in to twoo vpper garment*es* of twoe Nymphes to diana and so therof.	n*i*l but in the garment*es* *with*in said charged as p*ar*cell of the same.
	Blacke gold Tynsell broched xxix yard*es* q*ua*rter.	Imployed whoolie in to vj Clokes of Acteons Maske and therof	

* T Blagrave
* Iohn holtes marke †
* Rychard Leys

f° 8 v.

Charge.	Imploymente.	Remayne.
Purple cloth of Silver w*ith* work*es* x yardes.	Imployed whoolie in to twoo vpper garment*es* to twoo of Dianas Nymphes and so therof	
Blew clothe of gold playne Ten yardes.	Imployed whoolie in to twoo vpper garment*es* for Twoo of Dyanas Nymphes and so therof	
Clothe of Siluer w*ith* workes iij yard*es* quarter	Imployed whoolye in to the Cape and scarpler of Acteons hedpeces and xij dogg*es* Collers for the same Maske and so therof	not seruiceable nor chargeable
Crym*m*eson golde Bawdekynne twoo yardes. di. not Imployed to any vse		ij yard*es* q*ua*rter j nayle
white velvet raysed w*ith* copp*er* gold vij yard*es* iij q*ua*rters di	Imployed whoolie in to a doblett and a peire of hosen for Acteon and therof	n*i*l but in the same garment*es* w*hi*ch being all to Cutt in small panes and steyned w*ith* blood are no more serviceable nor chargeable
Sarcenett Tawney xxj yard*es*	Imployed into girdell*es* .16. and into lyning*es* of vizars and covering*es* of neck*es* .3. and so therof restethe	n*i*l seruiceable nor chargeable
Sarcenet yellowe lx yard*es*	Imployed in to torchebearers Sloppes 16. girdell*es* .18. head peces .6. pulling*es* oute 12. and tufting*es* .8. and so therof	
Taffita Towers white xix yardes	Imployed in to hedginge Mittons for the Cloynes .3. di. wherof nothinge	n*i*l chargeable.
	In to lyninge of parte of the patriark*es* gownes .12. and in to Scaplers to them .3. di. wherof.	

* T Blagrave
* Iohn holtes marke †
* Rychard Leys

fo 9 r.

Charge.	Imploymente.	Remayne
Damaske white lxxij yardes iij q*uar*ters.	Imployed in to lyninge and Ruffes of Eighte paire of Crymesen damaske Sloppes for the torche bearers of Acteons Maske. 36. Into the bodies of iij large gownes.18. and in to the vnder Sleves and panynge of longe Sleves.8. of the torche bearers to the Nusquams maske to *per*forme the greate Sleves of the torche bearers to the barbaryans Maske 8. and for turninge downe of Collers and Sleve handes .2. and so therof	n*i*l but in the garment*es* *with*in said charged as p*ar*cell of the same.
Damaske crymson. .c. yard*es* **Damaske** Murrey xij yard*es*	In the lynynge of Sixe gownes of the Nusquams. 60. In vj paire of Sloppes. 20. and vj paire of Sleves 10. of the torche bearers to Acteons Maske / In three gownes. 18. and paninge of three paire of Sleves. 3. of the torche bearers to Acteons maske wherof	
velvett Carnacion v yard*es* iij q*uar*ters.	Imployed whoollye in to vj paire of shorte buskyns for the Maske of Italyen wemen on twelf nighte and therof	n*i*l Chargeable.
velvett Orrenge coollo*ur* xiiij yardes di.	Imployed in to vj paire of longe buskyns for the hunters of Acteons Maske and therof	
velvett yellowe xxiij yardes.	Imployed whoollye in to vj cassockes of viij torche bearers to Acteons maske and so therof	n*i*l but in the garment*es* charged as p*ar*cell of the same
velvett Greene. xviij yardes. di. q*uar*ter	Imployed whoolie in to fflowers set vpon the lyninge of the Ierkins and Sloppes of the Hunters in Acteons Maske and so therof	n*i*l but in the garment*es* & that not chargeable

* T Blagrave
* Iohn holt*es* marke †
* Rychard Leys

f° 9 v.

	Charge.	Imploymente.	Remayne.
Quenes Maiestie **Elizabethe** that nowe is directed to the *Master* Officers there dated the xxvij[th] of Decembre .1558.	**Sarcenet** blacke xliiij yard*es*	Spente in girdles. 14. ffurnisshinge of Drom and ffyfe. 8. lyninge of visers. 10. tapes Tyes and Coveringe of neckes 9. and geven in rewardes. 3. so that therof	not chargeable. nor seruiceable.
	Sarcenet greene stripped w*ith* gold xxxv yardes.	Imployed in nether baces. 12. pendaunte Sleves. 12. and brode ruffed collers. 2. for the Patriarkes Maske. In tuftinge of the barbariens Maske. 8. and in lyninge of the Cloynes cappes 1. wherof	
	Crymsen gold Sarcenett xxxv yardes	Imployed in to the Sleves. 20. and p*er*forminge of the over tuftinge. 10. of the torche bearers to the barbarians maske and in to kirtells of two torche bearers to Diana. 5. besides a greate deale more pulled oute of the Swarte Rutters Sloppes. whereof.	nil but in the garment*es* not chargeable.
	white gold sarcenet. lj yard*es* q*uarte*r **white** Silu*er* Sarcenet. xl yard*es*	Imployed in to the lyninge of ye Ierkins and hoosen of the hunters in Acteons Maske. 48. in vpper and nether baces of kirtell Sleves and collers of the Italien women on twelf nighte. 18. in vnder kirtells of the Torche bearers to the Nymphes. 5. In the patriarkes head peces .6. and in girdells. 13. wherof	
	yellowe clothe of gold playne iiij yard*es* q*ua*rt*er*. **yellowe** clothe of gold playne xiiij yard*es*	Imployed whoollie in to vj middle garment*es* and Sleves of the patriarkes Maske and therof	nil but in the garment*es* charged as p*ar*cell of the same
	Blacke clothe of gold w*ith* work*es* iiij yardes q*ua*rter one nayle.	Imployed whoollie in Stertoppes for the patriarkes and therof	nil Chargeable.

* T Blagrave
* Iohn holt*es* marke †
* Rychard Leys

fo 10 r.

Charge.	Imployment.	Remayne.
yellowe clothe of gold w*ith* woorkes one yard	Imployed whollie in to Sixe Scaplers for the Nusquams Maske and therof	n*i*l but in the garment*es* charged as parcell of the same.
yellowe Clothe of gold w*ith* work*es* iij y*ar*d*es* iij *quar*t*er*s j naile		
purple Clothe of gold playne v. yard*es*.	Imployed to performe the Sleves of one of Acteons hunters.	
	In to vj head peces for the patriarkes	n*i*l chargeable nor Seruiceable.
Blacke cloth of gold .j. yard	Imployed all in to vj girdles for Dyanas Nymphes wherof	
Satten. purple al*ias* wattchett xxxvij yard*es* quarter	Imployed whollie in iiij greate longe garment*es* of the torche bearers to Dyanas Maske besides a greate deale more of old garmentes wherof	n*i*l but in the garment*es* and charged as p*ar*cell of ye same
Sarcenet redd lxxvj yard*es* iij quarters.	Imployed in pullinges oute of Sixe garmentes of the Italien Ladies on twelff nighte .24. and in furnisshinge of theire Drom and ffife .8. In pullinge oute in the half of viij torche bearers Sloppes 10. and cappes .4. for the Cloynes Maske and therof	n*i*l but in the garment*es* & that not chargeable nor seruiceable
Sarcenet redd more .vj yardes/ quarter/	In to a Cote a hoode a cappe and a girdle for a Shepp*er*d mynstrell to the Cloynes .7. in girdell*es* .10. in two paire of Sloppes & Scarfes for the womens Drom and ffife on Shroftuidaye at nighte .12. in tyeng*es* necke cou*er*inges and garnisshinges. 6. and geven in reward*es* one yard di.	n*i*l but in the garment*es* and that not chargeable nor seruiceable
Sarcenet whyte .lxxj. yardes.	Imployed in lyninges of the patriarkes gownes .12. In one Shepard*es* cote hood cappe and girdle .7. in girdles .24. in cappes and coyfes .7. in womens call*es* .2. in ffurniture of theire Drom and ffife .6. in tyeng*es* lyninge of vizers and garnisshinge .6. in ffurnisshinge of a pley by the children of the chapple .5. in reward one yard di. of all whiche	

* T Blagrave

.... holt*es* marke †

f° 10 v.

Charge.	Imploymente.	Remayne.
Satten Murrey xxx yardes.	Imployed into edginge of Stertvppes for the Patriarkes and in to viij paire of buskins for Acteons torche bearers .16.	
	In to twoo paire of Sloppes .6. and ij paire of Sleves .3. for two of Acteons torchberers and in to three paire of Sleves for the Nusquams Torche bearers .5. And so therof	n*i*l but in the garmen*tes* and charged as p*ar*cell of the same
Tawney Clothe of Silu*er* withe woorkes ij yardes.	Imployed whoolie in to turninge downe of Capes sleve hand*es* and toppes of buskins and therof	n*i*l chargeable.
Purple Clothe of Silu*er* withe woorkes ij yard*es* quarter di.	Imployed whoolie in to A paire of longe buskins for Acteon and therof	
Clothe of Silver playne v. yardes.	Imployed whoollie in to the brestes of the Nusquams for the devise of poco Apoco and in to the toppes of theire hedpeces & therof	n*i*l but in the garment*es* to be charged as p*ar*cell of the same
yellowe golde Sarcenett xxxvij. yardes.	Imployed in to twoo kirtell*es* of torche bearers to Dyana and her Nymphes .5. In gardinge and pullinge oute of vj vpper bodies .4. and p*er*forminge the gardes of the nether bodies .6. of the torche bearers to the Italyen Ladyes Maske on Twelff nighte. And in coveringe lyninge and garnisshinge of xlj head peces .21. wherof	n*i*l chargeable.

* T Blagrave
* Iohn holtes marke †
* Rychard Leys

f° 11 r.

Charge.	Imploymente.	Remayne.
Tawney clothe of Copper gold striped Sarcenett wise xxj yardes iij quarters di. narrowe.	Imployed whoolie in to the lyninge of the Ierkyn and Sloppes of Acteon beinge an odd garmente all to cutte in narrowe panes and steyned w*ith* blood and therfore therof in to vij girdell*es* for Dyana and her vj Nymphes and therof	n*i*l chargeable.
Purple clothe of gold playne xxv yardes quarter.	Imployed whoolye w*ith* a greate deale more in to vj Ierkins w*ith* Sleves and Sixe paire of Sloppes for the hunters in Acteons Maske and therof	n*i*l but in the garment*es* & charged as p*ar*cell of the same
Crymsen Satten xj. yardes.	Imployed in to the toppes and garnisshing of the torche bearers head peces to the Nusquams Maske and in to cappes edginge of Stertuppes and garnisshing of head peces wherof	n*i*l chargeable nor seruiceable

* T Blagrave
* Iohn holt*es* marke †
* Richard Leys

fo 11 v.

The Remayne of the Revell*es* in A*nno* Reginæ Elizab*eth* dei gra*cia* &c. | **Secundo** 1560. | **An Inventory** of Remayne in thoffyce of the queens Ma*ies*ties Revells Collected and made by the Righte woorshipfull S*ir* Thomas Benger knighte M*aster* of that office Richard Lee Clarke controwler and Thomas Blagrave Clerke of that office and Iohn Holte yeman of the same the 1560. in the seconde yeare of the Raigne of o*ur* moste dread Sou*er*egne Ladye Elizab*eth* by the grace of god Queene of Englande fraunce and Ierlande defendo*ur* of the faythe &c. of all the Maskes Stuffe and store w*ith*in that office Chargeable in the queenes p*re*sence taken vewed and p*er*vsed by the Righte honorable S*ir* Richard Sackevyle knighte one of the queenes Ma*ies*ties pryvye counsell and vndertreasuro*ur* of England and S*ir* walter Myldmey knighte Chaunselo*ur* of theschequer by vertue of A letter vnder IX of the Counsells handes her vnder mencioned

To o*ur* verye Lovinge frend*es* S*ir* Richard Sackevile knighte on*e* of the Queenes Ma*ies*-*ties* previe Counsell and vnderthresovrer of Englande and S*ir* walter Myldmaye knighte Chauncello*ur* of Thexchequer.

After o*ur* verye hartye come*n*dacions, where certaine pieces of Clothe of gowlde silv*er* and other silkes have been delyu*er*ed out of the queenes Ma*ies*ties greate wardrobe to S*ir* Thomas Benger knighte M*aster* of the Revell*es* to be employed in Maskes Interludes and other showes as have been p*re*sented before the Queenes Ma*ies*tie to gither w*ith* certeyne monye in p*re*ste toward*es* the makinge and p*re*paracion thereof the p*er*ticularities wherof the seid S*ir* Thomas Benger desireth that he maye declare and soe be dyscharged theyes be to signify vnto yowe that the Queenes Ma*ies*ties pleasor is ye do repayre to Thoffyce of the Revell*es* & there to see aswell howe the mony to hime delyuered hath ben disbursed & also how the stuff had owte of the wardrob is emploied & therevpon to take a sufficient Inventorie of suche Maskes as ar mete to be showed in her highn*es* p*re*sence, and to take order y[t] the rest being fees incydente to the saide office may be taken by y[e] M*aster* of y[e] Revell*es* & dystributed in soche sorte as have bene accostomed wherof wee praye yow not to fayle & soe we bed yow hartelye fayre well ffrom westm*inster* the .27. of Apryll 1560.

Yo*ur* asured loving frend*es*

N. Bacon | W. North*a*mpton. | E. Derby.
ff. Bedforde | E. Clynton/ W. Howard. | T. Parry.
f° 1 r. ff. Knoll[ys] | [W]ill Sicill/

Patryarkes vj.	vj Longe gownes of greene clothe of golde with woorkes .vj. payere of vndersleves of playne yellowe clothe of gowlde pulled oute vnder the armes with greene golde sarsenet. vj vnder garmentes of the same playne yellowe clothe of gowlde frenged and tasseled with Cullen sylver and vnder skirted with greene gowlde sarsenett frenged with cullen sylver the gownes lyned with white towres taffita & sarsenet stayned lyke Ermyns.	ſtayere and Sarvyshable.
	vj hedpeces of purple playne Clothe of gowlde edged with parcemane Lace of vennys gowld with rowles of redd gowlde sarsnett wrethed & tufted with whyte golde sarsenet with tuftes of redd and white fethers.	not Chargeable
	vj payere of Startopps of Blacke and yellowe golde.	not Chargeable
Acteons vj.	vj huntinge Clookes of blacke gowlde tynsell broched frenged abowte with golde & paris sylke. vj Ierkins with sleves and vj payer of sloppes of purple clothe of golde playne lined with white golde sarsenet enbrodered vppon with greane vellvet cutt in leaves scallopwise. vj payre of Buskins of orenge collerred vellvet buttoned with Copper buttons.	Servyshable.
	vj hedpeces of greane gowlde sarsnet cutt in Leaves the toppes of yellowe golde sarsenelt garnyshed with narrowe frenge of Cullen gowlde with tuftes of fethers yellowe and greane. vj bore speares of tree and paste paper foyld and paynted frenged withe cullen sylver and paris sylke.	not Chargeable.

* T Blagrave
* Iohn holtes merke †
* Rychard Leys.

fo 1v.

Hunters. torcheberers to the Actions. **viij.**	**viij** Cassockes of yellowe velvet with longe pendaunte sleves of the same paned with grene Satten with vj payere of vnder sleves of crimsen damaske and to payere of Murrey Satten the handes and skirtes ffrenged abowte with narrowe frenge of yellowe and greene paris sylke **viij** payer of sloppes wherof vj payere of crimmessen damaske and to payre of Murrye Satten all Lyned with whyte damaske.	Servishable.
	viij Hedpeces of white playne sarsnet covered with Ivye leaves of greene golde & sylver sarsnett lyned with greene taffita. **viij** payere of longe buskyns of Murrey Satten buttened with	not Chargeable.
Nusquams vj.	**vj** longe garmentes with sleves of white velvett cutt in frettes lyned with crimisen damaske frenged abowte with cullen sylver and redd paris sylke buttenned with **vj** Scaplers of yellowe clothe of gowlde the brestes of clothe of sylver stayned with the posye of poco A poco.	The Clothe of golde & Crymsen damaske Sarvyshable but the white velvet not sarvyshable any more.
	vj Hedpeces of paste paper stayned with asvre with pipes gylded the tapps of yellowe golde sarsnet lyned with Clothe of sylver tarcelled with cullen sylver.]	not Chargeable
Turkes Commoners torcheberers to the Musquams. **vj.**	**vj** longe gounes of damaske wherof three mvrreye & white with vnder sleves enterchaungehable & strayte pendaunt sleves partie payned of the same stuff frenged with shorte white & Murreye frenge of paris sylke.	Servyshable.
	vj hedpeces of yellowe golde sarsnet ye toppes of Crymmesen Satten stryped with sylver threedes with top tassells of cullen sylver.	not Chargeable.

* T Blagrave * Iohn holte †
* Rychard Leys

fo 2 r.

venecyans Commones torcheberers to the bar-baryans. **vj.**	**vj** gownes of white damaske with greate open sleves of the same vnder sleves of the same partie flamed with carnacion satten the open sleves lyned and the hole garmentes ouertufted with redd golde sarsnett	Servyshable.
	vj hedpeces of white damaske garnysshed with redd golde sarsnett greene damaske and yellowe satten with toppe tasselles of cullen sylver.	not Chargeable.
Colownes viij	**viij** Cotes of Crymmesen Satten garded with yellowe gowlde Laune with half sleves of the same and vnder sleves of greene damaske turned vp with yello gowlde Laune **viij** payere of playne hosen of greene damaske.	not servyshable.
	viij Aperns of white gowlde sarsnet edged with veniys gowlde frenge.	gyven awaye by the maskers in ye queenes presence
	viij broode hattes Crymmesen satten lyned with greene golde sarsenett. **viij** payere of Shewes of Blacke velvett Laced aboue the Ancle. **viij** flayles and viij Spades of tree foyled ouer.	not Chargeable.
Barbaryens vj	**vj** Streyghte gownes of owlde redd Cloth of gowlde taken owte of hanginges payned with olde enbrodered gardes ouertufted with greene golde sarsnett edged abowte with shorte frenge of Cullen sylver with vnder sleves of owlde red Cloth of gold rased **vj** Scaplers of Crymmesen satten Cutt in paines and lyned with yellowe gowlde sarsenett colored with greene damaske & edged abowte with shorte cullen sylver frenge.	not Servyshable but ffees
	vj hedpeces of redd and blacke golde sarsnet garnisshed with whyte silver Lane and Cullen sylver frenge topp tasselled with Cullen golde.	not Chargeable.

* T Blagrave
* Iohn holtes merke †
* Rychard Leys

fo 2v.

Almanes. vj.	vj Ierkyns of owlde clothe of gowlde with six payre of greate Ruff sleves of redd crimmesem and Carnacion velvet iagged and cutt lyned with yellowe sarsnett frenged with small silver freng. vj payere of Sloppes of lyke velvett lykewyse pulled owte Iagged and Cutt. vj payere of nether stockes of redd Clothe.	not servishable butt ffees.
	vj rounde hedpeces of owlde Clothe of tyssue with rowles of bace fethers.	not Chargeable
Moores vj.	vj vpper boddyes of owld clothe of gowlde & blewe velvet rayesed with wyde sleves of sylver sarsnet the nether baces of wode redd satten paynted & garnisshed with yellowe satten.	not servyshable butt ffees.
	vj Corled hed Sculles of blacke Laune wrether abowte with redd golde sarsnett and sylver Lawne.	not Chargeable.
	vj dartes of tree & paste paper gilded	————
Hindes Torcheberes to the Cloyens. viij.	viij Cassokes of owlde redd Sarsnett flamed with yellowe satten paynted with vnder sleves of owlde yellowe gowlde sarsnett. viij payre of sloppes of redd and yellowe playne sarsnett	not servyshable
	viij Capps of redd and yellow playne sarsnet	not Chargable
Swarte Rutters. viij.	viij Ierkyns & viij payere of longe breches soed to them of brode loome woorke & white & blacke with owte lyninge.	not servyshable
	viij longe hattes copper gowld Lawne garded garded with the seyed Lome worke viij dagges of tree sylver and paynted over. viij pertisauntes of tree & paste paper paynted and gylded.	no Chargehable.

* T Blagrave
* Iohn holtes merke †
* Rychard Leys

f° 3 r.

Odd garmentes and hedpeces of Men.

Toe Mvnkes kirtells of blacke taffita with sleves of purple Satten. **Toe** Mvnckes Cooles of black taffita with sleves of the same	not seruyshable
Toe vnder garmentes of Satten rufted stryped with wookes with sleves of the same	not servishable.
Toe gounes of blacke damaske for grasyers or gentillmen of the cvntrye with haulfe sleves of the same	not servishable
Toe ffryers garmentes of Russett velvet with sleves of yellowe velvett & purple satten partie payned.	not Sarvyshable.
vj Scaplers of yellowe damaske garnysshed withe blacke gowlde sarsnett.	Sarvyshable
viij hedpeces of crimsen satten whiche did serve for the ffryers that were torcheberers to the Moores.	not Chargehable

* T. Blagrave
* Iohn holtes merke †
* Rychard Leys

f° 4 v.

wemens Maskes.

Dyana and vj Nymphes Huntresses withe her.

one vpper garmente and one nether garmente of purple Clothe of sylver tyssued the blacke side tinsell the vpper garment frenged with narrowe frenge of Cullen golde and the nether garment frenged with frenge of vennys golde withe gylte bells.

Toe longe garmentes of carnacion Clothe of sylver edged abowte with narrowe cullen golde frenge and garnisshed with gilte bells.

Toe longe garmentes of purple Clothe of sylver with woorkes edged abowte withe narrowe Cullen frenge golde & garnysshed with bells

Toe longe garmentes of blewe Clothe of golde playne edged abowte with narrowe cullen golde frenge & garnisshed with gilt bells.

vj kirtells of purple Clothe of golde frenge withe Cullen sylver.

ffayere and Sarvyshable.

vij parteletttes of white taffita and vij payre of sleves of gloves on the same.

vij hed peces of paste paper gilded sylvered and paynted garnisshed with greene golde sarsnet and woovinge silke dyed and sett with counterfett stones.

vij gerdelles of blacke playne clothe of golde gylded & paynted with buckles

vij payre of taffita hosen with soles.

not Chargeable.

* T Blagrave
* Iohn boltes merke †
* Rychard Leys

f° 4 r.

Maydens Torcheberers to the Nymphes **viij**.	**viij** Longe garmentes of purple satten edged abowte the coller sleves and skirtes with frenge of cullen sylver and purple sylke.	Servyshable.
	viij kirtells of gold sarsnett wherof toe yellowe toe redd to whyte and toe greene edged abowte the skirtes with frenge of Cullen sylver.	
	viij partelettes and viij hole payere of sleves with handes of grograyne Chamlett flesshe cullour.	not Chargeable.
	viij payere of Buskyns of the same Chamlett.	
	viij hedpeces of paste paper gilded and paynted and of woovinge died garnysshed with redd gold sarsnet and sett with counterfett stones.	
Italyan wemen **vj**.	**vj** garmentes of Clothe of tyssve whyte ye vpper bodies pulled owte with redd sarsnett.	Servyshable.
	vj payere of vnder sleves vj collers vj middell baces and vj nether baces of crimesen velvet cutt in lozenges spangled and lyned with white golde sarsnett withe doble ruffes of white golde sarsnett spangled the baces and sleves edged abowte with cullen sylver freenge and tarseled with cullen Silver.	not Chargeable.
	vj payere of Buskyns of Carnacion velvett.	

* T Blagrave
* Iohn holtes merke †
* Rychard Leys

fo 4 v.

ffisherwyves vj

vj vpper boddyes of owlde red clothe of golde Scallopped barred ou*er* and garded w*i*th blewe vellvet and gowlde cheu*er*ned and frenged w*i*th narrow greene sylke frenge and frenge & tarsells of cullen sylver.

vj cumppased kertells of Clothe of golde clothe of Silver blewe velvet w*i*th threedes of silvu*er* and redd tynsell p*ar*tye payned in wrethes garded w*i*th crimesen satten cutt and pulled owte w*i*th yellowe gowlde sarsnet and frenged w*i*th narrowe cullen sylver frenge.

vj payer of vndersleves of the same stuff and sute

vj hedpeces of wycker silver and poynted ou*er* w*i*th redd and wrethed abowte w*i*th redd and blacke gowlde sarsnett and tasselled w*i*th cullen golde w*i*th hatt*es* w*i*th in them cou*er*ed w*i*th gowlde Laune.

Markett wyfes viij.

viij vpper bodies of sundrye sortes of Clothe of gowlde and sylv*er* cutt in to small scallopp*es* w*i*th small poynted baces of redd clothe of sylv*er* collered w*i*th purple clothe of silv*er* frenged w*i*th small cullen silver frenge.

viij kirtell*es* of tinsell cutt in Ruffes and pulled owte w*i*th white s*ar*snett p*ar*tye payned w*i*th redd satten enbrodred vppon w*i*th golde and sylv*er* threede.

vj hedpeces of wycker sylvered and paynted w th redd and tarseled w*i*th cullen gowlde and wrethed abowte w*i*th white and blacke golde s*ar*snett w*i*th hatt*es* w*i*thin them cou*er*ed w*i*th gold Laune.

not S*er*vyshable.

* T Blagrave

* Iohn holtes merke †

* Richard Leys

f°5r.

Od garmentes

and hedpeces for weemen.

vj hedpeces of wycker lyke Ruffes silvered over and wrethed betwene *with* white and blacke Lace.	not chargehable.

* T. Blagrave

* Iohn holtes merke †

* Rychard Leys

fo 5 v.

IV

A Survey of the Hospital of St John of Jerusalem, the seat of the Revels Office

British Museum. Lansdowne MSS. 86. Art. 60.

. . . . [Thomas Gra]ves gent*leman* Surveyo*ur* of her ma*ies*ties [works Thomas Fo]wler gent*leman* her ma*ies*ties Comptroller of the same . . . . . [Iohn] Colebrand gent*leman* *Master* Carpenter to her ma*ies*tie. Hum[frey] [Lovell] gent*leman* *Master* Mason to her Ma*ies*tie. And Will*iam* Necton gent*leman* . . towching the Surveye and state of her ma*ies*ties house or lat[e] Hospitall of St Iohnes Ierusalem in the saied Countie of M[iddlesex] By the com*m*aundement of the righte honorable S*ir* Will*iam* Cecyll knighte Lorde Treasorer of Englond/ viz.

	Iohn Dauntsey Porter	Twoo Roomes belowe occupied by warraunte to him graunted by the late marquex of winchester late lorde Treasorer of Englond S*ir* Ri*chard* Sackfylde knighte late vndretreasorer of her highnes Courte of Excheaquer vnder thier handes dated the xv^th of Iuly 1581 And w*i*th the yerlie ffee of lx^s x^d As I am enformed by Will*iam* ffuller Esquyo*ur* her ma*ies*ties Audito*ur* for the saied Countie/
The Gatehouse and other Roomes adioyning thervnto in the seuerall tenures of	Henry Middlemore Esquyo*ur* one of her ma*ies*ties gent*leman* of her highnes prevye Chamber holdeth at wyll by her ma*ies*ties appoint*ment* (as he saiethe)	viij Roomes in the saied Gatehouse. whereof vij Chambers And one Roome below on the west ende of the same gate. vsed for A Sello*ur*/ And certeyne other Roomes and Chambers lieng and adioyninge vnto theste ende and Northe syde of the same Gate viz. ij^o Chambers aboue One Butterye. One kitchien. One Larder. One yerde. One woodyerde. One lytell wood house to lye drye woode in. One wasshing house with lodging Chambers ouer the same And one Gardeyne/
[The] lodging lieng [ne]xte the saied [G]ate house & housez [a]dioyning And on theste syde of the Courte in the tenure of	Antho*ny* Wingfield Esquyo*ur* one of her ma*ies*ties gent*lemen* vsshers holdeth	One hall. One kytchien. One Coale house. One Larder. One Seller. having vj Roomes or Chambers ouer them. One large Gardeyne with one fayer ponde all whiche he saieth he hathe of her ma*ies*ties p*ro*mise for his lief withoute graunte of the same vnder any Seale of Offyce/
The Chappell or Churche in the vse of	Henry Sackforde Esquyo*ur* *master* of her ma*ies*ties pavilions hales and Tentes And Roberte Harvye yoman of the same hathe and vseth	The saied Churche or Chappell ys converted and vsed by the saied Officers of the hales and Tentes : To laye her ma*ies*ties Hales and Tentes in And for other necessaries to the same belonging And also for other necessaries : belonging to her ma*ies*ties Lodging*es* in the Charge of the saied Henry Sackford Esquyo*ur* duering her ma*ies*ties pleasure (as wee enformed).
Certeyne Roomes & Lodging*es* lienge nexte, on the North syde of the saied Chappell in the occupac*i*on of	Henry Sackford afore said Esquio*ur* holdeth.	One kytchien. One larder. One Coalehouse. iij^re woodhouses. One wasshing yerde. One Chamber. One Styllehouse in the passage leading to the garden : One fayer Seller for Beare and wyne. One fayer Gardeyne with one Orteyerde walled aboute havinge one doore newly made thoroughe the wall leading to Clerkenwell and Iselington : One lytell Roome on the syde of the Seller xiij Chambers. One hotehouse. One Butterey. Of which xiij Chambers one ys devided into ij^o Roome which serveth for A hall and great Chamber Or Dynyng Chamber/ All which premisses he claymeth to holde none otherwise. Then yt dothe appeare in A *Memorandum* here vndrewritten/

f° 152

Scyte [precink]te and Compasse [of th]e late dissolved [Hos]pitall of **St [Ioh]nes Ierusalem** [of] Englond in the [Cou]ntie of Midd*lesex*	**Certeyne Roomes and Chambers lieng nexte and on the Northe syde** of the saied Romes occupied by henry Sackford Esquy*our*. occupied by/	Edward kyrkh*am* yoman of the Revel*les* maskes and disguysing*es*. holdeth.	The Greate hall. iijre woorking housez. belowe. One Cutting house and one Greate Chambre vsed as Roomes for the Revell*es*. And are not graunted By patent otherwise. Then yt shall appeare herevnder emongest the Memorand*um*/
	Certeyne Roomes and lodging*es* lieng nexte to the Roomes in the tenure of the saied Edward kyrkh*am* And on the Northe syde And west ende of the saied Greate hall and Greate kytchien in the tenure of/	Edmond Tylney Esqui*our Master* of her ma*ies*ties Revell*es* holdeth as ffermo*ur* vnto william hunning*es* Clerke Comptroller of her ma*ies*ties hales and Tentes and of the Revell*es* &c.	One litell parlo*ur*. One lytell kytchen. One lytell Celler/ one littel larder/ one lytell hall/ One convenient Gardeyn/ one lytell Roome vsed for A Porters Lodge w*i*th one olde gate to passe thoroughe to Clerkenwell grene. One Greate kytchien at The west ende of the saied Greate hall/ One greate Seller at thende of the same hall ijo Larders One Coale house nexte to the saied greate kytchien. One lytell Courte at the west ende of the saied Greate kytchien/ One lytell Ten*emen*te adioyninge to the westende of the saied [Greate] hall lately in the occupac*i*on of one Thomas hall xiij Roomes or Chambers ouer all the saied lowe Roomes/ All which the saied Edmond Tylney Esquyo*ur* holdeth in ffourme of Will*iam* hunning*es* gent*leman* her ma*ies*ties Clerke Comptroller of the hales Tentes Revell*es* and Maskes. for the yerlie Rente of xvjli by yere/ And which the saied Clerkecomptroller. hadd. And holdeth as A manc*i*on house for his Offyce. As it will further appeare emongest the Memorand*um* hervnder written/
	Certeyne Roomes & Lodging sceated & adioyninge to the porche of the greate hall on the Righte hand goeng into the hall occupied by	Edw*ar*de kirkh*am* yoman of the Revell*es* holdeth	One kytchien one litell parlo*ur*/ One Coalehouse iiijre chambers and one Garrett. All which Roomes are sceated on the Southe syde of the greate hall : on the righte hand goeng into the hall And ouer the porche of the hall doore/ The certeyntie by what tytle he holdeth the premiss*es* shall appeare here vnder in the M*emorandum*.
	Certeyne Roomes lieng on the weste parte of Roomes in the tenure of the saied Edmond Tylney Esq*uiour* late in thoccupac*i*on of Thomas hall. And nowe occupied by	Rob*er*te harvye yoman of the Tentes and hales/	One hall one kytchien/ one p*ar*lo*ur*/ ijo lytell Chambers/ one litell Gardeyn. One greate house called the Toyle house somtyme the Brewhouse and Backhouse All seated belowe. w*i*th A Toyle yerde/ which Toyle house hathe A Backe doore of olde into Clerkenwell grene/ All which housez. speciallie his Lodging*es* he hathe bestowed greate Coste. not only in some newe buylding. But also in waynscotting and dealing the Roomes : his estate shall appeare emongest the Reste in the M*emorandum* herevnder written
	Certeyne Roomes & lodging*es* lieng on the west syde of the greate Courte Adioyninge to the saied Roomes in the tenure of the saied Rob*er*te Harvye occupied by	Thom*as* Blagrave *Esquier* Clerke of the Revell*es* hales Pavilions and Tent*es* holdeth	One hall/ one litell parlo*ur*/ One kytchien/ One Seller/ One Gardeyne. vij Chambers ouer the saied Roomes in p*ar*te And in p*ar*te over the saied Roomes in the tenure of the saied Rob*er*te Harvey/ his estate shall appeare herevnder in the Memorand*um*/
	One litell olde house stonding by him selfe towerdes the Stables occupied by	Iohn Dauntsey porter aforesaid holdethe the said Roome	conteynynge one lowe Roome and one upper Roome somtyme called the horsestable/ having one Backe doore to A house of Mr Thomas Sackford*es* Esquy*our* And so into his gardeyns/ who hathe no estate but at wille/

One Roome sceated emongest the Stables occupied by	Thom*as* Blagrave Esquyo*ur* aforesaid occupieth & is	vsed for A Stable
One Roome sceated nexte to the said Stable in the tenure of	Anth*ony* Wingfeld Esquyo*ur* aforeseid occupieth & is	vsed for A Stable
Two Roomes ioyninge toguyther Adioyninge to the seied former Stables occupied by	henry Sackford Esquyo*ur* aforseid occupieth & is	vsed for Stables which hathe Chambers ouer them/
One Shedd standing by him selfe newe buylded by	Edmond Tilney Esquyo*ur* aforseid occupieth & is	vsed for A Stable
One greate Barne sceated by him selfe within A greate Base Courte occupied by	Henry Middlemore & Henry Sackford Esquyo*urs* aforsaid And others the Officers of the hales & Tentes do occupie	One greate Barne and Barne yerde devided. The one halfe in the tenure of the Officers of hales and tentes/ And thother halfe. The saied gent*lemen* do occupie to laye haye in for thier horsez.

Memorand*um***.** That I haue seen euerye the patentes of the saied seuerall Officers of the Revell*es*. Hales. Pavilions. and. Tentes : abouementioned : In which (emongest other thing*es*) They haue Graunted. from her ma*ies*tie. seuerall houses. As dwellinge housez. And housez. for keping and exercisinge. thier seu*er*all offices/ But no one of them do clayme. ne yet can Clayme. by thier seuerall patent*es*. Any of thier saied seuerall Roomes. which any of them do occupie within the saied precinkte of the saied late dissolved house of St Iohnes/ As housez or Roomes graunted to them in that place/ And that her ma*ies*tie maye remove them from that place. At her highnes pleasure. To any other house/ Or otherwise to allowe them A yerlie Rente for thier saied seuerall houses, As was Accustomed to be allowed by the late king*es* of ffamous meomorye King henry the eighte and king Edward the
f° 154 vj^th^ (as I am enformed) | And as by some Accomptes shewed vnto ^mee^ appeareth. who did allowe vnto S*ir* Thomas Cawarden knight deceassed being then *Master* of the saied Revell*es* Hales and Tentes. after suche tyme As the same S*ir* Thomas Cawarden did purchace of the saied late king henrye the viij^th^ The howse in the Blackfriers in London : wheare the saied Offices wer then kepte He was allowed yerlie after certeyne money in the nature of A Rente. To sondrie the Officers of the saied Offices. for thier Lodging*es* and housez. vntill the Deathe of the saied S*ir* Thomas Cawerden. which Offices wer then removed. To the saied house of St Iohnes/ wherin yche offycer aboue named. hadd thier seu*er*all Offices and lodging*es* appointed to them : By the righte honorable late L*ord* Marquex of Winchester And late Lorde Treasorer of Englond And so from that tyme hythervnto ; the saied Rente allowed to them for thier housez susspended/ All which saied seu*er*all Roomes. They haue occupied successyvelye one after an other withoute any Rente yelded to her ma*ies*tie for the same Nevertheles euery of the saied Officers hathe well Repayred the same lodging*es*. which I fynde by viewe

f° 155 ***Examinatur per** me **Will*iam* Necton |**

[Endorsed, f° 151 :]
Certificate of ye Surveyor of Her Majesty's Board & Works &c.
[Endorsed, f° 155 v :]
Report of ye Surveyor of ye Queen's Board of Works concerning ye State of ye House or Hospital of St Iohn of Ierusalem in ye Blackfryars in ye County of Middlesex.

V

The Order of Precedence of the Master of the Revels

Bodleian Library. Tanner MSS. clxviii. p. 120 vo

The marshallinge of the *Master* of her Ma*ies*ties Reuells.

Whereas Mr Edmonde Tylney Esquier M*aster* of ye office of the Revells of the Queenes moste excellent ma*ies*tie vppon ye occasion of some doubte and question moved betweene him and others touchinge yer places and precedences by office, and dignitie at any honorable assemblies or companyes. And beinge verie vnwillinge (as he sayth) either to p*re*iudice his place and office, and so his Successors therby, or otherwise to Challendge yt w*hi*ch of right app*er*teyneth not vnto him, hath required me Garter princypall King of Armes of England together with Clarenceux K*ing* of Armes of the Southe, And Norrey K*ing* of Armes of ye North partes of this Realme That accordinge to the aucthority and Custome of our Office in all matters and causes of Armes, Honor and Chivalry, we would make suche search in ye Registers of o*ur* office, and signefie the same by way of Certificacon vnto all to whome it shall app*er*teyne : fforasmuch therefore as we finde by the auncient recordes and presidentes of o*ur* Office That especiall regard hath bin alwayes taken and observed for ye placinge and marshallinge of all officers of Dignitie p*er*teyninge to ye Imperiall Crowne of this Realme and estate of ye Kings ma*ies*ties moste royall p*er*son, takinge there places in all princly p*ro*ceedinge after the Dignities of yer Offices of estate and degrees, aswell at the Coronation of the Kings and Queenes of this Realme, and marriages of princes, as also at all solempne feastes Iustes Tryumphes and assemblies of Ho*nour* & Chivalry. And for yt ye said Edmond Tylney Esquier M*aster* of her ma*ies*ties Office called the Revells hath ye charge and direcc*i*on from her highnes for all her marciall Triumphes and princlie Revells in gen*er*all by patent vnder ye broade seale of England, with all rights and priviliges yer vnto belonging In as ample manner as any of his predecessors ever inioyed the same, and so by vertue of yt Office havinge place of Dignitie attendant vppon her ma*ies*ties moste royall p*er*son as well by example of forraine kingdomes, as in such like s*er*vices by himself and other his predicessors also exercised w*i*thin this Realme of England. It was in regard therof ordered and adiudged by the late right honorable W*illia*m L*ord* Burlie L*ord* H*igh* Treasurer of England and Deputed then for ye Office of Earle marshall of England assisted by S*i*r Christopher Hatton L*ord* Chauncellor of England and Henrie Lord Hunsdon, lo*rd* Chamberleyne to ye Queenes ma*ies*tie, with others then Commissioners assigned for ye orderinge and marshallinge of yt solempne p*ro*ceedinge before her royall ma*ies*tie to ye Cathedrall Church of St Paules in London Anno 1588 That the said Edmond Tylney Esquier M*aster* of ye Rlls should be placed and marshelled to take place and proceede together with other knightes and esquiers Officers and servantes to her highnes in like Dignities and Degrees as his saide predecessors had don, by minglinge with Bachelorknightes according vnto the Antiquitie of yt Office. vid*elicet* in order together with S*i*r Rob*ert* Constable knight livetena*unt* of the Queenes ma*ies*ties Ordinance and Artilery, S*i*r Owin Hopton knight liuetena*unt* of ye Tower of London and Mr Iohn Ashley Esquier M*aster* of her ma*ies*ties Iewellhouse with Mr Iohn fortescue then M*aster* of the Queenes wardrope and others, as doth appeare to vs in yt behalf. We therfore ye said Garter Clarenceux, and Norrey have herevnto subscribed accordinglie ffrom o*ur* office of Armes London ye xviijth Day of March 1600 and in the yeare of the Raigne of o*ur* sou*er*eigne Ladie Elizabeth by the grace of God of England ffrance and Ireland Queene Defender of ye faith &c. quadragesimo tercio

*Reuells

*W*illia*m Dethecke	*W*illia*m Camden	*W*illia*m Segar
Garter princip*all*	Clarenceux	Norrey Kinge
Kinge of Armes	Kinge of Armes	of Armes

VI

A Commission Touching the Powers of the Master.

Record Office. Patent Rolls 1606 (Watson's Rolls). m. 34. nº 46.

De Commissione speciali pro Edmundo Tylney Armigero Magistro Revellorum

Elizabeth by the grace of God &c To all manner our Iustic*es* Maiors Sheriffes Bayliff*es* Constables and all other our officers Ministers true liege men and Subiect*es* and to eu*er*y of them greetinge we lett you witt that we haue aucthorised licensed and co*m*maunded and by these p*re*sent*es* do aucthorise licence and co*m*maunde our welbeloved Edmunde Tylney Esquire Maister of our Revells aswell to take and retaine for vs and in our name at all tymes from hensforth and in all plac*es* within this our Realme of England aswell within ffrancheses and lib*er*ties as without at competent wages aswell all suche and as many painters Imbroderers Taylors Cappers Haberdashers Joyners Carders Glasiers Armorers Basketmakers Skinners Sadlers waggen makers plaisterers fethermakers as all other p*ro*p*er*tie makers and co*n*ninge Artificers and laborers whatsoever as our said Servant or his assigne bearers hereof shall thinke necessarie and requisite for the speedie workinge and fynisheinge of any exploite workmanshippe or peece of s*er*uice that shall at any tyme hereafter belonge to our saide office of the Revells As also to take at price reasonable in all places within our said Realme of England aswell within ffrancheses and lib*er*ties as without any kinde or kindes of stuffe ware or Marchandise woode or coale or other fewell tymber wainscott boarde lathe nailes bricke tile leade Iron wier and all other necessaries for our said workes of the said office of our Revells as he the said Edmunde or his assigne shall thinke behoofefull and expedient from tyme to tyme for our said s*er*uice in the said office of the Revells together with all carriages for the same both by land and by water as the case shall require And furthermore we haue by these p*re*sent*es* aucthorised and co*m*maunded the said Edmunde Tylney that in case any p*er*son or p*er*sons whatsoever they be will obstinatelie disobey and refuse from hensforth to accomplishe and obey our co*m*maundement and pleasure in that behalfe or withdrawe themselues from any of our said workes vpon warninge to them or any of them given by the saide Edmunde Tylney or by his sufficient deputie in that behalfe to be named appointed for their diligent attendance and workmanship vpon the said workes or devises as to their naturall dutie and alleigeance app*er*teineth that then it shalbe lawfull vnto the same Edmund Tilney or his deputie for the tyme beinge to attache the partie or parties so offendinge and him or them to co*m*mytt to warde there to remaine without baile or maineprise vntill suche tyme as the saide Edmunde or his deputie shall thinke the tyme of his or their imprisonment to be pu*n*nishement sufficient for his or their saide offenc*es* in that behalfe and that done to enlarge him or them so beinge imprisoned at their full lib*er*tie without any losse penaltie forfaiture or other damage in that behalfe to be susteined or borne by the said Edmunde Tilney or his saide deputie And also if any p*er*son or p*er*sons beinge taken into our said workes of the said office of our Revells beinge arrested co*m*minge or goinge to or from our saide workes of our said office of our Revells at the sute of any p*er*son or p*er*sons then the said Edmunde Tilney by vertue and aucthoritie hereof to enlarge him or them as by our speciall p*ro*tecc*io*n duringe the tyme of our said workes And also if any p*er*son or p*er*sons beinge reteyned in our said workes of our said office of Revells haue taken any manner of taske worke beinge bound to finishe the same by a certen day shall not runne into any manner of forfeiture or penaltie for breakinge of his day so that he or they ymediatly after the fynishinge of our said workes indevor him or themselues to fynishe the saide taske worke And furthermore also we haue and doe by these p*re*sent*es* aucthorise and co*m*maunde our said Servant Edmunde Tilney Maister of our said Revells by himselfe or his sufficient deputie or deputies to warne co*m*maunde and appointe in all places within this our Realme of England aswell within ffrancheses and lib*er*ties as without all and eu*er*y plaier or plaiers with their playmakers either belonginge to any noble man or otherwise bearinge the name or names of vsinge the facultie of playmakers or plaiers of Comedies Tragediès Ent*er*ludes or what other showes soever from tyme to tyme and at all tymes to appeare before him with all suche plaies Tragedies Comedies or showes as they shall haue in readines or meane to sett forth and them to p*re*sente and recite before our said Servant or his sufficient deputie whom wee ordeyne appointe and aucthorise by these p*re*sent*es* of all suche showes plaies plaiers and playmakers together with their playinge places to order and reforme auctorise and put downe as shalbe thought meete or vnmeete vnto himselfe or his said deputie in that behalfe And also likewise we haue by these p*re*sent*es* aucthorised and co*m*maunded the said Edmunde Tylney that in case if any of them whatsoever they bee will obstinatelie refuse vpon warninge vnto them given by the said Edmunde or his sufficient deputie to accomplishe and obey our co*m*maundement in this behalfe then it shalbe lawfull to the saide Edmunde or his sufficient deputie to attache the partie or parties so offendinge and him or them to co*m*mytt to warde to remaine without bayle or mayneprise vntill suche tyme as the same Edmunde Tylney or his sufficient deputie shall thinke the tyme of his or theire ymprisonment to be pu*n*nishement sufficient for his or their said offenc*es* in that behalfe and that done to inlarge him or them so beinge imprisoned at their plaine lib*er*tie without any losse penaltie forfeiture or other daunger in this behalfe to be susteyned or borne by the said Edmunde Tylney or his deputie Any Acte Statute ordynance or p*ro*uision heretofore had or made to the contrarie hereof in any wise notwithstandinge wherefore we will and co*m*maunde you and eu*er*y of you that vnto the said Edmunde Tylney or his sufficient deputie bearer hereof in the due execuc*io*n of this our aucthoritie and co*m*maundement ye be aydinge supportinge and assistinge from tyme to tyme as the case shall require as you and eu*er*y of you tender our pleasure and will answer to the contrarie at your vtt*er*most perills In witnesse whereof &c witnes our selfe at Westm*inster* the xxiiijth day of December in the xxiiijth yere of our raigne

per bre*ve* de priuat*o* Sigillo

VII

Royal Appointments of Masters of the Revels.

A. SIR THOMAS CAWERDEN APPOINTED 11 MARCH 1544-5.

Record Office. Patent Rolls. 36 Hen. VIII. p. 14. m. 23.

pro Thoma Cawerden milite de concessione ad vitam

Rex Omnibus ad quos &c. salutem. Sciatis quod nos de gracia nostra speciali ex certa sciencia et mero motu nostris necnon in consideracione boni veri et fidelis seruicij quod Dilectus et fidelis seruiens noster Thomas Cawerden Miles vnus generosorum priuate Camere nostre nobis antehac multipliciter impendit ac imposterum impendere intendit dedimus et concessimus prout per presentes damus et concedimus eidem Thome officium Magistri iocorum reuelorum et mascorum omnium et singulorum nostrorum vulgariter nuncupatorum reuelles and Maskes Ipsumque Thomam Cawerden Magistrum iocorum reuelorum et mascorum nostrorum predictorum facimus ordinamus et constituimus per presentes habendum gaudendum occupandum et exercendum officium predictum prefato Thome Cawerden per se vel per sufficientem deputatum suum siue deputatos suos a sexto decimo die Marcij vltimo preterito ante datam presencium pro termino vite sue cum omnibus domibus mansionibus regardis proficuis iuribus libertatibus et aduantagijs eidem officio quouismodo pertinentibus siue spectantibus vel tali officio pertinere siue spectare debentibus Et insuper de vberiori gracia nostra dedimus et concessimus ac per presentes damus et concedimus eidem Thome Cawerden pro exercicio et occupacione officij predicti vadium et feodum decem librarum sterlingorum per annum habendum et percipiendum sibi vel assignatis suis a dicto sexto decimo die Marcij vltimo preterito pro termino vite sue ad receptam Scaccarij nostri de Thesauro nostro per manus Thesaurarij et Camerariorum nostrorum pro tempore existencium ad festa sancti Michaelis Archangeli et Pasche per equales porciones annuatim soluendum Eo quod expressa mencio &c. In cuius &c. Teste Rege apud Westmonasterium xj die Marcij.

per breve de priuato Sigillo &c.

B. SIR THOMAS BENGER APPOINTED 18 JAN. 1559-60

Record Office. Patent Rolls. 2 Eliz. p. 5 m. 10.

De concessione ad vitam pro Thoma Benger

Regina Omnibus ad quos &c. salutem. Sciatis quod nos de gracia nostra speciali ac ex certa sciencia et mero motu nostris in consideracione boni veri et fidelis seruicij quod Dilectus et fidelis seruiens noster Thomas Benger Miles nobis antehac multipliciter impendit et imposterum impendere intendit Dedimus et concessimus ac per presentes pro nobis heredibus et successoribus nostris damus et concedimus eidem Thome Officium magistri iocorum reuellorum et mascarum omnium et singulorum nostrorum heredum et successorum nostrorum communiter vocatorum Revelles *and* Masques Ipsumque Thomam magistrum iocorum reuelorum et mascorum predictorum facimus ordinamus et constituimus per presentes habendum gaudendum et occupandum ac exercendum officium predictum prefato Thome Benger per se vel per sufficientem Deputatum suum siue deputatos suos sufficientes pro termino vite sue cum omnibus domibus mansionibus regardis proficuis iuribus libertatibus et aduantagiis eidem officio quouismodo pertinentibus siue spectantibus vel tali officio pertinere siue spectare debentibus Et insuper de vberiori gracia nostra dedimus et concessimus ac per presentes damus et concedimus pro nobis heredibus et successoribus nostris eidem Thome Benger Militi pro exercicio et occupacione officij predicti vadium et feodum decem librarum per Annum habendum et percipiendum dictum vadium et feodum sibi vel assignatis suis a tempore mortis Thome Carwarden Militis defuncti vltimi occupatoris dicti officij pro termino vite sue predicte ad receptam Scaccarij nostri Westmonasterij heredum et successorum nostrorum de Thesauro nostro heredum et successorum nostrorum per manus Thesaurarij et Camerariorum nostrorum heredum et successorum nostrorum ibidem pro tempore existencium ad ffesta Sancti Michaelis Archangeli et Pasche per equales porciones soluendum Eo quod expressa mencio &c. In cuius rei &c. Teste Regina apud Westmonasterium xviij die Ianuarij

per breue de priuato sigillo

C. EDMUND TYLLNEY APPOINTED 24 JULY 1579.

Record Office. Patent Rolls. 21 Eliz. p. 7. m. 8.

De concessione ad vitam pro Edmundo Tylney Armigero

Regina Omnibus ad quos &c. salutem Sciatis quod nos de gracia nostra speciali ac ex certa sciencia et mero motu nostris in consideracione boni et fidelis seruicij quod dilectus et fidelis seruiens noster Edmundus Tilney Armiger nobis antehac impendit et imposterum impendere intendit dedimus et concessimus ac per presentes pro nobis heredibus et successoribus nostris damus et concedimus eidem Edmundo Officium Magistri Iocorum Revellorum et mascarum omnium et singulorum nostrorum heredum et successorum nostrorum communiter vocatorum Revelles and Maskes ipsumque Edmundum Tilney Magistrum Iocorum Revellorum et Mascarum predictorum facimus ordinamus et constituimus per presentes habendum gaudendum occupandum et exercendum Officium predictum prefato Edmundo Tilney per se vel per sufficientem deputatum siue deputatos suos sufficientes pro termino vite sue cum omnibus domibus mansionibus regardis proficuis iuribus libertatibus et aduantagijs eidem Officio quouis modo pertinentibus siue spectantibus vel tali officio pertinere siue spectare debentibus. Et insuper de vberiori gracia nostra dedimus et concessimus ac per presentes damus et concedimus pro nobis heredibus et successoribus nostris eidem Edmundo Tilney pro exercicio et occupacione officij predicti vadium et feodum decem librarum per Annum habendum et percipiendum dictum vadium et feodum sibi vel Assignatis suis a festo Natalis domini vltimo ante datam presencium preterito pro termino vite sue predicto ad Receptam Scaccarij nostri Westmonasterij heredum et successorum nostrorum per manus Thesaurarij et Camerariorum nostrorum heredum et successorum nostrorum ibidem pro tempore existencium ad festa sancti Iohannis Baptiste et Natalis domini per equales porciones soluendum Eo quod &c. In cuius rei &c. Teste Regina apud Westmonasterium xxiiij die Iulij

per breue de priuato Sigillo &c.

VIII

Royal Appointments of Clerk-Controllers

A. RICHARD LEYS APPOINTED 17 MARCH 1550-1.

Record Office. Patent Rolls. 5 Edward VI. p. 2, m. 5

pro Richardo leys de concessione ad vitam

Rex omnibus ad quos &c. salutem/ Sciatis quod nos de gracia nostra speciali ac ex certa sciencia et mero motu nostris nominauimus assignauimus et constituimus Dicletum subditum nostrum Richardum leys Clericum contrarotulatorem omnium et singulorum pauilionum et tentorum nostrorum vulgariter nuncupatorum tentes hales and pavilions Necnon omnium et singulorum iocorum reuelorum masculorum nostrorum omnimodorum vesturarum reuelorum predictorum communiter vocatorum revelles maskes and maskyng garmentes infra regnum nostrum Anglie et alibi ac eidem Richardo leyes officium clerici contrarotulatoris pauillionum et tentorum nostrorum necnon revelorum et vesturarum predictorum dedimus et concessimus prout per presentes damus et concedimus habendum gaudendum occupandum et exercendum officium predictum prefato Richardo leyes per se vel per sufficientem deputatum suum siue deputatos suos sufficientes a primo die Septembris ultimo preterito ante datam presentium quo die Iohannes Barnard vltimus occupator eiusdem officij moriebatur ad terminum et pro termino vite ipsius Richardi leys vnacum omnibus vadijs feodis allocacionibus regardis proficuis iuribus libertatibus commoditatibus et aduantagijs predicto officio quoquomodo pertinentibus siue spectantibus aut imposterum spectandis siue debendis/ Et insuper de gracia certa sciencia et mero motu nostris predictis damus et concedimus eidem Richardo leyes pro exercicio et occupacione antedicti officij vadium et feodum octo denariorum bone et legalis mon[e]te Anglie per diem habendum gaudendum et percipiendum predictum vadium et feodum octo denariorum per diem prefato Richardo lewes et assignatis suis a predicto primo die Septembris durante vita sua de Thesauro nostro ad receptam Scaccarij nostri per manus Thesaurarij et Camerariorum nostrorum ibidem pro tempore existencium ad festa sancti Michaelis Archangeli et pasche per equales porciones annuatim soluendum/ Ac eciam damus per presentes eidem Richardo leyes pro liberatura et vestura suis pro officio predicto annuatim quatuor virgas lanei panni precij cuiuslibet virge sex solidos et octo denarios habendas et percipiendas eidem Richardo leys erga festum Natalis domini durante vita sua predicta ad magnam garderobam nostram per manus Custodis siue Clerici eiusdem garderobe nostre pro tempore existentis Et preterea sciatis quod nos de vberiori gracia nostra ac ex certa sciencia & mero motu nostris predictis c*eteris*q*ue* consideraci*on*ib*us* nos mouen*tibus* dedim*us* *et* concessim*us* ac p*er* p*re*sentes damus *et* concedim*us* p*re*fato Ric*hard*o leys bonam *et* conuenientem domu*m* siue mansione*m* vna cum Cameris cellar*ijs* solar*ijs* edific*ijs* stabulo ortu *et* gardino vbi pavillion*es* hale et tentor*ia* nos*t*ra posita sunt aut erunt p*er* M*agistru*m dict*orum* pavillionu*m* halar*um* *et* tentor*um* qui p*ro* tempore fu*er*it de tempore in tempus assignand*am* in qua ip*s*e Ric*hard*us *et* familia sua habitent h*ab*end*am* tenend*am* possidend*am* *et* gaudend*am* p*re*dict*am* domu*m* siue mansionem cum suis necessar*ijs* *et* p*er*tinenc*ijs* p*re*dict*is* p*re*fato Ric*hard*o leyes *et* assignat*is* suis p*ro* t*er*mino vite sue de dono n*os*tro absque redditu computo seu aliquo alio p*ro*inde nob*is* hered*ibus* vel successorib*us* n*os*tris aut alicui alij quoquo modo reddend*o* soluend*o* vel faciend*o* in tam amplis modo *et* forma p*re*dic*t*us Ioh*ann*es Bernard aut aliquis alius offic*ium* sup*ra*dict*um* occupans h*ab*uit *et* vnq*uam* gauis*us* fuit seu h*ab*ere *et* gaudere debuit r*aci*one ex*er*cicio p*re*missor*um* seu eor*um* alicuius Eo q*uo*d exp*re*ssa mencio &c. In cuius rei &c. T*este* R*ege* apud Westm*onasterium* xvij die Marci

p*er* bre*ue* de priuat*o* *et* Sigillo de dat*a* &c.

B. EDWARD BUGGYN APPOINTED 30 DEC. 1570

Record Office. Patent Rolls. 13 Eliz. p. 6. m. 12

De concessione ad vitam pro Edwardo Buggyn

* G. Gerrard

* Edwarde

* Buggyn

Regina. Omnibus ad quos &c. salutem. Sciatis quod nos de gracia nostra speciali ac ex certa sciencia et mero motu nostris nominauimus assignauimus et constituimus ac per presentes pro nobis heredibus et successoribus nostris nominamus assignamus et constituimus Dilectum subditum nostrum Edwardum Buggyn Generosum Clericum Contrarotulatorem omnium et singulorum Pavilionum et tentorum nostrorum heredum et successorum nostrorum vulgariter nuncupatorum Tentes hales and Pavilions. Necnon omnium et singulorum Iocorum Reuelorum mascorum omnimodorum vesturarum Reuelorum predictorum communiter vocatorum Revelles maskes and maskinge garmentes infra Regnum nostrum Anglie et alibi Ac eidem Edwardo Buggyn Officium Clerici Contrarotulatoris Pavilionum et tentorum nostrorum Necnon Reuelorum et vesturarum predictarum dedimus et concessimus ac pro nobis heredibus & successoribus nostris damus et concedimus per presentes. habendum gaudendum occupandum et exercendum officium predictum prefato Edwardo Buggyn per se vel per sufficientem deputatum suum siue deputatos suos sufficientes a tempore mortis Ricardi leys vltimi occupatoris euisdem officij ad terminum et pro termino vite ipsius Edwardi Buggyn vnacum omnibus vadijs feodis allocacionibus regardis proficuis iuribus libertatibus commoditatibus et advantagijs predicto officio quoquo modo pertinentibus siue spectantibus aut imposterum spectandis siue debendis. Et insuper de gracia certa sciencia et mero motu nostris predictis dedimus et concessimus ac per presentes pro nobis heredibus et successoribus nostris damus et concedimus eidem Edwardo Buggyn pro exercicio et occupacione antedicti officij vadium et feodum octo denariorum bone et legalis monete Anglie per diem. habendum gaudendum et percipiendum predictum vadium et feodum octo denariorum per diem prefato Edwardo Buggyn et assignatis suis a tempore mortis predicti Ricardi leys durante vita sua de Thesauro nostro heredum et successorum nostrorum ad Receptam Scaccarij nostri heredum et successorum nostrorum per manus Thesaurarij et Camerariorum nostrorum heredum et successorum nostrorum ibidem pro tempore existencium ad festa Pasche et sancti Michaelis Archangeli per equales porciones annuatim soluendum Aceciam dedimus et concessimus ac per presentes pro nobis heredibus et successoribus nostris damus et concedimus prefato Edwardo Buggyn pro liberatura et vestura suis pro exercicio officij predicti annuatim quatuor virgatas lanei panni precij cuiuslibet virge sex solidorum et octo denariorum . habendas et percipiendas eidem Edwardo Buggyn erga festum Natalis domini durante vita sua predicta ad magnam Garderobam nostram heredum et successorum nostrorum per manus Custodis siue Clerici eiusdem Garderobe nostre pro tempore existentis Et preterea sciatis quod nos de vberiori gracia nostra ac ex certa sciencia et mero motu nostris predictis ceterisque consideracionibus nos moventibus dedimus et concessimus ac per presentes pro nobis heredibus et successoribus nostris damus et concedimus prefato Edwardo Buggyn bonam et convenientem domum siue mansionem vnacum Cameris cellarijs sollarijs edificijs stabulis ortis et gardinis vbi Paviliones hale et tenta nostra posita sunt aut erunt per Magistrum dictorum pavilionum halarum et tentorum qui pro tempore fuerit de tempore in tempus assignandam in qua ipse Edwardus Buggyn et familia sua habitent. habendam et tenendam possidendam et gaudendam predictam domum siue mansionem cum suis necessarijs et pertinencijs predictis prefato Edwardo Buggyn et assignatis suis pro termino vite sue de dono nostro absque redditu compoto seu aliquo alio proinde nobis heredibus vel successoribus nostris aut alicui alio quoquo modo reddendo soluendo vel faciendo in tam amplis modo et forma prout predictus Ricardus leys aut aliquis alius officium supradictum occupans habuit et vnquam gauisus fuit seu habere et gaudere debuit racione exercicij premissorum seu eorum alicuius &c. Eo quod expressa mencio &c. In cuius rei &c. Teste Regina apud Westmonasterium tricesimo die Decembris.

per ipsam Reginam

vacant hee litteree patentes vnacum irrotulamento earumdem pro eo quod ix° die Octobris Anno regni domine Regine infrascripte xxvj° Edwardus Buggyn similiter infrascriptus venit coram dicta domina Regina in Cancellaria sua personaliter et sursumreddidit in manus dicte domine Regine totum ius titulum et interesse sua in litteris patentibus predictis contenta vnacum litteris patentibus predictis cancellandis Ideo ad requisicionem ipsius Edwardi littere patentes et irrotulamentum earumdem euacuantur cancellantur et omnino dampnantur.

C. WILLIAM HONNYNG APPOINTED 15 OCT. 1584.

Record Office. Patent Rolls. 26 Eliz. p. 13. m. 44 & 45.

De concessione ad vitam pro Willelmo Hunynge

*Thomas Egerton C. S.

*William *Honnyng

Regina &c. Omnibus ad quos &c. salutem Cum nos per litteras nostras patentes sub magno sigillo nostro Anglie confectas gerentes datam apud Westmonasterium tricesimo die Decembris Anno regni nostri terciodecimo nominauerimus assignauerimus et constituerimus Dilcetum Subditum nostrum Edwardum Buggin Clericum Contrarotulatorem omnium et singulorum Pavilionum et tentorum nostrorum Heredum et Successorum nostrorum vulgariter nuncupatorum tentes hales and Pavilions Necnon omnium et singulorum Iocorum revellorum Mascorum omnimodorum vesturarum Revellorum predictorum communiter vocatorum Revelles Maskes and Masking Garmentes infra Regnum nostrum Anglie et alibi Ac eidem Edwardo Buggin Officium Clerici Contrarotulatoris Pavilionum et tentorum nostrorum Necnon Revellorum et vesturarum predictorum pro nobis Heredibus et Successoribus nostris dederimus et concesserimus per easdem litteras nostras patentes Habendum gaudendum occupandum et excercendum officium predictum prefato Edwardo Buggyn per se vel per sufficientem deputatum suum siue deputatos suos sufficientes a tempore mortis Ricardi leys vltimi Occupatoris eiusdem Officij ad terminum et pro termino vite ipsius Edwardi Buggyn vnacum omnibus vadiis feodis allocacionibus regardis proficuis Iuribus libertatibus Commoditatibus et advauntagijs predicto officio quoquo modo pertinentibus siue spectantibus aut imposterum spectandis siue diliberendis Et insuper per easdem litteras patentes dederimus & concesserimus eidem Edwardo Buggyn pro exercitio et occupacione ante dicti officij vadium et feodum octo denariorum bone et legalis monete Anglie per diem Habendum gaudendum et percipiendum predictum vadium et feodum octo denariorum per diem prefato Edwardo Buggyn et assignatis suis a tempore mortis predicti Ricardi Leys durante vita sua de Thesaurario nostro Heredum et Successorum nostrorum ad receptam Scaccarij nostri heredum et successorum nostrorum per manus Thesaurarij et Camere nostre Heredum et Successorum nostrorum ibidem pro tempore existencium ad festa Pasche et sancti Michaelis Archangeli per equales porciones annuatim soluendum Ac etiam per easdem litteras patentes dederimus et concesserimus prefato Edwardo Buggyn pro liberatura et vestura suis pro exercitio officij predicti annuatim quatuor virgas lanei panni precij cuiuslibet virge sex solidorum et octo denariorum habendas et percipiendas eidem Edwardo Buggyn erga festum Natalis domini durante vita sua predicta ad magnam garde robam nostram Heredum et Successorum nostrorum per manus Custodis siue Clerici eiusdem garderobe nostre pro tempore existentis Et preterea cum nos per easdem litteras nostras patentes dederimus et concesserimus prefato Edwardo Buggyn bonam et convenientem domum siue Mansionem vnacum Cameris Cellarijs Sollarijs edificijs stabulis ortis et Gardinis vbi Paviliones hale et tenta nostra posita sunt aut erunt per Magistrum dictorum Paviliorum halarum et tentorum que pro tempore fuerit de tempore in tempus assignandam in qua ipse Edwardus Buggyn et familia sua habitarunt habendam et tenendam possidendam et gaudendam predictam domum siue mansionem cum suis necessarijs et pertinencijs predictis prefato Edwardo Buggin et assignatis suis pro termino vite sue de dono nostro absque Compoto reddendo seu aliquo alio proinde nobis Heredibus et Successoribus nostris aut alicui alij quoquomodo reddendo solue[n]do vel faciendo in tam amplis modo et forma prout predictus Ricardus leys aut aliquis alius officium supradictum occupans habuit et vnquam gauisus fuit seu habere et gaudere debuit racione exercitij premissorum seu eorum alicuius prout per easdem litteras patentes plenius liquet et apparet. Quiquidem Edwardus Buggyn predictas litteras patentes ac totum ius statum titulum interesse et demaundam sua que de et in officio predicto et ceteris premissis vigore dictarum litterarum patencium habuit nobis sursum reddit et restituit cancellandas Ea intencione quod nos litteras nostras patentes et aliam concessionem nostram de predicto officio vnacum predicto annuale feodo et ceteris premissis superius specificatis dilecto nobis Willelmo Hunynge Generoso in forma sequenti facere et concedere dignaremur Quamquidem sursum redditionem acceptamus per presentes Sciatis igitur quod nos pro diuersis causis et consideracionibus nos ad presens specialiter moventibus de gracia nostra speciali ac ex certa sciencia et mero motu nostris nominauimus assignauimus et constituimus ac per presentes pro nobis Heredibus et Successoribus nostris nominamus assignamus et constituimus prefatum Willelmum Hunyng Clericum Contrarotulatorem omnium et singulorum Pavilionum halarum et tentorum nostrorum Heredum|et Successorum nostrorum vulgariter nuncupatorum Tentes Hales and Pavilions Necnon omnium et singulorum Iocorum Revellorum Mascorum omnimodorum vesturarum Revellorum predictorum communiter vocatorum Revelles maskes and Masking Garmentes infra Regnum nostrum Anglie et alibi ac eidem Willelmo Hunyng officium Contra[ro]tulatoris Pavilionum Halarum et Tentorum nostrorum Necnon Revellorum et vesturarum predictarum dedimus et concessimus et pro nobis et Successoribus nostris damus et concedimus per presentes habendum gaudendum occupandum et excercendum officium predictum prefato Willelmo Hunyng per se vel per suffic[i]entem deputatum suum siue deputatos suos sufficientes a festo sancti Michaelis Archangeli vltimi preterito ad terminum et pro termino vite ipsius Willelmi Hunnyng vnacum omnibus et omnimodis vadijs feodis allocacionibus regardis proficuis Iuribus libertatibus commoditatibus et advauntagijs predicto officio quoquomodo pertinentibus siue spectantibus aut imposterum spectandis siue debendis. Et insuper de gracia nostra speciali ac ex certa sciencia et mero motu nostris predictis dedimus et concessimus ac pro nobis Heredibus et Successoribus nostris per presentes damus et concedimus eidem Willelmo Hunnynge pro exercitio et occupacione officij predicti vadium et feodum octo denariorum bone et legalis monete Anglie per diem Habendum gaudendum et percipiendum predictum vadium et feodum octo denariorum per diem prefato Willelmo Hunnynge et assignatis suis a predicto festo sancti Michaelis Archangeli vltimo preterito durante vita sua de Thesaurario nostro Heredum et Successorum nostrorum ad Receptam Scaccarij nostri Heredum et Successorum nostrorum per manus Thesaurarij et Camerariorum nostrorum Heredum et Successorum nostrorum ibidem pro tempore existencium ad festa Pasche et sancti Michaelis Archangeli per equales porciones annuatim Soluendum. Ac etiam dedimus et concessimus ac per presentes pro nobis heredibus et successoribus nostris damus et concedimus prefato Willelmo Hunnynge pro liberatura et vestura suis pro exercitio officij predicti annuatim quatuor virgas lanei panni precij cuiuslibet virge sex solidorum et octo denariorum habendas et percipiendas eidem Willelmo Hunnyng erga festum Natalis domini durante vita sua predicta ad magnam Garderobam nostram Heredum et Successorum nostrorum per manus Custodis siue Clerici eiusdem Gardrobe nostre pro tempore existentis Et preterea Sciatis quod nos de vberiori gracia nostra ac ex certa sciencia et mero motu nostris predictis ceterisque causis et consideracionibus nos ad presens specialiter moventibus dedimus et concessimus ac per presentes pro nobis Heredibus et Successoribus nostris damus et concedimus prefato Willelmo Hunnyng bonam et sufficientem domum siue mansionem vnacum Cameris Cellarijs Sollarijs edificijs Stabulis Ortis et Gardinis vbi Paviliones hale et tenta nostra posita sunt aut erunt per Magistrum dictorum Pavilionum halarum et tentorum qui pro tempore fuerit de tempore in tempus assignandam in qua ipse Willelmus Hunnynge et familia sua habitent habendam et tenendam possidendam et gaudendam predictam domum siue mansionem cum suis necessarijs et pertinencijs predictis prefato Willelmo Hunnynge et assignatis suis pro termino vite sue de dono nostro absque reddendo Compoto seu aliquo alio proinde nobis heredibus et successoribus nostris aut alicui alij quoquo modo reddendo soluendo vel faciendo in tam amplis modo et forma prout predictus Ricardus leys aut predictus Edwardus Buggyn aut aliquis alius siue al[i]qui alij officium predictum habens occupans et exercens habentes occupantes et exercentes habuit occupauit seu vnquam gauisus fuit habuerunt occupauerunt seu vnquam gauisi fuerunt vel habere occupare seu gaudere debuit vel debuerunt racione exercitij premissorum seu eorum alicuius Eo quod expressa mencio &c. In cuius rei &c. Teste Regina apud Westmonasterium decimo quinto die Octobris.

per breve sub priuato Sigillo

vacat istud Irrotulamentum harum litterarum patencium pro eo quod vicesimo primo die Iunij Anno regni infrascripte domine Regine xxxviij° Annoque domini 1596. infrauocatus Willelmus Hunynge venit coram dicta domina Regina in Cancellaria sua personaliter constitutus et predictas litteras patentes ac totum ius titulum et interesse sua de et in eisdem dicte domine Regine pure sponte et absolute sursumreddidit et restituit cancellandas Ideo ad requisicionem ipsius Willelmi Honinge cancellantur et omnino dampnantur ac tam istud Irrotulamentum quam littere patentes predicte evacuantur

D. EDMUND PAKENHAM APPOINTED 25 JUNE 1596

Record Office Patent. Rolls. 38 Eliz. p. 7. m. 35-6

De concessione officij pro Edmundo Pakenham

Regina Omnibus ad quos &c. salutem Cum nos per litteras nostras patentes sub magno sigillo nostro Anglie confectas gerentes datam apud Westmonasterium quinto decimo die Octobris Anno regni nostri vicesimo sexto nominauimus assignauimus et constituimus dilectum subditum nostrum Willelmum Hunninge Clericum Contrarotulatorem omnium et singulorum pauilionum halarum et tentorum nostrorum heredum et successorum nostrorum vulgariter nuncupatorum tentes hales and pauilions necnon omnium et singulorum iocorum revellorum mascorum omnimodorum vesturarum revellorum predictorum communiter vocatorum revells maskes and maskinge garmentes infra regnum nostrum Anglie et alibi Ac eidem Willelmo Huninge officium Clerici Contrarotulatoris pavilionum halarum et tentorum nostrorum necnon revellorum et vesturarum predictorum pro nobis heredibus et successoribus nostris dedimus et concedimus per easdem litteras nostras patentes habendum gaudendum occupandum et exercendum officium predictum prefato Willelmo Hunninge per se vel sufficientem deputatum suum siue deputatos suos sufficientes ad terminum et pro termino vite ipsius Willelmi Hunninge vnacum omnibus vadijs feodis allocacionibus regardis proficuis iuribus libertatibus comoditatibus et aduauntagijs predicto officio quoquomodo pertinentibus siue spectantibus aut imposterum spectandis siue debendis Et insuper per easden litteras patentes dedimus et concessimus eidem Willelmo Hunninge pro exercicio et occupacione dicti officij vadium et feodum octo denariorum bone et legalis monete Anglie per diem habendum gaudendum et percipiendum predictum vadium et feodum octo denariorum per diem prefato Willelmo Hunninge et assignatis suis duran[te] vita sua de thesauro nostro heredum et successorum nostrorum ad Receptam Scaccarij nostri heredum et successorum nostrorum per manus Thesaurarij et Camerariorum nostrorum heredum et successorum nostrorum ibidem pro tempore existencium ad festa Pasche et sancti Michaelis Archangeli per equales porciones annuatim soluendum Aceciam per easdem litteras nostras patentes dedimus et concessimus prefato Willelmo Huninge pro liberatura et vestura suis pro exercicio officii predicti an[n]uatim quatuor virgas lanei panni precij cuiuslibet virge sex solidorum et octo denariorum habendas et percipiendas eidem Willelmo Hunninge erga festum Natalis domini durante vita sua predicta ad magnam Garderobam nostram heredum et successorum nostrorum per manus Custodis siue Clerici eiusdem Garderobe nostre pro tempore existentis Et preterea cum nos per easdem litteras nostras patentes dederimus et concesserimus prefato Willelmo bonam et convenientem domum siue mansionem vnacum Cameris Cellarijs solarijs edificijs stabulis ortis et gardinis vbi pauiliones hale et tenta nostra posita sunt aut erunt per magistrum dictorum pauilionum halarum et tentorum qui pro tempore fuerit de tempore in tempus assignandam in qua ipse Willelmus Hunninge et familia sua habitarent habendam et tenendam possidendam et gaudendam predictam domum siue mansionem cum suis necessarijs et pertinencijs predictis prefato Willelmo Hunninge et assignatis suis pro termino vite sue de dono nostro ab[s]que compoto reddendo seu aliquo alio proinde nobis heredibus et successoribus nostris aut alicui alij quoquo modo reddendo soluendo vel faciendo in tam amplis modo et forma prout quidam Ricardus leys et Edwardus Buggyn et prefatus Willelmus Hunninge aut aliquis alius siue aliqui alij officium predictum habens occupans et exercens habentes occupantes et exercentes habuit occupauit seu vnquam gauisus fuit habuerunt occupauerunt seu vnquam gauisi fuerunt vel habere occupare seu gaudere debuit seu debuerunt racione exercicij·premissorum seu eorum alicuius prout per easdem litteras patentes plenius liquet et apparet Quiquidem Willelmus Hunninge predictas litteras patentes ac totum ius statum titulum interesse et demaundam sua que de et in officio predicto et ceteris premissis vigore dictarum litterarum patencium habuit nobis sursumreddit et restituit cancellandas Ea intencione quod nos litteras nostras patentes et aliam concessionem nostram de predicto annuali feodo et ceteris premissis superius specificatis dilecto seruienti nostro Edmundo Pakenham generoso in forma sequenti facere et concedere dignaremur quamquidem sursumredditionem acceptamus per presentes Sciatis igitur quod nos pro diuersis causis et consideracionibus nos ad presens specialiter moventibus de gracia nostra speciali ac ex certa sciencia et mero motu nostris nominauimus assignauimus et constituimus ac per presentes pro nobis heredibus et successoribus nostris nominamus assignamus et constituimus prefatum Edmundum Pakenham Clericum Contrarotulatorem omnium et singulorum pauilionum halarum et tentorum nostrorum heredum et successorum nostrorum vulgariter nuncupatorum tentes hales and pauilions necnon omnium et singulorum iocorum revellorum et mascorum omnium vesturarum revellorum predictorum communiter vocatorum revells maskes and maskinge garmentes infra regnum nostrum Anglie et alibi ac eidem Edmundo Pakenham officium Contrarotulatoris pauilionum halarum et tentorum nostrorum necnon revellorum et vesturarum predictarum dedimus et concessimus ac pro nobis heredibus et successoribus nostris damus et concedimus per presentes habendum gaudendum occupandum et exercendum officium predictum prefato Edmundo Pakenham per se vel per sufficientem deputatum suum siue deputatos suos sufficientes a festo sancti Michaelis Archangeli vltimo preterito ad terminum et pro termino vite ipsius Edmundi Pakenham vnacum omnibus et omnimodis vadijs feodis allocacionibus regardis proficuis iuribus libertatibus comoditatibus et aduantagijs predicto officio quoquo modo pertinentibus siue spectantibus aut imposterum spectandis siue debendis Et insuper de gracia nostra speciali ac ex certa sciencia et mero motu nostris predictis dedimus et concessimus ac pro nobis heredibus et successoribus nostris per presentes damus et concedimus eidem Edmundo Pakenham pro exercicio et occupacione officij predicti vadium et feodum octo denariorum bone et legalis monete Anglie per diem habendum gaudendum et percipiendum predictum vadium et feodum octo denariorum per diem prefato Edmundo Pakenham et assignatis suis a predicto ffesto sancti Michaelis Archangeli durante vita ipsius Edmundi

Pakenham de thesauro nostro heredum et successorum nostrorum ad Receptam Scaccarij nostri heredum et successorum nostrorum per manus Thesaurarij et Camerariornm nostrorum heredum et successorum nostrorum ibidem pro tempore existencium ad festa Pasche et sancti Michaelis Archangeli per equales porciones annuatim soluendum Aceciam dedimus et concessimus ac per presentes pro nobis heredibus et successoribus nostris damus et concedimus prefato Edmundo Pakenham pro liberatura et vestura suis pro exercicio officij predicti annuatim quatuor virgas lanei panni precij cuiuslibet virge sex solidorum et octo denariorum habendas et percipiendas eidem Edmundo Pakenham erga festum Natalis domini durante vita ipsius Edmundi Pakenham ad magnam Garderobam nostram heredum et successorum nostrorum per manus Custodis siue Clerici eiusdem Garderobe nostre pro tempore existentis Et preterea sciatis quod nos de vberiori gracia nostra ac ex certa sciencia et mero motu nostris predictis ceterisque causis et consideracionibus nos ad presens specialiter moventibus dedimus et concessimus ac per presentes pro nobis heredibus et successoribus nostris damus et concedimus prefato Edmundo Pakenham bonam et convenientem domum siue mansionem vnacum Cameris Cellarijs solarijs edificijs stabulis hortis et gardinis vbi paviliones hale et tenta nostra posita sunt aut erunt per Magistrum dictorum pauilionum halarum et tentorum qui pro tempore fuerit de tempore in tempus assignandam in qua ipse Edmundus Pakenham et familia sua habitent habendam et tenendam possidendam et gaudendam predictam domum siue mansionem cum suis necessarijs et pertinencijs predictis prefato Edmundo Pakenham et assignatis suis durante vita ipsius Edmundi Pakenham de dono nostro absque redditu compoto seu aliquo alio proinde nobis heredibus et successoribus nostris aut alicui alij quocumque modo reddendo soluendo vel faciendo in tam amplis modo et forma prout predictus Ricardus leys Edwardus Buggin et Willelmus Hunninge aut aliquis alius siue aliqui alij officium predictum habens occupans et exercens habentes occupantes et exercentes habuit occupauit seu vnquam gauisus fuit habuerunt occupauerunt seu vnquam gauisi fuerunt vel habere occupare seu gaudere debuit vel debuerunt racione exercicij premissorum seu eorum alicuius Eo quod expressa mencio &c. In cuius rei testimonium &c. Teste Regina apud Westmonasterium vicesimo quinto die Iunij

per breue de priuato sigillo.

IX

Royal Appointments of Clerks

A. THOMAS PHILLIPS APPOINTED 7 MAY 1546.

Record Office. Patent Rolls. 38 Henry VIII. p. 2. m. 16.

pro Thoma Philippys de concessione ad vitam.

Rex Omnibus ad quos &c. salutem. Sciatis quod nos de gracia nostra speciali ex certa sciencia et mero motu nostris dedimus et concessimus ac per presentes damus et concedimus Thome Philippes Officium clerici omnium et singulorum Pavillonum halarum et tentorum nostrorum vulgariter nuncupatorum tentes hales pavillions. Necnon omnium et singulorum iocorum revelorum et mascorum nostrorum omnimodorumque vesturarum reuellorum communiter vocatorum revelles maskes and maskinge Garmentes infra hoc regnum nostrum Anglie et alibi ipsumque Thomam Philippes clericum Pavillonum halarum tentorum iocorum revellorum et mascorum vesturarumque revelorum nostrorum et eorum cuiuslibet facimus ordinauimus et constituimus per presentes. habendum gaudendum et exercendum Officium predictum per se vel per sufficientem deputatum suum siue deputatos suos sufficientes pro termimo vite sue cum omnibus regardijs commoditatibus proficuis et aduantagijs dicto Officio debentibus siue accidentibus Et insuper de vberiori gracia nostra damus ac per presentes concedimus prefato Thome Philippes tam vadium et feodum octo denariorum per diem pro exercicio et occupacione dicti Officij quam viginti quatuor solidorum per Annum bone et legalis monete nostre Anglie sub nomine vesture et liberature sue. habenda et annuatim percipienda predicta vadium et feodum octo denariorum per diem ad festa Annunciacionis beate Marie virginis et sancti Michaelis Archangeli Necnon predictos viginti quatuor solidos per Annum pro vestura sua erga festum Natalis domini tantum singulis Annis prefato Thome Philippes vel assignatis suis ad receptam Scaccarij nostri per manus Thesaurarij et Camerariorum nostrorum ibidem pro tempore existencium per equales porciones. Sciatis preterea quod nos de gracia nostra predicta ac pro quibusdam alijs causis et occasionibus nos ad hoc specialiter mouentibus dedimus et concessimus prout per presentes damus et concedimus prefato Thome Philippes bonan et conuenientem domum siue mansionem infra limites et procinctus domus nuper fratrum predicatorum in Ciuitate nostra londonie existentis vbi pavillones hale et tentoria nostra ponantur cum edificijs cellarijs solarijs stabulo ortu et gardino sufficientibus per Magistrum dictorum pavillonum halarum et tentorum nostrorum qui pro tempore fuerit de tempore in tempus assignandam in qua ipse Thomas et familia sua habitent. habendam tenendam possidend*am* *et* gaudend*am* p*rēdictam* domu*m* siue mansionem cum suis necessarijs *et* p*er*tin*encijs* p*redict*is p*re*fato Thome vel assignatis suis p*ro* *ter*mino vite sue de dono n*ost*ro absque redditu compoto seu aliquo al[i]o p*ro*inde nob*is* hered*ibus* vel successorib*us* n*ost*ris quoquomodo reddend*o* soluend*o* vel faciend*o* Eo q*uo*d exp*r*essa mencio &c. In cuius rei &c. T*este* R*ege* apud Grenewiche vij die Maij

per breue de priuato Sigillo &c.

B. THOMAS BLAGRAVE APPOINTED 25 MARCH 1560.

Record Office. Patent Rolls. 2 Eliz. p. 15 m. 40

De concessione ad vitam pro Thoma Blagrave

Regina Omnibus ad quos &c salutem. Sciatis quod nos de gracia nostra speciali ac ex certa sciencia et mero motu nostris dedimus et concessimus ac per presentes pro nobis heredibus et successoribus nostris damus et concedimus Thome Blagrave generoso Officium Clerici omnium et singulorum Paviliorum halarum et tentariorum nostrorum quorumcumque communiter nuncupatorum tentes hales pauylions and hutes et huiusmodi consimilium Necnon omnium et singulorum Iocorum Reuellorum Mascorum et triumphorum vulgariter nuncupatorum lez Reuelles maskes Triumphes Iustes tyltes torneys Banketing howses sportes and pastymes ipsumque Thomam Blagrave Clericum pauilionum halarum tentoriorum et Iocarum Reuellorum mascorum et Triumphorum nostrorum ac ceterorum omnium et singulorum predictorum facimus ordinamus et constituimus per presentes. habendum gaudendum occupandum et exercendum Officium predictum tam per se quam per sufficientem deputatum suum siue deputatos suos sufficientes a tempore mortis Thome Phillippes vltimi Clerici omnium premissorum ad terminum et pro termino vite eiusdem Thome Blagrave vnacum omnibus allocacionibus regardijs proficuis commoditatibus et aduantagijs quibuscumque eidem Officio quouismodo pertinentibus siue spectantibus ac in tam amplis modo et forma prout dictus Thomas Phillipps aut aliquis alius siue aliqui alij dictum Officium ac omnia et singula premissa aut eorum aliquod habens occupans vel exercens habuit tenuit exercuit occupauit percepit vsus vel gauisus fuit aut habere tenere exercere occupare percipere vti vel gaudere consueuit vel debuit consueuerunt vel debuerunt Et insuper de vberiori gracia nostra dedimus et concessimus ac per presentes pro nobis heredibus et successoribus nostris damus et concedimus prefato Thome Blagrave pro exercicione et occupacione Officij predicti tam vadium et feodum octo denariorum per diem quam viginti quatuor solidos per annum pro liberatura et vestura sua. habendum et annuatim percipiendum predictum vadium siue feodum octo denariorum per diem ac dictos viginti quatuor solidos pro liberatura sua prefato Thome Blagrave et assignatis suis a tempore mortis dicti Thome Phillipps pro termino vite ipsius Thome Blagrave de Tesauro nostro heredum et successorum nostrorum ad Receptam Scaccarij nostri heredum et successorum nostrorum per manus Thesaurarij et Camerariorum nostrorum heredum et successorum nostrorum predictorum ad duos anni terminos videlicet ad festa annunciacionis beate Marie virginis et sancti Michaelis Archangeli p*er* equales porc*ion*es annuatim soluend*um* Ac p*reter*ea volum*us* *et* concedim*us* q*uo*d p*re*fat*us* Thomas Blagrave h*ab*ebit bonam *et* conuenientem domu*m* siue mansionem cum edificijs cellarijs solarijs Stabulo orto *et* gardin*o* sufficient*ibus* qua ip*s*e Thomas cum familia sua inh*ab*itent p*er* Mag*ist*ros tentorior*um* *et* reuelor*um* n*ost*ror*um* p*redict*orum aut eor*um* alter*orum* de tempore in tempus assignand*am* vbi Staurum eor*um*dem Officior*um* aut eor*um* alt*er*ius reponant*ur*. h*ab*end*am* tenend*am* possidend*am* *et* gaudend*am* d*ict*am domu*m* siue mansionem cum suis necessarijs p*er*tinen*cijs* p*re*fato Thome *et* assign*atis* suis p*ro* t*er*mino vite sue absq*ue* reddit*u* compoto seu aliquo alio p*ro*inde nob*is* hered*ibus* vel successorib*us* n*ost*ris quoquomodo reddend*o* soluend*o* vel faciend*o* Eo q*uo*d exp*re*ssa mencio &c. In cuius rei &c. T*este* R*egina* apud Westm*onasterium* xxv die Marcij

p*er* bre*ue* de priuato Sigillo &c.

X

Royal Appointments of Yeomen

A. *JOHN HOLTE APPOINTED 1 JULY 1550*

Record Office. Patent Rolls. 4 Edward VI. p. 5. m. 32

pro Ioh*anne* holte de conc*essione* ad vitam

Edwarde the sixte &c. / To all to whom &c. / greting / whereas our moste deaer father of famous memorie king henry theight late king of Englande by hys l*ett*res patentes vnder his great Seale of Englande bearing date at westm*inster* the xxvij daye of October in the xxxj^th^ yere of his mooste noble and p*ro*sperus Reigne did geve and graunte vnto his welbelouid Iohn Bridges the Office of yoman or keap*er* of his vestures or apparell of all and singuler his maskes Revell*es* and disguysing*es* and also of the apparell and Trappers of all and singuler his horses ordeyned and appointed and hereafter to be ordeyned and appointed for his Iustes and Turneis To haue holde occupie and enioye the said office to the said Iohn Bridges and his sufficient deputie or deputies for the terme of his lief withe the wages and ffees of vj^d^ sterling by the daye for the overseing and saufe keaping of the same To be had and yerely p*er*ceyuid of our treasuer at the recepte of our eschequier by the hand*es* of our treasourer and Chamberleynes for the tyme being at the feast*es* of seinte Michaell tharchaungell and Easter by evyn porc*i*ons And further gaue and grauntid vnto the said Iohn Bridges yerely during his said lieff one lyu*er*y Cote suche as yeoman officers of his howseholde had of hym to be yerely p*er*ceyuid and had at his great warde robe by thand*es* of the keaper or Clerke of the same for the tyme being And to haue and enioye one sufficient house or mancion to be assigned vnto the same Iohn for the sewer better and saufe keaping of his saide vestures apparell and trappers together withe all manner co*m*modities p*ro*ffitt*es* and aduantagies to the said office to be due and accustomed or in any wise apperteynyng as by the said l*ett*res patentes it dothe and maye more at length appeare fforasmuche as the said Iohn Bridges is contentid and fully mynded willinglye to yelde vppe and surrender the said l*ett*res patentes grauntid to hym in forme aforesaid into our Chaunc*er*y to be cancelled and as we vnderstande are all reddye cancellyd theyr to the intente that we wolde vouchesafe to graunte other l*ett*res patent*es* of the said office to our welbelouid s*er*uaunt Iohn holte one of the Sewers of our Chamber in manner and forme following / we let you wete that of our grace especiall and for c*er*teyne causes and considerac*i*ons vs specially moving withe thaduise and consente of our priuey Counseill we haue gevyn and grauntid and by theis p*re*sentes doo geve and graunte vnto the said

Iohn holte thoffice of yoman or keap*er* of our vestures or apparell of all and singuler our ma*s*kes Revelles and disguysing*es* and also of the apparell and Trappers of all and singuler our horses ordeynid and appointid and hereafter to be ordeynid and appointid for our Iustis and Turneys And we ordeyne constitute and make the same Iohn holte by theis *presentes* yeoman or kep*er* of our vestures or apparell of all and singuler our maskes Revelles and disguysinges And also of the apparell and Trappers of all and singuler our horses ordeynyd and appointid or hereafter to be ordeynid and appointed for our Iustes and Turneys To haue holde occupie an[d] enioy the said office to the saide Iohn holte and his sufficient deputie or deputies for the te*r*me of the lief naturall of the said Iohn holte withe the wages and fees of six pence sterling by the daye for the ou*er*seing and saufe keping of the same / To be had and yerely p*er*ceyuid of our treasourer at the Recepte of our Eschequyer by thand*es* of our Chamberlayns and Treasourer for the tyme being at the feast*es* of Seint Michaell tharchaungell And Easter by evyn porc*i*ons And further we geve vnto the said Iohn holte yerely during his said lief one lyu*er*ye Cote suche as yeoman officers of our householde haue of vs / To be yerely Receyuid and hadd at our great warderoppe by thand*es* of the keaper or Clerke of the same for tyme being And to haue and enioye one Sufficient howse or mansion to be assigned vnto the same Iohn holte for the sewer better and saufe keping of our said vestures Apparrell and Trappers to gether withe all manner co*m*modities p*r*offit*es* and aduauntagis to the said office to be due and accustomed or in any wise apparteynyng Albeit that exp*r*esse mencion &c. / In witnes whereof &c. / T*este* R*ege* apud leighes primo die Iulij /

p*er* bre*ui* de priuato Sigillo /

B. JOHN ARNOLDE APPOINTED 11 DEC. 1571

Record Office. Patent Rolls. 14 Eliz. p. 9 m. 18

De con*cessione* ad vitam p*ro* Ioh*anne* Arnolde.

Elizabeth by the grace of god &c. To all to whom theis our l*ett*res shall co*m*me greating we lett you witte that of our grace especiall and for certen causes and good consideracions vs speciallye movinge we have given and graunted and by theis p*re*sent*es* do give and graunt vnto our welbeloved Subiecte Iohn Arnold the Office of yeoman or keper of our vestures or apparell of all and singuler our maskes Revells and disguysing*es* and also of the apparrell and trappers of all and singuler our horses ordeyned and appoynted and hereafter to be ordayned and appoynted for our Iust*es* and Turneys And we doe ordeyne constitute and make the same Iohn Arnold by theis p*re*sent*es* yeoman or keper of our vestures or apparell of all and singuler our Mask*es* Revell*es* and disguysing*es* and also of the apparell and Trappers of all and singuler our horses ordayned & appoynted or hereafter to be ordayned and appoynted for our Iustic*es* and Tourneis To have holde occupye and enioye the said office to the said Iohn Arnolde and his sufficient deputye or deputyes for terme of the lyfe naturall of the said Iohn Arnold with the wages and fees of sixe pence sterlinge by the daye for the overseinge & saulfe kepinge of the same to be had and yerelye p*er*ceyved of our treasure at the receipte of our Exchequyer by the hand*es* of our Chamberlaynes and treasourer for the tyme beinge at the feast*es* of saynt Michaell the Archaungell and Ester by even porcyons And further we give vnto the said Iohn Arnold yerelye duringe his said lyfe one lyvery Cote suche as yeomen officers of our householde have of vs To be yerelye had & receyved at our greate warderobe by the hand*es* of the keper or clerke of the same for the tyme beinge And to have and enioye one sufficient house or mancion to be assigned vnto the said Iohn Arnold for the sure better and saufe kepinge of our said vestures apparrell and Trappers together with all maner co*m*modityes and aduantag*es* to the said office to be due and accustomed or in anye wise app*er*tayninge in as large ample and beneficiall manner and forme as Iohn holte deceassed or any other or others yeomen or kepers of all and singuler the p*re*mysses abovemencioned have had and enioyed or of right ought to have and enioye the same Albeit that expresse mencion &c. In witnes whereof &c. witnes our selfe at westm*inster* the eleventh daye of December.

p*er* bre*ue* de priuato sigillo &c.

C. WALTER FYSHE APPOINTED 29 JAN. 1573-4

Record Office. Patent Rolls. 16 Eliz. p. 4. m. 22

De conc*essione* ad vitam p*ro* Walt*ero* ffyshe

Elizabeth by the grace of god &c. To all to whome &c. greeting. wee lett you wytt that of our grace especyall *cer*teyne knowledge and mere moc*i*on and in considerac*i*on of the good and faythfull s*er*uice heretofore donne vnto vs by our welbeloued s*er*uaunte walter ffyshe wee haue giuen and graunted and by theis p*re*sentes for vs our heires and successors doe gyve and graunte vnto the said walter ffyshe thoffice of yoman or keper of our vestures or apparell of all and singuler our Maskes Revelles and disguysing*es* and also of the apparell and trappers of all and singuler our horses ordeyned and appoynted and hereafter to be ordeyned and appoynted for our Iustes and Turneys And wee doe ordeyne constitute and make the same walter ffyshe by theis p*re*sentes yoman or keper of our vestures or apparell of all and singuler our maskes Revelles and disguysinges And also of the apparell and Trappers of all and singuler our horses ordeyned and appoynted or hereafter to be ordeyned and appoynted for our Iustes and Turneys To haue holde occupye and enioye the said office to the said walter ffyshe and his sufficient deputie or deputies for t*er*me of the lyffe naturall of the said walter ffysshe with the waiges and ffees of sixe pence sterling by the daye for the overseing and salfe kepeing of the same to be had and yerely p*er*ceaved of the Treasure of vs our heires and successors at the Receipte of Thexchequier of vs our heires and successors at westm*inster* by thandes of the Th*reasu*rer and Chamb*er*leynes of vs our heires and successo*rs* ther for the tyme being at the feast*es* of tha*n*nunciac*i*on of our lady and saynt Michaell tharchaungell by evin porc*i*ons And further we giue vnto the said walter ffyshe yerely duringe his said lyffe one lyverye coate such as yeomen officers of our houshould haue of vs to be yerely had and p*er*ceaved at our greate warderobe by the handes of the keper or Clerke of the same for the tyme beinge And to haue and enioye one sufficiente house or manc*i*on to be assigned vnto the said walter ffysshe for the sure better and safe kepeing of our said vestures apparell and Trappers togeather with all mann*er* co*m*modities and adu*a*ntages to the said office to be dewe and accustomed or in any wise app*er*teyning in as lardge ample and benefyciall mann*er* and forme as Iohn Arnolde deceased or any other or others yeomen kepers of all and singuler the p*re*misses above mencyoned haue had and enioyed or of right ought to haue and enioye the same Albeit exp*re*sse mencyon &c. In wytnesse whereof &c. T*este* R*egina* apud westm*onasterium* xxix die Ianuarij

p*er* bre*ue* de priuato Sigillo

D. EDWARD KIRKHAM APPOINTED 28 APR. 1586

Record Office. Patent Rolls. 28 Eliz. p. I. m. 11.

De concessione ad vitam pro Edwardo kyrkham

Elizabeth by the grace of God &c. To all men to whome theyse presentes shall comme greeting knowe ye that we in consyderacyon of the diligent and faythfull servyce our welbeloved subiecte Edwarde kyrkham hathe donne vnto vs in the offyce of our Revelles and for other good causes vs herevnto specyallye moving have geven and graunted and by theyse presentes for vs our heyres and successors do gyve and graunte vnto the sayd Edward kyrkham the Offyce of yeoman or keper of our vestures or apparell of all and singuler our Maskes Revelles and disguysinges and also of the apparell and trappers of all and singuler our horses ordeyned and appointed and hereafter to be ordeyned and appoynted for our Iustes and Turneys And we doe ordeyne constytute and make the same Edwarde kyrkham by theyse presentes yeoman or keper of our vestures or apparrell of all and singuler our maskes Revelles and disguysinges and also of the apparrell and trappers of all and singuler our horses ordeyned and appoynted or hereafter to be ordeyned and appoynted for our Iustes and Turneys To have holde occupye and enioye the sayd Offyce to the sayd Edward kyrkham and hys Deputye or deputyes for tearme of the naturall lyfe of the sayd Edwarde kyrkham wyth the wages and fee of Syx pence by the daye sterling for the overseing and safe keping of the same To be had and yearelye perceyved of the treasure of vs our heyres and successors at the Receypte of the Exchequer of vs our heyres and Successors at westmynster by the handes of the Treasorer and Chambrelaynes of vs our heyres and successors there for the tyme being at the feastes of Thannuncyacyon of our ladye and Saynt Mychaell tharchangell by even porcyons from the daye of the deathe of walter ffyshe deceased And further we doe gyve vnto the sayd Edwarde kyrkham yerelye during hys sayd lyfe one lyverye Coate suche as the yeomen Offycers of our howseholde have of vs to be yearelye had and perceyved at our Greate wardrobe by the handes of the keper or Clarke of the same for the tyme being And to have and enioye one suffycyent house or mansyon as hereafter shalbe assigned vnto the sayd Edwarde kyrkham for the suer better and safe keeping of our sayd vestures apparrell and trappers together wythall manner of other commodytyes and advantages to the sayd Offyce to be due and accustomed or in anye wyse apperteynyng in as large ample and benefycyall manner and forme as the sayd walter ffyshe deceased or anye other or others yeomen kepers of all and singuler the premysses above mencyoned have had and enioyed or of ryghte oughte to have had and enioyed the same Althoughe expresse mencyon &c. In wytnes whereof &c. wytnes our selfe at westmynster the eight and Twentyth daye of Aprill

per breue de priuato sigillo &c.

PART II

ACCOUNTS

From Christmas 1558 to 30 September 1559

viz.

Loseley Mss.

Anno Primo Reginæ Elizabethæ et *Domini* 1558.

Translatinge newe makinge garnysshinge furnysshinge and fynysshinge of dyu*ers* and sundrye garment*es* Apparell vestures and *proper*tyes aswell of Maskes as for playes and other pastymes sett forthe and shewen in her M*aiesties* *pre*sence with the chaunge and Alteracion of the same to *ser*ve her Highnes pleasure and determynacion as occasion required from tyme to tyme upon comaundement to be in Areddines when it was called ffor.

vid*elicet* agaynste

***Chr*istmas Neweyeres tyde**/ & **Twelf tyde** / that yeare. and ageanste the **Coronacion** / foloinge aft*er* Twelftyde.

The Charges aswell of wages and hire of Artyfficers woorkemen and others woorkinge and attendinge thereon as otherwyse rysinge and growinge from the xjth daye of decembre vntyll the viijth daye of Ianuarye d*i*cto anno as Herunder the p*ar*ties names and Somes of mony dewe and wherefore p*er*ticlerlye ensue

vid*elicet*

Taylo*urs* workinge by the daye and nighte at like rate

	Dayes	Night*es*	
Iohn holte yeman at ij^{s} the daye	28	3	lxij^{s}
Thomas Clatterbocke at xij^{d}	28	3	xxxj^{s}
Thomas Emerye	20	2	xxij^{s}
Rob*ert* kyllicke	22	1	xxiij^{s}
Henrye Edneye	22	2	xxiiij^{s}
Thomas vaughan	28	3	xxxj^{s}
Davy Evans	28	3	xxxj^{s}
Iohn dyggins	28	3	xxxj^{s}
Thomas ware	18	1	xix^{s}
George daylye	19		xix^{s}

* T Blagrave
* Iohn holtės marke †
* Rychard Leys

f° 25 r.

	dayes	nightes	
Richard myllwo*or*the	28	3	xxxj^{s}
Thomas Bo*or*man	28	3	xxxj^{s}
Humfreye watson	28	3	xxxj^{s}
Thomas hardinge	16		xvj^{s}
George Gylbecke.	14	1	xv^{s}
Thomas norrys	13		xiii^{s}

Summa — xxj^{li} x^{s}

Hosyer working by greate

Hewe brise for the Makinge of vj payere of nether sockes of vellat — iij^{s} vj payre of sarsnett sloppes — iij^{s} viij payere of netherstock*es* — iiij^{s} vj pere of blacke vellat sleves — iij^{s} and for iij dayes woorkinge by ye daye — iij^{s} — xvj^{s}

Summa patet

Hatmaker by the greate

Rob*er*t Twesyll for the garnysshinge of iiij^{or} cardynalls hatt*es* at ix^{s} the pece — xxxvj^{s} for the Makinge of the same hatt*es* at ij^{s} vj^{d} the pece — x^{s} for v yard*es* of buckeram to the same hatt*es* at viij^{d} the yarde — iij^{s} iiij^{d} for the makinge of vj prestes cappes vj^{s} for the makinge of toe battyn cappes — v^{s} for the makinge of xliiij band*es* of collers at ij^{d} the pece — vij^{s} iiij^{d} for ij yard*es* of buckeram to put in the crymesen hatt*es* — ij^{s} for the keveringe of vj hatt*es* of wycker at ij^{s} vj^{d} the pece — xv^{s} for the makinge of vj satten nighte cappes — ij^{s} for to yard*es* of white cotten xvj^{d} and him and his mann woorkinge besydes that — iiij^{or} dayes — viij^{s} in ye hole — iiij^{li} xvj^{s}

Summa patet

* T. Blagrave
* Iohn holt*es* marke †
* Rychard Leys.

f°25v.

		dayes	night*es*	
paynters by the daye and nighte at lyke rate	**Richarde** Bosum warden at xx^{d} the daye	12	2	xxiij^{s} iiij^{d}
	George Bosom at xij^{d}	12	2	xiiij^{s}
	Iohn knighte	12	2	xiij^{s}
	Edmond Busshe	12		xij^{s}
	peter cutler	10		x^{s}
	Thomas Bysshopp at x^{d}	12	1	x^{s} x^{d}

S*um*ma — iiij^{li} iij^{s} ij^{d}

Karvers & p*ro*p*er*tye makers by the daye & by the greate w*i*th there stuffe

Iohn [carrowe] for the makinge of xx^{tie} hedd*es* at vj^{s} viij^{d} the pece — vj^{li} xiij^{s} iiij^{d} for xxiiij^{tie} swoord*es* lxxij^{s} for toe lambes — viij^{s} for vj dartes — xij^{s} viij hand bawles — viij^{s} viij doze*n* of bells — viij^{s} iiij^{or} crogerstaves — xij^{s} toe greate bells — viij^{s} vj dagg*es* — xviij^{s} xviij targett*es* — xxiiij^{s} vj staves of vj foote lengthe — ij^{s} vij visars w*i*th byrd*es* vpon then — viij^{s} and for him selfe at xx^{d} the daye and fyve others at xij^{d} the daye browghte w*i*th him woorkinge in the Revells one daye at xij^{d} the daye a pece — vj^{s} viij^{d} in the hole — nota xvj^{li} wherof is payede to him in p*re*ste by M^{r} carden but — vij^{li} & so resteth — ix^{li}

Rob*ert* Trunckewell for him sellfe at xx^{d} the daye & his man at xvj^{d} the daye woorkinge in his owne howse vppon toe modells of the M*asters* device for arowfe and A cobboo*r*de of a bancketinge howse by the space of ix dayes — xxvij^{s} and more alowede to him by the M*aster* for his manns hire cominge from westmynster to the blacke fryers at iiij^{or} sundry tymes beinge at eache tyme busyed there the moste parte of the daye — vj^{s} viij^{d} And alsoe alowed him more for waynescotte and other wood*es* and kind*es* of stuffe occupyed abowte the same — xij^{s} x^{d} — xlvj^{s} vj^{d}

S*um*ma — xviij^{li} vj^{s} vj^{d}

* T. Blagrave
* Iohn holt*es* marke †
* Rychard Leys

f° 26 r.

Basketmaker by greate with theire twigg*es*	**will*iam*** Madderstone for xviij. hedpeces ad ij^{s} the pece — xxxvj^{s} and for twoe lambes — v^{s} by him made w*i*th his owne stuffe in the hole	xlj^{s}

S*umm*a p*ate*t

		dayes		night*es*	
Officers.	The clerke at ij^{s} the daye	28	. . . . . .	3	lxij^{s}
	Clerke controwler	28	. . . . . .	3	lxij^{s}
	M*aster* at iiij^{s} the daye	28	. . . . . .	3	vj^{li} iiij^{s}

S*umm*a — xij^{li} viij^{s}

S*umm*a of all the wages } lxiiij^{li} viij^{d}

Em*p*tions

Merser

Henry bechere for viij peces of gowlde and and sylu*er*
con*teyning* cccxj yardes
sendalls narrowe at xx^{d} the yarde -- xxv^{li} xviij^{s} iiij^{d} vij peces
con*teyning* ciiij iij *yardes* (xx over ciiij)
narrowe gowlde sarsenett at ij^{s} the yarde — xviij^{li} vj^{s} three
con*teyning* lxviij yardes iij q*uarters*
peces more of narrowe gowlde sarsenett at iij^{s} the yarde —
con*teyning* cxlvj *yardes* & a q*uarter*
x^{li} vj^{s} iij^{d} vj peces of laune rewed with counterfete gowlde
narrowe at iij^{s} the yarde — xxj^{li} — xviij^{s} ix^{d} and for vij peces
con*teyning* clxix yardes
of fyne gowlde sarsenett*es* broode at vj^{s} the yarde — l^{li} xiiij^{s}
of him bowghte the fyrste daye of Ianuarye 1558. Anno p*ri*mo
reg*inæ* Elizab*eth* and spente in rowles and wrethes tuftinge
tyringe of hedpeces and gyrdells vsed in dyu*er*se Maskes
betwene *chr*istmas and shroftyde that yere in the hole } cxxvij^{li} iij^{s} iiij^{d}

S*umm*a p*ate*t

Haberdasshers p*ar*cells and necessaryes	**Symo** Scarce for ij doze*n* and one payre of calfes lether gloves at x^{d} the payere — xx^{s} xvj payere of coo*r*ce gloves at vj^{d} the payre — viij^{s}	xxviij^{s}

* T Blagrave
* Iohn holt*es* marke †
* Rychard Leys

f° 26 v.

phillipp Gunter for xiij bells for Maskinge apparrell at ij^{d} the pece of him bowghte } ij^{s} ij^{d}

Iohn holte for iij peces of buckeram to make patrons — xxij^{s} vj^{d} for patrons of hoodes and cappes — iiij^{s} for iij lb of blacke threede — vj^{s} for j lb di. of white threede — ij^{s} vj^{d} for j lb iij *q*uarter*s* of threed in colo*urs* — vij^{s} viij lb of candells — ij^{s} and for iij sackes of coles — ij^{s} by him bowghte and occupyed in the lower howse in the hole } xlvj^{s}

Rob*ert* Rogers for j bowlte of blacke threede — iiij^{s} viij^{d} and one hundred of nedells — xij^{d} by him bowghte and p*ro*vided } v^{s} viij^{d}

Iohn Sepam for j lb of packethreede — viij^{d} white threede j lb — ij^{s} viij^{d} / threede in colo*urs* j lb — iiij^{s} pecinge threede j lb — iiij^{s} tape and Inckle j lb — xx^{d} paper boorde j^{dd} — v^{s} poynt*es* and laces j groce — ij^{s} vj^{d} wooden candellstyck*es* j^{dd} [lynckes j doze*n* — vj^{s} candells ij^{dd} — vj^{s}] — xviij^{d} carte coles j lode — xviij^{s} tallwood ij lode — viij^{s} faggott*es* ij^{c} — vj^{s} viij^{d} billett*es* j M — xij^{s} Rysshes iij doze*n* — ix^{s} by him bowghte and p*ro*vided with reddy monye at sondrye tymes in the hole } iiij^{li} vij^{s} viij^{d}

The Clerke for j quyere of Ryoll paper — xij^{d} and one quyere of small paper — v^{d} Incke duste & quells — iij^{d} by him bowghte and spente } xx^{d}

S*um*ma — viij^{li} xj^{s} ij^{d}

S*um*ma of all the Emptions } cxxxv^{li} xiiij^{s} vj^{d}

watercariage w*i*th bote hiere } **will*iam*** Cleye for him and his companye to wayte with a barge of viij ores to carry and recarry the Revells stuffe and attendaunt*es* thereon betweene the blacke fryers and the corte when soe ever he was called betwene *chr*istmas day and twelfe daye by agreme*n*te w*i*th him by greate } xxxiij^{s} iiij^{d}

* T. Blagrave
* Iohn holt*es* marke †
* Rychard Leys

f° 27 r.

ffor the bote hire of the officers and dyu*er*s others passinge by water betweene the co*ur*te and the blacke fryers on arraunt*es* and othe busines at sondrye tymes as by acoleccion therof — iij^s^ iiij^d^

Thomas vaughan for his bote hire and other charges goinge one arraunt*es* and other busines of the M*aste*rs sendinge as by his byll therof — v^s^ j^d^

S*umma* — xlj^s^ ix^d^

S*umma* To*ta*lis of theis Charges — ccj^li^ xvj^s^. xi^d^

* T. Blagrave
* Iohn holt*es* marke †
* Rychard Leys

f° 27 v.

Att the **Coronacio*n*** and **Candellmas** anno p*redi*cto

The Charges aswell of wages and hire of Artyfficers woorkmen and others then woorkmen and attendinge as otherwyse rysinge and growinge from the viij^th^ of Ianuarye vntyll the ij^d^ of ffebruarye anno p*redi*cto as Herunder the partyes names and severall soomes of monye dewe and wherfore pertyclerlye ensue

Taylo*ur*s

	dayes	vid*elicet* night*es*	
Iohn holte yeman at — ij^s^ the daye	25	2	liiij^s^
Thomas Claterbocke at xij^d^	25	6	xxxj^s^
Roberte Rogers	25	6	xxxj^s^
Davy Evauns	25	6	xxxj^s^
Iohn Diggynns	25	6	xxxj^s^
Iohn weston	13	2	xv^s^
Thomas Burras	14		xiiij^s^
Iohn kinge	4		iiij^s^
Iohn pertriche	2		ij^s^
Edwarde Gryffynn	2	1	iij^s^
Henrye venables	10		x^s^
Richard Myllwoorth	25	6	xxxj^s^
Henry ffannyll	2		ij^s^
Richarde myll	25		~~xxv^s^~~

* T Blagrave
* Iohn holt*es* marke †
* Rychard Leys

f° 29 r.

	dayes	nightes	
Thomas Boorman	25	6	xxxj[s]
Humfrye watson	25	6	xxxj[s]
william Thomsons toe menn eyther of them iiij[or] dayes in y[e] hole	8		viij[s]
Thomas vernam	4		iiij[s]
Clemente Cotton	8		viij[s]
Symon Iardayne	1		j[s]
William kydwella	2		ij[s]
Tottey ffawkeye	1		j[s]
Iohn hodges	4		iiij[s]
George mvcklowe	3		iij[s]
*Christ*ofer lee	3		iij[s]
Iohn Robbynson	2		ij[s]
Martyn Hawdon	6		vj[s]
Henry williams	1		j[s]
Thomas Richardes	1		j[s]
william pele	1		j[s]
Thomas Streete	1		j[s]
Lewys Iames	4		iiij[s]
Richard Bamverte	5		v[s]
Thomas Bvrton	8		viij[s]
Iohn pennylberye	2		ij[s]
Nicholas Iohnson	4		iiij[s]

* T. Blagrave
* Iohn holtes marke †
* Rychard Leys

f[o] 29 v.

		dayes	nightes	
	Richard Slater	12		xij^s^
	George Bridges	3		iij^s^
	will*iam* Came	4		iiij^s^
	Richard Alee for him selfe[4] & for morrys 1 daye	5		v^s^
		Summa — xxj^li^ xix^s^		
Paynters by the daye and nighte at lyke rate	**Richarde** Bosum warden at xx^d^ the daye	12 di.	1	xxij^s^
	George Bosom at xij^d^	16	1	xvij^s^
	Iohn knighte	19	1	xx^s^
	George Breeke	16	1	xvij^s^
	Thomas Lame	11	1	xij^s^
	Robarte Harman	8 di.		viij^s^vj^d^
	Roberte Tompson	2		ij^s^
	Iohn Barber	7		viij^s^
		Summa — cvj^s^vj^d^		
Enbroderer by greate	**Nicholas** Marten for pynckinge of xxxv yardes di. of satten at ij^d^ the yarde in the hole			v^s^xj^d^
		Summa patet		
Haberdassher	**Peter** bonyvale at xx^d^	2		iij^s^iiij^d^
	His mann at xij^d^ ye daye	3		iij^s^
	and for the makinge of cccc^d^ di. & x strynges by greate			xv^s^
		Summa — xxj^s^ iiij^d^		

* T Blagrave
* Iohn holt*es* marke †
* Rychard Leys

f° 30 r.

		Dayes	nightes	
Basketmaker by greate with theire twigg*es*	**Iames** Sharlowe for vj doble hedpeces of wycker — xviij^{s} viij^{d} singell hedpeces — xvj^{s} and for twigg*es* for the same — xiiij^{d} in the hole			xxxv^{s} ij^{d}

S*umma* p*atet*

Officers		Dayes	nightes	
	The Clerke at ij^{s} ye daye	25	2	liiij^{s}
	Clerke controwler	25	2	liiij^{s}
	M*aster* at iiij^{s} the daye	25	2	cviij^{s}

S*umma* — x^{li} xvj^{s}

S*umma* To*talis* of the wages } xlj^{li} iij^{s} xj^{d}

Emptions

Mercer — **Henry** Becher for v Maste of cullen sylu*er* at xv^{s} the Maste — lxxv^{s}. toe Maste di. of cullen gowlde at xl^{s} the Maste — c^{s} & j ferdell of cullen gowlde and cullen sylu*er* con*teyning* xviij Maste myxed at xx^{s} the Maste — xviij^{li} of him bowghte } xxvj^{li} xv^{s}

S*umma* p*atet*

Haberdassher — **peter** Bonyvale for twelfe thowsand Spangells at ij^{s} the pece — xxiiij^{s} to oz di. of copper sylu*er* at iij^{s} the oz. — vij^{s} vj^{d} / xxv M spangells deliu*er*ed at another tyme at ij^{s} the M l^{s} / and more vj oz. di. of copper sylu*er* at iij^{s} the oz. — xviij^{s}. / di. doz*en* of fethers at ij^{s} the pece — xij^{s} / vj other fethers at xij^{d} the pece — vj^{s} for cullen sylu*er* frenge A small remna*n*te — ij^{s} for vj M of spangells delyu*er*ed more at Another tyme at ij^{s} the M — xij^{s} more j oz. di. of copper sylu*er* at iij^{s} the oz. — iiij^{s} vj^{d} of him bowghte at sundrye tymes in the hole } vj^{li} xvj^{s}

* T Blagrave
* Iohn holt*es* marke †
* Rychard Leys

f° 30 v.

Richarde lee for xxxix peces of cullen sylu*er* by him bowghte — xij^{s} and for mony by him Layede owte for the Makinge of vj p*ar*telett*es* of sylu*er* sarsenett and for copper gowlde to edge the same — iij^{s} and the hiere of A bote to fetche the same — viij^{d} in the hole } xv^{s} viij^{d}

***Christ*ofer** Myllener for ix payre of cutt gloves at xij^{d} the payere — ix^{s} and for ix payre of fyne gloves at vj^{d} the pere — iiij^{s} vj^{d}/ of him bowghte } xiij^{s} vj^{d}

S*umma* — viij^{li} v^{s} ij^{d}

Necessaries

Iames Sharlowe for iij greate hampyers for the Revells stuffe at — iij^{s} iiij^{d} the pece } x^{s}

Rob*er*t Harman paynter for one di. doze*n* of small pott*es* by him bowghte and lefte in the Revells } vj^{d}

Iohn Holte for toe lb di. of blacke threede — v^{s} j lb of white threede — xx^{d} j lb di. of threede in colo*ur* — iij^{s} and for viij lb of candells — ij^{s} by him bowghte and spente benethe in the Maske shewen the morowe after the Coronacion } xj^{s} viij^{d}

The same Iohn holte for j lb iij q*uarter*s of black threede — iij^{s} vj^{d} j lb of white threede — xx^{d} j lb q*uar*ter of threede in colo*urs* — v^{s} Seringe candell — vj^{d} ix lb of candells — ij^{s} iiij^{d} j q*uarter*ne di. of byllett*es* — vij^{s} j q*uarter*ne of ffaggott*es* — ij^{s} and for whighte Inckle and rounde laces — xvj^{d} by him bowghte and spente benethe abowte the Maske shewen on the sondaye seven nighte after the Coronacion } xxiij^{s} iiij^{d}

Iohn Sepam for j lb of white and blacke threede — v^{s} iiij^{d} pecinge threede j lb — iiij^{s} threede in colo*urs* j lb — iiij^{s} Rysshes iij doze*n* — ix^{s} candells ij doze*n* — vj^{s} coles vj Sackes — iiij^{s} byllettes j M — x^{s} faggott*es* ij^{C} — vj^{s} viij^{d}/ glewe — viij^{d} Syse toe pannes — iiij^{d} packthreede j lb — viij^{d} and tape and Inckle j lb — xx^{d} by him bowghte and p*ro*vided at sondrye tymes in the hole } lij^{s} iiij^{d}

* T Blagrave

* Iohn holt*es* marke †

* Rychard Leys

f° 31 r.

The Clerke for j *quyere* of Small paper — v^{d} di. pap*er* j q*uyere* — xij^{d} Incke quilles and duste — iij^{d} by hym bowghte and spente in The Hole } xx^{d}

S*um*ma — iiij^{li} xix^{s}·vj^{d}

S *umma* of all the Emptio*ns* } xxxix^{li} xix^{s} viij^{d}

Watercariage with bote Hiere

Will*iam* Cleye for him and his companye w*i*th A barge of viij ores to carrye and recarye the Revells stuffe and attendaunt*es* theron betweene the co*ur*te and the blackefryers and waytinge late theron toe sondrye nightes for for bothe } xiij^{s} iiij^{d}

ffor the bote hire of the officers and dyvers others passinge by water betweene the co*ur*te and the blackefryers at sondry tymes as by A coleccion therof did Amounte } iij^{s} viij^{d}

S*um*ma — xvij^{s}

Reward*es*

Iames Rob*ert* orras his man for cominge from westm*inster* to the blackeffryers by the M*aste*rs comaundeme*n*te at v sondry tymes and the occupyed moste parte of the dayes abowte the settinge owte of certeyne devices } vj^{s} viij^{d}

S*um*ma *patet*

S *umma* **Totalis** of theis Charges } iiij^{xx} ij^{li} vij^{s} iij^{d}

* T Blagrave
* Iohn holt*es* marke †
* Rychard Leys

fo 31 v.

Shrofftide anno p*redi*cto } **The Charges** aswell of wages and hire of Artyfficers woorkme*n* and others the*n* woorkinge and attendinge as other wyse rysinge and groinge w*i*thin the office from the ij^{d} vntyll the xxviijth of februarye anno p*re*-d*i*cto as herunder the p*ar*tyes names and seue*r*all somes of monye dewe and wherfore p*er*ticu*l*erly apere.

vid*elicet*

Taylo*urs* woorkinge by the daye and nighte at lyke rate

	dayes	night*es*	
Iohn Holte yeman at ij^{s} the daye	22	2	xlviij^{s}
Thomas Clatterbock at xij^{d}	22	2	xxiiij^{s}
Will*iam* Garrett	22	2	xxiiij^{s}
Davy Evauns	22	2	xxiiij^{s}
Iohn diggens	22	2	xxiiij^{s}
Richard mylwoorth	22	2	xxiiij^{s}
Thomas Boo*r*man	22	2	xxiiij^{s}
Humfrye watson	22	2	xxiiij^{s}
will*iam*	2 di.	1	iij^{s} vj^{d}
Nicholas Clerke	2 di.	1	iij^{s} vj^{d}
Iohn Lewys	2		ij^{s}
Richard davye	2 di.	1	iij^{s} vj^{d}
Iohn plu*m*mer	2 di.	1	iij^{s} vj^{d}
Iohn Hytche	2 di.	1	iij^{s} vj^{d}

* T Blagrave
* Iohn holt*es* marke †
* Rychard Leys

f° 33 r.

		dayes	nightes	
	Gilliam Crane for him selfe	5		v^{s}
	his toe men iiij^{or} dayes ye pere	8		viij^{s}
	Dyrycke Staffyn	4		iiij^{s}
	Mathewe pannell	4		iiij^{s}
	Iohn will*iam*s	3		iij^{s}
	Hewghe Iaxon	3		iij^{s}
	Rafe Harres	3		iij^{s}
	will*iam* vanberge	3		iij^{s}
	peter vandall	3		iij^{s}
	Thomas fferreye	1		j^{s}
	Arnold ferrye.	2		ij^{s}

S*umma* — xiij^{li} xiiij^{s} vj^{d}

Paynters	**Richarde** Bosu*m* warden at xx^{d} by the daye	12	1	xxj^{s} viij^{d}
	George Bosu*m* at xij^{d}	17	2	xix^{s}
	Iohn knighte	16	2	xviij^{s}
	Edmunde Busshe	16	1	xvij^{s}
	Thomas Busshe	15		xv^{s}
	peter Cuttler	15		xv^{s}
	Thomas Bysshoppe at x^{d}	17	2	xv^{s} x^{d}

* T Blagrave
* [Iohn holt*es*] marke †
* [Rychard Le]ys

f° 33 v.

S*umma* — vj^{li} xviij^{d}.

Haberdassher by the daye and by the greate w*i*th some stuffe

Peter Borrayne alias dorranger at xx^{d} the daye } 3 . . . . v^{s}

his man at xiiij^{d} ye daye 4 . . . . iiij^{s} viij^{d}

one other that he browghte to helpe him at xij^{d} ye daye } 1 . . . . xij^{d}

to hosyers that he browghte w*i*thim at xij^{d} ye daye apece ether of them A daye } 2 . . . . ij^{s}

The same peter for makinge of viij purses of Crymesen damaske at viij^{d} the pece — v^{s} iiij^{d} for makinge of v doze*n* of tassells of cullen sylu*er* at vj^{d} the doze*n* — ij^{s} vj^{d} for makinge of xxviij dd. of freenge of cullen sylu*er* at vj^{d} the dd. — xiiij^{s} for whyte and redd threede for the same — ij^{s} iiij^{d} for xiiij oz. of cullen sylu*er* by him bowghte at xvj^{d} the oz. — xviij^{s} viij^{d}/ for xiij doze*n* of freenge by him made of the same sylver at vj^{d} the doze*n* — vj^{s} vj^{d}/ for v dd. of tarsells by him made of ye same sylu*er* — ij^{s} vj^{d}. di. lb of redd threede for the same — ij^{s} for xxiiij^{tie} doze*n* of tarsells made of cullen gowlde at vj^{d} the doze*n* — xij^{s} in the hole as by his byll apereth } lxv^{s} x^{d}

S*umma* — lxxviij^{s} vj^{d}

Basketmakers by greate w*i*th theire twigg*es*

Thomas Ede Basketmaker for viij hedpeces — xvj^{s} vj doble hedpeces — xviij^{s} vj hedpeces more — xv^{s} j dd. of weemenns cappes — viij^{s} j di. doze*n* of small baskett*es* — ij^{s} and vj greate hampiers — xx^{s} by him made and delivered into the Revells in the hole } lxxix^{s}

S*umma* — p*atet*

Buskyn and shewe maker/ by greate

Genni*n*ge Shewemaker for xxxvij payre of Maskinge shewes made before the xjth of februarye 1559 at vj^{d} the payre and not entred tyll nowe } xviij^{s} vj^{d}.

S*umma* p*atet*

* T Blagrave
* Iohn holt*es* marke †
* Richard Leys

f° 34 r.

Ioyners and karvers — **Robert** Trunckewell for him selfe at xx^{d} the daye and his man at xvj^{d} the daye alteringe of to modells by them before made and nowe ageane turnede to Another purpose by the space of viij dayes woorkinge and cominge and goinge from westmynster to the blacke fryers — xxiiij^{s} and for dyu*ers* small *par*cells of sundry kyndes of stuffe for *per*formaunce of the same — x^{s} in the hole } xxxiiij^{s}.

S*umm*a patet.

		dayes	nightes	
Officers.	The Clerke at ij^{s} ye daye	22	2	xlviij^{s}
	Clerke Controwler	22	2	xlviij^{s}
	M*aster* at iiij^{s} the daye	22	2	iiij^{li}. xvj^{s}.

S*umm*a — ix^{li} xij^{s}.

S*umm*a of all the wages } xxxix^{li} xviij^{s}

Emptions

Mercer — **Henry** Becher for ij peces of gowlde sarsenet brode ye one redd and thother yellowe *conteyninge* lxv yardes iij *quarters* at — vj^{s} the yarde — xix^{li} xiiij^{s} vj^{d}/ and for one pece of white bullonye *conteyninge* xxviij and a *quarter* sarsenett at iiij^{s} ij^{d} the yarde — cxviij^{s} ix^{d} of him bowghte and spente in attyres of hedpeces gerdells tuskyng*es* pull*inges* owte and other garniture in the hole } xxv^{li} xiij^{s} iij^{d}.

S*umm*a patet

Silkewooma*n* — **An Mallerye** for iiij^{lb} and iiij^{or} oz. di. silke twyste at xiiij^{d} the oz. and xviij^{s} viij^{d} the lb — lxxix^{s} vij^{d} and for ij^{od} xj oz of cullen gowlde and cullen sylu*er* made in frenge and tarsells at ij^{s} ij^{d} the oz. — xxij^{lb} xvij^{s} ij^{d} in the hole } xxvj^{li} xvj^{s} ix^{d}

* T Blagrave
* Iohn holt*es* marke †
* Richard Leys

f° 34 v.

	Henry Stable for l^{tie} oz. di. of cullen sylver frenge of him bowghte as by A byll of his hande aperethe	vj^{li} vj^{s} iij^{d}
	Summa — xxxiij^{li} iij^{s}	
Gowld beter	**fforeste** valendone for M M M j^{c} di. of perty gowlde at ij^{s} vj^{d} the c^{d} — lxxviij^{s} ix^{d} and for M M M M viij^{c} of syluer at xviij^{d} the hundred — lxxij^{s} by him deliu*er*ed in to the Revells at sondry tymes before this daye in ye hole	vij^{li} x^{s} ix^{d}
	Summa patet	
Grosers p*ar*cells	**Iohn** Sepam for ij lb of Spanysshe white and blacke — xx^{d} glewe ij lb — xvj^{d} Syse iiij pannes — viij^{d} oyell one pynte — iiij^{d} byce j lb — iiij^{s} Rosset j lb — viij^{d} verditer — xiiij^{d} lytmose — xij^{d} paynters pott*es* ij dd — iij^{s} paynters toles — xiiij^{d} by him bowghte and p*ro*vided in the hole	xv[illegible]
	Summa patet	
ffeltemaker	**Iohn Horse** for viij Russett feltes at xij^{d} the pece by him delyvered in to the Revells	viij^{s}.
	Summa patet	
Haberdasshers	**Anthony** dolyn for liiij^{ti} yardes of lynnen clothe wroughte with silke and threede in loomewoorke at xiij^{s} iiij^{d} the yarde of him bowghte for the p*er*formaunce of A Maske of swart-rutters shewen on shrovesondaye at nighte amountinge in the hole to	xxxvj^{li}
	Thomas ffowler for xij calles of silke the silke poz. iiij^{or} oz. di. at xx^{d} the oz. — vij^{s} vj^{d} and for the makinge of them — vj^{s} for A heye of xij faddom longe — v^{s} iiij^{d} for ij doze*n* of pursenett*es* — ij^{s} viij^{d} for A doze*n* of foxnett*es* — vj^{s} and for A pottell of Inke to coler the same pursenet*es* blacke — ij^{s} viij^{d} of him bowghte for the ffysshermen and fysshwyves on Shroftuesdaye nighte	xxx^{s} ij^{d}
	Summa — xxxvij^{li} x^{s} ij^{d}.	

* T Blagrave
* Iohn holt*es* marke †
* Rychard Leys

f° 35 r.

necessaryes

Iohn holte for iij lb of blacke threede — vj^{s} ij lb iij q*uarte*rs of white threede — iiij^{s} vij^{d}/ j lb of Colored threede — iiij^{s}/ xvj lb of candells — iiij^{s}/ seringe candell — v^{d}/ yellowe caddas Rybben — xij^{d}/ and for viij doze*n* of greate buttons at ij^{d} the doze*n* — xvj^{d}/ by him bowghte p*ro*vided and spente benethe in the hole } xxj^{s} iiij^{d}.

The same Iohn holte for j doze*n* of viserdes with shorte berdes yellowe and blacke haulfe a doze*n* of the one and half A doze*n* of the other at xx^{d} the pece } xx^{s}.

Iohn Sepam for j lb of white and blacke threede — v^{s} di. lb of pecinge threede — ij^{s}/ di. lb of threede in colo*u*rs — ij^{s} Rysshes iij doze*n* — vj^{s} candells ij doze*n* — vj^{s} coles vj Sackes — iiij^{s} faggott*es* ij c^{d} — vj^{s} viij^{d}/ poyntes and laces — xiiij^{d} by him bowghte and p*ro*vided at sondrye tymes } xxxij^{s} x^{d}

The Clerke for j q*uyer*e of small paper — iiij^{d} one q*uye*re of di. paper — x^{d} Incke quells and duste — iij^{d} by him bowghte and spente } xvij^{d}

Summa — lxxv^{s} vij^{d}

S*umm*a of all the **Emptions** } cviij^{li} xv^{s} ix^{d}

Watercariage with bote hire

Will*ia*m Cleye for the hire of A barge with iiij^{or} ores one Shrove sondaye at nighte — vij^{s} one shrove mondaye — v^{s} and one Shrove tewesdaye — viij^{s} to carry and recarrye the Revells Stuff and attend*aunte*s theron betweene the blacke fryers and the co*urt*e & for A whirry to carrye the stuffe that woold not into the barge — ij^{s} } xxij^{s}

* T Blagrave
* Iohn holt*es* marke
* Rychard Leys

f° 35 v.

ffor the bote hire of the Officers and others passinge by water betweene the blackefryers and the co*u*rte one arraunt*es* & other busines at sondry tymes as by A coleccion therof } v[s]

S*um*ma — xxvij[s]. iiij[d]

S*um*ma Tot*a*lis of theis charges } cl[li] ix[d]. 5

* T Blagrave
* Iohn holt*es* marke †
* Rychard Leys

f° 36 r.

Maye 1559 d*ic*to anno P*ri*mo Reg*i*næ Elizab*ethæ*

The Charges aswell of wages and hire of Artyfficers woorkmen and others woorkinge and attendinge vppon the translatinge newe makinge furnysshinge and fynysshinge of dyu*er*s garment*es* apparrell vtensiles & p*ro*p*er*ties for Amaske of Astronon*er*s and A banckett howse at westm*inster* then made as other wyse rysinge and groinge betweene the seconde and the xxvth of of Maye that yere as Herunder the partyes names and seu*er*all somes of mony dewe and wherfore p*er*ticlerly apere vid*elicet*

Taylo*ur*s by the daye and nighte at lyke rate

	dayes	night*es*	
Iohn holte yeman at — ij^{s} the daye	12	1	xxvj^{s}
Thomas Clatterbocke at xij^{d}	12	1	xiij^{s}
Thomas vaughan	12	1	xiij^{s}
Iohn diggyns	12	1	xiij^{s}
will*iam* Garrett	12	1	xiij^{s}
henry keler	6		vj^{s}
Rob*er*t Beyner	8		viij^{s}
Richard myllwo*or*the	12	1	xiij^{s}
Richarde Iones	4		iiij^{s}
Thomas Bo*or*man	12	1	xiij^{s}
Rob*er*t wheler	5		v^{s}
Humfrey watson	12	1	xiij^{s}
Rob*er*t horsam	3	1	iiij^{s}

Summa — vij^{li} iiij^{s}.

* T Blagrave
* Iohn holt*es* marke †
* Rychard Leys

f° 37 r.

		dayes	nightes	
Paynters by the daye and nighte at lyke rate	**Richarde** Bosum at xx^{d} the daye	4	I	viij^{s} iiij^{d}
	George Bosum at xij^{d}	5	I	vj^{s}
	Rob*ert* Reduyrge at x^{d}	5	I	iiij^{s} ij^{d}
	Thomas Retuyap at xij^{d}	5		v^{s}
	peter Cuttler	2		ij^{s}

Summa — xxv^{s} vj^{d}

Baskettmakers by the daye and nighte woorkinge on wyndowes for A Bancketinge howse at westm*inster*	**will*iam*** howcros	12	xij^{s}
	will*iam* Etherson	12	xij^{s}
	Anthonye de vallaye	12	xij^{s}
	Nicholas devall	12	xij^{s}
	nicholas Crooketacke at viij^{d}	12	viij^{s}

Basketmakers by greate for the Maske — **will*iam*** Madderson for vj hedpeces at ij^{s} the pece — xij^{s} vj hedpeces at xij^{d} the pece — vj^{s} vj hole hed peces at viij^{d} the pece — iiij^{s} and for viij globes at viij^{d} the pece — v^{s} iiij^{d} by him made and delyu*er*ed into the Revells ... xxvij^{s} iiij^{d}

Summa — iiij^{li} iij^{s} iiij^{d}

Officers	The Clerke at ij^{s} ye daye	12	I	xxvj^{s}
	Clerke controwler	12	I	xxvj^{s}
	M*aster* at iiij^{s} ye daye	12	I	lij^{s}

Summa — ciiij^{s}

Summa of all the wages } xvij^{li} xvj^{s} x^{d}

* T Blagrave
* Iohn holt*es* marke †
* Rychard Leys

f° 37 v.

Emptions

merser **Henry** Becher for three peces of gowlde sarsenet thone purple An other redd and thother yellowe at vj^{s} [*conteyninge* lj *yardes* iij *quarters*] the yarde — xv^{li} x^{s} vj^{d} / one pece of white bullonye [*conteyninge* xxxix *yardes*] sarsentt at iiij^{s} iiij^{d} the yarde — viij^{lb} ix^{s} spente in girdells tuftinge pullinges owt attyre of hedpeces and other garniture and for j pece of white normaundye ca*n*vas conteyninge xxxv ells and A halffe at xviij^{d} the ell spente in makinge of armes and legg*es* steyned flesshe colo*ur* — liij^{s} iij^{d} / of him bowghte into the Revells — xxvj^{li} xij^{s} ix^{d}

Iulian hick*es* wydowe for iij yardes iij q*uarter*s di. redd sarsenet at v^{s} the yarde — xix^{s} and for cxij yard*es* of white and blacke sarsenet at iij^{s} viij^{d} the yarde — xxvj^{li} ij^{s} viij^{d} / j ell di. q*uartern* of white taffita — xvj^{s} x^{d} ob. and j ell di. q*uarter* of blacke taffita at xij^{s} vj^{d} — xiiij^{s} j^{d} and for ij yardes of blacke vellvat at xv^{s} vj^{d} the yarde xxxj^{s} of hir bowghte & spente in lyninge attyres and for furnysshinge of tunbborde and other p*ar*ties of the banc̃ketinge howse at westmynster — xxx^{li} iij^{s} vij^{d} ob.

Summa — lvj^{li} xvj^{s} iiij^{d} ob.

Sylkewooman **Henrye** Stableye for v oz. di. of blacke and sylu*er* tweyst at xx^{d} the oz. — ix^{s} ij^{d} / xx oz. q*uarter* of white and blacke twiste at xiiij^{d} the oz. — xxiij^{s} vij^{d} ob. for twistinge & vntwystinge yo*ther* lace wayinge v oz. — xx^{d} one pounde depe freenge of blacke silke and sylver at ij^{s} the oz. — xxxij^{s} viij oz. of narrowe frenge of red sylke and sylver at ij^{s} vj^{d} the oz. — xx^{s} j lb ij oz. of narrowe frenge of redd threede and sylver at ij^{s} vj^{d} the oz. — xlv^{s} viij oz. narrowe frenge of redd and sylu*er* at ij^{s} vj^{d} the oz. — xx^{s} xiiij oz. q*uarter* depe freenge of blacke and sylu*er* at ij^{s} the oz. — xxviij^{s} vj^{d} x oz. di. narrowe frenge of redd sylke and sylver at ij^{s} vj^{d} the oz. — xxvj^{s} iij^{d} / j lb iiij^{or} oz. q*uartern* depe frenge of blacke and sylu*er* at ij^{s} the oz. — xl^{s} vj^{d} / vj oz. di. narrowe frenge of redd — xviij^{li} xiiij^{s} ix^{d} ob.

Summa *patet*

* T Blagrave

* Iohn holtes marke †

* Rychard Leys

and sylu*er* at ij^{s} vj^{d} the oz. — xvj^{s}. iij^{d}. ij lb ij lb lackinge one q*uarter*ne depe freenge of blacke redd and sylu*er* at ij^{s} the oz. lxiij^{s} vj^{d} x oz. narrowe freenge of redd and sylu*er* at ij^{s} vj^{d} the oz. — xxv^{s}. and for xx^{tie} oz. of white and blacke twyste at xiiij^{d} the oz. — xxiij^{s} iiij^{d}/ of here bowghte and spente p*ar*te in garnyture of Maskes and parte in furnysshinge of the banketinge howse at westm*inster* in the hole

ffeltmaker — **Iohn** de horse for iij doze*n* of hatt*es* at xij^{s} the doze*n* by him delyu*er*ede into the Revells at sondrye tymes } xxxvj^{s}

S*umma* p*atet*

Grocers p*ar*cells } **Iohn** Sepam for j lb of glewe — viij^{d} j lb spanysshe white and blacke — x^{d} syse ij pannes — iiij^{d} oyle j pynte — iiij^{d} bice di. lb — ij^{s} Rossett j lb — viij^{d} verdyter — x^{d} lytmose — x^{d} p*ar*tye gowlde j C — ij^{s} vj^{d} sylu*er* j C^{d} — xviij^{d} for payntes pott*es* and tooles — xij^{d} by him bowghte sett and p*ro*vided at sundrye tymes in the hole } xj^{s} vj^{d}

S*umma* p*atet*

Necessaryes — **Iohn** Sepam for ij lb of whyte and blacke threede — v^{s} j lb of pecinge threde — iiij^{s} j lb of threede in colo*urs* — ij^{s} Rysshes ij doze*n* — iij^{s} iiij^{d}. Candells j doze*n* — ij^{s} vj^{d} coles v sack*es* — iij^{s} iiij^{d} faggott*es* j C^{d} — iij^{s} viij^{d} by him bowghte & p*ro*vided } xxiij^{s}. x^{d}.

The Clerke for j q*uy*ere of di. paper — x^{d} j q*uy*ere of small pap*er* — iiij^{d} Incke quylls and duste — iij^{d} by him bowghte & spente in the hole } xvij^{d}.

S*umma* — xxv^{s} iij^{d}

S*umma* of all the Emptions } lxix^{li} iij^{s} xj^{d}

* T Blagrave
* Iohn holt*es* marke †
* Rychard Leys

f° 38 v.

Botehire **ffor** the bote hiere of the officers and others passinge by water betweene the co*ur*te and the blacke fryers at sondry tymes as by Acoleccion therof amounteth } ij^{s} iiij^{d}.

S*umma* pa*tet*

S*umma* **To*ta*lis** of theis charges } iiij^{xx} xvij^{li} iij^{s} j^{d}

* T Blagrave
* Iohn holt*es* marke †
* Rychard Leys

f° 39 r.

Iune 1559 in d*i*cto anno **pr*i*mo** Reg*i*næ pr*æ*-dict*æ*

Eyringe repayringe lainge abroode turninge sowinge mendinge tackinge Spunginge wypinge brusshinge makinge cleane foldinge and lainge vp of the Maskes garment*es* vesturs and other Stuffe Store and Implement*es* of the office for the Safegarde and refresshinge of the same with the gatheringe and compylinge of the Imployment*es* and remayne of the Stuffe and Store of the office betweene the laste daye of maye and the xiiijth daye of Iune d*i*cto anno The charg*es* wherof with the p*ar*tyes names and seu*er*all dewties and wherfore hereunder p*er*tyclerlye ensue

vid*elicet*

		dayes	night*es*
Taylo*urs* and others woorkinge and attendinge theron by the daye at lyke rate	**Iohn** holte yeman at ij^{s} the daye	10	xx^{s}
	Thomas Clatterbocke at xij^{d}	10	x^{s}
	Rob*ert* Rogers.	10	x^{s}
	davy Evauns	10	x^{s}
	will*iam* Garrett	10	x^{s}
	myles hatter	10	x^{s}
	Roger Barnes	10	x^{s}
	Humfreye watson	10	x^{s}
Officers	The Clerke at ij^{s} ye daye	10	xx^{s}
	Clerke controwler	10	xx^{s}
	M*aster* at iiij^{s} ye daye	10	xl^{s}

S*umma* of all the wages } viij^{li} x^{s}.

* T Blagrave
* Iohn holt*es* marke †
* Rychard Leys

f° 39 v.

Emptions

Necessaries

Iohn Sepam for ij doze*n* of Rysshes — vj^{s} iiij^{d} nedells di. C^{d} — iiij^{d} white threede di. lb — xvj^{d} blacke threede di. bowlte — ij^{s} threede in colo*urs* di. lb — ij^{s} toe rubbing brusshes — iiij^{d} toe hand brusshes — xx^{d} byllett*es* di. M — v^{s} coles iij sackes — ij^{s} & seringe candell — ij^{d} by him bowghte and p*ro*vided } xxj^{s} ij^{d}

The Clerke for j q*uye*re of Ryoll paper — xij^{d} j q*uye*re of small pap*er* — iiij^{d} Incke quells and duste — iij^{d} & for A sett of castinge counters — xx^{d} } iij^{s} iij^{d}

S*umma* of the Emptions } xxiiij^{s} v^{d}

S*umma* **Tot***a***lis** of theis charges } ix^{li} xiiij^{s} v^{d}.

Rent*es*

The yeman of the Revells for the rente of his howse hired within the late blacke ffryers from the Anunciac*i*on of *our* Ladye .1558. in anno quarto et quinto Reg*is* et Reg*in*æ p*rædictorum* vntyll Thanunciac*i*on of *our* Ladye .1559. in anno p*ri*mo Reg*in*æ Elizabe*thæ* sup*radictum* by the space of one hole yere for } C^{s}.

The Clerke of bothe tentt*es* and Revells for the rente of his howse at C^{s} by yere lykewyse hired for the same tyme for w*hi*ch is alowed in the bookes of the tent*es* l^{s} and here } l^{s}

The Clerke controwler of bothe the tent*es* and Revells for the rente of his howse at C^{s} by yere lykewyse hired and for his lyu*ery* at xxvj^{s} viij^{d} by yere behinde for the same tyme for w*hi*ch is alowed in the bookes of the tent*es* lxiij^{s} iiij^{d} and here } lxiij^{s} iiij^{d}.

* T Blagrave

* Iohn holt*es* marke †

* Rychard Leys

f° 40 r.

The M*aster* of bothe the tent*es* and Revells for the rente of his howse at x^{li} by yere lykewyse behynde for the same tyme for w*hi*ch is alowed in the bookes of the tent*es* C^{s} and here	C^{s}.
ffor the rente of v greate large roomes within the seide late blacke fryers for the woorke and Store howses of the Revells behynde for y^{e} same tyme	vj^{li} $xiij^{s}$ $iiij^{d}$.

S *um*ma **Tot*a*lis** of all the Rent*es*	$xxij^{li}$ vj^{s} $viij^{d}$

* T Blagrave
* Iohn holtes merke †
* Rychard Leys

f° 40 v.

Auguste September 1559 in d*icto* anno p*rimo* reg*inæ* Elizab*ethe* sup*radict*ie

The Charges aswell of wages and hire of Artyfficers woorkemen and others woorkinge and attendinge vpon the translacion garnysshinge and fynysshinge of dyvers garment*es* Aparrel*es* vtensiles and p*ro*pertyes of A Maske of Shypmenn and maydes of the cuntrye then made and shewen at horseleye as otherwyse rysinge and gowinge betweene the xxiiij[th] daye of Iulye and the laste daye of September that yeare as herunder the p*ar*tyes names and seu*er*all somes of monye dewe and wherefore p*er*ticlerlye apere.

vid*elicet*

Taylo*urs* by the daye and nighte at lyke rate

	dayes	night*es*	
Iohn holte yeman at ij[s] the daye	14	2	xxxij[s]
Thomas Claterbocke at xij[d]	14	2	xvj[s]
Henry keler	10		x[s]
davye Evauns	14	2	xvj[s]
Thomas vaughan	14	2	xvj[s]
Iohn diggins	14	2	xvj[s]
Rob*ert* Reyuer	9	1	x[s]
Richarde Iones	9	1	x[s]
Richard myllwoorthe	14	2	xvj[s]
Rob*ert* wheler	6	1	vij[s]
Thomas Boo*r*man	14	2	xvj[s]
humfrye watson	14	2	xvj[s]
Rob*ert* Horsam	5	1	vj[s]

S*umma* — ix[li] — vij[s]

* T Blagrave
* Iohn holt*es* marke †
* Rychard Leys

f° 41 r.

Paynters woorkinge vpon the Bancketing-howse at horsleye by the daye and the greate	**Richard** Bosum at ij^{s} the daye his brother at xiiij^{d} the daye his man at xij^{d} the daye and Agrynder at x^{d} the daye xj dayes — lv^{s} for makinge of pyctures vpon clothe in the frunte and the gallerye by greate *with* theire owne stuffe — cviij^{s} in ye hole	viij^{li} iij^{s}

Summa patet

		dayes	nightes	
Officers	The Clerke at ij^{s} ye daye	14	2	xxxij^{s}
	Clerke comptrowler	14	2	xxxij^{s}
	Master at iiij^{s} ye daye	14	2	lxiiij^{s}

Summa **of all the wages — xxiij^{li} xviij^{s}**

Emptions.

necessaries	**Iohn** Sepam for j lb of packthreede — vj^{d} j lb of glewe viij^{d} j lb of white and blacke threede — v^{s} j lb of pecinge threede — iiij^{s} j lb of threede in col*ours* — ij^{s} Rysshes ij doz*en* — iij^{s} iiij^{d} candells j doz*en* — ij^{s} vj^{d} coles v sackes — iij^{s} iiij^{d} fagott*es* j c^{d} — iij^{s} viij^{d} by him bowght and p*ro*vided in the hole	xxv^{s}
	The Clerke for j q*ui*ere of small paper — iiij^{d} di. pap*er* j quiere — x^{d} Inke quylls and duste — iij^{d} by him bowghte and spente	xvij^{d}

Summa **of the Emptions** } xxvj^{s} v^{d}

Cariages

wat*er*cariage and landcariage with bote hire	**will*iam*** Cleye for the caryage of the same Maske and dyu*ers* other thing*es* concerninge A bancketing howse made at horsley and thattendaunt*es* theron from the blacke fryers to hampton co*ur*te in his Barge and thence backe ageane by water and awaytinge theron	xx^{s}

* T Blagrave
[* Iohn] holt*es* marke †
[* Rychar]d Leys

f^{o} **41 v.**

ffor the lande caryage of the same from hampton co*ur*te to horseleye and therence backe ageane to the water syde by carte — x^{s}

ffor the bote hyre of the officers and others within y^{t} tyme passinge betweene london and Hampton co*ur*te by water in whyrres and some in barge on arraunt*es* and other busynes concerninge the seide Maskes and Bancketinge howse as by Acoleccion therof — v^{s}

S*umm*a — xxxv^{s}

Rewa[r]**d*es*** To Thomas Tadnall in reward*es* for attendinge ye Gates & goinge one Arrauntes to fetche and by dyvers thing*es* & one other busines concerninge the Revells at *chr*istmas Shroftid & other tymes this yeare by discretion of ye M*aster* and the officers — xx^{s}

***Summa* Totalis** of theis charges — xxvij^{li} xxj^{s}. v^{d}.

Rent*es* **The** yeman of the Revells for the rente of his howse hired w*i*thin the late blacke fryers for c^{s} by yere behynde from the Anunciac*i*on of *our* ladye .1559. in anno p*ri*mo regin*æ* Elizab*ethæ* vntyll the feaste of seynte Mychell Tharchaungell then nexte folowinge in the same yere scil*ice*t by the space of one halfe yere — l^{s}.

The Clerke of bothe the tent*es* and Revells for the rente of his howse lykewyse hired and behynde forr the same tyme for w*hi*ch is alowed in the bookes of the tent*es* — xxv^{s} and here — xxv^{s}.

* T. Blagrave
* Iohn holt*es* marke †
* Rychard Leys

f° 42 r.

The Clerke controwler of both the Tent*es* and Revells for the rent of his howse at C^{s} by yere and for his lyu*er*ye at xxvj^{s} viij^{d} by yere behynde for the same tyme for w*hi*ch is alowed in the bookes of the tent*es* — xxxj^{s} viij^{d} and here } xxxj^{s} viij^{d}.

The M*aster* of bothe the Tent*es* and Revells for the rente of his howse at x^{li} by yere lykewyes behynde for the same tyme for which is alowed in the bookes of the tent*es* l^{s} and here } l^{s}

ffor the rente of v greate large roomes w*i*thin the seide late blacke fryers for the woorke and Store howses of the Revells by hynde for the same tyme } lxvj^{s} viij^{d}.

S*u*mm*a* Tot*a*lis of the Rent*es* } xj^{li} iij^{s} iiij^{d}.

S*UMMA* TOT*A*LIS of this booke and the charges of ye Revells in anno p*ri*mo Reg*in*æ nunc Elizab*eth*æ sup*ra*d*i*ctæ } vj^{c} ij^{li} xj^{s} x^{d}

* T Blagrave.
* Iohn holt*es* marke †
* Rychard Leys

f° 42 v.

From Christmas 1559 to 13 April 1567

Record Office. State Papers. Dom. Eliz. vol. XLII. n° 47

Somme Totall of all the provisions and paymentes (conteyned in Sixe bookes *with* the Booke of the progresse) of the Revelles from Christmas Anno Secundo Domine Regine nunc Elizabeth vntill the Thirtenth of Aprill. 1567. Anno Regni eiusdem domine Regine nunc Nono viz.			
	The ffirste booke .	v^{c} xxxvj^{li} xvj^{s} vj^{d}	
	The Second booke .	vij^{c} iiij^{xx} j^{li} vj^{s} vij^{d}	
	The Third Booke .	M viij^{c} xxxviij^{li}. xvj^{s}. iiij^{d} ob.	
	The ffourthe booke .	vij^{c} iiij^{xx} xv^{li} xij^{s} vij^{d}	iiij^{M}. v^{c} lxxviij^{li}. xxij^{d}.
	The ffiveth booke .	ccccxxxviij^{li}. x^{d}	
	The Progresse . .	ciiij^{xx} vij^{li} viij^{s} xj^{d} ob.	

Money Receyued of			
	The Threasorer and Chamberlaynes of Thexchequer at diuerse and sondrie tymes betwene the xvijth daye of Iulie Anno Secundo dicte domine Regine and Michaellmas Terme Anno Octavo eiusdem domine Regine	iij^{M}.v^{c}.vj^{li}.x^{s}.vij^{d} ob. qu.	iij^{M} vij^{c} xxxiiij^{li} x^{s} vij^{d} ob. qu.
	Sir William Damsell knighte generall Receyvour of the courte of Wardes and Liveries by a warraunte dated the xxiiijth daye of ffebruarie Anno Secundo domine Regine predicte	ccxxviij^{li}.	

And so Remayneth yeate to be Receyued viij^{c} xliij^{li}. xj^{s}. ij^{d}. qu.

Th. Beneger

Iohn holtes † marke

Rychard leys

* paid with in the compasse of this some *with* owt A pryncipall warrante xl^{li}

[Endorsed :]

from Christmas A°. 2° Elizabethe Regine ad .30. Aprilis 1567

The charges of the revelles for the same time

Christmas 1559 & Shrovetide 1559-60

Record Office. State Papers. Dom. Eliz. vol. VII. nº 50

The Revelles att Christmas and Shroftyde Anno Secundo regine Elizabethe

An Estymate of the Charges of the Maskes and other preparacions for pastymes to be showen in the presence of the queenes Maiestie att Cristmas and Shroftyde in the Seconde yeare of her highnes reigne Anno Domini 1559.

Videlicet of

ffower Maskes with there torche berers sett forthe and shewen before ye queenes maiestie at whyte Hawle on neweyeres even Neweyeres daye and Twelf daye att nighte the Charges in

Wages of taylours karvars propertie makers wemen and other woorking & attendinge theron as by the Colleccion of there dewes apereth at this presente — xxxvij^{li}. x^{s}.

Sylke for here of weemens heddes byllymente lace frenge buttons tarsells and other parcells bowghte of the Sylkewemen as by her billes aperethe — xxxij^{li}. xj^{s}. viij^{d}

ffeltes and pasteborde for hattes Buckeram for lyninges and patternes threed fuell lyghtes Rysshes and other necessaryes as by the parcells apereth at this presente — xij^{li}. ij^{s}.

Spangells Counterfett Stones with the gylding partie golde Colours mowlded woorke heres and other thinges for the furnyture and garnyture of the premysses to gether amountinge as aperethe at this presente — xiij^{li}. xv^{s}.

A remnaunte of greene Clothe of golde & A remnaunte of Crymsen vellatt sarsenett for performaunce of the Laste maskes with gloves laces & other Habberdasshers parcells as by ye merser & Habberdashers parcells apereth — xxj^{li}. xij^{s} vj^{d}.

— cxvij^{li}. xj^{s}. ij^{d}.

Thother Charges of theis maskes wherof none of ye parties have yet browghte in there parcelles billes and demaundes but ar vncollected will amounte by estymacion to eighte or ten poundes. — x^{li}.

Toe Maskes of men & one maske of women with there torche berers & A Rocke of founteyne and other furnyture thereto apertenente prepared to be sett forth & shewen in ye quenes presence at whighte Hall duringe ye tyme of Shroftyde whorof the Hole Charges will amounte by estymacion to — c^{li} at the leaste

Summa Totalis — ccxxvij^{li} xj^{s} ij^{d}.

verte

Memor*andum* that the Chargies for making of maskes cam never to so little a so*m*me as they do this yere for the same did ever amount aswell in the Quenes highnes tyme that nowe is, as at all other tymes hertofore, to the so*m*me of cccc^{li} alwaies when it was Leaste :

M*emorandum* also that it may please the Quenes Ma*ies*tie to appoint some of her highnes prevy Counsaile I*m*mediatly after Shroftyde yerely to survey the state of the saide office to thintent it may be knowne in what case I fownd it and how it hathe byn since vsed :

M*emorandum* also that the saide Counsailor*es* may haue aucthoritie to appoint suche fees of cast garment*es* as they shall think resonable and not the M*aster* to appoint any as hertofore he hathe done for I think it most for the M*aste*rs savegarde so to be vsed.

[Endorsed :]

Ea*rl* Marshall 1559
lievtena*un*t of ye towre. sollicitor. Revells
Grafto*n* S*ir* Roola*n*d hill.
Robotham. ye Recordor of Lo*n*do*n*.

10 Dec. 1560
Warrant for delivery of Stuff.

British Museum. Additional MSS. 5750.f.66.

Elizabeth R

By the Quene

We woll and co*m*maunde that Imeadiatly vppon the sight hereof ye delyu*er* or cause to be delyu*er*id vnto S*ir* thom*a*s Beng*er* knight m*aster* of o*ur* Revell*es*, for the making of certeyne masking garment*es*. thiese p*ar*cell*es* following. videl*icet*/ of Grene clothe of golde with w*or*k*es* — lxxj. yard*es*. iij q*uarters* di./ Purple golde tincell with knott*es* — xx^{ti} yardes di./ Purple Caffa striped with golde — xxviij yard*es* di. quarter./ Purple golde caffa Bawdkin — xxiiij yard*es*./ Purple Satten wrought with golde — xxiiij yard*es*/ Crymesen satten with w*or*k*es* of golde — xxj yard*es* di./ Incarnat satten wrought with golde — xvij yard*es* q*uarter* one naile/ Grene tyncell wrought with golde — xliij yard*es*/ Grene Caffa wrought w*i*th golde — xxxiiij yard*es* di. iij nailes/ Blacke satten. striped & wrought with golde — lxxij yard*es* di. di. q*uarter*/ Blewe satten with smalle thred*es* of golde — xvij yard*es* q*uarter* di./ Tawny Caffa wrought with golde — xvj yard*es* iij q*uarters*./ Russet vellat pirled with golde — xviij yard*es*/ Silke chamlett*es* crymesen striped with golde — xl yard*es* q*uar*ter di./ Silke chamlett*es* p*ur*ple striped with golde — xlvj yard*es* . . . . which p*ar*cell*es* remayne in yo*ur* custodye & chardge at our pallaice of westm*inster*, And thiese o*ur* Lett*r*es signed with our signemanuell shalbe yo*ur* sufficient warraunt and dischardge for the delyuerye hereof. Yeven at o*ur* said pallaice the xth day of decemb*er* in the thurd yere of oure reigne.

* exa*minatur* all the whole warr*ant*

To o*ur* trustie & welbeloued s*er*ua*u*nt George Bredyma*n* keper of oure said pallaice

[Endorsed :] A warraunt to George Bredyman

1560 & 1561

Record Office. State Papers. Dom. Eliz. vol. XXI. nº 23

Revell*es* in annis Tercio et Quarto *Regni* *Reg*inæ Elizab*ethæ*

<table>
<tr>
<td rowspan="2">A breefe Certifficathe of mony owinge by the Queenes Maiestie within that office above all prestes and soomes of monye payed for woorkes doone there within the tyme aforseide — ix^{c}. xix^{li}. iij^{s}. wherof dewe and growinge</td>
<td>Before Michellmas in dicto anno tercio Regni Reginæ prædictæ as by the perticuler bookes of the same delyuered and accompted for to the Auditours of the prestes and with them remayninge more playnely will apere.</td>
<td>v^{c}. iiij^{xx}iiij^{li}. iij^{s} iiij^{d}
for w<i>hi</i>ch the Queenes Ma<i>ies</i>tie graunted owte her highnes pryvie Seale dated the xxiijth of december laste paste but as yet no monye can be receyved vpon the same.</td>
</tr>
<tr>
<td>Sens the seide laste accompte and before the xxth daye of Ianuarye .1561. in dicto anno Quarto Regni Reginæ prædictæ for hallontyde and Christmas within that tyme.</td>
<td>cccxxxviij^{li}. xix^{s}. viij^{d}.</td>
</tr>
</table>

Memorand*u*m that the Charges for Shroftyde nowe nexte ensuinge is not conteyned w*i*thin this rekeninge w*hi*ch by estimacion will amounte to the some of one hundred poundes or thereabowtes.

Th. Benger
T. Blagrave
Iohn holtes † marke

[Endorsed :] 1561
The dett in ye Revells
20 Ianvarij 1561

iij^{c} xxxviij^{li} xix^{s} viij^{d}

10 May 1562

Warrant for Delivery of Stuff.

British Museum. Lansdowne MSS. 5. art. 40. n° 2.

We woll and commaund you that of soche *our* Silk*es* as remayneth in yo*ur* custodie in o*ur* great warderobe or otherwise to deliver or cause to be delyvered to *our* trustie and welbeloued S*ir* Thomas Benger knight m*aster* of o*ur* Revell*es* and Tryumphes for the better furnyshinge and settinge forthe of suche maskes and Revell*es* as shalbe shewed by hym in his saide office these p*ar*cell*es* of silk*es* followinge, that is to saye, first purple clothe of gold tysshewed w*i*th silver iiij yard*es* q*uarter*, cloth of Silver purple tysshiew iij yard*es* di. di. q*uarter*, black cloth of golde w*i*th woo*rkes* vj yard*es*, black clothe of golde plaine xxij yard*es* di., Russet clothe of golde plaine xxij yard*es* di. tawny cloth of golde plaine xj yard*es*, grene cloth of golde w*i*th work*es* ix yard*es* iij q*uarters*, grene cloth of golde plaine xxxij yard*es* q*uarter*. Russet cloth of golde xxvj yard*es* di., yellowe cloth of golde plaine xxx yard*es* iij q*uarters* di., purple clothe of golde plaine xxiij yard*es* di, cloth of silver xx yard*es* q*uarter*, cloth of silver white plaine xv yard*es*, velvet purple striped w*i*th golde vj yard*es*, velvet red xix yard*es* iij q*uarters*, velvet murrey v yard*es* di., veluet tawney w*i*th work*es* grounde satten xxix yard*es* iij q*uarters*, veluet russet w*i*th work*es* grounde satten lv yard*es* iij q*uarters*, veluet yelloe xxv yard*es* di. di. q*uarter*, veluet blue x yard*es* q*uarter*, veluet white striped ix yard*es* veluet black iij yard*es* iij q*uarters*, sattin crymosen lxxviij yard*es* di. di. q*uarter*, satten yellowe striped xxxvj yard*es* q*uarter*, Satten white striped xxiiij yard*es* iij q*uarters*, Satten yelloe vj yard*es*, damask white ciij yard*es*, damaske murrey capha xvij yard*es* iij q*uarters*, damaske murrey xliij yard*es* q*uarter* di., damaske purple $\overset{\text{xx}}{\text{iiij}}$ xij yardes di. damaske yelloe viij yard*es* di., taffyta yelloe cxvj yard*es* di., taffata carnation narrowe lxxviij yard*es* di., taffata tawney lj yard*es*, taffata russet xxiiij yardes di., taffata blue lv yard*es*, taffata white lj yard*es* q*uarter*, taffata grene lvij yard*es* q*uarter* di., taffata black lxj yard*es* q*uarter*, taffata crymsin xxxij yardes q*uarter* di., Sars*enet* red cciiij $\overset{\text{xx yardes}}{\text{iij}}$ q*uarter*, sars*enet* black xxiiij yard*es* di., sars*enet* tawney xxxvij yard*es* di., sars*enet* russet xxj yard*es* di., sars*enet* white ccxvij yard*es* di., sars*enet* yelloe ccxxiiij yard*es*, sars*enet* blewe $\overset{\text{xx}}{\text{iiij}}$ xvj yard*es*, sars*enet* crymsin doble xliij yard*es* iij q*uarters*, sars*enet* black double $\overset{\text{xx}}{\text{iiij}}$ iij yard*es*, sars*enet* purple lxxv yard*es*, Canvas siluer striped xvij yard*es*, lawne striped viij yard*es* q*uarter*, lawne striped single lx yard*es*, ...
And these o*ur* l*ett*res shalbe yo*ur* sufficient warraunt and dyscharge in this behaulf, yeven under o*ur* signet at o*ur* Palace of Westm*inster* the xth day of Maye in the fourthe yere of o*ur* Reigne.

To o*ur* trustie and welbeloued Iohn ffortescue
Esquire m*aster* of o*ur* great warderobe.

From Pentecost 1562 to 20 November 1563

Record Office. Warrants for Issue (Exch. of Receipt). Parcel 115.

Elizabeth by the grace of god Quene of England ffraunce and Ireland Defendor of the feith &c. To the Thr*easour*er and Cham*ber*laines of our Exchequier greeting We will and co*m*maund yow of suche our treasour as remaineth in yo*ur* custodie of the receipt of our said Exchequier to deliu*er* and paie or cause to be deliu*er*ed and paid vnto our trustie and welbeloved S*ir* Thomas Benger knight maister of our mask*es* revell*es* and plaies or to his deputie in full paiment to be made by him of the charges and arrerages due within his office for one whole yere and a half from the ffeast of Penthecost in the fowrth yere of our reigne vntill the twentie daie of November last past that is to saie for certaine provisions northward viz. hollantide in the said iiijth yere of our reigne, And Christmas Shroftyde and Alhallontyde in the ffifte yere of our reigne / And fromthens vntill the foresaid xx^{tie} of November last past the Some of Six hundreth threscore seventene pownd*es* nyne Shyling*es* a leven pence half peny being also the surplusage of the said S*ir* Thomas Bengers accompt touching his said office ended the said xx^{tie} of November last past / And theise our l*ett*res shalbe yo*ur* Sufficient warrant and discharge in that behalf / yeuen vnd*er* our Privie Seale at our Castell of wyndeso*ur* the ffirst daie of Marche in the Sixt yere of our reigne

Edw*ard*us Clerke

Mr Beng*er*

[endorsed :]

Sol*utio* { Term*ino* Mich*ael*is a*nno* v^{to} regine Eliz*abeth* per } { Stonley — Dxxvij^{li} ix^{s} xi^{d} ob Gardin*er* — c l^{li} } Dclxxvij^{li} ix^{s} xi^{d} ob

Irr*otulatur* p*er* Edmond*um*

From Christmas 1563 to Shrovetide 1564-5

Record Office. State Papers. Dom. Eliz. vol. xxxvi. n° 22

A Brief Estimat off all the Charges Agaynst Cristmas and Candellmas ffor iij Plays at wyndsor w*ith* thare necessaries and provicions ffor the Carrages and Recareges of the same stuf and all ordinarie charges and allsoo for the conveyinge of the Stuf in to the cleane ayre and save kepinge of the same in Anno Sexto Elizabeth. And allsoo in the same yeare the ixth of Iune Repayringe and new makinge of thre maskes with thare hole furniture and diu*ers* devisses and a Castle ffor ladies and a harboure ffor Lords and thre harrolds and iiij Trompetours too bringe in the devise with the men of Armes and showen at the Courtte of Richmond before the Quen*es* Ma*ies*tie and the ffrench Embassitours &c. And diu*ers* Eyrrings Repayringe and Translatinge of Sunderie garment*es* ffor playes And Cristmas and Shroftid in Anno Septimo Elizabeth and many thinges miaid and furneshed w*hi*ch ware nott Sene and much Stuf bought &c.

*1563	Cristmas wages or dieats of the officers & Tayllors payntars Silkwemen m*er*cers Lynen Drappars p*ro*pertie makers and other necessaries & provicions occupied and Bought ffor the same	xxxix^{li} xj^{s} iiij^{d} ob.
*1563	Candellmass ffollowinge wages or dieats of the officers and Tayllo*urs* Silkwemen m*er*cers Skynars and p*ro*pertie makers and other necessaries & provicions	x^{li} vj^{s} v^{d} ob.
*1564	Eyrringe and Repayringe in Aprill followinge wages or dieats of the officers and Tayllors p*ro*vicions and necessaries & other ordinarie Charges	viij^{li} v^{s} vj^{d}
*1564 *at Richmo*nt*. *Mos^{r} Gon*no*r	The ixth of Iune Translattinge new makinge of thre masks and other devisses Agaynst the french Embassitours cominge to Richmond wages or dieats of the officers and Tayllors payntars workinge vppon the Castle and other devisses & m*er*cers ffor Sarsnett and other stuf and Lynen drappars ffor canvas to cou*er* yt with all and Silkwemen for ffrenge & tassales to garnesh the old garments to make them seme fresh Agayne and other p*ro*vicions & necessaries.	iiij^{xx} vij^{li} ix^{s} vj^{d}
*1564	Eyrringe Repayringe in Agust followinge wages or dieats of the officers & Taylo*urs* Silkewomen, ffor frenge and tassels and other Necessaries	xj^{li} xviij^{s} iiij^{d}
*1564	Eyrringe in September ffollowinge wages or dieats of the officers and Taylo*urs* & other p*ro*vicions and necessaries	viij^{li} vj^{s} viij^{d}
*1564 *Edw*ardes* tragedy.	Cristmas Anno Septimo Elizabeth. wages or dieats of the officers and Taylo*urs* payntars workinge diu*ers* Cities and Townes carvars Silkewemen for frenge & tassells m*er*cers ffor Sarsnett & other stuf and Lynen drapars for canvas to cou*er* diu*ers* townes and howsses and other devisses and Clowds ffor a maske and a showe and a play by the childerne of the chaple ffor Rugge bumbayst an cottone ffor hosse and other p*ro*vicions and necessaries	iiij^{xx} vij^{li} vij^{s} viij^{d}

	Eyrringe in Ienevery ffor cayrtene playes by the gramar skolle of westmynster and the childerne of powles wages or dieats of the officers and tayllo*u*rs mercers and other p*ro*vicions	viij^{li} vj^{s} viij^{d}
* 1564 * S*ir* P*er*cyvall * hart*es* so*nnes*	The xviijth of fabruerie wages or dieats of the officers and Tayllors paynttars workinge vppon diu*er*s Cities and Townes and the Emperours pallace & other devisses carvars m*er*cers for Sarsnett and other Stuf & lynen drappars ffor canvas to cou*er* the Townes with all and other p*ro*vicions for A play maid by S*ir* percivall hartts Sones w*ith* a maske of huntars and diu*er*s devisses and a Rocke, or hill ffor the ix musses to Singe vppone w*i*th a vayne of Sarsnett Dravven vpp and downe before them &c.	lvij^{li} x^{s}
* 1564 * Gentillme*nne* * of ye Innes of * Court. Diana. * pallas	Shroftid ffollowinge wages or dieats of the officers and Tayllors payntars workinge vppon the Townes and charretts ffor the goodesses & diu*er*s devisses as the heuens & clowds and foure masks too of them nott occupied nor sene w*i*th thare hole furniture w*hi*ch be verie fayr and Riche of old stuf butt new garnished w*i*th frenge and tassells to seme new and diu*er*s showes made by the gentillmen of greys Ine m*er*cers ffor Sarsnett and other stuf Silkwomen for ffrenge and tasselles Lynen drapars for canvas p*ro*pertie makers and other p*ro*vicions and necessaries	cxv^{li} vij^{d} ob. q*u*.
	Eyrringe Repayringe in Aprill ffollowinge and Translatinge of diu*er*s garment*es* w*i*th thare p*ro*vicions and necessaries ffor the same	x^{l} viij^{s} iij^{d}

So*m*ma To*ta*lis — ccccxliiij^{li} xj^{s} v^{d} ob. q*u*.

[Endorsed :]

The Estimatt ffor the Reuell*es*
&c.

Estimat for y^{e}
Revells. for a^{o}
6°. 7°

1565-6 & 1566-7

Record Office. Warrants for Issue (Exch. of Receipt) Parcel 116.

Elizabeth by the grace of god quene of England ffr*au*nce and Ireland defend*our* of the faithe &c............ and Chambrelains of our Exchequier greating. Whereas vpon examyna*ci*on of the bookes for the charges of our Revells, from the seconde yere of our reign vntill this present it apperith that ther......... the said office the some of viij^{c} xliij^{li} xj^{s} ij ob viz. for anno viij^{o} ccxviij^{li} xvij^{d} And......... our progresse the said yere with stuf bought for the same whereof parte.......... $\overset{xx}{\text{c}}$iiij. vij^{li}. viij^{s}. xj^{d}. ob. And for A*nn*o IX° viz. Christmas shrovetide &c ccccxxxviij......... the somes aboue wrytton. And for that there hath byn payed by ord............ withe out o*ur* speciall warra*u*nt : We will and co*m*maunde yo*w* that of s........... remayneth in the Receipt of o*ur* Exchequier, or that hereaft*er* shall .... Exchequier yow content and paie, or cause to be contented and........ Benger knight m*aster* of o*ur* said Revells, or suche oth*er* as he shall......... the said office the some of eight hundred foure skore, and t........ two pence half pennye Whereof is p*ar*cell the xl^{li} allre........ maketh a even and clere Reckenyng with the sayd office........ l*ett*res shalbe yo*ur* sufficient warraunt and dischardge in that....... Seale at o*ur* Mano*ur* of Richemonde, the xxvth day of Iune........

Revells

[Endorsed :]

.... Sol*utio* per Gardiner Termino Mich*ael*is arch*angeli* a*n*no viij^{o} } xl^{li}

.... Sol*utio* per Pattent Termino Pasche Anno IX° } cc^{li}
....

From 14 July 1567 to 3 March 1567-8

British Museum. Harleian MSS. 146. f. 15 r.

Sir Thomas : Benger knight M*aster* of the Revelles

Elizabethe : by the grace of god Qvene of Englande ffraunce & Irelande Defendo*ur* of the faithe &c. To the Tre*asurer*e and Chaumberlaynes of o*ur* Exchequio*ur* gretinge. **Wheras** : yt apperethe by a Legiere Booke subscribede vnder the handes of the officeres of owere Revells, and remayninge withe the Audito*ur*s of owere prest*es*, that ther is growne due to ceartayne Creddito*ur*s Artifficeares and woorkmen, for stuffe deliu*er*de and woorke donne within thoffice of o*ur* Revells, from the xiiijth of Iulye in the ixth yeare of o*ur* Raigne, vntill the third daye of M*ar*che in the tenthe yeare of owre saide Raigne, the some of, Six hunderede fowre and thirtie poundes nyne shilling*es* and five pence ymployed vppon theis playes Tragides and Maskes following **viz. : Inprimis** for seven playes, the firste namede as playne as Canne be, The seconde the paynfull plillgrimage, The thirde Iacke and Iyll, The forthe sixe fooles, The fivethe callede witte and will, The sixte callede prodigallitie, The sevoenthe of Orest*es* and a Tragedie of the kinge of Scott*es*, to ye whiche belonged diu*ers* howses, for the settinge forthe of the same as Stratoes howse, Gobbyns howse, Orestioes howse Rome, the Pallace of prosperitie Scotlande and a gret Castell one thothere side Likwise for the altering and newe makinge of sixe Mask*es* out of ould stuffe w*ith* Torche beareres thervnto wherof iiij^{or} hathe byne shewene, before vs, and two remayne vnshewen **Wherefore** : o*ur* will and pleasure is y^{t} of suche o*ur* tresure as rem*ayneth* p*re*sentlie in ye Receipte of o*ur* Exchequio*ur* or that heraftere shall come into the same yo*u* contente and paye or cause to be contentede and payede vnto o*ur* trustie and welbelovede Searvaunte S*ir* Thomas Beng*er*e knight or his assigne the sayed some of — DCxxxiiij^{li} ix^{s} v^{d} to be payed ou*er*e vnto the sayed Creddito*ur*s and suche otheres as the same is owinge vnto **And theis owre L*ett*res** : shalbe yo*ur* sufficient warraunte and dischardge in this behalf yeven vndere o*ur* p*ri*vie Seale at o*ur* Manno*ur* of Grenwich the xjth daye of Iune in the tenth yere of o*ur* Raigne

[margin: ^{c}vj xxxiiij^{li} ix^{s}. v^{d}.]

Kerry :

From 19 February to 4 March 1567-8

British Museum. Lansdowne MSS. 9. n° 58.

Chardges Done for the Revells in the hall vppon Shrove sondaye and Shrove Tuisdaye at nighte. **Liber**

A Daye Booke made for the space of xiiij dayes Endinge the forthe daye of marche Anno Reg*ni* Regine Elizabethe Decimo. 1567.

f° 198.

Carpenters occupied not onelye in repayring of the old frame and Settinge of it vpp But alsoe in makinge of Certayne particions and Dore w*i*th diu*er*se other necessaries &c.

at xij^{d} the daye	Iohn Colbrande	x daies.	x^{s}
	Iohn Petter	xij daies.	xij^{s}
	Will*iam* Awstene.	xiij daies ij nig*htes*	xiij^{s} ix^{d}
	Will*iam* Clarke	xiij daies ij nig*htes*	xiij^{s} ix^{d}
at xj^{d} the daye	Iohn Awoode	vj daies.	v^{s} vj^{d}
	Humfreye Parker	ix daies.	viij^{s} iij^{d}
	Roger Bonner	x daies.	ix^{s} ij^{d}

Prentices to the Carpenters

	Thom*as* Wackfilde	x daies.	viij^{s} iiij^{d}
at x^{d} the daye	Gylbarte Beckvrstathe	x daies.	viij^{s} iiij^{d}
	Thoms ffynche	x dayes	viij^{s} iiij^{d}

Bricklayers occupied in newe pavinge of the hall in diu*er*se and sundrye places

at xij^{d} the daye	Wyll*iam* Emarton	vj daies.	vj^{s}
	Antonye Nealle	vj daies.	vj^{s}

S*umm*a Pag*ine* . . . . v^{li} ix^{s} v^{d}

f° 199 r

A Plomber occupied in makinge of Nosses of Lead for the Candellstyk*es*

at xj^{d} the daye	Wyllm Clarke	ij daies	xxij^{d}

A Plasterer occupied in Stoppinge of a Wyndowe at the vpper End of the Hall

at xij^{d} the daye	Pattrick Brandon.	ij daies	ij^{s}

Co*m*mon Labowrers occupied not onlye in helpinge of the Carpenters But alsoe in Servinge of the bricklayers and plasterers and Loadinge of cartes w*i*th bourdes q*uar*ter Iesse Rafters and vnloadinge of the same w*i*th diu*er*se other necessaries

	Iarman Ienkyne	x daies ij ni*ghtes* . .	viij^{s}
	Antonye vpprice	x dayes iij ni*ghtes* .	viij^{s} viij^{d}
	Wyll*iam* Dawnlyne	x daies one ni*gh*te .	vij^{s} iiij^{d}
	Thom*as* Howghton	x daies iij ni*ghtes*. .	viij^{s} viij^{d}
	Wyll*iam* Harper	x daies iij ni*ghtes*. .	viij^{s} viij^{d}
at viij^{d} the daye	Gregorye glasyer	x daies ij ni*ghtes* . .	viij^{s}
and viij^{d} the ni*gh*te	Thom*as* Rounde	vj daies	iiij^{s}
	Owene Thom*as*	vj daies	iiij^{s}
	Edward Percyvall	xij daies	viij^{s}
	Iames Harvye	x dayes iij ni*ghtes*. .	viij^{s} viij^{d}
	Richarde westbye	x daies	vj^{s} viij^{d}
	Iohn morris.	x daies	vj^{s} viij^{d}
		S*um*ma Pagi*ne*. .	iiij^{li} xj^{s} ij^{d}

f° 199 v.

A Kepper of the Store occupied in keppinge of the Chekboke and ou*er*seinge of the workmen and Labowrers

at x^{d} the daye & x^{d} the ni*gh*te	Iohn Whytwell	x daies iij ni*ghtes* . .	x^{s} x^{d}

Cartes by the daye occupied in caringe of the frame into the hall as alsoe in caringe of the saide fram from the Hall tothe storeyarde againe w*i*th diu*er*se other necessaries &c.

	Thom*as* Rogers	vj daies	xij^{s}
at ij^{s} the daye	Edwarde wyll*iams*	one daye	ij^{s}
	Wyll*iam* Ridgwaye	one daye	ij^{s}

Prouicions

pavinge tyles	To Iames Ancell for v^{c} of pavinge tyles of viij ynches broade at v^{s} the Hundrethe	xxv^{s}
Leade	To Henrye Deacon plomb*er* for one hundrethe of newe leade	xij^{s}
wodden platers	To Wyll*iam* Horner for iiij dossene of treene platers for the Light*es* at iij^{s} the doz*en*	xij^{s}
payntinge	To Nicholas Lyzarde for the paynting of iiij dozen of wodden platers at iiij^{d} the pece	xvj^{s}
Lyme	To Iohn marche Lymmane for ij^{c} of Lyme at vj^{s} the Hundrethe	xij^{s}
	S*umma* Pag*ine*	v^{li} iij^{s} x^{d}.

f° 200 r.

Nayles	To Hewghe Docksye Iron monger for one M of dowble x^{d} n*ai*lls — x^{s} for iij M of Sengle x^{d} n*ai*lls at v^{s} the M — xv^{s} for vj M of vj^{d} n*ai*lls at iiij^{s} the M — xxiiij^{s} And for one some of ij^{d} n*ai*lls — xij^{s}	iij^{li} xij^{d}
Lockes	To Gylbarte Polsone for v Lyverye Lockes at xiiij^{d} the pece	v^{s} x^{d}
plaunchebourde	To Robarte Edmondes for iij^{c} of planchbourd at iij^{s} iiij^{d} the hundrethe	x^{s}
plaunchbourde	To Wyll*iam* Beldam for viij^{c} di. & xxx^{ti} foote of plaunchebourde at iij^{s} iiij^{d} the hundrethe	xxix^{s} iiij^{d}
plaunchbourde	To Henrye Gylkynes for iij^{c} of planche bourde at iij^{s} iiij^{d} the hundrethe	x^{s}
q*uar*terbourde	To Thom*as* Butt*es* for v^{c} of q*uar*terbourd at iij^{s} iiij^{d} the hundrethe	xvj^{s} viij^{d}
q*uar*ters	To Iohn mowyer for one Loade of q*uar*ters . . .	xij^{s}
q*uar*ters Iesse Rafters	To Thom*as* Tomsone for ij Loades of Sengle q*uar*ters at xij^{s} the Load — xxiiij^{s} And for iiij Loades of Ieese and Rafters at xij^{s} the Loade — xlviij^{s}	iij^{li} xij^{s}

To Robarte Coxsone Sawyer for the Sawinge of one M foote of Elme bourde at xx^{d} the hundrethe Sawinge } xvj^{s} viij^{d}

Summa *Pagine* . . . xj^{li} xiij^{s} vj^{d}

f° 200 v.

Iron Worke — To Richarde Iefferies Smythe for one Dossene of Blacke boltes at vj^{d} the pece — vj^{s} and for one dozen di. of round Staples at j^{d} ob the pece — ij^{s} iij^{d} } viij^{s} iij^{d}

Basterope / Landcariage — To Iohn Whitwell for viij peces of Bastroppe at vj^{d} the pece — iiij^{s} And for the Landcariage of vij Loades di. of bourds q*uar*ters Rafters and Ieese from Sundrye places in London to the Storeyard in Scotlande at viij^{d} the Loade — v^{s} } ix^{s}

Glassinge — To Petter Nicollson glasyer for those p*ar*cells ffolowinge viz. In the Hall made of newe glase xxviij foote at vj^{d} ob the foote Sett in newe Leade xxxvj foote at iij^{d} the foote mended xiij panes at iiij^{d} the pece and stopte vij^{xx} xij q*u*arells at j^{d} the Quarrell } xlj^{s} ij^{d}

Summa *Pagine* — lviij^{s} v^{d}

f° 201 r.

SUMMA Totalis of This Booke } xxix^{li} xvj^{s} iiij^{d}

[Endorsed :] Chardges done for the Revelles vppon Shrovesonday and Shroftuisdaye at nighte

Christmas 1568 and Shrovetide 1568-9

British Museum. Harleian MSS. 146. f. 51 v°.

Sir **Thomas** Beng*er* knight M*aster* of the Revells

Elizabethe by the grace of god quene of England, ffraunce and Irelande defendor of the faithe &c To the Tr*easor*er and Chaumberlaynes of our Exchequio*ur* greetinge, Wheras it apperethe, by a Leiger book subscribed vnder the hand*es* of the M*aster* of our Revells, and other our officeares app*er*tayninge vnto the saied office, that theris growne due vnto certayne creddito*urs* for stuffe by them deliu*er*ed into the saied office, for the furnisshinge of suche playes, Tragidies, and Maskes as hathe byne shewed before vs at Christmas, and Shrovtide Last past in the eleventh year of our Raigne, As also for wag*es* and other necessaries due and oweinge for vnto diu*ers* and soundery Artifficeares and others for Woorkmanshipp therof, the some of fowre hunderethe fiftie three pound*es* v^{s} vj^{d}, as by the same booke committed by you o*ur* Tr*easor*er of England vnto the hand*es* of the Awdito*urs* of our prest*es* it appereth Theise therfore ar to signifie vnto you, that o*ur* will and pleasur is that of suche our treasur, as p*re*sentlye Remaynethe in the Receipte of our Exchequio*ur*, or that her-aftere shall come into the same, yow content and paye, or cause to be contented and payed, vnto o*ur* Right trustie and welbeloved searvaunt S*ir* Thomas Beng*er* knight M*aster* of our Revells, or his assigne the saied some of fowr hunderethe fiftie three pound*es* five shilling*es* and sixe pens, to be by him or them paied ou*er*e vnto suche Creddito*urs*, and other p*er*sons, as the same is oweinge vnto in full satisfacc*i*on, and paym*ent* of the saied Leiger booke And theis our L*ett*res shalbe yo*ur* sufficient war-raunt and dischardge in this behalf. Yeven vnder o*ur* p*ri*vie seale at o*ur* Manno*ur* of Grenw*i*ch the tenthe daye of Maye, in the eleventh yeare of our Raigne

Ry Osley

Christmas 1569 and Shrovetide 1569-70

British Museum. Harleian MSS. 146. f. 74 r.

Sir Thomas Benger knight *Master* of the Revells.

Elizabethe by the grace of God *Qvene* of Englande ffraunce and Irelande defendo*ur* of the ffaithe &c. To the treasorer and Chamberlaines of o*ur* Eschequier greteinge. Wheras it apperethe by a leidger booke subscribed vnder thand*es* of the M*aster* of our Reuells and other our officers appertayninge vnto our saide office that there is growne due vnto certeyne Creditors for stuffe by them deliu*er*ed into the saide office for the furnishinge of soche playes, tragedyes and maskes, as hathe bene shewed before vs at Christmas and Shrovetide Laste paste in the twelvithe yeare of our Raigne, As also for wages and other necessaries occupyed in the saide office aboute the same, as for kepeinge of the stuffe and suche other thinges as ar incident to thoffice, beinge due and oweinge for vnto diu*ers* and soundrie Artificers and other for worckemanshippe and attendinge therof, the some of foure hundred foure score nynetene poundes seaventene shillinges sixe pence halfpenny as by the same booke co*m*mitted by our Tre*asore*r vnto thandes of one of our Awditors of our prest*es* it more playnlie apperethe. Theis Therfore are to signifie vnto yo*u* that our will and pleasure is, that of soche our Treasure as p*rese*ntlie remaynethe in the Receipte of our eschequier or that hereafter shall come into the same, you Contente and paye or cause to be Contented and paide vnto our Righte trustie and welbeloueid servaunte S*ir* Thomas Benger knighte M*aster* of our Revells or his assigne, the saide some of foure hundred foure score nynetene poundes xvij^{s} vj^{d} ob, to be by him or his assigne paide over vnto soche Creditors and other persouns, as the same is oweinge vnto in full satisfaction and payment of the saide Leidger booke/ And theis our L*ett*res shalbe your sufficiente warraunte and dischardge in this behalf, yeven vnder our preuie seale at Chenyes the xxixth daie of Iulie in the xijth yeare of our Raigne.

P*er* me Anthonin*um* Pykeringe
Deput*atum* Edw*ard*i Clerke.

From Shrovetide 1569-70 to Shrovetuesday 1570-1.

Record Office. Imprest Certificate Books (Pells), vol. I [fol. 34 v. & 35 r.]

Elizabeth etc To the Treasourer and Chamblaynes of our Eschequire greting Wheras it appeareth in a lieger Booke subscribed with thandes of the master of our Revelles and other our officers app*er*teyning to our said office that there is growen dew vnto certayne Creditors for their Stuffe deliuered into the said office w*it*h such other necessaries and provisicons as are incident vnto the same / And for Wagies due vnto diuerse Artificers and workmen for working and attending theron ; especially about the new making furnishing and setting furth of soundrie Comodies Tragedies Maskes and Showes w*hi*ch were showen before vs this Last *christ*mas and Shroftyde; with other ordinarie chardg*es* rising by meanes of the said office and the safe keping therof during one hoole yere endid on Shroftewesday at night now Last past before the date hereof as by by the same Booke remayning w*it*h the Clerke of our said office aswell for the dischardge of the said M*aster* and officers as to pay the Creditors by at lardge appeareth vj^{c} lxvj^{li} xvj^{s} iij^{d} Theise are to signifie vnto you our Will and pleasure That of such our treasure as presentlie remayneth in the receipt of our Eschequire or that hereaftre shall come into the same you content and pay or cause to be contented and paied vnto our right trustie and welbeloued s*er*vaunt S*ir* Thomas Benger knight M*aster* of the said our office the some of Dclxvj^{li} xvj^{s} iij^{d} to be paied over vnto such p*er*sounes as by the said booke the same debtes shall appere to be owing vnto in full satisffacc*i*on and paym*ent* of all such chardges and allowaunces for that yere. And theise our l*ett*res shalbe your warraunt and dischardge in that behalfe / Yeven vndre our privay Seale at our Mannor of Richmound the xxiijth daye of Octobre in the thirtenth yere of our raigne.

From Shrovetuesday 1570-1 to 31 May 1572

viz.

Record Office. Audit Office. Accounts Various. Bundle 1213. Revels. nº 1

1571

Revells in One yeare Ending on Shrovetewsdaye : in the **xiiij**th yeare of oure Sovereaigne Lady Queene **Elyzabeth.**

The Contentes of this Booke.

The whole Charges of Thoffice aforeseide for one whole yeare. vid*elicet* ffrom Shrove Tewsday in the xiijth yeare vntill Shrovetewsdaie in the xiiijth yeare of her Ma*ies*ties reaigne.
Growing aswell by meanes of **Wages & allowaunc*es*** due to sundry persons woo*r*king and Attending w*ith*in the seide office & abowte thaffares therof : as Allso by meanes of sundry **Emptions & provizions** this yeare within the same tyme made & p*ro*vyded by S*ir* Thom*as* Benger knighte (being M*aster* of the seide office) for the Apparelling, Disgyzinge, ffurnishing, ffitting, Garnishing & orderly setting foorthe of men, woomen, & Children : in sundry Tragedies Playes, Maskes and sport*es* with theier apte howses of paynted Canvas & prop*er*ties incident suche as mighte most lyvely expresse the effect of the histories plaied & Devises in Mask*es* this yeare showen at the Coo*r*te for her Ma*ies*ties Regall Disporte & Recreac*i*on whose tytles & Numbers w*ith* the tymes wherin they were showen Breefely are sett owte in the ende of this booke. wherin first ffoloweth the ordinary chardge.

vid*elicet*

Within the tyme of ix monethes & for

Ayryng, Repayrng, Layeng abrode, Turning, sowing amending, Tacking, Spunging, wyping, Brushing, Sweeping, Caryeng, ffowlding, suting, putting in order & bestowing of the Garment*es*, vestures, Armo*ur*, prop*er*ties & other stuff, store and Impleme*n*tes of the seide office : for the safegarde, Refreshing, & Reddinesse therof at dyvers tymes as the necessitie therof required betweene the ende of the last Revells being as before is saide on Shrove tewsdaie in the xiijth yeare of her Ma*ies*ties reaigne : And the begynnyng of the new woork*es* for the next Christm*as* folowing which beg*anne* the first of December in the xiiijth yeare of her Ma*ies*ties reaigne.

vid*elicet* in

.1.	.2.	.3.	.4.	.5.	.6.
Marche,	**Aprill,**	**May,**	**Iune,**	**Iuly,**	**August**

.7.	.8.	.9.
September,	**October,**	**November.**

fo 2 r.

	Alowed ffor :		Dayes :	Night*es*.	Wages.
	Thom*a*s Clatterbooke	at xx^{d} the daie	56	04	c^{s}
	Robert Holmeden	at xij^{d} the daie	56	04	lx^{s}.
	Thom*a*s Booreman	at xij^{d} the daie	60	00	lx^{s}.
	Iohn Drawater	at xij^{d} the daie	60	00	lx^{s}.
	Richarde Mundaye	at xij^{d}.	60	00	lx^{s}.
	Hénri price.	at xij^{d} the daie	60	00	lx^{s}
Taylers & Attendant*es* woorking & attending on the premisses together with the **Travellers & attendant*es*** that followed the M*aster* of this office in the **progresse** on the Busynesse & affares of the same office. vide*licet*	Edwarde Grace	at xij^{d} the daie	60	00	lx^{s}.
	Wyll*iam* Hitchcock.	at xij^{d} ye daie	60	00	lx^{s}.
	Henri Calleweye & Huet		60	06	lxvj^{s}.
	Will*iam* Iennyn & his wyfe.		13	02	xxx^{s}.
	Robert Sayll & Thom*a*s Lowen		18	02	xl^{s}.
	Iohn Ollyf, & Angell Gyles :		26	04	lx^{s}.
	Ieffery yonge & his s*er*va*un*t*es* With iij Horses & Waggon. s*er*ving in the progresse				iiij^{li}.iij^{s}.

* S*umma* . . xxxix^{li} xix^{s}

porter.	Iohn Dawncye	at xij^{d}. the daie	56	04	lx^{s}.

* S*umma* pat*e*t

Offycers in Respect of diett as foloweth.	The Master : now, S*ir* Thom*a*s Benger knighte. at iiij^{s} the daie	60	00	xij^{li}
	The Clerkcomptrowler : now, Edward Buggyn esquier. at ij^{s} the daie.	60	00	vj^{li}.
	The Clerke : now, Thom*a*s Blagrave esquier. at ij^{s} the daie.	60	00	vj^{li}.
	The Yoman : now, Iohn Holte by Will*iam* Bowll his deputie at ij^{s}	60	00	vj^{li}.

* S*umma* xxx^{li}.

f° 2 v.

Necessaries. — **William Bowll** deputie vnto Iohn Holte yoman of this office for mony by him disbursed for Threade of sundry coollers: for Brushes, rubbers, Broomes bask*ettes*, Lock*es*, keyes, Hookes, Henges, Boord*es*, Nayles, ffewell [lightes] & suche other things as neede required within this tyme (of ix moneths before set owte) to be vzed & imploied *with*in the seide office in all — lxxiij^{s}.

ffrom Shrovetewsdaie in a*nno* r*egni* r*eg*in*æ* Elizab*eth* **xiij**^{o} **vntill** the ffirst of December in a*nno* r*egni* r*eg*in*æ* p*ræ*d*ictæ* **xiiij**^{o}

S*UMMA* of all the **ordinary** allowaunc*es* & Charges of this office together with the [xiij^{li}. xix^{s}.] wages & al[l]owaunces of ix p*er*sons [laste] before mencioned that travelled and attended on the M*aster* in the **progresse** abowte thaffares of the same office. **In all** amou*n*ting to — lxxvj^{li}. xij^{s}.

* *examinatur per* * Edwardum Buggyn
* T. Blagrave
* Iohn Arnold

f° 3 r.

1571

December : January : & ffebruary anno *R*egni *R*egin*æ* Elizabeth p*rædictæ* **xiiij**^{to} ffor

Christmas
Newyearesdaye :
Twelfedaye : and
Shrovetyde

Devyzyng, provydyng, preparing, Newmaking, Translating, Repayring ffytting, ffurnishing, Garnishing, setting foorthe Attending, well ordering, Taking in agayne, safebestowing, and safekeeping, of all **Thaparell & Implement***es* of the seide office (of her Ma*ies*ties Revells) with the Propertyes, Howses, and Necessaries incident therunto cheefely for Thapparelling, disguysing, fitting, ffurnishing & setting foorthe of sundry Menn, women & Children in the **vj. playes & vj. maskes.** mencioned more at lardge in the ende of this Booke. together with Thimployme*n*t of suche stuf as the same M*aster* of this office delyvered (vnto the yoman) being p*er*cells of themptions ffollowing. after the entrye of the wages.

vid*elicet*

Wages and Allowaunc*es* due to the partyes folowing

ffor woorkes doone and **Attendaunce** geaven within the seide Office. **Betweene** the ffirst of December aforeseide : on which daie, the New woork*es*, & preparac*i*ons, ffor playes, & Maskes, agaynst the tymes aforeseide, did begyn : **And** the aforeseide Shrove Tewsdaye : on which nighte the Revells for that yeare did ende. according to the concluzion of this booke.

	Dayes	**Nightes.**	
Thom*as* Clatterbooke at xx^{d} ye daie	55	15	cxvj^{s}. viij^{d}.
Richarde Bryan & all the rest at xij^{d}	34	06	xl^{s}.
Humphrie Smallman	20	04	xxiiij^{s}.
Henri kelleweye	55	15	lxx^{s}.
Will*iam* Lewis.	55	15	lxx^{s}.
Edward Iones	20	10	xxx^{s}.
Iohn Walker	32	15	xlvij^{s}.

fo 4 r.

Taylers and Attendant*es* woo*r*king attending & travelling in the woo*r*k*es*, buzinesses & affares of the seide office. daie & Nighte as foloweth vid*elicet*

Gryffyn Iones	18	13	xxxj^{s}.
Iohn Harper	43	12	lv^{s}.
Iohn Cleyton	33	15	xxxviij^{s}.
Geordge Haukynson	15	09	lxiiij^{s}.
Robert Garton.	55	07	lxij^{s}.
Thom*as* Lambe	40	06	xlvj^{s}.
Will*iam* Woodd	33	15	xlviij^{s}.
Thom*as* Kylforde.	40	10	l^{s}.
Randall Owley	23	15	xxxviij^{s}.
Iohn Rice.	20	10	xxx^{s}.
Bryan Will*is* for w*alte*r cock.	39	03	xlij^{s}.
Henri White	15	07	xxij^{s}.
Gryffyn Browne	37	03	xl^{s}.
ffraunc*es* Vanheydon	37	03	xl^{s}
Thom*as* Robothom	10	05	xv^{s}.
Richarde Snowzell	08	06	xiiij^{s}.
Edmund Owgle.	23	13	xxxvj^{s}.
Richarde Warmingham	60	10	lxx^{s}.
Richarde Gurnell.	60	10	lxx^{s}.
Thom*as* Birde.	80	15	iiij^{li} xv^{s}.
Richard Colleye	80	15	iiij^{li}. xv^{s}.
Thom*as* Booreman	80	15	iiij^{li}. xv^{s}.
Iohn Drawater	80	15	iiij^{li} xv^{s}.
Richard Mundaye	80	15	iiij^{li} xv^{s}.
Henri price.	80	15	iiij^{li}. xv^{s}.
Will*iam* Benger	80	15	iiij^{li} xv^{s}.
ffugall			
Stephan Bonde	80	15	iiij^{li}. xv^{s}.
Edwarde Grace	80	15	iiij^{li} xv^{s}.
Will*iam* Hitchcock	80	15	iiij^{li}. xv^{s}.
Will*iam* Bowll	36	04	xl^{s}.
Robert Holmeden	30	06	xxxvj^{s}
Robert Carr	20	00	xx^{s}
Iohn ffawnce	08	06	xiiij^{s}

* S*umma* — cxiij^{li}. viij^{s}. viij^{d}

f°4v.

Propertymakers Imbroders and Habberdashers *with* theier servauntes working vpon thapparell properties & headpeeces with strange hattes & garnishinges.	at ijs the daie	Iohn Carrowe	55	15	vijli.
	xxd.	William Pilkington.	80	15	vijli xviijs. iiijd
	xviijd.	Christopher Munford.	42	15	iiijli. vs. vjd.
	xvjd.	Iohn ffarrington	55	15	iiijli. xiijs. iiijd.
	at xijd the daie	Androw Hewett.	55	15	lxxs.
		Iohn Bashforde	49	15	lxiiijs.
		Iohn Davye	49	15	lxiiijs.
		Ione pilkington	80	15	iiijli. xvs.
		peeter Morris for hog.	06	05	xjs.
					* *Summa* — xxxixli xiiijd
Paynters and theier servauntes that wrowghte & attended in thoffice & at the Coorte vpon the Canvas that made all the howses for the plaies	at xxd the daye	William Lyzarde	55	15	cxvjs. viijd.
		Nicholas Sutton.	08	05	xxjs. viijd.
		Lewes Lyzarde	17	08	xljs. viijd.
		Balthazer	04		vjs viijd.
		Romyn	06	04	xvjs. viijd.
		Iacob Michell.	06	04	xvjs viijd
		Iacob Townce	02	01	vs.
		pangras Inglish	02	01	vs.
		Androw perry	02	01	vs.
					* *Summa* — xjli. xvs
	xvjd the daie	Christopher lulock	18	05	xxxs. viijd.
		Richarde Baker	10	04	xviijs. viijd.
		Nicholas knighte	01	01	ijs viijd.
		Iohn Barker	10	04	xviijs. viijd.
		Ioyce ffrolick	10	03	xvijs iiijd
		Iohn Lyzarde.	10	04	xviijs viijd
		Nicholas Lyzard	07	04	xiiijs viijd.

f° 5 r.

playes & devices for the Mask*es* & p*ro*p*er*ties therto incidente as cap*ar*isons & furnit*ure* for the challeng*er*s & def*enders with* theier horses &c. & vpon the targett*es* weapo*ns* garlonds, cronett*es*, & sundry other things. vid*elicet*

	Thom*as* Lymbye	02	01	iiij^{s}.
	Iohn Michell	03	01	v^{s}. iiij^{d}.
	Will*iam* Walton	03	01	v^{s}. iiij^{d}.
	Iohn Sam	06	02	x^{s} viij^{d}.
	Iohn Inglish	02	01	iiij^{s}.

* S*umma* — vij^{li} x^{s} viij^{d}

xiiij^{d} the daie	Anthony parke	28	08	xlij^{s}.
	Iohn ffian.	19	08	xxxj^{s}.vj^{d}.
	Henri Sharpe	08	05	xv^{s}. ij^{d}.
	Iohn Walton	03	02	v^{s}. x^{d}
	Iohn Nich*ol*as	03	01	iiij^{s}. viij^{d}.

* S*umma* — iiij^{li} [illegible]x^{s} ij^{d}

xij^{d} the daie	Iohn perkyns	29	08	xxxvij^{s}.
	Anthony Godfrie	27	08	xxxv^{s}.
	Iohn Debare	02	01	iij^{s}
	Harvie Chrispia*n*.	20	05	xxv^{s}. 29/4/10/

* S*umma* — c^{s}

Wyll*iam* Hearns for woorkmanshipp done in sundry places: and attendaunce geven at sundry tymes by him & his s*er*ua*un*tes at the seide M*aste*rs commandeme*nt* and for his golde, sylver, & other coollers Imploied in thoffice — vj^{li}.xiij^{s}.iiij^{d}.

* S*umma* paynters — xxxv^{li} xviij^{s} ij^{d}

Porter. Iohn Dawncye . . . . . 80 . . . 15 . . . iiij^{li} xv^{s}.

* S*umma* pat*et*

Officers in Respect of theier **Dyettes** vid*elicet.*

The M*aster* at iiij^{s} the daye	80	15	xix^{li}.
The Clerkcomptrol*er* at ij^{s} ye daie	80	15	ix^{li}. x^{s}.
The Clerke at ij^{s} the daie	80	15	ix^{li}. x^{s}.
The yoman now Iohn Arnolde (at ij^{s}.)	80	15	ix^{li}. x^{s}.

* S*umma* — xlvij^{li} x^{s}

ffrom the first daye of Desember. **vntill** Shroveteusdaie in *anno regni reginæ Elizabeth prædictæ* **xiiij**^{to}.

S*UMMA* **of** all the **Wages** for woork*es* doone & Attendaunce geven wi*th*in the seide office and abowte thaffares therof then — ccxl^{li}. xiij^{s}.

f°5v.

December : Ianuari : ffebruari : *anno Regni Reginæ* Elizabeth *prædictæ* **xiiij**^{to}.

By the *Master* of thoffice — **Emptions and provizions** made agaynst (and within) the same tymes browghte into this office : and delyvered (by the partyes following) vnto the handes and custody of the same S*ir* Thom*as* Benger knighte being M*aster* therof. to be employed vpon the ffurnishing of the vj playes : & the Newmaking, & translating, of the vj Maskes : now within this tyme sett foorthe (more at lardge appeering in the end of this booke) or otherwyse the Remayne then vnemployed (by him reserved) for the like vse, another tyme, to be likewise yelded : when the like service, owte of this office, sholde happen to bee (by her M*aies*tie) expected : or other wise required.

vide*licet*

Iohn Lacy for dyvers percells of wares by him delyvered vnto the seide M*aster* of this office as by A bill therof subscribed by the seid S*ir* T*homas* Benger knighte more at lardge appereth

Wares	Amount	Total
Taffita of sundry coollers and prices in all. cclxxiij yardes.	cxxx^{li}. vj^{d}.	
Sattyns of sundry cullers & p*ri*ces in all cclij yerdes	cxxxviij^{li}. xiiij^{s} v^{d}	
Sarcenett*es* of sundry cullers & p*ri*ces in all. DCCCxiiij yerd*es* di	c^{xx}iiijv^{li}. v^{s}. iiij^{d}	
Cloth of golde of sundry cullers &c in all. xxx yard*es*	xxxj^{li} xvj^{s} viij^{d}	
Tynsells of sundry cullers & p*ri*ces in all. cij yardes	xlv^{li}. ij^{s}. vj^{d}.	DCCxxiiij^{li}.xvj^{s}x^{d}
Velvett*es* of sundry cullers & p*ri*ces in all. cxxvij yardes	cvj^{li}. iij^{s}.	
Damask*es* of sundry cullers & pric*es* in all. lxxiiij yardes	lxiij^{li}. xiij^{s}. ix^{d}	
Sackclothe Stripte *with* sylver in all .v. yardes	l^{s}.	
Chamlet ane remn*au*nte greene contayning x yard*es*	lxvj^{s}. viij^{d}.	
Buckerams of sundry coollers vj peec*es* in all yard*es*	iiij^{li}. iiij^{s}.	
Tukes in all cxl yard*es*	xiiij^{li}	

Mercers and theier p*ar*cells. — **All w*hi*ch** his mony amounteth vnto

* S*umm*a pagine — pa*te*t

fo 6r.

	Will*iam* Ro for Cloth of Gowlde by him delyvered vnto the seide S*ir* Thom*as* Benger as by A bill therof by him the seide M*aster* subscribed may appeere in all xliiij yard*es* at xxj^{s} the yarde being of Crimsen$^{:15.}$ p*ur*ple$^{.15.}$ & greene$^{.14.}$ coolor price	xlvj^{li}. iiij^{s}.
	Iohn Will*ia*mson for sundry percells of his wares delyvered vnto the seide S*ir* T*homas* Benger to the vse likewise of the seide office as by his bill more at lardge appereth. vid*elicet*	
	Sarcenett*es* of sundry cullers and prices In all ciiij^{xx}xv ells price — lxj^{li}. xix^{d}. Vellvett xxvij yard*es* at xvij^{s} le y*ar*d — xxij^{li}. xix^{s}. Chaungeable Taffita j yarde . . — xj^{s}. viij^{d}. Loomewoorke liij ells at v^{s}.vj^{d} thell — xiiij^{li}. xj^{s}. vj^{d}. **All which** his mony amounteth vnto	iiij^{xx}xix^{li}. iij^{s}. ix^{d}.
	Iohn Browne, for dyvers percells of his wares delyvered vnto the seide S*ir* Thom*as* Benger to the vse aboveseide as by his bill vid*elicet*	
	Cloth of golde of Redd cooll*or* xvj yard*es* q*uarter* / of greene culler xxiij yard*es* iij q*uarter*s di. / of Blew culler xiij yard*es* di. & di. q*uarter* In all at xvj^{s} the yarde liij yard*es* iij q*uarter*s — xliij^{li}. Cloth of Tyssue of white culler xxxix yard*es* di./ of greene culler xxiij yard*es* di./ in all at viij^{s} the yarde lxiij yardes amou*n*ting vnto — xxv^{li}. iiij^{s}. **All which** his mony amounteth vnto	lxviij^{li}. iiij^{s}.
the Draper.	**Will*iam* Dane** alderman of London for One peece of Cloth of golde — xx^{li}. / ffor Canvas Diiij^{xx}vij ells di — xxix^{li}. vij^{s}. ix^{d}. And for vandelas lxvij ells di — lxvij^{s} vj^{d} / In all delyvered by his wyfe & s*er*vaunt*es* vnto the hands of the seide S*ir* T*homas* Benger to the vse afore saide	lij^{li}. xv^{s}. iij^{d}.

* S*um*m*a* pagine — cclxvj^{li} vij^{s}

f° 6 v.

Thupholster. **Philipp Gunter** for sundry percells of wares namely Buckerams of sundry cullers and sundry pryces by him browghte into thoffice and delyvered vnto the seide *Master* and others by him appointed to receive the same to be employed for lynyngs & patternes &c. in all as by his bill clxj peec*es* price } xxxij^{li}. v^{s}. viij^{d}.

Sylkwomen & wares bowghte of them vid*elicet*

Ione Bowll for sundry percells of ware by her delyvered into this office to the vse aforeseide by the commaundement of the seide Master as more at lardge appereth by her bill.

vid*elicet*

ffrynge of Copper sylver & silk in all xxxix lb. & iij q*uarter*s of an ounce	xlv^{li}. xix^{s}. j^{d}. ob.	} lvij^{li}. xij^{s}. ob
Silk ffyve ounc*es* & an halfe	xj^{s}.	
Buttons of Copper Sylver (324)	xviij^{s}. iiij^{d}.	
Tassels with Calles xij. price	xij^{s}. x^{d}.	
Lace ffyve pownde vij ounces	iiij^{li}. xj^{s}.	
Twist iiij lb. ij ounc*es* di.	iiij^{li}. xix^{s}. ix^{d}.	

All wh*i*ch her mony amounteth vnto

Wever of Saint Martyns for mony to him due for sundry percells of his ware, namely of Copper sylver frenge at xxiiij^{s} the .8. lb lb. — ix^{li}. xij^{s}./ ffor gold yolo Oving at xxx^{s} the lb. iiij lb. x ounc*es* — vj^{li}. xviij^{s} viij^{d}. And for buttons and lace of greene silke and golde — xj^{s} viij^{d}. in all as by his bill subscribed by the yoman y^{t} imploied it within this office on the matters ensuing appereth } xvij^{li}. ij^{s}. iiij^{d}.

Mr Buggyn for mony by him disburced for vj grose of Buttons by him browghte into thoffice — xij^{s} And for fyne Lawne for Mercuries heade — viij^{s}. in all } xx^{s}.

* S*um*ma pagine — cviij^{li} ob.

f° 7 r.

Willyam Bowll deputy to Iohn Holte late yoman of this office for mony by him disburced at sundry tymes at the M*aste*rs comaundem*ent* for sundry things following for the vse aforeseide. vid*elicet*

	^Stones called (240)^ Sitterines & Topiass*es* w*ith* ^dyvers^ enamellings	xij^{li}. vij^{s}. iiij^{d}.	
	Gylding and setting ^the seid^ of stones &c	cij^{s} vj^{d}.	
	Canvas .lv. ells price in all	lxx^{s}.	
	Vyzardes of the ffinest xviij p*r*ice	xxxv^{s}.	
	Gloves for maskers xij paier	vj^{s}.	
	Raw sattin silke for heare	xvij^{s} vj^{d}.	
	Threade iij lb ij bowlt*es*	xvj^{s} x^{d}.	
	Tape both fyne and Coorse	ij^{s}. ix^{d}	
	pacthreade and buttons togethers.	iij^{s} vi^{d}.	
	Orsedue.	iiij^{s}. iiij^{d}.	
	Lace of Crowne purle	ij^{s} viij^{d}.	
	Lambeskins for moores	iij^{s}. ix^{d}.	lj^{li}. j^{d}.
	past boordes ix dozen	xvij^{s} iiij^{d}.	
	ffelt*es* ij doozen & ix	xxij^{s}.	
	fflowers wrowghte w*ith* needle wo*r*ke wherof iij were preasented to her M*aies*tie the residue garnished maskers heads	iiij^{li}. xij^{s}.	
	Heare for Hozen.	iiij^{s}. xj^{d}.	
	ffewell & Rushes.	xj^{s}.	
Provizions of sundry kynd*es* of stuf & **Expences** sundry wayes disbu*r*sed by the yoman of this office his deputie for the tyme being. vid*elicet*	And for monye by him at sundry tymes disbursed in Reward*es* & payment*es* by him made at the speciall request of the seide S*ir* T*homas* Benger for sundry s*er*vic*es* by him vzed & sundry emptions by him had to his owne p*r*ivate implovme*n*t within this yeare in thaffares herof by the affirmacon of the seide M*aste*r	xviij^{li}. viij^{d}.	
	All which his mony amounteth vnto		

* *Summa* pagine — *patet*

Iohn Arnolde yoman of this office for mony by him disburced at sundry tymes for sundry things requisit to the vse aforesaide as by his bill viz.

Gilt Bugles [M] and Rubies [300] . . . . c^{s}.
Thread [.26. lb & .7. bolt*es*] of sundry cullers & sort*es* . . . . . . cij^{s}. viij^{d}.
Lace of sundry sort*es* ij lb. . . . . xxxiiij^{s}.
ffethers of sundry sort*es* . . . . xxiij^{s}.
ffewell spent in thoffice. . . . . iiij^{li}. xvij^{s}. iiij^{d}.
pasted paper & other pap*er* . . . . xxxvij^{s}. j^{d}
Gloves for players & maskers . . . . lj^{s}.
pinnes and tape togethers. . . . . ix^{s}. ij^{d}.
Rushes for the w*or*kehowses. . . . . vj^{s}. viij^{d}.
ffelt*es* [39^{s}] poynt*es* [.20^{d}.] and corde [.18^{d}.] in all . . . . xlij^{s}. ij^{d}
Curtyn Ringes & heare for hoz*en* . . . . . . iiij^{s} ij^{d}
Cariages and Reward*es* by him paid as occazions in s*er*vice required : and the seide M*aster* com*m*aunded sundry tymes in thaffares herof in all together w*ith* necessaris for Carow [35^{s}. ij^{d}.] imploied by the M*aster* } iiij^{li}. ij^{s} x^{d}

All wh*i*ch his mony amounteth together unto } xxix^{li}. xj^{s}. j^{d}.

Implement*es* for **p*ro*pertyes** suche as sundry playes req*ui*red p*ro*vided & employed by

Iohn Carow for sundry percells of stuf by him bowghte and provyded for the use of this office & [for] the plaies mask*es* & showes sett foorth therof by the seide M*aster*s com*m*aundement. vid*elicet*. Sparres, Rafters, boord*es*, punchyns, Nayles, vices, Hookes, Hing*es*, Horstayles, hobby horses pitchers, paper, Braunches of sylke & othe*r* garnit*ure* for pageant*es*, fethers, ffagbroches, Tow, Trenchers, gloves, septers, wheate sheaves, Bodyes of men in tymber, Dishes for devells eyes, devices for hell, & hell mowthe [black] staves for banners &c. Bowes, bills, daggs, Targett*es*, swordes, daggers, fawchins fierw*or*ke, Bosses for bitt*es*, speares, past, glew, pacthrede, whipcorde, Holly, Ivy, & other greene bowes, bayes & strewing erbes & such like Implem*entes* by him employed at the coo*r*te & in thoffice to acceptable purposes w*ith* cariag*es* & Reward*es* by him paid in all } xiiij^{li}. xj^{s}. j^{d}.

* S*umma* pagine — xliiij^{li} ij^{s} ij^{d}

f° 8 r.

The ffurryer.	**Sachary Benett** for x dosen of Kydd*es* skynnes together with the woorkma*n*ship by him and his servaunt*es* doone vpon the Hobby horses that s*er*ved the children of Westminster in the triumphe (where parris wan the Christall sheelde for vienna. at the Turneye and Barryers.) in all	xlij^{s}. vj^{d}.
The Cullo*rs*	**Willyam Lyzard** for Golde, sylver and sundry other Cullors by him spent in paynting the howses that s*er*ved for the playes, & players at the Coo*r*te : w*ith* theier p*ro*perties & necessaries Incident the p*er*ticcula*rs* wherof appeere at lardge in his bill.	xiij^{li} xvj^{s}. j^{d}.
Wyerdrawe*r* and his pa*r*cells.	**Thom*as* Leverett** for mony to him due for wyer, plates, Lanntornes, canstik*es* staples, snakes pack needls, Ropes, bitt*es* & suche like trinkett*es* w*ith* his attendaunce as more at lardge appereth in his bill amou*n*ting to	vj^{li}. xvj^{s}.
vizardes.	**Thoms Gyles** for mony to him due for xxj ffyne vyzard*es* with long Berdes lxx^{s}. And for vj Turk*es* vizard*es* xv^{s}. In all as by his byll therof appereth	iiij^{li}. v^{s}.
hunters.	**Iohn Tryce** for mony to him due for Leashes, & Doghookes, w*ith* staves, & other necessaries : by him provyded for the hunters that made the crye after the fox (let loose in the Coorte) with theier hownd*es*, hornes, and hallowing, in the playe of narcisses. w*hi*ch crye was made, of purpose even as the woord*es* then in vtteraunce, & the parte then played, did Requier. for the whiche the same s*ir* T*homas* Benger also appointed him to geve certeyne Reward*es* the whole amounting to	xxj^{s}. viij^{d}.

* *Summa* — xxvij^{li}. xv^{d}.

f° 8 v.

Thunder & Lightning	**Iohn Izarde** for mony to him due for his device in counterfeting Thunder & Lightning in the playe of Narscisses being requested thervnto by the seide M*aster* of this office And for sundry necessaries by him spent therin in all	xxij^{s}.
The Chaundler	**Barnard ffabian** for mony to him due for sundry percells of his ware Namely Torches, Linck*es*, other light*es* Seringcandle Corde &c in all as by his bill appereth	cxv^{s}.v^{d}.
Armour.	**Morris pickering** and Will*iam* Iening for mony by them disbursed for the hier of certeine Arm*our* for the playe of parris & vienna to furnish the triumphe therin and for Reward*es* by them geven to the armorers that attended by thappoyntment of the seide M*aster*	lj^{s} vj^{d}
	Roger Tyndall for mony to him due for certeyne Arm*our* by him lent for the same purpose with his s*er*vaunt*es* wages for wayting and attending on the same in all	xviij^{s}. ij^{d}.
Buskynmak*er*	**Iohn ffarington** for mony to him due for making of vij payer of Buskins at his howse & for sowling lether in all	xj^{s} iiij^{d}.
	Bryan Dodmer for mony by him disbursed for A Christall sheelde & certaine Bumbaste by him delyvered into thoffice & for his expenc*es* travell & dilligence in thaffares of this office by the speciall appoyntment of the seide S*ir* T*homas* Benger	lx^{s}.

* S*umma* pagine — xiij^{li}. xviij^{s}. v^{d}.

f° 9 r.

Iorneyeng charges and other necessary **Expences** and Rewardes. &c. alowed by the M*aster* &c. to	**Rycharde Mundaye** for mony by him disbursed in Reward*es* & for bothier, Linck*es* and other necessary expenc*es* at the commaundement of the Clerkcomptrowler of this office this yeare in all	xx^{s}.
	Iohn Drawater for mony by him disbursed in Reward*es* & for botehier Lynk*es* & other necessarye expenc*es* at the commaundement of the Clerke of this office this yeare in all	xx^{s}.

Greenecloth & ffor the Clerke.	**Thomas Blagrave** esquier Clerke of this office for his Greene Cloth, with pap*er*, Ink, Cownters, & suche other Necessaries as to his office appertayneth & is incident to the devices plott*es* orders, Bills, Reckonings, & Bookes, by him devysed, framed, sett owte, compiled, conferred, cast vpp, concluded & preferred for this whole yeare ending on shrovetewisdaie in the xiiijth of oure seide sovereaigne Lady Queene Elizab*e*th.	lxvj^{s}. viij^{d}.

* S*um*ma pagine — cvj^{s} viij^{d}

S*UMMA* **of** all the **Emptions** & provizions with the other expenc*es* before mencyoned Amounteth vnto	MCCxlj^{li}. xij^{s}. v^{d}. ob.

f° 8 v.

S*UMMA* **tot*a*lis of** this whole **Booke** conteyning all the whole Charges of this office any way growen within this yeare vid*elicet*. **ffrom** Shrovetewsdaye in the xiijth yeare of o*ur* sovereaigne Lady Queene Elizabeth **vntill** Shrovetewsdaie in the **xiiij**th yeare of her M*aies*ties Reaigne as before appeereth amounteth vnto } MD. lviij^{li}. xvij^{s}. v^{d}. ob.

* *examinatur per* nos

* T. Blagrave
* Edwarde Buggyn
* Iohn Arnold

f^{o} **10 r.**

Playes vj. vid*elicet* of

Lady Barbara showen on Saint Iohns day at nighte by S*ir* Robert Lanes Men.

Effiginia A Tragedye showen on the Innosent*es* daie at nighte by the Children of powles.

Aiax and vlisses showen on New yeares daie at nighte by the Children of Wynsor.

Narcisses showen on Twelfe daye at Nighte by the Children of the Chappell.

Cloridon and Radiamanta showen on Shrove sundaye at Nighte by S*ir* Robert Lanes Men

Paris and vienna showen on Shrovetewsdaie at Nighte by the Children of Westminster

All whiche .vj. playes being Chosen owte of many and ffownde to be the best that then were to be had. the same also being often p*er*vsed, & necessarely corrected & amended. (by all thafforeseide officers) Then, they being so orderly addressed : were lykewise Throwghly Apparelled, & ffurnished, with sundry kindes, and sutes, of Apparell, & furniture, ffitted and garnished necessarely : & answerable to the matter, person, and parte to be played : Having also apt howses : made of Canvasse, fframed, ffashioned & paynted accordingly : as mighte best serve theier severall purposes. Together with sundry properties incident: ffashioned, paynted, garnished, and bestowed as the partyes them selves required & needed. **wherevpon**, somuche of all manner of the Emptions & p*ro*visions aforeseide, as was expedient, & requizite : was aptly Employed. together with [parte of] the woo*r*kmanshipp & attendaunc*es* aforeseide. **And** the Residue of the Emptions not then employed theron : was by the seid M*aster* of this office & others whome he did put in trust reserved for farder service in thoffice. the most parte wherof was also Employed (together w*ith* the rest of the wo*r*kmanshipp done) vpon the Maskes ffollowing.

fo 11r.

Mask*es* vj. vid*elicet* of

Cloth of Golde .ij. of whiche one [maske] was yolow, garded with black velvett garnished with sylver Lace & fringe viz. vj. long gownes having vj. hatt*es* of Black velvett edged with golde lace & for theier Torchebearers .vj. long Gownes of Changeable Taffata red & yolow garnished with ye lyke lace & frenge w*ith* [.vj.] hatt*es* answerable & vizard*es*, skarfes, ffawchions, buskins, wrestband*es* & suche like necessaries incident The tother [maske] was of [3] Crymsen [3] purple & [2] greene cloth of golde. viz. viij Long Gownes garnished with silver frenge & lace & buttons. whose torchebearers had viij Long Gownes of Redd Damask likewise garnished & all furnished with [.xvj.] straunge heades. vyzard*es* skarfes fawchins Buskins garters & wrestbands according.

Loomewoorke white & black braunched .vj. long Gownes garded [*with*] black velvett Imbrodred w*ith* lace lyned w*ith* Tynsell & edged with ffrenge : whose Torchebearers had .vj. longe Gownes of Changeable Taffata blew & yolo garnished w*ith* sylver lace and frenge having likewise [.xij.] strange heades & [12] vizards w*ith* skarfes ffawchins buskins &c.

Murre Sattyn one of vj Long Gownes & for the Torchebearers vj long gownes of Chaungeable Taffata garnished w*ith* sylver Lace & frenge having [xij.] straunge head*es* curiusly decked with vyzard*es* skarfes ffachyns buskins &c.

The other .ij. mask*es* were but translated & otherwise garnished being of the former Nu*m*ber. by meanes wherof the Chardge of w*or*kmanshipp & attendaunce is cheefely to be respected

Item one of the forenamed Mask*es* had going before it A Childe gorgevsly decked for Mercury, who vttered A speeche : & p*re*sented iij fflowers (wroughte in silke & golde) to the Queenes Ma*iest*ie signefieng victory, peace, & plenty, to ensue. he had also ij torchebearers in Long gownes of changeable Taffata with him

vpon wh*i*ch .vj. Maskes. the Residue of all Themptions this yeare broughte into thoffice : for the moste parte was Employed.

The Remayne of all the forenamed stuf not on theise plaies & Mask*es* Employed. Resteth in the hands of the seide M*aster* of this office & suche as he comytted the custody therof vnto. till farder service Required the same.

* Edwarde Buggyn. * T. Blagrave. * Iohn Arnold.

f° 11 v.

Marche, Aprill & Maye in anno *R*egni *R*eginæ Elizabeth **xiiij^{to}**. *pr*ædicto.

Allowaunces Due vnto the Wo*r*kmen & Attendaunt*es* folow-i*ng* for Wo*r*kmanshipp doone and attendaunce geve*n* *with*in the seide office **Betwene Shrovetewsday** and the last daye of **Maye** a^{o} xiiij^{to} *pr*ædict*o* vid*elicet* vpon	**Ayryng, Repayryng** Layeng abrode, Turning, sowing, amending, Tacking, spunging, Wyping, Brushing, sweeping Caryeng, ffowlding, suting, putting in order and safe bestowing of the **Garment*es*, vestures, Armo*u*r. p*ro*perties,** and other stuf, store & Implement*es* of the seide office for the safegarde Refreshing and Reddynesse therof & **Agaynste** the Coommyng of **Duke Mommerancie** Embassado*ur* for ffraunce. In all (Betweene Shrovetewsdaie in the seide xiiijth yere and the last daye of May in the seide yeare) **xx^{ti} dayes** wherin the partyes herevnder written dilligently wrowghte and attended within the seide Office. vid*elicet*

Wages

Taylers and others. woorking & attending the premisses those xx^{ti} daies vid*elicet*	Thoms Clatterbooke at xx^{d} the daye only	xxxiij^{s}. iiij^{d}.
	Iohn Davyes & the residue at xij^{d} the daie	xx^{s}.
	Thom*as* Booreman.	xx^{s}.
	Iohn Drawater	xx^{s}.
	Richarde Mundaye	xx^{s}.
	Henri Price	xx^{s}.
	Will*iam* Benger	xx^{s}.
	Edwarde Grace	xx^{s}.
The porter.	Iohn Dawncye	xx^{s}.
The Officers in respect of dyett during those xx^{ti} daies.	The M*aster* of thoffice viz. S*ir* Thom*as* Benger knighte at iiij^{s}. by the daye	iiij^{li}.
	The Clerkcomptrowler viz. Edward Buggin esq*ui*er at .ij^{s}. the daie	xl^{s}.
	The Clerke viz. Thom*as* Blagrave esquier at ij^{s}. the daie	xl^{s}.
	The Yoman viz. Iohn Arnolde at ij^{s} the daie	xl^{s}.

ffrom Shrovetewsday vntill Iune a*nno* *R*eg*ni* *R*eg*inæ* E*lizabeth* *pr*ædict*æ*	**xiiij^{to}**.	***Summa*** of all theise wages Amou*n*teth vnto	**xix^{li}**. xiij^{s}. iiij^{d}.

* Edwarde Buggyn * T. Blagrave * Iohn Arnold

f^{o} **12** r.

Emptions & p*ro*vizions. made
within the same tyme. vid*elicet*

Iohn dauncy for ffewell by him bowghte of will*iam* Newman by the appoyntment of the seide S*ir* Thom*as* Benger & to him delyvered in Marche aforeseide viz. iiij M & an halfe of Billett*es* at xiij^{s} the thowsande — lviij^{s}. Tallwood iiij Lodes at v^{s}. iiij^{d} the lode — xxj^{s}. iiij^{d} And ffagott*es* iiij Lodes at v^{s} the Lode— xx^{s}. In all } iiij^{li}. **xix^{s}**. x^{d}.

Henri Callewaye for A Table with A frame & sundry other necessaries by him delyvered into thoffice by the comaundement of the seide M*aster* } xxx^{s}.

S*umm*a of all Themptions } vj^{li}. ix^{s}. x^{d}.

ffrom Shrovetewsdaye vntill Iune in a*nno* R*egni* Reg*in*æ p*rædictæ* **xiiij**^{to} { S *UMMA* **tot*a*lis** of all the **Charges** of this office any way **Growen** from shrovetewsdaie vntill Iune aforeseide } xxvj^{li}. iij^{s}. ij^{d}.

* Edward Buggyn * T. Blagrave * Iohn Arnold

f° 12 v.

From 31 May 1572 to 31 October 1573

viz.

Record Office. Audit Office. Accounts various. Bd. 1213. Revels. N°2

Revells

One yeare Ending the last of Maye Anno R*egni* R*eg*in*æ* Elyzabeth **xv^{to}.**

The Booke of Charges growen *with*in Thoffice of the Queenes M*aiesties* Revells aforesaide in One whole yeare scil*icet* / **ffrom** the Laste daye of Maye (1572) in the xiiijth yeare of her M*aiesties* Reaigne **vntill** the ffirst daye of Iune 1573 in the **xvth** yeare saving the Warderobe stuf which is not here mencyoned bycawse it was not bowghte by any officer of the seide office but delyvered to thoffice by Iohn fforteskue esq*uie*r M*aster* of the Queenes M*aies*ties greate Warderobe

And ffyve Monethes. Ending the Last daye. of October a^{o} xv^{to} præ*dicto*.

There is added also in the ende of this Booke the Charges that grew within .v. Monethes as afore is saide. vid*elicet* Iune, Iuly, August, September, and October in the saide xvth yeare. *with*in which tyme there was work*es* & Attendaunc*es* especially Against & in the **Progresse** into Kent as there in thend of this Booke at Lardge appereth.

Title-page r.

Monye Received in prest towardes the Charges following as may appeare by the certificat of Robert Peeter esquier Clerk of the Peale the coppy whereof hereafter ensueth. *videlicet*

Inter Exitus Ricardi Stoneley vnius Numeratorum Recepte Scaccarij de termino Pasche anno Regni Regine Elizabeth Quartodecimo continetur Sic.

Denarij prestiti extra Receptam Scaccarij

Iohanni fforteskue armigero magistro magno guarderobe Dominæ Reginæ in prestito tam pro diuersis necessarijs providendis et fiendis infra Officium predictum quam infra officium Revellorum magistrorum et alterorum erga adventum Ducis Mountmomerancey et alterorum dominorum ffranciæ per breve Dominæ Reginæ datum xvij^{mo} die Iunij anno Decimo Quarto regni Reginæ Elizabeth.

ccc^{li}. he added also this that foloweth *videlicet*

Memorandum there hath bene paide owte of the Receipte vnto the saide Iohn fforteskue the soome of **One Thowsand ffyve Hundred. ffower skore and ffyve powndes & vij^{d}.** *videlicet* by Richard Stoneleye MCCiiij^{xx}v^{li}. vij^{d} and by Richard Hodgeson deputie vnto Henri Killigrew ccc^{li}. by vertue of a privay seale dated the vijth of Iune in the xvth yeare of her highnesse Reaigne by him to be Issued in dischardge of suche debptes as were owing in the office of the Revells for parte of the tyme that Sir Thomas Benger deceassed was Master of the same that is to saye from Shrovetyde in the xiijth yeare of the Queenes Reaigne vnto the last daie of maye in the xiiijth yeare of the saide Queenes Reaigne.

Title-page v.

Iune Anno R*egni* Reg*in*æ Eliz*abeth* pr*æ*-d*ictæ* } **xiiijto.** { **Wook*es* doone & Attendaunc*es* geven** within the seide Office and on thaffares therof within the same tyme **ffor & vpon** the **Devyzing, Newmaking Translating, Repayring, ffyttyng, ffurnishing, Garnishing, & setting foorthe** of sundry kind*es* of Apparell properties and ffurnyture for **One Maske** showen at White hall before her Ma*ies*tie & Duke Mo*m*merancie Embassador for ffraunce **Together w*ith* the Emptions & p*ro*visions** bowghte and provyded for the same **And all other Charg*es*** growen by meanes therof within this Office (the Warderobe stuf as before is saide only excepted) p*er*ticulerly ensueth. with the partyes names to whome any mony is due.

fo 1 r.

Iune *anno Regni Reginæ Elizabeth prædictæ* xiiij^to^.		**Dayes & Nightes**		**Wages.**
Taylers & others woorking & attending vpon the premisses viz	Thomas Clatterbooke at xx^d^ the daye only the rest at xij^d^	30	10	lxvj^s^.viij^d^.
	Henri Callewaye	20	12	xxxij^s^.
	Robert Garton.	20	12	xxxij^s^.
	William Wood	20	10	xxx^s^.
	Richard Bryan	20	10	xxx^s^.
	Richard Wardman	20	10	xxx^s^.
	Thomas Dod	17	10	xxvij^s^.
	Edmund Owgle	20	10	xxx^s^.
	Henri White	20	08	xxviij^s^
	Thoms Lambe	20	10	xxx^s^.
	Thomas Kilforde.	20	10	xxx^s^
	Iohn Chippson	20	08	xxviij^s^.
	Iohn ffawnce	18	10	xxviij^s^.
	Royden Ede	17 1/2	08	xxv^s^. vj^d^
	Richarde Legatt	30	10	xl^s^.
	Richarde Gurnell	20	10	xxx^s^.
	Richard Warmingham.	20	10	xxx^s^
	Richarde Payne	20	04	xxiiij^s^.
	Geordge Watkinson.	17 1/2	06	xxiij^s^. vj^d^
	Barthillmew ffoster	17	04	xxj^s^.
	Ellis Sumner	17 1/2	03	xx^s^ vj^d^.
	Randall Owleye	23	09	xxxij^s^.
	George Haukynsonl.	30	10	xl^s^.
	Nicholas Turner	20	10	xxx^s^.
	Iohn Davyes	30	10	xl^s^.
	Thomas Byrde	30	10	xl^s^
	Iohn Drawater	30	10	xl^s^
	Thomas Booreman	30	10	xl^s^
	Richard Mundaye	30	10	xl^s^
	Henri Price	30	10	xl^s^
	Willyam Dodd	30	10	xl^s^
	Thomas Jenkyns	30	10	xl^s^
	Willyam Symons	30	10	xl^s^
	Iohn Cooke	30	10	xl^s^
	Iohn Dawncye	30	10	xl^s^.

* *Summa* . . lviij^li^ xviij^s^ ij^d^

fo 2 r.

		Dayes & Night*es*.		Wages.
propertymakers	Iohn Caro at ij^{s} *per* die*m*.	24 1/2 .	10 .	lxix^{s}.
Habberdasheres	Iohn Davy (for Caro) at xij^{d} *per* die*m*	18 . .	10 .	xxviij^{s}.
Imbroderers &c.	Iohn Owgle thelder at xvj^{d} *per* die*m*.	11 3/4 .	04 .	xxj^{s}.
	Iohn ffarrington at xvj^{d}	20 . .	10 .	xl^{s}.
	Will*iam* Bowll at xvj^{d}	20 . .	10 .	xl^{s}.
	Christopher Mu*n*forde at xviij^{d} . .	20 . .	10 .	xlv^{s}.
	Peeter Morris at xij^{d} *per* die*m*. . .	20 . .	03 .	xxiij^{s}.
	Will*iam* Pilkington at xx^{d} *per* die*m*.	22 . .	10 .	liij^{s}. iiij^{d}
	Ione Pilkington at xij^{d} *per* die*m* . .	20 . .	10 .	xxx^{s}.
	Iohn Owgle the yonger at xvj^{d} . .	11 3/4 .	04 .	xxj^{s}.

* *Summa* — xviij^{li}. x^{s} iiij^{d} viz. { ij^{s} — lxix^{s}. / xij^{d} — iiij^{li}. xij^{d}. / xvj^{d} — vj^{li}. ij^{s}. / xviij^{d} — xlv^{s}. / xx^{d} — liij^{s} iiij^{d}.

Officers in Respect of Diett	The M*aster* at iiij^{s} the daie	30 . .	10 .	viij^{li}
	The Clerkcontrowler at ij^{s} *per* die*m*.	30 . .	10 .	iiij^{li}
	The Clerke at ij^{s} *per* diem	30 . .	10 .	iiij^{li}
	The Yoman at ij^{s} *per* diem	30 . .	10 .	iiij^{li}.

* *Summa* — xx^{li}.

Ivne. xiiij^{to}.

S *UMMA* of all theise **Wages**. } iiij^{xx} xvij^{li}. viij^{s}. vj^{d}

*Iohn fortescue
*Henry Sekeforde
*Edwarde Buggyn
*Thomas Blagrave
*Iohn Arnold

f° 2 v.

Iune. .1572. xiiij^{to}.

Emptions &c.

The silkweaver & her p*ar*cells	Ione Bowll for Copp*er* Sylver ffrenge Twist and bone Lace .lix. lb & x oz. q*uarter* at xviij^{d} thounce — lxxj^{li}. xj^{s}. iiij^{d} ob. Golde ffrenge at ij^{s} vj^{d} thounce ij lb. j. oz. q*uarter* iiij lb xiij *ounces* di. — iiij^{li}. iij^{s}. j^{d}. ob. Copp*er* silver & silk Buttons and loopes at .ij^{s}. the ounce — vij^{li} xv^{s}. in all	iiij^{xx} iij^{li}. ix^{s}. vj^{d}.
The silkwoman	Ales Mowntague for Bone Lace wrowght w*ith* sylver and spangells. vij ounc*es* at ix^{s} thounce — lxiij^{s}. Golde plate .j. oz. iij q*uarte*rs at vij^{s} thou*n*ce — xij^{s}. iij^{d}. Lawne of fine white Netwoorke at xij^{s} the yarde iij yardes di. — xlij^{s}. It*em* delyvered to M*ist*ris Swegoo to garnishe ix heades and ix skarfes for the .ix. Muzes owte of thoffice. vid*elicet* Spanish silke of sundry cullers. w*eigh*ing iiij o*unces* iij q*uarte*rs at ij^{s} vj^{d} thounce — xj^{s}. x^{d}. ob. Heads of Heare drest and trymmed at xxiij^{s}. iiij^{d} the peece in all ix. — x^{li}. x^{s}. Sisters threade .j. oz — ij^{s}. Lawne for skarfes white & open xiiij yard*es* di. at iij^{s} iiij^{d} the yarde — xlviij^{s} iiij^{d}. White Sipers for skarfes xxvj yardes at ij^{s} iiij^{d} the yarde — lx^{s} viij^{d}. ffrenge of golde twisted for the same skarfes xiiij o*unces* at vij^{s} viij^{d} the oz. — cvij^{s} iiij^{d} Bone Lace cheyne ffrenge & edging lace of golde & silu*er* with spangles xxvij o*unces* di. at viij^{s} the ounce — xj^{li}. Poynting Ribbon of syluer golde and sylke. 102. yardes at viij^{d} the yarde — iij^{li}. viij^{s}. Ribon of penny brode silke .j. oz. q*uarter* at iij^{s} thounce — iij^{s}. ix^{d}. parchement Lace of watchett and sylver at vij^{s} viij^{d} the ounce ij o*unces* q*uarter*. — xvij^{s} iij^{d}. Laces of Crymsen ij/ at xvj^{d} the peece — ij^{s} viij^{d}. Spanish Lace & white heare lacyng .v. doozen at ij^{s} the doozen — x^{s}. Boxes to put the headest and skarfes in .ij. at ij^{s} the peece — iiij^{s}. in all	xliiij^{li}. iij^{s}. j^{d}. ob.
Silkewever & his p*ar*cells.	Will*iam* Bowll for xxxij long flowers iiij stalkes the peece at 32 viij^{d} the stalke — iiij^{li}. v^{s}. iiij^{d}. strigg*es* of bay Leaves for twigg head*es* at vj^{d} the peece — xvj^{s} single Roses at ij^{d} the peece xviij dozen — xxxvj^{s}. fflowers in Branches xj doze*n* at viij^{d} the braunche — iiij^{li}. viij^{s}. Reedes — ij^{d} Canvas x ells at x^{d} the ell — viij^{s} iiij^{d}/ Vandelas iiij ells di. at xiij^{d} thell — iiij^{s} x^{d} ob. single panc*es* iiij dozen — iiij^{s} viij^{d}/ fflowers of needlework & golde xxvij & iiij labells p*r*ice — iiij^{li} xij^{s} viij^{d}. Rose headeded Nayles M — xx^{d}. in all	xvj^{li}. xvij^{s}. viij^{d}. ob.

* S*umm*a — cxliiij^{li} x^{s} iiij^{d}

p*ro*p*er*tymaker.	Iohn Rosse (gent) for mony to him due for making of A Chariott of xiiij foote Long & viij foote brode *with* a Rock vpon it & A fowntayne therin *with* the furnishing and garnishing therof for Apollo and the Nine Muzes. by the composition & appoyntment of thaforeseide Iohn fforteskue esquier & Henri Sackford esquier	lxvj^{li}.xiij^{s}.iiij^{d}.
p*ro*p*er*tymaker	Iames Macredye for making of A Castell for Lady peace to sytt & be browghte in before the Queenes Ma*ies*tie & for dyvers things by him bowghte, and employed on the same : together *with* the wages by him demaunded for payment of suche as wroughte vpon the same. in all xxj^{li} But alowed only	xiij^{li}. xv^{s}.
patternemaker	Robert Trunkye al*ias* Arras for patternes by him made and plott*es* for sundry devices requizite in this office & at this tyme employed in all	xxx^{s}.
The Ioyner & p*ro*p*er*tymaker & his parcells	Iohn Carow for vj dozen of golde Lether at ij^{s} viij^{d} the dooze*n* — xvj^{s}. for xviij felt*es* at xij^{d} the peece — xviij^{s}/ for iiij staves at vj^{d} the peece — ij^{s}/ for ij felt*es* for woomen — xvj^{d}/ Nayells — iij^{d} ffelt*es* at viij^{d} the peece xij—viij^{s}/ One Turky Bowe and iij arrowes—xv^{d}. packthred—ij^{d}./ Bannarstaves vj at iiij^{d} the peece — ij^{s}/ for making of vj yard*es* of cheyne *with* the golde lether — vj^{s} for Another cheyne of xv yard*es* — viij^{s} for ffyne fflower for past — ij^{d}/ Glew — iiij^{d} for xv felt*es* more at viij^{d} the peece — x^{s} for iiij dozen more of golde lether — ix^{s}. ij^{d} ./ for A Bolte shackles & a coller for Discorde — ij^{s}. for boordes for the ffloore & shelves in the cou*n*tinghowse — xvj^{s} for Rafters & grunsells — xiiij^{s}. for wenskot — xiij^{s}. ffor Nayles of sundry sort*es* — vj^{s}. viij^{d}. for frames for wyndowes — x^{s}/ for ioynt*es* staples hook*es* & henges for windowes & doores — ix^{s} viij^{d} for making of A portall, shelves, dores, boxes & mending the floore & seeling in the same — x^{s}. viij^{d}./ In all as by one of his bill*es* iiij^{li} iiij^{s}.viij^{d} And by the other entred by [& paid by Dodmer] the Clerk*es* appointm*ent* iiij^{li}	viij^{li}.iij^{s}.viij^{d}.

* *Summa* — iiij^{xx}x^{li} iij^{s}

f° 3 v.

painter &c. — Will*iam* Lyzarde for xviij pencells at viij^{d} the peece — xij^{s}. for Banners iiij at vj^{s} viij^{d} the peece — xxvj^{s} viij^{d}/ Crownes ij — v^{s}./ for paynting ij Marshalls staves — ij^{s} for paynting A castell — x^{s} the Rock & churchein the Castle — x^{s}./ The pillers Arcatrye frize cornish & the Roofe gilt *with* golde and ffine silver — c^{s}./ the Armes of England and ffraunce vpon it — x^{s}/ the wing*es* — iiij^{s}./ certeyne garlond*es* — xx^{s}./ Ollyff Braunches and snakes — vij^{s}./ A vizard for Argus — ij^{s}/ Candelstick*es* likwise by him paynted ij dozen — iiij^{li}./ A prison for discord — v^{s}./ for drawing of divers Hedpeeces — vj^{s} viij^{d} for gilding iiij pillers of A waggon — iij^{s} iiij^{d} } xv^{li}. iij^{s}. viij^{d}

vpholster &c. — Philipp Gunter for xxx^{ti} peeces of Buckerams viz/ xxvj. at xj^{s} the peece — xiiij^{li}. vj^{s}. One pee[ce] more of Bridg*es* Buckeram — xij^{s} And iij peec*es* of Rownde Buckerams at iiij^{s} iiij^{d} the peece — xiij^{s} In all } xv^{li}. xj^{s}.

Chaundler — Barnarde ffabyan for seering Candell vj. lb at xvj^{d} the lb — viij^{s}. Weeke and Cotten Candell xij lb — ij^{s} ix^{d}. vj peeces of corde and Lyne — iij^{s}. viij^{d}./ In all } xiiij^{s}. v^{d}.

haberdasher — Gyles for ij dozen di. of fyne weemens vizardes at xxiiij^{s} the doozen — iij^{li}. It*em* .vj. fyne Turkes vizardes after xxiiij^{s} the doozen — xij^{s} In all iij doozen vizard*es* } lxxij^{s}.

Coffermaker
* *pro* le Charrott — Thomas Greene the Cofer maker for covering the seate of the chariot wheron the Muzes sate & for him & his ij *seruauntes* attendaunce & woork*es* doone within this tyme in all } xxij^{s}. vj^{d}.

* S*umma* — xxxvj^{li} iij^{s} vij^{d}

f° 4r.

propertymaker.	Iohn Ogle for Curling of Heare made of Black silk for Discord*es* heade (being lx ounc*es*) price of his woorkmanshipp theron only is	vij^{s}. viij^{d}.
Messengers.	Rychard Bryan &c. for mony by him disbursed & to him p*ai*d by Brian dodmer for horshier & expences in travelling abowte thaffares of this office at this tyme by thappoyntment of M^{r} fforteskue & Mr Sackforde sundry tymes in all	xxvj^{s}. viij^{d}.
Buskinmaker.	Iohn ffarrynton for inking viij payer of white startops of cloth of sylver & for theier sowles — viij^{s}. for making & sowling ix paier of sattyn — ix^{s} yolow caffa xij paier — xij^{s}/ of iij paier of Buskins one being cloth of golde for Allphonse the other .ij. of Caffa at xx^{d} the paier *with* theier solling lether — v^{s}. Rybbon for Laces ij ounc*es* q*uarter* — ij^{s}. vj^{d}. And for Tagging of Laces — iiij^{d} In all	xxxvj^{s}. x^{d}.
Necessaries & reward*es*.	Bryan Dodmer for mony by him disbursed for sundry Necessaries at dyvers tymes and for his contynuall attendaunce & s*er*vice during the tyme aforeseide in this office	xl^{s}.
Wyerdrawers	Thom*a*s Leverett for white Rownde plates turnde in with a crest for xxiiij braunches eche bearing iiij (for light*es*) at viij^{d} the peece — lxiiij^{s}. Wyer iiij to hang them by vj lb at xvj^{d} the lb — viij^{s} Greate wyers that went crosse the hall. *weighing* iiij lb the peece at xvj^{d} the lb — xxj^{s} iiij^{d}/ A lighte for the churche — xij^{d}/ Nailes ij^{d}. M — xvj^{d}. j lb more of fyne wyer — xvj^{d}/ ij lb of drawen wyer — iij^{s} iiij^{d}/ iiij lb. q*uarter* greate wyer at xvj^{d} the lb — v^{s} viij^{d}/ Doobble plat at viij^{d} the peece xv pee*ces* — x^{s}/ CC payer of clapses — xij^{d} And for wag*es* for vj of his s*er*vaunt*es* that attended & wroute at the Coo*r*te and in thoffice this tyme in all — xx^{s} viij^{d}. All which his mony for theise p*ar*cells amounteth vnto	vj^{li}. xvij^{s}. viij^{d}.

* S*umma* — xij^{li} viij^{s} x^{d}

f°4v.

The Maske yet in Iune **1572** xiiij^{to}.

paynter * for the Charriott	Haunce Eott*es* for drawing and paynting of dyvers & sundry patternes/ viz/ of the Chariott & mownte (w*hi*ch Rose made) *with* all the p*er*sonages apparell and Instrume*ntes* & setting [them] owte in apte cooll*ours* & such like s*er*vice by him doone in this office at this tyme at the request & apoyntment of Mr Alphonse & thofficers as by his bill x^{li} xv^{s} reduced by thofficers to	iiij^{li}. xix^{s}.
Reward*es* &c.	[34^{s}. 5^{d}.] Petrucio for his travell & paynes taken in p*re*parac*i*on for the same mask & for recompense to M*ist*ris Swego [40^{s}.] & for the [.8^{s}.] Muzisian that towghte the ladies In all iiij^{li}.ij^{s}.v^{d}. [as by his bill.] But alowed for all only	lxiiij^{s}. v^{d}.
Necessaries.	Thom*as* Booreman for mony by him disbursed for Lynkes, Torches, & other necessaries with Botehier & Reward*es* geven to dyvers porters Messengers and woorkemen by the clerk*es* appointm*ent*.	xx^{s}.
sylkwever	Iohn weaver for mony to him due for Buttons of greene silke and golde & for lace of the same employed by Iohn Arnolde vpon a skarfe for one of the gentlewemen Maskers. price	xj^{s}. viij^{d}.

* *Summa* — ix^{li} xv^{s} j^{d}

Edwarde Buggin esquier clerkcomptrowler of this Office for mony by him disbursed and taken vpon him to dyvers p*er*sons for sundry p*ar*cells of ware & s*er*vices following vid*elicet*

Merser. * no*ta* that will*iam* Row hadd for the lyke Tyncell but vj^{s} viij^{d} le yard/	To Pecock for ij peec*es* of blew and Crimsen Tyncell cont*eyning* xxxiiij yardes di at viij^{s} the *yar*de — xiij^{li}. xvj^{s}. Black Tyncell v. yard*es*. — xlj^{s}. And for yolo Sattyn ij yardes di. — xxj^{s}. iij^{d} in all	xvj^{li}.xviij^{s}.iij^{d}.
Mercer	Iohn Will*ia*mson for xlj ells white Tyncell at vij^{s} thell	xiiij^{li}. vij^{s}
Lynnendraper	M*ist*ris Dane for xlij ells canvasse at xiiij^{d} thell .	xlix^{s}.

f° 5 r.

Mercer	To Will*iam* Rowe for Blew tyncell x. yardes at vj^{s} viiij^{d} the yarde — lxvj^{s} viij^{d}/ Crimsen sattyn iij yard*es* — xxxj^{s}. Crimsen Tyncell xx yardes — vj^{li}. xiiij^{s}. iiij^{d} Blew Tyncell & crimsen lxxvij *yar*des q*uarter* at vj^{s} viij^{d}. the yarde — xxv^{li}. xiiij^{s} x^{d}./ In all.	xxxvij^{li}. v^{s}. x^{d}.
sylkwoman	M*ist*ris Wyett for carnac*io*n and sylver Lawne xxj yard*es* iij q*uarters* at the yarde — vij^{li} xij^{s} iij^{d}. Sylver Tyncell xviij yardes at the yerde — xlv^{s}./ Ribbon of Silver & golde iiij doze*n* di. at the doze*n* — xj^{s} iij^{d}	x^{li}. viij^{s}. vj^{d}.
sylkwever	Iohn Wever of Saint Martins for Copp*er* silver frenge xvij *ounces* at the ounce — xxv^{s}. silk heare ij lb price — lx^{s}. Copp*er* silver purled and laced ffrenge *ounces* at the ounce — viij^{s} vj^{d}.	iiij^{li}. xiij^{s}. vj^{d}.
Million*er*	To the Millioner for one yard qu*arter* of cou*n*terfete cloth of golde p*ri*ce	xxij^{s}.
habberdasher	To Hobson for iij doze*n* gold ski*n*nes.	viij^{s}.
Stacion*er*	To the stacyon*er* for a lidg*er* booke &c.	v^{s}. ij^{d}.
Mercer * not*a* that will*iam* Rowe had but vj^{s} viij^{d} le yard	To Barnes for v *yar*ds di. tincell . . . . iuxta Rat*am* xj^{s} j^{d} ob. le yard	lxiij^{s}.
gylder	To Dyrick for gilding .8. hedpeec*es* . -	xl^{s}.
fethermaker	To the ffethermaker for ffethers	x^{s}.
Mercer	To Iohn Lacye ror di. *yar*de tyncell.	xxij^{d}
Smyth	To the smith for lock*es* and keyes &c.	xij^{s} viij^{d}.
Basketmaker	To the Basketmaker for viij mold*es* for heade peec*es* xvj^{s} One greate Baskett — ix^{s} for bringing and mending the other baskett*es* & hamp*ers* in thoffice — v^{s}.	xxx^{s}.
Cariage	To A Bargeman for cariages by wat*er*.	x^{s}.
		cx^{li}. xv^{s}. iiij^{d}

f° 5 v.

	To Iohn ffarrington for ij ffelt*es* (for Mu*n*forde)	xx^{d}.
Reward*es*	To the porters that watched all nighte at the black ffryars brydge for the cummyng of the stuf from the Coorte	ij^{s}.
Reward*es*	To the woo*r*kmen that wayted on the Mask all nighte who had no tyme to eate theyer supper. xvj of them by way of Rewardes in all	vij^{s}.
ffewell	To Thom*as* Clatterbooke for billet*es* (vj^{s}.) for Coles (iiij^{s}.) & for Nayles (ij^{d}) for a chariot	x^{s}. ij^{d}
Botehier & Necessaries.	ffor his owne & his servant*es* expences in botehier Lynk*es* & sundry other necessaries boughte & reward*es* geven to Messeng*ers*, *with*in this tyme in all	xx^{s}.
Necessaries.	To Mr Arnolde yoman of thoffice for Threade of sundry sort*es* cullers and pric*es* su*m* in Bowlt*es* & su*m* by lb. — c x^{s}. x^{d}./ Tape j lb v^{s} & iij pec*es* iij^{s} — viij^{s}. past pap*er* — xxiij^{s} pack threade — iij^{d} Nailes — vj^{d} Hookes and eyes — vj^{d}/ silke — xij^{d}/ Corde — ij^{s}. Bent*es* — iij^{s}./ Cotten to make Rowles — vj^{s}. Rybbon for poyntyng — ix^{s}. pinnes a thowsand — xij^{d} Gloves — lix^{s}. vj^{d}. Sweete water — iij^{s}. iiij^{d}/ Billett*es* — vj^{s}./ Rushes — vij^{s} iiij^{d}/ Bote hier — xx^{d}. Cariages — iij^{s}. Seering Candell — iiij^{d} other light*es* — vj^{d} Rewardes — iij^{s}. In all	xij^{li}. ix^{s}. ix^{d}.
	All whiche mony Amounteth vnto	
Waggonmaker.	Walter Rippon for A chariett *with* all manner of Necessaries therto belonging w*hi*ch s*er*ved at the Tryumphe in the nighte at whitehall & there broke and spoyled as the clerk was enformed.	v^{li}. vij^{s}.

June. xiiij^{to}.

SUMMA of all theise **Emptions** and provisions for the seide Maske *with* (all) thexpenc*es* & alowaunc*es* (besides the wages afore sett owte) Amounteth vnto. — ccccix^{li}. iij^{s}. ij^{d}.

* *examinatur*

Iohn fortescue
Henry Sekeforde
Edwarde Buggyn
Thom*as* Blagrave
Iohn Arnold

f° 6 r.

Iune yet in Anno *Regni Reginæ* **Elizabeth** *prædicta* } **xiiij^{to}** {

The Banketting Howse made at White Hall (then) for Thentertaynement of the seide duke did drawe the Charges ens[v]ing for the Covering therof with Canvasse ; The decking therof with Birche & Ivie : And the ffretting, and garnishing therof, with fflowers, & Compartement*es*, *with* pendent*es* & armes paynted & gilded* for the purpose The ffloore therof being all strewed with Roze leaves pickt & sweetned *with* sweete waters &c. **The wages** for the dooing wherof : **Themptio*ns*** and provizions therefore : Together *with* **Rewardes, and Alowances** Incident. As also the partyes Names to whome, by whome, & wherfore the same was payde (& is to be alowed) *per*ticculerly ensue. vid*elicet*

wages to thartifficers & garnishers.

Iohn Drawater for mony by him paide vnto .30. **Basketmakers** that made the frett*es* 3. drawers of the patternes for them according to the measure of the walls, Roofe, & windowes, 17. **Plasterers** & others that Lathed the howse all the Inside to fasten the birche vnto 66. Labowrers or rather **Deckers** of the howse with Birche & Ivie in all **.116.** *per*sons — xxj^{li}. xvij^{s}. / And for Botehier, Reward*es* to messengers & expenc*es* in vittelling him selfe & iij of his ffellows — xxv^{s}. vj^{d}. In all } **xxiij^{li}. ij^{s}. vj^{d}.**

Byrche and fflowers to garnish &c.

Nycholas Stubbe for iiij^{xx} viij Lodes of Birche — xv^{li}. viij^{s}. ffor flowers — lix^{s} vj^{d}./ Ivye .v. Lodes with the Cariage — l^{s}./ And for Horshier, botehier, & Reward*es* to him selfe & others travelling and attending aboute the provision aforeseide — xxxv^{s}. viij^{d}. all } **xxij^{li}. xiij^{s}. ij^{d}.**

* ***Summa* — xlv^{li} xv^{s} viij^{d}**

f° 7 r.

ffIowers &c. to garnyshe

Iohn Sepeh*am* for flowers and other necessaries by him p*ro*vyded at kingston & browght to white hall. viz. Base Rope & Lyne bounde rownde aboute with fflowers 1560 ffadam — cvj^{s}./ fflowers xij baskett*es* full — x^{s} packthreade xxx lb — xv^{s} Crowne garland*es* of Roses. x. — vj^{s} viij^{d}./ Roses x bushells — viij^{s}. iiij^{d}./ Strewing herbes & sweete flowers — xj^{s}. viij^{d} Torches lynk*es* & other light*es* — viij^{s}vj^{d} Reward*es* by him paid to sundry w*or*kemen & women that wroughte nighte & daye — xviij^{s}. x^{d} His owne Rewarde for all his paynes — xl^{s}./ Bote hier & other Cariages in all — viij^{s} vj^{d}. all as by his booke appereth. p*aid* by M^{r} fforteskue. } xj^{li}. xiij^{s}. vj^{d}.

fflowers &c. to garnish together w*ith* Wages &c.

* wageIs

Iohn Robinson for flowers broughte in to the Cockpitt at white hall w*ith* other necessaries viz. fflowers of all sort*es* taken vp by comyssion & gathered in the feeldes — ix^{li} xiiij^{s} iiij^{d} Base Rope xxx fadom — xx^{s}./ sandwiche corde, packthreade, twyne, bynding threade & Needells in all — lxx^{s} ij^{d}/ fflaskett*es* & Baskett*es* to carry the flowers — ix^{s}. for Bote hier from Brayneforde and abowte the same preparac*i*ons — x^{s}/ Wages by him payd to .214. woorkfolkes the most of them being women that gathered bownde and sorted the flowers w*ith* ^{8s} reward*es* by him pa*i*d in all — xj^{li}. xij^{s}. vj^{d}./ Lynk*es* and other light*es* by him bowghte — iiij^{s} And for his owne Rewarde for all his paynes travell & attendaunce — xxvj^{s}. viij^{d}. In all } xxviij. vj^{s}. viij^{d}.

Cariage of Birche &c.

Iohn whitwell for Cariage of iiij^{xx}ix Lodes of Byrche from sundry places browghte to white hall by sundry persons at sundry rates as the p*ur*veior compounded and as appereth more Lardgely in his booke } xj^{li}. xv^{s}.

* S*umma* — lj^{li} xv^{s} ij^{d}

f° 7 v.

fflowers &c. * bothyre	Will*iam* Hunnys for Rozes xlvj Bushells — xlvj^{s} pink*es* and privett fflowers in all — xiij^{s} iiij^{d}./ Hu*n*ny suckells vj bushells — xij^{d}/ more Roses xxxiij bushells *with* basketes —. xxxiiij^{s}. x^{d}./ privett flowers xix bushells — xij^{s} viij^{d}./ Strewing herbes xij bushells — v^{s}./ Baskett*es* — ij^{s} viij^{d}./ Glasse Bottells ij of iiij gallons — iiij^{s}/ Rose water iiij gallons — xl^{s}./ Botehier & portage — v^{s} viij^{d}./ In all	viij^{li}.v^{s}.ij^{d}.
Reward*es*	Henri Sackforde esquier for Reward*es* by him geven vpon the necessitie of expedic*i*on emongs the Men & women w*or*king all Nighte vpo*n* the premiss*es* & for making kleane the banketting howse & keeping the dores in all	xlix^{s}. vj^{d}.
cariage &c. Reward*es*.	Will*iam* Boorne for mony by him paide for cariage of vj Lodes of Ivye fro*m* skotland to white hall & for flowers with tables and tressells & his owne paynes ij daies & one nighte In all	x^{s}. ij^{d}.
victualls. Botehier. Horshier. & Reward*es*.	Bryan Dodmer for Breade and Cheese &c. to serve the plasterers that wro*u*ghte all the nighte & mighte not be spared nor trusted to go abrode to supper & for ij greate steanes & iiij drinking pott*es* in all — xiiij^{s} and for his owne attendaunce & service w*i*th his s*er*vant*es* travell to & fro abowte the p*re*miss*es* : theier horshyer Botehier, expenc*es* of diet & for Lynck*es*, & Reward*es*, vnto messengers runnyng for betweene saint Iones & the Coorte &c. sundry times & cariage of dyvers necessaries to & fro in all — xl^{s}. paid by M^{r} fforteskue	liiij^{s}.

* S*umma* — xiij^{li} xviij^{s} x^{d}

f° 8r.

Basketmakers	Awdryan Awdrianson for Wicker Roddes [.7. bolts] to make frettes — xxxv^{s} the Cariage from estchepe to white hall — xx^{d}./ In all	xxxvj^{s}. viij^{d}.
Basketmaker	Vander valloy for mony by him disbursed for Roddes of seasoned wyckers 30 bundells—lxv^{s}. Hoopes. 200. — viij^{s}/ Nayles — xij^{d}/ Cariages by water and Land — ij^{s} vj^{d}./ wages for him selfe besides viij^{s} before paid by I. Drawater — iiij^{s} vj^{d}.	iiij^{li}. xij^{d}.
painter & his parcells	William Lyzarde for x peeces and pendentes fastned to them of iiij foote over — iiij^{li}/ iiij pendentes of xiiij inches over — xv^{s}/ xvj pendentes of .x. Inches — xxxij^{s}/ viij doozen Roses — iiij^{li}/ ij dozen di. of fflowerdeluces — xv^{s}./ for patternes — x^{s} all paynted gylded & bestowed on the seide howse for the better garnishing & setting foorth therof	xj^{li}. xij^{s}.
Ironmonger	Thomas Mathew for Nayles of all sortes delivered to M^{r} fortescue then & there employed and for ij peececes of base Rope in all	lxxviij^{s}. x^{d}.
Rewardes & Necessaries	Iohn Capp & Richard Warmingham for Theier service daye & nighte whiles the birche was browghte in vntill it was employed & for mony by them disbursed for iiij greate knyves to cutt the Birche. & vj Linckes, iij canvas baggs to conteyne [& cary] the Nailes & certeyne packthrede [to the deckers] & for kepping the byrche from stealing & serving the birchers [& lathers &c.] in all	xx^{s}.

* Summa — xxij^{li} viij^{s} vj^{d}

f° 8v.

Lynen drap*er*	M*ist*ris Dane for xx^{ti} peec*es* of Vandelas to cover the Banketting-howse conteyning in the whole 1006 ells at xiij^{d} thell — liiij^{li}. ix^{s}. x^{d}. It*em* more for xvij ells of the same rate viz. xiij^{d}. — xviij^{s} v^{d}./ And for 130 ells Canvas at xij^{d} the ell — vj^{li} x^{s} In all.	lxj^{li}. xviij^{s}. iij^{d}.
Wages * of * Taillers	Robert Welton for his owne wages & the wages of xvij Taylers by him paid for w*or*kmanshipp doone vpon the same Canvas to Coover the howse in all	xlij^{s}. xj^{d}.
Wages or Reward*es*.	Thom*as* Hales for cutting owte of the Canvas & fitting the same for the howse & for his attendaunce & ordering therof	xx^{s}.
fflowers Necessaries & Reward*es* *with* Botehier &c.	Iohn fforteskue esquier for mony by his owne hand*es* disbursed dyvers & sundry waies for thexpedic*i*on furnishing & garnishing therof To Iohn Barber for flowers — lxx^{s}. To W*illia*m Rowden and Rowlande for flowers & rewarde for s*er*vice done — lvj^{s} Iohn Trice for fflowers & Rose water — cxj^{s}. vj^{d}./ To Robert Iones for Ivie — xviij^{s} for Candelstick*es* *with* light*es* — xxvj^{s} viij^{d} for Thred & lyer — xvj^{s} viij^{d}/ Cariages sundry tymes of sundry things incident to the p*re*misses — xxiij^{s} iiij^{d}/ Botehier — xxvj^{s} viij^{d}. To gregory Glazier for flowers & w*or*k*es* — iiij^{li} To Iohn Browne for setting vp & taking downe the canvas — xij^{s}. And to sundry other p*er*sons by him vzed in the seide s*er*vice as the necessitie of aid therin Required — lxvj^{s} viij^{d} In all as by his notes therof appeereth.	xxv^{li}. vij^{s}. vj^{d}.

* *Summa* — iiij^{xx}x^{li}. viij^{s} viij

f° 9 r.

S*umma* **of theise Charg*es* for the Bankettinhowse** made in **Iune** aforesaide. — ccxxiij^{li}. vj^{s}. x^{d}.

Iune anno R*egni* Reg*in*æ Eliz*abeth* p*r*ædict*æ* } **xiiij**^{to}.

S*um*ma **of all** The Charges growen *with*in the tyme aforesaide Bothe for the **Maske** and also for the **Bankettinghowse** Amounteth together vnto — DCCXXX^{li}. xviij^{s}. vj^{d}.

* Iohn fortescue
* Henry Sekeforde
* Edwarde Buggyn
* Thom*as* Blagrave
* Iohn Arnold

f° 9v.

Iuly, August, September, & October
5 Anno R*egni* Reg*in*æ E*lizabeth* præ*dictæ*
and
November Anno
Regni Reg*in*æ Eliz*abeth* p*rædictæ*

xiiij^{to} xv^{to}

Ayryng, Repayryng, Layeng abrode Turning, sowing, Amending, Tacking, Spunginge, wyping, Brushing, Making Cleane, ffowlding, suting, putting in order, Layeng vp and safe Bestowing of the Garment*es*, Vestures, & ffurniture *with* the stuf, store and Implement*es* of the saide Office for the safegarde, Refreshing and Redynesse thereof doone at sundry tymes as the Necessitie thereof Required **Betwene** the first of Iuly and the last of November aforesaide wroughte & attended vpon by the parties ffollowinge as theier Nu*m*ber of daies severall wages & Alowaunc*es* here after appere vid*elicet*

Taylers and others woo*r*king, and attending the premiss*es*.

	Daies,	Wages
Thom*as* Clatterbooke at xx^{d} p*er* die*m*	40	lxvj^{s} viij^{d}.
Iohn Davies & the Residue at xij^{d}.	40	xl^{s}.
Richarde Mundaye	40	xl^{s}.
Henri Price.	40	xl^{s}.
Thom*as* Booreman	40	xl^{s}
Iohn Drawater.	40	xl^{s}
Will*iam* Dodd	40	xl^{s}
Thom*as* Ienkyns	40	xl^{s}
Isack Iones	40	xl^{s}
Iohn percye	40	xl^{s}
Richard Hawklyf.	40	xl^{s}
Peeter Marow	40	xl^{s}
Iohn Dauncye at xij^{d} p*er* diem	40	xl^{s}
Iohn Yanes	40	xl^{s}.

* *Summa* — xxix^{li} vj^{s} viij^{d}

Offycers for theier diett vid*elicet*

The M*aster* at iiij^{s} by the daye.	40	viij^{li}.
The Clerkcomptrowler at ij^{s} p*er* die*m*	40	iiij^{li}.
The Clerk at ij^{s} by the daie	40	iiij^{li}.
The Yoman at ij^{s} by the daie	40	iiij^{li}

S*umma* of all theise Wages. } xlix^{li}. vj^{s}. viij^{d}.

f° 10r.

Necessaries	Iohn Arnolde Yoman of this office for mony by him disbursed for Thredd of sundry cullers — vj^{s} viij^{d} Brushes of sundry sort*es* redd & white — v^{s} iiij^{d} ffewell — xxvj^{s} viij^{d}. Nayles, Ha*m*mers, pincers & other necessaryes from the Ironmunger — vj^{s} Lyght*es* Corde & other chaundry ware — vij^{s}. Glew & A melting pott — xiiij^{d} A hatchett — xvj^{d} Dust baskett*es* — xvj^{d}/ A shovell — viij^{d} Broomes — xij^{d} Boordes Rafters & Waynskott to mend the small presses & to make shelves & p*ar*ticions — xx^{s} Bowlt*es*, Hookes, Henges Lock*es* & keyes — viij^{s} Rubbers & spunges — ij^{s} Rushes — vj^{s} viiij^{s}.	iiij^{li}.xiij^{s}.x^{d}.

Summa patet

Iuly **August September** **& October** Anno *Regni* Reginæ Eliza*beth* præ*dictæ* **and** **November**	**xiiij^{to}** **xv^{to}.**	S*UMMA* **of all** the Charg*es* growen wi*th*in the same .v. Monethes	liiij^{li}. vj^{d}.

* Iohn fortescue

* Edwarde Buggyn
* Thom*as* Blagrave
* Iohn Arnold.

f° 10 v.

December Ianvary & ffebruary } **xv.**^{to} *Regni Reginæ* Eliz*abeth*

New making, Translating, Repayring ffytting, ffurnishing, Garnishing and attending the Wares, Apparell, properties, stuf, Store, and Implement*es* of the seide Office for the apte setting foorthe of Sundry playes and Mask*es with* other sport*es* & pastymes for her Ma*iesties* Recreac*i*on showen this yeare in Christm*as* & Shrovetyde at hampto*n* Coorte and at Greenewitche the Charg*es* wherof growen aswell by meanes of Wages as Emptions & provizions over and besides the warderob stuf hereafter p*er*ticculerly ensueth.

vid*elicet*

Tayler & others woorking & attending the premisses the first at xx^{d} *per* die*m* and all the rest at xij^{d}.

	Dayes & Night*es*		Wages	
Thom*as* Clatterbooke	63	17	vj^{li}.xiij^{s}.iiij^{d}.	cxvij^{li}.ix^{s}.iiij^{d}.
Richard Bryan	46	10	lvj^{s}.	
Humphrie Smallman	40	16	lvj^{s}.	
Iohn Price	46	10	lvj^{s}.	
Henri Kellawaye.	46	10	lvj^{s}.	
Nich*o*las ffrawnces	06	06	xij^{s}.	
Robert Garton	52	10	lxij^{s}.	
Edmund Owgle	46	10	lvj^{s}	
Iohn Cleyton	48	10	lviij^{s}.	
Geordge Haukinson	56	14	lxx^{s}.	
Thom*as* Kilforde.	46	10	lvj^{s}	
Iohn ffawnce	53	13	lxvj^{s}.	
Will*iam* Gallande	46	10	lvj^{s}.	
Will*iam* Wood	46	10	lvj^{s}	
Iohn Walker	46	10	lvj^{s}.	
Richard Wardman	46	07	liij^{s}	
Alexander Thewell	46	10	lvj^{s}	
Thom*as* Lambe	50	10	lx^{s}	
Richard Keyzer	46	10	lvj^{s}	
Iohn Harper	36	04	xl^{s}	
Iohn Daves.	80	17	iiij^{li}. xvij^{s}.	
Thom*as* Birde.	80	17	iiij^{li} xvij^{s}.	
Richard Mundaye	80	17	iiij^{li} xvij^{s}.	
Henri Price	80	17	iiij^{li}. xvij^{s}.	
Thom*as* Booreman	80	17	iiij^{li}. xvij^{s}.	
Iohn Drawater	80	17	iiij^{li} xvij^{s}.	
Will*iam* Dod	80	17	iiij^{li} xvij^{s}.	
Thomas Ienkins	80	17	iiij^{li}. xvij^{s}.	
Will*iam* Dawnce.	80	17	iiij^{li}. xvij^{s}.	
Nicholas Storye	80	17	iiij^{li} xvij^{s}	
Iohn Dawncye	80	17	iiij^{li}. xvij^{s}	
Vryan Dod	46	10	lvj^{s}.	
George Arnolde	46	10	lvj^{s}	

f° 11 r.

		Daies & Nyght*es*		Wages	
paynters	Will*iam* Lyzarde . .	40 . . .	10 . . .	iiij^{li}. iij^{s} iiij^{d}.	
	Lewes Lyzarde. . .	4	2 . . .	x^{s}	
at xx^{d}	Iohn Lyzarde . . .	8	3 . . .	xviij^{s} iiij^{d}	
	Pangrace Inglishe. .	6	0 . . .	x^{s}	
	Robert Hudson. . .	8	3 . . .	xviij^{s} iiij^{d}.	
	Henri Lambarde . .	8	3 . . .	xviij^{s} iiij^{d}.	
	Balthazer . .	3	3 . . .	x^{s}	
	Andro Depree . . .	3	3 . . .	x^{s}	
	Iacob Townce . . .	3	3 . . .	x^{s}	
	Hawnce Kisbye . .	8	3 . . .	xviij^{s}. iiij^{d}.	
xvj^{d}	Richard Baker . . .	10	3 . . .	xvij^{s} iiij^{d}.	
	Iohn ffyaunce . . .	12	3 . . .	xx^{s}.	xxij^{li}. iiij^{s}. iiij^{d}.
	Anthony Parke . . .	20	9 . . .	xxxviij^{s}. viij^{d}	
	Nich*o*las Knighte . .	8	2 . . .	xiij^{s} iiij^{d}.	
	Ioyce ffrolyk	30 . . .	10 . . .	liij^{s} iiij^{d}.	
	Iohn Clement . . .	8	2 . . .	xiij^{s} iiij^{d}.	
	Robert Bond. . . .	8	2 . . .	xiij^{s}. iiij^{d}.	
	Nich*o*las Kisbye . .	8	2 . . .	xiij^{s} iiij^{d}.	
& xij^{d} p*er* die*m*	Will*iam* Mark*es*. . .	8	3 . . .	xj^{s}	
	Anthony Godfrye . .	8	3 . . .	xj^{s}	
	Harvy Chrispian . .	8	3 . . .	xj^{s}	
	Iohn Barthillmew. .	8	3 . . .	xj^{s}	
	Iohn Sharpe	8	3 . . .	xj^{s}	

Will*iam* Lyzard for gilding & paynting sundry thing*es* at his howse vid*elicet*/ Patternes for p*er*sonag*es* of Men & Women in strange attyer, Hedpec*es* dishes for frutes & ffishes in all — xx^{s}. iiij^{d}. *** ultra iiij^{li} iij^{s} iiij^{d} antea**

Bryan Dodmer for his Attendaunce & service doone in the seid Office dyvers and sundry waies within the same tyme & in full satisfacc*io*n for all his disbursement*es* for necessaries imployed in the seide office & expenc*es* in the affares therof for .C^{s}. by him demaunded In the whole Alowed but — lxvj^{s}. viij^{d}.

* S*um*ma — xxvj^{li} xj^{s} iiij^{d}

f^{o} **11 v.**

property-makers Imbroderers Habberdasheres and theier *servauntes* & attendant*es* by the daye at	ij^{s}.	Iohn Carow	63	17	viij^{li}.	xlv^{li}. viij^{s}. x^{d}.
	xx^{d}.	Will*iam* Pilkington	43	10	iiij^{li} viij^{s}. iiij^{d}.	
		Will*iam* Bowll	43	10	iiij^{li} viij^{s}. iiij^{d}.	
	xviij^{d}.	Christopher Mumpherd	40	10	lxxv^{s}.	
		Iohn Tuke	36	9	lxvij^{s}. vj^{d}.	
	xvj^{d}.	Iohn ffarrington	58	14	iiij^{li}. xvj^{s}	
		Iohn Owgle Iunior	30	10	liij^{s} iiij^{d}.	
		Thom*as* Leverett for ij me*n*	4	4	xxj^{s} iiij^{d}.	
	xij^{d}.	Iohn Davyd for Carowe	63	17	iiij^{li}.	
		Ione Pilkington	40	10	l^{s}.	
		Richard Ball for Tuke	20	9	xxix^{s}.	
		Robert ffernollye	40	10	l^{s}.	
		Peeter Moris for Hay	42	8	l^{s}.	

Offycers for theier diett*es*. vid*elicet*	The M*aster* at iiij^{s} p*er* diem	80	17	xix^{li}. viij^{s}.	xlviij^{li}. x^{s}.
	Clerkcomptrowler at ij^{s}.	80	17	ix^{li} xiiij^{s}.	
	The Clerke at ij^{s}	80	17	ix^{li}. xiiij^{s}.	
	The Yomen at ij^{s}	80	17	ix^{li} xiiij^{s}.	

S*UMMA* of all the **Wages** in December, Ianvary, and ffebruary *anno* R*egni* R*eginæ* Eliz*abeth* p*rædictæ* **XV**^{to}. } ccxxxvij^{li}. xix^{s}. vj^{d}.

* Iohn fortescue
* Henry Sekeforde
* Edwarde Buggyn
* Thom*as* Blagrave
* Iohn Arnold

f° 12 r.

Emptions & provizions for Christmas &c. as before *anno Regni Reginæ Elizabeth* **xvto.**

vide*licet*

thupholster — Philipp Gunter for [xx] iiij. iiij. peec*es* of Buckeram at iiijs the peece Amounting vnto } **xvjli. xvjs.**

Necessaries — Iohn Arnolde for iiij lb Redd Thred — xiijs. iiijd./ for iij lb Blew Thred — xs./ for ij lb di. of yolo thred — viijs. iiijd/ iij lb di. of greene thred — xjs. viijd./ iij lb Black Thred — vjs. x lb di. white thred — xxxiijs iiijd./ ffor Cariage of Rubbish owte of the howses — xijd/ ffor fflower to make paste — vjd/ Pap*er* — iiijd/ ij oz. di. of sylke — vs Tape iij q*uarter*s of lb — iijs/ Bumbast to make snoballs — vs. vjd./ Lynnen cloth to lyne a Ierken & slops for ffarant*es* soon — ijs iiijd./ ffor Glew & paste — xijd/ Crvell to cut for frozen head*es* — vjs/ Arsedue to cut for the same head*es* — ijs/ Bumbast to stuf Rowles for the Turk*es* head*es* — ijs vjd/ Cotten to lyne the Ierken & slopps aforeseide — ijs. ijd/ Gloves for the Children of Eaten [dozen] .ij. — xs./ Gloves for Maskers vj paier — iiijs./ Gloves for Torchebearers vj paier — iijs/ Pinnes M — xijd/ Tape di.lb — ijs./ Cariage of Basket*es* to & fro the water syde — ijs Rewards to the Taylers — iiijs./ Horshyer & charges at hampton Coorte in the Christmas — xs./ ffor Bent*es* for fardngales — vs iiijd/ Red thred j lb — iijs iiijd./ Blew thred j lb — iijs iiijd white thred iiij lb di. — xvs./ Cotten to lyne [3 *yards*] .ij. p*aire* of hoze*n* for M*u*nkesters playe — ijs./ yolow & greene thred ij lb — vjs viijd/ ffellt*es* [xij] for women [xijs] & felt*es* [xij] for men [viijs] [& for maskers xvj *paire*] — xxs./ more bent*es* — iijs iiijd./ Gloves for the children of wynsor ij doze*n* — xxs iiijd Black thred j bolte [pinnes & tape — xvd] — iiijs/ fflower & past — vjd Reward*es* to the Taylers & habberdashers — iiijs [white thred iij lb — xs] botehier & charg*es* at Kingston on newyeres daie — vs./ The charg*es* there on twelf daie w*ith* botehyer — vijs ijd/ Billet*es* M — xiijs iiijd./ Coles for thimbroderer — vjd/ Bumbast to stuf the Rowles of the hatt*es* for the weme*n* maskers — ijs viijd Coles — xijs/ shethes for maryners — xijd./ white Thred ij lb — vjs viijd/ pynnes & Tape — xiijd Redd thred [di. lb] — xxd/ j lb blew thred — iijs iiijd./ more Red threde j lb di. — vs/ other coollerd thred — ijs vjd/ Gloves for Munkesters boyes ij doze*n* — xs Black gloves xij paier — iijs pinnes & tape — iiijs vjd/ Gloves [j dozen] for the Ladye Maskers — xs for the Lord*es* gloves — vjs vjd for the torcheberers gloves — iijs. Past pap*er* — iiijs cariage & recariage of basket*es* — ijs } **xviijli. xijs.**

fo 13 r.

Propertymaker & his parcells

Iohn Carow for sparres to make frames for the players howses — ix^{s}. vj^{d}/ Canvas ⸢at x^{d} thell⸣ for A monster vij ells — v^{s}. x^{d}./ A nett for the ffishers maskers — x^{s} vj^{d} for ⸢3 lb⸣ wooll to stuf the fishes — xij^{d}/ ij speares for the play of Cariclia — xvj^{d}/ A tree of Holly for the Duttons playe — iij^{s} iiij^{d}/ other holly for the forest — xij^{d} A Traye for the ffishermen — vij^{d} A mace — xij^{d}/ Turky bowes — ij^{s}/ ⸢13⸣ Arrowes — xij^{d} sparres caryed to hampton coorte — ij^{s} packthred — iiij^{d}/ A planke — xij^{d}. A new fawchyn — iij^{s} iiij^{d}/ the mending of v ffawchins — v^{s} A palmers staf — xij^{d}/ A desk for farrantes playe — iij^{s}/ Boordes to brace the skaffoldes — vj^{d} A vyzarde for an apes face — iij^{s} iiij^{d}/ Glew j lb — iij^{d}/ A keye for Ianvs — ij^{s} A Monster — xx^{s}/ An Awlter for theagines — iij^{s} iiij^{d}/ Dishes — iiij^{d}. Egges counterfet vij doozen — xiiij^{s}/ ⸢xxiiij⸣ Roches counterfet — vj^{s} Whitings xxiiij — vj^{s} knyves for marryners — xij^{d}/ Thornebackes — iiij^{s} Smeltes iij dozen — iij^{s} Mackerells — iij^{s}/ fflownders — iij^{s} ⸢an⸣ Image of canvas stuft — iij^{s} Boordes to beare lightes for the hall — iiij^{s}/ cariage of the Awlter from the warderobe to powles wharf — iiij^{d} A Ladder — xviij^{d}/ A ffootepace of iij stepps with Iointes — x^{s}/ Nayles v⸢c⸣ of single tenns — iiij^{s} ij^{d}/ Dubble tens — xviij^{d}/ ⸢300⸣ syxpeny nayles — xviij^{d}. three peny nayles — ix^{d} twopeny nayles — viij^{d} Tackes — vj^{d}/ hoopes for the monster — x^{d} In all } vij^{li}.xj^{s}.iij^{d}.

thappoticary & his parcells

Robert Moorer for suger plate — xij^{s}. viij^{d} Musk kumfettes j lb — ij^{s} iiij^{d}/ Corianders prepared j lb — xx^{d}. Clove Cumfettes j lb — ij^{s} iiij^{d} Synamon kumfettes — iij^{s} Rose water j quarte & j pynte of spike water — iij iiij^{d}/ Gynger Cumfettes j lb — ij^{s} All whiche served for fflakes of yse & hayle stones in the maske of Ianvs the Roze water sweetened the balls made for snowballes presented to her Maiestie by Ianvs } xxvij^{s}. iiij^{d}.

paynting

Iohn Arnolde yoman of thoffice for mony by him paid to Arnolde the paynter for the picture of Andromadas — x^{s} & To Anthony the basketmaker for patternes — x^{s} in all } xx^{s}

f° 13 v.

Banketting frutes necessaryes Botehier & Rewardes

Thomas Blagrave esquier for mony by him disbursed in Rewarde to Muzitians that plaide at the proofe of Duttons play — ij^{s} vj^{d}/ To Robert Baker for drawing of patternes for the playe of fortune & altering the same — vj^{s} viij^{d}./ ffor suger for Marchepane stuf at xiij^{d} ob. the lb viij lb — ix^{s} Almons .v. lb — v^{s}./ ffyne Cakes iij doozen — vij^{s}. vj^{d}./ Gum dragacanth — iiij^{d} Rose water j pynte — xiiij^{d} Baskettes ix & A mace wickerd by vandervaloy — x^{s}/ Gowlde leaves to gilde the Marchepane stuf — xij^{d}./ Almonds againe iij lb. di. — iij^{s} vj^{d}/ Baskettes boughte of Adrianson ij — ij^{s} ffrutes for Banketting — ij^{s}. ix^{d} Lynkes & botehier — xx^{d}/ portage to & fro the water syde — xiiij^{d} Banketting frutes iij lb di. at iij^{s} iiij^{d} the lb — xj^{s} viij^{d}/ Dishes of suger vj — xij^{s}/ ffor Marmellad — xij^{d} Cloves & saferne — ij^{d}/ preserved Quinces j lb — ij^{s} viij^{d} Cloves — iiij^{d}/ Botehier to the Coorte with & for M^{r} forteskue — xviij^{d}/ the hier of A Bardge for A Maske — vij^{s} for portage paid to Lam — iij^{s} vj^{d}./ A whirey to & fro grenewiche — ij^{s} paper for the baskettes of ffrute — xiiij^{d}./ Cariage of A hamper to & fro Billingsgate — iiij^{d} To Thomas Booreman for spices by him provided — iij^{s} To Boorne for lending his skales & weightes — iiij^{d} Botehier to & fro grenewiche — ij^{s} vj^{d}/ Egges.c. — ij^{s} ix^{d} synamon & gynger — xxij^{d}./ to Mr Buggyn for mony by him paid for botehier & barge hier to the Coorte on shrovetewsdaie — x^{s}./ ffrutes counterfete bowghte of Brayne thappoticary — x^{s}. to william Buston for his Bardge iij nightes at shrovtide — xxvj^{s} horshyer & waggonhier with charges at hampton Coorte — liiij^{s}./ Lynkes & torches there — iij^{s} iiij^{d} Rewardes there — iiij^{s} x^{d} Billettes .ij. Thowsand di. bowghte of Newman — xxxiij^{s} iiij^{d}/ A Table — v^{s}. wyer & hookes — ij^{s} vj^{d} Rewardes to boyes — viij^{d}./ To Benbow for playeng in the Monster — ij^{s}. vj^{d}. And to Robinson for workemanship & necessaries — vj^{s} viij^{d}

> xiij^{li}. vj^{s}. x^{d}.

Wierdrawers percells

Thomas Leveret for small Candelstickes iiij dozen — viij^{s}./ ffor xij high Candelstickes — vj^{s}/ vice candelstickes xij — xij^{s}/ Dubble plate (ix) 3 candlestickes — ij^{s} viij^{d}./ Bellowes ij payer — vj^{s} viij^{d}/ Lanthornes of Middle syze — x^{s}./ One greate Lanthorne — v^{s}./ Bastard wyer ij lb — ij^{s}/ Lattyn wyer j lb — xx^{d}./ Come brushes to dresse the heares — ij^{s}/ Lattyn Rings — xij^{d}./ one quarter of Lattyn — vj^{d}/ Rose nayles — viij^{d}./ spanish Needells — xx^{d}/ Another greate lanthorne — v^{s}./ A chayne & hooke to hang it by in an entery — xiiij^{d} long spanish needells ij — iiij^{d}/ packneedells — ij^{d} square packneedells — viij^{d}/ One shipp for frankensens — iij^{s} iiij^{d}./ One greate rownde plate — xij^{d} ffyne wyer di. lb — viij^{d}/ keye cheyne xij yerds — viij^{s} Rownde plates for sockettes — xxxij^{s} wyer di. lb to hang them by — iij^{s}/ Nayles M — xx^{d} Bynding wyer — xij^{d}.

> cxvij^{s}. x^{d}.

Mouldes for the frutes

Thomas Blagrave esquier for more mony by him payde for Mowldes to cast the frutes & ffishes in/ & to the weemen that tempred the stuf & made vp the same

> xx^{s}.

thimbroderer &c.

Will*iam* pilkington for ij peec*es* of greene garding for ij patternes — iij^{s} iiij^{d}/The patterne of A heade peece with leaves of Cloth of golde — vi^{s} viij^{d}/ Thimbrodring of iiij yard*es* di of yolow garding Imployed on the mores head*es* — xv^{s}./ pasting & tyting of sattyn for vj head peec*es* — iij^{s} iiij^{d}/ for iiij yard*es* garding for ij Mytẽrs — xiij^{s} iiij^{d}/ A patterne for A hed peece with comp*ar*tem*entes* — vj^{s}. viiij^{d}/ for making of a yarde di. more of yolo garding to p*er*forme the ffysshers capps — v^{s}/ } iiij^{s}. iiij^{d}.

Necessaries Botehier Cariag*es* & Reward*es*

Thom*as* Clatterbooke for Nayles — iiij^{d}/ Browne Thredd [7 lb] for the paynters — ij^{s} Lock*es* for the basket*es* vj — ij^{s} p*ar*chement for Meazures — ij^{d}/ Buttons for Buskins & Ierkyns — iij^{s} Botehier to kingsto*n* on twelfe Nighte — ij^{s}. Thred at kingsto*n* — xvj^{d} Cariage of stuf from kingston to the Coo*r*te & back agayne — iij^{s} A Bardge to cary all the stuf fro*m* kingston to Brydewell — xij^{s} vj^{d} fro*m* Bridewell to saint Iones — xvj^{d}/ vyzard*es* vj — xv^{s}./ Butto*ns* j groce — xij^{d}/ foyle for vyzard*es* — viij^{d}/ Billet*es* & Coles — x^{d} } xlv^{s}. ij^{d}.

Buskinmaker

Iohn ffarrington for making of vj payer of w*hi*te velvett Buskins at xx^{d} the payer fynding lether him selfe for the sowles — x^{s}/ for making of iij payer more of Rone [1] lether & [2] w*hi*te velvett at xvj^{d} the payer — iiij^{s} for one Rone skin — xx^{d}/ for Buckles — ij^{d}/ And for making of iij payer of crymsen satin Buskins — iiij^{s} } xix^{s}. x^{d}.

habberdashers for Beard*es* & heare &c.

Iohn Owgle [senior] for viij long white Berd*es* at xx^{d} the peece — xiij^{s} iiij^{s}/ Aberne Berd*es* ij & j blackfyzicians bearde — xiiij^{s} viij^{d}/ Berds White & Black vj — viij^{s}/ Heares for palm*ers* ij — ij^{s} viij^{d} Berd*es* for fyshers vj — ix^{s} Curled heare for fyshers Capps — xij^{d} Redd Berd*es* vj — ix^{s}. } vij^{s}.viij^{d}.

f° 14 v.

silkwaver William Bowll purveyour of ffrenge &c. & Lace &c. for mony by him disbursed for ffrenge & bone Lace of fyne copper sylver at xviij^{d} the oz M iiij oz. di. quarter di — lxxv^{li}. vij^{s}. iiij^{d} ob ffreng of cullerd sylk & thred at xij^{d} the oz. xv ounces — xv^{s}. .1. Ream. Paper Riall & other .ij. Reams paper for patternes &c. — xxxij^{s}./ Spangles at xij^{d} the M .8. M — viij^{s} Buttons & tassells of Copper silver at ij^{s} the oz. cc. lxiij oz. di. quarter — xxvj^{li} vj^{s}. iij^{d}./ Spangles at viij^{d} the M. 10000 — vj^{s} viij^{d} Buttons at 8^{d} the dozen ij dozen di. — xx^{d} fflowers — xiij^{s} iiij^{d}/ ffyne white Lam to make snoballs 8 skinnes at v^{d} the peece — iij^{s} iiij^{d} ffethers for hattes at xvj^{d} the pece .4. — v^{s}. iiij^{d}./ Boxes Lardge iiij — iiij^{s} iiij^{d}./ Lace at xx^{d} thoz. clxxviij oz. di. — xiiij^{li}. xvij^{s} viij^{d}./ Buttons fyne wroght of Copper sylver for heades & deepe frenge at .2^{s}. 6^{d}. the oz. xxv oz. quarter — lxiij^{s} j^{d} ob/ One Tassell — xxij^{d} ob/ Tyncell Ribbon at iij^{s} iiij^{d} the dozen v dozen — xvj^{s} viij^{d}/ Aglettes 600 — iij^{s}/ Stones at ix^{d} the peece. 48 — xxxvj^{s}./ for Setting the seide stones in Leade at iiij^{d} the pece — xvj^{s}./ An Irish hedpece of Crimsen velvett all garnished with frenge & lace — xiij^{s} iiij^{d}/ A greate hanging lock with a keye to it — ij^{s} vj^{d}./ A payer of Ballans with ij lb quarter of Brazen waightes — iiij^{s} viij^{d} A dozen of Buttons — viij^{d} In all } cxxviij^{li}.xviij^{s}.ix^{d}.ob.

painter &c. Wylliam Lyzarde for syze — xxvj^{s}. vj^{d}./ Black — xv^{s}. viij^{d} Redd — x^{s} iiij^{d}./ Vert — v^{s}. vj^{d}./ Sapp — iij^{s} viij^{d}./ Crymsen — v^{s}./ white — xv^{s}/ Browne — xij^{d} Yolow — iiij^{s}/ Smalt — xlij^{s}/ Pottes & Nayles — viij^{s} ij^{d}/ spruce yolow — xxij^{d}./ Gowlde — xv^{s}. x^{d}/ Silver — iiij^{s} ix^{d}/ Oker de Rowse — ij^{s} Glew — iij^{s} iiij^{d} ffoyle — vij^{s} vj^{d}/ fflorrey — iiij^{s} Copper culler — xx^{d} shave russet to smoothe the egges — viij^{d}./ Assedew — iij^{s} iiij^{d}./ Cullers for the sugerworke — xij^{d}/ the hier of A horse v daies & his meate by the waye to hampton Coorte &c. — xiiij^{s} vj^{d}./ Reduced by the Clerk Comptrowler in all to } viij^{li}.

f° 15 r.

Rep*ara*c*i*ons on the Leades &c.

Henri Sekeforde esquier for mony by him disbursed for Rushes in the hall & in the greate chambere where the w*or*k*es* were doone & the playes Rezited — xx^{s} for ij greate tables in the hall — xxxiij^{s} iiij^{d} for hanging vp Tent*es* to keepe away the wynde & snow from dryving into the hall & taking downe the same agayne — vj^{s} viij^{d}/ Two long peec*es* of Tymber of xx foote appeece to make A frame for the paynters — x^{s}./ and for ij M of Billett*es* & Coles where the playes were rezited in the greate chamber — xxvj^{s} viij^{d}/ I*te*m more for w*or*k*es* doone by Rowland Robynson for the w*hi*ch were bowghte cccc di. of Boordes to cloze vpp the hall & other necessary plac*es* aboute the same am*oun*ting to — xxvj^{s}. vj^{d}./ One dubble Rafter — viij^{d}/ di. M of vj^{d} nailes — iij^{s} di. c. of dubble x^{ns} — xvj^{d}. Two mennes woo*r*ke .x. daies in boording vp the hall & doing of other Necessary things — xx^{s} for setting vp of Tables & Boording vpp of wyndowes aboute the howse wher the Taylers wrawghte — iij^{s}. iiij^{d}./ Three quarters of a hundred of Boordes for the windos — iij^{s} iiij^{d}. A ffootepace to sett before the chimney where the Taylers wrowghte — xij^{d}/ for iiij woorkemen on saint Stevens daie & iiij w*or*kmen the same nighte & the morrow after & for ij men going to the Coo*r*te to sett vp [frames for] the seide Revells at ij sundry Tymes amownteth in all to the su*m* of — xxx^{s}. To Rowland Robynson for vj. daies at xx^{d} the daie — x^{s}./ and for ij of his men xv daies at xiiij^{d} the daie — xxxv^{s}./ It*e*m more for Leade bowghte of Sr *Chris*topher Drap*er* — xviij^{li}/ and for Bestowing the same vpon the Roofe of the howse adioyning to the greate hall & for sowdering & mending dyvers other places — xlvj^{s} In all as by iij severall Bills subscribed only by the seide Henri Sekeforde Amou*n*teth vnto } xxxj^{li}. xvj^{s}. x^{d}.

Chaundeler

Barnarde ffabyan for Seering candle at xvj^{d} the lb 9 lb — xij^{s} Cotten Candle 282 lb at .3^{d}. le lb — lxx^{s} vj^{d}/ Corde and Lyne xv peec*es* — viij^{s}. iiij^{d}. staf Torches x. — xij^{s} Lynkes .18. — vj^{s}/ and for ij pannes and A pott — xij^{d}./ in all } cix^{s}. x^{d}.

It*e*m more to him for iij dozen light*es* of cotten & weeke . . . . . viij^{s}. vj^{d}.

Thom*a*s Masters for Imbrodring of vj vellvett hatt*es* at his owne howse — xxx^{s} } xxx^{s}

Iohn Davyson for glasse — ij^{s} the tother glasier for his glasse — iiij^{s}./ In all for them bothe } vj^{s}

f° 15 v.

Necessaries. Botehier. Cariages. & Rewardes.

Edward Buggin Clerkcomptrowler for mony by him disbursed videlicet/ for Botehier & other charges coomyng to the Coorte [at hampton] at the begynnyng of the woorkes by thappoyntment of M^{r} fforteskue — x^{s}./ for charges & wages of Thomas Lambe [for going] to wynsor abowte M^{r} ffarrantes playe by M^{r} forteskues appointment — iiij^{s} vj^{d}./ for xx^{tie} sackes of Coles — x^{s} iiij^{d}. for iij M of Billettes — xl^{s} One dozen of Childrens ffeltes — viij^{s}./ ffeltes for Maskes .6. — vj^{s}./ past paper lardge iiij dozen — xij^{s}./ A Waggen for the first playe of my Lord of Leisters men — xviij^{s}./ Rewardes to the headpeecemakers working on Christmas Nighte — ij^{s}/ ffirr powles xvj & the cariage of them — vj^{s} Item more [viij^{d}] xxiiij^{ti} ffirr powles & for the cariage of them — xj^{s}./ To Henri Cellaweye for provizion & cariage of trees & other things to the Coorte for A wildernesse in A playe — viij^{s}. vj^{d}./ Rewarde more to Lambe — vj^{d} To clatterbooke for [iij dozen] greene Lace for A Ierken — iij^{s}/ The hier of A Waggon for cariage to the Coorte at the second play of my Lord of Leicesters men — xviij^{s}/ vyzardes with black Berdes .v. — xv^{s}./ Vizardes with [.4.] Redd Berdes — xij^{s} vyzardes [In ernest for] for Turkes vj. — xij^{d}/ To Iohn Bettes [&] his wyfe for one daye & one nighte spangling of the headpeeces — iij^{s} Item more to ij Maides — ij^{s} To pilkington for xij feltes for hedpeeces — x^{s}/ To Anthony the Basketmaker for vj hedpeeces for Turkes — xij^{s}/ Rewardes to the paynters — iij^{s} Lynkes for the paynter — xij^{d}/ ij Squirtes for the playe of the children of powles — viij^{s}./ To the Waggenner for cariage of the stuf to hampton Coorte the sunday next after Christmas daie — xviij^{s}./ A lock, A keye & A staple for the hall doore next the stayer foote — xx^{d}./ ij M Billettes — xxvj^{s}/ viij^{d}./ To lambe for spunges for snoballs — v^{s} iiij^{d}/ To Robynson for vj quarters & A plank of iiij yeardes longe — iij^{s}/ Tymber for the forest — ij^{s} vj^{d}/ ffirr powles caried to the Coorte — ij^{s} ix^{d}/ Boordes — ij^{s} Baskettes to serve for the Maske on New yeres daye — ix^{s}/ To Calleweye for one that gathered Mosse — xij^{d}/ Coles ij bushells — ix^{d}. To pilkington for iiij dozen lace — iiij^{s} Aglettes for the topps of headpeeces — viij^{d} Muskovie [& M bugles] glasse — iiij^{s} viij^{d} To the Waggenner for cariage on New yeres daie — xviij^{s} Coles x sackes — vj^{s} viij^{d}/ To pilkington for ix dozen & x yardes of silke Lace for headpeeces — ix^{s} iiij^{d}/ To henri kelleweye to go to the Coorte abowte the dubble Mask — iij^{s} To pilkengton for turned pynnes for hedpeeces v dozen — xvj^{d}/ To pilkington for vij dozen lace more for hedpeces — vij^{s} To Clatterbookes dawghter for cloth for Ruffs apornes Neckerchers & Rayles for Eldertons playe — xj^{s} vj^{d}/ for making them — xij^{d} Rewardes to the hedpeece makers — ij^{s} viij^{d} Item

> xix^{li}. xix^{s}. x^{d}.

f° 16 r.

	Item for .v. Tuffes of Bugles to sett on the Ianizes hattes bowghte of William Pilkington — iij[s] iiij[d]/ To M[r] Arnolde for his Botehier & cariage to the Coorte at hampton on twelf daie — viij[s]/ fflower for past — vj[d] Nayles of sundry sortes at sundry tymes — vj[s]./ Gloves for Maskers & children ij dozen, di. — xij[s] Pinnes & Tape — ij[s]	
Painting	Item more for mony by him paid to Arnolde the paynter for & in full payment for Andramadas picture — xx[s] & To haunce Eottes for painting of patternes for maskes — xiij[s] iiij[d]./ In all	xxxiij[s].iiij[d].
Greenecloth &c. or Necessaries.	The Clerke of thoffice for his ordinary greenecloth Paper Inck and suche other Necessaryes as to the same Office is Incident for the devices, plottes, bills & Bookes of this yeare	lxvj[s]. viij[d].

S *umma* of all theise **Emptions** — cclxxiiij[li]. xvij[s]. ob.

December Ianuary & ffebruary Anno *Regni Reginæ* Elizabeth *prædictæ* — **xv[to].**

S *UMMA* **of all** the Charges growen in the said office *within* the saide tyme aswell of **Wages as Emptions** Amounteth vnto — v.[c] xij[li]. xvj[s]. vj[d]. ob.

* Iohn fortescue
* Henry Sekeforde
* Edwarde Buggyn
* Thomas Blagrave
* Iohn Arnold

f° 16 v.

Marche, Aprill, Maye, Iune, Iuly, August, September, & October, Anno Regni Reginæ **Elyzabeth** **xv^{to}**

Ayrynges & preparacions made against the **Progresse** into kent *with* **Translatyng Repayring, ffurnishing,** garnishing setting foorth, Cariage, conduction & Attending of the best and most ffyttest ffurniture of the same Office to Cawnterbury & there Remayning by the space of vij daies & then Returning with the same stuf to saint Iohns & there safely bestowing therof as appertayned The whole Charges whereof together *with* the Ordinary Charges and alowaunc*es* of the officers & what soever ells *with*in the same tyme of **viij Monethes** ending the Last of October in the yeare aforesaide together with the parties Names to whome any mony is due hereafter pertyculerly ensueth. vid*elicet*

		Daies	& Nightes	Wages.	
Taylers. and others *wor*king & attending the premiss*es* at sundry tymes *with*in the saide viij monethes.	Thom*as* Clatterbooke at xx^{d} p*er* die*m*	40	5	lxxv^{s}.	*xxix^{li}.xv^{s}.
	Iohn Davyes at xij^{d} p*er* die*m*	40	5	xlv^{s}.	
	Henri price at xij^{d}.	40	5	xlv^{s}.	
	Richard Mundaye at xij^{d}.	40	5	xlv^{s}.	
	Thom*as* Booreman at xij^{d}.	40	5	xlv^{s}.	
	Iohn Drawater at xij^{d}.	40	5	xlv^{s}.	
	Will*iam* Dod at xij^{d}.	40	5	xlv^{s}.	
	Thom*as* Ienkens at xij^{d}.	40	5	xlv^{s}.	
	Iohn Dawncye at xij^{d}.	40	5	xlv^{s}.	
	Thom*as* Kilforde at xij^{d}.	11	2	xiij^{s}.	
	Iohn Walker at xij^{d}.	15	5	xx^{s}.	
	Henri kelleway at xij^{d}.	11	2	xiij^{s}.	
	Nich*ol*as Michell at xij^{d}.	15	5	xx^{s}.	
	Iohn Clayton at xij^{d}.	3	1	iiij^{s}.	
	will*iam* Symons.	40	5	xlv^{s}	
	Iohn Cooke	40	5	xlv^{s}.	
Prop*er*tymakers Haberdashers & others *with*in that tyme against the Progresse.	Will*iam* Pilkington at xx^{d} p*er* die*m*	15	5	xxxiij^{s}. iiij^{d}.	* vj^{li}. xvj^{d}.
	Iohn ffarrington at xvj^{d}	10	0	xiij^{s} iiij^{d}.	
	Iohn Tuke at xvj^{d}.	10	0	xiij^{s}. iiij^{d}.	
	Will*iam* Bowll at xx^{d} p*er* die*m*.	15	5	xxxiij^{s} iiij^{d}.	
	Iohn Ogle the yong*er* at xvj^{d}.	3	0	iiij^{s}	
	Iohn Bett*es* at xvj^{d} p*er* die*m*	3	0	iiij^{s}	
	Iohn Carow at .ij^{s}. p*er* die*m*	10	0	xx^{s}.	

* S*umma* xxxv^{li}. xvj^{s} iiij^{d}

f° 17 r.

		Daies &	Nightes	wages
Thoffycers for theose viij monethes theier diett & wages	The *Master* at iiij^{s} *per* diem	40	5	ix^{li}
	The Clerkcomptrowler at ij^{s}.	40	5	iiij^{li} x^{s}.
	The Clerke at ij^{s} *per* diem	40	5	iiij^{li}. x^{s}.
	The yoman at ij^{s} *per* diem	40	5	iiij^{li}. x^{s}.

S*umma* — xxij^{li}. x^{s}.

S*umma* of all these wages — lviij^{li}. vj^{s}. iiij^{d}.

Emptions & provizions against the **progresse** aforesaide. vid*elicet*

Necessaries Cariages botehier and Reward*es*

Edward Buggin esquier clerkcomptrouler of this Office for mony by him disbursed for A lock & A staple — xxij^{d} ffor ffoyle for vyzard*es* & ffawchins — xx^{d} another padlock — xij^{d} ffethers for hedpeeces viij — ij^{s} iiij^{d}/ A dosen of very good washt gloves for the Ladyes — xvj^{s}/ Three dosen of Spanish gloves — xviij^{s} ffor Cranage of stuf at Billingsgate — vj^{d}. the portage of stufe that folowed the progresse — iiij^{d} the Hyer of A Bardge from London to gravesende w*ith* the same stuf — v^{s}. for the w*or*kmens breakefast at Billingsgate after theier Night*es* watching — ij^{s} ffor one thowsand of pynnes — xij^{d} in Rewarde — xij^{d} for Horshyer sundry tymes within the same viij Monethes — xx^{s} } lxx^{s}. iij^{d}.

silkweaver.

Will*iam* Bowll for vij dosen di. of Lardge sylke fflowers at viij^{d} the peece — lx^{s} for xiiij ounc*es* iij quarters of tassells & frenge greate & small of Copp*er* sylver at xviij^{d} the ounce — xxij^{s}. j^{d}. ob. And for his Botehier & horshier to and fro caunterbury — xiij^{s} iiij^{d}. / In all } iiij^{li}. xv^{s}. v^{d}.

wyerdrawer.

Thom*as* Leveret for wyer — xij^{d} spanish needells ij dosen — xx^{d} Long Quilting Needells — xij^{d} Chaynes for the Marriners knives — iij^{s} iiij^{d}. / ij dozen of Redd Ring*es* — xvj^{d} And for his owne daies travell — xx^{d} In all } x^{s}.

fo 17 v.

Necessaries. Cariag*es*. botehier & expenc*es* in progresse	Iohn Davyes for mony by him disbursed for Tape j lb — iiij^{s}/ A quarterne of Cullred thredd — x^{d} di. lb of white thredd — xx^{d}/ a nother quarter of tape — xij^{d} A quarter of Cullered thredd — x^{d} ffagott*es* — viij^{d} Bumbast — xij^{d}/ halfe a lb more of cullered thredd — xx^{d} Cranage of stuf — iiij^{d} for Cariage from the waterside at gravesende to the wagon — viij^{d}. the hier of ij hackneies fro*m* gravesende to Rochester to overtake the Carte & gett another for speede — ij^{s} for horsemeate & victualls at Rochester for the carters & theier horses — xvj^{d}/ for horsemeate and the car*ter*s meate at Cittingborne — iij^{s} for ij hackneies from Rochester to Cittingborne — iiij^{s} the Carters wages fro*m* gravesende to caunterbury — vij^{s} vj^{d} the hier of ij hackneies from sittingborne to caunterbury — iiij^{s} for Rushes at Caunterbury — ij^{s} vj^{d} ffuell to ayer the howse & the stuf & to serve during viij daies there — ij^{s} Lyght*es* there that tyme — vj^{d} the Rent of the howse & hier of Necessaries there then — x^{s} Cariage from Caunterbury to Cittingborne — ij^{s} from Cyttingborne to gravesend — ij^{s}. vj^{d}. the hier of ij hackneies from caunterbury to gravesend — x^{s} portage at gravesend to the bote — vj^{d} Cariage by water to London — iiij^{s} Cariage from the water syde to saint Iohns — vj^{d}.	lxix^{s}.
thupholster	Philip Gunter for iiij peec*es* of Buckeram.	xvj^{s}.
habberdasher	Thom*as* Gyles for xij vyzard*es* for women & vij Turk*es* vyzard*es* at xxiiij^{s} the dosen In All amounting vnto	xxxviij^{s}.
Necessaries botehier. horshier & Reward*es*	Bryan Dodmer for his attendaunce & s*er*vice doone within the Office *with*in those viij monethes aforesaide & for his horshyer botehier and attendaunce in the progresse with sundry Necessaries by him emploied	lxx^{s}.

f° 18 r.

Necessaries Iohn Arnolde yoman of this Office for mony by him disbursed *with*in the tyme aforesaide for yolow Cotton to lyne the Monark*es* Gowne at viij^{d}. the yarde xij yard*es* — viij^{s}/ To lyne his gerkin iiij yard*es* ij^{s} viij^{d} To lyne his hose iij yard*es* — ij^{s}. Canvasse for his gerkin — xvj^{d} Carsy Lyning & hollon for his hosen — iij^{s} sylke to sett on the gard*es* — v^{s} Thredd to sowe those iij garment*es* — iij^{s} the wages of iij Men iiij daies — iiij^{s} for cariage of certeyne peec*es* of the wagon & Mownte from the warderob to saint Iones — ij^{s} The wages of A Ioyner & his Man *with* iiij others that tooke downe the greate press*es* & saving the wainskott — xiiij^{s} for caryeng foorth the Rubbish & making cleane the howse — ij^{s} for Rushes — iiij^{s} ffewell — vj^{s} Thredd & other small Necessaries — v^{s}. } lxij^{s}.

S*umma* of all theise Emptions &c. } xxj^{li}. x^{s}. viij^{d}

Marche Aprill Maye Iune, Iuly August September & October. } SUMMA of all the charg*es* growen *with*in those viij monethes } **lxxix^{li}. xvij^{s}.**

* Iohn fortescue
* Henry Sekeforde
* Edwarde Buggyn
* Thom*as* Blagrave
* Iohn Arnold

f° 18 v.

The Ioyner for Presses &c.

Item more for new presses to be made thorowowte the whole storehowse for that the olde were so Rotten that they coulde by no meanes be Repayred or made any waye to serve agayne. The Queenes Maiesties store lyeng now on the ffloore in the storehowse which of necessitie must preasently be provyded for before other workes can well Beginne. which presses being made as is desyred by the Officers wilbe a greate safegarde to the store preasently remayning and lykewise of the store to coome whereby many things may be preserved that otherwyse wilbe vtterly lost & spoyled contynually encreasing her Maiesties charge. } lli.

* not allowid for so moche as the said presseis ar not begonn

Summa — patet

SUMMA **Totalis of this whole volume** contayning all the Charges growen within this Office **Betweene the Last of Maye** in the xiiijth yeare of the Reaigne of our Sovereaigne Lady Queene Elizabeth **And the Last of October** in the xvth yeare of her Maiesties Reaigne Being **One whole yeare and ffyve Monethes** Amounteth vnto } **M. cccc xxvijli. xijs. vjd. ob.**

*Iohn fortescue
*Henry Sekeforde
*Edwarde Buggyn
*Thomas Blagrave
*Iohn Arnold

fo 19 r.

12 July 1572

A Warrant for Delivery of Stuff

British Museum. Additional MSS. 5751. B. f° 4

ELIZABETH R.

We will and Commaunde you that Immediatlie vppon the sighte herof ye deliuer or cause to be deliuered vnto oure welbeloued seruantes vndre named all suche parcells of stuf for our vse and service as herafter followeth That is to saie . . . .

Item to Sir Thomas Benger knighte Master of our maskes Revells and tryumphes for the better furnyture and settinge forth of the same these parcells followinge That is to saie Of clothe of gold yellowe plaine thirtie fyve yardes and a half Of cloth of golde yellowe with workes ffoure score foure yardes & three quarters/ Of cloth of gold crimsin plaine thirtie two yardes three quarters/ Of cloth of Siluer plaine ffyvetie yardes half and half quarter/ Of cloth of siluer russet with workes twenty and seaven yardes/ Of veluet Purple Twentie yardes/ Of veluet white Thirtie nyne yardes and a half/ Of veluet Reade thirtie and sixe yardes/ Of veluet Orrendge coloure eightene yardes three quarters/ Of veluet Carnacion twentie fyve yardes and three quarters/ Of veluet Carnacion Lighte coloure fouretie and fyve yardes/ Of veluet reade Bard with gold thirtie seaven yardes quarter/ Of veluet Blewe Bard with gold seaventene yardes/ Of veluet Grene twentie one yardes and a half/ Of veluet blewe thirtie nyne yardes quarter/ Of veluet yellowe Twentie and one yardes/ Of veluet black thirtie and foure yardes/ Of veluet Black with workes the grounde satten sixe yardes/ Of satten crimsin fouretie foure yardes and a half/ Of Satten Purple Twentie and eighte yardes and three quarters/ Of Satten Black threescore fouretene yardes and a half/ Of Satten yellowe one hundred yardes and a half/ Of Satten white fouretie and nyne yardes and a half/ Of Satten Grene ffyvety and foure yardes/ Of Satten Blewe striped fyvety and two yardes/ Of Satten Blewe twentie yardes and an half/ Of Satten Tawnie twelue yardes/ Of Satten chaungeable striped fouretie and seaven yardes/ Of Damask Purple thirtie eighte yardes and three quarters/ Of Damask white Two hundred three score and foure yardes/ Of Damask yellowe thirtie yardes quarter/ Of Damask Black Twelve yardes/ Of Taffata crimsin thirtie two yardes/ Of Taffata Tawnie Towers thirtie and sixe yardes/ Of Taffata Tawnie thirtie nyne yardes and a half/ Of Taffata Black one hundred eighte yardes quarter/ Of Taffata yellowe narrowe fyvetie and eighte yardes/ Of Sarcenet striped with gold and siluer one hundred threscore eleven yardes and an half/ Of Sarcenet purple one hundred sixtene yardes and an half/ Of Sarcenet Crimsin three hundred twentie and one yardes three quarters/ Of Sarcenet white one hundred fourescore and eightene yardes/ Of Sarcenet reade two hundred threscore and sixtene yardes and iij quarters/ Of Sarcenet yellowe three hundred and fyvetie yardes iij quarters/ Of Sarcenet Tawnie one hundred and fyve yardes/ Of Sarcenet Black one hundred and seaven yardes/ Of Sarcenet Russet one hundred thirtie three yardes and three quarters/ Of Sarcenet grene one hundred and fouretie yardes/ and of Lawne threescore two yardes and a half . . . .

. . . . **And these** oure Lettres shalbe youre sufficiente Warraunte and dischardge for the premisses **Yeven** vndre oure Signet at oure Pallace of Westminster the xij^th Daie of Iulie in the xiiij^th yeare of oure Reigne. 1572.

To our trustie And welbeloved Iohn ffortescue Esquire Master of oure Greate Warderobe.

[Endorsed :] A warraunte to M^r ffortiscue Master of the greate wardrobe for stuff by him deliuered to Sir Thomas Benegar knight & others.

From 31 October 1573 to 1 March 1573-4.

viz.

Record Office. Audit Office. Accounts various. Bd. 1213. Revels n° 3.

[Betweene the] Laste [of October afo]resaide } **xvto.**

[And the xxth] **of** [December **157**]**3.** } **xvjto.**

Woorkes doone & Attendaunce geven by the parties herevnder Named Abowte the Traslating, ffytting, ffurnishing, garnishing, setting ffoorth and Taking in agayne of ij Sutes of Apparell & furniture for Choyce of A Mask showen at Greenewitche after the Mariage of Willyam Drurye esquier. And lykewyse for the Ayring, Repayring, sspungyng, Wyping, Brushing, sorting, suting, putting in order and safe bestowing bothe of thapparell aforesaide and also of all the residue of thapparell propertyes, ffurniture, & Necessaries incident to the same.

Item for pervsing the whole store of thoffice pertycculerly after the death of Iohn Arnolde late yoman therof, comparing the Inventoryes & likewise orderly & safe bestowing therof againe.

Item agayne Lykewise pervsing the store pertycculerly and delyvering therof by Inventory in chardge to Walter ffysh yoma*n* of the same now remayning.

Item sundry other tymes for calling together of sundry Players, and for pervsing, fitting, & Reformyng theier matters (otherwise not convenient to be showen before her Ma*ies*tie)

And finally vpon the entraunce of the saide Blagrave into the execucon of the Masters office, for Collecc*i*on & showe of eche thinge prepared for her Ma*iesties* Regall disporte & Recreac*i*on as also the store wherewith to ffurnish garnish and sett foorth the same wherof as also of the whole state of thoffice the L*ord* Chamberlayne according to his honou*rs* appointment was throughly advertised.

The Charges wherof together w*ith* the parties names that wroughte & attended thervpon; eche mannes nu*m*ber of dayes; & p*er*tycculer dett due for the same ensueth. vid*elicet*

[T]aylers & others the first at xxd the daye daye &c. the residue at [x]jid the daye & the [l]ike for [the] Nighte.

	Dayes.	Night*es*.	Wages.
Thom*as* Clatterbooke	20	2	xxxvjs. viijd.
Nich*olas* Michell	4	2	vjs
Iohn Davyes	20	2	xxijs
Iohn Browne	20	2	xxijs
Richard Warmingh*am*	20	2	xxijs
Geordge Arnolde	20	2	xxijs.
Richard Mundaye	20	2	xxijs.
Henri price	20	2	xxijs.
Lewes Iones	10		xs
Rober[t] Reeve	10		xs
Iohn Drawater	20	2	xxijs
Nich*olas* story	20	2	xxijs
Thom*as* Booreman	20	2	xxijs
Will*iam* Dawnce	22	2	xxijs
Iohn Dawncy	20	2	xxijs

f°4 r. *Summa* — xvli. iiijs viijd

Prop*er*tymakers & Habberdashers.	Iohn Caro at ij^{s} by the daye	4	2	xij^{s}
	Will*iam* Pilkington at xx^{d}.	4	2	x^{s}
	Iohn ffarrington at xviij^{d}.	4	2	ix^{s}
	Iohn Davy for Caro at xvj^{d}.	4	2	viij^{s}
	Robert ffernollye at xij^{d}	2	0	ij^{s}
	Peeter Morris at xij^{d}.	2	1	iij^{s}

Summa — xliiij^{s}

Offycers.	The M*aster* at iiij^{s} by the daie.	20	2	iiij^{li}
	Clerkcomptrowler at ij^{s}.	20	2	xliiij^{s}.
	The Clerke at ij^{s}.	20	2	xliiij^{s}.
	The Yoman at ij^{s}.	20	2	xliiij^{s}.

Summa — xj^{li}

Emptions. and other charges incident vid*elicet*

Necessaries, Cariag*es*, Conductions & Reward*es* — Edward Buggin Clerkcomptrowler of this office for mony by him disburced for Gloves for the Maskers & Torchebearers at Mr Druries wedding — ix^{s} And for Cariag*es*, Light*es*, Botehier, expenc*es* & Reward*es* then & sundry other tymes vpon sundry occasions incident — xxxj^{s}. In all *with*in the tyme aforesaide } xl^{s}.

Rep*ar*acions. — Iohn Dawncy for mony by him disburced for tyling & Mending the stable and other plac*es* incident to the Clerk of this office } xlviij^{s}. ij^{d}.

Iorneyeng charg*es* & Reward*es*. — Bryan Dodmer for mony by him disbursed for fetching and bringing by water from Greenewitche certeine gilt pillers & fframes — iiij^{s} Horshier and Ryding Chardges for ij men*ne* that Rode post into wilshere & somersetshere for Mr Blagrave by the comaundement of my L. Chamberleyne a[n]d in recompence for his owen s*er*vice this tyme togeth[er a]llowed by thofficers — lx^{s} In all } lxiiij^{s}.

Summa — vij^{li}. xij^{s} ij^{d}

Betweene the last of October 1573 } **xv^{to}** — **wages of** { **Artifficers &c.** — xvij^{li} viij^{s}. viij^{d}. / **Officers** — xj^{li}. } xxviij^{li}. viij^{s} viij^{d}

And the xxth of December 1573. } **xvj^{to}.** — **Emptions** and other charg*es* incident & alowed for that tyme amou*n*teth to } vij^{li}. xij^{s} ij^{d}

The whole chardges aforesaide, is. } xxxvj^{li}. x^{d}.

* T. Blagr[ave]

* Edwarde Buggyn
* walter fysshe

f° 4 v.

Christmas, Newyeares tyde, & Twelfe tyde.

Betweene the xx[th] of December And the xj[th]. of Ianuary Anno *Regni* Reginæ *Elizabeth* præ*dictæ*

xvj[to].

Woorkes doone & Attendaunce geven Abowte the new making, Translating, ffytting, ffurnishing, garnishing, setting owte & Taking in againe, Making cleane & safe bestowing of sundry kyndes of Apparell, properties, ffurniture, & Implementes for the playes and Maskes ffollowing set foorthe & showen before her Maiestie *with*in the tyme aforesaide for her Regall disporte & Recreacion The Charges wherof together with the partyes names to whome any mony is due or hath bene paid for the same perticculerly ensueth.

Playes shown **at whytehall** vid*elicet*

Predor : & Lucia. played by Therle of Leicesters servauntes vpon Saint stevens daye at nighte at whitehall aforesaide/
Alkmeon, playde by the Children of Powles on Saint Iohns daye at nighte there/
Mamillia. playde by therle of Leicesteres seruauntes on Innosentes daye at nighte. there/
Truth, ffaythfullnesse, & Mercye, playde by the Children of westminster for Elderton vpon New yeares daye at nighte there/
Herpetulus the blew knighte **& perobia** playde by my Lorde klintons servantes the third of Ianuary being the sunday after Newyeares daye there/
Quintus ffabius playd by the Children of wyndsor ffor M[r] ffarrant on Twelfe daye at nighte lykewise at whitehall.

vj. all fytted and ffurnyshed with the store of thoffice and *with* the woorkmanshipp and provisions herein expressed as followeth hereafter orderly. ffirst the wages and then the Emptions with the other charges incident

Maskes shown **at white Hall.** *with*in the tyme aforesaide/ vid*elicet*

Lanceknightes .vj. in Blew sattyn gaskon cotes & slopps &c.
Torchebearers .vj. in Black & yolo Taffata &c. showen on Saint Iohns daie at nighte.
fforesters or hunters **.vj.** in Greene sattyn gaskon cotes & slopps &c.
Torchebearers .vj. attyred in Mosse & Ivye &c. showen on New yeres daye at nighte.
Sages .vj. in long gownes of Cownterfet cloth of golde &c.
Torchebearers .vj. in Long gownes of Redd damask showen on Twlfe daye at Nighte.
In all

iij all fytted & throughly ffurnyshed with all manner of properties & Necessaryes incident/ & garnished and sett foorth accordingly.

f° 5r.

Christmas ; Newyeares tyde ; & twelfe tyde.

		Dayes,	Nyghtes,	Wages.
Taylers & others the first at xx^{d} the residue at xij^{d} the daie and the like for the nighte. *videlicet*	Thomas Clatterbooke	19	12	lj^{s}. viij^{d}
	Nicholas Michell	19	12	xxxj^{s}
	Iohn Lvn	19	12	xxxj^{s}.
	peeter Conawaye	8	5	xiij^{s}
	Geordge whitledell	10	7	xvij^{s}.
	peeter Banbridge	10	7	xvij^{s}.
	Iohn ffiauncer	11	6	xvij^{s}.
	Robert Bokes	7	3	x^{s}
	Edmund Ogle	12	6	xviij^{s}
	Robert Garton	14	9	xxiij^{s}
	Richard Snozell	12	9	xxj^{s}.
	Symon Harison	10	7	xvij^{s}.
	William wood	12	7	xix^{s}
	Geordge Haukinson	13	9	xxij^{s}
	Iohn Harper	10	6	xvj^{s}
	Alexander Thuell	13	9	xxij^{s}
	Geordge wrighte	15	9	xxiiij^{s}
	Iohn Cleyton	13	9	xxij^{s}
	Iohn walker	12	9	xxj^{s}
	Randall Owley	12	7	xix^{s}
	Geordge Corkes	12	5	xvij^{s}
	Robert Iones	4	2	vj^{s}
	Robert Iones iunior	1	0	xij^{d}
	Thomas Lambe	15	8	xxiij^{s}
	Richard Wardman	11	8	xix^{s}
	Henri Callewaye	15	6	xxj^{s}
	Thomas kilforde	13	8	xxj^{s}
	Iohn payne	4	5	ix^{s}
	Gryffin Iones	14	8	xxij^{s}
	Geordge Dytten	6	5	xj^{s}
	Tymothye Stevens	1	0	xij^{d}
	Iohn pynnyng	1	0	xij^{d}
	Iohn Iewell	1	0	xij^{d}.
	George Eden	1	0	xij^{d}.
	Iohn willson	1	0	xij^{d}.
	Iohn Browne	19	12	xxxj^{s}
	Women spanglers xxvj	1	0	xvj^{s} vj^{d}
	Iohn ffawnce	18	10	xxviij^{s}
	Randall Bredge	18	10	xxviij^{s}
	Thoms Browne	12	8	xx^{s}
	Iohn Davy	21	14	xxxv^{s}.
	Lewes Iones	21	14	xxxv^{s}
	Robert Reeve	21	14	xxxv^{s}
	Richard warmingham	21	14	xxxv^{s}
	Geordge Arnolde	21	14	xxxv^{s}.
	Richard Mundaye	21	14	xxxv^{s}.
	Henri price	21	14	xxxv^{s}
	Iohn Drawater	21	14	xxxv^{s}
	Thomas Booreman	21	14	xxxv^{s}
	william Dawnce	21	14	xxxv^{s}
	Nicholas Storye	21	14	xxxv^{s}
	Iohn Dawncye	21	14	xxxv^{s}

Summa — lvj^{li}. x^{s}. ij^{d}

f° 7 r.

Paynters.	at xx^{d}.	William Lyzard	19	15	lvj^{s} viij^{d}
		Haunce Bonner	13	7	xxxiij^{s} iiij^{d}
		Iohn Lyzarde	14	12	xliij^{s} iiij^{d}
		Thomas Bushe	14	12	xliij^{s} iiij^{d}
		Richard Baker	1	2	v^{s}
		pangrace Inglish	1	2	v^{s}
	at xviij^{d}.	Robert Hudson	14	11	xxxvij^{s} vj^{d}
		Roger Poole	1	2	iiij^{s} vj^{d}
		Thomas Bush senior	13	5	xxvij^{s}.
		Iohn ffyaunce	14	12	xxxix^{s}
		Thomas Tyler	4	6	xv^{s}
		Iohn Clemence	3	4	x^{s} vj^{d}
		Iames Cooke	4	5	xiij^{s} vj^{d}
		William Gates	2	1	iiij^{s} vj^{d}
	at xvj^{d}.	Robert Tayler	14	12	xxxiiij^{s} viij^{d}
		Iohn Streter	17	13	xl^{s}
	at xij^{d}.	Thomas Tyler	4	5	ix^{s}
		Geordge Melling	14	6	xx^{s}
		Thomas Reade	4	1	v^{s}.
		william wilkins	17	13	xxx^{s}
				Summa — xxiij^{li}. xvj^{s} x^{d}	
Propertymakers.		Iohn Caro at ij^{s} the daie	19	14	lxvj^{s}
	at xx^{d}.	Iohn Rosse	10	3	xxj^{s} viij^{d}
	at xviij^{d}.	Nicholas Rosse	10	4	xxj^{s} vj^{d}.
	at xvj^{d}.	Iohn Rosse Iunior	7	2	xij^{s}.
		Thomas Sturley	4	2	viij^{s}
		Iohn Ogle	11	5	xxj^{s} iiij^{d}
		Iohn David for Caro	19	14	xliiij^{s}
				Summa — ix^{li} xiiij^{s}	
Basketmakers.	at xvj^{d}.	Iohn Ollyff	3	0	iiij^{s}
		Angell Gyles	3	0	iiij^{s}
	at xij^{d}.	Robert willson	2	0	ij^{s}
				Summa — x^{s}.	

f° 7 v.

Ioyners./	at xvj^{d}	Christopher Harison	13	8	xxviij^{s}
		Albert Harison	13	6	xxv^{s} iiij^{d}
		Iohn Basforde.	13	6	xxv^{s}. iiij^{d}.
				Summa — lxxviij^{s} viij^{d}	
Carpenters.	at .xvj^{d}.	Rowland Robinson	10	6	xxj^{s} iiij^{d}.
	at .xiiij^{d}.	Gyles Hayes	12	7	xxij^{s}. ij^{d}.
		Iohn Collins	16	7	xxvj^{s}. x^{d}
		Will*iam* Barker	9	7	xviij^{s}. viij^{d}.
		Alexander brokson	12 1/2	6	xxj^{s} iiij^{d}
				Summa — cx^{s}. iiij^{d}.	
Imbroderers. & Habberdashers.	at xx^{d}.	Will*iam* Pilkington.	19	14	lv^{s}.
	at xviij^{d}.	Iohn Tuke.	14	10	xxxvj^{s}.
		Richard Moorer	10 1/2	4	xxj^{s} vj^{d}.
		Iohn ffarrington	19	14	xlix^{s} vj^{d}.
	at xij^{d}.	Gilbert Sheperd	11	3	xiiij^{s}
		peeter Morris	11	3	xiiij^{s}.
		Davy Axson	6	3	ix^{s}.
		Ellin Morgan	1	0	xij^{d}
		Awdery Moorer	6	0	vj^{s}.
		An*ne* pryn*ne*	1	0	xij^{d}
		Davy Evance	2	1	iij^{s}.
		Thom*as* Blore	4	2	vj^{s}
		Ione pilkington	14	10	xxiiij^{s}
		Iohn payne	2	1	iij^{s}
		Hugh Tuke	3	3	vj^{s}
		Ales Tayler	1	0	xij^{d}.
		Robert ffernolly	14	10	xiiij^{s}
The wierdrawer		Thom*as* Leveret the wyerdrawer & his servunt*es* that attended sundry tymes & wrowght vpon sundry propertyes & specially to hang vpp the light*es* in the hall at xij^{fe} tyde.			x^{s}.
				Summa — xiiij^{li}. iiij^{s}.	
Officers.		The M*aster* at iiij^{s} the daye	21	14	vij^{li}.
		Clerkcomptrowler at ij^{s}.	21	14	lxx^{s}.
		The Clerk at the like	21	14	lxx^{s}.
		The Yoman at ij^{s}.	21	14	lxx^{s}.
				Summa — xvij^{li} x^{s}.	

All the Wages afore saide amo*un*teth to { Artifficers &c. — cxiiij^{li}. iiij^{s}. vj^{d}. / Officers . . . xvij^{li}. x^{s}. } cxxxj^{li}. xiiij^{s}.

* T. Blagrave.

* Edwarde Buggyn.

* walter fysshe.

f° 8 r.

Christmas, Newyeares tyde, & Twelftyde.

Emptions *pro*vizions, Cariages, & other Charges incident to the Affares of the said Office.

The Mercer.	Mark Iarard for Crimsen sarcenet branc̦hte all over with silver at iiij^{s} the yarde lxvj yard*es* boughte cheefely to make Clokes for the foresters mask.		xiij^{li}. iiij^{s}.
The Sylkweaver.	Will*iam* Bowll for mony to him due for sundry *per*cells viz.		
	Bonelace of Copp*er* sylver xxvij lb viij• *ounces* di. at xviij^{d} the ownce.	xxxiij^{li}. ix^{d}.	
	ffrenge of like stuf at the lyke rate 28^{lb} .12.^{ounces} 1/4 . . .	xxxiiij^{li}.x^{s}. iiij^{d}.	
	ffrenge at ij^{s} viij^{d} the ownce ij$^{lb.}$ .v. *ounces*	iiij^{li}.xviij^{s}.viij^{d}.	
	ffrenge at xvj^{d} thounce xj *ounces* di..	xv^{s} iiij^{d}	
	Twist & Tassells of lik̦e stuf ij lb ix^{ounces} *quarter* at xviij^{d} the ownce.	lxj^{s}. x^{d}. ob..	
	Boxes^{3} to contayne the premiss*es*^{2} & for the ffethers^{1} .	iij^{s} iiij^{d}.	
	Pap*er* for patternes & for leaves of trees & other garnishing*es* iiij Reames	xxiiij^{s}.	^{xx}iiijv^{li}. v^{i}ij^{s}. ij^{d}
	Ballence & wayght*es* for thoffice	vj^{s} x^{d}.	
	past Boordes x doozen price	xxxvj^{s}.	
	ffelt*es* at viij^{d} the peece .12.	viij^{s}	
	Sylke at xviij^{d} thounce 8 ounc*es*	xij^{s}	
	Tables to wryte in	ij^{s} vj^{d}.	
	ffethers white and Longe .7.	xxiij^{s} iiij^{d}.	
	ffethers Curled .6.	xv^{s}.	
	A standish for the yoman *with* cou*n*ters &c. . . .	iiij^{s} v^{d}.	
	Buttons of Copper sylver x ounc*es* di. at xviij^{d} the ownce.	xv^{s}. ix^{d}.	
	A Chest *with* a trebble Lock.	xxx^{s}	
	In all as by his Bill &c. appereth amou*n*ting to		
The Lynnen drap*er*	M*ist*ris Dane for Canvas to paynte for howses for the players & for other properties as Monsters, greate hollow trees & suche other ^{xx}xij ells at xij^{d} the ell		xij^{li}.

* *Summa* pagine — cx^{li} xij^{s} ij^{d}.

f° 9r.

The yomans provision of Sundry kindes of wares

Walter ffysh for mony by him disburced for vid*elicet*
42 pec*es* Redd, yolo, & Russet — vij^{li}. viij^{s}.
Buckerams Greene at iiij^{s} iiij^{d} the peece xiiij peeces — lx^{s} viij^{d}/ Black at .v^{s}. the peece — v^{s} And one peece of very fyne Buckeram — xiiij^{s} in all } xij^{li}. vij^{s} viij^{d}

Tyncell sarcenett Blew xj y*ar*ds iij quarters at xij^{s} the yarde — vij^{li} xij^{d}/ iij quarter [yerdes] of white tincell at xij^{s} the yarde — xxxix^{s}. Gowlde Tyncell for vj bande*s* for Maskers — xv^{s}/ in all am*oun*ting vnto } ix^{li}. xv^{s}

Thred of sundry Cullers/ viz/ white .vj^{lb}. q*uarter* at iiij^{s} the lb — xxv^{s}. ffyner white di. lb — ij^{s} viij^{d}/ Blew at iij^{s} iiij^{d}. the lb ij^{lb} di. — viij^{s} iiij^{d}/ Red at like rate ij lb di. p*ri*ce — viij^{s} iiij^{d}/ Greene at iij^{s} iiij^{d} the lb iij lb di. — xj^{s} viij^{d} yolo at like rate ij lb di. — viij^{s} iiij^{d}/ Browne at ij^{s} viij^{d} the lb iij lb — viij^{s}/ Black j bowlte & iij quarters — viij^{s} ij^{d}. } iiij^{li}. vj^{d}.

ffelte*s* xxx^{ti}. xxiiij^{s}.
Past pap*er* . . . . xij^{d}
Sarcenet white iij y*ar*ds iij q*uarter*s for a shirte . . . xv^{s}.
Gloves washt & poynted for Maskers xij paier — xij^{s} for Torchebearers xij payer — viij^{s}/ ffor Children v dozen — xxviij^{s} vj^{d}/ It*em* more for Maskers vij payer — ix^{s} iiij^{d}/ for Torchebearers xij payer — vij^{s}/ } lxiii^{s}. x^{d}.
Hear for Hosen iij lb . . . . xv^{d}
[3 lb] Tape and Buttons . . . . xiij^{s} vj^{d}
Coles and Billette*s* . . . . xlj^{s} iiij^{d}
fflannell viij yardes at ix^{d} the yerde . . . . . . vj^{s}.
fflocke*s* to stuf hattbande*s* . . . . xij^{d}
fflower and paste . . . . xx^{d}.
Spangells lvj thowsand at vj^{d} the thowsand . . . xxviij^{s}.
Locke*s* keyes and Bowlte*s* . . . . vij^{s} viij^{d}.
Corde to trusse the Baskette*s* . . . . xiiij^{d}
Vrinalls to vse at the Coorte. & one Ink glasse . xv^{d}
Dryeng of Mosse & Rose water for it . . . . . iij^{s} ij^{d}
Rushes — xx^{s} x^{d}./ Nayles — xj^{s}. x^{d}. . . . . . . xxxij^{s} viij^{d}
Cariages & Rewarde*s* . . . . viij^{s} vj^{d}.
Brushes & Rubbers & a coleshovell . . . . . . viij^{s} j^{d}.
In all as by his bill &c. appereth } xxxix^{li}. iij^{s}. iij^{d}

* S*umma* pagine pat*et*

f° 9 v.

The Mercer.	Iohn Robynson for iij yard*es* iij quarters of Narow Tyncell at iij^s the yarde.	xj^s iij^d
The Grocer for Confect*es* in the Mask of Wyldemen.	Robert Moorer for dyvers p*er*cells of his wares, viz. Suger xliiij lb .j. ounce at xiiij^d the lb . . . . . . lj^s v^d Rosewater three pynt*es*. . . . . iij^s vj^d Gu*m* tragachant ij ounc*es* . . . . xij^d Almons xx lb at xiiij^d the lb . . . . xxiij^s iiij^d Quinc*es* preservde ij lb q*uarter* . . . . ix^s Wallnutt*es* reddy made ij lb . . . . vj^s Cloves to stick in the peares . . . . xij^d Synamon and gynger .3. o*unces*. . . . . xiiij^d Peares reddy made of Marchpane stuf j lb . . . . iij^s. Apples & Lemans of Like stuf di. lb. . . . . xvj^d. Marmilade to temp*er* *with* the suger. . . . . . . ij^s A pott for the Quinc*es* . . . . iij^d. the hyer of A Cearce . . . . iiij^d In all Amounting vnto	ciij^s. iiij^d.
Reward*es* geven to The Carver and others	for the Mowldes & for Mowlding the frutes made of the stuf aforesaide *with*in this office in the preasence of the saide Blagrave vid*elicet* Apples, peares, peaches, peascodd*es*, Mulberies ffilberd*es*, Plummes, Akornes, Cherries &c.	xl^s.
The Basketmakers	Iohn Ollyf for iij small Baskett*es* made for patternes & for iij Bundells of Rodd*es* to make vj more for the Maskers to cary the frute in — viij^s for iij Hampers to carry thapparell — xiiij^s One Baskett with iiij Eares to hang Dylligence in/ in the play of p*er*obia/ & for ij other Browne Baskett*es* for thoffice — ij^s vj^d	xxiiij^s.vj^d
Beard*es* and heare	Iohn Owgle for vij Long Aberne beard*es* at xvj^d the peece — ix^s iiij/ vij other berd*es* ottett at xiiij^d the peece for the haunc*es* Mask at xvj^d the peece — viij^s ij^d/ xij beard*es* Black & Redd for the fforesters Mask at like rate — xvj^s/ Heare for the wylde Men at xvj^d the lb iij lb — iiij^s/ One Long white Bearde — ij^s viij^d.	xl^s. ij^d

* S*umma* pagine — x^li xix^s iij^d

f° 10 r.

P*ro*p*er*ty. *per*cells	Henri Calleway for mony by him disburced for		xx^{s}. vj^{d}
	Mosse and yong Okes for wylde me*n*	vj^{s}	
	Poles & Wand*es* for the Lictors	ij^{s}	
	Bayes for the prologg*es* & p*ro*p*er*ties	iij^{s} viij^{d}	
	Ivy for the Wylde men*ne* & tharbo*ur*	v^{s}x^{d}	
	Armes of Okes for the hollo tree	xij^{d}	
	Expenc*es* at higate one nighte & ij daies for p*ro*vision hereof	ij^{s}	
	In all as by his bill amounting vnto		
	Iohn Rosse for poles & shyvers for draft of the Curtins before the senat howse	ij^{s}	viij^{s} v^{d}.
	Curtyn Ring*es*	viij^{d}	
	Edging the Curtins w*ith* ffrenge	xij^{d}	
	Tape and Corde for the same	x^{d}	
	fflower & past w*ith* A pott for the same	vij^{d}	
	A Iebbett to hang vp diligence.	iij^{s} iiij^{d}	
	In all amounting vnto		
Necessaries.	Iohn Lam*be* for j dozen of past boorde — iij^{s} iiij^{d}/ pynnes & Nayles — ij^{s} iiij^{d} & for a porter y^{t} brought Canvas — iij^{d}./ all		v^{s} xj^{d}
The Chaundler.	Barnard ffabyan for sundry p*er*cells of his ware		vj^{li}. xviij^{s}./ix^{d}
	Sering candells j lb	xvj^{d}	
	White light*es* at iij^{s} vj^{d} the doze*n* xxvj dose*n*	iiij^{li} xj^{s}	
	Lynk*es* at iiij^{d} the peece lxxij	xxiiij^{s}	
	Corde iiij peeces	iiij^{s}	
	Lyne viij peec*es*	v^{s}. iiij^{d}	
	packthred.	v^{s}. j^{d}	
	with Torches	viij^{s}.	
	In all amounting vnto		

* *Summa* pagine — viij^{li} xiij^{s} vij^{d}

f° 10 v.

Paynters *per*cells	Will*iam* Lyzard for mony by him disbrced for		
	Syze & pott*es* for the same	xxxviij^{s}.vj^{d}.	
	Nayles to strayne the Canvas	xxij^{d}.	
	Browne Culler at xviij^{d} the lb 2 1/2^{lb}.	iij^{s} ix^{d}	
	Synop*er* di lb price	xviij^{d}	
	White iiij^{xx} xiij lb at iij^{d} the lb	xxiij^{s} iij^{d}	
	Lamp black xj lb at xvj^{d} the lb	xiiij^{s}. viij^{d}.	
	Masticote j lb	iij^{s} vj^{d}	
	Smalt xv lb at iij^{s} vj^{d} the lb	lij^{s} vj^{d}	
	Dark sinop*er* j lb	iiij^{s}	
	Vert iiij lb	x^{s} iiij^{d}	
	Redd xiij lb at vj^{d} the lb	vj^{s} vj^{d}	
	Vermillion di lb	iiij^{s}	
	fflurry at vij^{s} the lb j lb iij q*uarters*	xij^{s} iij^{d}	
	ffyne Black j lb	ij^{s}	
	Gowlde .v. c. at ij^{s} viij^{d} the c.	xiij^{s} iiij^{d}.	xiiij^{li}.
	Sylver at xviij^{d} the c m viij^{c}	xxvij^{s}	
	Glew iiij lb	xvj^{d}	
	Cotten to gilde with iij q*uarters* of lb	xij^{d}	
	Tyn*ne* ffoyle	ij^{s}	
	Assedue at iij^{s} the lb vj^{lb}iij q*uarters*	xx^{s} iij^{d}	
	Past and fflower	viij^{d}	
	Yolo coorse and Oker de Rooce	iiij^{s} vj^{d}	
	Past pap*er* iiij dozen for pendent*es* to the light*es*	viij^{s}	
	Copper cullor	iiij^{s}	
	Knopps of wood Turnde	xij^{d}.	
	Vert agayne	iij^{s} vj^{d}	
	Sinoper paper	xij^{d}	
	ffyne Black more j lb	iiij^{s}	
	Pencells & other necessaries	ij^{s} x^{d}	
	sape j lb	vj^{s} viij^{d}	
	In all as by his bill appereth Amou*n*ting unto		
Buskinmaker.	Iohn ffarrington for the making & solling of vj paier of Startopps — viij^{s} / vj paier of Mossy buskins — viij^{s} And vj payer of paynted buskins ^{all}for Maskers — xij^{s}/ in all		xxviij^{s}.

f°11r. * S*umma* pagine — xv^{li} viij^{s}

The wyerrawer	Thoms Leverett for sundry pecell*es*	vid*elicet*	
	Wyer xxvj lb to hang the light*es*	xxvij^{s} iiij^{d}	
	Candellstick*es* at ij^{s} the dozen iiij dose*n*	viij^{s}	
	Vice ^{12} Candellstick*es* at xij^{d} the peece	xij^{s}	
	High Candelstick*es* at vj^{d} the peece 6	iij^{s}.	
	Plates for small Canstick*es*	xij^{d}.	
	Plates for $^{vj.}$ walls & for $^{ij.}$ hatt*es*	viij^{s}.	
	ffunnells for hatt*es* with long pypes	iij^{s}	
	Rownde duble plates for the branches that hunge in the hall & bare light*es* viij doozen at x^{d} the peece	iiij^{li}	
	Launthornes iiij at vj^{s} the peece — xxiiij^{s} & ij at xvj^{d} the pece — ij^{s} viij^{d}	xxvj^{s}. viij^{d}	viij^{li} xvij^{s}. iij^{d}.
	for plating iiij ffawchyns	x^{d}	
	staples vj price	x^{d}	
	Lyne xxxvj yard*es*	xij^{d}.	
	Ring*es* for Curtyns	viij^{d}	
	Pack Needells greate & longe ij	viij^{d}	
	Bodkyns & dowt*es* for light*es*	xiij^{d}	
	Nayles of sundry sort*es*	ij^{s} ij^{d}	
	A greate hart Lock	xij^{d}	
	In all amownting vnto		
Tharmerer.	Roger Tyndall for Lending his Armor and for his *seruauntes* Attendaunc*es* to arme & vnarme the children in the play of *Quintus* ffabivs		xlvj^{s} viij^{d}.
Hunters hornes	Will*iam* Elom for vj Hornes garnisht with sylver by him delyvered into thoffice for the hunters Mask on New yeres Nighte which hornes the Maskers detayned & yet dooth kepe them against the will of all the officers		xviij^{s}.

* S*mma* pagine — xij^{li} xxiij^{d}

f° 11 v

Propertymaker	Iohn Caro for mony to him due for sundry percells		
	Holly & Ivye for the play of predor	iiij^{s}	
	ffyshes Cownterfete for the same viz. whiting, playce, Mackarell, &c.	iiij^{s}	
	A payle for the castell topp	vij^{d}	
	Bayes for sundry purposes	iiij^{d}	
	Lathes for the Hollo tree	xvj^{d}	
	Hoopes for tharbour & topp of an howse . . .	iiij^{s} xj^{d}	
	A Mace for the sargeant at armes.	xij^{d}	
	A Trunchin for the dictator	xx^{d}	
	Past & paper for the dragons head	xviij^{d}	
	Deale boordes for the senat howse	ij^{s} viij^{d}	
	Glew & glew pott	iiij^{d}	
	ffaggbroches for the knobbes of the tree. . . .	ij^{d}	
	A long staf to reache vp & downe ye lightes . .	viij^{d}	lxix^{s} ix
	ffawchions for ffarrantes playe iiij	iiij^{s}	
	Pynnes styf & greate for paynted clothes . . .	ix^{d}	
	Nayles viz. tenpeny nayle c di. — xv^{d}/ syxpeny nale vij c di. — iij^{s} ix^{d} fowerpeny Nayles .v. c — xx^{d}. threepenny Nayles vij c — xxj^{d}/ twopeny Nailes M — xx^{d} Tackes vj c — ix^{d} / Item more sixpeny Nayle cc — xij^{d}. ffower peny Nailes iiij c. — xvj^{d} In all	xiij^{s}. ij^{d}.	
	ffoormes ij [v^{s} iiij^{d}] & stooles [xiiij^{s}] xij. in all	xix^{s} iiij^{d}	
	knobbs for the senat howse	xvj^{d}	
	Item more for Nayles of sundry sortes by him browght in & imployed in thoffice	viij^{s}	
	In all as by [his] bill appereth		
The Carpenter	Rowland Robinson for stuf by him provided viz.		
	Rafters at xiiij^{d} the peece lviij	lxvij^{s} viij^{d}	
	Dubble Quarters at vj^{d} the pece 12	vj^{s}	
	singell quarters at iij^{d} the peece 38	ix^{s}. vj^{d}	
	Boordes iiij c di. at vj^{s} the .c.	xxvij^{s}	viij^{li}. iij^{s}. iiij^{d}.
	Seeling Boorde .j. c price	vj^{s} viij^{d}	
	Nayles by him employed	xj^{s}	
	ffirr poles lx price	xxx^{s}	
	Plankes ij. price	ij^{s}	
	Cariages to & fro.	iij^{s} vj^{d}	

* Summa pagine — xj^{li}. xiij^{s}. j^{d}.

fo 12 r.

Patternes & leaves Cutt. Will*iam* Pilkington thimbroderer for cutting of lxxij leaves w*hi*ch were cutt iij tymes duble vid*elicet* ij tymes in pap*er* & ones in sattin — xviij^{s} for making of vj patternes & for cutting therof for samples for the gownes of Cloth of golde — iij^{s} In all } xxj^{s}

Cariages &c. Richard Gryme & others for cariage of the fframes for the howses that served in the playes & other stuf & apparell for the play*ers* & Maskers / w*ith* theier attendanc*es* daye & Nighte sundry tymes at S*ain*ct Iohns & at the Coorte betwene Christm*as* and the Munday after twelfe daye — xxvj^{s} / Richard Tayler & Roger Atkenson — ij^{s} Geordge haukinson & sundry others — vj^{s} } xxxiiij^{s}

Lock*es* keyes Hasp*es* & henges. Iohn Collins for hing*es* to the Colehowse dore in thoffice — xij^{d} & to others for Lock*es* keyes haspes & henges for dores & windos — xiij^{s} iiij^{d} / in all w*ith* Nailes — ij^{s} } xvj^{s} iiij^{d}

Botehier. Lynk*es* Coles, Reward*es* &c. Iohn Drawater for Lynk*es* & botehier betwene the beginnyng & end of the w*orkes* — xvij^{s} viij^{d} / One Lode of Coles — xxij^{s} / in Reward*es* by the speciall appointm*ent* of M^{r} Io*hn* forteskue to be geven to Mr Nicholas Nudigate — xl^{s} / And by thappointm*ent* of the M*aster* — xij^{s} And for Taynterhookes & other necessaries — iij^{s}. vj^{d}. } iiij^{li}. xv^{s}. ij^{d}.

Reward*es*. Bryan Dodmer for Botehier & charges in suyng owte the privie seale, w*ith* sundry Reward*es* by him geven for expedic*ion* in obtayning the cc^{li} afore charged as prest and for his owne travell & attendaunce in sundry affares of this office to him comitted at this tyme before mencioned in all } lx.

* S*umma* pagine — xj^{li}. vj^{s}. vj^{d}.

f° 12 v.

ffvell. William Newman for vj .M. Billettes — lxxij^{s} and for vj^{c}. ffagottes — xxx^{s}. And to William Wood for ij Lodes of Coles — xl^{s} in all } vij^{li}. ij^{s}.

Necessaries Iohn Okes for A close stoole for the Maskers & Players &c. to vse at the Coorte — viij^{s} / for Lyer to strengthen the hangings with workes done by him & his servauntes at the Coorte & sundry other Necessaries by him there vsed — xij^{s} x^{d}. } xx^{s} x^{d}

Betwene the xxth of December 1573 And the xjth of Ianuary 1573 Anno Regni Regine Elizabeth predicte } xvj^{to}. { All Themptions for Christmas, New yeres tyde & Twelftyde, with the other charges besides the wages is } ccxxviij^{li}.vij^{d} * T. Blagrave

* Edwarde Buggyn

* walter fysshe

f° 13 r.

ffor Candellm*as*
Betweene the xj[th] of Ianuary aforesaide and the ffyft of ffebr*uary* 1573 Anno R*egni* R*egi*ne *Eliza-beth* p*re*dicte

xvj[to].

Woorkes doone & Attendaunce geven vpon the New making, Translating, ffytting, ffurnishing Garnishing setting foorth and taking in agayne of sundry kindes of Apparell prop*er*tyes and Necessaries Incident for **One Playe** [Timoclia at the sege of Thebes. by Alexander.] showen at Hampton Coo*r*te before her Ma*ies*tie by M[r] Munkesters Children **And One Maske** [of Ladies *with* lightes being vj vertues] likewyse prepared & brought thither in Redynesse but not showen for the Tediusnesse of the playe that nighte. The Charges of all which with the parties Names to whome any [mony] is due or hath bene payde for the same pertyculerly ensueth.

vid*elicet*

Taylers & others the first at xx[d] and all the Rest at xij[d] the daye & the lyke for the nighte.

	Daies	Night*es*	Wages.
Thom*as* Clatterbooke	15	8	xxxviij[s]iiij[d]
Nich*ol*as Michell	15	8	xxiij[s]
Iohn Lvn	15	8	xxiij[s]
Iohn fflauncer	14	4	xviij[s]
Geordge write	14	4	xviij[s]
Richard wardman	10	3	xiij[s]
Edmund Owgle	10	3	xiij[s]
Iohn Cleyton	10	3	xiij[s]
Geordge whitledell	8	3	xj[s]
Richard Moorecroft	7	0	vij[s]
Henri Callewaye	15	8	xxiij[s]
George Haukinson	10	3	xiij[s]
Thom*as* Lam*be*	12	6	xviij[s]
Robert Reeve	15	8	xxiij[s]
Iohn Browne	15	8	xxiij[s]
Iohn Davies	20	10	xxx[s]
Lewes Iones	20	10	xxx[s]
Richard warmingh*am*	20	10	xxx[s]
George Arnolde	20	10	xxx[s]
Richard Mundaye	20	10	xxx[s]
Henri price	20	10	xxx[s]
Iohn Drawater	20	10	xxx[s]
Thom*as* Booreman	20	10	xxx[s]
Will*iam* Dawnce	20	10	xxx[s]
Nich*ol*as Story	20	10	xxx[s]
Iohn Dawncy	20	10	xxx[s]
Iohn Bett*es* & his wyfe	1	0	ij[s]
Women spanglers .xj	1		vij[s].

S*umma* — xxx[li] xvj[s] iiij[d]

f[o] 14 r.

Prop*er*ty Makers.	at ij^{s}	Iohn Caro	16	4	xl^{s}.
Imbroderers &.	at xx^{d}.	Will*iam* Pilkington.	12	6	xxx^{s}
Habberdashers		Iohn Sharpe	6	2	xiij^{s} iiij^{d}
	at xviiij^{d}.	Iohn ffarington	16	4	xxx^{s}
		Iohn Tuke.	9	5	xxj^{s}
	at xvj^{d}.	Iohn Owgle	7	2	xij^{s}
		Iohn David for Caro	12	4	xxj^{s} iiij^{d}
	at xij^{d}	Ione Pilkington	8	6	xiiij^{s}

Summa — ix^{li}. xx^{d}.

Paynters.	at xx^{d}.	Will*iam* Lizard	16	4	xxxiij^{s}iiij^{d}.
		Iohn Lyzarde.	14	4	xxx^{s}.
		Haunce Bonner	10	4	xxiij^{s} iiij^{d}
		Pangrace Inglish	6	4	xvj^{s} viij^{d}
	at xviiij^{d}	Iohn ffyance	14	4	xxvij^{s}
		Thom*as* Tyler	5	4	xiij^{s}. vj^{d}
	at xvj^{d}.	Robert Tayler	6	4	xiij^{s} iiij^{d}
		Iohn Streter	13	4	xxij^{s} viij^{d}
	at xij^{d}	Thom*as* Tyler Iunior	4	2	vj^{s}
		Will*iam* wilkins	11	4	xv^{s}
		George Melling	11	4	xv^{s}
		Thom*as* Reade	4	2	vj^{s}

Summa — xj^{li}. xxij^{d}.

Officers.	The M*aster* at iiij^{s} the daie	20	10	vj^{li}
	Clerkcomptrowler at ij^{s}	20	10	lx^{s}
	The Clerk at ij^{s}	20	10	lx^{s}
	The Yoman at ij^{s}	20	10	lx^{s}

Summa — xv^{li}.

All the wages for Candellmas is { Artiffic*ers* &c — l^{li}. xix^{s}. x^{d}. / Officers — xv^{li}. } lxv^{li}. xix^{s}. x^{d}.

* T Blagrave

* Edwarde Buggyn

* walter fysshe

f° 14 v.

Candellm*as*, Emptions, and provisions *with* other charges incident

The yomans p*ro*visions.	Walter ffish for mony by him disburced for	vid*elicet*	vij^{li}. vij^{s}. x^{d}.
	Buckerams vj pece*es* at iiij^{s} the peece	xxiiij^{s}	
	Gloves for the Ladyes Maskers vj paier	xij^{s}	
	Glooves for the torchebearers vj paier	viij^{s}	
	It*em* ij dozen for children	xij^{s}	
	Thredd of sundry sort*es*	xvij^{s} ix^{d}	
	Tape di. lb.	ij^{s}	
	ffellt*es* for Boyes hat*es* vj — iiij^{s} vj^{d} for womens hatt*es* vj — iiij^{s} vj^{d} and for Men vj — iiij^{s} vj^{d} in all for felt*es*.	xiij^{s} vj^{d}	
	Hookes & eies *with* thackbroches	ix^{d}	
	Keyes for the entry dore iij	xviij^{d}	
	Coles one Lode	xxij^{s}	
	Cariages by Land	xvj^{d}	
	Barge & Botehier to & fro*m* ham*p*to*n* co*or*te	xxviij^{s}	
	Reward*es* to the wo*r*kmen to buy vittell at hampton Coorte.	v^{s}.	
	In all as by his bill		
The Wexchaundler	Richard sharp for the wax and woorkmanshipp of vj personages with the rest of the prop*er*ties on vj candellstick*es* at viij^{s} the peece — xlviij^{s} vj sweete light*es* of white wex for the same — vij^{s} In all with ij^{s} toward*es* his expence*s* at the Coorte.		lvij^{s}
The Basketmaker	Iohn Ollyf for vij Baskett*es* (ij^{s}. 8^{d}) made of purpose to cary the candellstick*es* & p*ro*p*er*ties & for certeine small (ij^{s} viij^{d}) Baskett*es* & iij greate hampers (xij^{s}) in all		xxvj^{s}. iiij^{d}
Matches & powder	Robert Moorer for perfvmes to burne at thende of the Matches — vj^{s} & for sweete powder made of Musk & Amber — xj^{s} viij^{d}/ in all		xvij^{s} viij^{d}
patternes for Mask*es*	Hawnce Eott*es* for sundry patternes by him made		vj^{s}.
The Turner	for vj Candellstick*es* of wood specially framed & turned for the p*ur*pose to beare the p*ro*p*er*ties & light*es* in the Ladyes Mask		xvj^{s} iiij^{d}
The Habberdasher	for sylver paper for the Maskers sleeves iiij doze*n* di. at iiij^{s} the dozen		xviij^{s}

* *Summa* pagine — xiiij^{li} ix^{s} ij^{d}

f° 15 r.

Silkwooman	for Buttons and flowers for Maskers hedd*es* vij & one silk tree for A device in one of the Candellstick*es* & a box to put them in — xvj^{s} A Border of edging for A womans hed — viij^{s}.	xxiiij^{s}.
Upholster	for pendent*es* of burnished golde for the Maskers garment*es* vij dozen — xiiij^{s} silk for tassells & setting them on — ij^{s}. Item mor iij doze*n* — vj^{s}.	xxij^{s}.
The skrivener	for writing in fayer Text the speches [viij above the line] d*elivere*d to her Ma*ies*tie	vij^{s} x^{d}
Cariages. to hampton Coo*r*te.	for Cariage of fframes for the players hows*es* & brynging them back from the Coo*r*te to saint Iones & for A tilt bote besides in all	xx^{s} viij^{d}.
Reward*es* and Expenc*es* at H*ampton* Coorte.	To the paynters & others that went to hampton Coo*r*te & stayed there that nighte as also the fellow that kept the stuff iij daies	xx^{s}.
Prop*er*ty p*er*cells	Iohn Caro for viij bills . . . . xvj^{s} Target*tes* vj . . . . x^{s} Gunnes vj . . . . xij^{s} fflask*es* [6] & tuchboxes [6] . . . . x^{s} Armyng swordes vj . . . . ix^{s} Truncheons xj . . . . iij^{s} viij^{d} Bowes vj . . . . vj^{s} Arrowes xij . . . . xx^{d} Bord*es* for the light*es* . . . . ij^{s} viij^{d} Long poles to hang them . . . . ij^{s} viij^{d} Daggers. iij . . . . iij^{s} In all Amounting vnto	lxxvj^{s}viij^{d}.
The Chaundler	Barnard ffabian for di. lb seering candells — viij^{d}/ xiiij doze*n* of Candells at iij^{s} vj^{d} the dozen — xlix^{s}/ Pack thread j lb — xij^{d} Lyne one peece — x^{d}/ a greate Corde — xij^{d}. Lynk*es* — ij^{s}. In all	liij^{s} x^{d}
Horshyer	Thom*as* Booreman for horshier [ij above the line] iij daies to hampton Coo*r*t *with* expenc*es* there	xiij^{s} iiij^{d}.

* *Summa* — xj^{li} xviij^{s} iiij^{d}

f° 15 v.

Paynters p*er*cells.	Will*iam* Lyzarde for mony to him due for sundry cullers viz.		
	Syze & pott*es*	vij^{s}	
	White x lb at iij^{d} the lb	v^{s}.	
	Black iij lb at xvj^{d} the lb	iiij^{s}	
	Nayles	viij^{d}	
	smalt iij lb/ at iij^{s} vj^{d} the lb	x^{s} vj^{d}	
	Masticote j lb.	iij^{s}	
	Ende di. lb.	ij^{s} viij^{d}	
	sinop*er* j lb	ij^{s}	
	Browne di. lb.	ix^{d}	
	Vert j lb	ij^{s} viij^{d}	
	sape .j. q*uarter*ne	xx^{d}	
	Gold culler.	iij^{s}	iiij^{li}. j^{d}
	Glew	viij^{d}	
	Wex	vj^{d}	
	Golde.	v^{s}.	
	sylver.	vj^{s}	
	ffyne golde.	vj^{s} viij^{d}	
	Vermillion	ij^{s}	
	Byce .3. *ounces*	iij^{s}	
	A canstick of wood.	xij^{d}.	
	fflower & past.	viij^{d}	
	shells of golde ij.	ij^{s} viij^{d}	
	shells of Sylver	iij^{s}	
	fyne cullers for wex w*or*ke	vj^{s}	
	In all as by his bill appereth amounting to		
Silk weaver	Will*iam* Bowll for mony to him due for ffrenge of fine copp*er* silver at xviij^{d} thounce vj lb xix ownc*es*	viij^{li} xij^{s} vj^{d}	
	Past boorde lardge iij dozen di.	xiiij^{s}	
	Bawderick*es* & Tassells of ffyne copp*er* sylver & black silk xij for the flask*es* & tucheboxes. price	iiij^{li} iiij^{s}	xiij^{li}. xix^{s}. vj^{d}
	Tassells more vj ounc*es*.	ix^{s}.	
	In All Amounting as by his bill		
Thimbroderer	Will*iam* Pilkington for Tufting vj lardge kirtells of greene Sattin w*ith* golde sarcenet all over wrought—iiij^{li}/ iij samples wrought—xiij^{s} iiij^{d}/ A felt — xij^{d} vij sylver buttons for hatt*es* — v^{s}. x^{d} / A paier of Ioyned tressells — ij^{s} / in all		cij^{s}. ij^{d}.
The Buskinmaker	Iohn ffarrington for making ij paier of painted Buskins — iiij^{s} A paier of yolo & Redd velvett — xx^{d} A paier of Russet taffata startopps — xvj^{d}		vij^{s}

* S*umma* — xxiij^{li} viij^{s} ix^{d} f° 16 r.

The wexchaundler	Iohn Izard for A proofe of p*er*fvmed light*es*	ij^{s} vj^{d}
P*ro*p*er*ty p*er*cells	Iohn Carow for seeling boorde .C. — vj^{s} viij^{d} It*em* for Nayles by him d*elivere*d to the Clerk*es* custody x^{s}. in all	xj^{s} viij^{d}
Perles & flowers	Martyn Hardrett for perles sett vpon silver bonelace for the Ladys Maskers head*es* ccc & odd	xxx^{s}.
	It*em* for vj greate Roses at xij^{d} the peece — vj^{s} A smaler sorte xviij at viij^{d} the peece — xij^{s} & for vij doze*n* di. at ij^{d} the peece — xv^{s}. in all	xxxiij^{s}.
planche boorde & sparres	Iohn Carowe for c plancheborde — iij^{s} iiij^{d} and for vj sparres — iij^{s} iiij^{d} in all	vj^{s} viij^{d}
Spangles & pinnes	Iohn Lam for spangles for the Ladyes Mask — v^{s} & for pynns d*elivere*d to Caro for the Clothes — x^{d}	v^{s}. x^{d}
Cariages by land and water to the Coo*r*te.	Granger the Bargeman for his Bardge &c. w*hi*ch caried the fframes & su*m* of the stuf to hampto*n* Coorte — xij^{s} viij^{d} & for Land cariage paid to I. hutten by M^{r} buggins appointme*nt* — iij^{s}	xv^{s}. viij^{d}
Iourneyeng charg*es* & expenc*es* at H*ampton* Coo*r*te & Kingston w*ith* Rewarde*s*	Bryan Dodmer for the chag*es* of him selfe & others viz. Mr Nudigate & the wexchandler &c before candellm*as* whiles the chamber for the Revells was prepared & the stuf bestowed — vj^{s}/ And farder likewyse remayning there till the Revells of candellm*as* was past & things safe Returned againe — x^{s} And for his owne s*er*vice during the tyme of the w*o*rk*es* aforesaide — xl^{s} / in all	lvj^{s}
Botehier	To Thom*as* Lam*be* for his & the wexchandlers Botehier to hamton Coo*r*te in post w*ith* the white light*es* — v^{s}/ theier Returne — iiij^{s}.	ix^{s}.
expenc*es* at H*ampton* Coorte.	Geordge Arnolde for his expenc*es* at the Coo*r*te & at Kingston during all the tyme that the stuf Remayned at the Coo*r*te in the chamber till her Ma*ies*tie came thorow that the same was bestowed in the clozet &c. and for sundry necessaries by him bowghte all	x^{s} iiij^{d}

* S*um*ma — ix^{li} v^{s} viij^{d}

f° 16 v.

ffvell.	**Will*iam* Newman for ij M billett*es* — xxvj^{s} viij^{d} / It*em* more to Will*iam* Wood for A lode of Coles — xxij^{s}**	**xlviij^{s}. viij^{d}.**
Bothier Riding charg*es* & Expenc*es*.	**Edward Buggin Clerkcomptrowler of thoffice / for Botehier and horshier *with* other expenc*es* at hampton Coo*r*te & at kingston &c. at this tyme**	**xx^{s}.**
	Bryan Dodmer for botehier to & fro hampton coo*r*te after Candellm*as* to know my L*ord* Chamb*er*leyne his pleasure for mony due by this booke & likewise his pleasure for preparac*io*ns to be made against Shrovety — viij^{s} and for his expenc*es* at the Coo*r*te & at kingston during that iij daies & iij nightes attendaunce for that matt*er* — vj^{s}	**xiiij^{s}**

***4. 2. 8**

All Themptions &c at Candellm*as*. is **lxiij^{li}. iiij^{s}. vij^{d}** *** T. Blagrave**

*** Edwarde Buggyn**
*** walter fysshe**

f° 17 r.

ffor Shrovetyde. at Hampton Coo*r*te

Beweene the .v^te^. of ffebruarye And the ffyrste of Marche a° R*egni* R*egi*ne E*lizabeth* p*re*d*ic*te — **xvj^to^.** — **Woork*es* doone, & attendaunce, geven.** & provisions made for the playes and Mask*es* showen at shrovetide aforesaide New making, Translating, Repayring, ffitting ffurnishing Garnishing & setting foorth of sundry kindes of Apparell p*ro*p*er*ties furniture & Necessaries Incident therevnto. And likewise the Taking in againe making cleane & safe bestowing therof & of the whole store of The office. The charges wherof as also for all other Business*es* therevnto belonging & *with*in that tyme issued & due to the parties herevnder written p*er*ticulerly ensueth. vid*elicet*

Playes Playde at Hampton Coo*r*te as ffolloweth.	**Philemon & philecia** play by the Erle of Lecesters men on Shrove Mundaye nighte **Percius & Anthomiris** playde by Munkest*er*s Children on Shrovetewsdaye at Nighte.	**ij.** Throughly furnished garnished & fytted with the store of thoffice and p*ro*visions following.
Maskes. showen at Hampto*n* Coo*r*te.	**Warriers vij** *with* one shippm*aster* that vttered speche **Torchebearers vj.** the warriers had hargabuss*es*. **Ladyes .vij.** *with* one that vttered a speeche. **Torchebearers .vj.** both w*hi*ch Mask*es* were showene on Shrovetewsdaye nighte.	**ij.** furnished & garnished *with* the store of thoffice & provisions following

f° 18 r.

ffor Shrovetyde	aforesaide.	**Dayes**	**& Night*es***	**Wages.**
Taylers and others the first at xx^{d}. the residue at xij^{d} the daie & asmuche for the nighte.	Thomas Clatterbooke	9	5	xxiij^{s} iiij^{d}
	Nich*ol*as Michell	9	5	xiiij^{s}
	Iohn Lvn	9	5	xiiij^{s}.
	Iohn fflauncer.	9	5	xiiij^{s}.
	Geordge wrighte	9	5	xiiij^{s}
	Edmund Owgle	9	5	xiiij^{s}
	Geordge Haukinson	9	5	xiiij^{s}
	Richard wardman	9	5	xiiij^{s}
	Will*iam* Wood	9	5	xiiij^{s}
	Robert Garton	9	5	xiiij^{s}.
	Richard Moorecrost	8	2	x^{s}.
	Symon Harison	8	5	xiij^{s}
	Iohn Walker	1	0	xij^{d}
	Thomas Lamb*e*	9	5	xiiij^{s}
	Iohn Cleyton	7	5	xij^{s}
	Henri Calleway & his man	6	5	xxij^{s}.
	Robert Bookes	6	4	x^{s}
	Iohn Browne	9	5	xiiij^{s}
	Robert Reeve	9	5	xiiij^{s}
	Iohn Davies	23	10	xxxiij^{s}
	Lewes Iones	23	10	xxxiij^{s}.
	Geordge Arnolde	23	10	xxxiij^{s}.
	Richard warmingh*am*	23	10	xxxiij^{s}.
	Richard Mundaye	23	10	xxxiij^{s}
	Henri price	23	10	xxxiij^{s}
	Iohn Drawater	23	10	xxxiij^{s}
	Thom*as* Booreman	23	10	xxxiij^{s}
	Will*iam* Dawnce.	23	10	xxxiij^{s}
	Nich*ol*as story	23	10	xxxiij^{s}
	Iohn Dawncy	23	10	xxxiij^{s}

Summa — xxxj^{li}. ij^{s} iiij^{d}

Carpenters at xiiij^{d} p*er* diem.	Gyles Hayes	4	3	viij^{s} ij^{d}
	Iohn Collyns	4	3	viij^{s} ij^{d}

Summa — xvj^{s} iiij^{d}

* *Summa* pagine — xxxj^{li}. xviij^{s}. viij^{d}. f° 19r.

Paynters. at xx^{d}. per diem	William Lyzard	9	8	xxviij^{s} iiij^{d}
	Iohn Lyzard	9	8	xxviij^{s}. iiij^{d}.
	Pangrace Inglish	8	7	xxv^{s}.
	Richard Baker	8	7	xxv^{s}
	Thomas Bush	7	6	xxj^{s} viij^{d}
	Haunce Bonner	8	7	xxv^{s}
at xviij^{d}	Iohn ffyance	8	7	xxij^{s} vj^{d}.
	Robert Hudson	8	7	xxij^{s} vj^{d}
	Iohn Clemence	6	5	xvj^{s} vj^{d}
at xvj^{d}	William Gates	8	7	xx^{s}.
	Robert Tayler	8	7	xx^{s}.
	Iohn Streter	9	8	xxij^{s}. viij^{d}.
at xij^{d}	William wilkins	8	7	xv^{s}
	Iohn Stevenson	6	5	xj^{s}
	Robert Gardner	6	5	xj^{s}
	Geordge Melling	8	6	xiiij^{s}

Summa — xvj^{li} viij^{s} vj^{d}

Propertymakers Imbroderers & Habberdashers.	Iohn Carowe at ij^{s} per diem	10	5	xxx^{s}
	William Pilkington at xx^{d}	9	8	xxviij^{s} iiij^{d}.
	Iohn ffarrington at xviij^{d}	9	8	xxv^{s}. vj^{d}
	Iohn Tuke at xviij^{d}	9	6	xxij^{s} vj^{d}
	Ione pilkington at xij^{d}	8	4	xij^{s}.
	Thomas Tysant at xij^{d}	9	3	xij^{s}.
	Iohn David for Caro at 16^{d}.	10	5	xx^{s}.
Wyerdrawers	Thomas Leveret & his servantes all together			xvj^{s}

Summa — viij^{li} vj^{s} iiij^{d}

Officers.	The Master at iiij^{s} per diem	23	10	vj^{li}. xij^{s}.
	Clerkcomptrowler at ij^{s}.	23	10	lxvj^{s}.
	The Clerk at ij^{s}.	23	10	lxvj^{s}
	The Yoman at ij^{s}	23	10	lxvj^{s}

Summa xvj^{li} x^{s}

All the Wages for Shrovetide { Artifficers &c — lvj^{li}. xiij^{s}. vj^{d} / Officers — xvj^{li}. x^{s}. } lxxiij^{li}. iij^{s}. vj^{d}.

* T. Blagrave

* Edwarde Buggyn
* walter fysshe

f° 19 v.

ffor Shrovetyde aforesaide **Emptions** provisions & other charges incident.

The Yomans p*ro*vision	Walter ffysh for mony by him disburced vid*elicet*	for	
	Buckerams xij peeces at iiij^{s} the peece	xlviij^{s}	
	Bladders	xvj^{d}	
	ffelt*es* vj.	iiij^{s} vj^{d}.	
	Thread of sundry cullers. & prices	xij^{s} viij^{d}.	
	Golde Sarcenett for one odd head. 1 q*uarter*. . . .	iiij^{s} ij^{d}	
	Glooves washte for (vj paier) Maskers — x^{s} (vj p*aire*) Torchebearers viij^{s} & ij dozen di. for children — xv^{s}.	xxxiij^{s}.	
	Buttons j groce	xij^{d}	
	Calles at viij^{d} the peece vij.	iiij^{s} viij^{d}	
	Band*es* and Ruff*es* for children all spangled .8. . .	xxvj^{s} viij^{d}	xj^{li}. xiiij^{d}.
	A Booke of Riall paper for ye yoman	vj^{s}	
	Tape j lb	iiij^{s}	
	A Whissell of Sylu*er* for A shipp M*aster* hiered . .	ij^{s} vj^{d}	
	Ink for the yoman	vj^{d}	
	Coles j Lode	xxij^{s}	
	Reward*es* & expenc*es* at hampton Co*or*te	vij^{s} viij^{d}	
	Barge & Botehier to & fro hampto*n* Co*or*te . . .	xxij^{s}	
	Cariag*es* by Land	xxij^{d}	
	Horshier for him selfe & his man	vj^{s} viij^{d}	
	In all as by his bill w*ith* iiij fardngalls	xij^{s}	
The Wyerdrawer & his percells.	Thom*a*s Leverett for sundry p*er*cells of his wares. vid*elicet*		
	Plates for the Braunches that bare the light*es* in the hall at Hampton Co*or*te .cx. at x^{d} the peece in all	iiij^{li}. xj^{s}. viij^{d}	
	Wyer to strayne (24 lb at x^{d} the lb) crosse the hall & to hang the braunches with the light*es* viij lb. (at xij^{d} the lb) price	xxviij^{s}	vj^{li}. vij^{s}. iiij^{d}.
	Nayles. M	xx^{d}	
	Candellstick*es* of dubble plate xij/ price	iij^{s}.	
	Plates with holes for hatt*es*.	iij^{s}.	
	In all as by his bill appereth Amounting vnto		
Sylk Weaver	Will*iam* Bowll for sundry p*er*cells of ware viz.		
	Bone Lace of ffyne Copp*er* silver x lb at xviij^{d} the ownce	xij^{li}	
	ffrenge & Buttons of like stuf & Rate. ij lb	xlviij^{s}	
	Ollyff branches. & trees of silk	viij^{s} ij^{d}	xv^{li}. xvj^{s}. ij^{d}.
	A Box to contayne the p*re*miss*es*	ij lb	
	In Reward for speciall s*er*vic*es* by him done . . .	xx^{s}	
	All which amounteth vnto		

* *Summa* — xxxiij^{li} iiij^{s} viij^{d} f° 20 r.

Paynters *per*cells for the clotes & *pro*p*er*ties.	Will*iam* Lyzard for sundry Cullers by him *pro*vided vid*elicet*		vij^{li}. xiiij^{s}. x^{d}.
	Syze.	vj^{s}	
	smalt	x^{s} vj^{d}	
	Byce	iiij^{s}	
	Ende	xvj^{d}	
	Masticot	iij^{s}	
	sinop*er*.	ij^{s}	
	vert	ij^{s} viij^{d}	
	sape.	xx^{d}	
	white	xij^{d}	
	Black	xvj^{d}	
	Vermillion	ij^{s}	
ffor Maskhead*es* Weapons gvnnes flask*es* tuchboxes and branches for light*es*	Sylver / 2200.	xxxiij^{s}	
	ffyne golde 200	xiij^{s}. iiij^{d}	
	Glew	xij^{d}.	
	Syze.	vj^{s}	
	vermillion.	ij^{s}	
	sinop*er* j lb di.	iij^{s}	
	ffyne white j lb	xvj^{d}	
	ffyne Black j lb.	ij^{s} viij^{d}	
	xij shells of silu*er*	xij^{s}.	
	viij shells of sinop*er* pap*er*.	ij^{s} viij^{d}	
	Goulde iiij^{c} at ij^{s} viij^{d} le c.	x^{s} viij^{d}	
	past pap*er* .v. dozen	x^{s}	
	Glew.	xij^{d}.	
	Assedue. iiij lb	xij^{s} viij^{d}	
	Golde culler j lb di.	vj^{s}.	
	the Grinding of iiij p*air*e of sheeres	viij^{d}	
	Yron cullers	xvj^{d}	
	In all as by his bill		
Buskinmaker.	Iohn ffarrington for making and selling of vj paier of purple buskins w*ith* Males painted on them — xij^{s} Redd paynted Buskins ij paier — iiij^{s} Yolow gold Taffita .8. paier — xiij^{s} iiij^{d}.		xxix^{s}. iiij^{d}.
The Millioner	Martin Hardrett &c. for iiij Braunches of Ollyffs/ made of greene sylk — iiij^{s} / ffor the Tronchwomans Heade & for vij Hatband*es* for the men Maskers &c. — xlvj^{s} viij^{d}. In all		l^{s}. viij^{d}.
ffvell.	Will*iam* Newman for iij M billett*es* — xl^{s} & to Dawncy for j Lode of Coles — xxij^{s}		lxij^{s}.

f° 20 v. * S*umm*a — xiiij^{li} xvj^{s} x^{d}.

The ffethermaker.	for vj bandes of ffethers for the Men maskers & one for the Tronchewoman in all vij price	liij^{s}. iiij^{d}.
The Carpenter	Rowland Robynson for iij Elme boordes & vij Ledges for the fframes for the players & for Nayles &c.	iij^{s} viij^{d}.
	Item for vyces & wrestes to draw the wyers tighte wheron the lightes did hang crosse the hall	iiij^{s}.
Horshier & Iorneyeng charges.	Thomas Booreman for mony by him layd owte sundry tymes for the hier of Horses and for theier meate whiles they travelled & remayned at Kingston &c. ffirst the xxth of ffebruary for ij Geldinges to osterly & to hampton Coorte to know my Lord Chamberlens pleasure & back againe to saint Iones & likewise to the Coorte againe & there remayning vij daies at xx^{d} the daye & theier charges at Kingston &c. together	xxxix^{s} iiij^{d}.
[C]ariages by land & by water	Iohn Drawater for Cariage of fframes & painted Clothes for the players howses to hampton Coorte attending the same there till service therwith was past and so returning the same In all with the Carters and Carpenters expences there whiles thay wayted & the Carmens wages & horshier for him selfe — xxxv^{s} iiij^{d} And for boote and bardgehier to & fro the Coorte with certayne other stuf — xvj^{s}. 8^{d} In all with his botehier sundry tymes to westminster / for the children that served the Mask.	lj^{s} iiij^{d}.
[Diett] for Children. [(Mas]kers) before [Shrov]etide.	Item for the diettes & Lodging of dyvers children at saint Iones whiles they Learned theier partes & Iestures meete for the Mask in which ix of them did serve at hampton Coorte	xxxiij^{s}. iiij^{d}.
The vy[z]ardmaker	Iohn Owgle for xiiij Beardes Marquesotted at xvj^{d} the peece — xviij^{s} viij^{d} & for egges to make cleane vizardes curing heares &c. — iiij^{d}. And for his Wages or Reward for his service at this tyme before omitted — x^{s} viij^{d}. In all	xxix^{s} viij^{d}.
Land Cariages	Thomas Lamb for the Carmen &c. that caried certayne of the stuf in hampers to the water &c. with iiij^{d} by him paid for bladders in all	xx^{d}.

Summa — x^{li} xvj^{s} iiij^{d}

f° 21 r.

Bardgehier & Botehier to Hamton co*or*te	To Bruton of Powles wharfe for A Barge & vj ores with ij Tylt whirreyes that caryed The Masking geare, & Children *with* theier tuto*r*s and An Italian Woman &c. to dresse theier head*es* as also the Taylers p*ro*p*er*tymakers & haberdashers	xxiiij^{s}.
Expenc*es* at the Co*or*te on shrove Mundaye	To W*illia*m Skarboro for ffyer & vittells for the Children & theier attendant*es* whiles they wayted to know whether her Ma*ies*tie wolde haue the Mask that nighte	ix^{s}. vj^{d}.
Expenc*es* at Kingston on Munday Nighte. aforesaide &c.	Lodging, ffyer, & vittells for the children & Women y^{t} wayted tattyer them *with* others y^{t} were appointed to stay till the Mask were showen and for theier dynners the next daye being Shrovetewsdaye there	xiiij^{s}. viij^{d}.
The Barber.	for trymmyng the Children on shrovetuisdaye —	xij^{d}
Expenc*es* at the Co*or*te on Shrovetwisdaye	To Skarboro for the childrens supp*er*s & the Womens supp*er*s *with* the Rest of th*eier* attendant*es*	ix^{s} x^{d}
Expenc*es* at Kingston on shrovetwisdaie nighte	To Mother sparo for the childrens lodging*es* *with* ffyer & ffoode that nighte & in the Morning whiles thay staied for botes	xij^{s}
Bardge and botehier from the Co*or*te	To Bruton for his Bardge & ij whirreyes to cary the children & stuff back to Londo*n* and for his wayting daie & nighte to cary the Children betwene the Coorte & kingston	xxv^{s} vj^{d}
Expenc*es* at the black ffryers on ash Wednisdaie	To Thom*as* Totnall for ffyer & vittells for the Children when they Landed su*m* of them being sick & colde & hungry	vij^{s} vj^{d}
Reward*es* & hier of womens heares for the Children.	To the Nine Children that served at ye Coorte — ix^{s} To the Italian woman & her dawght*er* for Lending the Heares &c. & for theier s*er*vice & attendaunc*es* — xxxiij^{s} iiij^{d}/ To N. Nudigate by thappointm*en*t & at the request of M^{r} fforteskue in respect of his s*er*vice & paines *with* the childre*n* and otherwise — xl^{s}. And to Bryan dodmer for his paynes sundry waies imployed — xl^{s}.	vj^{li}. ij^{s} iiij^{d}

* *Summa* pag*ine* — xj^{li} v^{s} x^{d}

f° 21 v.

Horshier and Botehier.	Edward Buggin clerkcomptrowler for mony by him disburced for the hier of ij Horses to hampton Coorte theier expences there & at Kingston & likewise for his Botehier sundry tymes *with* rewarde*s* geven & other expence*s* in thaffares of this office	xx^{s}.
Necessaries for	The Clerk for his ordinari Greene cloth, pap*er*, Ink Cownters & other Necessaries incident to his office.	lxvj^{s}. viij^{d}.

* *Summa* — iiij^{li} vj^{s} viij^{d}

All **Themptions &c. for Shrovetyde.** is lxxiiij^{li}. x^{s}. iiij^{d}. * T. Blagrave

* Edwarde Buggyn
* walter fysshe

The Totall Sum of this whole Volume according to the devision thereof

videlicet

	Betweene the last of October 1573 and the xxth of Decemb*er* 1573 anno *Regni Regine Elizabeth predicte* xvj^{to}.	wages of	Artifficers &c. — xvij^{li} viij^{s} viij^{d}. / Officers — xj^{li}.	xxviij^{li} viij^{s} viij^{d}.	Mr Druryes wedding &c. xxxvj^{li}. x^{d}.	
			Emptions & other charges y^{t} tyme	— vij^{li}. xij^{s}. ij^{d}		
[ffrom] y^{e} [last da]y [of] October [1]573. Anno [*Regni Regine*] [Eliz]abeth [*predicte* **xv^{to}**] **[vntill] [th]e ffyrste of Marche 1573** / Anno *Regni Regine* Elizabeth *predicte* **xvj^{to}.**	Betweene the xxth of Decemb*er* aforesaid & the xjth of Ianuary dicto anno Including Christm*as* Newyeres tyde & Twelfe [t]yde that yere	wag es of	Artifficers &c. — cxiiij^{li} iiij^{s} vj^{d} / Offycers. — xvij^{li} x^{s}	cxxxj^{li} xiiij^{s} vj^{d}.	Christmas &c ccclix^{li}. xv^{s}. j^{d}.	**Dclxxij^{li}. xiiij^{s}. ij^{d}.** as followeth more breefely
			Emptions and other charges then	— ccxxviij^{li}. vij^{d}.		
	Betweene the xjth of Ianuary afore saide & the v^{te} of ffebruary y^{t} yere for Candellmas.	wages of	Artifficers &c. — l^{li}. xix^{s}. x^{d}. / Officers — xv^{li}.	lxv^{li}. xix^{s}. x^{d}.	Candelmas cxxix^{li} iiij^{s} v^{d}.	
			Emptions & other charges then	— lxiij^{li} iiij^{s} vij^{d}.		
	Betwene the v^{te}. of ffebr*uary* aforesaide and the fyrst of Marche y^{t} yeare for Shrovetyde.	wages of	Artifficers &c. — lvj^{li} xiij^{s} vj^{d}. / Officers — xvj^{li}. x^{s}.	lxxiij^{li} iij^{s} vj^{d}.	Shrovetyde cxlvij^{li}. xiij^{s}. x^{d}.	
			Emptions and other charges then	— lxxiiij^{li} x^{s} iiij^{d}.		

In all as more p*er*ticculerly by the same booke appereth Amounting vnto

f° 22 r.

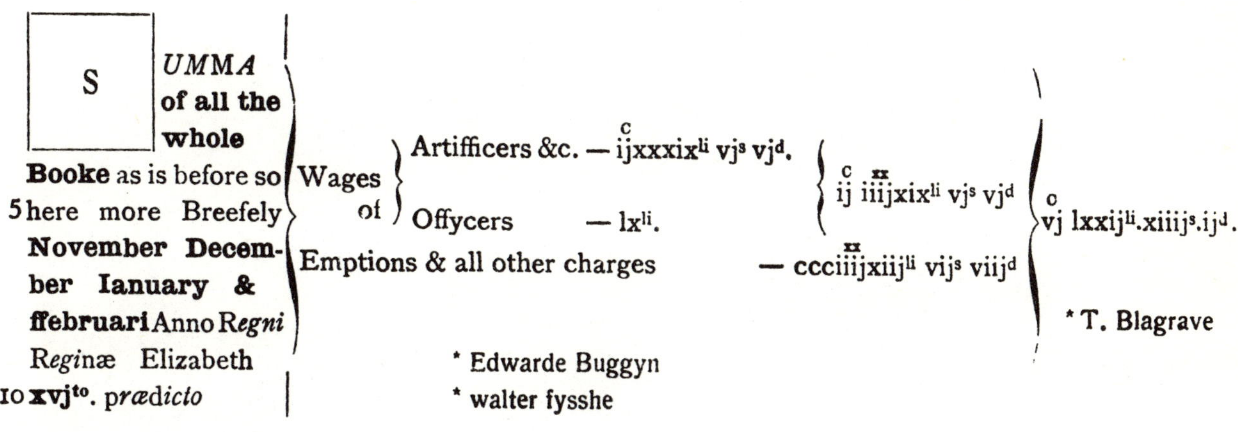

SUMMA of all the whole Booke as is before so here more Breefely November December Ianuary & ffebruari Anno *Regni Reginæ* Elizabeth xvj^{to}. *prædicto*

Wages of Artifficers &c. — ij^{c}xxxix^{li} vj^{s} vj^{d}.
Wages of Offycers — lx^{li}.
ij^{c} iiij^{xx}xix^{li} vj^{s} vj^{d}
Emptions & all other charges — ccciiij^{xx}xiij^{li} vij^{s} viij^{d}
vj^{c} lxxij^{li}.xiiij^{s}.ij^{d}.

* Edwarde Buggyn
* walter fysshe
* T. Blagrave

Canvas at shrovetyde forgotten before.	Herevnto is to be Added A peece of Canvas *conteyning* xl ells which was browght into thoffice by M^{ris} Danes *seruaunt* at xij^{d} the ell it was for the howses made for the players then	xl^{s}.

f° 22 v.

From 1 March 1573-4 to 28 February 1574-5

viz.

Record Office. Audit Office. Accounts Various. Bd. 1213. Revels. N° 4.

Revells in One Yeare. **vid*elicet***

ffrom the Last of ffebruary .1573. **Anno** R*egni* R*egi*næ Elizab*eth*e — **xvj^to^.**
Vntill the Last of ffebruary 1574. **Anno** R*egni* R*egin*æ Elizab*eth*e p*rædic*tæ — **xvij^mo^.**

The Booke of all Charges growen w*ith*in the said Office, And by meanes of thaffares therevnto belonging, for that tyme. Thom*as* Blagrave esquier being appoynted Master of the same. (as by svndry Letters from the Lorde Chamberlayne maye appeare) He proceded therein. Geving Attendaunce, and making preparac*i*on, with other service, Incident therevnto, as Occasion required : ffor her Magestyes Regall Disporte and Recreacion, at tymes convenyent. Wherein the charges arose, and did grow as ffolloweth. Aswell for him selfe; as also for others hereafter ensving.

ffirste.

Betweene the Last of ffebrua[r]y aforesaide .1573. **And** the ffirst daye of November in the said yere Anno R*egni* R*egi*ne Elizab*eth*e. — **xvj^to^.**

ffor the Progresse to Reading &c. And Lykewyze ffor The Ayrynges, Repayryngs Translatynges, preparing, ffytting, ffurnishing, Garnishing Attending, and setting foorth, of svndry kynd*es* of Apparell propertyes & ffurnyture for the Italyan players that ffollowed the progresse and made pastyme fyrst at Wynsor and afterward*es* at Reading. As also for the whole charges of those viij Moneths any waye Ryzing by the saide Office and thaffares therto belonging p*er*tycculerly ensueth

vid*elicet*

Taylers & others woorking & attending the premiss*es* the first at xx^d^ & the Rest at xij^d^ the daie & asmuche for the nyghte.

	Dayes	**&** **Night*es*.**	**Wages.**
Thom*as* Clatterbooke	35	5	lxvj^s^ viij^d^
Iohn Davyes	40	5	xlv^s^.
Lewes Iones	40	5	xlv^s^.
Iames Michell	40	5	xlv^s^
George Arnolde	40	5	xlv^s^
Iohn Browne	40	5	xlv^s^
Will*iam* Lvmleye	40	5	xlv^s^
Richard Mvndaye	40	5	xlv^s^.
Iohn Drawater	40	5	xlv^s^.
Goodlak Drawater	40	5	xlv^s^

	Thomas Booreman	40	5	xlv^{s}
	Nich*ol*as Storye	40	5	xlv^{s}
	Iohn Dawncy	40	5	xlv^{s}
	Izack Iones	40	5	xlv^{s}
	Iohn Percy	40	5	xlv^{s}
	Richard Hawklyf	40	5	xlv^{s}
	Peeter Marow	40	5	xlv^{s}
	Iohn Yanes	40	5	xlv^{s}

S*umma* — xlj^{li}. xj^{s} viij^{d}.

Propertymakers.	Iohn Carow at ij^{s}	10	5	xxx^{s}.
	Will*iam* Pilkington at xx^{d}	10	5	xxv^{s}.
	Iohn ffarrington at xviij^{d}	10	5	xxij^{s}. vj^{d}.
	Iohn Davy for carow at xij^{d}	10	5	xv^{s}.

S*umma* — iiij^{li} xij^{s}. vj^{d}

Offycers.	The M*aster* at iiij^{s} the daye	40	5	ix^{li}.
	Clerkcomptrowler at ij^{s}	40	5	iiij^{li}. x^{s}
	The Clerke at ij^{s}	40	5	iiij^{li}. x^{s}.
	The Yoman at ij^{s}	40	5	iiij^{li}. x^{s}.

S*umma* — xxij^{li}. x^{s}

S*umma* of all the **Wages** those viij Monethe*s* ending the last of October .1574. anno R*egni* R*egine* Eliza*bethe* xvj^{to}.	Artyfic*ers*	xlvj^{li}. iiij^{s} ij^{d}	lxviij^{li}. xiiij^{s}. ij^{d}.
	Offic*ers*	xxij^{li}. x^{s}.	

f° 2 v.

Emptions, provizions, And
Expences within the
viij Monethes
aforesaide
vid*elicet*

Canvas.

Mis*tr*is Dane for fforty ells of Canvas at xij^{d}. the ell whiche shoulde haue bene alowed in the last booke (before this) according to the entry there. but, bycause it was entred after the Totall soom*me* : and not subscribed by any Officer. Therefore the Auditor wolde not alow it there. Neverthelesse she was paide for that among the residue of her soommes in that booke due as by her acquittance remayning w*ith* Bryan Dodmer maye appere so y^{t} now her dett for this must be payd to the said dodm*er* — **xl^{s}.**

Implement*es* and Expenc*es* in the **Progresse** for the Italyan Players at Wynsor & Reding.

Thom*as* Blagrave esquier for mony by him disburced for sundry Implement*es* & occazions vid*elicet*

To Iohn Carow for a plank of ffyrr & other peeces of sawen wood. — xvj^{s} viij^{d}.
It*em* for Iron woorke for A frame for A seate in A pageant. — xv^{s}.
It*em* for the woorkmanship of the Seate or Chayer. &c. — xviij^{s} iiij^{d}
It*em* for A hamp*er* to carye the same together and for cariage of it from Suthwarke w*ith* Rewarde to carowes man in all. — vij^{s}.
In all by him paid to Carowe then — lvij^{s}.

It*em* for Ladles & Dishes to beare the light*es* at wynsor for the Italyans and for payntyng & garnishing of them w*ith* Reward*es* geven to dyvers whose Necessaryes and s*er*vic*es* were then vsed — xj^{s}. vj^{d}.

It*em* for preparacons &c. at Reading the xvth of Ivly. 1574 *anno Regni Regine Elizabethe* xvj^{to}.
Golde Lether for cronet*es* . . . iij^{s}. iiij^{d}.
Thred & sheperd*es* hookes . . xiiij^{d}
Horshyer vj daies .3. . . . . . xxxiij^{s}
Horsemeate at Reading . . . xj^{s} vj^{d}
The vitteller at Reading for the dyet of su*n*dry p*er*sons — xv^{s}.
Lamskynnes for Shepperds .8. . . iiij^{s}.
Horstayles for the wylde mannes garment — iiij^{s}. viij^{d}
Arrowes for Nymphes . . . . vj^{d}.

— **viij^{li}. xv^{s}. iiij^{d}**

f° 3 r.

Light*es* and shepperd*es* staves . . vij^{d}.
Hoopes for Garland*es* . . . . . iiij^{d}.
Pott*es* for the Paynter . . . . . ij^{d}.
ij^{d} iij^{d} iiij^{d} ij^{d}
Pacthredd, Glew, Lyne, Tack*es*
iiij^{d} iiij^{d}
Wyer & Coles } xix^{d}.
6
Plates for the Candlestick*es* . . . iiij^{s}
Boordes for the plates . . . . . xvj^{d}
Wyer to hang the light*es* . . . . xvj^{d}
Baye Leaves & flowers. . . . . xij^{d}.
for paynting sundry devic*es* . . . ij^{s}
Reward*es* to .vj. Taylers there . . vj^{s}.
Howseroome for the stuf . . . . v^{s}.
The hyer of A Syth for saturne . . iiij^{d}.
Cariage of Stuf fro*m* Reding . . . ij^{s} vj^{d}
The hier of A Trunk. . . . . . ij^{s}. vj^{d}
svndry Necessaries & Reward*es* disburced by Iohn drawat*er* there } v^{s}.
In all for his disburcem*entes* at Reading. } cvj^{s}. x^{d}.

In all by him the said T*homas* Blagrave disburced *with*in those viij Moneth*es* aforesaide amou*n*teth vnto.

ffewell and Necessar ies *with* Botehier &c. — Walter ffish yoman of the saide office for mony by him disburced for ffewell — xxvj^{s} viij^{d} ffor Thredd of svndry Cullers & svndry other small necessaries — xiij^{s} iiij^{d} And for Botehier horshier & Riding charges *with* other expenc*es* — xx^{s} } lx^{s}.

Iorneyeng charges. — Edward Buggin gent*leman* Clerkcomptrowler of this office for his Botehier, horshier Riding charg*es* and other expenc*es* *within* that tyme in all } xx^{s}

Iorneyeng charg*es* & Reward*es* — Bryan Dodmer for his Botehier, horshier, Riding charges and expenc*es* *with*in this tyme of viij moneths as also for his owne s*er*vice and attendaunce vpon theise matters & Reconyng*es* vntill thaccou*n*te hereof be past } lxvj^{s} viij^{d}

The hyer of apparell — Thom*a*s Clatterbooke for hier of iij devells cotes and head*es* & one olde mannes fries cote for the Italian prayers at Wynsor } v^{s}.

S*UMMA* of all the Emptions p*ro*visio*n*s and Expenc*es* for the Progresse & those viij Monet[h]*es* ending the last of Octob*er* a*nno* Reg*ni* Regi*ne* Elizab*ethe* xvj^{to}. p*re*d*icte* } xviij^{li}. vij^{s}.

f° 3 v.

SUMMA of those viij Monethes Ending the Last of October .1574. Anno Regni Reginæ Elizabethe .xvj^{to}. Amounteth to

Wages of	Artifficers &c. xlvj^{li}. iiij^{s} ij^{d}		
	Offycers . xxij^{li}. x^{s}.	68^{li}. 14^{s}. 2^{d}	
			iiij^{xx} vij^{li}. xiiij^{d}.
Emptions &c. . . . xviij^{li}. vij^{s}.			
In all amounting to.			

* T Blagrave
* Edwarde Buggyn
* walter fysshe

f° 4 r.

ffor Christmas And Twelftyde : Candellmas & Shrovetyde. $^{1574.}$ **Anno** ***Regni*** **Reginæ Elyzabethe.** } **xvij^{mo}**

Woork*es* doone and Attendaunce geaven **Betweene** the ffyrst of November (1574) Anno R*egni* R*egi*ne Elizab[*e*]the **xvj^{to}. And** The last of ffebrvary (1574) Anno R*egni* R*egi*ne E*lizabethe* p*re*dict*e*. **xvij^{mo}.** By meanes of **Preparing, Newmaking, Translating Repayring,** ffytting, ffurnishing, Garnishing, and Attending of the Playes, Maskes, Apparell, flurniture, Wares, P*ro*pertyes Stuf store and Implement*es* of the saide Office for the apt setting foorthe of the same at the tymes aforesaide. The whole charges wherof aswell or the Wages as for Wares, Cariages, Iorneyeng charges & all fother expenc*es* therevnto incident hereafter p*er*tyculer[l]y ensveth. vid*elicet*

Taylers & others. The fyrst at xx^{d} & all the Residue at xij^{d} the daye and asmuche for the Nighte

	Dayes	**& Night*es*.**	**Wages.**
Thom*a*s Clatterbooke	81	19	viij^{li}.vj^{s}.viij^{d}
Richard Wardman	25	11	xxxvj^{s}
Thomas Lam*be*	38	20	lviij^{s}
Thom[*a*]s Wrighte	35	17	lij^{s}
Will*iam* Woodd	25	12	xxxvij^{s}
George Gybbon	39	18	lvij^{s}
Robert Garton	18	15	xxxiij^{s}
Iohn fflawncer	31	20	lj^{s}
Richard Moorecrost	10	5	xv^{s}
George Wryte	28	10	xxxviij^{s}
Iohn Cleyton	18	13	xxxj^{s}
Henri Callewaye	4	4	viij^{s}
Iohn Dayton	4	4	viij^{s}
Peeter Banbridge	5	3	viij^{s}
Iohn Walker	8	7	xv^{s}
Thom*as* Yonge	2	2	iiij^{s}
George Haukynson	4	4	viij^{s}
Richard Brian for clatterbooke	18	9	xxvij^{s}
Iames Michell$^{.54'.}$ & Reeve$^{.46'.}$	81	19	c^{s}
Alexander Thewell	1	1	ij^{s}
Harman Burcott	5	2	vij^{s}
Will*iam* Galland	1	1	ij^{s}
Iohn Huntley	1	1	ij^{s}
Iohn Machyn	1	1	ij^{s}

f° 5 r.

	Iohn Davy the yonger	1	1	ij^{s}
	Iohn Owgle	6	5	xj^{s}.
	Iohn Davyes thelder	81	19	c^{s}.
	Lewes Iones.	81	19	c^{s}.
	George Arnolde.	81	19	c^{s}.
	Iohn Browne	81	19	c^{s}.
	Will*iam* Lvmleye	81	19	c^{s}.
	Richard Mvndaie	81	19	c^{s}.
	Iohn Drawater	81	19	c^{s}.
	Goodlack Drawater	81	19	c^{s}.
	Thom*as* Booreman	81	19	c^{s}.
	Nich*ol*as Storye	81	19	c^{s}.
	Iohn Dawncy	81	19	c^{s}.

S*umm*a of the Taylers &c. } iiij^{xx} xiiij^{li}. viij^{d}

Paynters at xx^{d}. the daye & xx^{d} the nighte.	Will*iam* Lyzard.	44	14	iiij^{li} xvj^{s} viij^{d}.
	Richard Baker	26	11	lxj^{s} viij^{d}
	Richard Blackborne	40	9	iiij^{li} xx^{d}
	Thom*as* Bushe	33	14	lxxviij^{s} iiij^{d}
at xviij^{d}.	Robert Hudson.	17	7	xxxvj^{s}.
	Iohn Clemence	24	13	lv^{s}. vj^{d}.
	Nich*ol*as Sutton	12	6	xxvij^{s}
	Thom*as* Tyler thelder	25	14	lviij^{s}. vj^{d}
	Thom*as* Bush the elder.	3	3	ix^{s}
at xvj^{d}.	Nich*ol*as Knyghte.	18	5	xxx^{s} viij^{d}
	Anthony sparke.	44	20	iiij^{li} v^{s} iiij^{d}
	Iohn Cordell.	14	7	xxviij^{s}
	Iohn Hall	3	3	viij^{s}
at xij^{d}.	Richard Symons	19	9	xxviij^{s}
	Thom*as* tyler the yonger	4	3	vij^{s}
	Will*iam* Wilkyns	41	11	lij^{s}.

S*umm*a of the paynters } xxxvij^{li} iij^{s} iiij^{d}

f° 5 v.

Prop*er*tymakers Habberdasher*es* Ioyners, and Carpenters.	Iohn Carow at ij^{s} by the daye and ij^{s} the night	20	1	xlij^{s}.
	Iohn Rosse after Iohn Carow his deceace at the same Rate	30 1/2	3	lxvj^{s} viij^{d}.
	Richard Rowland at xx^{d} the daye &c.	29	12	lxviij^{s}
	Will*iam* Pilkington at xx^{d}.	32	15	lxxviij^{s} iiij^{d}
	Iohn Tuke at xviij^{d}	32	15	lxx^{s} vj^{d}
	Iohn ffarrington at xviij^{d}	38	19	iiij^{li}. v^{s}. vj^{d}
	Richard Morer at xviij^{d}	11	3	xxj^{s}
	Thom*as* Butler at xviij^{d}	3	2	vij^{s} vj^{d}
	Christopher Harryson at xvj^{d} the daie &c.	7	0	ix^{s} iiij^{d}
	Henri Price at xvj^{d}	30	12	lvj^{s}
	Trustram Hudson ye like	33	13	lxj^{s} iiij^{d}
	Iohn Edward*es* at xvj^{d}	27	13	liij^{s} iiij^{d}
	Albert haryson at xvj^{d}.	2	0	ij^{s} viij^{d}
	Alexander Cockleye at 16^{d}	6	3	xij^{s}
	Iohn Wayne at xvj^{d}	2	0	ij^{s} viij^{d}
	Rowland Robynson at xvj^{d}	7	2	xij^{s}
	Nich*ol*as Rosse ye like	39	10	liij^{s} iiij^{d}
	Bastian Vicars at xvj^{d}	20	10	xl^{s}
	Iohn Richardson at xvj^{d}	13	8	xxviij^{s}
	Robert Blaze at xvj^{d}.	17	10	xxxvj^{s}
	Richard Moorers man ^{at} xvj^{d}	3	0	iiij^{s}
	Henri Devenish at xvj^{d}	5	1	viij^{s}
	Will*iam* Barker at xiiij^{d}	16	12	xxxij^{s} viij^{d}
	Iohn Collyns at xiiij^{d}	16	12	xxxij^{s} viij^{d}
	Iohn Morris at xiiij^{d}.	6	3	x^{s} vj^{d}
	Alexander Broxson at 14^{d}	5	3	ix^{s} iiij^{d}
	Will*iam* Greenefelde at 14^{d}	5	3	ix^{s} iiij^{d}
	Richard Colleye at xiiij^{d}	6	3	x^{s} vj^{d}
	Iohn Parratt at xiiij^{d}	14	7	xxiiij^{s} vj^{d}
	Edward Beachamp 14^{d}.	3	1	iiij^{s} viij^{d}
	Nich*ol*as Harp*er* at xiiij^{d}	5	1	vij^{s}

f° 6 r.

	William Gossen for Iohn Caro at xij^{d}	28	8	xxxvj^{s}.
	Ione Pilkington at xij^{d}	3	0	iij^{s}
	Edward ffrees at xij^{d}	15	7	xxij^{s}.

Summa of the *proper*tymakers &c. } lj^{li}. iiij^{d}.

Offycers.	The *Master* at iiij^{s} *per* diem.	81	19	xx^{li}.
	Clerkcomptrowler. ij^{s}.	81	19	x^{li}.
	The Clerk at ij^{s}	81	19	x^{li}
	The Yoman at ij^{s}.	81	19	x^{li}.

Summa of Thoffic*ers* } l^{li}.

S*UMMA* of those **Wages** for November December Ianvary & ffebruarye viz. ffor preparac*i*on of Playes, & Mask*es* and for Woork*es* doone at Christm*as* Twelfe tyde, Candellm*as* & Shrovetyde Anno *Regni Regine* Elizab[e]the **xvij**^{mo}. Amou*n*teth to } ccxxxij^{li}. iiij^{s}. iiij^{d}.

f° 6 v.

Emptions, provizions, And
Expenc*es* with all other Charges
for Chrystmas Twelftyde
Candellmas and
Shrovetyde
Anno *Regni Regine*
Elizabethe
xvij^{mo}
*p*redict*o*
vid*elicet*

Thymbroderers *per*cells.

Will*iam* Pylkyngton for woork*es* by him doone and mony by hym disbursed ffor Stytching A Cote and a payer of Buskyns with a hatt made all over with sylver coyne and for sylk for the same — xv^{s}. A patterne for A Bande — ij^{s}/ The Imbrodering of vj band*es* for hatt*es* for Maskers ritchly wroughte with venys sylu*er* and for sylk and sylver for the same — iiij^{li} and for his fferriage at putneye — iiij^{d} — iiij^{li}. xvij^{s} iiij^{d}.

Propertymakers *per*cells.

Richard Rowlande for mony by him disburced

for Nayles of sundry sort*es*	xxxvij^{s}. vj^{d}.	
skynnes to cover horses	xxj^{s}	
Glew and Hoopes	iiij^{s} viij^{d}	
Horstayles & Manes	xij^{d}	
Corde and a halter for an asse	xij^{d}	
Turning of pyllers	iiij^{s}	iiij^{li}. iiij^{s}. xj^{d}.
Leaves and Mosse	v^{s}.	
Cyzers & Taynterhookes	xix^{d}	
ffirr poles 12. at iiij^{d} the peece	iiij^{s}.	
Hunters staves	iij^{s}	
Cariages	ij^{s} ij^{d}.	
In all Amownting vnto.		

Chaundler*es* *per*cells.

Barnard ffabyan for sundry percells of his ware

fyrst for white light*es* 416 lb. at iiij^{d} the lb	vj^{li}. xviij^{s}. viij^{d}.	
Seering Candell iij lb at xvj^{d} the lb	iiij^{s}.	
Packthread iij lb at xij^{d}. the lb	iij^{s}	viij^{li}. ix^{s} .iiij^{d}.
Corde & Lyne of severall sort*es*	xiij^{s} viij^{d}	
Lynkes xxx at iiij^{d} the peece	x^{s}.	
In all as by his bill more at lardge apereth		

f° 7 r.

Propertymakers *per*cells.	**Henri Devenish** for mony to him due		**xlj^{s}. iij^{d}**
	for iiij plates for the Rock	ij^{s}. x^{d}	
	Post*es* at xiiij^{d} the peece iiij price.	iiij^{s}. viij^{d}	
	Vpper peeces for the topp iiij	xxij^{d}	
	Quarters for the dore ij price	vj^{d}	
	Eves boorde .159. foote. price.	xij^{s}	
	Elme Boorde .76. foote price	iiij^{s} viij^{d}	
	seeling Boorde 113 foote price.	viij^{s}	
	Nayles of sundry sort*es*	xiiij^{d}	
	Light*es* by him bowght & spent there	vij^{d}	
	Eves boorde more 47 ^foote^ price	iij^{s} iiij^{d}	
	seeling Boord more 17 foote	xiiij^{d}	
	Transoms ij price	vj^{d}	
	In all by him *delivere*d & Imployed in thoffice		

Carpenters *per*cells	**Will*iam* Tayler**. for mony to him due for		**lvij^{s}. viij^{d}.**
	Oken Inche boorde 200 foote 1/2	xvj^{s} viij^{d}	
	Dubble Quarters xxiiij	xij^{s}.	
	syngle Quarters .10. at iij^{d} the peece	ij^{s} vj^{d}	
	It*em* more xxiiij single quarters	vij^{s} vj^{d}	
	A planck & Beeche for a ladder	ij^{s} viij^{d}	
	It*em* more for oke Inche boorde 100 foote & iij quarters of a hundred and .x. foote in all am*oun*ting to	xij^{s} viij^{d}	
	syngle boorde di. c & .v. foote.	iij^{s} viij^{d}.	
	In all Amownting together vnto		

Mercers *per*cells	**Will*iam* Harding** for xxvj ells iij q*uarter*s of yolow Sarcenet at .v^{s}. the ell — vj^{li} xiij^{s} ix^{d} And for Russett Sarcenet xxxix ells at v^{s} the ell — ix^{li} xv^{s}.	xvj^{li}.viij^{s}.ix^{d}.
Mercers *per*cells	**Richard Barne** for cclxj ells q*uarter* *sar*cenett of sundry Cullers at v^{s}. the ell lxv^{li}. vj^{s}. iij^{d}. Greene velvett iij quarters of a yard xij^{s}. ix^{d}/ Whit sarcenett xxv ells at v^{s} thell vj^{li} v^{s}/ Black velvett xvij yard*es* iij q*uarter*s at .15^{s}. xiij^{li} vj^{s} iij^{d}. It*em* more for .j. yarde di. of the same xxij^{s} vj^{d}/ Black Buckeram of the fynest j ^pece^ — xiij^{s} iiij^{d}.	iiij ^xx^ vij^{li} vj^{s}. j^{d}.

f° 7 v.

Sundry kyndes of wares provyded by the yoman & his expenc*es* at this tyme		**Walter ffyshe** for mony by him disburced	vid*elicet*	
	necc*essaries*	for Rushes, Brushes, and Rubbers	xxiij^{s}. iiij^{d}.	
		Thredd of sundry cullers & prices	liiij^{s}. ij^{d}	
	necc*essaries*	Paper for patterns &c. iij quiers	xij^{d}.	
		Tyncell [.ij^{s}. viij^{d}.], ffelt*es* & stock*es* [xvj^{s} iiij^{d}]	xix^{s}.	
		Damask iiij yard*es* q*uarter* di. being greene . . .	xliij^{s} ix^{d}	
		Taffata orengeculler of levant .5. y*ar*ds . . .	xj^{s} viij^{d}	
		Copper lace ij lb xv ounc*es*	lxij^{s} viij^{d}	
		Gloves for Players & Maskers	cix^{s} iiij^{d}	
	necc*essaries*	Tape for tyeng*es* and strengthning	vij^{s}	
		ffurres of woolvering*es* for pedlers capps . . .	xxxiij^{s}	
		Past boorde	iij^{s} iiij^{d}	
		ffewell by him provyded	xxviij^{s} ij^{d}	
		Light*es* besides the chaundlers p*er*cells . . .	ij^{s} iiij^{d}	
	necc*essaries*	Egg*es* to trymme the vizard*es*	ij^{d}	
	necc*essaries*	Sylk and Needells	xvj^{d}	xlij^{li}. vj^{s}. vij^{d}.
	necc*essaries*	Breade to make cleane headpeec*es*	vj^{d}	
		Cutting of Gard*es*	xij^{s}	
		Beardes	x^{s}	
		Lynnen Lynyng*es*	v^{s} x^{d}	
		Cotten Lynyng*es*	xj^{s}. viij^{d}	
		Vizard*es* 27 price	iiij^{li}. x^{s}	
		The hyer of a Marryners whissell	iij^{s}. iiij^{d}.	
	necc*essaries*	A sack for the players	ij^{s} iiij^{d}	
	necc*essaries*	Heare to stuff Bootes for the horses / And for ij payer of Spurres . . .	iij^{s}. iiij^{d}.	
	necc*essaries*	Bottells for Pilgrymes ij	xij^{d}	
	necc*essaries*	Styck*es* ij Bundells	viij^{d}	
		Barge hyer and Botehier	ciiij^{s}. x^{d}.	
		Cariages by Land	lxiiij^{s} vj^{d}	
		Ryding charges	xvj^{d}	
		Reward*es*	viij^{s}	
		Buckerams of [30 peeces] sundry prices	vj^{li}. vij^{s}	
		In all Amowntyng vnto		

ffewell.	**Iohn Hill** for Ten*ne* Thowsand of Billett*es* by him delyvered into the said Office at xij^{s} viij^{d} the thowsand paid by Bryan Dodmer at thappoyntment of Mr Blagrave. Therefore vpon payment of this Booke the said Dodmer is to Receive his mony againe namely	vj^{li}. vj^{s}. viij^{d}.

f° 8 r.

Wyerdrawers p*er*cells & theier Wag*es* or Reward*es*. **Thom*a*s Leverett** for mony to him due for Wares and for service done by him & his *seruauntes*

ffirst at Christm*a*s & Twelftyde aforesaide for		
Stock Candellstick*es* iiij doosen	x^{s} vj^{d}	
Vyce Candellstick*es* .vj. price	vj^{s}	
Bodkyns halfe a doozen price	xij^{d}	
Cases halfe a doosyn price	ij^{s}	
Wyer xlj lb. di. and ij lb	xliij^{s} vj^{d}	
Curtyn Ring*es* iij dozen	xij^{d}	
A greate Lanthorne	ij^{s}.	
Rownd plates for the Branches at x^{d} the peece viij dozen and ij greate plates for pillers at iij^{s} iiij^{d} the pece in all	iiij^{li}.vj^{s}.viij^{d}.	
Small spykers .j dozen &c	ij^{s} ij^{d}	
Tack*es* One Thowsand price	xx^{d}.	
Botehier to Hampton coorte	iiij^{s}	
Reward*es* or wages for him & his *ser*u*au*nt*es* Namely for Iohn Collarde, Edmvnd Birchall, Iohn Will*ia*ms, & *Wil*l*ia*m Dawson, for all theier Attendaunces & *ser*vice this Christm*a*s & Twelftyde aswell at hampton coorte as in thoffice.	xlvj^{s} viij^{d}.	xviij^{li}.xviij^{s}.vj^{d}.
At Candellm*a*s for .2. Bitt*es* *with* bosses for the hobby horses.	iiij^{s}.	
Cownters to cast awaye by players.	iij^{s}	
Buckles with penners vj paier.	iiij^{d}	
Bellowes one payer price	iij^{s} iiij^{d}.	
Wyer for the horses legg*es* iiij lb.	iiij^{s}.	
Clavant wyer ij lb price	iij^{s}	
Two pe*n*ny Nayles .j. M	xx^{d}	
Wyer ix lb price	ix^{s}	
Plates ij price	xij^{d}	
Reward*es* or wages for him selfe & ij other then.	xxiiij^{s} vj^{d}	
At Shrovetyde for xix branches to beare the light*es*	iij^{li}.iij^{s}.iiij^{d}.	
Wyer of the greate sorte to hang or to strayne crosse the hall at H*ampton* Coort*e*	xxv^{s}	
Clavant wyer viij lb.	viij^{s}	
Nayles vij C.	xiiij^{d}.	
Reward*es* or Wag*es* for him & his iij *ser*vant*es* woo*r*king and attending then	xx^{s}.	
In all Amownting vnto		

f° 8 v.

	Thomas Blagrave esquier for mony by him disburced vpon sundry occazions concerning this Office and Thaffares therof as foloweth videlicet	
	26° Novembris. 1574	
Iorneyeng charg*es*	.3. Horshyer and charges by the waye at Wynsor stayeng there ij dayes in November iiij daies for p*er*vzing & Reformyng of ffarrant*es* playe &c.	xlij^{s} vj^{d}
	.5°. Decembr*is* 1574	
	.3. Horsehyer to hampton Coorte to conferr w*ith* my L*ord* Chamberlayne the L*ord* Haward, & Mr Knevett vpo*n* certayne devices & to p*er*vze ffarrant*es* playe there againe iij daies the charg*es* wherof w*ith* horsemeate at kingston is	xxvij^{s} viij^{d}
	.13°. Decembr*is* .1574.	
ffewell.	Coles j Lode & v sack*es*	xxiij^{s}. iiij^{d}.
Necessaries.	for A keye & mending of a lock	xij^{d}
	Lynk*es* ij .viij^{d}. & to Rosse for a xvj^{d} patterne . . .	ij^{s}
	14° Decembr*is*	
Pervzing and Reforming of plaies	The expenc*es* & charg*es* where my L*ord* Chamberlens players did show the history of Phedrastus & Phigon and Lucia together amou*n*teth vnto	ix^{s}. iiij^{d}.
	15° Decembr*is*.	
ffewell.	Coles .j. Lode and vj sack*es*	xxiiij^{s}.
	18° Decembr*is*.	
Pervzing and Reformyng of playes	The expenc*es* and charg*es* wheare my L*ord* of Leicesters men*n*e showed theier matter of Panecia.	x^{s}
	It*em* for A dozen ot Lether poynt*es*	iiij^{d}
	It*em* for iij Torches that nighte	iij^{s}
	23° Decembr*is*	
ffewell.	Coles xx sack*es* at viij^{d} the sack	xiij^{s} iiij^{d}.
Habberdash small ware.	Mirors or lookingglasses for the pedlers Mask xij small at ij^{s} the peece and vj. viij^{d} greater at .iiij^{s}. the peece and for ffrenche pynnes in all	xlviij^{s} viij^{d}.
	26° Decembr*is*.	
Cariag*es*	The Hyer of .j. Wagon & syx horses from London to Hampton coorte the mony was p*aid* to Thom*as* Smyth	xl^{s}
	20° Die	
Pervsing and Reforming of playes	The Charg*es* and expenc*es* where my L*ord* Clyntons players rehearsed a matter called pretestus	xiij^{s}
	21° Die	
	The Charg*es* and expenc*es* where the showed ij other playes with iij^{s} for torches & iiij^{d} for an howerglasse	xiij^{s} iiij^{d}

f° 9 r.

	27° Decembr*is*.	
Habberdash small ware.	The same Thom*as* Blagrave for mony by him disbursed for Gloves for my *Lord* of Lesters boyes y^t plaied at the coorte	ij^s
	for Cariage of theier stuf & for the Carters attendaunce that nighte	xvj^d.
	Reward*es* to the Carpenters & painters	ij^s vj^d
	29° Decembr*is*.	
Iorneyeng charges.	.3. Horshyer and expenc*es* iiij daies from London to Hampton Coorte and there Remaynyng *with* the Revells	xxxj^s. vj^d.
Habberdash small ware for the pedlers Mask.	ffrenche pynnes & greate pynnes	ix^s
	Sylk poynt*es* Brayded 18 dozen	xxj^s
	White & sweete Inglish balls j dozen	vj^s
	Gloves perfvmed ij dozen price	xxviij^s
	sylk Twyst to tye the papers	xij^d
	Laces of sylke iiij doozen price	xij^s.
	Venis Balls sweete j doozen	xvj^s
	Staves bowght of Carow j dozen	ij^s vj^d
	ffayer wryting of pozies for the Mask	vj^s viij^d
	1° Ianvarij 1574	
Iorneyeng charges	.3. Horshier on New yeares daie to Hampton Coorte & theier charg*es* there & at kingston iiij daies	xxxij^s
P*ro*perty p*er*cells	fflowers vj dozen at ij^d the peece	xij^s.
	fflowers at iij^d the peece iij dozen	ix^s.
	Long poles with brushes for chymney sweepers in my *Lord* of Leycesters mennes playe & for Mosse & styck*es* and other implement*es* for them	ij^s vj^d
	6° Ianvarij	
Iorneyeng charg*es*	.3. Horshyer & expenc*es* iij daies Resting at Kingston —	xxv^s. vj^d
Yron woorke for fframes and devic*es*	lxvj^{s}iij^d & .vj^s. ij^d. To Vlrick Netsley for vyces viij doozen and .v. price together	xxxiij^s viij^d.
	for keyes for vices xvj price	ij^s. x^d.
	Hinges xviij price together	vj^s.
	The mending of vic*es* & nvtt*es*	iij^d.
	Plates 13. at iij^d the peece	iij^s iij^d
	A greate plate for the Rock	ij^s vj^d
	The mending of wyers & staples	x^d
	ij Barrs of Iron ix foote longe	xviij^d
	sheepe hookes & other hookes	ij^s xj^d
	haspes & henges for the stock*es*	xij^d
	New nvtt*es* & plates	xviij^d
	v. Balls at. xvj^d. the peece	vj^s viij^d
	viij stepps & xvj pynnes	iij^s iiij^d
	It*em* more to him for mending of vic*es* and Nutt*es* *with* other Iron woorke	vj^s ij^d

f° 9 v.

Hier of Armo*ur*	To Roger Tyndall tharmerer for Lending of Armor for ffarrant*es* playe and for attending the same . .	xj^{s}. iiij^{d}.	
The Basketmaker.	To Iohn Ollyf [xxix^{s} viij^{d}] for A hamper to pack the vardngales in—	ij^{s}.	
	Another greate hamper to carry A fframe in . .	viij^{s}.	
	ix. Little hampers at xx^{d} the peece for the pedlers Mask	xv^{s}.	
	x Browne Baskett*es*	iij^{s} iiij^{d}.	
	Rodd*es* for Lictos Bvndells in ye playe . . .	xvj^{d}	lxxj^{li}. iiij^{s}. ix^{d}.
The Glazier	To Will*iam* Davyson for viij square peces of glasse for the Rock — viij^{s} for iiij other peeces at xvj^{d} the peece for the same Rock — v^{s} iiij^{d}/ for ij peec*es* to make shild*es* — iij^{s} iiij^{d} Other glasse for other plac*es* — ij^{s} And for his owne paynes & his *seruauntes* ij daies & ij Night*es* — vij^{s}. in all	xxv^{s}. viij^{d}.	
Wexchaundler	Wax for A Cake in ffarrant*es* playe.	iij^{s} vj^{d}.	
ffewell	Coles j Lode bowght of .T. daye	xx^{s}.	
Prop*er*tymaker.	To Iohn Rosse for vj branches of flowers made of ffethers — vj^{s} fflowers for Garland*es* iiij dozen — viij^{s}. Long boordes for the Stere of a clowde — vj^{s} Pulleyes for the Clowd*es* and curteynes — iiij^{s} Bote hier to & fro the Coorte — viij^{s} Lynk*es* to rec*eive* the stuf — viij^{d}/ Dubble gyrt*es* to hange the soon in the Clowde — xij^{d}/ for sowing the curtyns & setting on the frenge for the same — iij^{s}./ Wyer to hang the urtyns — vj^{d} vyces for the pulleyes &c. — iiij^{s}.	xlj^{s}. ij^{d}	
Carpenter	To Rowland Robynson for Elme Boordes cc — xiiij^{s} Oken boordes vj^{c} — xl^{s}. One Elme boorde — xx^{d}/ Oken boorde lxx foote — iiij^{s} iiij^{d}. / Oken [15.] Rafters of xiiij foote long [at] xvj^{d} the peece — xx^{s}/ Beechen Rafters at xiiij^{d} the peece vj p*r*ice — vij^{s} It*em* more iiij beechen Rafters — iiij^{s} viij^{d} Cariage of Rafters — viij^{d}/ single quarters xxiiij at iij^{d} the pece — vj^{s}/ ij more Rafters of beeche — ij^{s}. iiij^{d}. A peece of Tymber xiiij foote — iij^{s} Nayles of Sundry sort*es* — xij^{s} vij^{d} A peece of Elme boorde for the clowde — xviij^{d} fyrr poles xij at vj^{d} the pece — vj^{s}/ It*em* more to w*illiam* barker for xviij firr poles — ix^{s}/ Cariage of Poles &c. — xij^{d}/	vj^{li}. xiij^{s}. ix^{d}	

f° 10 r.

The Propertymaker	To Iohn Carow in his lyfe tyme not long before his death — vj^{li} And to his wyfe after his deathe in full satisfaccon for all the wares by him delyvered this yeare into the said office or is to be by him the saide Carow his executors or admynistrators demawnded for any dett due before the third of ffebruary 1574 or not entred in this booke — vj^{li} xiiij^{s}. iiij^{d}. as which grew by propertyes videlicet Monsters, Mountaynes, fforrestes, Beastes, Serpentes, Weapons for warr as gvnnes, dagges, bowes, Arowes, Bills, holberdes, borespeares, fawchions daggers, Targettes, pollaxes, clubbes headdes & headpeeces Armor counterfet Mosse, holly, Ivye, Bayes, flowers quarters, glew, past. paper. and suche lyke with Nayles hoopes horstailes dishes for devells eyes heaven, hell, & the devell & all the devell I should saie but not all	xij^{li}. xiiij^{s}. iiij^{d}
The furryer.	To Thomas Garlyk for iiij dozen of Coony skynnes at iij^{d} the peece	xij^{s}.

.2°. februarij.

Iorneyeng charges	.3. Horshier for iij daies to Hampton Coorte with theier charges at kingston &c.	xxvj^{s}. ij^{d}
Watercariage &c.	Barge hier paid to .T. white for ij ffares of Tymber from Hampton Coorte to London at x^{s} the peece	xx^{s}.
	Land Cariage from the waterside	xij^{d}.
The fethermaker	A Cote, A hatt, & Buskins all ouer covered with ffethers of cvllers for vanytie in sabastians playe with xij^{d} geven in Rewarde to ye bringer	xxvj^{s}

13° februarij being shrovesvndaye

Iorneyeng charges	.3. Horshier iiij dayes with theier charges at kingston in the meane tyme	xxxiiij^{s}.
Iron woorke	To Vlrik Netsleye for vices & nuttes . . .	xv^{s}
expences & botehier	To Lambe for the french womans dyner that went with the heares to dresse childrens heades in M^{r} hunyes his playe & for pynnes & Botehier	ij^{s}. ij^{d}.
The Hyer of Heares for headdes and Rewardes.	To the french woman for her paynes and her Dawghters paynes that went to Richemond & there attended vpon M^{r} hunnyes his Children & dressed theier heades &c. when they played before her Magestye	xxiij^{s} vj^{d}

f° 10v.

Buskynmaker	To Iohn ffarrington for making of ffyve payer of Buskyns and one payer of Startopps w*ith* the Lether that sowled them in all	xj^{s}. viij^{d}.
The Plummer	To Dvnstone Braye for Leade and sowlder w*ith* woorkmanshipp by him bestowed over the Cowntynghowse at saynt Iohns where it Rayned in	xlvj^{s}. j^{d}.
The Millioner	Martyn Hardrett for iij Borders — vj^{s}/ for iij partlett*es* — x^{s} vj chaines — iiij^{s}/ ij Heares — iiij^{s}/ fflowers ix dozen — xxj^{s} in all	xlv^{s}.
Iron woork	To Iohn Rosse for Longe vices to Ioyne fframes together iij dozen & viij — xvj^{s} for his Botehier &c. — xx^{d}	xviij^{s} iiij^{d}
Reward*es*	Reward*es* geven by the prop*er* hand*es* of the saide Mr Blagrave to sundry persons at sundry tymes for sundry services vpon sundry occazions concerning the premiss*es* in all	lx^{s}.
	In all Amownting vnto	

Rewarde	To for his paynes in p*er*vsing and Reformyng of playes svndry tymes as neede required for her Ma*iesties* Lyking p*aid* by Dodmer by the speciall appoyntm*ent* of the saide Mr Blagrave	xl^{s}.

Silkweaver. & his p*er*cells	**Will*iam* Bowll.** for mony to him due for	
	25°. Decembr*is*. 1574	
	Past paper halfe A dozen	xij^{d}
	26°. Die.	
	Paper for patternes Leaves of trees & such other necessary vzag in thoffice one Reame and one Quier price	vj^{s}. iiij^{d}.
	Paste Boorde of the largest syze j doze*n* . .	iiij^{s}
	27°. Die.	
	Buttons of Copper sylver ij dozen wayeng ix oun*ces* at xviij^{d} thounce	xiij^{s} vj^{d}
	Lace of Copp*er* sylver .v/ ounc*es* di. at 18^{d} . .	viij^{s} iij^{d}.
	Brayded Lace of Sylver & black silk vij ounc*es* di. at .18. the ounce	xj^{s} iij^{d}.
	30°. Die. ffrenge & twyst .11. ounces.	xl^{s} vj^{d}
	31°. Die	
	ffringe & Twist .j. lb .xiiij. o*unces* q*uarter* at .18^{d}. .	xlv^{s}. iiij^{d} ob.
	Paned sylk at .16^{d}. the ounce ij o*unces* q*uarter* p*r*ice	iij^{s}.
	frenge of Red silk & copp*er* sylver v o*unces* . .	vij^{s} vj^{d}
	ffringe & Tassells of copp*er* sylu*er* .xvj. o*unces* .	xxiiij^{s}
	sylk frenge at xvj^{d} thou*n*ce xiij ounc*es* . . .	xvij^{s}. iiij^{d}.

fo 11 r.

	.j°. Die Ianvarij 1574		
	ffringe of Copper sylver and silk v ounc*es* at xviij^{d} the ounce	vij^{s} vj^{d}	xxxviij^{li}. xiij^{s}. iiij^{d}.
	A lardge Box for the premiss*es*	xviij^{d}	
	ffrenge of Copper sylver vij *ounces* di.	xj^{s}. iij^{d}.	
	2°. Die.		
	ffrenge of sylver and sylk iij *ounces*. di. at 18^{d} . . .	v^{s}. iij^{d}.	
	Bone Lace of Copp*er* sylu*er* & silk .j. lb ij. *ounces* .	xxvij^{s}.	
	Brayded Lace at .18^{d}. iij lb .j. *ounce* di. price . .	lxxiiij^{s}. iij^{d}.	
	4°. Die.		
	Pasted paper of the Largest sorte ij. doze*n* . . .	viij^{s}	
	Brayded Lace .j. lb iiij. *ounces* di. at. 18^{d}. thou*nce* .	xxx^{s}. ix^{d}.	
	5°. Die.		
	Brayded Tassells & frenge .ij. lb ix. *ounces* iij q*uarters*.	lxij^{s} vij^{d} ob.	
	Lace at xviij^{d} .15. *ounces* *quarter* price at 18^{d} thou*nce* .	xxij^{s}. x^{d}. ob.	
	ffrenge and Lace .ij. lb vij. *ounces* at xviij^{d} . . .	lviij^{s} vj^{d}.	
	Topp Buttons & frenge Lace at .18^{d}. j lb j ounce quarter	xxv^{s}. x^{d}. ob.	
	30° Die.		
	Crymsen Sylk & sylver frenge at ij^{s} vj^{d} thou*nce* .x. ounc*es* di.	xxvj^{s}. iij^{d}.	
	Black sylk & sylver frenge at xviij^{d} the ownce j lb .v. ounc*es* q*uarter*	xxxj^{s}. x^{d}. ob.	
	31°. Die.		
	Past boorde [ij dozen] of the Largest sorte	viij^{s}.	
	j° Die februarij .1574		
	Crimsen silk & sylver frenge ij. lb vj. *ounces* at ij^{s} vj^{d} the ownce	iiij^{li}. xv^{s}.	
	Black sylver ffrenge xiiij *ounces* *quarter*. at 18^{d} . .	xxj^{s}. iiij^{d}. ob.	
	10°. Die /& 14° die		
	Crimsen silk frenge .j. lb v. *ounces* di. at. 2^{s} 6^{d}. . .	liij^{s}. ix^{d}.	
	Black sylk & sylver frenge at .18^{d}. v. *ounces* di. . .	viij^{s} iij^{d}	
	Black sylk & silver frenge viij *ounces* at 18^{d} . . .	xij^{s}	
	In all Amownting vnto		
Canvas	Henri Sekford esquier for Canvas by him d[e]lyvered into the saide Office. cl^{ti}. ells/ at xiiij^{d} the ell Imployed vpo*n* the howses & propertyes made for players at Christm*as*, Twelftyde, Candellm*as*, and shrovetyde aforesaide in All am*oun*ting vnto		viij^{li}. xv^{s}.

f° 11 v.

	Edward Buggyn gent*leman* clerkcomptrowler of Thoffice for mony by him disburced vid*elicet*		ix^{li}. v^{s}. ij^{d}.
	25° Decembris		
	Cariage of iiij Lodes of Tymber for the Rock (w*h*ich Mr Rosse made for my L*ord* of Leicesters menns playe) & for other frames for players howses	ij^{s}. iiij^{d}.	
	Cariage of one hundred seeling boorde to make Branches to beare lyght*es*	.iiij^{d}.	
	.27°. Decembris.		
	The hier of a wagon to carry a Lode of stvf to hte Coorte for the ⸢playe⸣ Duttons	xx^{s}.	
neccessaries	It*em* for A standish cou*n*ters & Ink	vj^{s} vj^{d}	
	j^{o}. Die Ianvarij.		
	for Spangles xxiiij Thowsand	xij^{s}	
	Cariage of one hundred of Boorde from saint pulkers to thoffice	vj^{d}	
	xj^{o}. Ianvarij.		
	for A perwigg of Heare for king xerxces syster in ffarrant*es* playe	iiij^{s}.viij^{d}.	
	for Cariage of iij Lode of stuf (for the playe &c. on twelfe Nighte) to the watersyde at the Blackfryers	iij^{s}.	
	xviij^{o}. Die.		
	ffor ffelt*es* one doozen at vj^{d} the pece	vj^{s}.	
	.j^{o}. ffebruarij .1574.		
neccessaries	for ij ells of Canvas to make frenge for the players howse in farrant*es* play	xx^{d}.	
	Cariage of Stuff for Candellmas Nighte to the watersyde.	ij^{s}. ij^{d}.	
	Barge hier to hampton Coorte then	xiiij^{s}.	
	skynnes to furr the hoode in sabastians playe . .	ij^{s}.	
neccessaries	ffor making of ij sarcenet hoodd*es* for Cyttyzens in the same playe	ij^{s}.	
	Holly, Ivye, firr poles & Mosse for the Rock in M^{r} hvnnyes playe	x^{s}.	
	Hornes iij. Collers iij, Leashes iij & dogghookes iij/ w*ith* Bawdrick*es* for the hornes in hvnnyes playe	x^{s}.	
	13. februarij.		
	Cariage of Tymber woork for the same M^{r} hvnnyes his playe downe to the watersyde.	ij^{s}. vj^{d}	
neccessaries	To Iohn Tuke for going to the Coo*r*te in a Message	xij^{d}	
	14°. Die		
	for A Lode of Coles	xix^{s}	
neccessaries	A ffelt y^{t} was covered w*ith* mony	vj^{d}	

f° 12 r.

	Item more for mony by him disburced for Sylver Lawne xliiij yerd*es* di.		xliiij^{s}.
Reward*es*	Bote hier for him selfe & others sund*r*y tymes *with* Reward*es* by him geven to sundry p*er*sons not before mencioned		xxj^{s}.
Paynters p*er*cells	Will*iam* Lyzarde for mony to him due for		viz.
	20° Die Decembris		
	White xxx lb at iij^{d} the lb	vij^{s} vj^{d}	
	Syze	vj^{s}	
	Nayles	xij^{d}	
	Pott*es* iij doozen	ij^{s}	
	Black xij lb	xij^{s}	
	Smalt	xxiij^{s} iiij^{d}	
	Masticot	iij^{s} iiij^{d}	
	Inde .j. lb.	vj^{s} viij^{d}	iiij^{li}. v^{s}. iiij^{d}.
	Synaper j lb	ij^{s}	
	Browne j lb	xviij^{d}	
	Vermillion di. lb	iiij^{s}	
	sape di lb	iij^{s} iiij^{d}	
	Vert .j. lb.	liij^{s}	
	Dark synap*er* j lb	iij^{s}.	
	Redd iiij lb	ij^{s} viij^{d}.	
	Yellow iij lb	iij^{s}.	
	24°. Die		
	White xxx lb at iij^{d} the lb	vij^{s} vj^{d}	
	Black xij lb	xij^{s}	
	smalt iij lb	x^{s}	
	Syze	vj^{s}	
	Synaper dark di. lb	xviij^{d}	xlij^{s}. vij^{d}
	sylver cc.	iij^{s}	
	ffoyle	xvj^{d}	
	Pott*es*	xij^{d}	
	Past	iij^{d}	
	26°. Die.		
	ffyne gowlde	vj^{s} viij^{d}	
	Golde 200	v^{s}. vij^{d}	
	Byse q*uarter* of lb	iij^{s}.	

f° 12 v.

Item	Amount	Subtotal	Total
for shells of fyne sylver	xv^s. ij^d.		
White Lead grownde	ij^s. vj^d.		
ffyne Black for the lott*es*	v^s.	lij^s. v^d.	
Vert	iiij^s.		
Glew ij lb	viij^d		
Inde	iij^s. iiij^d.		
ffyne yolow to wryte vpon the Mirrors	ij^s.		xvj^{li}. xviij^d
Sylver 300	iiij^s.vj^d.		
29°. Decembr*is*. 1574.			
Syze	iiij^s.		
Smalt ij lb	vj^s viij^d		
Stayning cvllers for s*ar*cenet . . .	vj^s		
Past Boordes iij dozen	vj^s vj^d		
Synaper	iij^s		
Cvller for iij dozen light*es*	vj^s	xlviij^s. x^d.	
Assedue iiij lb	xij^s		
Glew	xvj^d		
Golde	ij^s viij^d		
Grynding of Sheeres to clypp the Assedue	viij^d		
15° Ianvarij 1574			
Syze	iiij^s		
Assedue	xviij^d	xv^s. x^d.	
Gowlde	iij^s iiij^d		
sylver paper to make mony. . . .	vij^s.		
28° Ianvarij			
White	iiij^s. vj^d.		
Black	iij^s.		
Gowlde	vj^s	xxij^s x^d.	
Masticot	iij^s iiij^d		
Assedue .j. lb. di	iiij^s vj^d		
Sylver to wryte names	xviij^d		
12° die ffebruarij			
Syze	v^s.		
White	ij^s.	xvij^s vj^d	
sylver	iiij^s. vj^d		
Patternes.	vj^s.		
13° februarij			f° 13 r.

13° ffebruarij

Assedue iiij. lb	xij^{s}.	
Past paper iij dozen	vj^{s}. vj^{d}.	
Golde	vj^{s}	
Glew .v. lb	xx^{d}	xxxvj^{s}. ij^{d}.
Patternes for light*es* ij	v^{s}.	
A pattern for A helmett	v^{s}.	

Reward*es* & Iorneyeng charg*es*.

Bryan Dodmer for his Botehier, horshier, Iorneyeng charg*es* and expenc*es* betwene the saide first of November in the xvjth yeare and the Last of ffebruary in the xvijth yere specially To Hampton Coorte and there attending vpon the Lorde Chamberlayne, the Lorde Treasaurer ^and^ Mr Secretary Walsingh*a*m for mony ^in prest^ to be Imployed vpon the premiss*es* being after longe attendaunce (and that none of the aforenamed coulde get the Queenes M*aies*tie to resolve therin). Dryven to trouble her M*aies*tie him selfe & by ^speciall^ peticion obtayned aswell the grawnt for cc^{li} in prest as the dett*es* to be p*aid*. In consideracon wherof, as also for the Rest of his s*er*vice done in this office, & to be doone abowte theise Reckonyng*es* vntill thaccou*n*te herof be past. In all for xx mark*es* demaunded alowed but — vj^{li} xiij^{s} iiij^{d}.

Necessaries for the clerk.

The Clerk of thoffice for his ordinary Greene cloth, Paper, Ink, Cownters Tooles and Necessary Implement*es* for the Making ^& coserving^ of Bills Bookes Plott*es* & Modells — lxvj^{s} viij^{d}

S*umma* of all the **Emptions** and p*ro*vyzions for **Christmas Twelftyde Candellmas** and **Srovetyde** aforesaide. — cccxlix^{li}.xvj^{s}.x^{d}.

f° 13 v.

S *umma* **for Christm*as* Twelfe Tyde, Candellm*as* & Shrovetyde** 1574 / Anno R*egni* R*egin*æ Elizab[e]the **xvij**^{mo}. } $\overset{xx}{\text{D}}$iiij. ij^{li}. xiiij^{d}

* T Blagrave
* Edwarde Buggyn
* walter fysshe

S *UMMA* TOT*A*LIS **of this whole Booke** Being all the Charges of This Office **ffor one yeare Endyng** the Last daye of februari 1574. Anno R*egni* R*egin*æ Elizab*e*the **xvij**^{mo}.

Wag*es* of	**Artiffic*ers* & others.**	ccxxviij^{li}:viij^{s}: vj^{d}	**Dclxix**^{li}. **ij**^{s}. **iiij**^{d}
	300^{li}/18^{s}/6^{d}/ **Offic*ers*** — lxxij^{li}. x^{s}.		
Emptions provizions & other expenc*es* with Reward*es* &c.		ccclxviij^{li} iij^{s} x^{d}	

* T Blagrave
* Edwarde Buggyn
* walter fysshe

f° 14 r.

Revell*es*	xvj^to^		xix^no^ Aprilis 1575
Anno		Anno xvij^mo^	Anno xvij^mo^ D*omi*ne *Elizabethe* Regine

From 1 March 1573-4 to 11 March 1575-6

Record Office. Warrants for Issue (Exch. of Receipt). Parcel 120

Elizabeth by the grace of god Queen of England ffraunce and Ireland defendo*ur* of the faythe &c. To the Thr*easur*er and Chamberlains of our Exchequier greetinge. Whereas it apperith by a declaration subscribed by Will*iam* Dodington one of thauditors of our prest*es* that there is remayninge vnpayed in thoffice of our Revells for wares and wag*es* growen due in two yeeres and elevyn dayes ending the xjth of Marche nowe laste paste seavyn hundred sixe pound*es* twelve shilling*es* fowre pence. These therefore are to signefye vnto you our will and pleasure is of suche our treasure as presently remayneth in the receipte of our Exchequier, or hereafter shall come into the same That you delyver, or cause to be delyvered vnto our trustie and welbeloued *ser*vant Thomas Blagrave esquier clerke of our sayd Revells the said some of vij^{c} vj^{li}. xij^{s} iiij^{d} in full satisfaction of the sayd debte, to be by him payed over vnto suche p*er*sons as to whom the same or any p*ar*te thereof shall appere to be due by the bookes of the said office compyled for the tyme aforesaid. And these o*ur* *lett*res shalbe yo*ur* sufficient warrante and discharge in that behalfe. Gevin vnder o*ur* pryvie Seale at our Mano*ur* of Haveringe the fifte day of Auguste, in the eightenth yeere of our reign.

*p*er* W^{m} packer deput*atum*
Hug: Alington

[Endorsed :]

Quinto Die August*i* 1576

Thome Blagraue — vij^{c}. vj^{li}. xij^{s}. iiij^{d}. Sol*ucio* p*er* Taillor et allo*catio* ei Term*in*o Pasche 1576

From 11 March 1575-6 to 21 February 1576-7.

viz.

Record Office. Audit Office. Accounts Various. Bd. 1213. Revels. Nº 5.

Revelles : 1576 : Anno R*egni* R*eg*ine Elizabeth xix^{o} : The Lidgeard or Perticuler Booke of all the Charges rysing and growing w*i*thin the Office of the Quenes Ma*ie*sties Revell*es* aforsaid **Betwene the xjth of March 1575 : And the xxjth of ffebruarie 1576 : A***nno* R*egni* R*egi*ne Eliz*abeth* predict*e* xix^{o} : w*i*thin w*hi*ch tyme. There were work*es* don and Attendaunces given as foloweth vid*elicet*

Title-page r.

Betweene the xjth of Marche 1575 *Anno Regni Regine* Eliz*abeth* predict*e* xviij^{o} **And** the xxth of December : Anno Regni Regine Eliz*abeth* xix^{o} : The Charges of this Office grew by meanes of Ayringe Repayringe, pervsing, amending, Brusshing, Spunging, Rubbing, wyping, sweeping, making cleane putting in order, and safebestowinge, of the garment*es*, Vestures, Apparell, Disguisinges, Properties, and furniture of the same, from tyme to tyme (w*i*thin those ix monethes) as the necessitie thereof fro*m* tyme to tyme requyred, to keepe the same in Redynes for service, w*hi*ch els wold be mowldy, mustie, motheten, and rotten, by meanes of the Dankenes of the howse, and want of convenyent Presses, and places requysite. The parties who Co*m*monlie attende the said Office for the same purpose w*i*th their severall names, (allowed for this tyme) particulerlie hereafter ensueth.

vid*elicet*

		Daies	**Wages**
Taylours and others workinge and attending the premiss*es* at th'officers Co*m*maundement the first at xx^{d} the daie and all the rest at xij^{d} as in the former president*es*. 6^{li}/13^{s}/4^{d}/	Thomas Clatterbuck	20	xxxiij^{s} iiij^{d}
	Thomas Wright sen*ior*	20	xx^{s}
	Iohn Davys	20	xx^{s}
	Iohn Stagar	20	xx^{s}
	Iohn Drawater	20	xx^{s}
	Iohn Dawncye	20	xx^{s}

Th'officers	The M*aster* at iiij^{s} the daie	20	iiij^{li}
	The Clerk Comptroller at ij^{s}	20	xl^{s}
	The Clerk at ij^{s}	20	xl^{s}
	The yeoman at ij^{s}	20	xl^{s}

f° 1 r.

S *umma* of all the wages betwene the xjth of Marche 1575 : Annoq*ue* R*egni* R*eg*ine Eliz*abeth* xviij^{uo}. **And** the xxth of December 1576 Anno Regni Regine Elizabeth xix^{o} — xvj^{li} xiij^{s} iiij^{d}

ffewell Walt*er* ffysshe gent*leman* for 30 sack*es* of coales by him p*ro*vided for the said Ayring*es* — xxij^{s} vj^{d}

S *umma* **totalis** of the whole Ayringes . . . . xvij^{li} xv^{s} x^{d}

* T Blagrave
* Edwarde Buggin
* walter fysshe

f° 1 v.

Chrystmas Newyerestide Twelftide & Candlemas Anno R*egni* R*egi*ne Eliz*abeth* pred*icte* — **xix°** **1576.**

The Charges of those tymes vid*elicet* **Betweene** the xxth of [1576] December Anno Regni Regine Eliz*abeth* predict*e* xix° at w*hi*ch tyme the woorkes began for the providing, apting, preparing, furnishing, and setting fourth of divers plaies or showes of Histories, and other Inventions and Devyces folowinge. **And** the [1576] iiijth of ffebruarie in the said xixth yere of her M*aiesties* Reigne, at w*hi*ch tyme the woorkes and attendaunces did ende, together w*i*th all Th'emptions and Provisions of stuff and Necessaries, Cariadges, and other Incident*es*, bought p*ro*vided done and attended by divers p*er*sons whose seu*er*all names rates and wages w*i*th their Rewardes and allowaunces do p*ar*ticulerlie in their apt places ensue

Histories & Invenc*i*ons showen w*i*thin the tyme aforesaid — **vj.** viz.

The Paynters daughter showen at Hampton Court on St Stevens daie at night, enacted by th'erle of warwick*es* *seruauntes*

Toolie showen at Hampton Court on St Iohns daie at night enacted by the L*ord* Howard*es* *seruauntes*.

The historie of the Collyer showen at Hampton Court on the Sundaie folowing enacted by th'erle of Leicesters men.

The historie of Error showen at Hampton Court on Newyeres daie at night, enacted by the Children of Powles.

The historye of Mutius Sceuola showen at Hampton Court on Twelt daie at night, enacted by the Children of windsore and the Chappell

The historye of the Cenofall*es* showen at Hampto*n* Court on Candlemas day at night, enacted by the L*ord* Chamb*er*leyn his men.

		Dayes	**Nightes**	**Wages**
Taylours and others working and attending the premiss*es* the first at xxd the daie and asmuch for the night, the Residew at xijd vid*elicet*	Thomas Clatterbuck	21	14	lviijs iiijd
	Thomas Wright sen*ior*	21	14	xxxvs
	David ffludd	21	14	xxxvs
	Robert Smyth	21	14	xxxvs
	Will*iam* Lumley	21	14	xxxvs
	Iohn Stagar	21	14	xxxvs
	Iohn ffludde	17	8	xxvs

f° 2 r.

		Daies	Nightes	Wages
	George wright	16	7	xxiij^{s}
	William Boydon	13	7	xx^{s}
	Richard wardeman	16	8	xxiiij^{s}
	George warton.	20	8	xxviij^{s}
	Thomas wright Iunior	8	5	xiij^{s}
	Thomas Byrd	8	4	xij^{s}
	Iohn Cleyton	11	6	xvij^{s}
	William woode	6	3	ix^{s}
	Iohn ffaunsham	5	4	ix^{s}
	Iohn Eavans	5	4	ix^{s}
	Robert Haies	4	4	viij^{s}
	Danyell Wye	3	3	vj^{s}
	William Homes	3	3	vj^{s}
	Iohn walker	5	4	ix^{s}
22^{li}/11^{s}/4^{d}/				
The Porter and other Attendauntes at xij^{d} the daie ech one and asmuch for the night viz.	Iohn Dawncye.	21	14	xxxv^{s}
	Iohn Drawater.	21	14	xxxv^{s}
	Iohn Davys.	21	14	xxxv^{s}
	Thomas Lambe	19	10	xxix^{s}
6^{li}/14^{s}/				
Paynters and others working and attending the premisses daie and night at sundrie Rates viz.	william Lyzard at ij^{s} by the daie and asmuch for the night	20	11	lxij^{s}
	Lewys Lyzard at xx^{d}.	11	8	xxxj^{s} viij^{d}
	Thomas Tyler senior at xviij^{d}	15	14	xliij^{s} vj^{d}
	Robert Peake at the like	8	7	xxij^{s} vj^{d}
	Iohn Rows at the like	8	6	xxj^{s}
	Richard Gilmond at xvj^{d}	3	4	ix^{s} iiij^{d}

f° 2 v.

		Daies	Nightes	Wages
	Robert Cotes at xvj^{d}	20	13	xliiij^{s}
	Iohn kelsey at the like	1	0	xvj^{d}
	Charles Reeder at the like	1	0	xvj^{d}
	Iohn Lymbie at xij^{d}	12	11	xxiij^{s}
12^{li}/19^{s}/8^{d}/				
Hab*er*dasshers and Propertymakers at sundrie rates viz.	Iohn ffarrington at xvj^{d}	21	9	xl^{s}
	Iohn Ogle at xvj^{d}	10	6	xxj^{s} iiij^{d}
	Richard Moorer at xvj^{d}	2	2	v^{s} iiij^{d}
	Adam Cowper at xvj^{d}	2	3	vj^{s} viij^{d}
	Thomas Stronge at xij^{d}	21	14	xxxv^{s}
5^{li}/8^{s}/4^{d}/				
Ioyners Carvers and Propertymakers at sundrie rates viz.	Richard Rowland at ij^{s}	6	4	xx^{s}
	Sebastian vycars at xvj^{d}	11	10	xxviij^{s}
	Thomas Booreman at xij^{d}	21	14	xxxv^{s}
	Thomas Tyler Iun*ior* at xij^{d}	9	8	xvij^{s}
5^{li}/				
Carpenters at xvj^{d} the daie and asmuch the night viz.	Will*iam* Barker at xvj^{d}	14	10	xxxij^{s}
	Edward ffurres at xvj^{d}	13	9	xxix^{s} iiij^{d}
	Iohn Collyns at xvj^{d}	8	7	xx^{s}
	Iohn Lawrence at xvj^{d}	11	8	xxv^{s} iiij^{d}
5^{li}/6^{s}/8^{d}/				
Wyerdrawers at sundry rates. viz.	Thomas Leverett at xx^{d}	3	1	vj^{s} viij^{d}
	Edmunde Byrchall at 18^{d}	3	1	vj^{s}
	Simon Powle at xvj^{d}	3	1	v^{s} iiij^{d}

f° 3 r.

		Daies	Nightes	Wages
Th'offycers	The M*aster* at iiij^{s} the daie . .	23 . .	14 . .	vij^{li} viij^{s}
	The Clerk Comptroller at ij^{s}. .	23 . .	14 . .	lxxiiij^{s}
	The Clerke at ij^{s}	23 . .	14 . .	lxxiiij^{s}
	The Yeoman at ij^{s}.	23 . .	14 . .	lxxiiij^{s}
18^{li}/10^{s}/				

S*umma* of all the **Wages** due in this Office for workemanship and attendaunces don therein and vpon the Affaires thereof for **Christmas** and **Candlem*a*s** ending the iiijth of ffebruarie 1576 : A*nn*oq*ue* R*egni* R*egi*ne Elizabeth xix^{o} } lxxvij^{li} viij^{s}

* T Blagrave
* Edwarde Buggin
* walter fysshe

f° 3 v.

Emptions. Prouisions & Cariadges
w*i*th Reward*es* and other Charges Incident.

The Mercer	**Will*iam* Roe** for Sarcenett*es* by him delivered into the Office viz. 6° : die Ianuarij one peece of yelow sarcenett conteigning 30 : elles at vj^{s} the ell, and one pece of red sarcenett conteigning 25 : elles at the same rate	xvj^{li} x^{s}
Sylkewevers parcelles	**Guillaime Tien** for xj li. xv ounces of copp*er* silver lace at xviij^{d} the ounce	xiiij^{li} vj^{s} vj^{d}
The lynnen Draper	**Richard Busshe** for Canvas by him delivered into th'office at sundrie tymes viz. 26° : Decembr*is* [1576] one pece of Canvas conteigning 36 : elles iij q*uar*ters at xij^{d} the ell — xxxvj^{s} ix^{d} : 31° : Decembr*is* 25 : elles iij q*uar*ters at xij^{d} the ell — xxv^{s} ix^{d} In the whole 62 : ell*es* : 1/2	iij^{li} ij^{s} vj^{d}
The vpholster	**Iohn Okes** for buckram by him delivered into the Office at sundrie tymes viz. 3° : Decembr*is* : 6 : peeces of purple buckram at iiij^{s} the peece — xxiiij^{s}, and 4° : Ianuarij : 6 : peeces of yelow buckram at iiij^{s} the peece — xxiiij^{s} amounting vnto	xlviij^{s}

Paynters p*ar*cell*es*

William Lyzard for col*ou*rs and Necessaries folowinge

ffoure gallons of Size	iiij^{s}
White 15 li. at iij^{d} the pound	iij^{s} ix^{d}
Black 3 li. at xij^{d} the pound	iij^{s}
Syneper j li.	ij^{s}
Browne j li.	xviij^{d}
Vert dimid. pound	ij^{s} iiij^{d}
Smalt iij li. at iiij^{s} the li.	xij^{s}
Inde dimid. pound	v^{s}
Red ij li. at viij^{d} the li.	xvj^{d}
Pottes for coloures	xij^{d}
Nayles	xij^{d}
Glue j li.	iiij^{d}
Gold 100	ij^{s} viij^{d}
Sylver 200	iij^{s}
Syze	iiij^{s}
Masticott j li.	iij^{s} iiij^{d}
Gold 100	ij^{s} viij^{d}

36^{li}/7^{s}/

f° 4 r.

	Size	iij^{s}	v^{li} v^{s}
	White xij li. at iij^{d} the li.	iij^{s}	
	ffyne white ij li. at xij^{d} the li.	ij^{s}	
	Size	iij^{s}	
	Masticott j li.	iij^{s} iiij^{d}	
	Syneper j li. dimid. at xvj^{d} the li.	ij^{s}	
	Byce iij oz. at xij^{d} the oz.	iij^{s}	
	Vermelyon iiij oz. at vj^{d} the oz.	ij^{s}	
	Pottes for coloures	vj^{d}	
	Vert dimid. pound	ij^{s} iiij^{d}	
	Gold 100	ij^{s} viij^{d}	
	Arsidew 4 li. at iij^{s} vj^{d} the pound	xiiij^{s}	
	Glue ij li. at iiij^{d} the li.	viij^{d}	
	Tynfoyle	xij^{d}	
	Syze	xviij^{d}	
	White	ix^{d}	
	Black	ij^{s}	
	Gold	xvj^{d}	
	Vert a q*uarter* of a li.	xiiij^{d}	
	Byce ij oz.	ij^{s}	
	Yelow a q*uarter* of a pound	x^{d}	
Smythes p*ar*cell*es*	woolrick Netesley for xiiij vices at vj^{d} the peece	vij^{s}	xiiij^{s} vij^{d}
	Nyneteene nuttes w*i*th plates vnder them at iij^{d} the pece	iiij^{s} ix^{d}	
	ffive keyes to them at ij^{d} the peece	x^{d}	
	ffive pynnes and a plate	ij^{s}	
Propertye makers p*ar*cell*es*	Richard Rowland for j c of plaster of Paris	iij^{s}	xiiij^{s} x^{d}
	Browne paper	xij^{d}	
	fflowre to make past	xij^{d}	
	Allom ij li.	viij^{d}	
	Glue ij li.	vj^{d}	
	Lynnen Ragges	xij^{d}	
	Claye to mowlde w*i*thall	viij^{d}	
	A bowle to beat browne paper in	vj^{d}	
	ffoure penie nailes vj c at iiij^{d} ye c	ij^{s}	
	Two peny nailes j c	ij^{d}	
	waynscott to make blades for rapio*ur*s &c	iiij^{d}	
6^{li}/14^{s}/5^{d}/	One dozen of pasteboordes	iiij^{s}	

f° 4 v.

Lightes and other neccessaries	Barnard ffabyan for xv dozen pound dimid. of candell*es* at iiij^{s} the dozen	lxij^{s}	
	Item xxiiij staffetorches at xiiij^{d} the pece. . .	xxviij^{s}	
	Item foure dozen of lynkes at iiij^{s} the dozen . .	xvj^{s}	
	Item two pound of packthreed at xij^{d} the pound	ij^{s}	vj^{li} ij^{s} iiij^{d}
	Item iij li. of glew at iiij^{d} the li.	xij^{d}	
	Item iiij peces of great cord at ij^{s} the pece . .	viij^{s}	
	Item ix peces of small cord	iiij^{s}	
	Item foure peeces of whipcord at iiij^{d} ye pece.	xvj^{d}	
	In the whole amounting vnto		
Boordes quarters Nailes and other Necc*essar*ies	Rowland Robynson for xiij doble q*uar*ters at vj^{d} the pece	vj^{s} vj^{d}	
	Plench boorde ij C dimid. at vij^{s} ye C	xvij^{s} vj^{d}	
	Single q*uar*ters 32 : at iij^{d} the pece	viij^{s}	
	Seelinge boorde a q*uar*tern.	xx^{d}	
	ffirre poles ten at vij^{d} the pece.	v^{s} x^{d}	
	for Cariadge of them	vj^{d}	
	Rafters xj at xvj^{d} the peece	xiiij^{s} viij^{d}	
	Beechen plankes ij at viij^{d} the pece.	xvj^{d}	
	Vyces xij and wynches ij	v^{s}	
	ffor the turnyng of foure postes and for xx^{tie} foote of tymber w*hi*ch made them	xviij^{s}	v^{li} xvj^{s} ij^{d}
	Elme boorde CC dimid. at vj^{s} viij^{d} ye C	xvj^{s} viij^{d}	
	ffor Tymber to make a frame	v^{s}	
	Sixpenie nailes 1900 at vj^{d} the C	ix^{s} vj^{d}	
	Tenpenie nailes CC at viij^{d} the C	xvj^{d}	
	Doble tenpenie nailes CC at xiiij^{d} ye C	ij^{s} iiij^{d}	
	Two penie nailes CCCC dimid.	ix^{d}	
	Threepenie nailes CC	vj^{d}	
	Single x^{d} nailes one C	vij^{d}	
	Sixpenie nailes one C	vj^{d}	
	In all to the said Robynson		
The Buskynmaker	Iohn ffarrington for xij sheepe skynnes at vj^{d} the pece	vj^{s}	
	ffor paring and russeting of them	ij^{s}	xx^{s}
	ffor the soles and making of vj paire of buskins of those skynnes	xij^{s}	

12^{li}/18^{s}/6^{d}/

f° 5 r.

The Hab*er*dasher	Richard Moorer for two hangers w*i*th girdles of black freesed lether	v^{s} iiij^{d}	xxij^{s} ix^{d}
	ffor v wastes of the same	v^{s}	
	ffor the making of 3 : cappes of tyncell sarcenett .	iij^{s}	
	for a yard dimid. of buckram to lyne the same Cappes w*i*thall	xv^{d}	
	ffor 2 : p*er*wick*es* at iij^{s} iiij^{d} the pece.	vj^{s} viij^{d}	
	ffor dimid. yard of cotton.	x^{d}	
	ffor dimid. thousand of great gold spangles . .	viij^{d}	
Wyerdrawers p*ar*celles	Thomas Leverett for one dozen dimid. of candlestick*es*	iiij^{s} vj^{d}	iiij^{li} xiij^{s} vj^{d}
	vj vicecandlestick*es* at xij^{d} the peece	vj^{s}	
	One hundreth of Claspes	iiij^{d}	
	v pulleys	iij^{s} iiij^{d}	
	xv hundreth of ij^{d} nayles	ij^{s} vj^{d}	
	Dimid. c of spykers	xvj^{d}	
	An hundreth of vj^{d} nayles.	vj^{d}	
	Three dozen of rownde plates	xviij^{s}	
	viij dozen of sockett*es*	xvj^{s}	
	ffor Repairing of two braunches	v^{s}	
	ffor xxx pound of wyer	xxx^{s}	
	ffor a great Lanterne	iiij^{s}	
	ffor botehire.	ij^{s}	
ffewell &c.	Will*iam* Humfrey for xlv sack*es* of coales at ix^{d} the sack . .		xxxiij^{s} ix^{d}
	Will*iam* Iurdane for xxvj sack*es* of coales after the same rate .		xix^{s} vj^{d}
	Will*iam* kynge for one thowsand of billett*es* — xiij^{s} iiij^{d} ffor an hundreth of ffaggott*es* — v^{s} iiij^{d}		xviij^{s} viij^{d}
Necessaries	Iohn Ogle for curlyng of heare	viij^{s} vj^{d}	ix^{s} ij^{d}
	ffor v cow tailes to curle	vj^{d}	
	ffor egges to try*m*me vyzerdes	ij^{d}	
	Will*iam* Lyzard for a whirrey to cary stuff to the Court and 4 men	iij^{s} viij^{d}	viij^{s} viij^{d}
	ffor lether for 2 : shieldes.	v^{s}	

10^{li}/6^{s}/

f° 5 v.

Necessaries

Thomas Wright for viij paire of gloves for Torchebearers at viij^{d} the paire	v^{s} iiij^{d}	vj^{s} ij^{d}
ffor mending of two lockes and setting them on againe	viij^{d}	
ffor openyng of a lock	ij^{d}	
Iohn Davys for money by him disbursed as foloweth		v^{li} xj^{s} x^{d}
ffor mosse	vj^{d}	
for a pound of threed of divers colo*urs*	iij^{s}	
for a dozen of round trenchers w*i*th a box for them	xij^{d}	
for a quyer of pap*er*	v^{d}	
for pynnes	ix^{d}	
for glue	ij^{d}	
for small tack*es*	ij^{d}	
for foure pasteboordes	xij^{d}	
for tape	x^{d}	
for a dozen of Childrens gloves	vj^{s}	
for pastpaper	iiij^{s}	
for dimid. pound of threede	xiiij^{d}	
for 9 : horsetayles and 35 : cowtailes	v^{s} xj^{d}	
for Cariadge of them	iij^{d}	
for pynnes	ij^{d}	
for broomes	ij^{d}	
for a pound dimid. of threed of sundry coloures at iij^{s} iiij^{d} the li.	v^{s}	
for browne paper	ij^{s} ij^{d}	
for a dozen of gloves	v^{s}	
for a quyer of paper	vj^{d}	
for heare to Iohn Ogle	ij^{s} vj^{d}	
for a q*uar*tern dimid. of tape	xvj^{d}	
for dimid. pound of coloured threede	xx^{d}	
for 4 : dozen of pasteboordes	xvj^{s}	
for two pound of white threede at iij^{s} viij^{d} the pound	vij^{s} iiij^{d}	
for two sheepe skynnes for flayles	viij^{d}	
for a q*uar*tern of black threede	vij^{d}	
for dimid. li. of red threede	xx^{d}	
for allom	iij^{d}	
for past	j^{d}	
for a quyer of paper	v^{d}	
for 4 : dozen of white buttons	iiij^{d}	
for dimid. pound of coloured threede	xvj^{d}	
for iij dozen of gloves	xvj^{s}	
for a dozen of gloves for Maskers	viij	
for drinke for players	vij^{d}	
for a Car to cary stuff for the Earle of Leicesters men	viij^{d}	

5^{li}/18/^{s}

f° 6 r.

ffor a Carr to cary stuff to the waterside on Christmas daie at night . . . xvj^{d}
for dimid. pound of coloured threede . . . . xv^{d}
for a Panyer . . . . xiiij^{d}
for a Calves skynne . . . . xiij^{d}
for dimid. pound of tape . . . . xxij^{d}
for Pomgranett*es* orenges and pipens . . . . iij^{s}
for bayes . . . . ij^{d}
for q*uar*tern of black threede . . . . vij^{d}
for black tape . . . . iiij^{d}
for 4 : dozen of poyntes . . . . x^{d}
for nailes . . . . ij^{d}
for candell*es* . . . . ij^{d}
for threede. . . . . ij^{d}
for buttons. . . . . ij^{d}
for a whirrey to Hampton Court . . . . . . ij^{s}
In all amounting vnto

Will*iam* Maye for holie and Ivie . . . . v^{s}

Rowland Allen for vj feltes for the Cenofalles headepeeces— v^{s}

The Mowldeman for a houndes heade mowlded for a Cenofall . . . ij^{s}

The Turno*ur* for a boxe for Myrre . . . . iiij^{d}

Wydow leafe for two dozen of russhes w*ith* vj^{d} for the Cariadge . . . v^{s} x^{d}

Iohn Davys for lynkes at sundrie nightes for cariadges of the fframes from the Revell*es* to the waterside and to and from the Court . . . xvj^{d}

Edward Buggyn gent*leman* for Ynke paper wexe quilles pindust Rewardes and other Necc*essar*ies . . . xx^{s}

Thom*as* Blagrave Esquyer for a Realme of wryting paper — viij^{s}
ffor two quyer of Royall paper . . . . ij^{s}

50^{s}/8^{d}/ Thomas Wright for drynking at Branford going to the Court and from the Court for the waggener and others . . . xiiij^{d}

f° 6 v.

Cariadges with horshier and ryding Charges.

Edward Buggyn gent*leman* for money by him disbursed as foloweth vid*elicet* — vij^{li} vij^{s} viij^{d}

ffor a barge to cary stuffe to the Court 26 : Decembr*is* for therle of warwick his mens plaie — xij^{s}

ffor 2 : Waggons 27 : Decembr*is* for the Cariadge of stuff for the L*ord* Howard*es* seru*a*unt*es* at xviij^{s} the waggon — xxxvj^{s}

ffor Cariadge by water of a paynted cloth and two frames for the Earle of Leicesters to the Court 28 : Decembr*is* — v^{s}

ffor one waggon 26° Decembr*is* to cary stuff to the Court for the Earle of Warwick his mens plaie — xviij^{s}

ffor a waggon to the Court two or three daies after (for that their plaie was deferred vntill the Sundaie folowing) to bring their stuff to the Revell*es* — x^{s}

ffor a barge to cary two fframes to the Court for the Children of windso*urs* plaie on Twelf daie — xj^{s}

ffor two Waggons to carie stuff for the Mask, and to carie the Children that shold have s*e*rved in the Maske and to carie some other stuffe to s*e*rve in the Children of Windso*urs* playe, 6° : Ianuarij — xxxvj^{s}

ffor a bote to bring certein stuff that came back from the Court concerning the Lightes for the hall 8° : Ianuar*ij* — xx^{d}

ffor a waggon to cary stuffe to Hampton Court for the L*ord* Chamb*er*lyn his mens plaie on Candlemas daie — xviij^{s}

Thomas Blagrave Esquyer for money by him disbursed as foloweth vid*elicet*

ffor the hier of a horse and a man from London to Bedwyn for that Mr Blagrave was sent for vpon my L*ord* Chamb*er*leyn his Co*m*maundement going and retorning by the space of 4 : daies and at xx^{d} the daie for the horsehier, and for his horsemeate and his owne meate at ij^{s} the daie and night w*ith* vj^{d} for horshowinge being the 4 : 5 : 6 : and 7 : of November [1576] — xv^{s} ij^{d}

7^{li}/7^{s}/8^{d}/

f° 7 r.

Tewsdaie[18] Wedensdaie[19] Thursdaie[20] and ffrydaye[21] of December for the hier of 3 : horses at xx^{d} the daie a peece from London to Hampton Court and tarying there about conference for the Charges in the office and and retorning that while — xx^{s} and for the hier of one horse to Hampton Court and back againe to London 2 : daies at xviij^{d} the daie — iij^{s} about the warrant and order for the Prest. And for ye meate of those horses that tyme at xij^{d} daie and night a horse — xiiij^{s}	xxxvij^{s}	
ffor the hier of a horse from London to Hampton Court the xxiiijth of December for the warrant and carying a note to the Chamberleyn of alteracion of the plaies and retornyng on the morow at xx^{d} the daie — iij^{s} iiij^{d} and for horsemeate — ij^{s} in all	v^{s} iiij^{d}	
ffor the hier of 3 : horses from London to Hampton Court on St Iohns daie and retorne on the morowe to London being the 27 : and 28 : of December 1576 at xx^{d} the daie apece — x^{s} and for their meate at xij^{d} daie and night a pece for those two daies — vj^{s}	xvj^{s}	viij^{li} iij^{s} vj^{d}
ffor the hier of a horse the xxixth of December for 4 : daies last before at xx^{d} the daie — vj^{s} viij^{d} the same horses meate those foure daies — iiij^{s} in all	x^{s} viij^{d}	
ffor the hier of a horse the 29 : of December for 2 : daies last before at xx^{d} the daie, to the Court and back for the plaie of Powles on Newyeres daie — iij^{s} iiij^{d} and the horsemeate — ij^{s}	v^{s} iiij^{d}	
ffor the hier of a horse to the Court the third of Ianuarie 1576 : and for two daies last before with garmentes for a Maske to my Lord Chamberlyn for 3 : daies at xx^{d} the daie — v^{s}, and for the horsemeate — iij^{s} at xij^{d} the daie	viij^{s}	

8^{li}/3^{s}/6^{d}/

f° 7 v.

	ffor the hyer of a horse for 4 : daies viz. the 5 : 6 : 7 : and 8 : daies of Ianuarie at xx^d the daie — vj^s viij^d and his meate for that tyme — iiij^s	x^s viij^d
	ffor the hyer of 3 : horses the 6 : of Ianua*rie* for 3 : daies viz. the 6 : 7 : and 8 : of Ianuarie at xx^d the daie — xv^s & their meate — ix^s	xxiiij^s
	ffor Cariadge of the new frames to Paules Wharf by Carr the 4 : of Ian*uarie*	xij^d
	ffor the hier of 3 : horses for 2 : daies viz. the 2 : and 3 : of ffebruarie at xviij^d the daie a horse from London to hampton Court — ix^s and for their meate — vj^s	xv^s
	ffor the Cariadge of all the fframes & stuff from hampto*n* Court to london by barge : 3° : ffebruar*ij*	xiij^{s}iiij^d
	ffor Cariadge of the same from the water side to St Iohns	ij^s
	Thomas Tyler for the Cariadge of stuff for fferrant*es* playe, and furnyture for the lightes to Hampton Court on Twelf daie by Tilt bote	v^s
Rewardes	To Nich*ol*as Newdigate gent*leman* for his paynes in hearing and trayninge of the boyes[7] that should have spoken the speeches in the Mask, and for their Charges and Cariadge back againe	xliij^s viij^d
	To those boyes[7] viz. to everie one of them for their paynes — ij^s vj^d	xvij^s vj^d
	To the Tayl*ours* in Reward to drinke because they should not go from their woorke	xij^d
	To Stafferton the 4 : of Ianuar*ie*, [1576] for his botehire to and fro Westm*inster*	xij^d
	To the Paynters in Reward to keepe their woorke that night–	xij^d
	To Groome of the Chamber comyng with a letter from my L*ord* Treasaur*our* from the Court in Reward on Christmas even at night the 24 : of December 1576	ij^s
	To Mr Tayl*ours* man for the doble Quyttaunce the 25 : of December 1576	xij^d
	To Mr Giles his man for bringing vyzerdes to the Office twise in Reward	vj^d

3^{li}/12^s/8^d/ * suma p*artialis*

f° 8 r.

To Iohn kelsey for vsing of his Dro*m*me in the Duttons plaie } ij^{s} vj^{d}

ffor openyng the Chamber dore of the Revell*es* house at Hampton Court the 5 : of Ianuar*ie* } vj^{d}

To Iohn Ragats for divers and sundrie *tra*nscriptes and billes of deliverie by him written and for other paynes by him taken in deliverie & Induccion of p*ar*cell*es* of stuff caried out and brought into the office at sundrie tymes to him in Reward } xiij^{s} iiij^{d}

16^{s}/4^{d}/

S*um*ma of all the **Emptions Prouisions Cariadges** Rewardes and other Charges beside the wages aforesaid, for Christm*as*, Newyeres tide, Twelftide and Candlemas 1576 : Annoq*ue* Regni Regine Eliz*abeth* xix° } iiij^{xx} xiiij^{li} xiiij^{s} ix^{d}

S*um*ma of all the **Wages** together w*i*th the **Emptions Prouisions Cariadges** Rewardes and other Charges for Christm*as* Newyeres tide Twelftide and Candlemas, *Anno*q*ue* r*egni* r*egine* p*redicte* xix°. } clxxij^{li} ij^{s} ix^{d}

* T Blagrave
* Edwarde Buggin
* walter fysshe

f° 8 v.

Shrovetide Anno *Regni Regine* Elizabeth predic*te* — **xix° : 1576 :**

Preparacions made : and **workes** don **Betw[eene** the] xijth of ffebruarie 1576 : Anno Regni Regine Elizabeth xix° p[redicto at] w*hi*ch tyme the woorkes began for p*ro*vidinge, preparing, hearing, a[ptly] furnyshinge and setting foorth of divers playes or showes of histor[ies] and other Inven*ci*ons and Devyces folowinge. **And** the xxjth of the same moneth 1576. Anno R*egni* Reg*in*e xix° predi*cto*, at w*hi*ch tyme the woorkes and attendaunces did ende, and the garmentes, vestures, Properties and other furnyture, w*i*th the stuffe store and other Implementes of the said Office, were suted put in order, laid vp, and safebestowed for the view and preserva*ci*on thereof. The Charges whereof together w*i*th all the Emptions and Provisions of stuff and Necce*ssar*ies Incident w*i*th the Cariadges and all other expences for in and about the same particulerlie ensue

vid*elicet*

Histories and Inven*ci*ons showen w*i*thin the tyme aforesaid viz. — **iij** : viz.

The Historie of the Solitarie knight showen at whitehall on Shrovesundaie at night, enacted by the L*ord* Howardes *seruauntes*

The Irisshe Knyght showen at whitehall on Shrovemundaie at night enacted by the Earle of warwick his *seruauntes*.

The historye of Titus and Gisippus showen at whitehall on Shrovetuysdaie at night, enacted by the Children of Pawles.

Maskes — j viz.

A longe Maske [6] of murrey satten crossed all over w*i*th silver lace w*i*th sleves of gold tyncell, w*i*th headepeeces full of pipes of white silver lawne laid bias very rich, prepared for Twelf night, w*i*th a device of 7 : speeches framed correspondent to the daie. Their Torchebearers vj : had gownes of crymsen Damask, and headepeeces new furnished, showen on Shrovetuysdaie night, w*i*thout anie speeche.

Taylours & others working and attending the premiss*es* the first at xxd the daie and asmuch for the night the residew at xijd vid*elicet*

	Daies	**Nightes**	**Wages**
Thomas Clatterbuck	8	6	xxiijs iiijd
Thomas wright sen*ior*	8	6	xiiijs
David ffludd	8	6	xiiijs
Robert Smyth	8	6	xiiijs
Will*iam* Lumley	8	6	xiiijs
Iohn Stagar	8	6	xiiijs
Iohn ffludde	7	4	xjs
George wright	7	2	ixs
George warton	7	3	xs.

f° 9 r.

		Daies	Nightes	Wages
	Iohn Cleyton	7	4	xj^{s}
	Iohn fflaunsham	7	4	xj^{s}
	William woode	3	2	v^{s}
	Richard wardeman	2	1	iij^{s}
7^{li}/13^{s}/4^{d}/				
The Porter and other Attendauntes at xij^{d} the daie ech one and asmuch for the night viz.	Iohn Dawncye.	8	6	xiiij^{s}
	Iohn Drawater.	8	6	xiiij^{s}
	Iohn Davis	8	6	xiiij^{s}
	Thomas Lambe	8	4	xij^{s}
54^{s}/				
Paynters and others at sundrie rates viz.	William Lyzard at ij^{s}	7	5	xxiiij^{s}
	Lewys Lyzard at xx^{d}	6	3	xv^{s}
	Thomas Tyler senior at xviij^{d}	6	3	xiij^{s} vj^{d}
	Robert Peake at xviij^{d}	3	3	ix^{s}
	Iohn Rows at xviij^{d}	3	3	ix^{s}
	Richard Gilmond at xvj^{d}	2	2	v^{s} iiij^{d}
	Robert Cotes at xvj^{d}.	6	5	xiiij^{s} viij^{d}
	Iohn Lymbie at xij^{d}	6	5	xj^{s}
5^{li}/18^{d}/				
Haberdasshers and Propertymakers at sundrie rates viz.	Iohn ffarryngton at xvj^{d}	8	5	xvij^{s} iiij^{d}
	Iohn Ogle at xvj^{d}.	2	0	ij^{s} viij^{d}
	Richard Moorer at xvj^{d}	3	0	iiij^{s}
	Adam Cowper at xvj^{d}	1	0	xvj^{d}
	Thomas Stronge at 12^{d}.	8	6	xiiij^{s}
39^{s}/4^{d}/				
Wyerdrawers at sundrie rates viz.	Thomas Leverett at xx^{d}.	5	1	x^{s}
	Edmunde Byrchall at xviij^{d}	4	1	vij^{s} vj^{d}
	Simon Powle at xvj^{d}	4	1	vj^{s} viij^{d}
24^{s}/2^{d}/				

f° 9 v.

		Daies	Nightes	[Wages]
Carvers Ioyners and Propertymakers at sundrie Rates	Richard Rowland at ij^{s} the daie .	7 . .	. 2 . .	[xviij^{s}]
	Sebastian vycars at xvj^{d} . . .	4 . .	. I . .	[vj^{s} viij^{d}]
	David woode at xvj^{d}.	3 . .	. 2 . .	[vj^{s} viij^{d}]
	Thom*as* Booreman at xij^{d}. . .	8 . .	. 6 . .	x[iij^{s}]
	Thom*as* Tyler Iun*ior* at the like.	4 . .	. I . .	v^{s}
l^{s}/4^{d}/				
Carpenters at xvj^{d} the daie viz.	Will*iam* Barker at xvj^{d}	7 . .	. 2 . .	xij^{s}
	Edward ffurres at xvj^{d}	8 . .	. 3 . .	xiiij^{s} viij^{d}
	Iohn Lawrence at the like. . .	I . .	. I . .	ij^{s} viij^{d}
29^{s}/4^{d}/				
Th'offycers	The M*aster* at iiij^{s} the daie . .	10 . .	. 6 . .	lxiiij^{s}
	The Clerk Comptroller at ij^{s} . .	10 . .	. 6 . .	xxxij^{s}
	The Clerke at ij^{s}	10 . .	. 6 . .	xxxij^{s}
	The Yeoman at ij^{s}	10 . .	. 6 . .	xxxij^{s}
8^{li}/				

S*um*m*a* of all the **Wages** due in this Office for workmanship and attendaunces done therein, and vpon the affaires thereof for **Shrovetide** ending the xxjth daie of ffebruarie 1576 : Annoq*ue* R*egni* R*egi*ne Elizabeth xix^{o}. } xxx^{li} xij^{s}

* T Blagrave
* Edwarde Buggin
* walter fysshe

f° 10 r.

Emptions Prouisions & Cariadges w*it*h Reward*es* and other Charges Incident.

[The M]ercer — **Will*iam* Roe** for silkes by him delivered into thoffice viz. 18:^{o} ffebruar*ij* one ell dimid. of crymsen Taffita at xiiij^{s} the ell — xxj^{s} and 19°: ffebruarij one peece of yelow sarcenett cont*eigning* 16 : elles and iij q*uar*ters at vj^{s} thell — v^{li} vj^{d} } vj^{li} xviij^{d}

[T]he lynnen drap*er* — **Richard Busshe** for 20 : elles of Canvas 12°: die ffebruar*ij*, at xij^{d} the ell } xx^{s}

The vpholster — **Iohn Okes** for one peece of grene buckram by him delivered into the Office — iiij^{s} vj^{d} and 18°: ffebruar*ij* for one pece of red buckram — iiij^{s} and the same daie a close stoole w*it*h a large tynne panne — x^{s} In all } xviij^{s} vj^{d}

Paynters parcelles. — **William Lyzard** for coloures and necc*essar*ies folowing } iiij^{li} xiij^{d}

Size	v^{s}
Black v lb at xij^{d} the li.	v^{s}
White 30: li. at iij^{d} the li.	vij^{s} vj^{d}
Smalt ij li. at iiij^{s} the li.	viij^{s}
Masticott li.	iij^{s} iiij^{d}
Red j li.	viij^{d}
Browne j li.	xviij^{d}
Size	vj^{s}
Sineper j li.	ij^{s}
Sape a q*uar*tern	x^{d}
Bysse iij oz.	iij^{s}
Vermelyon iiij oz.	ij^{s}
Vert j li.	iiij^{s} viij^{d}
Pottes for coloures	x^{d}
White xxx li. at iij^{d} the li.	vij^{s} vj^{d}
Copper colo*ur*	iiij^{s}
Arsidew iij li. for the great braunches at iij^{s} vj^{d} the li.	x^{s} vj^{d}
Arsidew ij li. dimid. for the xxiiij small lightes w*it*h v: pendentes to everie light at iij^{s} vj^{d} the li.	viij^{s} ix^{d}

12^{li}/13^{d}/

f° 10 v.

Paynters *parcelles* and other neccessaries occupied at the Court	**Lewis Lyzard** for Size	iiij^{d}	iiij^{s} j^{d}
	White ij li.	vj^{d}	
	Red	vj^{d}	
	Rosett	v^{d}	
	Black	iiij^{d}	
	Packthreede	iiij^{d}	
	Browne threede	iiij^{d}	
	A ffier panne	iiij^{d}	
	Coales	vj^{d}	
	Botehier	vj^{d}	
	In all		
Propertymakers *parcelles*	Richard Rowland for plaister ef Parrys	iij^{s}	vj^{s} ij^{d}
	fflower to make paste	vj^{d}	
	Browne paper	vj^{d}	
	Ragges to mowlde withall	vj^{d}	
	Two penie nailes CC	iiij^{d}	
	Clay to mowlde withall	xij^{d}	
	Allom j li.	iiij^{d}	
	In all		
Lightes and other neccessaries	Barnard ffabyan :3: dozen of candelles at iiij^{s} the dozen	xij^{s}	xxviij^{s} iiij^{d}
	Two dozen of lynkes at iiij^{s} the dozen	viij^{s}	
	Small corde 4: peeces at vj^{d} ye peece	ij^{s}	
	Packthreede j li.	xij^{d}	
	Great cord 4 : peeces at xvj^{d} the pece	v^{s} iiij^{d}	
Wyerdrawers *parcelles*	Thomas Leverett for the furnishing of ix : small braunches with rownde plates and wyer	xxiiij^{s}	ij^{li} x^{s} v^{d}
	ffor the furnishing of two great braunches with wyer and plate	xxvj^{s} viij^{d}	
	Ten pound of wyer for the Coming vp of the small lightes at xij^{d} the li.	x^{s}	
	ffoure quilting needles at iij^{d} the pece	xij^{d}	
	ffoure bodkyns at ij^{d} the pece	viij^{d}	
	Three dartes heades at viij^{d} the pece	ij^{s}	
	half a hundreth of spikers	xvj^{d}	
	Two penie nailes D	x^{d}	
	Threepenie nailes j C	iij^{d}	
	Two Ropes at xvj^{d} the pece	ij^{s} viij^{d}	
	ffor a Carr to the Court to carie stuff for lightes	xij^{d}	

5^{li}/9^{s}/ f° 11 r$^{•}$

[**Boordes** qu]arters [ ]es	Rowland Robynson for xj single *quarters* at iij^{d} the pece	ij^{s} ix^{d}	xxvj^{s} viij^{d}
	Doble *quarters* five at vj^{d} the peece.	ij^{s} vj^{d}	
	Elme boorde one hundreth.	vij^{s}	
	Seeling boorde xxxvj foote	ij^{s} vj^{d}	
	Doble x^{d} nailes j c	xvj^{d}	
	Sixepenie ix c dimid.	iiij^{s} ix^{d}.	
	Threepenie nailes iij c	ix^{d}	
	Two penie nailes dimid. thowsand	viij^{d}	
	Doble englishe x^{d} nailes j c.	xx^{d}	
	Single x^{d} nailes j c	x^{d}	
	v^{d} nailes j c	v^{d}	
	Tack*es* c c c	vj^{d}	
	ffor Cariadge of boordes and *quarters* at sundrie tymes	xij^{d}	
	In all to the said R : Robynson		
The Haberdasher	Richard Moorer for the making of vj : Senat*ours* Cappes of Crymsen Taffita	vj^{s}	xij^{s}
	ffor the making of a large ffrenche Cappe of blue tyncell sarcenett	xij^{d}	
The Armorer	Iohn Edwyn for the lone of certeine Armour *with* a base and Targett*es* *which* the *Lord* Howardes *seruauntes* vsed in their plaie of the Solytarye knyght	vij^{s}	viij^{s}
	ffor Cariadge of the same	xij^{d}	
Necessaries	Richard Rowland for one dozen of small paste-boorde	ij^{s}	ij^{s} iiij^{d}
	for ij c of ij^{d} nailes	iiij^{d}	
	Iohn Drawater for money by him disbursed as foloweth viz.		vj^{d}
	ffor two glasse voyall*es* for the *Lord* Howard*es* *seruauntes* on Shrovesunday	ij^{d}	
	ffor a lyne to draw a curteyne. . . . . . , .	iiij^{d}	
	Richard Moorer for vj paire of syzars at vj^{d} the paire for the clipping of arsidew : 18° : ffebruar*ij*		iij^{s}

47^{s}/6^{d}/

f° 11 v.

ffewell &c. Robert Collyer for 3o : sack*es* of coales at ix^{d} the sack the 14 :th of ffebruarie } xxij^{s}

Necessaries Iohn Davys for money by him disbursed as foloweth

ffor a whirrey to whitehall	xij^{d}
ffor dimid. li. of grene threede.	xx^{d}
ffor a quyer of paper	vj^{d}
ffor a dozen of small pasteboord	ij^{s}
ffor vj Lambes skynnes	ij^{s}
ffor dimid. q*uar*tern of black threede	iiij^{d}
ffor white threede	vj^{d}
ffor Moores Dartes and Irishe Dartes	ij^{s}
ffor pynnes	ij^{d}
ffor a q*uar*tern of tape	x^{d}
ffor Ynckle	iij^{d}
ffor two dozen of small pastboorde	iiij^{s}
ffor dimid. pound of coloured threede	xx^{d}
ffor holy and Ivie	ij^{s}
ffor egges	j^{d}
ffor two formes for the Senat*ours* in the historie of Titus and Gisippus	vj^{s}
ffor the Cariadge of the same	ij^{d}
ffor the Cariadge of the Maske from St Iohns to the Courte	xij^{d}
ffor pynnes	vj^{d}
ffor tape	iiij^{d}
ffor a dozen of Childrens gloves	v^{s}
ffor vj paire of gloves for Maskers	iiij^{s}
ffor vj paire of gloves for Torchebearers . . .	ij^{s} ij^{d}
ffor the mending and spangling of 4 : fethers. .	viij^{d}
ffor breade w*hi*ch was vsed in the Historie of the Solitarye knight	j^{d}
ffor a Car from the Revell*es* to the waterside to cary stuff for the L*ord* Howard*es* seru*auntes*	xij^{d}
ffor a Carr to cary stuff for the Erle of Warwick his men	xij^{d}
ffor two Carres to Cary stuff for the Mask and for the Children of Powles from the Courte to St Iohns	iiij^{s}

In all to the said Iohn Davis } xliiij^{s} xj^{d}

3^{li}/7^{s}/5^{d}/ f° 12 r.

[**Cariadge**]**s**	Iohn Drawater for mony by him disbursed as foloweth **viz.**	
	ffor the Cariadge of the Earle of Warwick his mens stuffe from the Revell*es* to whitehall and back againe to recyte before my L*ord* Chamb*er*leyn — ij^{s}	
	ffor the hier of a barge the 14 : of ffebr*uarie* for the Cariadge of the Earle of warwick his men and stuff for them to the Court and back againe for the 14 : and 16 : of ffebruar*ie* for recytall of playes, and the 17 : and 18 : for the playes before ye Quene — xxij^{s}	xxiiij^{s} x^{d}
	ffor the Cariadge of the partes of ye well counterfeit from the Bell in gracious strete to St Iohns to be p*er*formed for the play of Cutwell — x^{d}	
Botehire	Thomas Blagrave Esquyer for botehire to the Court and from the Court at sundrie tymes	v^{s} iiij^{d}
Neccess*ar*ies	ffor the repayringe of the nether Roome of the Clerk*es* Office beside next the yard as by the bill of the p*ar*cell*es* appeereth	xj^{s} vj^{d}
	The Clerke for his grene Cloth, and pap*er*, Inke, Count*ers* Deskes, standishes and Tooles, for the making, compiling and cons*er*vinge of the Billes, Plott*es*, Patternes, and Modell*es* &c. for and concerninge this Office	lxvj^{s} viij^{d}
Rewardes	To the Paynters and other woorkemen for victuall*es* because they shold not go from their woork in Reward — ij^{s} and to the Porters at the gate attending at sundrie tymes — xviij^{d}	iij^{s} vj^{d}
5^{li}/11^{s}/10^{d}/	ffor myne owne charges co*m*ming from Bedwyn the 13 : of November 1576 : vp to the Court and from thence to London and there Remayninge till the workes began being the xxxjth of December viz. by the space of 5 : wekes and 3 : daies w*hi*ch everie waie standes me in	

S*umma* of all the **Emptions provisions Cariadges** Rewardes and Charges beside wages for **Shrovetide** vid*elicet* from the xijth of ffebruarie 1576 vntill the xxjth of ffebruarie 1576 : Anno R*egni* R*egi*ne Eliz*abeth* predi*cte* **xix**^{o} — **xxviij^{li} xvj^{s} x^{d}**

* T Blagrave
* Edwarde Buggin
* walter fysshe

S*umma* of all the whole woorkes for Shrovetide 1576 : *Anno regni regine predicte* pred*icto* xix^{o} — lix^{li} viij^{s} x^{d}

f^{o} **12 v.**

The Totallis **Summ**a **of this whole Booke** vid*elicet* **[from the]** xjth of 1575 March Anno *Regni* *Reg*ine Elizabeth xviijuo. **vntill** the xxjth of [ffebruarie 1576] Annoq*ue* *Regni* *Reg*ine Elizabeth predict*e* **xixo** hereafter ensueth.

Ayring*es* from the xjth of March 1575 vntill the **xx**th of December 1576 : A*nno* *Regni* *Reg*ine Eli-*zabeth* **xixo**	**Wages** of	**Artificers** . . . . vjli xiijs iiijd	xvjli xiijs iiijd	xvijli xvs xd	ccxlixli vijs vd
		Officers. xli			
	Emptions Provisions &c. . , ...		xxijs vjd		
Christm*as* Newyeres tide Twelftide and Candlem*as* viz. from the xxth of December 1576 : vntill the iiijth of ffebrua-*rie* 1576 : A*nno* *Regni* *Reg*ine Elizab*e*th **xixo**	**Wages** of	**Artificers** . . . . lviijli xviijs	lxxvijli viijs	clxxijli ijs ixd	
		Officers. . . . . . xviijli xs			
	Emptions Provisions &c.		iiijxx xiiijli xiiijs ixd		
Shrovetide viz. from the xijth day of ffebruar*ie* 1576 : vntill the xxjth of ffebruar*ie* 1576 : *Anno* *regni* *regine* Eliza*b*eth xixo	**Wages** of	**Artificers** . . . . xxijli xijs	xxxli xijs	lixli viijs xd	
		Officers. . . . . . viijli.			
	Emptions Provisions &c.		xxviijli xvjs xd		

Iohn Drawater for money by him disbursed aswell about the Charges of makinge th'accomptes of the Audit*our* of the prestes, and Declarac*ion* of the same before my *Lord* *Treasur*er and *Sir* walter mildmay as also for the Charges of the Q*ue*enes warrant, the privie seale, direcc*ion* of the payment of the money, and Receipt of the same } viijli xs.

[S] *umm*a **tot***a***lis** of the whole **Wages Emptions Prouisions Cariadges** Rewardes and other Charges for the severall tymes aforesaid } **cclvijli xvijs vd**

* T Blagrave

fo 13 r.

* The Book of the Revelles Anno xix^{no}

* Anno xix^{no}

f° 14 v.

From 21 February 1576-7 to 14 February 1577-8

Record Office. Imprest Certificate Books (Pells), vol. 2 [fol. 47 v.]

Inter Exit*us* Ric*ard*i Stonley vnius Numerator*um* Recept*e* Scaccar*i*j D*omi*ne Regine de Termi*no* Mich*ael*is anno xx^{mo} regni Regine Eliz*abethe* finiente et xxj^{mo} incipiente inter al*ia* continet*ur* vt sequit*ur*. viz.

Denar*ij* prestit*i* extra Recept*am* Scaccar*i*j pro causis infrascript*is* Termi*no* suprad*icto*

Thome Blagrave ar*migero* Capital*i* Officiar*io* Revellor*um* D*omi*ne Regine tam — ccxliiij^{li} ix^{s}. j^{d}. ob. in plena*m* exoneraci*on*em et soluci*on*em Debitor*um* D*omi*ne Regine in d*ict*o officio crescenc*ium* inter xxj^{um} diem ffebruarij 1576 et xiiij^{tum} diem eiusdem mensis ffebr*uarij* 1577. Quam — cc^{li} in prestit*o* p*er* ips*um* soluend*a* et exponend*a* in et circa onera d*ict*e D*omi*ne Regine in officio pred*icto* fiend*a* anno 1578 p*er* Bre*u*e sub priuato Sigillo dat*um* xxx^{mo} die Decembr*is* anno xxj^{mo} regni Regine anted*ict*e in toto

iiij^{c} xliiij^{li}. ix^{s}. j^{d} ob.

Which So*mm*e of fower hundred fortie and fower poundes nyne shilling*es* and one penny halfepenny, is all the money that hath bene paied to the saide Office of the Revelles from the aforesaide xiiijth Day of ffebruarie 1577 vntill this viijth Day of November 1579.

From 14 February 1577-8 to 1 November 1579.

viz.

Record Office. Audit Office. Accounts Various. Bd. 1213. Revels. N° 6.

Revell*es*. 1578. Anno Regni
Regine Elizabethe. **xxi**^{o} the Lidgerd
p*ar*ticuler Booke of all the Chardg*es*
Rising and growing w*i*thin the
said office **Betwene**
the xiiijth of ffebruarie
1577. And the vjth
of march . 1578 .
A*nno* Regni R*eg*ine Eliz*abethe*
pred*icte*
viz..

Title-page r.

Betwene the xiiijth of ffebruarie. 1577. Anno regni Regine Elizabeth **xx^{mo}. And** the xxth of december .1578. Anno regni Regine Elizabeth xxj^{o}. The chardges of this office grewe by meanes of Ayreing Repairing p*er*vsing amending brushing, Spunging Rubbing, wiping, Sweeping, making cleane Putting in order, folding laying vpp, and safe bestowing of the garment*es* vestures apparrell, disguysing*es* prop*er*ties and furnyture of the same from tyme to tyme (w*i*thin those monethes) as the necessitie therof from tyme to tyme Required to keepe the same in Readines for service, which ells would be mowldie, mustie, motheaten, and Rotten by meanes of the dancknes of the howse and wante of convenient presses And plac*es* requisite/ The p*ar*ties whoe co*mm*only attend the said office for the said purpose w*i*th their severall names Allowed for this tyme p*ar*ticulerly hereafter ensueth. viz.

Taylors and others working & attending the p*re*misses at the officers comaundm*ent* the first at xx^{d} the daie and the rest at xij^{d} as in form*er* p*re*sident*es*

	Daies	
Thomas Clatterbooke	24	xl^{s}.
Thomas Wrighte	24	xxiiij^{s}.
Will*iam* Tyldesley	24	xxiiij^{s}
Thomas Stronge	24	xviiij^{s}
Iohn Drawater	24	xxiiij^{s}
Iohn Davyes	24	xxiiij^{s}
Iohn Dawncey	24	xxiiij^{s}

The officers.

The m*aster* at iiij^{s} the daie	24	iiij^{li}xvj^{s}
The clerk comptroller at ij^{s} the daie	24	xlviij^{s}
The clerk at ij^{s} the daie	24	xlviij^{s}
The yoman at ij^{s} the daie.	24	xlviij^{s}

ffewell and other necessaries.

Iohn Lucas for ffewell and other necessaries by him bought provided and brought into the office and vsed at sondrey tymes in the said Ayring*es* amending &c. w*i*thin the tyme aforesaid. viz.

Coales xxx. sackes	xxij^{s} vj^{d}	lviij^{s} viij^{d}.
Browne thred di. li.	xiiij^{d}.	
white thred [2s. 10 d.] one pound black thred one [2s. 4 d.] li.	v^{s}. ij^{d}.	
Cullered thred .3. q*uar*ters of A pounde	ij^{s} viij^{d}.	
Tape one pound.	iij^{s} viij^{d}.	
Brushes iiij [8s.]. Rubbing brushes. iij [xd.].	viij^{s} x^{d}	
whitebrushes Longe and shorte for Cobwebbes .4.	ij^{s}.	
Billett*es* one thowsand	xij^{s}viij^{d}.	

* Ed: Tyllney S*umma* **totalis** of all the whole Ayring*es* w*i*thin the tyme aforesaid } xxiiij^{li} ij^{s} viij^{d}.

* Edwarde Buggyn * T Blagrave
* walter fysshe

f° 1 r.

Christmas Newyeares tide **Twelftide** and the sonday folowing. *Anno Regni Regine* Elizabethe pred*icte* xxjmo. 1578.

The Chardges of those tymes. viz. **Betwene** the xxth of December 1578. Anno regni Regine Elizabeth p*redicte* xxjo, at w*hi*ch tymes the work*es* beganne for the providing preparing hearing devising furnishing and setting forth of diu*er*se plaies or showes of histories and other speciall Invenc*i*ons devises and showes for that tyme incidente **And** the xvth of Ianuarie. in the said xxjth yeare of her ma*iesties* Raigne at w*hi*ch tyme the work*es* and attendaunc*es* did end. Together w*i*th all themptions, provisions of stuffe, and necessaries, caryag*es* and other incident*es* bought provided done and attended by diu*er*se p*er*sons whose severall names rat*es* and wag*es* w*i*th their Reward*es* and allowaunc*es* doe p*ar*ticulerly in their apte plac*es* ensue.

Histories and Invenc*i*ons shewen w*i*thin the tyme aforesaid vj. viz.

An Inventyon or playe of the three Systers of Mantua shewen at Richmond on St Stephens daie at night enacted by thearle of warwick his s*er*vaunt*es*) furnished in this office w*i*th sondrey thinges as was requisite for the same.

The historie of shewen at Richmond on St Iohns daie at night enacted by the children of the Quenes ma*iesties* chappell furnished in this office w*i*th verie manie thing*es* aptly fitted for the same.

An history of the creweltie of A Stepmother shewen at Richmond on Innocent*es* daie at night enacted by the Lord Chamberlaynes s*er*vaunt*es* furnished in this office w*i*th sondrey thing*es*.

A Morrall of the marryage of Mynde and Measure shewen at Richmond on the sondaie next after Newe yeares daie enacted by the children of Pawles furnished somthing*es* in this office.

A pastorell or historie of A Greeke maide shewen at Richmond on the sondaie next after Newe yeares daie enacted by the Earle of Leicester his servaunt*es* furnished w*i*th some thing*es* in this office.

The historie of the Rape of the second Helene shewen at Richmond on Twelf daie at night well furnished in this office w*i*th manie thing*es* for them.

A Maske of Amasones in all Armore compleate p*ar*cell gilte gilded w*i*thin this office w*i*th Counterfett Murryons silvered ou*er* and p*ar*cell guylte (besides their head peec*es* belonging to their Armoure) and A creste on the toppe of every .6. of them having longe heare hanging downe behind them, their kirtles were of Crymson cloth of gold being indented at the skirte and Laied w*i*th silver Lace and frindge w*i*th pendaunt*es* of golde Tassells gold knobbes and set on w*i*th Broches of golde plated vppon the skirte ~~w*i*th~~ plates of silver lawne w*i*th tassells of gold Laid vnder belowe in steed of petticot*es* w*i*th white silver rich tincle fringed w*i*th golde fringe Buskins of oringe cullor velvet Antick ffawcheons and shield*es* w*i*th A devise painted theron and Iavelinge*s*

fo 2 r.

Maskes shewen before her ma*ies*tie the ffrench Imbassado*ur* being p*rese*nte the sonday night after Twelfdaie whereof one was.

ij. in their hand*es* one w*i*th A speach to the Quenes ma*ies*tie delivering A Table w*i*th writing*es* vnto her highnes comyng in w*i*th musitions playing on Cornett*es* apparrelled in longe white taffeta sarcenett garment*es* torche bearers w*i*th the troocheman wearing longe gownes of white taffeta w*i*th sleaves of the same and vppon them had longe crymson taffeta gownes w*i*thout sleaves Indented at the skirte and frindged Laced and tasselled w*i*th silver, and gold tucked vpp w*i*th the girding almoste to the knee bowes in their hand*es* and quivers of Arrowes at their girdles head peec*es* of gold Lawne and woemens heare wrethed verie faire and after the Amasons had dawnced w*i*th Lord*es* in her ma*iesties* presence in came.

An other Maske of knight*es* all likewise in Armoure compleate p*ar*cell guilte also guilte w*i*thin this office w*i*th like counterfett Murryons vppon their head*es* silvered and p*ar*cell guylte w*i*th plomes of ffeathers in the toppes of every of them. w*i*th bases of Rich gold Tyncell frindged w*i*th gold frindge garded w*i*th riche purple silver Tyncell Lardge Bawdrick*es* about their neck*es* of black gold Tyncell having truncheons in their hand*es* guylte and guylded sheild*es* w*i*th A posey written on every of them their showes of gold Lawne tyncell and co*m*myng in w*i*th one before them. w*i*th A speach vnto her highnes and delivering A table written their torch bearers being Rutters apparrelled. in greene satten Ierkines panned Laid w*i*th silver Laice and drawne owte w*i*th Tincell sarcenet their hose being verie Longe paned of rased velvet ground yealowe and rasing greene likewise Laid w*i*th silver Lace and drawne owte w*i*th tincell sarcenett, their hatt*es* of crymson silk and sylver thro*m*med and wreythed band*es* w*i*th ffeathers the Amasons and the Knight*es* after the Knightes had dawnced A while w*i*th Ladies before her ma*ies*tie did then in her ma*iesties* p*re*sence fight at Barriars.

Taylors and others attendaunt*es* working and Attending the p*re*misses the first at xx^d the daie and as much the night and the reste at xij^d

	Dayes	**Nightes**			
Thomas Clatterbooke. . . .	26 . .	3. dobble	11. .5. single.		lxj^s. viij^d.
Thomas Wrighte	26 . .	3. dobble.	11. 5. single.		xxxvij^s
Willyam Tyldesley. . . .	26 . .	3. dobble.	11. .5. single		xxxvij^s.
Edward Griffith.	26 . .	.3. dobble	11. .5. single		xxxvij^s.
Thom*as* Boreman	26 . .	3. dobble	11. 5. single		xxxvij^s.
Thomas Stronge	26 . .	3. dobble	11. 5. single.		xxxvij^s
Will*iam* Snewde	26 . .	3. doble.	11. .5. single.		xxxvij^s
Beniamyn Edward. . . .	26 . .	3. doble.	11. 5 single.		xxxvij^s.
Thom*as* Lambe	10 . .	2. doble.	4. . . .		xiiij^s.
George Wrighte.	10 . .	2. doble.	4. . . .		xiiij^s.
Iohn Davyes	26 . .	3. doble.	11. .5. single		xxxvij^s.
Iohn fflawncer	4 . .	2. doble	5. 1. single		ix^s
Iohn Clayton.	7 . .	2. doble	5 1. single		xij^s.
Iohn Tipsley.	13 . .	2. doble.	6. 2. single		xix^s
David Lloid. . . , ...	26 . .	3. doble	11 5 single		xxxvij^s

f° 2 v

	Dayes.		Nyghtes		
Iohn Harris	6	2 doble	5	1. single	xj^{s}
Iohn Pynnynge	2	1 doble	2		iiij^{s}
Cutbert Wannop	2	1 doble	2		iiij^{s}
Thomas Russe	2	1 doble	2		iiij^{s}
Thomas Skott	4	2. doble	5	1. single	ix^{s}
Thomas Iohnson	3	2. doble	4		vij^{s}.
Richard Smyth	2	1. doble	2		iiij^{s}
Richard Wardman	5	2. doble	5	1. single	x^{s}.
Richard Angell	8	2. doble	6	2. single	xiiij^{s}.
william Bould	3	2. doble	4		vij^{s}.
william Boyden	4	2. doble	5	1. single	ix^{s}.
william Buck	2	2. doble	4		vj^{s}.
Iohn Lucas	26	3. doble	11	5. single	xxxvij^{s}
Ieromy Bland	4	2. doble	4		viij^{s}
Iohn Evans	4	2. doble	4		viij^{s}

30/4/8

xxx^{li} iiij^{s} viij^{d}

Paynters and others working and attending vppon the *pre*misses the daie & night at sondrey rat*es* viz.

	Rate	Dayes		Nyghtes		
will*iam* Lyzard	at ij^{s} *per* diem	17	3. doble	8	2 single	l^{s}.
Iohn Bett*es*.	at xx^{d} *per* diem.	3	3. doble	6		xv^{s}
Robert Peake	at xx^{d}.	3	3 doble	6		xv^{s}.
Iohn Tyrris	at xviij^{d}.	3	3. doble	6		xiij^{s} vj^{d}
Edward Gefferson	at xviij^{d}.	7	3. doble	6		xix^{s}. vj^{d}
willyam Rumley	at xviij^{d}.	6	3. doble	6		xviij^{s}
Thom*as* Thompson	at xvj^{d}.	7	3. doble	7	1. single	xviij^{s} viij^{d}
Iohn Beamond	at xvj^{d}.	3	3. doble	7	1. single	xiij^{s}. iiij^{d}.
Robert Bridgewell	at xvj^{d}	2	1. doble	2		v^{s}. iiij^{d}
Iames Turner	at. xviij^{d}.	2	1 doble	2		vj^{s}
Will*iam* Kennys	at xviij^{d}.	2	1. doble	2		vj^{s}.
Tobie Randall	at. xviij^{d}	3	2 doble	4		x^{s}. vj^{d}
Iohn Mullens	at xviij^{d}.	3	2 doble	4		x^{s}. vj^{d}
Iohn Cordwall	at xviij^{d}	3	2 doble	4		x^{s}. vj^{d}
Richard Evans	at xij^{d}.	3	3. doble	6		ix^{s}
Robert Clement	at xij^{d}.	3	3 doble	6		ix^{s}
Lewys Lyzard	at xx^{d}.	0		1	single	xx^{d}.

11/11/6

x^{li} xj^{s} vj^{d}

f° 3 r.

The Porter and other Attendaunt*es* at **xij**^{d} the daie.	Iohn Dawncie	26	2. doble	11	5 single	xxxvij^{s}
	Iohn Drawater	26	2 doble	11	5. single.	xxxvij^{s}.
	Willyam Stone	12	4. doble	8		xx^{s}
4/14^{s}						iiij^{li} xiiij^{s}
wyerdrawers at sondrey rat*es*	Edmond Bircholl (at xx^{d} *per* diem.)	5	2. doble	4		xv^{s}.
	Henry Watt*es* (at xij^{d}.)	1	1. doble	2		iij^{s}
	Symon Powle. (at xij^{d})	5	2. doble	4		ix^{s}
27^{s}						xxvij^{s}
prop*er*ty makers.	w*illiam* Pilkington. (at ij^{s})	2	1. doble	2		viij^{s}.
	Richard morer (at xvj^{d})	5	2. doble	4		xij^{s}
	Iohn Ogle (at xvj^{d})	5	1. doble	2		ix^{s} iiij^{d}
	Iohn ffarrington (at xvj^{d})	6	2. doble	4		xiij^{s} iiij^{d}
	Adam Cowper (at xvj^{d})	3	2. doble	4		ix^{s} iiij^{d}
52^{s}						lij^{s}
Carpenters at xvj^{d} the daie and as much the night.	Will*iam* Barker	15		7	single	xxix^{s} iiij^{d}.
	Edward ffurrys	15		7	single	xxix^{s} iiij^{d}.
	Robert Towe	6		2	single	x^{s} viij^{d}.
3^{li} 9/4						lxix^{s} iiij^{d}
Thofficers	The m*aster* at iiij^{s} the daie	27		11	single	vij^{li}. xij^{s}.
	The clerk comptroller at ij^{s}.	27		11	single	iij^{li}. xvj^{s}
	The clerke at ij^{s}	27		11	single	iij^{li} xvj^{s}
19^{li}	The yeoman at ij^{s}	27		11	single	iij^{li}. xvj^{s}
						xix^{li}

S *UMMA* of all the wages due w*i*thin this office aswell for workmanship and attendaunc*es* done there in and vppon thaffaires therof for ***Christmas*** **Neweyeares** tide and **Twelftyde** as vppon the ij **Maskes** shewen before her ma*ie*stie the Imbassado*ur* being there on sondaie nyght the xjth of Ianuary. 1578. ending the xvth of the same Ianuary in the xxjth yere of her ma*iesties* raigne } lxxij^{li} xviij^{s} vj^{d}

f° 3 v.

The Mercers *par*cells.

Will*iam* Roe for taffeta sarcenet by hym delivered into this office viz. the 11th of Ianuary 1578. blewe taffetie Sarcenet at viij^{s} the ell .16. ell*es* q*uar*ter — vj^{li}. x^{s}. Yealowe taffeta sarcenet at viij^{s} the ell, ell*es* 17. q*uar*ter — vj^{li}. xviij^{s}. Crymson taffata sarcenet at ix^{s} the ell vij ell*es* di. — lxvij^{s}. vj^{d}. white taffeta sarcenet at viij^{s} the ell iij ell*es* Quarter — xxvj^{s} in All — xviij^{li}. j^{s} vj^{d}.

Wal^t^er ffyshe for money by him disbursed as followeth. ffor viij ell*es* of taffata sarcenet white at — ix^{s} the ell. — lxxij^{s}. for an ell. di. of white taffata at xij^{s} the ell. — xviij^{s}. And for ij yard*es* of white Buckerome ij^{s}/ All for the musitions of the Amasons and xiij. yard*es* Quarter of Copper silver white tincell byrd*es* eyes at — x^{s} the yard — vj^{li} xij^{s} vj^{d}. In all — xj^{li} iiij^{s} vj^{d}.

Will*iam* Bowell for xxj. yard*es* Quarter of blewe tyncell sarcenet at viij^{s} the yard brought into the office the ixth of Ianuarie.1578. in the whole Amounting to — viij^{li}. x^{s}.

vpholsters *par*cells. for vj. dozen of guylte Belles for the Amasons — vj^{s}. for vj. peec*es* of Buckromes at iiij^{s} viij^{d} the peece — xxviij^{s}. for A close stoole — x^{s}. for one peece of verie good Buckrome — v^{s}. — xlix^{s}.

Sylkmans *par*cells. **Trott** for ij li. quart*er* of silk to make heares for the Amasons at xxij^{s} the pownd — xlix^{s} vj^{d}.

Walter ffyshe for mony by him paid for A yard of gold Tyncell of the Narrowest sorte — ij^{s}. And for A yard three Quarters di. of silu*er* Lawne tyncell of the Narrowest sorte — v^{s}. in all. — vij^{s}

f° 4 r.

Gyllam Tyen for p*ar*cells by him brought into the office. viz. Silver copper frindge at xviij^{d} .v. oz. di. — viij^{s} iij^{d} Longe frindge of golde copp*er* at xx^{d}. the oz. xiij. oz. di. xxij^{s} vj^{d}. ffrindge and Tassells of gold copp*er* .v. oz. — viij^{s} iiij^{d} Deepe gold copper frindge xij ounc*es* — xx^{s}. ffor iiij^{o} .oz. di. of copp*er* gold frindg at ij^{s} iiij^{d} ye oz. x^{s}. vj^{d} } lxix^{s} vij^{d}.

Will*iam* Bowle for sondrey p*ar*cells brought into the said office. viz.

Deepe frindge of copper gold at ij^{s} the oz. q*uarter* v oz. } x^{s} vj^{d}
ffrindge of copp*er* silver at xviij^{d} the oz. 14.oz. di.—xxj^{s} ix^{d}
Tassells of copp*er* silver ix oz. di.. . . . . . xiiij^{s} iij^{d}
Deepe ffrindge and tassells of copp*er* gold .xj. oz.—xxij^{s}
ffrindge and tassells of copp*er* silver. x. ounc*es* Quarter } xv^{s}. 4^{d}. ob.
Deepe ffrindge. Copp*er* gold iij oz. di. . . . . vij^{s}
ffrindge of Copper silu*er* viij oz. . . . . xij^{s}
ffrindge of Cop*er* sylver viij .oz. q*uar*ter. . . . xij^{s} iiij^{d} ob.
Deepe ffrindge and tassells of copp*er* gold 16. oz.—xxxij^{s}.
xij tassells for Iavelynes of Crymson silk and copp*er* silver xij ounc*es* Quarter } xviij^{s} iiij^{d} ob.
Deepe ffrindge and tassells of gold xij oz. q*uarter*—xxiiij^{s} vj^{d}
ffrindge of copp*er* silver xiij oz. . . . . xix^{s} vj^{d}
Deepe ffrindge and tassells of copp*er* gold xxxij ounc*es* } lxiiij^{s}
ffrindge of copp*er* silver vj. oz. di. . . . . . ix^{s} ix^{d}
ffrindge of crymson silk and silu*er* xiij oz.. . . xix^{s} vj^{d}
Tassells of copp*er* gold vj. oz. Quarter. . . . xij^{s} vj^{d}
ffrindge and tasselll̃s of crymson silk and silver xiij ounc*es* } xix^{s} vj^{d}
Deepe frindge and tassells of copp*er* gold viij ounc*es* Quarter } xvj^{s} vj^{d}
Small tassells of copp*er* silu*er* vij. oz. . . . . . x^{s} vj^{d}
Deepe ffrindge of copp*er* gold iij oz. . . . . vj^{s}
Calles for tassells of copp*er* golde one oz. q*uar*ter—ij^{s} vj^{d}.

} xviij^{li} x^{s}.iiij^{d} ob.

f° 4 v.

	Item	Amount	Total
	Hughe ffayreclough for sondrey *par*cells by him brought into the office videlicet.		viij^{li}. xij^{s}. x^{d}.
	Gold Lawne Tincell at iij^{s} viij^{d} the yard 31. yard*es* di.	cxv^{s} vj^{d}	
	Sylver tyncell at ij^{s} vj^{d} the yard.iij. yard*es* . .	vij^{s} vj^{d}	
	ffrindge of copp*er* silu*er* at xvj^{d} the oz. 13.oz. .	xvij^{s} iiij^{d}.	
	Sylu*er* Lawne tyncell at ij^{s} vj^{d} the yarde xiij. yard*es*	xxxij^{s} vj^{d}	
Propertymakers *par*cells	**Pawle Sytolyn** for vij head peec*es* of silver and gold Lawne and woemens heare at xiij^{s} iiij^{d} the peece for torch bearers for the Amasons	iiij^{li}.xiij^{s} iiij^{d}.	vj^{li}. xiiij^{s}
	Iohn Ogle for the cullering the yealow heare and stuffe to curle it iiij^{s} and for vj. beardes for the vizard*es* for the Knight*es*. x^{s}.	xiiij^{s}.	
	George Ioyner for xij ffawchions for the Amasons	xxvj^{s} viij^{d}	
	Willyam Lyzarde for sondrey *par*cells by him brought into the office viz.		vij^{li}.x^{s}
	ffor xij. murryons counterfeicte mowlded and guilt at vj^{s} viij^{d} the peece	iiij^{li}.	
	ffor xij. Lyons head*es* counterfeicte moulded and guylt at ij^{s} vj^{d} the peece	xxx^{s}.	
	ffor xxx^{tie}.dozen of Roases mowlded and guylded at xvj^{d} the dozen	xl^{s}.	
	Willyam Earpe for sondrey *par*cells brought into the office. viz.		xxx^{s}.
	ffor xij. sheild*es* at xvij^{d} the pece xvij^{s} vij Turkie Bowes at xij^{d} the peece vij^{s} vj speares at vij^{d} the peece iij^{s} vj^{d}. for fitting of vj. trunchions xij^{d} ffor translating of vj. sheild*es*. xij^{d}. and for glewing A ffawchion vj^{d} in the whole	xxx^{s}.	

f° 5 r.

Barnarde ffabyan for sondrey p*ar*cells by him provided and brought into thoffice at sondrey tymes in mann*er* and fforme following. viz.

The xxjth of December. 1578. A pound of Cearing Candle	xij^{d}.
ffor vj. linck*es* at iiij^{d} the peece	ij^{s}.
A peece of greate cord.	xvj^{d}
A peece of small cord.	vj^{d}
Cotten Candles at iiij^{d} the pound. xij li. . . .	iiij^{s}.
The xxvth of December.1578. A dozen of cotten candles at iiij^{d} the pound xij li.	iiij^{s}.
A pownd of Packethread	xij^{d}.
The xxviijth of the same December. ij dozen cotten candles	viij^{s}.
A pound of Cearing candle	xij^{d}.
A peece of small corde	vj^{d}
A pound of Packthread	xij^{d}.
The iiijth of Ianuarie .1578. two dozen cotten candles	viij^{s}.
A pound of glewe	iiij^{d}.
A peece of great corde	xvj^{d}.
A peece of Small cord	vj^{d}
A pound of cearing candle	xij^{d}.
The vjth of Ianuarie .1578. for A dozen li. of cotten candles	iiij^{s}
The viijth of Ianuarie A dozen pound of Cotten candles	iiij^{s}.
The xth of Ianuarie, A dozen pound of Cotten candles	iiij^{s}
The xjth of Ianuarie two dozen of cotten Candles —	viij^{s}.
The xiijth of Ianuarie .1578. for three pownd*es* of Cowtten candles	xij^{d}
In all	lvj^{s} vj^{d}

f. 5 v.

Paynters p*ar*cells. **Wyllyam Lyzarde** for cullors and Necessaries by him p*ro*vided and brought into this office videl*icet*.

ffor Sise	xiij^{s} vj^{d}.	ix^{li} xvij^{s} vj^{d}
ffor pott*es* and nayles.	ij^{s}	
ffor redd two pownd	xvj^{d}	
ffor vermyllion viij oz.	ij^{s} vj^{d}	
ffor Synep*er*	iij^{s}.	
ffor Smalt iij li. at — di. iij^{s} the pound.	x^{s} vj^{d}	
Black three pound at xvj^{d} the li.	iiij^{s}	
white xxxij li. at iij^{d} the pound	viij^{s}	
yealowe	xvj^{d}	
Verte A pownd	iiij^{s}.	
masticott j li.	iij^{s}.	
Sape greene q*uar*ter li.	ij^{s}.	
Blewing q*uar*ter li.	iij^{s}	
Browne	xviij^{d}.	
Assidue iij li.	x^{s} vj^{d}	
Shells of gold at xvj^{d} the peece/ ix/	xij^{s}	
Shells of silu*er* at x^{d} the pece .vij/.	v^{s} x^{d}	
ffine cullors for paterns and for the sheild*es*	x^{s}.	
Bisse iiij oz.	viij^{s}	
ffyre pannes .ij.	vj^{d}	
Gilte Belles iij dozen	iij^{s} vj^{d}	
ffatt oyle and fine gold size for the Armors and Sword*es*	vj^{s} viij^{d}.	
ffine gold for the Armor and Sword*es*	lxxviij^{s}	
p*ar*tie gold for sheild*es* trunchions & fawchions	xxx^{s}.	
Syluer for the Bowes and ffawchions	iiij^{s} vj^{d}	
dymme black	viij^{d}.	

In all xj^{li} ix^{s} x^{d}. wherof the m*aster* and clerkcomptroller have Abated for excessive prices xxxij^{s} iiij^{d}. And so remayneth.

To Iohn white/ [xxxiij^{s}. iiij^{d}.] and Boswell [xxxiij^{s} iiij^{d}] for the p*ar*cell gilding of two Armors compleat for m^{r} Tresham and m^{r} Knowles being two of the Knightes in the Amasons maske — lxvj^{s} viij^{d}.

Carpenters p*ar*cells. **Rowland Robinson** for xvj. furre poles

Rowland Robinson for xvj. furre poles	viij^{s}.	lxxvij^{s} vj^{d}.
Rafters at xiiij^{d} the peece viij.	ix^{s} iiij^{d}	
Bord*es* at vij^{s} vj^{d} the c/ v. c. di.	xlj^{s} iij^{d}	
single q*uar*ters for Rayles at iij^{d} the peece. ix.	ij^{s} iij^{d}	
ffor A dore and dore postes hookes hyng*es* Bolte and staple to the same for the Lead*es* in the m*aster* his Lodging.	xvj^{s} viij^{d}	

f° 6 r.

Ironmongers *par*cells.	**Rychard Warby** for sondrey *par*cells by him brought into this office	viz.	
	One thowsand of vj^{d} nayles.	v^{s}.	
	Doble x^{d} nayles iiij [6^{s}. 8^{d}.] C. single. x^{d}. nailes v [4^{s}. 2^{d}.] C	x^{s}. x^{d}.	xviij^{s} iiij^{d}.
	ffor great spikes to straine the wiers in the hall	xvj^{d}	
	ffor mending two Lockes for A cheste in the office.	xiiij^{d}.	
Necessaries	**Walter ffyshe** for money by him disbursed	viz.	
	ffor the washing and glacing of vj. sarcenet shirt*es*.	viij^{s}.	
	ffor half A yard of cotton.	v^{d}.	
	ffor ij linck*es* [viij^{d}] and his mans supp*er* [vj^{d}] when he wente to my Lo*rd* Chamberleynes being sente for	xiiij^{d}.	xiij^{s} vij^{d}.
	To iiij^{or}. men for making garm*en*t*es* at the courte for the musitions of the Amasons	iiij^{s}.	
	Edwarde Buggyn gent*leman* for mony by him p*aid*.		
	ffor half A Reame of fine Lardge pap*er*	v^{s}.	
	ffor half A Reame of courser sorte	iij^{s} iiij^{d}.	xiiij^{s}. ix^{d}
	ffor A hundred of choice quills	v^{d}.	
	ffor A bottle and A pinte of Inck	xij^{d}.	
	ffor ij lardge pap*er* bokes to remayne in the office	v^{s}.	
	Thomas Wright for money by him disbursed.	viz.	
	ffor thread	xij^{s} x^{d}.	
	Tape	vij^{s} xj^{d}	
	Paste borde iij dozen and one	vij^{s}	
	Rushes ij dozen Bundles [vj^{s} vj^{d}] & the cariage [viij^{d}.]	vij^{s} ij^{d}.	xlv^{s}. v^{d}.
	Holly and Ivie	xij^{d}	
	Three yard*es* of gray cloth to make my Lo*rd* of Leicesters men A fishermans coat	v^{s}.	
	Bromes [j.^{d}], small nayles [iiij^{d}] A brushe [ij^{d} vj^{d}].	ij^{s} xj^{d}	
	ffor ij. peec*es* of cord and A chalk lyne	xix^{d}	
	John Davyes for sondrey thing*es* by him brought into thoffice.	viz.	
	ffor tape occupied when the children of the chappell plaid before the Queene	x^{d}.	
	ffor thred [vj^{d}] & silk and A dozen of past bord*es* [xviij^{d}]	ij^{s}.	v^{s} vj^{d}.
	ffor iiij^{or}. pullies [xij^{d}.] ij yard*es* of cotten [xx^{d}.] to make Rolles for the head peec*es*	ij^{s} viij^{d}	

f. 6 v.

	Iohn Drawater for money by him disbursed.	viz.	
	ffor ij Lynes to drawe curtens with . . .	xij^{d}	
	ffor A rope [xvj^{d}] A pulley [viij^{d}.] A basket [ij^{s}.] to serve in the Earle of warwickes men plaie	iiij^{s}	
	ffor iiij quire of Royall paper [iiij^{s}.] and A Reame of small paper [vj^{s} viij^{d}.]	x^{s} viij^{d}	
	ffor A standishe. iij^{s} iiij^{d}. Inck. ij^{d}. quills .ij^{d}. pennes ij^{d}. waxe iiij^{d}. counters .xvj^{d}. pindust vj^{d} and penknife xij^{d}.	vij^{s}	
	ffor ij peeces of small cord for pendauntes at the Courte being verie fine and lardg for the purpose	iiij^{s} vj^{d}	lxxj^{s} ij^{d}.
	ffor A Little cheste [v^{s}.] with Lock and key to put papers and paterns for diuerse causes in the office and ij paire of compasses [xvj^{d}]	vj^{s} iiij^{d}.	
	A dozen and A half of gloves for maskers at xvj^{d} the paire xxiiij^{s}. & A dozen and A half of gloves for torche bearers at viij^{d}. seruing the doble maske shewing at the courte the Imbassadour being there xij^{s}	xxxvj^{s}	
	To Greene the coffermaker for lynnyng A cheste with Buckrome for thoffice	ij^{s}.	
Armorers parcells.	**Roger Tyndall** for the making of xij Skabordes to be vsed in the Amasons maske	viij^{s}	xij^{s}
	ffor xij. chapes guylte for the same scaberdes —	ij^{s}.	
	ffor covering of xij handles and garnishing them with nayles	ij^{s}	
ffethermaker	**To Bastyan** for the hier of vj. plomes of feathers [xij^{s}] for Knightes in the Amasons maske and iiij^{s} geven to take Agayne iiij of the falles of the same feathers which otherwise by composition should have coste viij^{s}. Because they were dropte with torches. and vj^{d} for ij hearons toppes which were burnte with Torches. In all		xvj^{s} vj^{d}
Cariage by water and Land. with horse-hier and riding chardges.	**Thomas Wrighte** for mony by him disbursed	viz.	
	The Cariage of A basket from Barmesey to the Reavelles when the stuffe were shewen to my Lord Chamberlen	xx^{d}.	iij^{s} viij^{d}.
	ffor the cariage of A hamper with stuffe to whitehall & back againe	ij^{s}.	

f° 7 r.

Iohn Davyes for money by him laid owt.	viz.	
Boate hier to and from the courte to carry the stuffe for the children of the chappell to Recite before my Lord Chamberleyne	xij^{d}.	iiij^{s}
Boate hier iij tymes to Barmesey and Back agayne to waight my Lord chamberlaines comyng thither	xij^{d}	
Boate hier to the courte to carry my Lord Chamberleyne Patorns of the maske	vj^{d}	
Two Carres to carry the maske from Pawles wharfe to St Iohns	xviij^{d}.	

Walter ffyshe for mony by him disbursed.	viz.	
ffor Boate hier to Barmesey to speake with my Lord Chamberleyne	iiij^{d}.	x^{s} iiij^{d}
ffor A Carre the next daie to carry ij Baskettes of stuffe to Barmesey to shewe my Lord Chamberleyne	ij^{s}.	
ffor his owne boate hyer the same day	iiij^{d}.	
Boate hier to m^{r} Brydemans to see what stuffe was there	viij^{d}.	
ffor A Carre to fetche home the same stuffe. . . .	ij^{s}.	
ffor his boate hier when he wente to meete my Lord Chamberleyne there	iiij^{d}.	
ffor his bote hier when he wente to fetche Awaie the same stuffe	viij^{d}.	
ffor his boate hier to and from the Courte when he wente to make the garmentes for the Amasons Musitions	iiij^{s}.	

Thomas Blagrave esquier for money by him disbursed.	videlicet	
ffor his chardges with. ij men. the 20. and 21th of december. 1578. from Bedwin in wilteshire to London —xx^{s}. The chardges of iij horses in London and backe — x^{s}.	xxx^{s}.	

f° 7 v.

ffor his boate hier from London to Richmond. the xxijth of the same December .1578. to speake *w*ith my Lo*rd* Chamberlayne and back agayne — v^{s}. his boate hier the .28th of December .1578. to the court to shew my Lo*rd* Chamberlaine A patorne for A maske and back againe. v^{s}. his boate hier from London to the courte the second of Ianuarie /1578. — ij^{s} .vj^{d}/ ffor ij wherries from London to the Courte the xjth of Ianuarie for him self and others that wente to sett forth the maske — v^{s}. And for boate hier to Whitehall ffor choice of Stuffe to Barmesey for choice of plaies and conference about mask*es* and diu*er*se other plac*es* in London. and sondrey tymes as occasion served.— v^{s} viij^{d} in all

xxiiij^{s} ij^{d} liiij^{s}.ij^{d}.

Iohn Drawater for money by him disbursed as followeth. videl*ice*t

The xxiiijth of December .1578. for his bote hier to the courte and back againe to get the warrante signed — iij^{s} iiij^{d}. 26. of December for ij Carres to carry the fframes to the water side — xx^{d}. his owne botehier and ij wheries to carry the frames to the courte — vij^{s} for cariadge of the stuffe from the courte by water the 27th of December that served in my Lo*rd* Chamberleynes men plaie — iij^{s} vj^{d}. The same daie for cariage of the stuffe that served the plaie for the children of the chappell to the courte and back agayne — vj^{s} viij^{d}. the 29th of December for his boate hier when he carried the privie seale to m^{r} Peeter from the courte — xx^{d}. 30. of December for his bote hier *w*ith others from Powles Wharf to m^{r} Brydemans from thence to Lambeth and so to the courte when my Lo*rd* Chamberleyne toke A viewe of the stuffe at m^{r} Brydemans — iij^{s}/ The ffirste of Ianuarie for cariage of A frame for master Sabastian to the courte — iij^{s} vj^{d}/ ffor his Bote hier to the courte the same daie — xvj^{d} ij^{o} of Ianuarie. 1578. when I came to m^{r} Peeter to have receaved the money But could nott *w*ithout further order from my Lo*rd* Treasorer — xvj^{d}/ 4. of Ianuarie. 1578. ffor the hier of A horsse ij daies to the courte to ffurnishe my Lo*rd* of Leicesters players the ffrost being so greate no bote could goe and come back againe at xij^{d} the daie — iij^{s} iiij^{d} for his meate those Two daies — ij^{s} viij^{d}. ffor holly and Ivie for my Lo*rd* of Leicesters servaunt*es* — xij^{d} .5. of Ianuary for my bote hier to and from westmester to receave the money — xij^{d}. The Sixte of Ianuarie for m^{r} Blagraves bote hier to and from the courte being sent for by my Lord Chamberlayne — v^{s}. ffor boate hier of diu*er*se workemen that wente to conferre w*i*th my Lord Aboute the maske to the Courte and back agayne w*i*th xij^{d} bestowed on them At mortlack the same daie — v^{s}. .6. Ianuarie for cariage of the Revells stuffe to the courte and back agayne that served my L*ord* Chamberleynes players second plaie — vij^{s}. 7. of Ianuarie for the carriage of the .ij. frames from the courte to London in A carte — vij^{s}. 8. of Ianuarie/ ffor m^{r} Blagrave and m^{r} Buggins botehier to and from Whitehall when they fetched the cloth of gold and silkes from m^{r} Brydemans — xij^{d}. 11. of Ianuary to Iohn Garret and Dwaryns Martyn for carryage of the Armoure from Greenewitche to St Iohnes to be guylded/ [2 s.] And from St Iohns to the water side/ [.16 d.] And from thence to Richmond in iij wherries. [.9 s.] — xij^{s} iiij^{d}. The same daie. iij carres to carry the hampers w*i*th candlesticks and the mast*es* to the water side — ij^{s} vj^{d}. ffor A wherry to carry the candlestick*es* to the courte — iiij^{s}. The same daie for A Bardge [.16 s.] to carry the mask*es* to the courte by water and back agayne. And xij^{d} to the water men for expedic*i*on — viij^{d} bestowed vppon them in drinck and xvj^{d} to carry them to the courte from Mortlack. on mens showlders Because tyme would not serve to go by water — xix^{s} .13. of Ianuarie ffor ij wherryes to carry the greate cheste and the two hamp*er*s w*i*th candlestick*es* from the courte to London — v^{s}. And from the waterside to Sainte Iohnes — viij^{d}. — v^{s}. viij^{d}. The same daie ffor m^{r} Blagrave his botehier from the courte w*i*th ij^{d} bestowed in bread and drinck vppon the watermen — ij^{s} viij^{d}. 9. of Ianuarie 1578. to will*iam* Lyzard for his boate hier to the courte to shewe certen patterns to my L*ord* Chamberleyne — ij^{s} vj^{d}. 29. of December .1578. for the carriage of A greate chest and A close stoole by water to the courte — ij^{s} viij^{d} } cxvij^{s}. iiij^{d}.

Habberdashers p*ar*cells. **Rychard Morer** for sondrey p*ar*cells brought into the office. viz.

ffor xij Armyng girdles/ vj. of gold tyncle and vj. of red tissue all w*i*th guylte Buccles and harnesse at ij^{s} viij^{d} the peece	xxxij^{s}.	xxxv^{s}
ffelt*es* to Lyne the counterfecte head peec*es* in the Amazons maske vj/ at vj^{d} the peece	iij^{s}.	

f° 8 v.

ffewell **Thomas Wright** for money by him disbursed
for A Load of Coales . . . . xxij^{s}.
ffagott*es* ij C. . . . . xj^{s} iiij^{d}.
Billett*es* one thowsand and A half. . . . . . . xix^{s} iiij^{d}.
} **lij^{s} viij^{d}.**

Thomas Stronge for money by him paid
ffor A Load of Coales . . . . xxij^{s}.
ffagott*es* ij C. . . . . xj^{s} iiij^{d}.
Billett*es* ij thowsand . . . . xxv^{s}. iiij^{d}.
} **lviij^{s} viij^{d}.**

Wyerdrawer. **Edmond Byrcholl** for sondrey p*ar*cells by him brought into the office. viz.
Stocke candlestick*es* ij dozen . . . . iiij^{s}.
Pricke Candlestick*es*.vj. . . . . xij^{d}.
Compasses one paire . . . . iiij^{d}.
Quylting needles ij . . . . iiij^{d}.
Heades for the Javelines sixe . . . . iij^{s}.
A great braunche for light*es* . . . . xl^{s}
ffyne wyer one Pound . . . . xij^{d}.
Greate wier xij pound*es* . . . . x^{s}.
Plate one dozen . . . . iiij^{s}.
Lanthornes ij . . . . iiij^{s}.
wyer vj. yard*es* . . . . vj^{d}.
In the whole — lxviij^{s} ij^{d}. whereout abate vj^{s}. viij^{d}. by the m*aster* and clerk comptrolle*r*. for excessive prices and so remayneth.
} **lxj^{s} vj^{d}**

Reward*es* **John Drawater** for money by him disbursed as followeth. viz.
To m^{r} Nichasius for the privie seale and the signet for the Revells money } x^{s}.
To Harris A grome of the chamber for bringing A Lettre to the m*aster* the 31. of December .1578. } ij^{s}.
To m^{r} Peter for making the orders for my L*ord* Theasorer should signe for the paym*ent* of the Revells money } x^{s}.
To m^{r} Stoneley for paym*ent* of 344^{li}. 9^{s} . . . . . . x^{s}.
To his men for their paine for paym*ent*. . . . . ij^{s} vj^{d}.

f° 9 r.

To the Keep*er* of the gardeyne at whitehall when the m*aster* viewed the stuffe to serue this torne for his attendaunce at sondrey tymes	xij^{d}.	iiij^{li}. viij^{d}.
To the Porter of Thexchequo*ur* at the receipte of the money.	xij^{d}.	
To Will*iam* Bowles man for going on Errand*es* at the m*aster* his comaundem*ent*	xij^{d}.	
To the painters to buy victualls for that they should not go from their work	xij^{d}.	
To Patruchius Vbaldinas by the comaundm*ent* of the Lord chamberleyne for the translating of certen speaches into Italian to be vsed in the maske the making the Tables for them the writing faire in the same Tables and for his chardges in travelling About the same	xlij^{s} ij^{d}.	

Thomas Blagrave esquier for mony by him disbursed. vidháli*cet*

The xixth of December to Harris groome of the chamber comyng from Richmond to Bedwin by the Lo*rd* Chamberleyne his comaundem*ent*	iij^{s} iiij^{d}	xvij^{s} x^{d}
To the prope*r*tie makers working on the head peec*es* for the Amasons torche Bearers to send for victualls because they should not goe from their worke.	ij^{s}	
To the painters at will*iam* Lyzard*es* Lyzard*es* working on the murryons head*es* to send for victualls for that they should not goe from their work*es*	ij^{s}.	
To m^{r} Skynn*er* my Lo*rd* Treasorers clerk. for newe making the orders sent by m^{r} Peeter and his furtheraunce therin	x^{s}	
To Pawle Sytolons his mayde	vj^{d}.	

The Clerke for his ordynary grene cloth pap*er* Incke counters deskes standishes and tooles for the making compiling and conseruing of the Billes plott*es* patornes and modells &c. ffor and concernyng this office	lxvj^{s} viij^{d}.

S*umma* **tot*a*lis** of the emptions p*ro*visions cariag*es* Reward*es* &c. besides the wag*es* afores aid	cxlvij^{li} vj^{s} ij^{d}.

f. 9 r.

* Ed. Tyllney

Summa **totalis** of all the emptions provisions cariages Rewardes together with the wages and attendaunces of workemen and Attendauntes wrought and attended within the tyme aforesaid } ccxliiij^{li}. vij^{s} iiij^{d}.

* T Blagrave

* Edward Buggyn

* walter fysshe

The totall somme of the whole booke viz. from the xiiijth of ffebruarie: 1577. Anno Regni Regine Elizabeth xx^{o} vntill the xiiijth of Ianuarie . 1578 . Anno xxj^{o} Regni Regine Elizabeth predicte .1578. videlicet.

Ayringes from the .14 of ffebruarie /1577. vntill the 20. of December .1578.	**wages** of	Artificers . . . ix^{li} iiij^{s}	xxiiij^{li}. ij^{s} viij^{d}.		ccxliiij^{li} vij^{s} iiij^{d}
		Officers . . . . xij^{li}.			
	Emptions, and provisions,—lviij^{s} viij^{d}.				
Christmas Neweyeres tide twelf tide and the sonday after when the maskes were shewen.	**wages** of	Artificers . . . liij^{li}. xviij^{s} vj^{d}	ccxx^{li}.iiij^{s} viij^{d}		
		Officers . . . . xix^{li}			
	Emptions provisions Rewardes Cariages &c.	cxlvij^{li} vj^{s} ij^{d}			

f° 10 r.

Candlem*as* Shrovetide Anno Regni Regine Elizabethe .xxj^mo^. 1578.

The Chardges of the tymes vid*elicet*. **Betwene** the firste of ffebruary. 1578. Anno Regni Regine Elizabeth pred*icte* xxj°. At w*hi*ch tyme the work*es* beganne for the p*ro*viding apting p*re*paring furnishing and setting furth of diu*er*se plaies comodies or shewes of histories and other Inventions and devises incident. **And** the vj^th^ of Marche .1578. Anno Regni Regine pred*icte* xxj°. At w*hi*ch tyme the work*es* and Attendaunc*es* did end Together w*i*th all the emptions p*ro*visions of stuffe and necessaries cariag*es* and other incident*es* bought, p*ro*vided done and attended by diu*er*se p*er*sons whose seu*er*all names rat*es* and wages w*i*th their Reward*es* and Allowaunc*es* do p*ar*ticulerly in their apt plac*es* ensue.

Histories and Invencions p*re*pared for and furnished shewen and to be shewen w*i*thin the tyme aforesai*d* .iiij. viz.

The history of .provided to have ben shewen at whitehall on candlemas daie at nighte by the Earle of Warwick*es* servaunt*es* furnished in this office w*i*th sondrey garm*entes* and prop*er*ties in redines Being At ye place to have enacted the same. But the Quenes ma*ies*tie wold not come to heare the same and therefore put of.

The history of the Knight in the Burnyng Rock shewen at Whitehall on shrovesondaie at night enacted by the Earle of warwick*es* s*er*vaunt*es* furnished in this office w*i*th sondrey garm*entes* and p*ro*p*er*ties.

The history of Loyaltie and bewtie shewen at Whitehall on Shrove monday at night enacted by the children of the Quenes ma*iesti*cs chappell furnished in this office w*i*th verie manie Riche garm*entes* and prop*er*ties aptly fitted for the same.

The history of murderous mychaell shewen at Whiteh all on shrovetuesdaie at night enacted by the L*ord* Chamberleynes s*er*vaunt*es* furnished in this office w*i*th sondrey thing*es*.

Taylors and others working and attending the p*re*miss*es* the first at xx^d^ the daie and as much the night the reste at ij^d^.

	Daies	Doble night*es*		
Thom*as* Clatterbooke	10	5	single	xxv^s^.
Thomas wrighte	10	5	single	xv^s^
will*iam* Tyldesley.	10	5	single	xv^s^
Edward Griffeth	10	5	single	xv^s^
Thom*as* Boreman.	10	5	single	xv^s^
will*iam* Snewde	10	5	single	xv^s^
Beniamyn Edward*es*.	10	5	single	xv^s^
Edward Lucas.	10	5	single.	xv^s^
Iohn Tupsley	10	5	single	xv^s^
Thom*as* Lambe	6	3	single	ix^s^
George Wright.	3	2	single	v^s^
Richard Angell.	4	3	single	vij^s^
David Lloid.	10	5	single	xv^s^.

ix^li^ xij^d^

f° 11 r.

Paynters and others working and Attending vppon the *pre*misses the day and night at sondrey rat*es*.	Will*iam* Lyzard at ij^{s} *per* die*m*	8	4	single	xxiiij^{s}
	Thom*as* Thompson at xvj^{d}	6	3	single	xij^{s}
	John Teres at xvii^{id}	5	2	single	x^{s} vj^{d}
	will*iam* Rumley at xviij^{d}	5	2	single	x^{s} vj^{d}
	Iohn Beamount at xviij^{d}	3	2	single	vij^{s} vj^{d}
	will*iam* Kynns at xviij^{d}	3	2	single	vij^{s} vj^{d}
	Edward Jefferson at 18^{d}	3	2	single	vij^{s} vj^{d}
	will*iam* Reeles at xviij^{d}	3	2	single	vij^{s} vj^{d}
					iiij^{li} vij^{s}
The porter & Attendaunt*es* at xij^{d} the daie.	Iohn Dawncey	10	5	single	xv^{s}
	Iohn Drawater	10	5	single	xv^{s}
	Iohn Davies	10	5		xv^{s}
					xlv^{s}.
wyerdrawers at sondrey rat*es*	Edward Bircholl at xx^{d} *per* die*m*.	5	3	single	xiij^{s} iiij^{d}
	Henry watt*es* at xvj^{d}	2	1	single	iiij^{s}
	Symon Powle at xij^{d}	5 .3: doble.	6		xj^{s}
					xxviij^{s}. iiij^{d}.
prop*er*ty makers ye one at ij^{s} *per* diem the rest at xvj^{d} the daie	Will*iam* Pilkington at ij^{s}.	2	2	single	viij^{s}
	John Rose Iunior	5	3	single	x^{s} viij^{d}
	Iohn Glymson	2	1	single	iiij^{s}
	Iohn ffarrington	5	3		x^{s} viij^{d}
	John Ogle	5 .3: doble.	6		xiiij^{s} viij^{d}
					xlviij^{s}
Carpenters at xvj^{d} the daie asmouch the night.	Edward ffurres	5	3	single	x^{s} viij^{d}.
	Thom*as* Sylvester	5	3	single	x^{s} viij^{d}
	Iohn Berry	5	1	single	viij^{s}
	Iames Berry	2	1	single	iiij^{s}.
	Henry Waplett	3	2		vj^{s} viij^{d}
					xl^{s}

f° 11 v.

Joyners at sondrey Rat*es*.	George Ioyn*er* at xx^{d} *per* die*m*. . . .	6 . . .	3. single	xv^{s}.
	Patrick Dale at xvj^{d}	6 . . .	3. single	xij^{s}.
	Thomas Hinckson at 16^{d}.	6 . . .	3. single	xij^{s}
	Thom*as* Ioyner at. 16^{d}.	4 . . .	1. . . .	vj^{s} viij^{d}.
			xlv^{s} viij^{d}	
Thofficers.	The m*aster* at iiij^{s} the daie	12 . . .	6 single	lxxij^{s}.
	The Clerk comptroll*our* at ij^{s}	12 . . .	6. single	xxxvj^{s}
	The Clerk at ij^{s}.	12 . . .	6 single	xxxvj^{s}
	The yeoman at ij^{s}. . . . . . . , ...	12 . . .	6. single	xxxvj^{s}.
			ix^{li}	

SUMMA of all the wag*es* due w*i*thin this office aswell for workemenship & Attendaunc*es* done in and vppon thaffaires therof for Candlem*as* and shrove tyde ending the Sixte of march .1578. in the xxjth yere of her ma*iesties* Raigne } xxxij^{li}.xv^{s}.

f° 12 r.

Emptions Provisions and cariages w*i*th Reward*es* and other chardg*es* incident.

The Lynen Drap*er*. — **M*is*tres Dane** for canvas by her deliu*er*ed into this office at sondrey tymes. viz. the xxvjth of ffebruary .1578. one peece of canvas cont*eyning*. xxxix. ells. at xiiij^{d} the ell. — xlv^{s}. vj^{d}/ And the second of marche. 1578. one peece of canvas cont*eyning*. xxxix. ells at xiiij^{d} the ell — xlv^{s}. vj^{d} the whole amounting vnto lxxviij. ell*es*. — iiij^{li}. xj^{s}

vpholsters p*ar*cells. — for one peece of yealowe Buckerham — vj^{s}. white Buckram.ij yard*es* di. iij^{s} iiij^{d}. Black buckram iiij. yard*es* — v^{s}. iiij^{d}. in all. — xiiij^{s} viij^{d}.

Chaundlers. p*ar*cells. — **Barnard ffabyan** for sondrey p*ar*cells by him brought into the office. viz.

Greate cord. vj. peec*es*	v^{s} iiij^{d}
Cotten candles at iiij^{d} the li. iiij. dozen	xvj^{s}
Glewe one pownd	iiij^{d}.
Lynck*es* at iiij^{d} the peece. xiiij	iiij^{s} viij^{d}.
Pack thred iij li.	iij^{s}.
Searing candles one pound	xij^{d}
Small cord .v. peec*es*	ij^{s} vj^{d}
Staffe bromes iij	vj^{d}.

— xxxiij^{s} iiij^{d}.

Carpenters. p*ar*cell — **Iohn Rose senyor** for certeyne p*ar*cells by him bestowed in and About A rock at the courte for A plaie enacted by the Earle of warwick*es* servaunt*es*. viz.

Longe sparre poles of ffurre	vj^{s}x^{d}.	x^{s} x^{d}
peec*es* of Elme cutt compasse	iiij^{s}	

Rowland Robynson for sondrey thing*es* by him brought into the office viz.

Oken bord three hundred — xxj^{s}. Elme bourd xxj. foote. xviij^{d}. ffurre poles xxj. wherof xiiij. for altering the lightes on Shrovetuesdaie and the rest for the frames — x^{s}. vj^{d}/ single quarters. x/ & for cariage of them. and the rest to the court. — iij^{s} in all — xxxvj^{s}.

Gybsonne for certeyn p*ar*cells by him bestowed about the rock at the court for A play enacted by the Earle of warwick*es* servant*es*. viz.

Dobble quarters iiij — ij^{s}. single quarters ij vj^{d}/ Deale bourd*es* xxxij — xxxij^{s} Elme bord*es*. 153. foote xij^{s} in all — xlvj^{s} vj^{d}

[Carpenters total:] iiij^{li}. xiij^{s} iiij^{d}

f° 12 v.

Ironmongers or Smythes pa*r*cells.

Vlryck Netsley for certeyne pa*r*cells by him wrought and delyvered into the office viz.
ffor an Iron for the wagon that s*er*ued in the plaie of Loyaltie and bewtie — ijs vjd and for mending A scalling Ladder that s*er*ued at the Rock. — viijd. In all } iijs ijd.

Rychard Warby for sondrey pa*r*cells by him brought into the office. viz.
Doble xd. nayles to alter the light*es* in the hall on shrovetuesdaie and to have lightes in the p*re*sence and for setting vpp of the frames 425 — vijs jd. Single xd nayles for the same Cause iiij c — iijs iiijd. vjd nayles for the same cause v c — ijs vjd/ iijd nayles one. c. — iijd. In all } xiijs ijd

George Ioyner for sondrey pa*r*cells by him boughte and brought into the office to be spente about the rock viz.
Dobble xd. nayles 425. — vijs jd single xd nayles 800. — vjs viijd. Two penny nayles [xd.] 500. & iijd nayles [xijd.] 400. for the same cause And for the wagon of Loyaltie [xvjd] and bewtie — iijs. ijd/ vjd nayles/ 400. — ijs Sparres viij. — iiijs. hoopes and packthread — xiiijd. In all } xxiiijs jd

Iohn Rose senio*ur* for nayles of sondry [*sortes*] vsed about the Clowde and drawing it vpp and downe. } vjs viijd

} xlvijs jd

ffewell

Thomas Stronge for mony by him disbursed ffor A Load of Coales — xxijs vjd.
Iohn Davyes for money by him disbursed. viz.
ffor Coales at the courte to drie the Painters worke on the Rock } vjd.

} xxiijs

Necessaries

Thomas Wright for sondrey thing*es* by him p*ro*vided and brought into the office. viz.
Paste bord*es* iiij. dozen — xijs. Tape ij li. quarter di. — xjs ijd. Thred of sondrey Cullors ij li. iij q*uar*ters di. — xjs vjd Browne thread j li. Quarte*r* — iijs iiijd. Ivie ij bundles — ijs. A painted cheste for my Lo*rd* Chamb*er*leyns men — xvjd/ for the hier of foure feathers — ijs In all } xliijs iiijd.

Ion Rose senio*ur* for mony by him disbursed. viz.
for Lead for the chaire of the burnyng Knight — ijs vjd Candlestick*es* to work by at the court — ijs. for A coard & pullies to drawe vpp the clowde — iijs in all } vijs vjd

f° 13 r.

Iohn Davyes for certeyne thing*es* by him *pro*vided and brought into the office. viz.

Ivie and holly for the Rock in the play enacted by the Earle of warwick*es* *ser*vaunt*es* — iiij^{s} ij^{d}. Aquavite to burne in the same Rock — iij^{s}. Rosewater to Alay the smell therof — xij^{d}. glasses to carry the same and other for the vse therof — xij^{d}/ thred expended at the courte — ij^{d}. Bladders j^{d} and Beares feete — xviij^{d}. } x^{s} xj^{d}

Iohn Drawater for sondry thing*es* by him provided and brought into the office. viz.

Gloves for the children of the chappell xviij^{ten}. paire — x^{s}. A garland of grapes and Leaves for Baccus and other of roses for vsed in the play of Loyaltie and Bewtie — ij^{s} iiij^{d}. for ij li. of Sises to have served in the play that should have ben shewed on Candlem*as* daie at night — ij^{s} iiij^{d}. for the hire of iij vizars that should have served that night — xviij^{d}. ffor A hoope and blewe Lynnen cloth to mend the clowde that was Borrowed and cut to serve the rock in the plaie of the burnyng knight and for the hire therof and setting vpp the same where it was borowed — x^{s} } xxvj^{s} ij^{d}.

} iiij^{li}. vij^{s}. xj^{d}

Paynters p*ar*cells. **Willyam Lyzard** for cullors and other necessaries by him *pro*vided and brought into the office viz.

Three masking coat*es* made of doble pap*er* there hatt*es* covered w*i*th the same iij broomes painted v. staves and A Quinten. painted w*i*th A fool*es* head } xx^{s}.

for ffyne Cullers gold and silu*er* for patorns for the mores maske that should have served on Shrovetuesday } iiij^{s}.

Syse xiiij. gallons . . . . . xiiij^{s}.

Copper culler for the Light*es* in the hall . . . . . iij^{s} iiij^{d}.

masticott j li. . . . . . iij^{s}.

Browne j li. . . . . . xviij^{d}.

Blewe di. li. . . . . . iiij^{s}.

verte iiij li. . . . . . xvj^{s}.

Smalt iiij li. . . . . . xvj^{s}

white l li. . . . . . xvij^{s} viij^{d}

Assidewe v li. . . . . . xvj^{s} viij^{d}

Red ij li. xvj^{d}. Sape di. li. xx^{d} . . . . . iij^{s}.

Black. v li. v^{s}. glewe ij li. viij^{d}. . . . . . v^{s}. viij^{d}.

Trashe nayle xiiij^{d}. pott*es* vj^{d} & botehy xij^{d} er at sondrey tymes . ij^{s} viij^{d}.

In all — vj^{li}. vij^{s} iiij^{d}. wherof the m*aster* and clerk comptroller have abated for excessiue pric*es* — xij^{s}. And so resteth.

} cxv^{s}. iiij^{d}.

f° 13 v.

Wyerdrawers *parcells*

Edmond Burcholl for sondrey p*ar*cells by him provided and brought into the office. viz.
Doble. x^{d}. nayles to strayne wyers .c.. . . . . . . xiiij^{d}
Packnedles vj. iij^{d}/ pullies ij — viij^{d} . . . . xj^{d}
ffyne wyer j li. xiiij^{d} great wyer xxij li — xxij^{s} . . . xxiij^{s} ij^{d}
Small braunches viij newe. . . . . xxxij^{s}.
Newe mending of xiiij. old braunches of the same . ix^{s} iiij^{d}
for iij great braunches . . . . vj^{li}.
for his going by water iiij. tymes . . . . xvj^{d}
In all — ix^{li} vij^{s} xj^{d} wherof Abated by the m*aster* and clerk comptroller xvj^{s} viij^{d} & so resteth } viij^{li}. xj^{s} iij^{d}.

Botehier and cariage by water and Land and Reward*es*.

John Davyes for money by him disbursed viz.
Boate hier to the courte the xxvijth of ffebruary. 1578 to set vpp the candlestick*es* . . . . iiij^{d}
Cariage of the rock from Bridewell to the court the first of march . 1578. . . . . xiiij^{d}.
his owne bote hier agayne. . . . . iij^{d}. } xxj^{d}.

George Ioyn*er* for money by him disbursed viz.
ffor his bote hier from Sowthwarke to the courte and back agayne on sonday [8^{d}.] monday [10^{d}.] and tuesday [12^{d}.] the first of march. 1578. } ij^{s} vj^{d}

John Rose senio*ur* for money by him disbursed. viz.
ffor his botehier to the courte to take measure of the bignes of the Rock. and back agayne and after into London for provision of stuffe } xx^{d}.

Thomas Stronge for money by him disbursed. viz.
ffor bote hier for the m*aster* to and from the courte the 23 of ffebruary. 1578. being sent for by m^{r} Threasorer viij^{d}. ffor bote hier for the m*aster* to the court and back agayne the 25. and 26. of ffebruary 1578. being sent for by the Lo*rd* Chamberleyne about patornes of maske — xviij^{d}. ffor the m*aster* his bote hier to and from the courte the firste second third and ffowrth of march — iiij^{s}. ffrom the courte to Leicester howse to speake w*ith* my Lo*rd* Chamb*er*leyn — viij^{d}. geven to the Porters for Late comyng owte at the Water gate the said ffirst second and third of marche — ij^{s} In all } viij^{s} x^{d}.

f° 14 r.

Iohn Drawater for mony by him disbursed. viz. ffor his bote hier to and from the courte sondrey tymes at the making readie and setting vpp the frames Rock*es* and lightes in the hall against Shrovesondaie and to and from the court the first second. third and fowrth of march. 1578. for the safe bestowing of the furnyture in the hall ffor the players their enacted — v^{s} vj^{d} geven to the porter for late comyng owte the gate xij^{d}. to the painters on shrove tuesdaie to send for victualls because they should not go from their worke. — vj^{d} ffor Caryage A hamp*er* w*i*th stuffe to shewe my Lo*rd* Chamberleyne to the courte and back agayne — xviij^{d}. ffor cariage of two fframes to the courte the 28 of ffebruary .1578. xx^{d} ffor cariage of them and the rock from the court in two Carres — iij^{s} viij^{d}. To Roger Atkinson for carying Stuffe at two seu*er*all tymes that served the children of the Quenes chappell and my Lo*rd* Chamberleynes men to the court and back agayne — iiij^{s}. In all } xvij^{s} iiij^{d}.

Howse rent **Edmond Tilney** Esquier m*aster* of the said office having by graunte from her ma*ie*stie by her L*ett*res patent*es* dated the of Iulie in the xxjth yeare of her ma*iesties* Raigne the office of the mastership of the said office, and A mansion howse w*i*th thapp*er*ten*aunces*/ The same office being specially appointed continued and vsed w*i*thin the howsing and p*re*cincte of St Iohnes where all the store and furniture of the said office have bene and is kept and remaynyng/ The howsing and romes there app*er*teynyng to him being Imploied that he cannot yet convenyently have the same, But is driven to hire an other He is to be allowed for the rent wherof from Christmas.1578. A*nno* 21°. *Regni* Regine pred*icte* vntill mydsom*er* .1579. *Anno Regni Reg*ine p*redicte* 21°. by the space of one half yeare after of xxiij^{li}. vj^{s} viij^{d} p*er* An*num* } vj^{li} xiij^{s} iiij^{d}.

Item for money disbursed and to be disbursed aswell about the chardg*es* for making the accompt*es* to the Audito*ur* of themprest*es* and declarac*i*on of the same before my Lo*rd* Threasorer and S*ir* walter myldmey. As also for the chardg*es* in suyng furthe the Quenes warrante the privie seale order for the money and receipt of the same } viij^{li}.

S*UMMA* of all the **Emptions provisions** cariag*es* reward*es* and other necessaries besides the wag*es* aforesaid for Candlem*as* and Shrovetyde/ Anno R*egni* R*eg*ine Elizabeth pred*icte* xxj^{mo}. } L^{li}. ij^{s} iiij^{d}.

S*UMMA* TOT*A*LIS of the whole boke viz. from the xiiijth of ffebruary 1577. Anno regni Regine Elizab*eth* xx°. At w*hi*ch tyme the boke of the Laste yeare ended. vntill the vjth of march.1578. Annoq*ue* R*egni* R*eg*ine Elizabeth pred*icte* xxj^{mo}. } cccxxvij^{li} v^{s}. ij^{d}.

*Ed. Tillney

*Edward Buggyn *T Blagrave

*walter fysshe

f° 14 v.

The Totall Su*mma* **of the whole booke viz. from** the xiiijth of ffebruary .1577. Anno **R*egni* R*eg*ine** Elizabeth. **xx^{mo}.** vntill **the** vjth **of marche 1578. Anno** R*egni* R*eg*ine Elizabeth pred*icte* xxj^{mo}.

Ayring*es* from the 14 of ffebruary.1577.vntill the xxth of December then next	Wages of.	Artificers	ix^{li} iiij^{s}.	xxiiij^{li}. ij^{s} viij^{d}.	ccc xxvij^{li} v^{s}. ij^{d}.
		officers	xij^{li}.		
	Emptions and provisions . . .		lviij^{s}. viij^{d}.		
Christmas Newyeres tide tweftide and the sonday after when the mask*es* were shewen.	Wages of.	Artificers	liij^{li}. xviij^{s} vj^{d}.	ccxx^{li}. iiij^{s} viij^{d}.	
		officers	xix^{li}.		
	Emptions & p*ro*visions		cxliiij^{li}. vj^{s} ij^{d}		
Candlemas and Shrovetyde.	Wages of.	Artificers	xxiij^{li}. xv^{s}.	iiij^{xx}. ij^{li}. xvij^{s} iiij^{d}.	
		officers	ix^{li}.		
	Emptions and provisions . . .		L^{li}. ij^{s} iiij^{d}		

f° 15 r.

Betwene the vjth of marche/ 1578. *Anno* xxj^{mo}. *Regni Reg*ine Elizabethe And the ffirste of November. 1579/ *Anno* xxj^{mo}. *Reg*ni *Reg*ine Eliz*abethe* being viij. monethes The chardges of this c*ffice grewe by meanes of Ayring*es* Repairing Laying abroad Turnyng tacking sowing Brushing Rubbing spunging folding Laying vpp and safe bestowing of the garment*es* vestures apparrell disguising*es* prop*er*ties and furnyture of the same from tyme to tyme (w*i*thin those monethes) as the necessitie therof required to keepe the same in reydines for service w*hi*ch ells wold decay and be Rotten by meanes of the dancknes of the howse and want of convenient presses and plac*es* requisite to bestowe the same in the p*ar*ties names who Attended the office for the same purpose hereafter Ensueth. viz.

		Daies	
Taylors and others working and Attending the p*re*misses at thofficers comandem*ent* the first at xx^{d} the day the rest at xij^{d} as in form*er* p*re*sedent*es*	Thom*as* Clatterbook.	20	xxxiij^{s} iiij^{d}
	Thom*as* wright	20	xx^{s}.
	will*iam* Tyldesley	20	xx^{s}.
	Iohn Davies	20	xx^{s}.
	Iohn Sherborne	20	xx^{s}.
	Iohn Drawater.	20	xx^{s}.
	Iohn Dawnesey	20	xx^{s}.
			vij^{li} xiij^{s} iiij^{d}
Thofficers	The m*aster* at iiij^{s} the day	20	iiij^{li}
	The clerk comptroller At ij^{s} the daie	20	xl^{s}.
	The Clark at ij^{s} the day	20	xl^{s}.
	The yeoman at ij^{s} the day	20	xl^{s}.
			x^{li}

ffewell and other necessaries — Henry Dyson. ffor sondrey ffewell and other necessaries by him bought and brought into the office and vsed at sondrey tymes in the said Ayring*es* w*i*thin the tyme Aforesaid. viz.

Coles xxx. sack*es* — xxv^{s}. Billet*es* one M. — xiij^{s} iiij^{d} ffagot*es* one hundred — v^{s} iiij^{d}. Browne thread. di. li. — xiiij^{d} white thred j li. — ij^{s} x^{d}. Black thread j li. — ij^{s} iiij^{d} cullered thred iij q*uarters* li. — ij^{s} viij^{d}. Tape j li. — iij^{s} viij^{d}. Brushes iiij. — viij^{s}. Rubbing brushes. iij. — x^{d}. white brushes Longe and shorte for cobwebbes iiij. — ij^{s}. } lxvij^{s} ij^{d}.

S*UMMA* to*ta*lis of all the whole Ayring*es* w*i*thin the tyme Aforesaid } xxj^{li} vj^{d}

S*UMMA* To*ta*lis of the whole booke viz. from the xiiijth of ffebruary. 1577. *Annoque Regni Reg*ine Eliz*abethe* xx^{o}.(At w*hi*ch tyme the booke of the Last yeare ended) vntill the ffirst of November. 1579. Annoq*ue* *Regni Reg*ine Elizabeth*e* pred*icte* xxj^{mo} } ccc xlviij^{li}.v^{s}.viij^{d}.

* T Blagrave
* walter fysshe

* Ed Tillney
* Edwarde Buggyn

f° 15 v.

Extract from a Declared Account (1577/8-1579)

British Museum. Lansdowne MSS. 27. n° 86.

Memor*andum* there were not any kyndes of Silkes delyuered out of Thoffice of the Qu*enes* ma*iesties* greate wardrobe in london vnto Thofficers of the Revell*es* duringe the tyme of this declarac*i*on As by Certificatt subscribed by Anthony Walker Clarke of the said great wardrobe may appeare

But there hathe bene sondrie kyndes of cloth of gold & other silk*es* receued by Thofficers of the said Office, of her ma*iesties* Stoare vnder the Chardge viz. of

George Bredyman kep*er* of y^{e} wardrobe at y^{e} white haule viz. — Crymsyn cloth of gold w*i*th woo*rkes* — xxv yard*es* di . di . q*uarter*, Crymsyn gold bodkine raysed — $iiij^{er}$ yard*es* q*uarter* Cloth of sylu*er* striped w*ith* blacke silke — iij^{s} (yardes) q*uarter* Russett gold Tyncell — xx yard*es* q*uarter* p*ur*ple syluer Tyncell mailled — vij yard*es* and velvett of Orrendge Culler — xij yardes di.

Raphe Hope yeoman of the Robes in the Tower of london viz. — Tyncell chamlett of gold — x yard*es* di. Tyncell playne of blacke gold — v yard*es*/ Taffata white — xxxvij yard*es*/ Taffata Crymsyn — xxxj yard*es* di., Taffata S*ar*cenett Crymsyn — v yard*es*, and Taffata S*ar*cenett yallowe — viij yardes quarter di.

All w*hi*ch p*ar*cell*es* ar conteyned in two seuerall Certificatt*es* subscribed by the before named George Bredyman & Raphe Hope here vppon shewed/ And the imploym*ent* of the same is to be aunswered in a Reere Accompte to be made by Thofficers of the Revell*es*

7-10 January 1578-9

Warrant for Delivery of Stuff & Letters relating to the Same.

British Museum. Additional MSS. 5750.

Elizabeth R*egina*

By the Quene.

We will and commaund you, that furthw*ith* vpon the receipt herof you deliure or cause to be deliurid vnto the officers of our revels such and so much of our cloth of gold and of siluer and peces of Silk*es* remayning in yo*ur* custodye as shalbe namid in a bill subscribid by our right trusty and right Welbilouid cousin and counseler the Erel of Sussex *our Lord* chambrelain. taking a bill of the said officers or officer of o*ur* sayd revels to whom you shall deliure the same mentioning the receipt therof to o*ur* vse and seruice And thies o*ur* Lett*res* shalbe your sufficient warraunt and dischardge in this behalf Geven vndre o*ur* Signet at our Manour of Richemond the vij^th^ day of Ianuary 1578 in the xxj^th^ yere of o*ur* reign

To our trusty and welbilouid s*er*vaunt George Bredyman esquier kepar of o*ur* palais of Westm*inster*

* Examinatur per yetsweirt

f° 71.

M^r^ brydeman The q*uene* ma*iestye* hathe sent vnto you her warrant for the delyverye to her officers of her revell*es* such p*ar*cell*es* as shalbe specyfyed in a byll subscrybed w*ith* my hand & bycause it is not yet certenly known nor wylbe before the garmen*tes* be made what stuffe shall suffyce I do hartely pray you to delyver to them all such stuffe as they shall requyre to have of the old store & when all thing*es* shalbe fynyshed I wyll delyver vnto you a byll of the p*ar*tyculars sygned w*ith* my hand for *your* dyscharg and so I byd you hartely well to fare

ffrom the court .7. Ianurij 1578

f° 69.

Mr Bredyman wee hartelie pray you to send by this bearer a peece of the stuffe wheareof wee send the patrone vnto you : the whiche wee are constrayned by necessitie to send vnto [you] for/ for that wee cannot make so good shifte with all the stuff wee haue for one purpose as with some small porcion of that peece. And this *our* writing wee hope wilbe sufficient for you to lay the charge vpon vs for *your* deliuerye of the same. Written from St Iohns of Ierusalem the xth of Ianuarye 1578

Yo*ur* very louing freend*es*

It is a peece of black
and silver stryped

* T Blagrave

* Edwarde Buggyn

* walter fysshe

* non allo*catur*

f° 70.

From 1 November 1579 to 1 November 1580

viz.

Record Office. Audit Office. Accounts Various. Bd. 1213. Revels. N° 7.

Revelles. 1580. Anno *Regni* R*egi*ne Elizabeth*e* xxij^{do} The Lydgeard or Pertyculer Booke of the Chardges rysinge and growinge w*i*thin the saide Offyce Betwene the ffirste of November .1579. A*nno* xxj^{o} R*egni* R*egi*ne pred*icte* & the firste of November 1580 Anno xxij^{do} R*egni* R*egi*ne pred*icte* w*i*thin w*hi*ch tyme there were workes done & Attendaunc*es* geven as followeth videl*ice*t

Title-page r.

Christmas
Twelvtyde
Candlemas
& Shrovetyde
and makinge Choyse of playes Anno Regni *Reg*ine Elizabeth*e*

The Chardges of theis tymes viz. **ffrom** the firste daie of November 1579 Anno xxj° *Regni Reg*ine Elizabeth*e* (at whiche tyme the Booke for the Last yeare ended) The begynnynge was of makinge choise of sondrye playes comodies and inventions at dyu*ers* and sondrye tymes for the tymes aforesaid vntill the xix[th] daie of December then next followinge at whiche tymes the workes began aswell for furnyshinge & settinge forthe of sondrye of the said playes comodies and Inventions As also in Emptions and provisions made togeather w*i*th the Workes done and Attendaunc*es* geven by dyu*ers* Artyficers Workemen and Attendant*es* Workinge and Attendinge the same at sondry tymes from the said xix[th] of December vntill the xx[th] of ffebruary .1579. Anno xxij° *Regni Reg*ine predict*e* At whiche tymes the workes and Attendanc*es* for those tymes did end) for the newe makinge translatinge Repairinge fyttinge furnyshinge & settinge forth of sondrye payntinges howses vestures garment*es* vtencells and prop*er*ties incydent and requysite for the showe of the said playes comodies pastymes Inventions and devises prepared made sett forthe and shewen before her Ma*ies*tie for her Regall disporte and pastyme w*i*thin the tyme aforesaid The whole chardges whereof togeather w*i*th the p*ar*ties names to whome and wherefore the same is due hereafter ensueth

histories and Inventions shewen w*i*thin the tyme aforesaid viz. **ix.**

A history of the Duke of Millayn and the Marques of Mantua shewed at Whitehall on S[t] Stephens daie at nighte enacted by the lord Chamberlaynes s*er*u*aunt*es wholie furnyshed in this offyce some newe made and moche altered whereon was Imployed for iiij[or] newe head Attyers with traynes Scarfes, garters and other Attyers, xiij Ells of Sarcenett a Countrie howse a Cyttye and vij paire of gloves

A history of Alucius. shewed at white hall on S[t] Iohns daie at nighte enacted by the Children of her Ma*ies*ties Chappell wholly furnyshed in this offyce with many garment*es* newe made manye altered and translated whereon was Imployed for head Attyers sleeves Canyons Cases for hoase Skarfes garters and other rep*ar*acions tenne Ells of Sarcenett A Cittie a Battlement and xviij paire of gloves.

A historye of provided to haue bene shewen at Whitehall on Innocent*es* daie at nighte by the Earle of Leicesters s*er*u*aunt*es beinge in Readynes in the place to haue enacted the same whollye furnyshed w*i*th sondrye thinges in this offyce But the Queenes Ma*ies*tie coulde not come forth to heare the same/ therefore put of.

A history of the foure sonnes of ffabyous shewed at Whithall on Newe Yeares daie at [ni]ghte enacted by the Earle of Warwick*es* s*er*va*unt*es wholie furnyshed in this offyce w*i*th garment*es* some newe some altered and repaired whereon was Imployed for newe lynynge translatinge and alteringe of the Senatours gownes iij head Attyres w*i*th traynes for womens skarfes and girdles xiij ells of Sarcenett A Cytie a Mounte & vj paire of gloves

p. 1.

The histor of Cipio Africa*nus* shewen at whitehall the sondaye night after newe yeares daie enacted by the Children of Pawles furnyshed in this Offyce w*i*th sondrie garment*es* and tryumphant ensignes & bann*ers* newe made and their head peec*es* of white sarcenett scarfes and garters whereon was ymployed ells of Sarcenett A Citie a Battlem*ent* and xviij^{ne} payre of gloues

The history of shewen at white hall on Twelvedaye at nighte by the Earle of Leicesters s*e*ru*au*nt*es* furnished in this offyce with many garment*es* vtensells and prop*er*ties some made newe some translated and made fitt whereon was ymployed for head Attyers scarfes and garters ells of Sarcenett, A Citie a Countrye house and vij paire of gloves.

The history of Portio and demorantes shewen at whitehall on Candlemas daie at nighte enacted by the Lord Chamb*er*leyns s*e*ru*au*nt*es* wholly furnyshed in this offyce whereon was ymployed for scarfes garters head Attyers for women & Lynynges for hatt*es* vj ells of Sarcenett A cytie a towne & vj payre of gloves

The history of the Soldan and the Duke of shewen at Whitehall on Shrovesondaye at nighte enacted by the Earle of Derby his s*e*ru*au*nt*es* wholly furnyshed in this offyce whereon was ymployed for two Robes of blacke sarcenett, head Attyers and scarfes ells of Sarcenett A Citie and xij payre of gloves.

The history of Serpedon shewen at whitehall on Shrovetwesdaye at nighte enacted by the lord Chamb*er*leyns s*e*ru*au*nt*es* wholly furnyshed in this offyce whereon was ymployed for head Attyers for women and Scarfes xj ells of Sarcenett a greate Citie a wood, A wood A Castell and vj payre of gloves.

Taylors and other Attendant*es* workinge and attendinge the p*re*mysses the first at xx^{d} the daie and asmoche the night and the rest at xij^{d}.

	Daies	Night*es*	
Thomas Clatterbooke	37	19	iiij^{li} xiij^{s} iiij^{d}
Iohn Davyes	37	19	lvj^{s}
Thomas Wrighte	37	19	lvj^{s}
Davyd lloyd	37	19	lvj^{s}
Will*iam* Tildeslay	37	19	lvj^{s}
Edward Griffith	37	19	lvj^{s}
Thomas Stronge	37	19	lvj^{s}
Iohn Lucas	37	19	lvj^{s}
Iohn Digges	37	19	lvj^{s}
Iohn Sherbourne	37	19	lvj^{s}
Iohn Hilton	37	19	lvj^{s}
Thomas Peacock	37	19	lvj^{s}

p. 2.

	Name	Daies	Nightes		
	Edward Blacknoll	37	19		lvj^{s}
	Iohn Tipsley	36	18		liiij^{s}
	Thomas Lambe	23	6		xxix^{s}
	George Wrighte	1	0		xij^{d}
	Richard Wardman	4	0		iiij^{s}
	William Wood	4	0		iiij^{s}
	Iohn Cleiton	14	7		xxj^{s}
	Thomas Rayner	22	14		xxxvj^{s}
	Iohn ffauncer	32	17		x^{li}x^{s}
	Iohn ffarryngton	6	3		ix^{s}
	William Bonde	3	1		iiij^{s}
	George Whitledell	1	0		xij^{d}
Paynters the first at ij^{s} the daie as moche the nighte the second at xx^{d} the rest xviij^{d} the daye & asmoch the nighte	William Lyzard	21	9		lx^{s}
	Pangrasse Englishe	1	2	1 doble	v^{s}
	William Reeles	21	12	2 single 5 doble	xlix^{s} vj^{d}
	William Keenes	24	14	4 single 5 doble	lvij^{s}
	Thomas Tyler	21	21	11 single 5 doble	lxiij^{s}
	Edmonde Iefferson	8	5	5 single	xix^{s} vj^{d}
	Richarde Woode	20	16	6 single 5 doble	liiij^{s}
	Iohn Terres	13	11	7 single 2 doble	xxvj^{s}
	Abraham Kernell	3	1	1 single	vj^{s}
	Iohn Birde	11	8	4 doble	xxviij^{s} vj^{d}
Wyerdrawers the first at xx^{d} the daye and as moche the nighte the rest at xvj^{d}.	Edmond Byrchell	9	6	2 single 2 doble	xxv^{s}
	Symon Powle	3	4	2 single 1 doble	ix^{s} iiij^{d}
	Henry Wattes	1	3	1 single 1 doble	v^{s} iiij^{d}
	Thomas Hall	5	3	1 single 1 doble	x^{s} viij^{d}

34 — 16 — 10.

p. 3.

		Daies	Nightes	
Carpenters at xvj^{d} the daye and asmoche the nighte	William Barker	18	6	xxxij^{s}
	Edward ffurres	19	6	xxxiij^{s} iiij^{d}
	Anthony Lizon	5	0	vj^{s} viij^{d}
	Robert Bunbery	14	3	xxij^{s} viij^{d}
	Robert Cranwell	11	4	xx^{s}
The Porter at xij^{d} the daye and asmoche the nighte	Iohn Dawncye	37	19	lvj^{s}
Thoffycers the first at iiij^{s} the daie and asmoche the nighte the rest at ij^{s} the daye & asmoche the nighte	The Master	39	21	xij^{li}
	The Clarke comptroller	39	21	vj^{li}
	The Clarke	39	21	vj^{li}
	The Yeoman	39	21	vj^{li}

S*umma* **of all** the Wages due within this offyce for Workmanshipp and attendaunc*es* in the same within the tyme aforesaid } cviij^{li} xvj^{s} x^{d}

* Ed : Tyllney

* Edwarde Buggyn

* walter fysshe

p 1. 38-10-8.

Emptions & prouisions.

Mercers and Lynnen drap*ers* p*ar*cells and other necessaryes

Iohn digges for sondrye thinges by him bought provided and brought into the said offyce viz.		xx^{li} v^{s} j^{d}
White sarcenet xxvj ells at vj^{s} the elle	vij^{li} xvj^{s}	
Canvas fower peec*es* contayninge in the whole elles 142 at xij^{d} the ell	vij^{li} ij^{s}	
Paste bordes one dosen.	iiij^{s}	
A standishe brought into the store howse of the office	ij^{s} iiij^{d}	
ffirre poles vj.	iij^{s}	
Coles one loade	xxvj^{s}	
ffaggott*es* one hundred	viij^{s}	
Billett*es* [18 s] one thowsand and the Carryage [2 s.] thereof.	xx^{s}	
Carryage of stuffe to the Court at sondry tymes	ij^{s}	
Hoopes to make a Mounte	iij^{s}	
Nailes of sondry [sortes] ix hundred and 4 pillers [20 d.]	ix^{s} ix^{d}	
Bote hier to and from the Court at sondry tymes	ij^{s} iiij^{d}	
Coullers vsed at	xij^{d}	
Ropes three Bundells	vj^{s}	
Holly Ivy and Baies.	xx^{d}	
Russett Ieyne ffustian xviij yard*es*	xviij^{s}	

Chandelors p*ar*cells

Barnard ffabyan for sondrie p*ar*cells by him broughte into the offyce. viz.		xl^{s} ij^{d}.
Cotton candells at iiij^{d} the li. vj dosen di.	xxvj^{s}	
Packthread iiij li. at xij^{d} the li.	iiij^{s}	
Glew j li.	vj^{d}	
Searinge candell ij li. di.	ij^{s} vj^{d}	
Great cord v peec*es* at xvj^{d} the peece	vj^{s} viij^{d}	
Small cord at vj^{d} the peece vij peec*es*	iij^{s} vj^{d}	
Lynck*es* vj.	ij^{s}	

Thom*as* Wright for sondry thinges by him bought provided & brought into the offyce viz.	
ffyne collored thread at iiij^{s} the pound iij li. iij quarters —	xv^{s}
Paste bord*es* of sondry sort*es* ij dosen di.	ix^{s}
ffyne white thread at vj^{s} the pound iij quarters of a pound	iiij^{s} vj^{d}
Browne threade at ij^{s} viij^{d} the pou[n]d one pound and one Quarter	iij^{s} iiij^{d}
Tape of sondry cull*ou*rs and prizes three pound*es*	xij^{s} x^{d}
Gloves at vij^{s} the dozen vij dozen di.	lij^{s} vj^{d}
Tainter Hookes at viij^{d} the c / ij^{c}	xvj^{d}
Nayles at iiij^{d} the. c. cc.	viij^{d}

27-9-5.

p. 5.

Necessaries

Carryage and recaryage to and from the courte sortes of stuffe and garmentes at sondry tymes	xvij^{s} vj^{d}	vj^{li} vj^{s} x^{d}
Baskettes ij — xij^{d} glasse Bottells ij — x^{d}	xxij^{d}	
Silke one ounce	ij^{s}	
Mendinge a locke for the store howse dore	xvj^{d}	
Pynduste one pound	xij^{d}	
Blacke thread of sondry sortes iij quarters [le pounde]	ij^{s} j^{d}	
Hoppes one pound	xij^{d}	
Bromes [ij d] Rubbing Brushe [iij d]	v^{d}	
Milke and Butter	vj^{d}	

Iohn Sherborne for sondrye thinges by h[i]m boughte provided vsed expended & brought into the Masters Lodginge for the rehearsall of sondrie playes to make Choise of dyuers of them for her Maiestie viz.

Cotton candells at sondry prices xv dozen	iij^{li} j^{s} iij^{d}	xij^{li} v^{s} vij^{d}.
Plates for to hange vpon Walles to sett .v Candells in .vij	vj^{s}	
Torches ij^{o} dozen at xiiij^{s} the dozen	xxviij^{s}	
Billettes iiij thowsand at xvj^{s} the thowsand	lxiiij^{s}	
Coales ij loades at xxvj^{s} the Loade	lij^{s}.	
Rushes [v s vj d] yncke [x s] and paper [ij s] ij^{o} Lockes and the amendinge of one Locke [vj d.] Hookes [vj d.] nayles [18 d.] iiij^{or} Wheeles [16 d.] and fflowres [12 d.] paterns for head attyers [vj s.]	xxviij^{s} iiij^{d}	
Lawne Ruffes for head Attyers vj	vj^{s}	

Edmonde Tylney esquier Master of the said Offyce for dyver provisions by him made and his Chardges in the seruice of the said Offyce at sondrye tymes viz.

ffor his Attendaunce botehyer and other Chardges to and from the Court at Greenewich by the space of ij monethes and more by Commaundement for settinge downe of dyverse devises to Receave the ffreenche	c^{s}
ffor his botehier and other Chardges to and from thence About the declaracion of the laste yeares Accompte to my Lord Treasorer and my Lord Chamberleyne	xxx^{s}

ffor his Chardges with the Chardges of the players the Carriage and recariage of their stuffe for examynynge and Rehersinge of dyuers plaies and Choise makinge of x of them to be showen before her Maiestie at Christmas twelfetide Candelmas and Shrovetide and their sondry rehersalls afterwardes till to be presented before her Maiestie — x^{li}

To one Porter and iij other Attendauntes at severall tymes after the rate of xij^{d} a pece A day for their Attendaunce and service at the rehersalls and Choise makinge of the said x plaies — x^{li}

ffor v yardes of greene clothe at $viij^{s}$ the yard and for A deske — xlix^{s}

ffor his Attendaunce at the Court xij weekes after Ashewedensday to sue out the warrant and for horse hier and Ridinge Chardges dyuerse tymes to Nonesuche to Satisfie her Maiestie my Lord Treasorer and my Lord Chamberleyne in matters concernynge the offyce — c^{s}

} $xxxiij^{li}\ xix^{s}$

William Barker. for sondry thinges by him provided and browght in to this offyce to be vsed at shrovetyde .viz.

Rafters [v s. iiij d] iiij^or ffirre poles [ij s] /iiij/ Bordes one hundreth [vij s] . . . $xiiij^{s}\ iiij^{d}$

Doble Quarters fower . . . . ij^{s}

Doble x^{d} nayles one hundread [xx d] single x^{d} nayles ij hondread [xx d] six peny Nayles three hundread [xviij d] tw[o]peny Nayles one hundred [ij d.] — v^{s}

ffor Carriage of the thinges above said to the Court — xvj^{d}

} $xxij^{s}\ viij^{d}$

Iohn Davyes for sondry thinges by him provided and vsed in the said office viz.

ffor Ivy [viij d.] nayles [iij d.] Collored thred and tape [vj d.] Browne thred [xij d.] Caryage of Stuffe into the Masters Chamber [ij d.] — $ij^{s}\ vij^{d}$

ffor Carryage of a Load of tymber from the Court to St Iohns bote hier for the straunger that Brought Cawles — xvj^{d}

} $iij^{s}\ xj^{d}$.

28-15-7.

p. 7.

Edmonde Bircholl for sondry thing*es* by him bowght provided and browght into the offyce } x^{li} vj^{s} iiij^{d}.

Hande Candelstyckes iiij dozen . . . . viij^{s}
Sȣcke Candelstickes [one dozen] for painters [ij s] /vj bodkins [vj d] . . . . ij^{s} vj^{d}
plate Candelstick*es* one dozen . . . . ij^{s}
Dowt*es* [vj d] for Candells vj snuffers vj paire [ij s.] . . . . . . ij^{s} vj^{d}
Lantornes [xj s viij d] vj, one paile/ [v d] hookes and eyes one thowsand [xx] xiij^{s} ix^{d}
A hollowe knife [xij d] of plate, head*es* of wier/ [iiij s] iiij. . . . . . v^{s}
Bowles [xij d] for A speare iiij^{or}, white wandes [vj d]. . . . . } . . . . ij^{s} viij^{d}
Soder two pounde [xiiij d.] . . . .
Botehier to the Court w*i*th the stuffe twise . . . . . viij^{d}
Wier [xxxij s] xxxij li A Pole [iiij d] Rosin [ij d] Bayes [viij d]. . . . . xxiij^{s} ij^{d}
Light*es* of Plate in Braunches xxiiij. . . . . vj^{li}
White Plates [xij d] iij, nayles [x d], quiltinge needles [ij d]. . . . . . ij^{s}
Rubbinge Brushes [viij d] ij Heath brushe one [iij s] . . . . . . iij^{s} viij^{d}
Light*es* of Plate in Braunches more ij^{o} . . . . x^{s}
Red Incke and a Bottell . . . . v^{d}.

Iohn Drawater for money by him disbursed for sondry thing*es* .viz. } xxxvij^{s} v^{d}.

Nayles at vj^{d} the hundred, [ij s] iiij^{c}/ doble x^{d} nayles [v s] iij^{c}/ single x^{d} nayles [xx d] cc fower peny nayles [viij d] ij^{c}/ iij^{d} nailes ij^{d}/ j^{c}/ bordes [vj s.] j^{c} } xvj^{s} vij^{d}

ffurre poles to make Rayles for the battlem*entes* and to make the prison for my *Lord* of Warwick*es* men at vj^{d} the peece — v^{s} single Quarters to enlardge the Scaffolde in the hall one Twelfe night vj xviij doble quarters for the same Cause ij — xij^{d} } vij^{s} vj^{d}

ff*or* a Reame of pap*er* to make Counterfeit flowers patterns and other wise vsed in the offyce for foldinge of sondry thing*es* } vj^{s} viij^{d}

ffor his bote hier to and from the Court at sondry tymes during Christmas Twelfetyde Candellmas and Shrove and many tymes in the night after the plaies were ended } vj^{s} viij^{d}

The Clerke. for his Ordynarye Greene cloth pap*er* Incke Quilles waxe Counters Deskes Standishes and tooles fo[r] the makynge Compiling and cons*er*vinge of the Bookes bylles plot*es* paternes and models &c. for and concernynge this Offyce } lxvj^{s} viij^{d} } lxvj^{s} viij^{d}

Thomas Skynn*er* for sundry parcells by him deliu*er*ed in to the offyce viz. — viz. — xiiij^{li} xviij^{s} iiij^{d}

Chaungeable sarsenett at vj^{s} viij^{d} the ell xxxj ells . . .	x^{li} vj^{s} viij^{d}
White sarsenett at vj^{s} viij^{d} the ell iij elles di.	xxiij^{s} iiij^{d}
Yelowe sarsenett at vj^{s} viij^{d} the ell j ell and a quarter . .	viij^{s} iii^{d}j
Blacke sarsenett at vj^{s} viij^{d} the ell vj ell*es*	xl^{s}
Greene sarscenett at vj^{s} viij^{d} the el liij ells	xx^{s}

Will*iam* Lyzarde for sondry thing*es* by him browght into the offyce — x^{li} xvj^{d}.

Syse cullers pottes nayles and pensills vsed and occupyed vpon the payntinge of vij Cities one villadge one Cuntrey howse one Battlement iiij axes a Braunche lillyes and a mount for Christmas iij Holidaies	iiij^{li} xv^{s} viij^{d}
Syse cullers pott*es* Assydewe golde and silver vsed and occupied for the Garnyshinge of xiiij titles iiij facynges. of sarsenett powdered with Ermyns A Backe of Armo*ur* a paier of wyng*es* a banner a penndaunt and foure guilte balls againste new yeares day the sonday after Twelfe day and Candelmas	lij^{s} iiij^{d}
Syse cullers Assidew and other necessaries vsed and occupied aboute the ffurnyshinge and garnyshinge of three greate braunches of Leight*es* in the hall fower and Twenty small braunches all twise garnyshed for Twelfe tyde and Shrove tyde	liij^{s} iiij^{d}

Edwarde Buggyn gent*leman* for money by him disbursed. for standyshe pap*er* wax Quilles Bookes Counters botehier and in Reward*es* at sondry tymes duringe the workes — xx^{s}

Summa of the Emptions provisions and Carryages &c. . . . cxvi^{li} xviij^{s} iiij^{d}.

S*UMMA* total*is* of all the Emptions provisions carryages and reward*es* w*i*th the wages & Attendanc*es* w*i*thin the tyme aforesaid — ccxxvj^{li} xv^{s} ij^{d}.

* Ed : Tyllney

* walter fysshe

* Edwarde Buggyn

25-19-8.

p. 9.

Betwene the twentith of ffebruary .1579. Anno Regni Regine Elizabeth*e* xxij^{do} at w*hi*ch tyme the workes for the tymes aforesaid did end **And** the first of October **1580** Anno Regni Regine Elizabeth*e* p*redicte* **The Chardges** of this offyce grewe at sondry tymes by meanes of Ayringe reparyinge amendinge Brushinge spungeinge Rubbynge Wypinge swepinge Cleane puttinge in order foldinge layinge vpp and safe bestowinge of the garment*es* vestures apparell dysguisinges prop*er*ties and furniture of the same from tyme to tyme w*i*thin the tyme afore said as the necessitie thereof at sondry tymes required to kepe the same in redynes for s*er*vice w*hi*ch els wolde be mowldy musty mothe eaten and rotten by meanes of the dancknes of the howse and wante of Convenient presses & places requier togeathe w*i*th the oldnes of the stuffe and store within the said offyice The p*ar*ties who comonly attend att the said office for the same purpose w*i*th their severall names allowed for this tyme togeather w*i*th suche Emptions & necessaries as was expended at and aboute the same p*ar*ticulerlie hereafter ensueth viz.

Taylors and others workinge and attendinge the p*re*mysses the first at xx^{d} the daye the rest at xij^{d}.	**Thomas Clatterbooke**	20	xxxiij^{s} iiij^{d}
	Iohn Davies	20	xx^{s}
	Will*iam* Tyldesley	20	xx^{s}
	Ioh[n] Dygg*es*	20	xx^{s}
	Iohn Sherborne	20	xx^{s}
	Iohn Lucas	20	xx^{s}
	Iohn Dawncye	20	xx^{s}

Offycers	The M*aster* at iiij^{s} the day	20	iiij^{li}
	The Clerke comptroller at ij^{s} the day	20	xl^{s}
	The Clerke at ij^{s} the day	20	xl^{s}
	The Yeoman at ij^{s} the day	20	xl^{s}

ffewell & other necessaryes

Iohn Lucas for fewell and other necessaries by him bought and browghte into the offyce & vsed at sondry tymes in the said Ayringes &c. w*i*thin the tyme aforesaid viz.

Coales twenty sack*es* — xx^{s} Byllett*es* one thowsand — xvj^{s} 8^{d}/ ffaggott*es* one hundreth — v^{s} viij^{d} Browne thredd di. li. — xvj^{d} White thred three quarters of a lb — ij^{s}. Blacke thred a lb — ij^{s} iiij^{d} Thred of sondry Coll*ou*rs three quarters of a lb — ij^{s} vj^{d} Tape j lb — iij^{s} iiij^{d} Brushes iij — vj^{s} Rubbinge Brushes iij — x^{d} white Brushes longe and shorte for Cobbwebbes iiij — ij^{s}/ in all — lxij^{s} viij^{d}

p. 10.

20^{li} - 16^{s}.

Edmond Tilney Esquier for money by him dysbursed and to be disbursed aswell about the Charges for makynge the accomptes to the Auditour of themprest and declaracion of the same before my Lord Treasourer and Sir walter Myldmay As also for the Chardges in suynge on the Queenes Warraunte the privy seale order for the payment of the money and receipte of the same } viij^li^

S umma totalis of the Chardges Last aforesaid } xxviij^li^ xvj^s^

October 1580 Anno xxij^do^ Regni Regine Elizabethe

Layinge. abroade turnynge mending brushing spunginge Rubbinge and puttinge in order and redynes of the Maskes vestures players garmentes properties stuffe store and ymplementes of this offyce for the shewe thereof to & before Thomas Sackford Esquier Master of the Requestes and Sir Owen Hopton Knight liefe Tenaunte of her Maiesties Tower of london especially appointed and aucthorised to viewe and devide the store theire Remaynynge with the waitinge workynge and attendaunce of the officers of the same office and others workinge fframynge Compillinge and declarynge the state ymplementes and remayne vntill the full pervse and determynacion of the same by vertue of a warrante vnder six of the Counsells handes beneath mencioned The Chardges from the said first of October vntill the first of November Anno predicto as here vnder the persons names with their seuerall duetyes and wherefore particularly ensueth viz.

To our lovinge frendes Mr Seckford Master of the Requestes Sir Owyn Hopton knight Leife tenaunte of her Maiesties Tower of London

After our harty Comendacions Whereas the Queenes Maiestie hath lately by her lettres Patentes bestowed the Office of the Master of the Revells theis are to signify vnto you her highnes pleasure is That you doe Repaire vnto the said Office & theire to take a view and pervse the stuffe which remayneth theire in what estate it is in and so takinge a sufficient Inventory of suche of the same stuffe as shalbe found remayninge making a dyvision in the same Inventory of suche stuffe as shall seeme serviceable from the rest not serviceable and deliver the same by Indenture to Edmond Tylney nowe Master of the said Offyce And so fare you well from the Courte at Oteland this eighte day of Awgust

Thomas Bromley (Cancellarius), William Burleighe Thomas Sussex R Leicester ffrancis Walsingham, Iohn Wylson

p. 11.

Taylo*urs* & others workinge and Attendinge the p*re*mysses the first at xx^{d} the daye the rest at xij^{d}	Taylo*urs* Thomas Clatterbooke	5	viij^{s} iiij^{d}
	Iohn Digges	5	v^{s}
	Iohn Davyes	5	v^{s}
	Davyd Lloyd	5	v^{s}
	Will*iam* Tildesley	5	v^{s}
	Will*iam* Sone	5	v^{s}
	Thomas Stronge	5	v^{s}
	Iohn Lucas	5	v^{s}
	Iohn Sherbourne	5	v^{s}
	Iohn Hilton	5	v^{s}
	Thomas Peacock	5	v^{s}
	Edward Blacknoll	5	v^{s}
	Iohn Dauncye	5	v^{s}
Thoffycers the ffirste at iiij^{s} the daye the rest at ij^{s}	The *Master*	5	xx^{s}
	The Clerk Comptroller	5	x^{s}
	The Clerk	5	x^{s}
	The yeoma*n*	5	x^{s}

S*umma* of the wages . . . . cxviij^{s} iiij^{d}.

Emptions and Provisions

Iohn Digges for ffewer and sondrye other necessaryes by him bought brought and vsed in thoffyce for the tyme & purpose aforesaid viz. Rushes — v^{s} x^{d} Coales xxx sackes — xxvj^{s} viij^{d} Billett*es* one thowsand — xvj^{s} Lock*es* and keyes of Vlricke Netsey for the store howse Chest*es* and presses and for hinges and staples for the same Chest*es* & press*es* for the safe kepinge and bestowinge of the stuffe menc*i*oned in the Inventoryes — xxxiij^{s} iiij^{d}. Paper p*ar*chement Counters Standishe pyndust pens quylls wax & tooles for makinge compilinge & examynge the same Inventoryes — xiij^{s} iiij^{d}. Thred Tape bodkyns brushes & Rubbers for settinge thinges in Readynes for the tyme and purpose aforesaid — xvj^{s} x^{d} in all — v^{li} xij^{s}.

ffor the Ingrossinge of three paire of Indentid Inventories — xl^{s}.

S*umma* **Total***is* of the Chardges aforesaid — xiij^{li} x^{s} iiij^{d}.

The totall of this booke viz. from the firste daye of November 1579. Anno xxj *Regni Reg*ine Elizabethe vntill the firste of Novemb*er* 1580 Anno xxij^{do} *Regni Reg*ine predi*cte* — cclxix^{li} j^{s} vj^{d}.

Chrystmas Candlemas and Shrovetyde	Wages of: Artyficers — lxxviij^{li} vj^{s}; Offycers — xxx^{li} x^{d}	ccxxvj^{li} xv^{s} ij^{d}	cclxix^{li} j^{s} vj^{d}
	Emptions & provisions — cxvij^{li} xviij^{s} iiij^{d}		
Eyringes from the xxth of ffebruary .1579. vntill the firste of October 1580	Wages of: Artyfycers — vij^{li} xiij^{s} iiij^{d}; Offycers — x^{li}	xxviij^{li} xvj^{s}	
	Emptions and provisions with the Chardges of the Accompte — xj^{li} ij^{s} viij^{d}		
The Chardges of the Survey.	Wages of: Artyficers — lxviij^{s} iiij^{d}; Offycers — l^{s}	xiij^{li} ix^{s} viij^{d}	
	Emptions & provisions — vij^{li} xj^{s} iiij^{d}		

* Ed: Tyllney

* Edwarde Buggyn

* walter fysshe

p. 13

From 1 November 1580 to 31 October 1581

viz.

Record Office. Audit Office. Accounts Various. Bd. 1213. Revells. N° 8.

Revell*es* .1580. Annoq*ue* Regni Regine Elizabeth*e* xxiij°.

Title-page r.

Christmas Twelftide Candlemas & Shrovetide twoe challendges & the choise making of playes. Anno regni Regine Elizabethe **xxiij° 1580.**

Attendaunce geven and worke done betwene the firste of November .1580. Anno regni Regine Elizabethe .xxij°. and the laste of october .1581. Anno regni Regine Elizabethe pred*icte* .xxiij°. By meanes of choise making reformyng and attending of such plaies comodies and invenc*i*ons as were presented and set furth before her ma*ies*tie At the tymes aforesaid. The whole chardges wherof aswell for wages as for wares Iournig chardges and all expenc*es* thervnto belonging herafter p*ar*ticulerly ensueth.

The Earle of Leicesters men — **A Comodie called delighte** shewed at white hall on S[t] Stephens daie at nyght wheron was ymploied newe, one cittie, one battlement and .xij. paire of gloves.

The Earle of Sussex men. — **A storie** of enacted on S[t] Iohns daie at night wheron was Imploied newe one howse one battlement and thirtene paire of gloves.

The Earle of Derbies men — **A storie** of shewed at white hall on newe yeres daye at nyght wheron was ymployed newe one cittie one battlement and .xiij. paire of gloves.

The children of Pawles — **A storie of Pompey** enacted in the hall on twelf nighte wheron was ymploied newe one great citty, A senate howse and eight ells of dobble sarcenet for curtens and .xviij. paire of gloves.

A Challendge. — **A Challendge** at the Tilte proclaymed on twelf nighte and performed by therle of Arundle the xxij[th] of Ianuary following during all w*hi*ch tyme the m*aster* of the Revells attended for the p*re*senting of diuerse devises w*hi*ch happened in that meane season.

The earle of Sussex men — **A storie** of shewed on Candlemas daie at night wheron was ymploied newe, one cittie, one battlement and xij. paire of gloves besides other furniture out of thoffice

The children of the Quenes ma*ies*t*ies* chappell — **A Storie** of enacted on shrovesondaie night wheron was ymployed .xvij. newe sutes of apparrell .ij. newe hat*es* of velvet xx[tie] Ells of single sarcenet for facing*es* band*es* scarfes and girdles one citty, one pallace and xviij. paire of gloves.

The Earle of Leicesters men. — **A Storie** of shewed on shrovetuesdaie at night in the hall wheron was ymploied one great citty and .xij. paire of gloves.

f° 1 r.

wages

		Daies	Nightes	
The Yeoman & certen taylors for worke doing	The yeoman of the Revells at ij^{s} the day	40	10	v^{li}.
	His twoe men at xij^{d} A peece by the daie	40	10	v^{li}.
	Thomas Clatterboke at xx^{d} the daye	13	10	xxj^{s}.
	Iohn Tuppesley at xij^{d} the daye.	20	8	xxviij^{s}
	Thomas Rayner at xij^{d} the daye	14	0	xiiij^{s}.
* Porter	Iohn Dauncey at xij^{d} the daye	18	0	xviij^{s}.

The maister one porter and .iij. other servitors for Attendaunc*es* geven in the said servic*es*

The Maister of the Revells aswell for his attendaunce at the tymes aforesaid As also for the choise making of playes at iiij^{s}. the daie from All Hollan Eve vntill Ashewednesdaie. *being cx dayes . . . . xxij^{li}.
Iohn Hilton during the said tyme at .xij^{d}. the day . . . . c.x^{s}.
Iohn Sherborne at .xij^{d}. the daie. . . . . c.x^{s}.
Robert Reaklidge at xij^{d} the daie. . . . . c.x^{s}.
Thomas Reaklidge at xij^{d} the daie . . . . c.x^{s}.

wierdrawers. the firste at xx^{d} the day and the reste at xvj^{d}.

Edmond Burchall and his .ij. men him self at xx^{d}. the daie and as much the night and his men At xvj^{d} the day A peece .vj. daies and .viij. nightes . . . . iij^{li}. viij^{d}.

Carpenters at xvj^{d} the day and as much the night

Iohn Taylor and his three men at xvj^{d} A peece the daie and as much the night .16. daies and .7. nightes . . . . iiij^{li}. xv^{s}.

SUMMA of all the wages due within this office for workemanship and Attendaunce at the tymes aforesaid . . . . lxv^{li}. xvj^{s}. viij^{d}.

* Ed : Tyllney
* walter fysshe

* The M*aster* allouans from Allhallotid vntell ashwedsneday as well for ye choyse making of playes & attendantt*es* att ij seuerall triuphes during the sayd time as also for his wagis at cristmas candell-mas & shroue tid at iiij^{s} the Daye — xxij^{li}

f° 1 v.

Emptions and Provisions

Parcels	Item	Sum	Total
Paynters p*ar*cells.	* willia*m* lizard Paynting by greate of .vj. small citties & three battlement*es*	ix^{li}	**xx^{li}.**
	Paynting by great of twoe great clothes at iij^{li}. x^{s}. the peece	vij^{li}.	
	Sylvering of one herault*es* coate . . .	x^{s}.	
	Painting and working the braunches in the hall by greate	lv^{s}.	
	Painting of .ix. titles w*i*th cop*ar*tment*es*—	xv^{s}.	
Wierdrawers & Ironmong*ers* p*ar*cells.	Candlestick*es* .iiij. dozen.	viij^{s}.	xviij^{li}. ij^{s}.
	stock candlestick*es* .ij. dozen	ij^{s}.	
	wyer greate and small.	xxxvj^{s}	
	Lanterns .iij.	vj^{s}.	
	Small lightes of plate in braunches .xxvj. at .v^{s}. the peece	vj^{li}. x^{s}.	
	one greate newe lighte	xl^{s}.	
	for mending the old great lightes . . .	xij^{s}.	
	Pulleys	xij^{d}.	
	Ropes sixe greate and other small cord—	xij^{s}. 15. 14^{s}.	
	for mending agayne the .iij. greate lightes and vj. small	x^{s}.	
	Bodkyns	xij^{d}.	
	small lightes three for them w*hi*ch were stollen at twelftide	xv^{s}.	
	A Iron cradle to make fire in for the players	xx^{s}.	
	one locke	xij^{d}.	
	nayles and hookes of all sort*es* . . .	xx^{s}.	
	Arsedewe xij li. at iiij^{s} the pound . . .	xlviij^{s}.	
mercers p*ar*cells. * The duble Sarcenett maid into Curtyns and Implowid aboute Storie of pompay plaid by the Childring of powles/ The single Sarcenett was Implowid for fasinges bandes Scarffes & Girdles whan the Childring of the Chapell plaid before her Ma*ies*tie	* Thom*as* Skiner Orendge taffeta sarcenet at x^{s} the ell viij. ells	iiij^{li}.	**xj^{li}.xiiij^{s}.iiij^{d}.**
	single sarcenet of diu*er*se cullors at vj^{s} viij^{d} the ell. xx. ells	vj^{li}. xiij^{s} iiij^{d}.	
	Buckeram red at xij^{d} the yard. xxj^{tie}. yard*es*	xxj^{s}	
haberdash*ers* p*ar*cells.	Twoe broad copher bond*es* for hat*es* at iij^{s} iiij^{d} the peece	vj^{s} viij^{d}.	xxij^{s} viij^{d}
	fethers .ij. at .v^{s}. the peece	x^{s}.	
	The making of ij. velvet hat*es*	vj^{s}.	

f° 2 r.

Carpenters parcells.	Bordes. vj^{c}. at vij^{s}. the hundred	xlij^{s}.	iiij^{li}. ij^{s}.
	Rafters	xij^{s}.	
	firre polles	x^{s}	
	dobble quarters	viij^{s}	
	Single quarters	vij^{s}	
	Cariage	iij^{s}.	

Iohn Sherbourne for diuerse thinges by him brought and Provided for the office vsed and expended aswell for the Rehersalls of playes as at the courte in the hall and other places. viz.

Lightes.	Cotten candle at sondrey prices. xvj. dozen.	lxv^{s}. iiij^{d}.	xix^{li}. ij^{s}. iiij^{d}.
	Torches.ij. dozen at .xiiij^{s}. the dozen.	xlij^{s}.	
	Linckes.ij. dozen at .iiij^{s}. the dozen	viij^{s}.	
ffewell.	Billettes. iiij. thowsand at xvj^{s} the thousand	lxiiij^{s}	
	Coles .iiij. load at xxvj^{s} the load	v^{li}.iiij^{s}.	
	ffagottes twoe hundred at vj^{s} the hundred	xij^{s}.	
necessaries cariage.	Rushes — viij^{s}. pastebordes — xij^{s}. glewe — ij^{s}. Tape — x^{s} Threed of diuerse cullors and prices — xxv^{s}. botehier v^{s}. — cariage and Recariage of stuffe — xv^{s}. and for A close stoole — x^{s}.	iiij^{li}. vij^{s}.	

Edmond Tylney esquire master of the said office for diuerse thinges and provisions by him made and his chardges in the service of the said office at sondrey tymes. viz.

Canvas	*Iohn Digges for Canvas. c.xl. ells at xij^{d} the ell	vij^{li}.	xxiij^{li}. vij^{s}.
Gloves	Gloves viij. dozen at vij^{s} the dozen	lvj^{s}	
	Twoe yardes of velvet dying	v^{s}.	
botehier	botehier at sondrey tymes	xxvj^{s}	
ordinary allowaunce	for his ordinarie grene cloth, standishe Inck and paper —	iij^{li}.	
	for his attendaunce and chardges at the courte after Ashewednesdaie.vij weekes to sue out her maiesties warrante.	vj^{li}.	
	for the examyning compiling and twice writing of this booke	iij^{li}.	

Summa of the emptions provisions & cariages — iiij^{xx} xvij^{li}. x^{s}. iiij^{d}.

SUMMA totalis of all the emptions provisions and cariages with the wages and Attendaunces within the tyme aforesaid. — clxij^{li} xix^{s} iiij^{d}

* Ed Tyllney

* walter fysshe

f° 2 v.

Attendaunce geven and worke done betwixt the **xviij**th daie of marche and the firste of Aprill Anno pred*icto* at the Comaundement of the Lord Chamberleyne for setting downe of paterns for maskes and making vp of some of the same for the Receaving of the ffrench Comissioners w*i*th the provision of certeyne stuffe prop*er*ties and making of modells for A mownte and for the edifying of A greate p*ar*te of the said mounte The p*ar*ticularities wherof herafter ensueth viz.

		Daies	
Tailors and other attendaunt*es* the firste at **xx**^{d} the daie the reste at xij^{d}	Thomas Clatterbooke	8	xiij^{s} iiij^{d}
	Iohn Tuppesley	12	xij^{s}.
	Iohn Davis	12	xij^{s}
	David lloid	12	xij^{s}
	Will*iam* Tyldesley	12	xij^{s}
	Edward Griffith	12	xij^{s}.
	Thom*as* Stronge	12	xij^{s}.
	Iohn Lucas	12	xij^{s}.
	Iohn Sherbourne	12	xij^{s}.
	Iohn Hilton.	12	xij^{s}.
	Thom*as* Chapman	12	xij^{s}.
	Thom*as* Ruckledge	12	xij^{s}.
	Thomas Rayner	8	viij^{s}.
	Iohn Dauncy	12	xij^{s}.
Porter.	Iohn digges.	10	x^{s}.
Painter at ij^{s} the day	Will*iam* Lizard	12	xxiiij^{s}.
The officers the firste at iiij^{s} the reste at ij^{s}	The maister	12	xlviij^{s}.
	The clerk comptroller	12	xxiiij^{s}.
	The clerke	12	xxiiij^{s}.
	The yeoman	12	xxiiij^{s}

Iohn Rose for the tymber and workmanship of A mounte to take it agayne into his owne hand*es* because it was not vsed } xlvj^{s} viij^{d}.

Iohn Bowles for copper lace frindge tassells and buttons deliu*er*ed into the offic*es* for the workes w*hi*ch should haue ben done for paterns } x^{li}. x^{s}

will*iam* Lyzard for cullors gold and silu*er* for painting of paterns and such like } xxxvj^{s}

Edward Buggen clerk comptroller of the said office for certen paterns of maskes brought into the office } xl^{s}.

Iohn Sherborne for.ij load*es* of billet*es* — xxvij^{s}. threed — v^{s}. tape. v^{s}. paper for paterns — ij^{s} } xxxix^{s}

f° 3 r.

Edmond Tylney esquier *master* of the Revells for his chardges and certen provision. viz.

ffor his Attendaunce at the proclaymyng of the challendge and the ij. daies of the tryumphe him self and his men	xxiiij^{s}
ffor botehier for him self and his men at diu*er*se tymes during the laste work*es* of the Revells vnto the lord Chamberleyne and the lord of Leicester for showing of paterns	x^{s}.
ffor A head attire of A woman of lawne florished w*i*th gold and silver w*i*th longe pendent*es*	xx^{s}
ffor A paire of winges of Estrichfeathers to have ben vsed in the maske	xxx^{s}

38. 15^{s}. **Su*mma*** . . . . . xxxviij^{li}. xv^{s}.

Ayreinges

Betwene the firste of Aprill 1581. Anno regni Regine Elizabethe xxiij^{o}. at w*hi*ch tyme the work*es* & attendanc*es* for the tymes aforesaid did end. And the firste of october. 1581. Anno regni Regine Eliz*abethe* .xxiij^{o}. the chardges of this office grewe at sondrey tymes by meanes of ayring repairing brushing spunging rubbing sweeping, putting in order, laying vp, and safe bestowing of the garment*es* vestures disguising*es* properties and furniture of the same from tyme to tyme w*i*thin the tyme aforesaid as the necessity therof at sondrey tymes required to kepe the same in redines for her *maiesties* service. The whole chardges wherof aswell for wages as for other necessaries herafter p*ar*ticulerly ensueth. viz.

		Daies	
Taylors and other workmen & attending the p*re*misses one at xx^{d}. the day and the reste at xij^{d}	Will*iam* Tyldesley	20	xx^{s}.
	Iohn Lucas	20	xx^{s}.
	Thom*as* Clatterbooke	20	xxxiij^{s}. iiij^{d}.
	Iohn Davis	20	xx^{s}.
	Iohn Digges	20	xx^{s}.
	Iohn Hilton	20	xx^{s}.
	Iohn Sherborne	20	xx^{s}.
*porter	Iohn Dauncy	20	xx^{s}.
Officers.	The m*aster* at iiij^{s}. the day	20	iiij^{li}.
	The comptroller at ij^{s} the daye	20	xl^{s}.
	The clerke at ij^{s}. the day	20	xl^{s}.
	The yeoman at ij^{s}. ye day	20	xl^{s}.

f° 3 v.

Iohn Sherbourne for fewell and other necessaries vsed at sondrey tymes in the said Aireing.

ffewell and other necessaries	Coles .xx. sack*es*. xx^{s}. Billett*es* one thousand xvj^{s} threed and tape of all sort*es* — vij^{s}. brushes and Rushes — v^{s}.	xlviij^{s}.
	Edmond Tylney esquire for money by him disbursed and to be disbursed aswell about the chardges for making the accomptes to the audit*our* of the Imprest and declarac*i*on of the same before the Lord Treasorer and S*ir* walter Myldmey And also for the chardges of the priuie seale order for payment of the money and receipt of the same w*i*th certificat*es*	viij^{li}.
29^{li}. 16^{d}.	Su*mm*a of the chardges laste aforesaid	xxix^{li}. xvj^{d}.

The totall of this booke viz. from the firste of November 1580. Anno .xxij^{o}. Regni Regine Eliz*abethe* vntill the firste of November. 1581. Anno xxiij^{o}. Regni Regine pred*icte*

Christmas twelftide candlemas & Shrovetide w*i*th one challendge.	wages of	artificers & attendant*es*.	xxxviij^{li}. xvj^{s} viij^{d}.	clxiiij^{li}. xiiij^{s}.	ccxxxj^{li} iiij^{s}.
		officers	xxvij^{li}.		
	Emptions & provisions		lxxxxviij^{li}. vj^{s} iiij^{d}.		
The chardges of the work*es* begonne & lefte vnfynished for the receaving of the ffrenche Comissioners.	wages of	artificers and attendant*es*	ix^{li}. xix^{s}. iiij^{d}	xxxviij^{li}. xv^{s}.	* Ed Tyllney
		officers	vij^{li}. iiij^{s}.		
	Emptions & provisions		xxj^{li}. xj^{s} v^{d}.		
Ayringes from the first of Aprill 1581. vntill the firste of octob*er* then next following	wages of	artificers & attendant*es*.	viij^{li}. xiij^{s}. iiij^{d}	xxix^{li}. iiij^{s} iiij^{d}.	* walter fysshe
		officers	x^{li}.		
	Emptions & p*ro*visions w*i*th the chardges of the accompte		x^{li}. xj^{s}.		

f° 4r.

* The priuie seale . . . . x^s
* for y^e order . . . . x^s
* for y^e receipt . . . . . . xl^s
* m^r peters certificatt . . . $x^s v^d$
* tow other certificatt*es*. . . j^s

f° 5 r.

[Note. — The following bill has been sewed on the right margin of f° 3 r.]

D*elivere*d into thoffice of the Revells in severall p*ar*cells in ij dayes as vnder

the 27 of m*ar*che 1581

Item .v. oz. naro. frenge of fyne cop*er* gold
Item iiij oz. & d. brode p*ar*sment lace of fyne cop*er* gold
Item j oz j q*uarter* p*ar*sment lace Crymzen silk & silver

The xxviijth day as vnder

Item vj. oz. j q*uarter* naro frenge of cop*er* sylver
Item iiij oz. iij q*uarter* naro frenge of fyne cop*er* gold
Item .v. oz. j q*uarter* deep frenge of cop*er* gold
Item iiij oz. j q*uarter* deep frenge of cop*er* gold
Item iij oz. & d. & d. q*uarter* depe frenge cop*er* gold
Item vj oz. of Tassells w*it*h Calls all cop*er* sylver

R*eceived* by me w*illiam* bowll of ye right worshipfull Mr Tylney Esquyer M*aster* of her ma*iesties* Revells in full payment of all the stuff w*hi*ch I d*elivere*d into thoffice of the Revells to her ma*iesties* vse in march Last before this xxviijth of november 1581 the some of

xv^{li} xvij^{s} iij^{d}

p*er* me will*iam* Bowll.

April 1581

Money to be Allowed in Prest

British Museum. Lansdowne MSS. 31. n° 46.

The Mounte, Dragon *with* ye fyer woorkes, Castell *with* ye falling sydes Tree *with* shyldes, hermytage & hermytt, Savages, Enchaunter, Charryott, & incydentes to theis.	cc markes	
Braunches for lightes in the hawle *with* there garnyshinge.	xx^{li}	
ffrenge Lace tarsells lawne sylke flowers fethers & other garnyture —	lxvj^{li} 13 4.	
visers Targates Tape threede sylke fuell lightes carriages conduccions rewardes & other insident*es* to p*ro*p*er*ties & necessaries	xl^{li}	
Wages of Taylers paynters & Inbroderers habberdasshers & other p*ro*p*er*tie makers officers & attendandes	cxx^{li}.	
Dewe of the old accou*n*tt	lxx^{li}	$\overset{c}{ij}$ xxx^{li}
Dew for the last Cristmas	clxx^{li}	
$\overset{c}{iij}$ $\overset{xx}{iiij}$ ij^{s}		cccccc xix^{li} xiiij^{s}

[Endorsed :] 1° Apr*ilis* 1581
what monnie is to
be allowed in prest

for certayne shewes
to be had at whitehal.

1581.

British Museum. Lansdowne MSS. 31. n° 49.

A brief note of the provisions emptions and wages for her *maiesties* Revells this yeare. 1581.

	Iohn Rose for A mounte *w*ith A castle vppon it A dragon and artificiall tree	c^{li}.
	Vnto diu*er*se p*er*sons for .xlvj. sheildes the tymber worke Iron worke, and leathering of them, *w*ith the painting and gilding, of the Impresseis at xv^{s}. A peece	xxxiiij^{li}. x^{s}.
	Serieant painters bill for painting, mowlding, and gilding	xxxviij^{li}.
	Will*iam* Boles bill for cop*er* frindge, lace, tassells buttons, and such like	xxxvj^{li}. iij^{s}.
Lacie Stone	Twoe m*er*cers billes for cloth of golde, counterfect cloth of silver, tincells, taffeta [tafleti], sarcenet*es*, and single sarcenet*es*.	cv^{li}. iij^{s}.
	The carpenters bill for bord, tymber, & nayles —	v^{li}. xiiij^{s}. x^{d}.
	The buskenmaker, haberdasher, Ioyn*er*, & Lizard*es* bills	v^{li}. xij^{s}.
	The fethermaker	ix^{li}.
	The wierdrawer for braunches, plat*es*, and other garnishing*es* for the hall	xxvj^{li}.
	Iohn Digges bills for threed, silke, tape, candle, fewell, ropes, paste bord*es*, buckram, ribbond and artificiall lyon, and horse.	xxj^{li}. xj^{s}.
	Iohn Sherbornes billes, for carrell, baies, hamp*ers* lock*es*, fewell, candles, gloves, buckerham, lynnen cloth, heares, beard*es*, brushes, tenter hook*es*, cariage of stuffe, and botehier	xix^{li}. x^{s} viij^{d}.
	The yeomans bill for golde tincell, fustian cotten, baies, and botehier	iij^{li} ix^{s} v^{d}.
	The clerke comptrollers bill for silke floures fruytadge, counterfecte p*e*rle, silu*er* tincell, botehier and other, such ordinarie chardges	xiiij^{li}. iiij^{s}. j^{d}.
	Laid out by the m*aster* of the Revells for canvas, visard*es*, fewell, reward*es*, and other his ordinary allowaunc*es*.	xxij^{li}. iij^{s}.
	Wages to artificers and attendaunt*es*	lxxxvij^{li}
	Officers wages	xlix^{li}. *w*ith the airing*es* for this yeare.

S*UMMA* TOTALIS — ccccc lxxvij^{li}. x^{s}.

* Ed. Tyllney * Edwarde Buggyn * Edwarde Kirkham

[Endorsed :] Charge of ye Reuels A^{o}. 1581.

From 1 November 1582 to 31 October 1583.

viz.

Record Office. Audit Office. Accounts Various. Bd. 1213. Revels. N° 9.

Christmas Twelftide & Shrouetide and makeing choise of playes. Anno *Regni Regine* Eliz*abethe* **xxv^{to}. 1582.**

The Chardges of those tymes viz. Betwene the daie of 158 / Anno xx Regni Regine Elizabethe And the xiiijth of ffebruary 1582. Annoq*ue* R*egni* R*egin*e Eliz*abethe* xxv^{to}. did rise Aswell by meanes of makeing choise reformyng and attending of such plaies Comodies mask*es* and Inventions as were prepared set furth and presented before her ma*ies*tie at the tymes aforesaid : As also of wages, workemanship, Translations, Attendaunc*es*, wares delivered, Iurneying chardges, and expenc*es* therevnto belonging. The p*ar*ticularities whereof together w*i*th the p*ar*ties names to whom and wherfore the same is due hereafter at lardge ensueth. viz.

* from the first of November vnto the last of October Anno xxvth

A Comodie or Morrall devised on A game of the Card*es* shewed on St Stephens daie at night before her ma*ies*tie at Wyndesor Enacted by the Children of her ma*iesties* Chapple, furnished w*i*th many thing*es* w*i*thin this Office, whereof some were translated, and some newe made, and Imploied therein viz. Twoe clothes of canvas xx^{tie} Ells of sarcenet for iiij^{or} pavilions and girdles for the Boyes and viij. paire of gloves.

A Comodie of Bewtie and Huswyfery shewed before her ma*ies*tie at Wyndesor on St Iohns daie at night enacted by the lord of Hundesdons servaunt*es*, for w*hi*ch was prepared newe one Cloth and one Battlement of Canvas, iij. Ells of sarcenet and Eight paire of gloves w*i*th sondrey other thing*es* out of this office.

A Historie of Loue and ffortune shewed before her ma*ies*tie at Wyndesor on the sondaie at night next before newe yeares daie Enacted by the Earle of Derbies servaunt*es*. ffor w*hi*ch newe provision was made of one Citty and one Battlement of Canvas iij Ells of sarcenet A of canvas, and viij. paire of gloves w*i*th sondrey other furniture in this office.

Sundrey feates of Tumbling and Activitie were shewed before her ma*ies*tie on Newe yeares daie at night by the Lord Straunge his servaunt*es*. ffor w*hi*ch was bought and Imploied xxj^{tie}. yard*es* of cotten for the Matachins. iij. ells of sarcenet and viij. paire of gloves.

A maske of Ladies presented them selues before her ma*ies*tie at wyndesor at Twelf Eve at night, wherevnto was prepared and Imployed (beside the stuff of this office) xv yard*es* of black and white Lawne or Cipres for head Attires & vizard*es* xj. ells of Sarcenet. viij paire of gloves for boyes and Torch bearers, and one paire of white shoes.

f° 2 r.

A historie of fferrar shewed before her ma*ies*tie at wyndesor on Twelf daie at night Enacted by the Lord Chamberleynes servaunt*es* furnished in this office w*i*th diverse newe thing*es* As one Citty, one Battlement of canvas, iij Ells of sarcenet and .x. paire of gloves, and sondrey other thing*es* in this office whereof some were translated for fitting of the p*er*sons &c.

A historie of Telomo shewed before her ma*ies*tie at Richmond on Shrovesondaie at night Enacted by the Earle of Leicesters servaunt*es*, for w*hi*ch was prepared and Imployed, one Citty, one Battlement of canvas iij. Ells of sarcenet and viij. paire of gloves. And furnished w*i*th sondrey other garment*es* of the store of the office &c.

A historie of Ariodante and Geneuora shewed before her ma*ies*tie on Shrovetuesdaie at night enacted by m^r^ Mulcasters children, ffor w*hi*ch was newe prepared and Imployed, one Citty, one battlem*ent* of Canvas. vij Ells of sarcenet, and ij. dozen of gloves. The whole furniture for the reste was of the store of this office, whereof sondrey garment*es* for fytting of the Children were altered & translated

A Maske of Sixe Seamen prepared to have ben shewed, but not vsed, made of sondrey garment*es* and store w*i*thin the office into vj. Cassock*es* of Carnac*i*on cloth of silver garded w*i*th greene cloth of gold laid w*i*th copper silu*er* lace and tassells w*i*th hanging sleves of Russet cloth of silu*er* .vj. paire of venetians of Russet gold tyncell w*i*th flowres/ Buskins of crymsen cloth of gold, and Caps of black gold tyncell playne lyned w*i*th white silu*er* tincell bird*es* eyes, And counterfecte pearles vpon them. The Torche bearers sixe Three in Cassock*es* and hanging sleeves of crymsen damaske garded w*i*th yeallowe damaske and three paire of venetians of yeallowe damaske garded w*i*th crymsen damaske. And three Cassock*es* w*i*th hanging sleeves of yeallowe damaske garded w*i*th crymsen damaske, And three paire of venetians of crymsen damaske garded w*i*th yeallowe damaske. wearing sleeves for all the said sixe Torche bearers of purple satten striped w*i*th silu*er*. And sixe cappes for the same Torch bearers of oringe cull*our* damaske. laid w*i*th silu*er* lace.

f° 2 v.

		Daies	Night*es*.	
Taylors and others working and attending the p*re*misses the firste at xx^{d} the daie and as much the night the reste at xij^{d}.	Thomas Clatterboke	37	6	lxxj^{s} viij^{d}.
	Iohn Digg*es*	44	16	lx^{s}.
	Iohn Davies	44	16	lx^{s}
	will*iam* Huyte	44	16	lx^{s}.
	will*iam* Steadman	44	16	lx^{s}.
	will*iam* Tyldesley	44	16	lx^{s}.
	will*iam* Sone	44	16	lx^{s}.
	Lawrence Dyson	44	16	lx^{s}.
	Iohn Lucas	44	16	lx^{s}.
	Iohn Sherborne	44	16	lx^{s}
	Raphe Knevett	44	16	lx^{s}
	Thomas Rewklidge	44	16	lx^{s}
	George Reading	44	16	lx^{s}.
	will*iam* Morgan.	37	6	xliij^{s}
	Iohn Tipsley	18	0	xviij^{s}
	Thomas Rayner.	18	0	xviij^{s}.
	Richard Angell	37	6	xliij^{s}.
	Thomas Hoye	11	0	xj^{s}
	Richard Wardman	15	1	xvj^{s}
	Iames Batten	6	0	vj^{s}
	Davie Eavans	8	0	viij^{s}

* S*um*ma — xlvij^{li} xiiij^{s} viij^{d}.

Carpenters at xvj^{d} the daie and as much the night.	Iohn Myldnayle.	20	3	xxx^{s} viij^{d}.
	will*iam* Padmer.	18	2	xxvj^{s} viij^{d}.
	Edward Gledden	16	2	xxiiij^{s}.
	Iohn Taylor	12	1	xvij^{s} iiij^{d}.

* S*um*ma — iiij^{li} xviij^{s} viij^{d}

* S*um*ma pag*ine* — lij^{li} xiij^{s} iiij^{d}

f° 3 r.

Propertymakers being **Paynters** the firste at ij^{s}. the day and as much the night and the reste at xviij^{d}	William Lyzard.	27	0	liiij^{s}.
	Ellis Sawtrye	9	0	xiij^{s} vj^{d}.
	Hugh Swayne	6	0	ix^{s}.
	Thomas Tyler	10	0	xv^{s}
	George Russell	20	4	xxxvj^{s}.

* *Summa* — vj^{li} vij^{s} vj^{d}

Wierdrawers the firste at xx^{d} the daie and as much the night the reste at xvj^{d}	Edmond Bircholl	20	6	xliij^{s} iiij^{d}.
	Amos Todde	8	0	x^{s} viij^{d}.
	Thomas Hall	4	0	v^{s} iiij^{d}.
	Symon Poole	3	0	iiij^{s}.

* *Summa* — lxiij^{s} iiij^{d}

The porter at xij^{d} the daie & as much the night	Iohn daunce	44	16	lx^{s}.

Summa — *patet*

The officers the *master* at iij^{s} the daie and as much the night and the reste at ij^{s}.	The Yeoman	44	16	vj^{li}
	The Clerke	44	16	vj^{li}
	The Clerke Comptroller	44	16	vj^{li}.

The *master* of the Revells for his Attendaunce from the laste of October 1582. vntill Ashewednesdaie, Aswell for the choise makeing of playes, As for his wages at Christmas and Shrovetide conteynyng in all .cvj. daies and xvj. night*es* at iiij^{s} the daie and as much the night.	xxiiij^{li} viij^{s}.
To one dore keep*er* and iij. other Attendaunt*es* for p*ar*te of the said tyme and during the Rehersalls at xij^{d} the daie	xij^{li} x[illegible]

* *Summa* — lv^{li}.

Summa pagi*ne* — lxvij^{li} x^{s} x^{d}.

f° 3 v.

Mercers p*ar*cells.	**William Stone** for sondrey p*ar*cells of silke by him deliu*er*ed into the office viz.		
	Orindge cull*our* taffeta sarcenet at ix^{s} thell di. ell	iij^{s} vj^{d}.	ix^{li} vij^{s} x^{d}.
	Watchet sarcenet at vj^{s} viij^{d} thell xx^{tie} Ells	vj^{li} xiij^{s} iiij^{d}.	
	Yeallowe sarcenet at vj^{s} viij^{d} the ell .vj. ells	xl^{s}.	
	Russet sarcenet at vj^{s} viij^{d} the ell one ell di.	x^{s}	
Hab*er*dashers p*ar*cells.	for sondrey p*ar*cells by him wrought & brought into the office. viz.		
	The makeing of sixe Cappes of cloth of gold at iij^{s} iiij^{d} the peece	xx^{s}.	xliiij^{s} vj^{d}
	for ij. yard*es* of buccram to stiffen them	ij^{s}.	
	for sixe white feathers at ij^{s} vj^{d} ye pece	xv^{s}.	
	for an ell and q*uarter* of white sarcenet for to lyne them at vj^{s} thell	vij^{s} vj^{d}.	
Wierdrawers p*ar*cells.	**Edmond Byrcholl** for sondrey p*ar*cells by him provided wrought and brought into the office viz.		
	hand Candlestick*es* .viij.	xvj^{d}.	xiij^{li} ij^{s} iij^{d}.
	ffyne wier one pound	xij^{d}.	
	ffor fowre small pulleyes	viij^{d}.	
	ffor whip lyne	iij^{d}.	
	ffor three greate pulleyes	ix^{d}.	
	ffor sixe bodkins	vj^{d}	
	ffor mending of A small braunch at St. Iohns	vj^{d}.	
	ffor A lyne for the same braunche	iiij^{d}.	
	ffor xxv li. quarter of Englishe wier	xxv^{s} ij^{d}.	
	ffor vj li. of basterd wier	iiij^{s}.	
	ffor xxvj. small braunches to hange light*es* in the hall at wyndesor	v^{li} iiij^{s}.	
	ffor iij. great braunches for the same purpose	vj^{li}.	
	ffor cariage of ij hamp*er*s to St Iohns	viij^{d}.	
	ffor A dozen of single white plate	iij^{s}	

* S*umma* — xxiiij^{li} xiiij^{s} vij^{d}

f° 4 r.

Sarcenet Canvas ffuell & other necessaries

Iohn Digges for sondrey *par*cells by him provided bought & brought into the office viz.

Billet*es* vij. thowsand at x^{s} the M	lxx^{s}.	xxvj^{li} j^{s}. viij^{d}.
Coles iiij^{or}. load*es* at xviij^{s} the load	lxxij^{s}.	
Canvas one hundred & forty ells.	vij^{li}.	
Buccrams vj. peec*es*	xxx^{s}.	
Sarcenet sent to the Courte of diu*er*se cullors at vj^{s} viij^{d} thell. xxx ells. . .	x^{li}.	
Three hampers to carry the stuff to Bircholls . .	vj^{s}	
for ij ropes	iij^{s} viij^{d}.	

ffuell chaundelors *par*cells and other necessaries

Iohn Sherborne for sondrey thing*es* by him provided and brought into the office viz.

Billet*es* at wyndesor for the office and for the m*aste*rs Chamber there ij thowsand at x^{s} the thousand .	xx^{s}.	xiij^{li} x^{s} iiij^{d}.
Coales one load	xviij^{s}.	
Cotten candles at sondrey pric*es* aswell for the rehersalls as for the work*es* in the office and at the Courte xv. dozen .	lv^{s}	
Torches iij dozen at xiiij^{s} the dozen	xlij^{s}.	
Lynck*es* one dozen	iiij^{s}.	
Gloves viij. dozen at vij^{s} the dozen.	lvj^{s}	
nayles & tenterhook*es* of diu*er*se sort*es*	ix^{s} ij^{d}.	
for horsehire from wyndesor to London in poste and back agayne for my lord Chamberleynes men .	vj^{s} viij^{d}.	
Botehire from Richmond & barne Elmes to London Twice .	iij^{s}.	
Billet*es* at Richmond for the office and the m*aste*rs chamber there one thowsand .	x^{s}.	
Coles there	vj^{s}	
Threed$^{5s\ 10d.}$ Rushes$^{6s\ 4d.}$/ searing candles$^{3s.}$ paper^{12d}. white shoes^{12d}/ glacing$^{3s\ 4d}$ at the Courte. buccram^{2s}/ bord^{12d}. vices$^{4d.}$.	xxvij^{s} vj^{d}.	
Twoe wedges of Iron to be gilded and A lock. .	iij^{s}.	
A close stoole	x^{s}	

*S*umma* — xxxix^{li} xij^{s}.

f° 4 v

Iohn Dauis for sondrey p*ar*cells by him brought into the office. viz.

for bromes vj^{d} ob. Nayles j^{d} / candles v^{li} xv^{d}. pease one peck vj^{d} searing candle — j^{d}	ij^{s} v^{d} ob.	v^{s} vj^{d} ob.
ffor cariage of stuff to m^{r} Mulcasters'& back agayne	xx^{d}.	
ffor carying of certen stuffe to Barnes Elmes .	xij^{d}.	
ffor holly and Ivie at wyndesor	iiij^{d}.	
ffor botehire for my self at Richmond	j^{d}.	

Edward Kirkeham for sondrey p*ar*cells by him brought into the office and for money by him otherwise disbursed viz.

ffor tape ij li. vj^{s} browne threed iij li. q*uarter* vj^{s} vj^{d}. white threed ij li. vj^{s} grene threed di.li. xvj^{d}	xix^{s} x^{d}.	lxxix^{s} x^{d}.
Russet fustian xiij. yard*es* at x^{d} the yard . . .	x^{s} x^{d}.	
Gold tyncell at ij^{s} viij^{d} the yard iiij^{or} yard*es* . .	x^{s} viij^{d}.	
Sylu*er* tyncell at iij^{s} the yard iij. yard*es* di. . .	x^{s} vj^{d}.	
ffor the hire of ij horses for him self & his man to wyndeso*ur* and back agayne to attend the stuff of the Revells thith*er* caried	xviij^{s}.	
for their ij horsemeate at wyndesou*r*	vj^{s}	
for botehire to & from Richmond	iiij^{s}	

Edward Buggyn gent*leman* for money by him disbursed. viz.

Botehire and in reward*es* at sondrey tymes during the worke	x^{s}.	lxx^{s}.
for sondrey patterns of mask*es* w*hi*ch he procured to be drawed and brought into the office by the m*aste*rs appointem*ent*	lx^{s}.	

* S*um*ma — vij^{li} xv^{s} iiij^{d} ob.

fo 5 r.

Edmond Tylney esquire for sondrey so*m*mes of money by him laid out viz.		
To diverse p*er*sons for payting by greate of ccx. yard*es* of Canvas at xij[d] the yard [* Will*ia*m Lezerdd]	x[li] x[s]	
for xxj[tie]. yard*es* of red and yeallowe Cotton . . .	xxiij[s]	
for the hire of iiij[or] horses to wyndesor at ij[s] the daie the peece for ij daies	xvj[s]	
for the hire of three cart*es* to remove the store of the office to Wyndesor	xx[s].	
ffor white and black Cipres at iij[s] iiij[d] the yard .xv. yard*es* for the Ladies maske	l[s].	
geven in Reward to the boye that pronounced the speeche before the maske of the Ladies	x[s].	
geven in reward to m[r] Cardell for devising the daunce w*hi*ch m[r] Cardell came in w*i*th	xx[s].	xxiiij[li] xv[s].
for the hire of iiij[or] horses ij daies from wyndesor to London at ij[s] the daie A peece	xvj[s]	
for horsemeate	xij[s].	
for three cart*es* to remove the stuff of the office from wyndeso*ur* to London	xx[s].	
for the hire of iiij[or]. horses from London to Richmond at Shrovetide one daye at ij[s] the daie A peece	viij[s].	
for the hire of one Carte to remove the stuff of the office from London to Richmond & back againe	x[s].	
for the hire of iiij[or] horses from Richmond to London one daie at ij[s] the daye A peece	viij[s].	
for makeing of vj. paire of buskins	xij[s].	
for .v. yard*es* of grene cloth at viij[s] the yard . . .	xl[s].	
for standishe ynck pap*er* and other necessaries . .	xx[s]	

* *Summa* — *patet*

f[o] 5 v.

Iohn Drawater for money by him disbursed. viz.

for A Reame of paper . . . . vj^{s} viij^{d}.
for sixe quire of Royall pap*er* . . . . vj^{s}.
for A standishe [3s. 4d], penknife [12d], pynduste [6d] j li . . . . iiij^{s} x^{d}.
for Counters [2s]. Inck [8d], quills [3d] botehire [2s 6d]. . . . . . . v^{s} v^{d}.

= xxij^{s} xj^{d}.

Silkemans par*cells*

William Bowle for sondrey par*cells* by him provided and brought into the office viz.

Sylver lace plated of copper xiiij oz. di. at ij^{s} the oz. xxix^{s}
Tassells and buttons of copper silu*er* at ij^{s} the oz. ij li. xj oz. di. iiij^{li} vij^{s}.
Bone lace brayded of copper silu*er* xxj. oz. di. xliij^{s}.
Laid worke buttons of copper silu*er* at vj^{d} the dozen xij. dozen vj^{s}

= viij^{li} v^{s}.

Carpent*ers* par*cells*.

Iohn Taylor for sondrey par*cells* by him brought into the office. viz.

Dubble quarters xlviij [24s]. single quarters xxxiiij [8s 6d] . . xxxij^{s} vj^{d}
punchions iiij [2s 8d]/ Deales ij [2s 8d]/ rafters v [5s]. . . . . x^{s} iiij^{d}.
Bord*es* cccc q*uar*ter [30s 10d] and xx^{tie} foote Ioyces v/ [6s 4d] planck*es* iiij [3s 6d]. xl^{s} viij^{d}.
Tymber xv [7s 6d] foote. Inche borde [8s 4d] . . . . xv^{s} x^{d}

= iiij^{li} xix^{s} iiij^{d}.

*S*um*ma* — xiiij^{li} vij^{s} iij^{d}

f° 6 r.

Reparations

Thomas Blagraue Esquire for money by him disbursed and laid out for the newe flowring of A chamber (fallen downe) being pa*r*te of his owne lodging, newe casting of all the lead ou*er* the same chamber, newe tymber and bord*es* vnder the same lead. And newe makeing A longe paire of staires w*i*th A house about and over them into the lead*es*, and mending the other lead*es* in many plac*es*. viz.

Somers [15 s] ij/ Iois*tes* [14 s] xiiij/ Beame [9 d] j / Entertice [12 d] j — xxxˢ ixᵈ
Bord*es* at sondrey pric*es* the C. fote viijᶜ di. — liiijˢ
half [8 d] pace j/ single quarters [8 s 9 d] xxxv. rafter vij. [4 s 8 d] paire — xiiijˢ jᵈ
hook*es* and hing*es* iiij. [3 s 4 d] paire/ lock*es* and [2 s] staples ij — vˢ iiijᵈ
Nayles at vjᵈ the C [x s] 2000 lath nayles [ix s] 6000 . . . xixˢ
lyme CC di. and [xvj s.] iiij sack*es*/ sand [iij s 4 d] iij load heare xiij [vj s vj d] bushells/ Tyles [ix s] vjᶜ. Tyle [viijᵈ] pyns } xxxvˢ vjᵈ
Brick to amend the harth/ furre [22 d] poll for the staires, lath x [x s v d] bundle, painting washing and p*er*uiting the [13 s] chamber } xxvjˢ iijᵈ
newe casting of vjᶜ and A quartern of [15 s] lead/ Soder [ij s] xix li. } xxvjˢ
Cariage & recariage of lead & tymb*er* . . . . ijˢ.
workemanship of [36 s] Carpenters, [4 s] Bricklaiers. [4 s 8 d] Tylers. [8 s 10 d] plaisterers [5 s 6 d] plumbers and [10 s 6 d] laborers } lxixˢ vjᵈ

} xiiijˡⁱ ijˢ vᵈ.

Plumbers pa*r*cells.

Dunstone Braye for work*es* done vpon the hall & office of the Revell*es*.

pipe lead to mend the m*aste*rs conduite lxxvj li. at ijᵈ. the li. } xijˢ viijᵈ.
sheete lead to make A spowte 305 li. at xiijˢ the hundred } xxxixˢ viijᵈ
Soder lj li. At vijᵈ the pound . . . . xxixˢ ixᵈ
for workemanship of Plumbers & laborers . . xxxijˢ iiijᵈ

} vˡⁱ xiiijˢ vᵈ.

* S*umma* — xixˡⁱ xvjˢ xᵈ.

f° 6 v.

The Clerke for his ordinarie grenecloth paper Inck Quills waxe Counters desk*es* standishes and Tooles for the makeing compiling and conserving of the Bookes Bill*es* plott*es* paternes modells &c. for and concernyng this office — lxvj^{s} viij^{d}.

Paynters *par*cells for the *pro*p*er*ty-makers

William Lizard for money by him laid out for sondrey thing*es* by him bought and brought into this office viz.

Paste bord, paper, and paste, white, sise, verte, Syneper, fyne gold, *par*tie gold, silu*er*, masticote, blewe Inde, Smalte blacke, vermylion, glewe, Assedewe browne, Tynfoyle, and pot*es* vsed and Imployed vpon the premisses Amounting vnto — iiij^{li} vij^{s} vj^{d}.

Edmond Tylney Esquire M*aster* of the office being sente for to the Courte by Letter from m^{r} Secreatary dated the xth of marche 1582. To choose out A companie of players for her ma*ies*tie for money by him laid out viz.
ffor horse hire to the courte and back agayne — x^{s}.
ffor his owne chardges his mens and horsemeate there ij daies — x^{s}
— xx^{s}.

SUMM*A* TOT*A*LIS of all the Emptions and Provisions cariag*es* Reward*es* wages and Attendaunc*es* w*it*hin the tyme aforesaid — cclix^{li} xix^{s} iiij^{d} ob.

* Ed : Tyllney
* Edwarde Buggyn

* T Blagrave
* Edward kirkham

f° 7 r.

Betwene the xiiijth of ffebruary 1582· Anno *Regni Regine* Elizabethe xxv^{to}. (At which tyme the workes and Attendaunces for the tymes aforesaid did end) And the firste of November 1583. Annoque *Regni Regine* Elizabethe predicte xxv^{to}. the chardges of this office grewe at sondrey tymes by meanes of Airing Repairing brushing, spunging Rubbing, sweeping, putting in order laying vp and safe bestowing of garmentes vestures disguysinges properties and furniture of the same from tyme to tyme within the tyme aforesaid as the necessity thereof at sondrey tymes required to keepe the same in Readines for her maiesties service· The whole chardges whereof, Aswell for chardges, As for other necessaries herafter particulerly ensueth viz.

Tailors and others workeing and attending the premisses the firste at xx^{d} the daie the reste at xij^{d}	Thomas Clatterboke	20	xxxiij^{s} iiij^{d}.	*vij^{li} xiij^{s} iiij^{d}
	Iohn Davies	20	xx^{s}	
	Iohn Lucas	20	xx^{s}	
	William Tyldesley	20	xx^{s}	
	Thomas Rewklidge.	20	xx^{s}	
	Iohn Sherborne	20	xx^{s}	
	Iohn Tipsley	20	xx^{s}.	
Porter.	Iohn Dawncy	20	xx^{s}	

*Summa — patet

Officers the firste at iiij^{s} the daie the reste at ij^{s}	The maister	20	iiij^{li}	*x^{li}.
	The clerke comptroller	20	xl^{s}.	
	The Clerke	20	xl^{s}.	
	The yoman	20	xl^{s}.	

Iohn Sherborne for fewell and other necessaries vsed at sondrey tymes in the said Airinges viz. Coles xx^{tie}. sackes — xv^{s}. billetes one thowsand — x^{s}. threed and tape of sondrey sortes — vij^{s}/ brushes and rushes — v^{s} } xxxvij^{s}.

Edmond Tylney Esquire for money by him disbursed Aswell about the makeing of Thaccompt to the Auditour of Thimpreste, and declaration of the same before the lord Treasorer and Sir walter myldmey : As also for the chardges of the privie seale, And for the payment of the money and receipt of the same with the certificat doth yearely Amount vnto Above } viij^{li}.

SUMMA of the chardges laste aforesaid } xxviij^{li} x^{s} iiij^{d}.

SUMMA TOTALIS of this whole booke } cc iiij^{xx} viij^{li}. ix^{s} viij^{d} ob.

*T Blagrave

*Ed Tyllney

*Edwarde Buggyn

*Edward kirkham

f° 7 v.

From 1 November 1583 to 31 October 1584

Record Office. Declared Accounts (Audit Office). Bundle 2045. Roll 8.

A Breife declaration of the Charges of the saide Office aswell for diverse kindes of Emptions and other neccessaries bought and provided for the same, As also for wages and Entertaynemente of Artificers Officers and others occupied aboute the ffurnishinge Makinge and settinge furthe of vj histories, one Comedie one Maske and other devises shewed before hir Maiestie And for Ayringe the stuffe belonginge to the saide office with other ordinarye Charges incidente to the same by the space of one whole yere beginning the ffirst of Nouember 1583 Annoque xxv^{to} Domine Elizabethe nunc Regine And endinge the laste of October 1584 anno xxvj^{to} eiusdem Domine Regine the Particularities whereof hearevpon caste tried, and examined more at large maie appeare — **xxvj^{to}. 1584 vidilicet**

The Superplusage of his laste Declaratione ended vltimo Octobris a^{o} xxv^{to} Elizabethe Regine as by the same here vpon seen appereth — **ccliij^{li} iiij^{s} iiij^{d}**

Thoffice of the Reuells viz.

Emptions & Prouisions viz.

- **Golde** assidew, and diverse other Coulers for the Painter . . . x^{li} xix^{s}
- **Mercers percells viz.**
  - **Taffita** sarcnet Blacke xxix ells, Chaungable iij elles — xiiij^{li} xiiij^{s}
  - **Satten** iij yardes quarter after viij^{s} j^{d} ob. the yarde — xlv^{s} vj^{d}
  - **Sarcnett** of sundrie Coulers iiij j elles di., di. quarter at vj^{s} viij^{d} the ell — xxvij^{li} iij^{s} x^{d}
  - **Buckram** bothe blacke and greene — lv^{s}
  - [total] xlvj^{li} xviij^{s} iiij^{d}
- **Sikeweauers parcells** viz. silver lace and buttons . . . . . v^{s}
- **Canvas,** Hollande clothe and bombaste, gloues, vizerdes berdes and heares — xvij^{li} ij^{s} vj^{d}
- **A paire** of Silvered ffoiles, Patrones Sise glew and pastboordes — vj^{li} xvij^{s}
- **wierdrawers parcelles viz.**
  - **wier** lxiiij^{s}, Braunches small xxviij vj^{li} greate braunches iij vj^{li}
  - Reparinge of Braunches lj^{s} iiij^{d} plates and Candlestickes
  - [total] xviij^{li} ij^{s} iiij^{d}
- **Carpenters parcells viz.**
  - **Timber** and Boordes, Rafters, quarters, Ioistes, postes . . . . Dealebordes ffirre pooles with ix^{s} for sawinge of boordes . . . . — xiij^{li} vij^{s}
- **fewell**
  - **Billettes** cx^{s} and Coales cviij^{s}. . . . . . x^{li} xviij^{s}
- **Diuerse other Neccessaries viz.**
  - **lockes** and vices xxiiij^{s} and nailes xlv^{s} — lxix^{s} iiij^{d}
  - **Ropes** Cordes, Lines Thredd and Tape — xxxviij^{s} iiij^{d}
  - **lathes,** lime, loame, and heare, — lxx^{s}
  - **Rushes** xxxj^{s} viij^{d} mosse, holie, and Ivie — xxxvj^{s} x^{d}
  - **Torches** xxxvj^{s} viij^{d} linkes viij^{s} and Candles lxij^{s} — cvj^{s}
  - **Hampers** iiij^{s} and pottes vj^{s} with x^{s} for a Close stole — xx^{s}
  - [total] xvij^{li} vj^{d}
- [total Emptions & Prouisions] cxlj^{li} x^{s} ix^{d}

Cariadges of diuerse percelles of the prouisions aforesaide, by lande, and by water with xviij^{s} x^{d} for boathier — xl^{s} ij^{d}

Wages

- **Artificers**
  - **Tailors** one at xx^{d} & the rest at xij^{d} per diem & asmuch per noctem — xlvj^{li} iiij^{d}
  - **Painters** Ioyners wierdrawers Carpenters iij attendants & one dore keaper xviij^{li}, at diuirs rates of xij^{d} xvj^{d} xviij^{d} xx^{d} and ij^{s} per diem and like seuerall rates per noctem — xli ij^{li} xij^{s}
  - [total] iiij^{xx} ix^{li} xij^{s} iiij^{d}
- **Officers**
  - **The maister** attendinge from the laste of October 1583 vntill Ashe wednesdaie next followinge for makinge Chose of plaies & other deuises to be shewen before hir Maiestie bye the space of cxxv dayes — xxviij^{li} iiij^{s}, and for xx^{tie} dayes within the saide time for Airinge the stuffe of the same office — iiij^{li} — xxxij^{li} iiij^{s}
  - **The Clerke** Comptroller for lxix dayes and xvj nightes at ij^{s} per diem & asmuche per noctem — viij^{li} x^{s}
  - **The Clerke** for the same time and at like rate — viij^{li} x^{s}
  - **The yeoman** for the same time & at like rate — viij^{li} x^{s}
- [total Wages] cxlvij^{li} vj^{s} iiij^{d}

Tasque woork viz. for glasinge the windowes of St Iohns Hall where the Rehersalls be made — vj^{li} for reparinge the leades there xl^{s} To william Lizerde for mendinge of iiij whelkes shelles and Couloringe them — vj^{s} for gildinge a wedge with ffine golde and an other with silver — ij^{s} vj^{d} ffor paintinge and gildinge vj shildes with impresses vpon them — l^{s} vj^{d} and for one vnicorns horne — xij^{d} in all for paintinge — lx^{s} and to diuers workemen for makinge iiij blew gownes a Cassocke & a hose — xvij^{s} — xj^{li} xvij^{s}

Rewardes to diuerse persouns for sundrie Causes. . . . . xj^{li} xj^{s}

Allowaunces, for greene Clothe, paper, inke penneknives, pinduste and other neccessaries belonginge to the saide office — viij^{li} vij^{s} viij^{d}

All which Charges are conteyned, and particlerelie entred in a legier thereof subscribed withe thandes of Edmunde Tilney esquier Maister of the Reuells Edward Buggin Comptroller & Edward kirkehame yeoman of the saide office as herevpon pervsed, cast, tried and Examined maie appeare — **cccxxj^{li} xij^{s}**

S UMMA TOTALLIS of the saide Superplusage, and all and singuler the paimentes and allowaunces aforesaide within the time of this Declaracion — **dlxxiiij^{li} xvj^{s} iiij^{d}**

Readie Money by the said Maister Receiued & had viz.

Theare hath been Received out of the Receipte of the Eschequier by Edmund Tilney esquier maister of the saide Reuells of Henrye Killigrew one of the Tellors of the saide receipte by vertue of a previe seale Dated the xv^{to} Martij a^{o} xxvj^{to} regni Regine Elizabethe predicte in full paimente of the fforesaide superplusage, and all Charges as had growen within the time of the preceadente Declaration, as by certificat of Robert Peter esquier appeareth, the some of — ccliij. iiij^{s}. iiij^{d}

There hathe also, beyn imprested and paide to the saide maister of the Revells by the saide Henrye Killigrew by vertue of the aforesaide previe seale Dated the xv^{to} Martij Anno xxvj^{to} Regine predicte towardes the satisfacion and paimente of the Chardges of the saide office for this yere as by certificat of the saide Roberte Peter esquier likewise appearethe the some of — c^{li}

An so the saide Accomptaunt resteth in Superplusage vpon this Declaracion the some of . . . . **cccxxj^{li}. xij^{s}**

Memorandum there hathe not ben any kinde of silkes or other stuffe deliuered to the saide officers of the Revells out of hir Maiesties greatewarderobe or out of hir Maiesties store at white hall as by twoe Certificates the one subscribed by Anthoney walker Clerke of the saide greate Guarderobe, and the other by Thomas knevett esquier keper of the saide stoore at whitehall appeethar.

Table III

From 1 November 1583 to 31 October 1584

Record Office Declared Accounts (Audit Office). Bundle 2045. Roll 8.

From 31 October 1584 to 31 October 1585.

viz.

Record Office. Audit Office. Accounts Various. Bd. 1213. Revels. N° 10.

[**Reuell*es* .1584. Anno** } **xxvij°.**]
[***R*egni *R*egine Elizabethe** }]

Title-page r.

Chrystmas Twelftyde & Shrouetyde and making choyse of plaies Anno *Regni Regine* Elizabeth*e* **xxvij**° **1584.**

The Charges of those tymes viz. betwene the laste daie of October 1584. Anno xxvj[to] Regni Regine Elizabeth*e* and the of ffebruary .1584. Anno*que* *Regni Regine* Elizabeth*e* pred*icte* xxvij° did rise aswell by meanes of attending making choyce, reforminge and altering of suche plaies Comodies maskes and inventions as were prepared sett furth and presented before her ma*ies*tie at the tymes aforesaid. As also of wages workmanshipp translac*i*ons attendaunc*es* wares deliu*er*ed Cariag*es*. Iorneying chardg*es* and expenc*es* therunto belonging. The p*ar*ticulers wherof together w*i*th the p*ar*ties names to whom and wherfore the same is due hereafter ensueth. viz.

Playes shewes & devises before her highnes in the tyme aforesaid .vij. viz.

A pastorall of phillyda & Choryn presented and enacted before her ma*ies*tie by her highnes servaunt*es* on S[t] Stephens daie at night at Grenew*i*ch whereon was ymployed yard*es* of Buffyn for Shepherd*es* coat*es* xxx[tie] ells of sarcenet. for fower matachyne sutes one greate curteyne and scarfes for the nymphes one mountayne and one great cloth of canvas and vj peec*es* of buccram.

The history of Agamemnon & Vlisses presented and enacted before her ma*ies*tie by the Earle of of Oxenford his boyes on S[t] Iohns daie at night at Grenew*i*ch.

Dyuers feates of Actyuytie were shewed and presented before her ma*ies*tie on newe yeares daye at night at Grenew*i*ch by Symons and his fellowes wheron was ymployed the pages sute of Oringe tawney tissued vellet w*hi*ch they spoyled yardes of white Cotten / a batlement and ij Ianes sutes of canvas and iiij ells of sarcenett.

The history of felix & philiomena. shewed and enacted before her highnes by her ma*iesties* servaunt*es* on the Sondaie next after newe yeares daye at nighte at Grenew*i*che wheron was ymployed one battlement & a howse of canvas.

An Inuention called ffiue playes in one presented and enacted before her ma*ies*tie on Twelfe daie at nighte in the hall at Grenew*i*che by her highnes servaunt*es* wheron was ymployed a greate cloth and a battlement of canvas and canvas for a well and a mounte .xv ells of sarcenet .ix yard*es* of sullen cloth of gold purple.

An Inuention of three playes in one prepared to haue ben shewed before her highnes on Shroue sondaye at night and to haue ben enacted by her ma*iesties* servaunt*es* at Somerset place. But the Quene came not abroad that night. yet was ymployed on the same one howse & a battlement.

An Antick playe & a comodye shewed presented and enacted before her highnes on Shrouetewsdaie at nighte at Somerset place by her ma*iesties* servaunt*es* wheron was ymployed one howse.

fo 1 r.

		Daies	Nicht*es*	
Taylors and others working and attending the p*re*misses the firste at 20^{d} the daie and as much the night the reste at xij^{d}.	Thomas Clatterbooke	32	14	lxxvj^{s} viij^{d}
	Iohn Davies.	51	14	lxv^{s}
	Iohn Digg*es*.	51	14	lxv^{s}
	Will*iam* huett	51	14	lxv^{s}
	Will*iam* Steadman	51	14	lxv^{s}
	William Phillippes	51	14	lxv^{s}
	Peter Gifforde	51	14	lxv^{s}
	Iohn Lucas	51	14	lxv^{s}
	Will*iam* kiffyn	51	14	lxv^{s}
	Iohn Sherborne	51	14	lxv^{s}
	Raphe knevett	51	14	lxv^{s}
	Thomas Rewklydge	51	14	lxv^{s}
	George Reading	51	14	lxv^{s}
	Iohn Tipsley	14	0	xiiij^{s}
	Iames Batton	12	0	xij^{s}
	Thomas Rayner	21	0	xxj^{s}
The porter	Iohn dawncye	51	14	lxv^{s}.
Prop*er*ty makers at sondrie rates	Will*iam* Lizard at ij^{s}.	44	15	cxviij^{s}
	Thomas ffringe at xij^{d}.	12	0	xij^{s}
	Thomas Tyler at xviij^{d}..	46	13	iiij^{li} viij^{s} vj^{d}.
	Richard Spicer	38	8	xlvj^{s}
	Richard Dykinson at xviij^{d}	10	0	xv^{s}
	Iohn Ougle. at xviij^{d}	2	1	iiij^{s} vj^{d}
Paynters at sondry rates the day. viz.	Baltezer at ij^{s}	8	0	xvj^{s}
	Toby Randall at xx^{d}.	7	0	xj^{s} viij^{d}
	Iohn Abbes at xviij^{d}	8	0	xij^{s}
	George Bynge at xviij^{d}	8	0	xij^{s}
	Iohn Salter at xviij^{d}	7	0	x^{s} vj^{d}.
	Thomas Rose at xij^{d}.	8	0	viij^{s}
	Iohn Leathe at xviij^{d}.	8	0	xij^{s}

* *Received per* George gower

wierdrawers at sondry Rat*es* viz.	Edmond Birchall at. xx^{d}	20	13	lv^{s}
	Thomas hall at xvj^{d}	4	4	x^{s} viij^{d}
	Iohn Palmer at xvj^{d}	10	10	xxvj^{s} viij^{d}
	Thomas Birchall at xij^{d}.	7	2	ix^{s}

Carpenters at xvj^{d} the day and as much the night.	Iohn myldnayle	23	0	xxx^{s} viij^{d}
	Richard westrop	24	0	xxxij^{s}
	Iohn maisters	8	10	xxiiij^{s}
	Richard Twycrofte	10	4	xviij^{s} viij^{d}
Ioyners at xvj^{d} the daye.	David hurley	7	0	ix^{s} iiij^{d}
	Garret Trayshe.	5	0	vj^{s} viij^{d}
	Thomas dyer	18	0	xxiiij^{s}
Plomers at xvj^{d} the daye	Iohn Peele	6	0	viij^{s}
	Iohn Trybeck	6	0	viij^{s}
The officers at ij^{s} the daye and as much the night in respect of their diet & expences.	The yomen	51	14	vj^{li} x^{s}
	The Clerke	51	14	vj^{li} x^{s}
	The Clerke controwler.	51	14	vj^{li} x^{s}.

fo 1 v.

The maister for his attendaunce from the laste of october 1584 vntill Ashewednesdaie then next following aswell for the choise making of plaies as for his wag*es* at Christmas Twelftide and Shrovetide conteyning in all. cxvij daies and xiiij^{ten} night*es* at iiij^{s} the daie and as much the night } xxvj^{li} iiij^{s}.

To one dore keeper and iij. other attendaunt*es* for p*ar*te of the same tyme and during the rehersall*es* at xij^{d} the daie and as much the night } xiij^{li} iiij^{s}.

Emptions and prouitions

Mercers p*ar*cell*es*.

Wyllyam Stone for sondrey p*ar*cells by him delivered in the office. viz.

Buffin of watchet cullor xxxviij. yard*es* at iij^{s} the yard — cxiiij^{s}.

Sarcenet some of yeallowe some greene some of crymsen, some blewe, and some white at vj^{s} viij^{d} thell in all. l. ell*es* } xvj^{li} xiij^{s} iiij^{d}

} xxij^{li} vij^{s} iiij^{d}

* Rec*eived* the .xxj of Aprill 1586 the some of Twenty tow pound*es* vij^{s} iiij^{d} P*er* me : Will*iam* Stone :

wyerdrawers p*ar*cell*es*.

Edmond Byrcholl for sondrey thing*es* by him p*ro*vided wrought and brought in this office. viz.

for xxiiij. small braunches	ciiij^{s}.
for iiij. greate braunches.	viij^{li}
for xij. bodkins	xij^{d}
for xxxij li. di. of wier of sondrey sort*es* at 22^{d} ye li	xxxij^{s} vj^{d}
for spanishe needles	iij^{d}
for vj. pulleis.	ij^{s}.
for iiij. lynes	iiij^{s}.
for hanging vp of the pulleis	xviij^{d}
for cc of x^{d} nayles	xx^{d}
for ij li. di. of Assidue	vij^{s} vj^{d}
for iij. vice candlestick*es*.	xviij^{d}
for vj. stock candlestick*es*	xij^{d}
for iij. prickt candlestick*es*	vj^{d}
for xviij. plates	iij^{s}.
for a pipe for water	v^{s}.
for working of the wier	x^{s}.
for cariage & recariage of the thing*es* aforesaid to Greenewiche & to Somerset place & back agayne	v^{s}.

} xvij^{li} v^{d}.

Carpenters p*ar*cells.

Iohn Taylor for sondrey thing*es* by him p*ro*vided and brought into the office. viz.

for xxx. doble quarters	xv^{s}.
for xvj. rafters	xvj^{s}
for vj. Ioyces.	vj^{s}
for ij. scantling peec*es*	iij^{s} iiij^{d}
for vj. greate rafters	viij^{s}.
for viij. post*es*	viij^{s}.
for cccc of bord*es*	xxviij^{s}.

} iiij^{li} iiij^{s} iiij^{d}.

f° 2 r.

Paynters parcelles. **Gower** for diuerse cullours paste bordes and other parcells by him provided and brought into the office viz. — vij^{li} xiij^{s}.
* *Received* George Gower

for cullors of all sortes . . . . xl^{s}.
for paste bordes greate & small . . . . xxvij^{s}.
for Orcedewe . . . . lx^{s}.
for pottes greate & small Size glewe needles threed fire candles traishe nayle &c. — xxiiij^{s} vj^{d}
for botehier . . . . xviij^{d}.

Property makers parcelles. **Willyam Lizard** for cullors and other thinges by him brought into the office viz. — liij^{s} viij^{d}

for cullors of sondrey sortes . . . . xxxj^{s}
for gold and siluer . . . . xx^{s} ij^{d}
for Orcedewe . . . . ij^{s} vj^{d}

Iohn Newdyck for fyve vizardes at iiij^{s} the pece by him provided and brought into the office. — xx^{s}.

Cutlers parcelles. **Beauis Tod** for sondrey thinges by him brought into the office and wrought for the office. viz. — vij^{s} ij^{d}

for ij. daggers . . . . v^{s}.
for a scabard. . . . . vj^{d}
for makeing cleane of ij blades. . . . . iiij^{d}
for making cleane of ij paire of hiltes . . . . . . xvj^{d}.

Skynners parcelles **Simond Tuke** for sondrey thinges by him bought wrought and brought into the office viz. — xxiij^{s} x^{d}.

for three half furres of white pever . . . . . . xviij^{s}.
for working of them into a Cassock . . . . . . iij^{s}.
for budge to make the spottes of a Cassock . . . xij^{d}
for making of the kydde skynne hose . . . . . . xviij^{d}
for a lardge white lambe skynne for the goates head iiij^{d}.

Plumbers parcelles. **Dunston Bray** for sondrey thinges by him brought and wrought in the office. viz. — xxvij^{s} iiij^{d}.

Caste pipes waying cxv li. at ij^{d} the pound . . . xix^{s} ij^{d}
Soder xiiij li. at vij^{d} the pound . . . . viij^{s} ij^{d}

Necessaryes **Iohn Ogle** for thinges by him provided & brought into the office. viz. — xxvij^{s} viij^{d}.

for fowre yeallowe heares for head attires for woemen — xxvj^{s} viij^{d}
for a pound of heare . . . . xij^{d}

Iohn Digges for sondrey somes of money by him disbursed for thinges bought & brought into the office. viz. — xvij^{li} vj^{d}

for clxxx. ells of canvas at xij^{d} thell. . . . . . ix^{li}
for wood & cole laid into thoffice at St Iohnes. . for rehersalles airinges & workes done — vij^{li}
for iiij. peeces of buccram . . . . xviij^{s}
for a standishe for thoffice . . . . ij^{s} vj^{d}.

willyam Huninges gentleman for money by him layd out for botehier to & from the court being then at Grenewich rewardes to workmen for expidicion and for victualls for them because they should not goe from their worke — xx^{s}].

f° 2 v.

Iohn Sherborne for sondrie thing*es* by him p*ro*vided and money laid out. viz.		xv^{li} vij^{s}
for fuell at the courte for the office and m*aste*rs Chamber there	lx^{s}.	
for torches and lynck*es*	xl^{s}	
for cotten candles of all sortes for the reherssalls & work*es* at St Iohns and for the m*aste*rs Chamber and office at the Courte.	lxvj^{s}	
for lock*es* keyes nayles hook*es* ropesrand mending of the vices for the frames.	xl^{s}	
for Rushes for the great hall at St Iohns the m*aste*rs Chamber and office at the court.	xxij^{s}	
for vj dozen of gloves	xlij^{s}	
for a Close stoole	x^{s}.	
for a plancke at Grenewiche	ij^{s}	
for Carying by land and by water and boatehier and otherwise of errand*es*.	xxv^{s}.	

Iohn Drawater. for money by him disbursed for a reame of paper — vj^{s} viij^{d} for di. Reame of Riall paper — x^{s}. for Inke quilles waxe pinduste and counters — vj^{s} x^{d} for boate hier at sondrie tymes .vj^{s} viij^{d}	xxx^{s} ij^{d}

Edward Kyrkham for money by him laid out viz.		lxxij^{s} x^{d}
for iij ells of iij q*uar*ter clothe at .xij^{d} the elle	iij^{s}	
for xxiiij^{ti} yardes of white playne at x^{d} the yarde . . .	xx^{s}	
for iij li. of thrid of all cullers at ij^{s} viij^{d} the li.	viij^{s}	
for a li. of tape	iij^{s} iiij^{d}	
for iiij doz*en* of lace of white & yalowe at xvj^{d} the doz*en* —	v^{s} iiij^{d}	
for ix yard*es* of welshe playne	ix^{s}	
for an ell of holland	ij^{s} vj^{d}	
for a peece of buccram	iiij^{s} viij^{d}	
for more tape Incle and threde	viij^{s}	
for boate hier to and from the courte at sondry tymes .	ix^{s}	

The Clarke for his ordinarie grene cloth paper incke quilles deske and for making compiling and conserveinge of the book*es* bills plott*es* paternes modells &c. for and concerning this office.	lxvj^{s} viij^{d}

Edmonde Tylney Esquire m*aster* of the office for sondry somes of money by him disbursed. viz.		xiij^{li} vij^{s} viij^{d}.
paid to Lizard Tiler and the carver for plaster of parris Claye paste bordes and other necessaries for prop*er*tie makers	xl^{s}	
for a dozen of goate skinnes	vj^{s}	
for botehier & horse hier at sondrie tymes during the servis and since in suing for money.	xlv^{s}	
Reward*es* to diuers p*er*sons at the courte at the Rehersalls there.	xx^{s}	
for five yard*es* of grene cloth — xl^{s}. standishe Incke pap*er* sand and quilles. — xx^{s}.	lx^{s}	
for a quarterne of deale bordes	xxv^{s}	

To the feather maker for iiij^{or} garland*es* of flowers	xxvj^{s} viij^{d}
for buskins and pumpes for nymphes & shepherd*es*	xxv^{s}
for Shepherd*es* hatt*es*	xx^{s}

S*umma* to*t*alis of the Emptions p*ro*visions Carriages Reward*es* wages and attendaunc*es* w*i*thin the tyme aforesaid. } ccliij^{li} v^{s} j^{d}.

* Ed Tyllney

* T Blagrave

* [Edward] kirkham

fo 3 r.

Betwene the xxvth of ffebruary .1584. Anno Regni Regine Elizabeth*e* xxvij^{o} (at w*hi*ch tyme the workes and attendaunc*es* for the tymes aforesaid did end). And the last of October .1585. A*nn*oq*ue* *nos*tre Elizabethe pred*icte* xxvij^{o}. The chardges of this office grewe at sondry tymes by meanes of Ayringe amending brushing Rubbing spungeing swepeing foulding laying vp and safe bestowing of garment*es*. both for maskers and players, disguisinges prop*er*ties and furniture of the same from tyme to tyme w*i*thin the tyme aforesaid as the necessity thereof at sondrie tymes required to kepe the same in Redynes for her m*aies*ties s*er*uice. The chardg*es* aswell for wages as for other necessaries hereafter ensueth.

Thomas Clatterbooke at. 20^{d}. p*er* diem	20	xxxiij^{s} iiij^{d}
Iohn Tipsley at .xij^{d} p*er* diem	20	xx^{s}
Iohn Davies at xij^{d} p*er* diem	20	xx^{s}
Iohn Lucas at the like	20	xx^{s}
will*iam* Phillippes at the like	20	xx^{s}
Thomas Rowkelidge. at the like	20	xx^{s}
Iohn Sherborne at the like	20	xx^{s}
Iohn daunsey at the like	20	xx^{s}
The M*aster* at iiij^{s} p*er* diem	20	iiij^{li}
The Clarke controwler at ij^{s}	20	xl^{s}
The Clarke at ij^{s} p*er* diem	20	xl^{s}
The Yomen at ij^{s} p*er* diem	20	xl^{s}

Iohn Sherborne for money layd out for necessaries vsed at sondry tymes in the said Ayreing*es* viz. Threde and tape of sondrie sort*es* — vij^{s}/ for brushes rubbing brushes and Rushes — vij^{s} viij^{d} } xiiij^{s} viij^{d}

Edmonde Tylney esquire for money by him disbursed and to be disbursed aswell aboute the making of the accompte to the Auditor of Thimpreste and declarac*io*n of the same before the L*ord* Treaseror and S*ir* walter mildmey. As also for the chardg*es* of the privie seale Order for the payment of the money and receipte of the same w*i*th the Certificat*es* doth yearly amounte vnto above. } viij^{li}

SU*MMA* of the chardg*es* last afore said. } xxvij^{li} viij^{s}

SU*MMA* TOT*A*LIS of this whole booke. } cclxxx^{li} xiij^{s} j^{d}.

* T Blagrave * E Tyllney

*Memorandu*m* that all this bouke was discharged by Edmond Tyllney *master* of the office In Ann*o* 1586 In the xxviij yere of her ma*ies*tes raygn At w*hi*ch time ther was Imprestid j c^{li} toward*es* the chardgis off y^{t} yere

E Tyllney

wheroff was disbursed as followithe

Edward kirkham

*The c^{li} in prest following vide*licet* xxviij Regn*i* Reg*ine* Elizabeth

*Inprimis ye previe seall & signett . . . . . iij^{li}

Itim to m^{r} peter & ye tellers for ye recept . . . . .

Itim payd for fuell. . . . . .

I[tim] payd for Canvas . . . . .

[Itim] In prest to Burchall ye wierd[rawer] . . . . . f° 3 v.

Itim f[or] wagis Dew vnto the *master* & his men Attendantses about her maiestes seruice from Ahollan eue vnteil Ashweddensday dayes & nightes } xlvjli
Itim for ye masters wagis Dew to him & his men for the ayringes . . . . vjli
Itim payd for torchis, Candells, & linkkes . . . . xli xs
Itim for ye *masters* grenclothe standish, Inke, & paper. . . . . iijli
Itim payd to ye plumber for repayring ye leads ouer ye haull & office. . . xxxs
Itim for bardghier & bothier to & from ye court to london diuers times . . xxxs
Itim payd for rushis . . . . xvs
Itim payd to ye Auditor & for certificat*tes* out off ye wardrops . . . . . viijli

fo 4 r.

From 31 October 1586 to 1 November 1589

Record Office. Privy Seal Books (Auditors), vol. I^{b}. f. 310 v.

Edmonde Tylney ar*miger* M*aster* of hir ma*iest*ies Revell*es* in full paym*ent* of the debt*es* due in the same Office vj^{c} iiij^{xx} vij^{li} xix^{s} j^{d} ob.

Elizabeth &c. To the Treasourer and Chamb*er*laines of o*ur* Exchequire greetinge : Wee will and Comande yo*u* that of such our treasure as is or shall come into the Receipt of o*ur* said Exchequire yow delyver or cause to be delyvered to o*ur* trustie and welbeloved s*er*vant Edmonde Tylney esquire M*aster* of the Office of our Revell*es* aswe'l the some of vj^{c} iiij^{xx} vij^{li} xix^{s} j^{d} ob. in full payment of the debtes due by vs to diuerse p*er*sounes for wares delyvered and workes doune w*i*thin the said office and for wages due to the Officers there, betwene the last day of Octobre in the xxviijth yere of o*ur* reigne and the fyrst day of Novembre in the xxxjth yere of our reigne beinge fower whole yeres to be by hym payed to the said p*er*sounes as appeareth in two Lydger bookes subscribed by the Officers of the same Office remayninge w*i*th the Auditors of our Imprestes, As also the some of one hundred powndes in prest to be by hym defrayed and Layed owt towardes the Chardges of our service for this yere Last past in our said Office : And theise o*ur* L*ett*res, shalbe yo*ur* sufficient warrante and discharde in this behalfe. Geven vndre o*ur* privey Seale at o*ur* Manno*ur* of Grenewiche the xviijth daye of Aprill in the xxxijth yere of our reigne.

as also in prest for the yere past — c^{li}

* Will*iam* Packer

From 31 October 1587 to 1 November 1588

Record Office. Audit Office. Accounts Various. Bd. 1213. Revels. N° 12.

Reuelles : .1.5.8.7. Anno
R*egni* R*egin*e Elizabeth } **xxx°**

Title-page r.

Christmas Twelfftid Shrouetide & choysmakinge of playes w*i*th the reforminge of them Anno Reg*ni* Elizabethe } xxx°

The chardgis of thos tymes viz.: from the last of October .1587. In Anno xxix° Reg*ni* Reg*ine* Elizabeth & the firste of November, 1588 Anno xxx° d*ict*e Reg*ine* ded rise aswell by means Attendinge makinge choyse p*er*vsinge reformi*n*ge & Alteringe of suche playes co*m*medies maskes and Inventions as were prepared set forthe & presented before her Ma*ies*tie In the tymes before said, As also of the wagis workmanship translations wares deliuered careagis Iorni*n*ge chardgis, & expencis therevnto belonginge w*i*th the Arringes, brushing*es* and salffe kepinge of the robes & other stuffe w*i*thin the sayd office. The particulars whereof together w*i*th the parties names to whom & wherefore the same is dewe hereafter Insuethe viz.

Anno xxx° Reg*ni* Regine

The Quenes Ma*ies*tie beinge At Grenew*i*ch ther were shewed presented and enacted before: her highnes betwixte Christmas & Shrouetid vij playes besides featt*es* of Activitie And other shewes by the Childeren of Poles her Ma*iesties* owne servant*es* & the gentlemen of grayes In on whom was Inployed dyverse rem*n*antt*es* of Clothe of goulde & other stuffe oute of the Store.

f° 1r.

Tayllors & others woorkinge & Attending the premeses during the foresayd tyme at xij^{d} the daye & as muche the Night

	Dayes	Night*es*	
Thomas Clatterbouke	28	14	xlij^{s}
	* iiiij^{s}	* lvij^{s}	
Iohn Davis.	40	14	lxiij^{s}
Richarde Oughton	2	1	iij^{s}
Thomas Tipslye	12	6	xviij^{s}

Two Attendancis for the Clarke controler Two for the Clarke and twoe for the yeoman 28 dayes and 14 Night*es* At xij^{d} the daye & asmuche the Night In all — xij^{li} xij^{s}

Lenarde Knight	2	1	iij^{s}
Robarte williamson.	2	1	iij^{s}
Iohn Plaute	6	3	xj^{s}

The Porter of St Ihons Gatt

Iohn Daunsie porter of St Ihons gatt for his Attendantt*es* duringe the rehersalles. & otherwise for Christmas and Shroutid at xij^{d} the daye and asmuche the Night 49 dayes and 14 Night*es* — lxiij^{s}

* *Summa* — xxij^{li} ix^{s}

The officers wagis for ther attendance duringe Christmas & Shrouetid At ij^{s} the daye and asmuch the Night.

	Dayes	Night*es*	
The Yeoman of the Revells	38	14	v^{li} iiij^{s}
The Clarke.	28	14	iiij^{li} iiij^{s}
The Clarke controler	28	14	iiij^{li} iiij^{s}

* *Summa* — xiij^{li} xij^{s}

The M*aster* of the office at iiij^{s} ye daye.

The M*aster* of the office for his attendance & chardgis from the laste of October vntil Ashewedensdaye aswell for choysmakinge & reforminge of playes and Commedies as Also for his and other attendant*es* duringe Christmas & Shrouetide Amontinge In all vnto cxvj dayes & xiiijth night*es* at iiij^{s} ye daye and asmuche the Night cometh to — xxvj^{li}

A dorekeper and iij other attendant*es* aswell duringe the rehersalls as also for ther attendance At the Courte In Christmas and Shrouetid at xij^{d} the daye.

	dayes	night*es*	
William Cooke	116	14	vj^{li} x^{s}
Roger Chamber	116	14	vj^{li} x^{s}
Thomas Carlton	116	14	vj^{li} x^{s}
Henry Cooke	116	14	vj^{li} x^{s}

Summa — lxxxviij^{li} x^{s}.

f° 1 v.

Wierdrawer	Edmond Burchall wierdrauer for wierworke & braunchis In the hall At Grenewich at Twelfftid and Shrouetid by greate aswell for wares as worckmanship	xvij^{li}.
Carpenter	Iohn Mildney carpenter for Tymber bordes and worckmanship In mendinge and settinge vpp of the howses by greate	iij^{li}
Mercer	Bartholomew hix mercer for xxx ells of Sarssnett of Sundery coullers at vj^{s} viij^{d} the elle delyvered Into the office	x^{li}

*xxxij^{li} Edward Kirkham yeoman of the Revells for diuerse thinges by him disbursed In service of the said office.

ffor xviij yerdes of Cotton	xxij^{s}
ffor vj pound of Assedew	xviij^{s}
And for cuttinge of ij pound thereof	iij^{s}
ffor vj dozen of pastebordes	vj^{s}
ffor ij yerdes of boukram	ij^{s} vj^{d}
ffor gloves geven to the Quenes players to ye tumblers & childeren of Poles	xxxvj^{s}
ffro threide of diuerse coullers	v^{s}
ffor Inkle	ij^{s}
ffor caryinge of stuffe from Grenewich to Tower wharffe	ij^{s} iiij^{d}
ffor botehyer dyuerse tymes duringe the said service	x^{s}

*cvj^{s} x^{d}. Summa — v^{li} vij^{s} x^{d}

f° 2 r.

The Clerke Thomas Blagraue clerke of the said office demandeth allowance for A grene clothe standishe Inke & paper — iij^{li} vj^{s} viij^{d}

And layde out for A pece of Canvas. . . . . . . xxx^{s}

Edmond Tyllney esquier and m*aster* of the said office for money by hym disbursed and allowanc*es* In the said office viz.

Inprimis Layde out vnto dyuers paynters for ther workes and couller as well of the clothe for howses as also for garneshinge of the branches In the hall At Twelfftid and Shrouetid — vij^{li}

It*em* for Canvas for the howse & Tumblers . . . l^{s}

It*em* for ffewell bothe for the rehersalls of playes In ye greate hall & for thearing*es* of the robes and other thing*es* In the office as also for the M*aster* lodginge & office At the Courte duringe the said service — vj^{li}

It*em* for light*es* of all sort*es* link*es* and torches . . iij^{li} vj^{s}

It*em* for rushis aswell for strawinge of the greate hall at St Ihons as also the office at the Courte — x^{s}.

It*em* for the M*aste*rs grene clothe standishe Inke paper & a close steole — iij^{li} x^{s}

It*em* for botehyer as well for him selfe as for his men sentt dyuerse Tymes In the service of the office from Grenewich to London & for cariage of the stuffe to & froe — xl^{s}

*xxvj^{li}. vj^{s}. *Summa* — xxix^{li} xij^{s} viij^{d}

f° 2 v.

The Porter — Dauncey porter of St Ihons gatte for Candlls & lanterne duringe the rehersalls } x^{s}

*lxviij^{li} xix^{s} vj^{d} — *Summa* — lxviij^{li} xix^{s} vj^{d}

Chardgis of the office growinge at sunderie tymes by meanes of Ayringes mendinge brushinge spunging layinge vp and salffe kepinge the robes & garmentes from tyme to tyme within the tyme afore said as the necessitie thereof requirethe to kepe ye same In redines for her Maiesties service the chardgis whereof as well for wagis as for other necessaris hereafter Insuethe.

	dayes	
Thomas Clatterbouke	20	xx^{s}
Iohn Davis at the leke	20	xx^{s}
Iohn Lucas	20	xx^{s}
william Huitt	20	xx^{s}
william Phillipes	20	xx^{s}
william Cooke	20	xx^{s}
Roger Chambers	20	xx^{s}
Iohn Dauncie porter of St Ihons	20	xx^{s}
The Master of the office at iiij^{s} a daye	20	iiij^{li}
The clarkecontroler at ij^{s} a daye	20	xl^{s}
The clearke At ye leke rate	20	xl^{s}
The yeomas At the leke rate	20	xl^{s}

Edward Kerkham yeoman of the office for money by him layde oute In the said Ayringes viz. threid rubbinge brushes rushis and bromes } x^{s}

* *Summa* — xviij^{li} x^{s}

f° 8 r.

Edmond Tyllney esquier for money by him to be disbursed about*es* the makinge vp of the Acco*un*tte to the Auditor of the Inprest & declartion of the same before the Lord Treasoror & S*ir* water Mildmey } viij^{li}

S*umma* — xxvj^{li} x^{s}

* S*umma* Tot*alis* — c$\overset{xx}{\text{iiij}}$^{li} vj^{d}

* c$\overset{xx}{\text{iiij}}$ iij^{li} x^{s} vj^{d}

S*umma* Totalys — clxxxiiij^{li} vj^{d}

* Ed Tyllney

* Edward kirkham

f° 3 v.

xv^{to} pro Anno & v Mensibus	Superplussage...... nihilo Empcion......... viij^{c} iiij^{xx} x^{li} xij^{s} iij^{d} ob. master xliiij^{li} viij^{s} Comptroler xxij^{li} iiij^{s} Clarke xxij^{li} iiij^{s} yeoman xxij^{li} iiij^{s} vadia — iiij^{c} iiij^{xx} vij^{li} iij^{d}	Miij^{c}lxxvij^{li} xij^{s} vj^{d} ob. which Summe is all paid

Iohn ffortescue & henry Sakford/ at this tyme Duke Memoranci was here

xiiij^{o}	nihilo MCCxix^{li} x^{s} ix^{d} ij^{c}xxxiiij^{li} xvj^{s} viij^{d} Rewardes & other perticulers — xxx^{li} xiij^{s} ij^{d}	MDiiij^{xx}v^{li} vij^{d} all paid
xvj^{o} M^{r} dodington	Superplussage ... nihilo Empcions....... cccxv^{li} xiiij^{s} iiij^{d} Wages .... cccxiiij^{li} ij^{s} Master xxiiij^{li} clarke xij^{li} Comptroler xij^{li} yeoman xij^{li} Rewardes — xxij^{li} ix^{s} iiij^{d}	vj^{c}lxxij^{li} xiij^{s} ij^{d}
xvij^{mo}	MDl^{li} v^{s} viij^{d} ob. cccvj^{li} xiiij^{s} vij^{d} cccx^{li} xv^{s} j^{d} Master xxix^{li} Comptroler xiiij^{li} x^{s} Clarke xiiij^{li} x^{s} yeoman xiiij^{li} x^{s} lj^{li} xij^{s} viij^{d}	MMCCxix^{li} viij^{s} ob. wherof paid MDCCl^{li} v^{s} viij^{d}
xix^{no}		
xx^{mo} m^{r} dodington	clvij^{li} xvij^{s} v^{d} lxxvij^{li} iij^{s} iiij^{d} ob. cxxviij^{li} xiij^{s} iiij^{d} Master xvj^{li} xij^{s} Comptroler viij^{li} vj^{s} Clark viij^{li} vj^{s} yeoman viij^{li} vj^{s} xxxviij^{li} xj^{s} vj^{d}	iiij^{c} ij^{li} vj^{s} vj^{d} ob. wherof paid clvij^{li} xvij^{s} v^{d} Remaining ccxliiij^{li} ix^{s} j^{d} ob.
xxij w dodington sub manu domini Thesaurarij & w Mildmaye	cxlj^{li} xj^{s} x^{d} iiij^{xx}xv^{li} xj^{s}. cxlij^{li} viij^{s} vj^{d} Master xvij^{li} Comptroler viij^{li} x^{s} Clark viij^{li} x^{s} yeoman viij^{li} x^{s} xxxj^{li} ij^{s}	iiij^{c} x^{li} xiij^{s} iiij^{d} wherof paid iij^{c}xlj^{li} xj^{s} x^{d} Remaining lxix^{li} viij^{d}

f° 7 r.

From 31 October 1587 to 31 October 1589

British Museum. Lansdowne MSS. 59. n° 21.

Reuells 1587. & 1588 annis regni Regine Elizabethe ·: } xxx^mo & xxxj^o.

f° 38 r.

Christmas Twelftide, & Shrouetide & choice making of plaies w*i*th the reforming of them Annis R*eg*ine Elizabethe

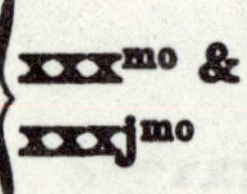

xxx^{mo} & xxxj^{mo}

The chardges of those tymes viz. from the last of October 1587 in A*nno* xxix^{no} regni R*eg*ine Elizabethe vntill the Last of October 1589 anno xxxj^{mo} d*ict*e d*omi*ne R*eg*ine being for twoe yeares did arise aswell by meanes of attending making choice perusing reforming & altering of suche plaies Comedies maskes and Inventions as [were p*re*pared set forthe & p*re*sented before her M*aies*tie in the tymes within the twoe yeares aforesaide as also of the wages workemanshipp translations wares deliu*er*ed caryages iourneyeng chardges and expences therevnto belonging w*i*th the ayring*es* brushing and safe keping of the Robes and other stuffe within the saide office. The p*ar*ticularities whereof together w*i*th the p*ar*ties names to whome and wherefore the same is dewe hereafter insueth

viz.

Anno xxx^{mo} regni R*eg*ine Elizabethe. 1587

The Quenes M*aies*tie being at Grenewiche there were p*re*sented shewed & enacted before her highnes betwixt *Christ*mas and Shrovetide seaven plaies besides feates of activity & other shewes by the children of Poules her M*aiesties* owne s*er*vant*es* & the gent*lemen* of Grayes Inne on whome was ymployed dyvers remnant*es* of cloth of gold & other stuffe out of the store.

Anno xxxj^{mo} regni R*eg*ine Elizabethe. 1588

The Queenes M*aies*tie being at Richemonde at *Christ*mas Newyearstide & Twelftide there were shewed p*re*sented & enacted before her highnes ffyve playes & her M*aies*tie being at white hall at Shrovetide there were shewed & presented before her twoe plaies All w*hi*ch playes were enacted by her M*aiesties* owne s*er*vant*es* the children of Paules & the Lord Admiralls men besides sondry feates of actyvity tumbling & Matichives shewed before her highnes w*i*thin the tyme & at the places aforesaide.

f° 39 r.

Taillours & others working & attending the premisses during the twoe yeares aforesaide the first at xxd the daye & as muche the night the rest at xijd.

	daies	nightes	
Thomas Clatterbooke	56	24	vjli xiijs iiijd
Richard Houghton	2	1	iijs
Iohn Davis	100	30	vjli xs
william Hewett	100	30	vjli xs
william Stedeman	100	30	vjli xs
william Phillipps	100	30	vjli xs
Peter Geofforde	100	30	vjli xs
Iohn Lucas	100	30	vjli xs
william kiffin	100	30	vjli xs
william Cooke	100	30	vjli xs
Roger Chambers	100	30	vjli xs
Thomas Carleton	100	30	vjli xs
Henry Cooke	100	30	vjli xs
Iohn Blackborne	9	3	xijs
Iohn Tipsley	12	6	xviijs
Leonard knight	2	1	iijs
Iohn Plowte	8	3	xjs
Roberte williamson	2	1	iijs

*Summa — iiij^xx li xiijs iijd.

The Portour of St Iohns gate

Iohn Dauncye Portour of St Iohns gate for his attendance during the rehearsalls & otherwise for Christmas and Shrovetide in the said twoe yeares at xijd the daye & as muche the night for 100 daies & 30 nightes — vjli xs.

*master — xxvjli
*Clark — xiijli
comptroller *Clark — xiijli
*yeoman — xiijli

The Master of the office, the Clarke, the Clarke Comptroller & the yeoman for there attendances & chardges aswell for choice making & reforming of playes & comedies as also for there other attendances during Christmas & Shrovetide amounting to 100 daies & 30 nightes the Master at iiijs the daye & as muche the night & thother officers at ijs whiche cometh to — lxvli.

The saide Master of the office demaundeth further allowance for wages for his owne attendance viz. for 64 daies in the xxxth yeare of her Maiesties raigne & for 57 daies in the xxxjth yeare of her Maiesties raigne for choice making & reforming of playes, viz. betwene the last of October 1587 & the last of October 1588 & Ashwednesdaye then followeng being in all 121 daies at iiijs ye daye — xxiiijli iiijs *for 121

He demaundeth further allowance for wages for ffoure of his men being one dorekeper and three other attendantes during the 121 daies aforesaid at xijd the daye a pece — xxiiijli iiijs.

200. 8. 4. *Summa — ccli xjs iiijd.

f° 39 v.

Vpholster	To Iohn Okes vpholster for twoe close stooles	xx^{s}.
Wyerdrawer	Edmonde Burchall wyerdrawer for wyerworke & braunches in the halles at Greenewiche & at Richemonde & whitehall at Twelftide and Shrovetide in the said twoe yeares by greate aswell for wares as workemanshipp	xxviij^{li} xix^{s} iij^{d} ob.
Mercer	Bartholomewe Hix m*er*cer for lx elles of sarcenet of sondry collors deliu*er*ed into the office, 3o elles in the 3o yeare & 3o elles in the 31 yeare of the quene at vj^{s} viij^{d} the ell	xx^{li}.
Carpenter	Iohn Mildney Carpenter for timber bordes and workemanshipp in mending & setting vp of the houses by greate in the said twoe yeares	vj^{li} xv^{s} vj^{d}.
	To Iames Huse for one pece of canvis deliu*er*ed into the office	xxv^{s} viij^{d}.
	Edwarde kirkham yeoman of the Revells for dyvers thing*es* by him disbursed in service of the saide office in the saide twoe yeares.	
Necessaries.	ffor gloves geven to the players the children of Powles & tumblers in the xxxth yeare of her ma*iestie*s raign	xxxix^{s}. } *iiij^{li} iiij^{s}
	ffor gloves geven to the players the children of Poules & tumblers in ye xxxjth yeare of her ma*iesties* raign	xlv^{s}.
	ffor a paire of fflannell hose for Symmons the Tumbler . . .	iiij^{s}
	ffor inckle & thredd	ix^{s} x^{d}.
	ffor six dozen of paste bordes	vj^{s}
*Taylors	ffor twoe men twoe daies for to make sarcenett sherth & hose for the Tumblers	iiij^{s}
	ffor Searing candles.	iiij^{d}
	ffor twoe yardes of Buckerome	ij^{s} vj^{d}
	ffor xviij yardes of Cotton.	xxij^{s}.
	ffor xij poundes of Assidewe and xviij dozen of paste bordes .	xlviij^{s}
	ffor the cutting of the Assedewe	vij^{s}
	ffor boatehire & for cariage of stuffe at sondry tymes to Grenewiche & to Richemonde during the said twoe yeares	xx^{s} vj^{d}

* S*umma* — lxviij^{li} viij^{s} vij^{d} ob.

68. 8. 7. ob. f° 40 r.

Edmonde Tilney esquier & M*aster* of the said office for money by him disbursed in the said office viz.	
Inprimis for the fayre writing of all the devises on the 17 daye of November A*nno* 31 Eliz*abethe* in two copies for the quene	x^{s}
ffor greeneclothe, Standishe hower glasse Inck & paper for the said twoe yeares	vj^{li}
ffor Roome for the office & Masters lodging at Grenewiche Richemounde & white hall in the said twoe yeares	xx^{s}
ffor carieng of the stuffe	x^{s}
ffor candles & other light*es* in y[e] said ij yeares	c^{s}.
ffor rushes	xv^{s}
ffor nayles	$ij^{s}\ vj^{d}$
ffor Coales & billet*es* in the said twoe yeares	$x^{li}\ xiiij^{s}$
Geven to Russell & dyvers other paynters for there worke & collo*u*rs for paynting of houses and garnishing of braunches at Grenewiche Richemond and white hall annis 30 & 31 regni R*eg*ine Elizabethe	$xiiij^{li}\ x^{s}$
paide to a painter for painting of a battlement by greate . . .	x^{s}
ffor a baskett to carry the stuffe	$iij^{s}\ iiij^{d}$
ffor botehire for him self & his men & for cariage of stuffe from London to Grenewiche & Richemonde & back againe for the saide s*er*vice in those twoe yeares	lx^{s}
ffor Canvis for the houses & Tumblers	$iiij^{li}$
The Clarke. — The Clarke of the said office for his ordenary greneclothe Standishe Inck & paper &c. for the twoe yeares aforesaide	$vj^{li}\ xiij^{s}\ iiij^{d}$
Iohn Dauncy Porto*ur* of S[t] Iohns gate for candles & Lanthornes during the rehearsalls & workes in the said twoe yeares	xx^{s}

*S*umma — $liiij^{li}\ viij^{s}\ ij^{d}$

34.3.2.

f° 40 v.

A maske sent into Scotland.

Betwene the   of September 1589 *anno* xxxj° regni R*egine* Eliz*abethe* and the   of the same September for newe making of dyvers garment*es* & altering & translating of sondry other garment*es* for the furnishing of a maske for six Maskers & six torchebearers and of suche p*er*sons as were to vtter speches at the sheweng of the same maske Sent into Scotland to the king of Scott*es* mariage by her M*aiesties* comaundement signified vnto the M*aster* & other officers of this office by the L*ord* T*reasor*er, the L*ord* Chamberleyn & M^r^ vicechamberleine. The chardges aswell for workmanshipp & attendance as for wares deliu*er*ed & brought into this office for & about the same hereafter p*ar*ticulerly insueth.

viz.

A maske of six coates of purple gold tinsell garded w*i*th purple & black clothe of silu*er* striped. Bases of Crimson clothe of gold w*i*th pendant*es* of maled purple silu*er* Tinsell, twoe paire of sleves to the same of red cloth of gold & ffoure paire of sleves to the same of white clothe of copper silu*er* six partlet*es* of purple clothe of silu*er* knotted, six hed peces whereof ffoure of clothe of gold knotted and twoe of purple clothe of gold braunched, six ffethers to the same hed peces, six Mantles whereof ffoure of Oringe clothe of gold braunched & twoe of purple & white clothe of silu*er* braunched, six vizardes & six ffawchins guilded.

Six Cassock*es* for torche bearers of damaske three of yellowe and three of red garded w*i*th red & yellowe damaske Counterchaunged, six paire of hose of damaske three of yellowe and three of red garded w*i*th red & yellowe damaske Counterchanged, six hatt*es* of Crimson clothe of gold & six fethers to the same, six vizardes.

ffoure heares of silke & ffoure garlandes of fflowers for the attire of them that are to vtter certeine speches at the sheweng of the same maske

Taill*ou*rs & others working & attending the p*re*misses the ffirst at xx^d^. ye day & the rest at xij^d^

	daies	
Thomas Clatterbooke	7	xj^s^ viij^d^
Iohn Davis	7	vij^s^
Clement Caliot	7	vij^s^
Abraham Bradford	4	iiij^s^
Lyson Phillipps	4	iiij^s^
Daniell Hall	4	iiij^s^
Richard Houghton	4	iiij^s^
will*iam* Hewet	10	x^s^
will*iam* Stedeman	10	x^s^
will*iam* Phillipps	10	x^s^
Peter Gifford	10	x^s^.

f° 41r.

	Iohn Lucas	10	x^{s}	
	will*iam* kiffin	10	x^{s}	
	will*iam* Cooke	10	x^{s}	
	Roger Chambers	10	x^{s}	
	Thomas Carleton	10	x^{s}	
	Henry Cooke.	10	x^{s}	
				*S*um*ma*—vij^{li} xx^{d}.
The Porto*ur*	Iohn Dauncye	10	x^{s}	
Officers	The M*aster* at iiij^{s} p*er* diem	10	xl^{s}	
	The Clarke Comptroller at ij^{s}	10	xx^{s}	
	The Clarke at ij^{s}.	10	xx^{s}	
	The yeoman at ij^{s}	10	xx^{s}	
				*S*um*ma—c^{s}.

Emptions & provisions

ffethermaker	Siluester Bonnefoy for washing tryming & putting in six ffethers into a plume for a hed pece — viij^{s} & for vij other fethers for hatt*es* x^{s} in all	xviij^{s}
Necessaries	Edwarde kirkham for black browne white and yellowe thredd — iij^{s} iiij^{d} Incle — xviij^{d} searing candle — iiij^{d} gilding of six ffawchins — x^{s} to a messinger for going to the M*aster* of the Revells into the countrye myles — ij^{s} to a messinger for going from London to the courte at Oatelandes to M^{r} vicechamberleyne — ij^{s} for xij vizardes xxiiij^{s} in all	xliij^{s} ij^{d}.
	Clement Calcott for xviij ownces of copper ffrindge at xx^{d} the oz. xxx^{s} for viij tassells of copper v^{s} iiij^{d} for painting of vj ffawchins ij^{s} in all	xxxvij^{s} iiij^{d}
Haberdasher	for tryming of six hatt*es* at viij^{d} the pece — iiij^{s} for making of twoe hatt*es* of clothe of gold & putting paste & buckerome into them — vj^{s} viij^{d} in all	x^{s} viij^{d}.

Chardges of the office groweng at sondrye tymes within the saide twoe yeares by meanes of ayring mending brushing spunging layeng vp and safe keping the Robes & garment*es* from tyme to tyme within the tyme aforesaid as the necessity thereof requiered to kepe the same in readines for her M*aiesties* service. The chardges whereof aswell for wages as for necessaries hereafter insueth

18. I. 8. *S*um*ma*–xviij^{li} x^{d}.

f° 41 v.

	Daies	
Thomas Clatterbooke at xx^{d}	40	lxvj^{s} viij^{d}
Iohn Davis at xij^{d}	40	xl^{s}
Iohn Lucas at xij^{d}	40	xl^{s}
will*iam* Hewet at xij^{d}	40	xl^{s}
will*iam* Phillipps at xij^{d}	40	xl^{s}
will*iam* Cooke at xij^{d}	40	xl^{s}
Roger Chambers at xij^{d}	40	xl^{s}

* *Summa* — xv^{li} vj^{s} viij^{d}

Iohn Dauncye Port*our* of s^{t} Iohns gate at xij^{d} 40 . . . . . . xl^{s}

The M*aster* of the office at iiij^{s} p*er* die*m*	40	viij^{li}	* xx^{li}
The Clarke comptroller at ij^{s} p*er* die*m*.	40	iiij^{li}	
The Clarke at the like rate	40	iiij^{li}	
The yeoman at the like rate	40	iiij^{li}	

Edward kirkham yeoman of the office for money by him laide out in the saide ayring*es* viz. Thredd Rubbing brushes, rushes and Broomes } xx^{s}.

Edmonde Tilney esquier for money by him to be disbursed about his making vp of the accompt to the Audit*our* of the imprest*es* & Declaration of the same before the Lord Tr*easor*er } xij^{li}.

* *Summa* — l^{li} vj^{s} viij^{d}.

* Ed Tyllney

*Sum*ma total*is* of all the chardges conteyned in this Booke amounteth vnto } ccc^{xx}iiij xj^{li} xv^{s} vij^{d} ob.

* T Blagrave * Edward kirkham

.5o. 6 . 8 .

f° 42 r.

1587 & 1588

Allowances to the Officers

British Museum. Lansdowne MSS. 59. n° 26.

---

for 2. yeres. The *Master* of the Thoffice for his attendance aswell for choise, makinge, and reforminge of plaies and Commedies as otherwise in Christmas & Shrovetide by the space of ccxxxj. daies and xxx. night*es* at iiij^{s} p*er* die*m* and asmuch p*er* noctem — lij^{li} iiij^{s} and for xl. daies w*i*thin the said time for airing the stuffe of the said office viij^{li} in all. } lx^{li} iiij^{s}.

The Clarke Comptroller cl daies & xxx. night*es* at ij^{s} p*er* diem & asmuch p*er* noctem. } xviij^{li}

The Clarke for the same time, and at the said Rate. . . . . xviij^{li}.

The yeoman for the same time and at the said Rate. . . . . xviij^{li}.

f° 52 r. S*umma* — cxiiij^{li} xiiij^{s}.

[Endorsed (f° 52 v.) :]

Allowances for daie and night seruices in the Office of ye Reuels.

An*n*is .1587. & 1588.

From 31 October 1589 to 1 November 1592

Record Office. Exchequer of Receipt. Warrants for Issue. Parcel 131.

Elizabeth by the grace of god Queene of England ffraunce and Ireland defendo*ur* of the faith &c. To the Treasorer and Chamberlains of our Exchecquer greeting. We will and co*m*maund you that of such o*ur* treasure as is or shall come into the Receipt of o*ur* said Exchecquer you deliu*er* or cause to be deliuered to o*ur* trustie and welbeloued servant Edmunde Tylney Esquier M*aster* of the office of our Revelles aswell the some of three hundred eleven poundes two shilling*es* and two pence in full payment of the debt*es* due by vs to divers p*er*sons for wares deliu*er*ed and woorkes done w*i*thin the said office And for wages due to the officers there betwene the last day of October in the one and thirtith yere of our reigne and the first daye of November in the fower and thirtith yere of o*ur* reigne being three whole yeres to be by him paid to the said p*er*sons as appeareth in one lidgier booke subscribed by the officers of the same office remayning w*i*th the Audito*urs* of our Imprest*es*. As also the some of one hundred pownd*es* in prest to be by him defrayed and layd out toward*es* the charges of o*ur* service for the yere last past in our said office. And these o*ur* l*ett*res shalbe yo*ur* sufficient warrant and discharge in this behalf. Gyven vnder our Privy Seale at o*ur* Manno*ur* of Grenewich the eight & twentith day of Maye in the six and thirtith yere of our reigne.

* Will*iam* Packer

M*aster* of the Revelles.

[Endorsed :]

* Mak an order
* W. Burghley

From 1 November 1593 to 31 October 1596 and from 31 October 1596 to 31 October 1597.

Record Office. Privy Seal Books (Auditors). Vol. 2^{b}. f° 127 v.

Master of ye Revell*es*.

Elizabeth &c. To the Tr*easur*er and Chamberlins of *our* Exchecque*r* greeting. We will & co*m*maunde yo*w* y^{t} of such *our* treasure as is or shall come into ye Receipt of *our* Exchecque*r*, yo*w* deliuer or cause tobe deliuered to *our* trustie and welbeloued seruaunt Edmond Tilney Esquie*r* M*aster* of the office of *our* Revell*es* aswell the some of twoo hundred pound*es* in full payem*ent* of all ye debt*es* due by vs vnto diverse p*er*sons for wares deliuered & workes done in ye said office, & for wages due vnto the officers there

for 3 yeares Arrerages.

behinde vnpaide for ye three whole yeares last past. viz. from ye first of November in the five & thirteth yeare of *our* raigne vnto the last of October in ye eight & thirteth yeare of *our* said raigne to be paid by him vnto the said p*er*sons according to the ratement of a late reformac*i*on and composic*i*on exhibited vnto vs for the ordinary charges of ye said office As also yearely thencforth from the said last of October in the eight and thirteth yeare of *our* raigne the some of three score sixe pound*es* six shilling*es* eight pence by waie of composic*i*on for ye defraying of *our* said ordinary service w*i*thin y^{t} office, concerning plays onely and according to the foresaid ratement. And theise *our* l*ett*res &c. Geuene vnde*r* *our* priuy Seale at *our* Pallace of Westm*inste*r the eleventh daie of Ianuary in the fortith yeare of *our* raigne.

* W. Packer

From 31 October 1597 to 31 October 1598.

Record Office. Order Books (Pells). Vol. I. f° 112 r.

M*aster* of the Reuell*es* for the chardges of playes only for the yeare endinge vltimo Oct*obris* 1598

Irr*otulatum* in pell*e* Exit*us* xxviij° Octo*bris* 1598

By order xxv° Oct*obris* 1598 To Edmund Tilney Esq*uier* M*aster* of the Office of Revell*es* the some of threscore six pound*es* six shilling*es* eight pence for defrayinge the ordinary chardg*es* and service within that office concerning plaies only accordinge to a late composic*ion* for the yeare endinge the last of Octobre 1598 p*er* bre*ue* Dat*um* xj° Ianuarij 1597.

lxvj^li^ vj^s^ viij^d^

Taillo*ur*

1598 (?)

Record Office. Order Books (Pells). Vol. I. f° 159 r.

Master of the Reuells vppon a yearely certeine composition for the chardges of Playes only.

By Order xxvj^{o} Martij 1599. To Edmund Tilney Esq*uier* M*aster* of the Revell*es* the some of threscore six pound*es* six shilling*es* eight pence allowed vnto him yearely by waie of Composic*i*on for defrayinge the ordinary service w*ith*in that office concerning playes onely p*er* breue dat*um* xj^{o} Ianuarij 1597. lxvj^{li} vj^{s} viij^{d}

Irrot*ulatum* in pell*e* Exit*us* xxx^{o} Martij 1599

Killigrew

From 31 October 1598 to 31 October 1599

Record Office. Order Books (Pells). Vol. 2. f° 34 r.

M*aster* of the Reuells. for defrayeng the ordinary chardge of playes within that office by composicion

Irr*otulatum* in pell*e* Ex*itus* xx° ffeb*ruarij* 1599.

By Order xiiij° ffeb*ruarij* 1599 To Edmund Tilney Esq*uier* M*aster* of the Reuell*es* the some of threscore six pounds six shilling*es* eight pence in prest for his yearely allowance by way of Composic*i*on for defraying the ordinary Chardge w*ith*in that Office ffor playes only for the yeare ended the last of Octobre in the xljth yeare of her Ma*iesties* raign p*er* br*eue* dat*um* xj° Ianu*a*rij 1599

lxvj^{li} vj^{s} viij^{d}

Taillo*ur*

From 31 October 1599 to 31 October 1600.

Record Office. Order Books (Pells). Vol. 2. f° 143 r.

M*aster* of the Reuells by way of composicion for playes only.	By Orde*r* vltimo ffebruarij 1600 To Edmund Tilney Esq*uier* M*aster* of the Revell*es* the some of lxvj^{li} vj^{s} viij^{d} for his yearelie allowance by waie of Composicion for defrayinge the ordinary chard*ges* within that office for plaies onely for this p*rese*nt yeare 1600 p*er* br*eue* Dat*um* xj° Ianuarij 1597.	lxvj^{li} vj^{s} viij^{d}
Irr*otulatum* in pell*e* Ex*itus* iij° Martij 1600		Tail*our*

From 31 October 1600 to 31 October 1601

Record Office. Order Books (Pells). Vol. 2. f° 253 r.

M*aster* of the Reuell*es* for the chardge of Playes by composic*ion* Irr*otulatum* in pell*e* xxij^{o} ffeb*ruarij* 1601	By Orde*r* xx^{o} ffebr*uar*ij 1601 To Edmund Tilney Esq*uier* M*aster* of the Reuell*es* the some of lxvj^{li} vj^{s} viij^{d} for his yearly allowance by way of Composic*ion* for defrayinge the ordinary chardg*es* *with*in that office for playes only for the year ended the last of Octobre last. *per* bre*ue* dat*um* xj^{o} Ianuarij 1597	lxvj^{li} vj^{s} viij^{d}

Taill*our*

From 31 October 1601 to 31 October 1602

Record Office. Order Books (Pells). Vol. 3. f° 106 r.

M*aster* of the Reuell*es* for the chardg*es* of playes by composic*i*on for the yeare ended vlt*imo* Oct*obris* 1602

Irr*otulatum* xxij^{o} Martij 1602.

By Order xxij^{o} Martij 1602. To Edmund Tilney Esq*uier* M*aster* of the Reuell*es* the some of lxvj^{li} vj^{s} viij^{d} for his yearly allowance by waie of composic*i*on for defraying the ordinary chardges for playes only for the yeare ended the last of Octobre last p*er* br*eue* dat*um* xj^{o} Ianu*ar*ij 1597.

lxvj^{li} vj^{s} viij^{d}

Bowier

APPENDIX

SUNDRY DOCUMENTS CHIEFLY RELATING

TO THE

BAD MANAGEMENT OF THE OFFICE.

A Petition of Richard Leys for the Office to be Surveyed

(Before 1570)

British Museum. Lansdowne MSS. 12. n° 54.

To the right honorable S*ir* Will*iam* Cecill knight
principall Secretarie to the Quenes most excellent ma*ies*tie,

In moste humble wise enformeth yo*ur* hono*ur* for the Quenes maiesties benefitt & better s*er*uice of her highnes, Richarde Leys Clerke Comptroller of her graces Revell*es*, tenthes and pavillions That where by the space of five yeres paste or there aboutes, he having ben required from tyme to tyme to consent and subscribe to thaccompt*es* and reckoning*es* of the Revell*es* as he before that tyme hadd alweys don and ought to doo / and he seing and verie well p*er*ceiving that in his conscience her maiestie hathe ben and is ouercharged in that behalfe, hathe vtterlie refused according to his bounden dutie & othe to subscribe or consent to any suche reckoning, And therfore dothe nowe moste humblye beseche yo*ur* hono*ur* that there maye be suche a *sur*vey or *sur*veio*ur*s appointed by yo*ur* hono*ur* as bothe can and will *sur*vey the office and the whole charge therof who also maye be autorised to call before them all and euerie the officers of the saide Revell*es* and to make p*ar*ticulerlie answere for their and euerie of their doing*es* according to their bounden dutie and office, as to her maiesties better s*er*uice app*er*teyneth, vpon which *sur*vey it will appere where and in whome the abuse is / And he according to his bounden duetie shall dailie pray for yo*ur* hono*ur* estate long to contynue ;

f° 118 r.

A Petition of William Bowll for the Office of Yeoman (Between 1 & 10 December 1571)

Record Office. State Papers. Dom. Eliz. Addenda xx. n° 101.

To the right honorable & my singuler good Lorde the Lorde of Burley

May it please yo*ur* hono*ur* to be adv*er*tised that whear as of Late I did delyv*er* to yo*ur* hono*ur* certen letters subscrybed w*it*h the handes of the right honorable ye lorde treasorer ye worshipfull S*ir* Thomas Benger knight and of Iohn holte late yoman of the queenes M*aies*tis Revells for yo*ur* Lordships Lawfull favo*ur* and furtheraunce/ for the obteyninge of ye said office in the names of the saide Iohn holte and of me yo*ur* humble Suppliant. sithens the delyvery whearof yt hath pleased god to call the saide holte to his m*er*cy. w*it*hout haveinge Done any further acte therin to the great Losse or rather vtter vndoeinge of yo*ur* said supplyant. his wyff & children onles yo*ur* Lordships favourable ayd bee to me in this behalf extended/ May it thearfore please yo*ur* hono*ur* accordinge to theffect of the said letters to shew me yo*ur* Lawfull favo*ur* and ayd And to stand my good Lorde for the obtayninge of the sayd office/ whearin. I haue longe tyme served as Deputie for the saide Iohn holte and haue also bene forssed to sell my lyvinge/ to make payment of mony w*hi*ch I payd holte vpon the composisio*n* wherof yo*ur* hono*ur* is advertysed and also to make payment to the workmen & other poore creditors for mony due vnto them in the said office accordinge to thear necessitees before any warant graunted as only for to mayntayn the credit of the said office as is very well known all w*hi*ch I beseech yo*ur* hono*ur* tenderly to consider/ And I accordinge to my Duty I will contynvally pray vnto god for the preservacion of yo*ur* Hono*ur*s as for thonly key of my well doinge

Yo*ur* Humble Suppliant will*iam* Bowll

f^o **240 r.**

[Endorsed (f° 241 v.) :] Will*ia*m Bowls Supplication
Holt. Revells.

A Complaint of Thomas Gylles against the Yeoman of the Revells

(c. December 1572)

British Museum. Lansdowne MSS. 13. n° 3.

In most Humble wysse shewythe to your honor your dayllye orator Thomas gylles/ wheras the yeman of the quenes Magestyes revell*es* dothe vsuallye lett to hyer her sayde hyghnes mask*es* to the grett hurt spoylle & dyscredyt of the same/ to all sort of parsons that wyll hyer the same/ by reson of wyche comen vsage the glosse & bewtye of the same garment*es* ys lost & canott sowell serve to to be often allteryde & to be shewyde before hyr hyghnes/ as otherwyes yt myght & hathe byn vsyde/ for ytt takythe more harme by ounce werynge Into the cytye or contre where yt ys often vsyd/ then by many tymes werynge In the cowrt/ by the grett presse of peple & fowlnes bothe of the weye & wether & soyll of the werer*es* /who for the most part be of the meanest sort of mene/ to the grett dyscredytt of the same aparell/ w*hi*ch afterwarde ys to be shewyd before her heyghnes & to be worne by theme of grett callynge/ & ytt ys allso to the doble charges of hyr grace/ Ande for truthe herof your sayde orator hathe a noett redy to be shewyde to your Honor for on yere last past conteynynge the tymes & places wher the sayd mask*es* hathe byn seen & vsyde/ allthoughe nott of all/ besyd*es* a grett nomber lent before tym In lyk sort/ And allthoughe your sayd orator hathe often complaynyde heroff to other*es* of the same offyce/ yett there hathe byn no redresse of the same/ by reson that the sayd yeman havynge alloen the costodye of the garment*es* /dothe lend the same at hys plesuer/ ffor remedy heroff yff ytt myght plesse your honor that there myght be some better ordor or reformacyon hade In the sayde offyce by surveye or other wysse In takynge the garment*es* a sonder after they haue ben shewyde before the quenes heyghnes vntyll the next shew they be allterede ageyne/ for theye never com before her heyghnes twysse In on forme/ or some other good order as maye best apere to your honor. And your orator shall praye vnto allmyghty gode for your honor*es* longe lyffe & prosspery-tye/ for your orator ys grettlye hynderyde of hys lyvynge herbye/ who havynge aparell to lett & canott so cheplye lett the same as hyr hyghnes mask*es* be lett/ as knowytt god who ever preserv you In honor & felycytye

f° 4 r.

A noett off certeyne maskes of the quenes magestyes w*hi*ch hathe byn lent by the offycer*es* of the revell*es* syns the fyrst of Ianvarye last past 1571.

1 In primis the gownes of red clothe of golde wyche was alteryd for lyncolnes In Ianvarye last

2 Ita*m* the yello clothe of golde gownes lent to greyes In In Ianarye

3 Lent the new mask of blak & whytt w*hi*ch was shewyd befor the quene In the crystmas holydayes the same mask was lent to the temple In the crystmas tyme

4 Lent the same mask of blak & whytt to my lord mayor*es* on twelff nyght last

5 Lent the yello clothe of golde gownes to the horshed tavern In chepsyde the 21 of Ianvary

6 Lent the yello clothe of gold gownes from the bullhed In chep to m^{r} blank*es* the 28 of Ianvarye

7 Lent the new mask*es* of blak & whyt gounes to edward hynd*es* maryage Into kent/ xth of february

8 Lent the changable taffyte gownes new the xiiij of febrarye/ from the seynt Ihon hede : to m^{r} ryves Into flett strett

10 11 Lent on shrove sondaye ij mask*es* of gownes Into the charhowse yarde

12 Lent the mask of blak & whytt gownes on maye yeve w*hi*ch came throw chepsyde

13 Lent the new morre satten gounes the vj of maye to my ladye champyons.

14 Lent the red clothe of gold gownes In to kent the 7 of Septembre beyng worn ij nyght*es*

15 Lent the red clothe of golde gownes to a taylor maryag in the blak fryer the 15 of Septembre

16 Lent the coper clothe of golde gownes w*hi*ch was last made & on other mask Into the contre to the maryage of the dowter of my lorde montague

17 Lent the red clothe of golde gounes Into bodgrowe the vj of Octobre

18 Lent the new maske of coper clothe of gold gounes to denmans marag the 14 of octobre

19 Lent the red clothe of gold gownes the 14 of Octobre to denmans maryage

20 Lent the 2 of novembre the yello clothe of golde maske Into flett strett by the churche

21 Lent the xj of novembre the blak & whytt gownes Into soper laen to m^{r} martyns maryage

[Endorsed :] of the dyssorder of the offyce
of the Revell*es*

fo 5 r.

A Note of Things to be redressed in the Revels.

British Museum. Lansdowne MSS. 83. n° 56.

A note of sarten thing*es* which are very nedefull to be Redressed in the offys of the Revelles

1 ffyrste the Romes or Loging*es* where the garment*es* & other thing*es*/ as hed peces and suche like dothe lye / Is in suche decaye for want of repracions that it hath by that meanes perished A very greate longe wall, which parte thereof is falne doune & hath brokenn doune A greate presse which stoode all Alongest the same / by w*hi*ch meanes I ame fayne to laye the garment*es* vppon the grounde to the greate hurt of the same so as if youre honoure ded se the same it woolde petye you to see suche stoffe so yll bestowed

2 Next there is no convenyent Romes for the Artifycers to worcke in but that Taylours Paynters Proparatiue makers and Carpenders are all fayne to worcke in one rome which is A very greate hinderaunce one to Another w*hi*ch thinge nedes not for theye are slacke anove of them selves

3 More there ys two whole yeares charg*es* be hinde vn payde to the greate hinderaunce of the poore Artyfycers that worcke there Insomvche that there be A greate parte of them that haue byn dryven to sell there billes or debentars for halfe that is deve vnto them by the same

4 More yt hath broughte the offyce in suche dyscredet with those that dyd delyuer wares into the offyce that theye will delyuer yt in for A thirde parte more then it is woorthe or ellce we can get no credet of them for the same / which thinge is A very greate hinderaunce to the Queenes ma*ies*tie and A greate discredet to those that be offecers in that place which thinge for my parte I Ame very sory to see.

f° 149 r.

[Endorsed (f° 150 v.) :] for the Reuels.

Matters to be redressed there.

A Petition of the Creditors of the Revels.

(1574)

British Museum. Lansdowne MSS. 83. nº 55.

To oure moste gracious sovereaigne Lady the Queenes moste excellent Maiestye.

In moste humble wyse. The poore Creadito*urs* and Artyffycers which serve thoffyce of yo*ur* Ma*ies*ties Revells : are dryven of necessitye, thus now to trouble yo*ur* Ma*ies*tie (more then otherwyze they wolde) by meanes of many evells which theye sustayne : through want of mony Due vnto them in the saide Offyce Especyally for One yeare and Nyne monethes ending the last of ffebruary in the xvjth yeare of yo*ur* Ma*ies*ties Reaigne (as maye appeare in the Bookes of the saide offyce, subscribed by Iohn fforteskue, and Henri Sekforde esquiers : together *with* the Offycers of the saide Revells : And also by ij Declaraci*o*ns thereof, breefely sett owte vnder the hand*es* of ij of yo*ur* Ma*ies*ties Awdito*urs* One Thowsand, ffyve hundred, and ffyfty pownd*es*, fyve shilling*es* and Eight pence. Wherof, onlesse it maye please yo*ur* Ma*ies*tie the sooner to graunt payment it cannot be but that the myseryes of many must needes be very daungerusly augmented, and soom vtterly vndoone. whiche they moste needefully beseeche yo*ur* Ma*ies*tie for god*es* cause to prevent accordyng to yo*ur* gracious compassion whose dayes of godly peace, and Ioye, they duly beseche almighty god in mercy long to encrese.

poore Bryan Dodmer a credito*ur* to saue the labo*ur* of a great Nu*m*ber whose exclamaci*o*n is lamentable

fº 147 r.

[Endorsed (**fº 148 v.**) :] The poore credito*urs* & Artifficers which serve thoffice of yo*ur* ma*ies*ties Revells moste needefully desyer payment of Dett*es* vnpaide ij yeares & more /1550^{li}/5^{s}/8^{d}/
As may appere by the Awdito*urs* declarci*o*ns d*elivere*d to Mr. Secretory Wallsingh*a*m.

A Supplication of Bryan Dodmer.

(May 1576.)

Record Office. Court of Requests Proceedings. Bundle 132. n° 54.

To the Queenes most exellent Magestye

In moste humble wyze complayning, showeth vnto yo*ur* highnes : yo*ur* true and faythfull subiect Bryan Dodmer. That whereas : by speciall sute which at his owne charges he made vnto yo*ur* highnes in the xvijth yeare of yo*ur* Reaigne, he obtayned yo*ur* highnesse*s* privay seale for payment of all suche dette*s* as then remayned vnpayde, in the Office of yo*ur* highnesse*s* Revells And afterwarde*s* (as deputy or s*er*vant vnto the w*or*shippfull Thom*as* Blagrave esquier clerk of the saide office) did Receive in prest owt of yo*ur* highnesse*s* treasure to be accompted for so muche mony as wolde aunswere all the same dette*s*, saving ccc^{li} whiche was before imprested vnto the woorshippfull Iohn fforteskue esquier in Iune in the xiiijth yeare of yo*ur* saide highnesse*s* reaigne for or towarde*s* the Charges thencefoorthe growing in the said Office. And whereas among other Creaditors contayned in the bookes of that office compiled Betweene the last of maye in the xiiijth yeare and the last of october in the xvth yeare of yo*ur* saide highnesse*s* reaigne, One Iohn Arnolde late yoman of the saide Office deceased, had certayne demaundes entred and allowed vnto him for wage*s* and wares then and there imployed. which is supposed to Amownte vnto the soom of lx^{li}./Towarde*s* the which lx^{li} or what so eu*er* it bee he the saide Arnolde Received therof in part of payment at the hande*s* of the saide Iohn fforteskue (and Edward Buggin clerkcomptrowler of the said Office) xxxiij^{li} xix^{s}. ix^{d}./ w*hi*ch was by them paid owt of the ccc^{li} w*hi*ch the saide fforteskue Received paid owte and in the saide xiiijth and xvth yeares of yo*ur* highnesse*s* said Reaigne therefore defalked by them as A deduccion which of equitie owght to be admitted (by the said Arnold) owte of his whole alowance*s*. and so consequently not to be demaunded at the hande*s* of yo*ur* highnesse*s* said subiect. for by this Reckoning there remayneth in the hande*s* of yo*ur* highnes said subiect for the saide Arnolde but only xxvj^{li} iij^{d}. which xxvj^{li}. iij^{d} and what soever ells can be Iustly demaunded and shall appere by certificat (or debenter) from thofficers of the said office of right to appertayne to the said Arnold or any other vnpaid in the said office (for that tyme) yo*ur* highnesse*s* said subiect is and allwayes hath bene redy to paye (his owne indempnitie provided for) as he is bownde to see yo*ur* highnesse*s* & the said officers discharged. But so it is most gracious sovereaigne ladye that withoute all good order equitie or good conscience One Iohn Weaver of Saint Martins le graund in London silkman by culler of A certayne dett w*hi*ch he saith was owing to him by the said Arnold at the tyme of his decease not being for any wares or matter Imployed in that office hath yet procured a letter of Atturney from thexecutor of the saide Iohn Arnold. wherby he saith he hath aucthoritie to receive as suche dette*s* as were due to the said Iohn Arnolde, especially the lx^{li} aforesaid. which he supposeth to be still due in yo*ur* highnesse*s* said office. But vtterly refuzeth to admit any deduccio*n*s though equitie & the order of thoffice requier the same (never so muche) where yet there is to be Deducted in equitie and by the order of the said office not only the saide xxxiij^{li} xix^{s} ix^{d} alredy paide as is aforesaide. But also v^{li} or vj^{li} more for xviij poore artificers whome the said Arnolde did sett to woorke in the said office and are yet vnpayde therfore exclamyng dayly against the said Arnold and the said weaver as also against yo*ur* highnesses said subiect. And besid*es* that There are sertayne other deductions to be admitted vnto yo*ur* highnes said subiect aswell for his expenc*es* in suing owte yo*ur* highness*es* privaye seale aforesaide : as also for other iust & Reasonable demaund*es* heere for tediousnes omytted. All which the premiss*es* notwithstanding : yet for quietnesse sake your highness*es* said subiect hath many tymes offered vnto the saide weaver (among other sooms by yo*ur* highness*es* saide subiect offered likewise for other respect*es*, then in eq*ui*tye or conscience he owght to yelde) the saide soom of xxvj^{li} iij^{d} w*hi*ch seemeth to Remayne vnpayde of the saide lx^{li}./ or otherwise tabyde the order of yo*ur* highness*es* L*ord* Treasawrer : or L*ord* Cheefe Iustice of Ingland : or thofficers of yo*ur* highness*es* saide Revells : or any other arbitrament for the same And yet neverthelesse the saide Iohn Weaver hath taken his coorse by the comon Lawe w*ith*owt brynging any certificat or debenter from yo*ur* highness*es* saide office, contrary to equitie, cvstom, and good conscience, and also contrary to thexprest order and presyes comaundement written vnto him in yo*ur* highness*es* name by yo*ur* highness*es* said L*ord* Treasurer. And hath long proceded so against yo*ur* highness*es* saide subiect for the whole lx^{li}. by ij severall acc*io*ns co*m*menced in the coorte of yo*ur* highnes benche at Westm*inster* Aledging very vntruly that there was lx^{li} delyvered owt of yo*ur* highness*es* treasure vnto the hand*es* of your highness*es* said subiect (in the said xvijth yeare) for the vse of the saide Iohn Arnold. w*hi*ch yf it were true. yet then the same xxxiij^{li} xix^{s} ix^{d} must be returned to yo*ur* highnes againe and wilbe fownd vpon thaccompt of yo*ur* Highness*es* said subiect : where he demaundeth alowance but of that w*hi*ch was vnpaid in the said xvijth yeare. and not of the xxxiij^{li} xix^{s} ix^{d} before paide by the said ffortescue and Buggyn yo*ur* H*ighnesses* officers in the said xiiij and xvth yeares of yo*ur* h*ighnesses* Reaigne. He very vntruly also aledgeth in one of his declarac*io*ns that yo*ur* H*ighnesses* said subiect did promys him to paye vnto him the said soom of lx^{li} where in troth yo*ur* h*ighnesses* said subiect did promys to paye only so much as then vpon pervsing & conference of the bookes should appere to remayne vnpayd (and to be due) vnto the said arnold, vpon his debenter. yet by sinister practice the said Weaver hath obtayned A verdict for that surmised assumtion of lx^{li} against yo*ur* highness*es* said subiect. And his second acc*io*n being browght against yo*ur* h*ighnesses* said subiect in the same yo*ur* highness*es* benche is also for the same lx^{li} but it is an acc*io*n of accompt layde in the Name of one Will*ia*m Arnolde executo*ur* to the saide Iohn Arnolde. which also yet dependeth to the great danger expenc*es* & wrongfull vexac*io*n of yo*ur* h*ighnesses* said subiect and is like to be the vtter vndooing both of him and his : except soom speedy order be taken by yo*ur* highnes for Remedye. In Tender considerac*io*n whereof : and forasmuche as yo*ur* highness*es* said subiect is but A s*er*vant & was a traveller to obtayne at yo*ur* highness*es* hand*es* the saide dett*es* w*hi*ch long had bene vnpaid (for want of a suter for the same) And now hathe also paide all suche other persons as wolde but bryng debenters from the said office and yelde sufficient dischardge for yo*ur* highnes and thofficers. Maye it therefore please yo*ur* highnes to graunt yo*ur* said subiet not only yo*ur* highness*es* wrytt of Privie seale to be directed to the said Iohn Weaver : and Will*ia*m Arnolde : co*m*maunding them and every of them thereby personally to appeare before yo*ur* highness*es* cowncell in yo*ur* high Coorte of Request*es* then and there to Awnswere to the premiss*es* : and furder to stand to and abyde suche order and decree herein as vnto yo*ur* highness*es* said cowncell shall seeme to stand most agreeable to Right equitye and good conscience. But also to graunt vnto yo*ur* highnesse*s* saide subiect yo*ur* most gracious writt of Eniunction to be directed to the saide Iohn weaver and wil*liam* Arnolde co*m*manding and enioyning them and either of them theier Cowncellors soliciters and atturneies and the cowncellers soliciters and atturneies of either of them to surceace and staye the said sutes co*m*menced as before is saide in yo*ur* highnesse*s* benche at Westm*inster* against yo*ur* sayde subiect and no furder to procede therein vntill such farder order also shalbe taken therein by yo*ur* highnesse*s* said cowncell as vnto them shall seeme to be agreable to equitie and good conscience. And yo*ur* highnesse*s* said subiect shall according to his most bownden duty pray to god for the prosperous and peaceable continewance of yo*ur* gracious Ma*ies*tie long in helth and Ioye to Reaigne over vs to his glory and yo*ur* owne everlasting cvmforte Amen.

Danyell

[Endorsed :]

Dodmer q*uerens*
Weaver def*endens*

xj° die Maij A*nno*
R*eg*ine Elizabeth xviij°
Def*endens* voce*tur* p*er* Nunnciu*m* Camer*e*
Do*m*ine R*eg*ine

A Petition of W. Bowll touching Sums due to him for Wares delivered to the Officers of the Revels.

British Museum. Lansdowne MSS. 83. n° 54.

To the right honorable Lorde Highe Th*r*easorer of Englande

In moste humble wyse beseecheth yo*ur* hono*ur* to be good vnto him your Humble supplyant will*iam* bowll one of thordonary yeomen of the queenes M*aie*sties Honorable chambre / whearas at the ernest request of thoffycers of the Revells he hath delyvered into the said office w*i*thin two yers & iij q*uarter*s laste paste/ dyvers p*ar*cells of wares ; for the which thear is due & owinge vnto yo*ur* sayd orato*ur* the some of ccxxxvj^{li}. ffor A great porcion whearof yo*ur* said suppliant is indebted to one Thomas bate / & dyvers others who do not only exclayme against yo*ur* said orato*ur* ; but do also sue & molest him in ye law by all extreme wayes & meanes. To the great dyscredyt hurt Hynderance & vtter vndoinge of yo*ur* said orator his wyff & children onles some spedy remedy may be had / In tendre consideracion wherof may yt please yo*ur* hono*ur* of yo*ur* accustomed cleamency & favourable goodnes : to graunt yo*ur* warant to some one who hath the custody of her M*aie*sties Threaso*ur* to be derected for the said some of ccxxxvj^{li} to be delyvered to thofficers of the Revells. ffor them to pay over vnto yo*ur* said supplyant for his Releeffe & in full payment of his due / And the said officers to stand charged as w*i*th so much d*elivere*d them in prest. for the w*hi*ch they ar to accompt in thear Tottall accompte / Or otherwyse to delyver the said some of ccxxxvj^{li} vnto yo*ur* said orato*ur* vpon his recognoysance to repay the same at such tyme as her Maie*s*tie shall assigne her warant for the payment of that office Tharearag*es* due by her M*aies*tie yet owinge / wherby yo*ur* honor shall bynde yo*ur* Said Supplyant & his whole famvly to pray vnto god for the prosperous preservacion of yo*ur* honor whome the almighty blis for ever.

f° 145 r.

[Endorsed (f° 146 v.) :] The humble peticion of will*iam* Bowll beseechinge yo*ur* Hono*ur* to defend him from Rwyn w*hi*ch is presently Enteringe vpon him
* for ccxxxvj^{li} due to him for wares delyvered to the officers of ye revells

A Petition of the Creditors and Servitors of the Revels

(Nov. 1597 — Jan. 1597-8)

British Museum. Lansdowne MSS. 83. n° 63.

To the right Honnorable ye Lord highe Tr*easor*er of Englande.

In most humble wise beseecheth yo*ur* good L*ordshippe* your poore Orato*ur*s Peeter wrighte wyer Drawer, Iames Clarke Chandler Ioseph Smith painter Richard Gotley Carpenter, Ihon Davys Taylo*ur* Richard Page Collyer Thomas Ihones woodbroker and Ihon Griffeth Porter of St. Ihons gate. Creditors and S*er*vitors of her Ma*iesties* office of ye Reuell*es* yt wheras wee be now v : yeares behinde, vnpayed for warres deliuered and service done w*ith* In yt : office. to our greate hindera*u*nce these deare yeares passed : deteyned as wee heare only throughe ye discention amoungest ye officers beinge longe sence signed by her Ma*ies*te and for yt ye M*aster* of ye office dothe still aunswere vs that ye faulte Is not in him beinge reddie to p*er*forme vnto ye other officers as he saithe all such allowances as either by yo*ur* L*ordshippes* formare orders Is dew vnto yem or yt In righte they can anie other waies Challenge but because wee can gett no other aunswere from ye M*aster* and for yt wee see no Likelyhoode of any agreement betweene yem ye M*aster* relyeinge wholly as he saith vppon yo*ur* Lordshipp*es* foresaide orders sett downe vnto him ye other officers vtterly reiectinge ye same wee therfore most humbly beseech yo*ur* Lordshippe In Tender Regard of our poore estatt*es* and of ye longe forbearinge of our Monney yt It will please your Lordshippe to Commaunde some order for ye Releiuinge of vs and wee shall be allwaies bounde to praie for your good Lordshipp

* All yt I can saye Is, yt yer Is A Composition layd vppo*n* me by Quens ma*ies*te & signed by her selff rated verbatimly by certayn orders sett down by my *Lord* Treasorer vnder his *Lordshippes* Hand whervnto I haue Appealed because ye other officers will nott be satisficed w*ith* ayni reason & wherto I am now teyd & nott vnto ther friuilus demandes wherfore lett yem sett down In writtinge ye speciall Causes why they shuld reiect ye forsayd orders & ye Compositio*n* gronded ther on /& then Am I to reply vnto ye same as I can/ for tell then yes petitioners can nott be satisficed.

Ed Tyllney

f° 170 r.

[Endorsed :] * 5. Novembe*r* 1597
* The Petic*io*n of ye Creditors and Seruitors of ye Reuells.
* They shewe y^{t} theie are vnpaid theise five yeares Last past for wares deliuered and service done in y^{e}
* office of ye Revells throughe ye dissencion amongest ye officers to y^{re} greate hinderance theise deare yeares
* beeing poore men
* Vppon y^{re} mocion to ye m*aster* of ye office his answere is y^{t} ye faulte is not in him but he is redy to satisfie
* y^{m} all such allowances as are dew vnto y^{m} either by yo*ur* *Lordshippes* forme*r* order or in righte theie can
* challeng. vppon w*hi*ch order ye m*aster* doth wholly relie but ye other reiect ye same.
* for y^{t} y^{re} is no lickelyhood of y^{re} agreeme*n*te whereby ye petecioners may be satisfied Theie Humbly
* pray yo*ur* L*ordshippe* to Command som order for ye releving y^{re} poore estates.

* One of the Awdito*urs* of the prest w*i*th one of the Barons of ye Eschecq*uer* to heare the officers of the
* Revels, and the petitioners, and either to ende the questions betwene them, or to certefie theyre opi-
* nions. * W Burghley

* quinto Ianuarij 1597
* Pleaseth it yo*ur* good Lordeship to be advertized that after longe travaile and paines taken betwene the
* *Master* of the Revell*es* and the Officers thereof, It is agreed by o*ur* entreaty that out of the xl^{li} by yeare
* allowed for ffees or wag*es* for their attendaunces the *Master* of the Revell*es* shall yearely allowe and paye
* the severall Somes of mony und*er*written

viz.

* To the Clarke Comptroller of that Office . . . . viij^{li}
* To the yeoman of the Revell*es* . . . . viij^{li}
* To the Groome of the Office . . . . xl^{s}
* To the Porter of St Iohns . . . . xx^{s}.
* whereof xx^{s}. p*ar*cell of the saide viij^{li} allowed to the yeoman is to be aunswered by the same yeoman after
* this yeare to the saide Groome.
* which yf it may stande w*i*th yo*ur* good Lordshippes lyking wee truste will bring contynuall quietnes &
* dutifull service to her M*aiest*ie.

* Iohn Sotherton
* Io Conyers

* My desire is to be better satisficed howe the Credito*urs* shall be payd.
* W. Burghley

f° 171 v.

A Collection of Payments out of the Receipt of the Exchequer from Easter Term 1560 down to 22 March 1602/3.

I add this List of Payments though it cannot, strictly speaking, be considered as a document; but it is a fitting addition to the documents contained in this Appendix since it tells the tale of the difficulty the Officers very often had in obtaining money from the Queen's Exchequer. The List, which is nearly complete, has been compiled from the following sources, all in the Public Record Office:

a) Books of Payments by Royal Warrant.
b) Imprest Certificate Books (Pells).
c) Issue Books (Pells).
d) Order Books (Pells).

In most cases, the facts supplied by these documents have been supplemented and checked by a reference to the Warrants for Issues.

In the first column of the following Table, E.T. = Easter Term; M.T. = Michaelmas Term; in the fifth column, P = In prest, and S = In full satisfaction.

DATE OF PAYMENT		SUM PAID	NAME OF PAYEE	KIND OF PAYMENT	PERIOD OF EXPENSES COVERED BY THE PAYMENT
ENTRY IN THE EXCHEQUER BOOKS	DATE OF THE WARRANT				
1	2	3	4	5	6
E. T. 1560[1]	17 July 1560[2] ?	100^{li} } 100^{li} } 200^{li} $109^{li}19^{s}9^{d}$ } $309^{li}19^{s}9^{d}$	Sir T. Benger	P S (?)	[From Michaelmas 1559 to Michaelmas 1560][3] } [1 year]
M. T. 1560[4]	28 Dec. 1560[4]	$740^{li}13^{s}10^{d}1/2$	W. More (Cawarden's executor)	S	In full payment of arrears due to Sir T. Cawarden till Michaelmas 1559[4]
M. T. 1560[5]	16 Dec. 1560[5]	200^{li}	Sir T. Benger	P	[From Michaelmas 1560 to Michaelmas 1561][6] } [1 year]
M. T. 1561[7]	23 Dec. 1561[7] 6 March 1561/2[7]	$581^{li}6^{s}7^{d}$ 500^{li}	Sir T. Benger Sir T. Benger	S (?)	
M. T. 1563[8]	1 March 1563/4[9]	$527^{li}9^{s}11^{d}1/2$ } 150^{li} } $677^{li}9^{s}11^{d}1/2$	Sir T. Benger	S	From Pentecost 1562 to 20 November 1563[9] } 1 year 6 months
E. T. 1565[10]	8 July 1565[10]	50^{li} } 110^{li} } 160^{li} }	Sir T. Benger	P	[From Christmas 1563 to Christmas 1565][13] } [2 years]
M. T. 1565[11]	8 July 1565[11] 19 Feb. 1566/7[12]	140^{li} } 300^{li} $248^{li}15^{s}1^{d}1/4$		S P	
E. T. 1566[14]	19 Feb. 1566/7[12]	200^{li} } $180^{li}5^{s}4^{d}$ } 40^{li} } 420^{li} $5^{s}4^{d}$	Sir T. Benger	P	
M. T. 1566[15]	19 Feb. 1566/7[12]	100^{li} } 100^{li} } $28^{li}13^{s}11^{d}$ } 228^{li} $13^{s}11^{d}$ } 897^{li} $14^{s}4^{d}1/4$		S	

1. Books of Payments by Royal Warrant. I. 18 v. — The $109^{li}19^{s}9^{d}$ were paid by a second warrant, the date of which is not given.
2. Warrants for Issues (Exch. of Receipt) Parcel 113.
3. See my note to page 109.
4. Warrants for Issues &c. Parcel 114 (see my note to page 105. line 1).
5. d° d°
6. See my note to page 109.
7. Books of Payments &c. II. 3 v.
8. Books of Payments &c. III. 4 v.
9. Warrants for Issues &c. Parcel 115 (cf. p. 115).
10. Books of Payments &c. IV. 14 v.
11. d° V. 9 v.
12. Warrants for Issues &c. Parcel 116.
13. See my note to p. 109.
14. Books of Payments &c. V. 20 v.
15. d° VI. 5 r.

DATE OF PAYMENT		SUM PAID		NAME OF PAYEE	KIND OF PAYMENT	PERIOD OF EXPENSES COVERED BY THE PAYMENT	
ENTRY IN THE EXCHEQUER BOOKS	DATE OF THE WARRANT		Total				
M. T. 1566[15]	25 June 1567[16]	40^{li}			P		
E. T. 1567[17]	25 June 1567[16]	200^{li}	$883^{li}11^{s}2^{d}$	Sir T. Benger	P	From Christmas 1565 to Shrovetide 1566/7[16]	ab. 1 year 2 months
M. T. 1567[18]	25 June 1567[16]	$243^{li}11^{s}2^{d}$	643^{li} $11^{s}2^{d}$		S		
		200^{li}					
		200^{li}					
E. T. 1568[19]	11 June 1568[20]	200^{li}	$634^{li}9^{s}5^{d}$	Sir T. Benger	S	From 14 July 1567 to 3 March 1567/8[20]	over 7 months
		100^{li}					
		$334^{li}9^{s}5^{d}$					
	10 May 1569[21]	$453^{li}5^{s}6^{d}$		Sir T. Benger	S	Christmas 1568 & Shrovetide 1568/9[21]	ab. 3 months
M. T. 1570[22]	29 July 1570[23]	$199^{li}17^{s}6^{d}$ 1/2	$499^{li}17^{s}6^{d}$ 1/2	Sir T. Benger	S	Christmas 1569 & Shrovetide 1569/70[23]	ab. 3 months
		200^{li}					
		100^{li}					
M. T. 1571[24]	23 Oct. 1571[25]	$666^{li}16^{s}3^{d}$		Sir T. Benger	S	From Shrovetide 1569/70 to Shrovetide 1570/1[25]	1 year
E. T. 1572[26]	17 June 1572[27]	300^{li}		John Fortescue	P		
E. T. 1573[28]	7 June 1573[29]	$1285^{li}7^{d}$	$1585^{li}7^{d}$	John Fortescue	S	From Shrovetide 1570/1 to 31 May 1572[29]	1 year 3 months
		300^{li}					
M. T. 1573[30]	23 Dec. 1573[30]	200^{li}		T. Blagrave	P	From 31 May 1572 to February 1573/4[33]	1 year 9 months
M. T. 1574[31]	25 Dec. 1574[32]	$1550^{li}5^{s}8^{d}$1/2	$1750^{li}5^{s}8^{d}$ 1/2	T. Blagrave	S		
		200^{li}			P		
M. T. 1575[34]	12 Dec. 1575[35]	200^{li}		T. Blagrave	P	From 1 March 1573/4 to 11 March 1575/6[37]	2 years 11 days
E. T. 1576[36]	5 Aug. 1576[37]	$706^{li}12^{s}4^{d}$		T. Blagrave	S		
M. T. 1576[36]	24 Dec. 1576[38]	100^{li}		T. Blagrave	P	From 11 March 1575/6 to 21 February 1576/7[39]	ab. 1 year
M. T. 1577[40]	22 Dec. 1577[41]	$157^{li}17^{s}5^{d}$		T. Blagrave	S		
M. T. 1578[42]	30 Dec. 1578[42]	$244^{li}9^{s}1^{d}$1/2		T. Blagrave	S	From 21 February 1576/7 to 14 February 1577/8[42]	ab. 1 year
		200^{li}		T. Blagrave	P	From 14 February 1577/8 to 1 November 1579[43]	1 year 8 months
E. T. 1580[43]	7 Aug. 1580[43]	$141^{li}11^{s}10^{d}$		E. Tyllney	S		
		200^{li}		E. Tyllney	P	From 1 November 1579 to 1 November 1580[44]	1 year
E. T. 1581[44]	1 April 1581[44]	$69^{li}18^{d}$		E. Tyllney	S		
		400^{li}		E. Tyllney	P	[From 1 November 1580 to 1 November 1581][45]	[1 year]

16. Warrants for Issues. &c. Parcel 116 (cf. p. 109 & p. 118). The original warrant is dated 25 June, but in the Book of Payments the date is given as 26 June.
17. Books of Payments &c. VI. 20 v.
18. d° VII. 4 v.
19. d° VII. 26 r.
20. Warrants for Issues &c. Parcel 116 (cf. p. 119).
21. d° Parcel 117 (cf. p. 124).
22. Books of Payments &c. IX. 3 r.
23. Warrants for Issues &c. Parcel 117 (cf. p. 125).
24. Imprest Certificate Books (Pells). I. 34 v.
25. Warrants for Issues &c. Parcel 117 (cf. p. 126).
26. Imprest Certificate Books (Pells). I. 42 v. (cf. p. 152).
27. Warrants for Issues &c. Parcel 118. (see my note to p. 152. line 11).
28. Books of Payments &c. X. 9 r. & Imprest Certificate Books (Pells). I. 42 v.
29. Warrants for Issues &c. Parcel 119.
30. Imprest Certificate Books (Pells). II. 2 r. & 17 v.
31. Books of Payments &c. XI. 2 r.; & Imprest Certificate Books (Pells). II. 10 & 17 v.
32. Warrants for Issues &c. Parcel 120.
33. Bryan Dodmer's Petition (p. 412).
34. Imprest Certificate Books (Pells). II. 17 v.
35. Warrants for Issues &c. Parcel 120.
36. Imprest Certificate Books (Pells). II. 29 r.
37. Warrants for Issues &c. Parcel 120 (cf. p. 250).
38. d° Parcel 121.
39. Cf. the total at p. 278, with the addition of 100^{li} in prest.
40. Books of Payments &c. XII. 2 v. & Imprest Certificate Books (Pells). II. 35. r.
41. Warrants for Issues &c. Parcel 121.
42. Imprest Certificate Books (Pells). II. 47 v. (cf. p. 280).
43. d° II. 65 r.
44. d° II. 82 r.
45. There was no full settlement that year; for the total expense was only $231^{li}4^{s}$ & « Theare Remayned in thandes » of Tyllney the sum of $168^{li}16^{s}$ (v. Table II. 76).

DATE OF PAYMENT		SUM PAID	NAME OF PAYEE	KIND OF PAYMENT	PERIOD OF EXPENSES COVERED BY THE PAYMENT	
ENTRY IN THE EXCHEQUER BOOKS	DATE OF THE WARRANT					
M. T. 1581[46]	22 Dec. 1581[47]	200^{li}	E. Tyllney	P	From 1 November 1581 to 31 October 1582[47]	1 year
E. T. 1582[48]	22 Dec. 1581[47]	300^{li}	E. Tyllney	P		
M. T. 1583[49]	15 March 1583/4[49]	$253^{li}4^{s}4^{d}$ } $353^{li}4^{s}4^{d}$	E. Tyllney	S	From 1 November 1582 to 31 October 1583[49]	1 year
		100^{li}	E. Tyllney	P	From 31 October 1583 to 1 November 1585[51]	2 years
E. T. 1586[50]	16 April 1586[51]	$502^{li}5^{s}1^{d}$	E. Tyllney	S		
		100^{li}	E. Tyllney	P	[From 1 November 1585 to 31 October 1586][52]	[1 year]
E. T. 1590[53]	18 April 1590[54]	$687^{li}19^{s}1^{d}1/2$	E. Tyllney	S	From 31 October 1586 to 1 November 1589[54]	3 years
		100^{li}	E. Tyllney	P	From 31 October 1589 to 1 November 1592[56]	3 years
E. T. 1594[55]	28 May 1594[56]	$311^{li}2^{s}2^{d}$	E. Tyllney	S		
		100^{li}	E. Tyllney	P	[From 1 November 1592 to 31 October 1593][57]	[1 year]
21 Feb. 1597/8[58]	11 Jan. 1597/8[59]	200^{li}	E. Tyllney	S	From 1 November 1593 to 31 October 1596[58]	3 years
		$66^{li}6^{s}8^{d}$	E. Tyllney	Composition	From 31 October 1596 to 31 October 1597[58]	1 year
25 Oct. 1598[60]	d°	$66^{li}6^{s}8^{d}$	E. Tyllney	d°	From 31 October 1597 to 31 October 1598[60]	1 year
26 March 1599[61]	d°	$66^{li}6^{s}8^{d}$	E. Tyllney	d°	?	
14 Feb. 1599/00[62]	d°	$66^{li}6^{s}8^{d}$	E. Tyllney	d°	From 31 October 1598 to 31 October 1599[62]	1 year
28 Feb. 1600/1[63]	d°	$66^{li}6^{s}8^{d}$	E. Tyllney	d°	From 31 October 1599 to 31 October 1600[63]	1 year
20 Feb. 1601/2[64]	d°	$66^{li}6^{s}8^{d}$	E. Tyllney	d°	From 31 October 1600 to 31 October 1601[64]	1 year
22 March 1602/3[65]	d°	$66^{li}6^{s}8^{d}$	E. Tyllney	d°	From 31 October 1601 to 31 October 1602[65]	1 year

46. Books of Payments &c. XIV. 4 v. & Imprest Certificate Books (Pells). II. 103 r.
47. Warrants for Issues &c. Parcel 124. Cf. also note to Table II. 81.
48. Books of Payments &c. XIV. 10 r. & Imprest Certificate Books (Pells). II. 103 r.
49. Books of Payments &c. XVI. 4 v. & Imprest Certificate Books (Pells) II. 125 v.
50. Imprest Certificate Books (Pells). II. 139 v.
51. Warrants for Issues &c. Parcel 126.
52. From the Imprest Certificate Books (II. 139 v., III. 7 r., 22 r., & 73 v.) it appears that this was the only sum paid for that year.
53. Imprest Certificate Books (Pells). III. 73 v.
54. Warrants for Issues &c. Parcel 129 (cf. p. 374).
55. Imprest Certificate Books (Pells). III. 96 r.
56. Warrants for Issues &c. Parcel 131 (cf. p. 396).
57. From the Imprest Certificate Books (III. 73 v. & 96 r.) & from a Docket of the Signet Office dated January 1596, it appears that this was the only sum paid for that year.
58. Issue Books (Pells). I. 121 v.
59. Warrants for Issues &c. Parcel 133 (cf. p. 397).
60. Order Books (Pells). I. 112 r. (cf. p. 398).
61. d° I. 159 r. (cf. p. 399).
62. d° II. 34 r. (cf. p. 400).
63. d° II. 143 r. (cf. p. 401).
64. d° II. 253 r. (cf. p. 402).
65. d° III. 106 r. (cf. p. 403).

NOTES

NOTES

5. DOCUMENT I. A duplicate of this document is among the Additional MSS. 19256 in the British Museum : it is a copy made for Sir Henry Herbert on the occasion of one of his lawsuits. This Herbert copy, together with several other documents concerning the Office of the Revels, was printed by Halliwell-Phillipps in a small volume bearing the following title : « *A Collection of Ancient Documents respecting the Office of Master of the Revels, and other papers relating to the Early English Theatre. From the Original Manuscripts formerly in the Haslewood Collection.* London : Printed by T. Richards, Great Queen Street, 1870 ». The edition was limited to eleven copies, and is extremely rare.

Two years later, Halliwell reprinted the document separately, and, this time, from the Lansdowne MS. : « *A Curious Paper of the Time of Queen Elizabeth respecting the Office of the Revels. Now first printed from the Lansdowne Manuscript N° 83, in the British Museum.* London : Printed by Thomas Richards. MDCCCLXXII. » Only twenty copies were printed ; one of which is in the Shakespeare Memorial Library, Birmingham, and another, presented by the editor, in the British Museum (11765. bb. 25). (This I presume is the reprint which Mr E. K. Chambers dates « about 1874 », and of which he could trace no copy. *Tudor Revels.* p. 30. *n.* 1). Collier mentions this document in his *History of Dramatic Poetry* (I. 290) and attributes it to the Clerk of the Revels. R. W. Bond extracted from it in the Introduction to his edition of Lyly's *Works*, and was the first to date it 1573, as it should be. Lastly, Mr. E. K. Chambers has lately reprinted it from the Original in his *Notes on the History of the Revels Office under the Tudors.* A. H. Bullen. 1906.

The date of the document is given by the passage in the « Articles and Ordynaunces », where it is stated that the said articles are to be enforced in the XVth year of Elizabeth's reign, *i. e.* between 17 November 1572 and 16 November 1573. Moreover, the paper must have been written before 25 March 1573, for the scribe would not have left the date of the Christian year blank, had there been no possibility of the proposals being accepted in 1572 (See p. 11 l. 7-8).

I thought at one time that the author of this memorandum was the same person who concocted the elaborate « platte » printed after page 16, that is to say, Blagrave, the Clerk of the Revels (Cf. note to Table I). I had been led into that belief by a striking similarity in thought and even expression, which I considered as pointing to one writer. I accounted for the differences (*e. g.* the creation of an office of serjeant, omitted in the « platte ») by supposing that the « platte » might be a revised form of the first memorandum after the Lord Treasurer had objected to some of the proposals submitted to his approval. And this hypothesis seemed to be supported by the date of the « platte » which, I think, must have been written a little later, in 1574 (See note to Table I).

But on further consideration, I adhere to Mr E. K. Chambers's opinion, that the two memoranda were drawn up by two different persons. At any rate, the author of the former cannot have been Blagrave, for he seems not to have known the office in the time of Sir Thomas Cawerden, whilst Blagrave had been acting as Clerk since 1550, at the latest. I find it less easy to attribute this plan of reform to Buggyn, as Mr E. K. Chamber does (*Tudor Revels*, 49). There is not the least positive evidence in favour of such an hypothesis, and there is, on the contrary, an improbability against it. Evidently the writer of the memorandum does not sympathise with the inferior officers; he unequivocally hints at their insubordination, and dogmatically states that « it is not for Inferiour officers to repugne the Master his doings hym selfe beinge in place albeit there be never so greate cause » (p. 10); he is particularly strict in the case of the Clerk-Controller, whom he sets under the incessant and absolute control of both the Master and the Serjeant. Now, Buggyn was Clerk-Controller and one of the severely treated « inferiour officers »; unless we assume he had an uncommon share of humility and abnegation, it is difficult to understand why he should have been so hard upon himself, and why he should have insisted so much upon offences which he had undoubtedly committed more than once. On the other hand, the writer speaks from the point of view of the Master; he thinks it advisable to create a new post, that of Serjeant, the result of which creation would have been to « ease » the Master, that is to say, to take all the disagreeable work off the Master's hands, and he insists upon the necessity of confirming the Master's authority over the other officers. All this points to some person of authority, to some high officer in one of the offices which often had to do with the Revels, such as the Tents, the Wardrobe, the Works, and even the Lieutenancy of the Tower. To choose between these different officers would be idle and dangerous.

12. *Iohn Houlte.* As will be seen at p. 70, John Bridges, Yeoman of the Revels, surrendered his patent on July 1, 1550, and on that day Holte was appointed Yeoman. Holte, however, had been acting as Yeoman ever since the beginning of 1547, for in a book of expenses (from February 1 to February 28, I Edward VI) he is styled « Yeoman », and on the « ffyrst daye of Aprill » of the same year, an inventory was taken by Sir Thomas Cawerden and John Barnard of « all suche the kinges Masking Garmentes with thappurtinaunces Riche Bassis & Couering of bardes as were delyueryd owte of the Custody of Iohn Briges Late yoman of the same into the Tuycion & Saff kep[ing] of Iohn Holte nowe yoman of the same Revelles » (Loseley MSS. Roll xxxi). Such deputyships seem to have been frequent. They were legitimate from the very terms of the patent (See *e. g.* p. 70 l.14). The person thus recognised received the wages in his own name, and in every way acted as the nominee of the office; but he could not be formally appointed to the post before the decease or the resignation of the patentee. Of course a deputyship had no other value than that of a private arrangement between the officer and his substitute; and the Crown remained free to appoint whomsoever it liked when the office became vacant. This is what happened when Holte died: Bowll had been acting as deputy for several years, but his hopes of a reversion were frustrated (S. p. 408 & 72).

This situation of Yeoman of the Revels was but one of the many posts which Holte accumulated during his lifetime. On 26 January 1546-7, he was granted, jointly with Richard

Nueport, the « office of Taylours to his [Henry VIII's] Sonne and the makinge of all the garmentes robes & apparell as well of his said sonne as also of the lyveries of his Gentlemen henchemen and fotemen with thapparell of his stable » (Cf. the Warrant made out in I Eliz. for the payment of arrears unpaid since the appointment. Record Office. Warrants for Issues. Parcel 112). On 14 October 1550, he was appointed by Edward VI, in survivorship with Richard Longman, « yeoman of our Pavyllyons and tentes » (Patent Rolls. 4 Edward VI. p. 3. m. 12). In this patent Holte is styled « one of the Sewers of our Chamber ». An entry of payments of fees by vertue of Holte's three distinct patents is to be found in Lansdowne MSS. 156. f° 99. He died between 1 December & 11 December 1571 (Cf. p. 130 l.26; 131 l.1, and Arnold's patent).

Mr E. K. Chambers suggests (*Tudor Revels*, 25) that the Yeoman of the Revels was the « John Holt momer » who helped the Westminster boys in their representations. This I very much doubt : the name was common at the time, and, besides, our officer of the Revels was a totally untaught man, not being even able to sign his name (See pp. 79 & sqq.) ; he, therfore, could scarcely have been an actor.

22. *Travers Seriaunt of the said office.* John Travers was a Gentleman Sewer of the King's Chamber. He was appointed Serjeant of the Pavilions and Tents on September 28, 1539, after the death of John Farlyon.

Sir Thomas Cawerden. For a life of Sir Thomas Cawerden, compiled from his own papers, see Hist. MSS. Commission, VIIth Report. Appendix, p. 596-7. He had been granted the Mastership of the Pavilions and Tents in survivorship with Sir Anthony Aucher. The latter was also Master and Treasurer of the Jewels and Plate (Record Office. Declared Accounts. Audit Office. Bd. 1533). For Sir Thomas Cawerden's appointment as Master of the Revels in March 1544-5, with retroactive effect from 16 March 1543-4, see p. 53.

6. 2. *Iohn Barnard.* His patent as Clerk-Controller of the Tents, Hales and Pavilions as well as of the Revels and Masks, was granted on the same day as Sir Thomas Cawerden's as Master (See Patent Rolls. 26 H. VIII. p. 14. m. 23).

18. *The Clerke of the workes beinge a straunger.* The Clerk of the Works was not quite a « stranger » to the Revels, for there was always a sort of connection between the Works and the Revels, even after the Clerk of the Works had ceased to make out the Accounts of the Revels. Cf. note to **148**. 22.

19. *Thomas Philippes.* Mr. E. K. Chambers is wrong when he says that « the first mention of Thomas Philipps as Clerk is on May 29, 1549 » (*Tudor Revels*, 10). His patent, dated 7 May 1546 is in the Record Office (see page 66 of this volume). In the account belonging to the year I Edward VI (already quoted) « Thomas Phelippes Clarke » receives a payment for « xxiiij daies at xviij^{d} [a] daie ».

21. *The Quenes Maiestye... devided the said Office....* The division was made in January 1559-60, after Cawerden's death. Sackford's patent as Master of the Pavilions, Hales and Tents is dated 20 January 2 Eliz. (Record Office. Patent Books. Auditors. vol. 9), that is two days after the patent appointing Sir Thomas Benger Master of the Revels was made out (See page 54).

23. *Sir Thomas Benger.* According to Chalmers (*Suppl. Apology for the Believers* &c., 194), Tho-

mas Berenger, or Benger, was the second son of Robert Berenger of Marlborough, in Wiltshire, by Agnes, the daughter of William Vavasor of Spaldington, in Yorkshire. He was made a knight of the Carpet in 1553 (Strype, *Memor.* iii. App. 7). In 1554, he was accused of witchcraft and committed to the Fleet *(Acts of the Privy Council*, N. S. vol. V, 139 & 143); on 7 July 1555, he was bailed (*Ibid.* 157). On the 27th of April 1557, he was again brought before the Privy Council, and once more committed to prison (*Ibid.* vol. VI, 81 & 82). Being sent to the Assizes at Oxford, he was probably acquitted (*Ibid.* 101 & 108). Again, in October 1557, Sir Thomas Benger and one Robert Runneger, were found indebted to the Queen « for xxx^{tie} foder of leade », and « the Lorde Tresourer was this daie [27 October] spoken to cause proces to be awarded out of theschequier against the said Bengier and his suerties for the payment of his parte » (*Ibid.* vol. VI, 191). Chalmers thinks (*Op. cit.* 195) that his sufferings under Mary were considered when he was appointed Master of the Revels by Elizabeth, but upon what ground I know not. The patent appointing him to the Mastership of the Revels in Jan. 1559-60 is printed at page 54 of this volume. A paper endorsed : « A liberate for Sir Thomas Benger knyght, dat. xxviij ffebr. 3 Eliz. » is to be found in Warrants for Issues (Parcel 113). Collier mentions (I. 185) a Warrant under the Privy Seal dated 18th of April 1566, by vertue of which Sir Thomas Benger was granted a license to purchase in England, and to export for his own advantage, 300 tons of beer.

Chalmers discovered more than a hundred years ago that Benger's will was proved on the 27th of March 1577, and he inferred therefrom that the Master of the Revels died in March 1577 (*Apology for the Believers* &c. 482); this statement has been accepted as an indubitable fact by all the historians of the stage down to Mr E. K. Chambers (*Tudor Revels*, 56). But this is an error which I am now able to disprove. It is true that the testament was proved in 1577 ; but it was made on 25 June 1572, and there is no doubt whatever that Benger was dead in 1573, as appears from a certificate made out by the end of that year, to be found in the Imprest Certificate Books (Record Office. Vol. 1. 1569-1573. f° 42 *v.*), and copied out, probably by one of the Officers of the Revels, on the back of the title-page of the Account Book for May 1572-October 1573 (See page 152 of this volume). In this document (omitted by Cunningham in his *Extracts from the Accounts of the Revels*), Benger is said to be « deceased ». The same mention occurs again in another certificate dated « xxth of January 1575 » (*i. e.* 1575-6), in the Imprest Certificate Books (Pells. vol. 2. 1573-1587. f° 17 *v.*), and it is confirmed by the privy seal of the 7th of June 1573, referred to in the foresaid certificate (See page 152 l. 19-20), where, again, we hear of the « last time of Sir Thomas Benger, knight, late master of the same office ». I give it in full (the italics are mine) : « Elizabeth by the grace of God queen of England ffraunce & Ireland defendour of the faythe &c. To the threasurer & Chambrelayns of our Exchequier greetinge. Whereas it apperith by a Lidger booke subscrybed with the handes of thofficers of our Revells that there is growen due vnto certen Creditors for stuf delyuered into the said office with suche necessaryes and prouicions as are incident vnto the same and for wages due vnto certen artificers & laborers woorking and attendinge thereon especially aboute the new makinge translating fittinge furnyshinge garnyshinge and settinge furthe of sondry Commodyties [*sic*] Tragedyes tryumphes maskes and shewes sett forthe of that office & *shewen before vs in the last tyme of Sir Thomas Benger knight late Master of the same office* with other ordenary chardges rysinge by meanes of the ayringe repayringe and safe kepinge of the furnyture thereof viz. from Shrovetewsday in the xiijth yere of our reign vntill the laste of May in the fouretenth yere beinge one yere quarter &c. as in the same booke remayninge with the Clerke of our said office at lardge apperithe, one thousand fyve hundred fowre score fyve powndes seavyn pence. These therefore are to signefy vnto you our will & pleasure is That of suche our treasure as presently remayneth in the Receipt of our Exchequier, or hereafter shall cumme into the same you content and paye, or cause to be contented and payed vnto our trusty & welbeloued Iohn ffortescughe & Henry Sackeford esquiers, or either of them the same somme of one thousand, fyve hundred fowre score & fyve poundes vij[d] of currant money, to be ymediatly paied over to suche persons as the same is owinge vnto accordinge to the Debenters gevin oute for the same by our clerke aforesaid in full satisffaction & payment of all the charges and allowaunces *due within the tyme of the said Sir Thomas Benger as aforesaid*. And these our Lettres shalbe your sufficient warraunt & discharge in that behalfe. Yevin vnder. our prevy Seale at our manour of Grenewich the seavinth day of June, in the fiftenth yere of our reign (*i. e.* 1573.) — (Record Office. Warrants for Issues. Parcel 119).

The date of this document can be taken as a downward limit for Benger's death. On the other hand, we know he was still living on 12 July 1572, for on that day stuff was delivered to him out of the Great Wardrobe (See page 187). This is the latest mention I have been able to discover concerning him, and we may therefore say that he died between 12 July 1572 and 7 June 1573. Moreover, if we remember that Benger says in his will, written on 25 June 1572, that he is « sick in body » (Somerset House. Prerogative Court. 11 Daughty), that Fortescue and Sackford signed the books of the Revels as early as June 1572 (See page 155), it is safe enough to surmise that by June 1572 Benger's days were numbered, and that his death must have taken place soon after.

Several suppositions have been made to explain Benger's secession. Collier remarked (I. 199) that « at his death, Benger was greatly in debt », and from this fact deduced that « probably his embarrassments might interfere with the discharge of his official duties ». Mr Fleay boldly conjectured that Benger retired because he could not agree with Sussex, the new Lord Chamberlain (*Chron. Hist.* 45). Mr E. K. Chambers, evidently influenced by Collier, reminds us of Benger's debts, and hints that his extravagant and unbusinesslike administration might be the cause why « temporary provision was made for the conduct of the Office » (*Tudor Revels*, 26). All these hypotheses are, of course, overturned by the new documents we now possess concerning Benger's death. There is no necessity to burden his character with the foibles of incapacity or extravagance : the simple reason why poor Benger had no longer to deal in the business of the office was that he was bringing « his boke of count » to a severer judge than the Queen's Auditors.

24. *Henrye Sakeford*. The patent appointing him Master of the Tents is dated 20 Jan. 2 Eliz. He was one of the Grooms of the Privy Chamber (See Signet Office. Docquets. Aug. 1587), and

Keeper of the Privy Purse. In August 1587, he was appointed to the Mastership of the Toils (*Ibid.*); but he had begun to perform the duties of Master of the Toils much earlier, for, in 1576, we find him thus denominated in a document in the Record Office (State Papers. Dom. Eliz. cx. 536), which fact is corroborated by a Warrant for Issue of 25 Eliz. (1582-3).

Among the State Papers (Dom. Eliz. cclxxix. 1601. 20 May) is a certificate, similar to the one printed in this volume at page 50, establishing Sackeford's order of precedence.

25. *Mr Tamworth of her Maiestics privie Chamber*. In a Warrant, the date of which is torn off, but which belongs to the year 1559-60, John Tamworth is styled «Groom of the Privy Chamber & master of our Toylles» (Record Office. Warr. for Issues. Parcel 113). He was also Keeper of the Privy Purse (Cunningham, *Extr. from the Acc. of the Revels*. xx). In 1561-2, he gave a New Year's gift to the Queen (Nichols. *Prog. Eliz.* I. 127). In a privy seal, dated 23 May 1572, one « Iohn Tamworthe arm. » is given as son to « Christopher, defunctus » (Record Office. Privy Seals. May. 14 Eliz.). «Among the Lansdowne Charters..... N° 16, is the « Account of John Tamworth, Esq. Executor of the late Lady Denny, widow » dated 1555-6 » (Madden, *Privy Purse Expenses of Pr. Mary*. p. 227). Lady Denny was the widow of Sir Anthony Denny, one of the gentlemen of the Privy Chamber to Henry VIII. See also Camden, *Annales*, p. 115, edit. 1616. Frankf.

35. *The Storehouses of theym all &c*. At the time when this document was written, the Revels were stored, together with the Tents and the Toils, in the dissolved hospital of St John of Jerusalem (See p. 47-9). Though the enumeration of the different storehouses of the Revels is outside the scope of this book, it will be useful to give here a brief account of the successive removals of the office. About 1540, we hear of the Revels being stored with the Tents at Warwick Inn. In June 1543, Warwick Inn no doubt proving too small for the safe keeping of such cumbersome affairs as the Royal Pavilions &c, these were transported to the Charterhouse. But the Charterhouse was alienated, the Tents had to be displaced again, and they were this time stored in a house which had lately been granted to Sir Thomas Cheyney, and which was situated in Blackfriars. The removal took place in March 1544-5. As this fact has been unknown till now, I give an extract from a Decree of 1 March 4 Edward VI, made by the Court of Augmentations and which is my authority for that statement: « Edwardus Sextus &c. Omnibus ad quos....... Memorandum for asmuch as it is duelie proved byfore the chauncellor of the Court of the Augmentacions that the Master and officers of the kinges maiesties Tentes doe occupie to the K. maiesties vse one howse within the precincte of the late Blacke fryers of London, belonging to Sir Thomas Cheyney Knight treasourer of the Kinges maiesties most honorable house for the lying of the Kinges maiesties Tentes there, and that the same house hath byn occupied to that vse withowt any Recompense or rent therfore poaed [paid] to the said Sir Thomas Cheyney from the feast of the Anunciacion of our Ladie which was in the xxxvjth yere of the late kinge henrie theight which house is of the yerelie rent of fyve poundes. It is therfore ordered and decreed by the said Chauncellor and councell the first day of marche in the iiijth yere of the raigne of our soveraigne Lorde King Edward the vjth That the said Sir Thomas Cheyney his heires executors and assignes during the tyme that the said howse shalbe and remayne in thandes of the said Master and Officers of the kinges maiesties Tentes

to thvse and intent before rehersed, shall haue of the kinges maiesties highnes the somme of fyve poundes yerelie to be paied by thandes of the Treasourer of the said court of Augmentacions....... In cuius rei testimonium has litteras nostras fieri fecimus patentes. Teste Ricardo Sackvile vij[mo] die marcij anno regni nostri quarto » (Loseley MSS. Parcel 244. N[o] VI). Stowe (*Survey of London*. p. 162, ed. W. J. Thoms), says that St John's « was employed as a store-house for the king's toils and tents, for hunting, and for the wars » ; this I am inclined to take as an error — Stowe is not free from errors — as it is difficult to reconcile such a statement with the facts supplied by the preceding documents.

All this time the Revels had remained at Warwick Inn ; but on his accession, Edward VI had them removed to Blackfriars, where they were again united to the Tents, though the two were in separate buildings (See Account of the « Charges as well of the Removing of the kinges highnes Revelles & maskes with thappertenaunces from Warwyck Inne vnto the late disolved howse of black ffryers..... from the firste daie of ffebruarij in the ffirste yere of our said Soueraigne lordes Reigne vnto the xxviijth daie of the same monythe », in the Loseley Collection, and to be published in my forthcoming volume on the Revels). The Revels and the Tents remained in Blackfriars until the death of Sir Thomas Cawerden, when they were again displaced and removed to the Hospital of St John's (See page 49 l.31), where they remained till the beginning of James I's reign.

38. *Syr Thomas Carden... hadde the dealinges of all three offices* **at once**. In the heading to the ledger containing the Accounts from 4 Edward VI to 1 & 2 Ph. & Mary, I find the Toils included among the various business that Cawerden had to superintend. It runs as follows : « Thoffyces of the Tentes & revelles with the Toyles lorde of Mysrule Maskes Playes and other Pastimes tryumphes Banketinghowses and other preparacions actes & devices therto incidente appartenente and accustomed made done furnished attended & setforthe of those offices ». (Loseley MSS. XII).

7. 23. *Banquetinge houses*. One may have an idea of the gorgeousness of such banqueting-houses from the following description given by Stowe (*Chron*., edit. 1615. p. 688) : « This yeere [1581] (against the comming of certaine Ambassadors out of France) by her maiesties appointment, on the sixt and twentith day of March in the morning (being Easter day) a banquetting house was begun at Westminster, on the Southwest side of her maiesties palace of White hall, made in manner & forme of a long square 332 in measure about, 30. principals made of great masts being 40. foote in length a peece, standing vpright, betweene euery one of the Masts, ten foote asunder and more, the wals of this house were closed with canuas, and painted all the outsides of the same artificially, with a worke called rustike much like stone. This house had two hundred, nintie and two lights of glasse. The sides within the same house was made with x heights of degrees for people to stand vpon : and the top of this house was wrought cunningly vpon canuas works of iuie and holly, with pendants made of wickar roddes, and garnished with Bay, Rue, and all manner of strange floures garnished with spangles of gold, as also beautified with hanging toscans made of hollie and iuie with all manner of strange fruits, as pomegranates, orenges, pompions, cucumbers, grapes, with such like spangled with gold and most richly hanged : betwixt these workes of baies & iuie were great spaces of canuas, which was most cunningly painted, the clouds with starres, the sunne and sun-beames, with diuerse other coates of sundry sorts belonging to the Queenes maiestie most richly garnished with gold. There were of all manner of persons working on this house, to the number of 375. two men had mischances, the one broke his legge and so did the other. This house was made in three weekes and three dayes, and was ended the eighteenth of Aprill, and cost 1744*l*. 19*s*. ».

Cf. the accounts for a similar banqueting-house at pp. 163-8 of this volume.

9. 18. It should be noticed here that the writer of this memorandum does not speak of the Yeoman's duties. No doubt he considered the Yeoman, not as a real officer, but as a kind of higher workman, which indeed he was, being as a rule a tailor. In Sir Thomas Cawerden's accounts, the Yeoman is never set among the officers, but always among the tailors (See *e. g.* 79; 84 &c., & 87).

25. *A platte forme of certen ordynaunces &c.* In a note to page 34 of his *Tudor Revels*, Mr E. K. Chambers suggests that this may be a reference to the « Constitucions howe the King's Revells ought to be usyd » preserved among the Cawerden papers (printed in Kempe, *Loseley Manuscripts*. 93). This is impossible since the writer says that the « platte forme » was « delyvered over to some of the *Quenes* Maiesties most honorable privye Counsell », whilst the « Constitucions » refer to a *King*. And, indeed, at page 12, Mr E. K. Chambers has rightly said that the said « Constitucions » must fall between 1544 and 1553.

40. *setto*. i. e. « set to ».

10. 3. *Vnderstande*. Mr. E. K. Chambers reads (*Tudor Revels*, 35) « vnderstanded ». This is not correct, for the word is not surmounted by any sign of abbreviation. « Vnderstande » is simply a variant of « vnderstonde » an old form of the past participle of « understand ». See, for one instance among many, Chaucer's *Works*, Group B. 520.

11. 41. *Sight of perspective*. This statement is a very important one for the history of the stage in England. Its meaning will be fully discussed elsewhere.

12. 19. *Prest monye*. The List of Payments, printed at page 419 & sqq., shows that from 1567 to 1572 no imprest was advanced ; but from 1573 onwards, impress occur quite regularly.

25. *Greate Warderobe*. The Great Wardrobe was situated near the parish church of St Andrew, on the east side of the Blackfriars precinct. There were minor wardrobes in the palaces of Westminster, Greenwich, Windsor, Richmond, in the Tower &c. For deliveries of stuff from the different wardrobes, see Subject Index, under « Wardrobe ».

32. *As as*. *Sic* for *as*.

13. 40. *Inuentorye*. For a specimen of such inventories, see pp. 18-46.

14. 2. *Other other*. *Sic* for *other*.

15. 1. *Concernynge the lendinge furthe &c.* See page 409.

14. *A Commission*. The commission here asked for was granted to Tyllney in 1581. See page 51.

TABLE I. The original consists of a folio sheet, written on one side, and of a smaller one, which is a kind of commentary on the former ; they have been numbered by the British Museum N° 1 & N° 2 respectively. This document is evidently by Blagrave, since the writer speaks of his « waiges and allowaunces » as Clerk (See page 17 l.32). Its date can be fixed approximately. It must have been written after Holte's death in 1571, for, had the old yeoman been living, Blagrave could not have boasted he was the « auncient of the office by at the leaste xxiiij of those yeres » (Page 17 l.30); nor can it have been written in Benger's lifetime, for the latter was appointed in January 1559-60, and twenty-four years' seniority over him would have implied that Blagrave had entered the office before January 1535-6, which is impossible (See note to **68.** 1). Benger, as I have shown, died between 12 July 1572 and 7 June 1573; this gives us 12 July 1572 as an upward limit for the date of the document. Now, after 1572, the most ancient officer of the Revels, next to Blagrave, was Buggyn, appointed on 30 December 1570 and Blagrave was therefore thinking of him (Buggyn) when he said he (Blagrave) was the « auncient of the office » by at least twenty-four years. As on the other hand he states that he had had « acquayntaunce with those thaffaires » of the Revels « and contynuall dealing therein by the space of xxvij or xxviij yeres », we are to conclude that when the document was written, Buggyn had been more than three and less than four years in the office of the Revels. In other words, if we bear in mind the date of his patent, the document was written at some intermediate date between 30 December 1573 and 30 December 1574. This agrees perfectly well with the date of Blagrave's entrance into Cawerden's service, that is in 1546, at which time, as I suggest in my note to **68.** 1, he must have begun to have that acquaintance with the affairs of the Revels of which he is so proud.

An objection could be made to the preceding argumentation. As I shall show in my note to **58.** 1, there is every probability that Buggyn began acting as deputy to Leys c. 1566; but then we should be obliged to admit that the document was written in 1570 at the latest, which date, as we have seen, is impossible. The discrepancy can easily be explained away. Blagrave amplified his own time of service by adding all the years of his deputyship and even of his informal assistance; but in his opinion, Buggyn could not be considered as having entered the office before he was formally appointed! This is perfectly human.

The object of this « Platte » of Orders, as well as of Document I, is now pretty clear. After Benger's death, the Lord Treasurer thought it was a convenient time to reform an office to which, as a man with puritanical tendencies, he surely had no liking, and especially to reduce expenses which weighed heavily upon the Queen's Exchequer. He seems to have considered that the best remedy was to grant the office to some one who would take it « in ferme after a rate » (See page 6 l.41), or, at least, to suppress some of the charges, such as the « airings » and to lessen the number of officers. He asked the opinion of some personage outside the Revels but who had some acquaintance with the working of the office; Blagrave being the most ancient among the remaining officers of the Revels was also consulted. Document I and the « Platte » of Orders were the answers to Burghley's questions. They must not have been much to his liking. The writer of Document I flatly disapproved of the idea of giving the office in ferm and of suppressing the airings: to the Treasurer's desire of reducing the number of officers, he coolly opposed the necessity of creating a new officer. Blagrave, who could not have spoken so freely to the Treasurer, prudently passed over the question of the ferm and of the officers, and confined himself to purely technical points, which were calculated to bring a little more order into the management of the office, but not to diminish the expenses very much. And he seized this opportunity to petition for the mastership. The opposition which seems to have been made to the Treasurer's efforts at reform, together with Blagrave's and Tyllney's adverse intrigues to obtain the mastership, were probably the cause why the vacancy was not filled till 1579.

18 & 30. The MS. offers a curious example of the use of the inverted semicolon (⁏) as a mark of punctuation. In mediaeval handwritings, the inverted semicolon held an intermediate position between our modern semicolon and our comma. I have preserved it in my transcript as it is interesting in a paleographical point of view.

17. 10. *Privye or speciall wardrops.* See note to **12.** 25.

14. *Hanginges.* In the Loseley MSS., I have found frequent mentions of hangings « cut into clothes for players or masquers ». See, for instance, pp. 21 l.15; 22 l.25; 40 l.18 of this volume.

28. *To bestowe the Mastership of the office vpon me.* Blagrave's wishes were not to be gratified, as we shall see later on (note to **68.** 1).

31. *I wolde be lothe hereafter to deale nor medle with it.* Blagrave was as good as his word : from 1579 (*i. e.* after Tyllney's appointment) to the end of 1581, he refused to sign the books; and in the Declared Account for 1 Nov. 1580 — 31 October 1581 (Record Office. Audit Office. Bd. 2045. Roll 6), we find Tyllney charging the Queen for « twice writing, ingrossing, compiling and keping of one lidgier boke of this office by reason there is no Clerke ». In the same Declaration, the Auditor has written the following note : « In former yeres the Clarke Comptroler and the Clerke of Thoffice were wontt to subscribe the said lidgeard Book with the M^r^ » ; from which it appears that the Clerk-Controller seems to have sided with Blagrave against Tyllney. Blagrave must then have been taken to task, for in the following year (1582-3) he began again signing the books ; but henceforth, the Accounts were more and more badly kept, to the loss of the historians of the drama.

18. DOCUMENT III. *Inventory of the Stuff of the Revels.* This valuable document containing the descriptions of a score of Masques, till now unknown to the dramatic historian, is one of the treasures preserved in the Loseley Collection. It forms part of one of the two ledgers indexed in the Historical MSS. Commission (VIIth Report. pp. 606 & 612), and in which are recorded all the expenses for the Tents and Revels from 4 Edward VI to 1 Elizabeth. As the papers are in a temporary arrangement, I have thought it best not to give this Inventory any reference number; but it should be said that the ledger is now marked XIII.

The extract here given consists of three parts : 1° a survey of the state of the Revels stuff in 1555 when the last inventory was taken, together with an account of the different masques in which the stuff was employed (pp. 19-22) ; 2° an enumeration of all the stuffs received from the Royal Wardrobe, with their employment (pp. 23-36) ; 3° a description of the state in which the masquing garments were found when the new inventory was taken, *i. e.* c. April or May 1560 (See page 37 l.35). Parts I & II form what was then called a rear-account (See note to **330.** 15) ; Part III is the inventory properly so called. Such inventories were made every time a new Master or a new Yeoman was appointed. This one was made at Benger's own request (See 111 l. 4-6). Similar documents are preserved in the Loseley Collection, and will be printed in my next volume.

The MS. is a good specimen of the office work of the period; only the scribe has a constant habit of surmounting his n's & m's with the sign (⌒); I thought at first this was the sign of abbreviation sometimes used in Latin MSS.; but after a closer study of the document I came to the conclusion that it is but a flourish, and therefore took no notice of it in my transcription.

4. *Sir Iohn Gage; Sir Robert Rochester; Sir Francis Inglefeld.* For the biographies of these three statesmen, see *Dictionary of Nat. Biography*, vols. xx. 350; xlix. 72; xvii. 372.

19. 34. *Rychard Leys.* He was the Clerk-Controller. The only facts I am able to bring touching his biography are: 1° a mention of him in Sir Thomas Cawerden's will: « Also I gyue and bequethe vnto Rycharde Leys of London twenty powndes by the yere.... Also I gyue and bequeth vnto the same Rycharde Leys all such offall stuffe and lumber of tentes and other old howses and tymber as ys now remaynyng within the place of offyce of the Tentes » (Loseley MSS.); 2° a « licentia Edmundo Harman alienandi Manerium de Thirrefeld & in Comitatu Buck Ricardo Leys » (Patent Rolls. 37 Henry VIII. p. 8). He died c. 1570 (See page 58 l. 17). Cf. also note to **56**.

21. 6. *Albomas.* This is a blunder for *Albonyes*, i. e. Albanese, as I have ascertained by a comparison with the inventory of 1555, preserved among the Loseley MSS., and which contains the original description from which this one was copied. As it is impossible to read Albonias, the scribe being unusually particular about the dotting of his i's, I have let the error stand.

22. 32. *Rewe.* i. e. rewed, as is clear from another description of the same masque in the Loseley Collection.

23. 9. *Of of. Sic* for *of.*

19. *They were all taken awey by the straungers.* Rifling was a not uncommon accident in Court festivities. Similar mentions occur at pp. 202 l.27; 338 l.24, and we have an account of the riotous onset of the « King's gard & other gentyllmen » who « by fors karryed away » a pageant & besides broke the heads of the poor men that were set to keep it (Brewer. II. 1495).

25. *Sir Edward Walgrave.* See *Dictionary of National Biography*, lix. 13. It is not known that Waldegrave, though he was soon to be sent to the Tower, superintended the preparations for Elizabeth's Coronation (See the Accounts of Sir Edward Waldegrave &c. for the Coronation of Q. Elizabeth among the Exchequer Papers, Queen's Remembrancer's Depart. Bd. 429. N° 4). A letter of Queen Katherine Parr, recommending Edward Waldegrave for a lease in reversion of the manor farm of Chipley in Suffolk, is printed in the Correspondence of Archbishop Parker (Parker Soc.) p. 19-20.

26. 16. *Eares.* A curious spelling for *hairs.*

22. *Fro.* The scribe wrote first *from*, then crossed out the *m.*

24. *Grasiers.* At page 28, they are called « Ientlemen of the contrey ». Since the extension of sheep-farming towards the end of the XIVth century, there had grown up a very active opposition to the gentlemen who took to what was called « enclosing », because it dispensed with the necessity of employing many servants, and therefore pauperized a great number of labourers. See Becon's *Jewel of Joy* (*Works*, 1564, II. f° xvi, quoted in Furnivall's Stubbes, I. p. 290); & William Stafford, *Examination of certayn ordinary Complaints* (New Shak. Soc.), p. 17 & *passim.*

28. 16. *Shroff Tuisdaye.* i. e. 1558-9 (See page 94 l.28).

30. 4. *Twelff night.* i. e. 1559-60, since the stuff was delivered «in the tyme of Sir Thomas Benger».

31. 27. *Mittons.* Fairholt (*Costume.* pp. 133-4) gives extracts from a «Tale of King Edward and the Shepherd» from which it appears that mittens and a staff were characteristic articles of a shepherd's dress.

32. 21. *Twelf nighte.* i. e. 1559-60. See page 19 l. 22 and note to **30.** 4.

34. 40. *A pley by the children of the chapple.* Since the stuff was delivered to Sir Thomas Benger, the play was performed between Christmas 1559 (the date when Benger entered the Office of the Revels) and April or May 1560, the approximate date at which the Inventory was made.

44. *Signatures.* The bottom of the page has been much injured by damp: Rychard Leys's signature has disappeared.

37. 12. *Sir Richard Sackevyle.* See *Dictionary of Nat. Biog.* vol. L. 95.

14. *Sir Walter Myldmey.* See *Dict. of Nat. Biography*, xxxvii. 374. As may be seen from the letter here printed, Mildmay was already acting as Chancellor of the Exchequer in 1560, though, according to *Dict. of Nat. Biography*, he was appointed only in 1566.

27. *Benger desireth that he maye declare &c.* Cf. page 111 l. 4-6.

33. *The rest being fees incydente.* Cf. page 111 l. 7-9.

39. 17. *Nusquams.* These probably were allegorical personages (Cf. the « posye of poco a poco »).

26. *Musquams. Sic* for *Nusquams.*

40. 12. *Gyven awaye by the &c.* The scribe had written first:

gyven awaye by the M[r]
in y[e] queenes presence.

He afterwards crossed out the word *M[r]* and interlined *maskers*; but he forgot to correct *by* into *to.*

41. 12. *Wrether. Sic* for *wreathed.*

21. *Garded garded. Sic* for *garded.*

42. 7. *Wookes. Sic* for *workes.*

45. 6. *Silvuer.* In the MS. the word is written : « silvu[r] »; I have expanded the overwritten « r » into « er » as usual; but I have a suspicion that the scribe did not mean any contraction here.

47. Document IV. Collier (I. 232 *n.* 1) and Mr E. K. Chambers (*Tudor Revels*, 20) maintain that this survey was made before 1571; and their reason is that, in the document, Burghley is styled « Sir William Cecyll ». But this is obviously a slip of the pen, since the writer has added «Lorde Treasorer of Englond » (See page 47 l.11). Besides, Tyllney, Honnyng and Kirkham are mentioned as « Master », « Clerk-Controller », and « Yeoman », respectively (See page 48 ll.9, 18 & 24). The mention of Kirkham's name gives 28 April 1586 as an upward limit for the date of the document; for though Kirkham began acting as yeoman in 1581 (see note to **48.** 2), Necton, who signed the survey, says (page 49 l.20) he has « seen euerye the patentes of the saied seuerall Officers of the Revelles », a statement which he could not have made before Kirkham was formally appointed. A downward limit is supplied by the fact that Thomas Graves, Surveyor of the Works, was present when the survey was made, for it is clear from a Declared Account of the

Works in the Record Office (Audit Office. 2414. N° 16) that Thomas Graves died between 31 March 1586 and 31 March 1587 (In the heading to the Account March 1586 — March 1587, it is said : « As by one greate Ligier Booke... subscribed partelie by thandes of Thomas Graves late Surveyor of her Maiesties saide woorkes deceased, and partelie by thandes of Thomas Blagrave nowe Surveyor of her highnes saide woorkes succeading the saide Thomas Graves.. »). We can therefore date this survey between 28 April 1586 and 31 March 1587.

4-5. *Graves; Fowler*. I had no difficulty in identifying the persons here meant, for the Accounts of the Works supply us with a complete list of all the officers of the Works, in the time of Elizabeth. Thomas Graves was appointed Surveyor on 10 November 20 Eliz., succeeding Lewis Stocket (appointed 11 March 6 Eliz.). As to his death, see preceeding note. Fowler died in 1589 (See Record Office. Declared Accounts. Audit Office. Works. 2414. N° 18).

6. *Colebrand*. He had been appointed Master Carpenter, in survivorship with John Russel, by a patent dated 8 February 7 Eliz.

7. *Lovell*. The name has been supplied by the Declared Account of the Works for 1586-7, already referred to.

Necton. Collier (I. 232) and Mr E. K. Chambers (*Tudor Revels*, 20) print *Norton*. The handwriting of the MS. is very legible, and I do not think there can be any doubt about the spelling of the name. Such is also the opinion of one of the superintendents in the MSS. Room of the British Museum, whom I consulted.

15. *1581*. This is a mistake for 1561, since Winchester died in 1572 and Richard Sackville in 1566. Probably, the scribe wrote «8» from habit, the document having been written in the « eighties ».

25. *Wingfield*. He was son to Sir Anthony Wingfield, the Controller of the Household to Henry VIII and Edward VI. In a Warrant for Issues (Parcel 117), dated 27 April 11 Elizabeth (1569), he is given as « gentleman usher ». He probably was the same Anthony Wingfield, who, on 28 May 1591, obtained the Office of verge-bearer « coram domina Regina ad festum sancti Georgij apud Castrum Windsore » (Record Office. Patent Books. Auditors. vol. 10). He died in 1593 (*Dict. Nat. Biog*. lxii. p. 182).

32. *Roberte Harvye*. He succeeded Holte as yeoman of the Tents on 11 December 1571 (Patent Books. Auditors. vol. 9). A document concerning a lawsuit between Robert Harvye and John & Andrew Richars about lands in Wakefield and Alverthorpe, is preserved in the Record Office among the Proceedings of the Court of Requests (Bdle 61. N° 80).

36. *Beare*. Read *beer*.

48. 2. *Kyrkham*. His patent is printed at page 74 of this volume. It is dated 28 April 1586; but therein it is expressly said that, at that time, Kirkham had already served in the office. In fact, he had begun acting as deputy to the yeoman in 1581-2 (See Table II 1.74). This can be taken as the exact date of his entrance into the office, since the book for Nov. 1580-Nov. 1581 is signed by Walter Fysshe (See page 342 l.28). All I can add to the biographical data already known (the most interesting of which are the documents published by Greenstreet in the *Athenæum*), is that Kirkham is mentioned in a Court of Requests document (Bdle 42. N° 53) concerning a pasture in the parish of St Giles, London.

14. *William Hunninges*. See his patent at page 60. Can the Clerk-Controller of the Tents and Revels be the same as the « Willelmus Huninge, clericus consilij » mentioned in Lansdowne MSS. (156. f° 99) ? or the Honnynge noticed in Cotton MSS. Otho. C. x. f° 177 (From Madden, *Privy Purse Expenses of the Princess Mary*. p. 283) ? In the volume last mentioned, there is an entry for the year 1536-7 of viij*d* « geuen to Honnynges seruante bringing a Carpe to my ladies grace » (page 17), and again, in July 1544, xx*d* were « geuen to mistress Honnyng seruaunte bringing Shrimpes » (p. 160). The Clerk-Controller resigned on 21 June 1596 (See page 62 l.25) but later on, in 1603, he returned to the Office of the Revels as successor to Blagrave (State Papers. Dom. Add. vol. ix. N° 58).

15. *Thomas Hall*. Evidently the same person with the Thomas Hale who was appointed « Groom of the Tents and Pavilions » by Henry VIII, and « serviens ad arma » on 2 January 1554-5 by Mary (Patent Books. Auditors. vol. 9). Thomas Hale still held the former post in 1572 for in an interrogatory written in that year he is given as « Grome of the Tentes Hales and pavilions » (Loseley Collection. vol. 243. p. 103). In the same document, he is said to have been « aged lxvj yeres or there aboutes », which makes the date of his birth c. 1506. If he is the same as the Thomas Hall to whom a privy seal was granted in July 1570 (Record Office. Privy Seals. July 12 Eliz.) concerning lands in co. Suffolk he may have been a native of this county.

16. *All*. Here ends the first part of the document as it is now bound. It formerly consisted of one single folio, made up of three pieces of paper pasted together ; these pieces have been separated by the binder, thus cutting lines 15 of page 48 and 26 of page 49 in the very middle of the letters ; but the reconstitution of the words is easy enough.

49. 25. *A yerlie Rente.... as was accustomed*. Cf. pp. 103 & 107.

27. *Enformed*. See note to **48.** 16.

50. Document V. I print this document from a contemporary transcript in the Bodleian. A similar document is preserved among the Chalmers Papers in the same library (MSS. Eng. Poet. d. 13. p. 157). It has the following note : « Extracted from the College of Arms London 25 March 1799. Fras Townsend Windsor ». It is more concise than the one I give, and is dated « xxvjth of December » 1600 ; but the import is the same. This Townsend transcript has been published by Chalmers (*Supplemental Apology*. 197*n*.).

4. *Edmonde Tylney*. See note to **55**.

38. *Iohn Ashley* ; *Iohn Fortescue*. See *Dict. of Nat. Biography*, vols ii. 206 and xx. 45.

51. Document VI. This document has been printed by T. E. Tomlins in the Shakespeare Society's Papers (vol. 3) and by Collier (*Hist. of Dram. Literature*. I. 247). Collier gives it as bearing on the formation of the Queen's Company. This, to use a favourite phrase of his, is « decidedly a mistake ». It is such a commission « for prouisione of necessaries and takeinge upp of woorckemen » as was given out as most necessary « for the better sarvice » of the Queen by both the authors of the plan of reform already mentioned. Mr. E. K. Chambers has been the first to draw attention to the importance of this document in the history of the Stage. As this is outside the scope of this work, I refer to his very good treatment of the question in his *Tudor Revels*, pp. 62, 73 & sqq.

53. Cawerden's patent has already been printed by Rymer (*Fœdera.* T. VI. P. III. 123) and by Halliwell (*Collection of Ancient Documents respecting the Office of Master of the Revels.* p. 1).

54. Benger's patent has already been printed in Rymer's (*Fœdera.* T. VI. P. IV. 93). As to his biography, see note to 6. 23.

8 & 10. *Mascarum ; Mascorum.* The scribe's incertitude as to the gender of this Latin word is curious but easily explained. The correct form was «masca»; but the proximity of the words « iocorum», « revellorum » frequently attracted the scribes into the wrong spelling « mascorum ».

55. A duplicate of Tyllney's patent is in the Patent Books (Pells. vol. 1), and a seventeenth century copy is preserved amongst the papers which Sir Henry Herbert used for his lawsuits. Halliwell printed it from the Herbert copy in his *Documents respecting the Office of Master of the Revels* already referred to. There seems to be a good deal of uncertainty as to the spelling of the name ; « Tyllney » is the form the Master of the Revels invariably used when he signed the books. For his biography, see *Dictionary of National Biography*, lvi. 399, and add the following data which may be interesting. There are in the Record Office amongst the Court of Requests Proceedings two Tyllney lawsuits ; the one (Bdle 56. N° 57) concerning lands in Stepney, Middlesex ; the other (Bdle 97. N° 46) concerning the stewardship of St Katherine's, Middlesex. Stowe (*Chron.*, edit. 1615, p. 675) mentions a « Master Tilney » among divers gentlemen who went to the siege of Edinburgh Castle « of their own free wils », in 1573. This pugnacious gentleman may have been the future Master of the Revels ; but he may, just as well, have been one of Edmund Tyllney's cousins. Tyllney was to be Elizabeth's last Master of the Revels. But in his lifetime several steps were taken to find him a successor. John Lyly, the dramatist, as is known from several of his letters, printed in R. W. Bond's edition of the *Works*, was a suitor for a reversionary grant of the Office ; but in spite of the Queen's promises he was disappointed, and in 1597, George Buck, Tyllney's nephew, obtained a promise of the reversion (See Lyly's letter to Cecil, *Works.* 1. 68). I say a promise, because there exists no enrolment of any reversionary grant to Buck before June 1603. So much so, that soon after James's accession to the throne a grant was made « vnto Edmond Tilney and Edward Glascock and the longer liver of them of thoffice of Master of the Revelles & Maskes with the fee of x*l.* per Annum & other duties belonging to the same. Subscribed by Mr Attorney generall » (Signet Office. Docquets. May 1603). But Buck, no doubt, succeeded in establishing his rights to the reversion, for the grant was « stayd » (See margin of the document just quoted), and three months after (June) the same office of « Master of his Maiesties Reuelles » was granted to « George Bucke esquire during his life in reuersion after the deceasse of Edmond Tilney now Master of the said Reuelles » (Record Office. Signet Office. Docquets. June 1603).

By the bye, it should be noticed that Chalmers, whose conscientious zeal cannot be too highly praised, had rightly assigned to the end of Elizabeth's reign John Lyly's solicitations for the Revels (*Apology for the Believers &c.* 487). But Collier, disregarding Chalmers's statement (which I believe must have been based on some document now lost), assumed that Lyly was « a petitioner to the Queen for the reversion of the place on the demise of Benger » (I. 231) ; and this error has been since adopted by all the historians of the stage till R. W. Bond found that

Lyly's first petition must be dated 1598, thus independently going back to Chalmers's statement of the truth.

Dr Furnivall reminds me that a specimen of Tyllney's annotations on manuscripts of plays, is to be found at p. 1 of the Old Shakespeare Society edition of *Sir Thomas More.*

56. This is the first time, I believe, that the date of Richard Leys's appointment is made known. Collier (I. 140) only notices that in May 1551 the Clerk (*sic*) of the Revels was Richard Lees. Mr E. K. Chambers simply says (*Tudor Revels*, 10) that « before the end of Edward VI's reign he (Barnard) had been succeeded by Richard Lees ». A study of the Loseley MSS. has made me pretty sure that Leys never acted as Clerk-Controller before his formal appointment; for in the account for Christmas, 3 Edward VI (1549), Iohn Barnard received xij days' wages ; and a few days after the latter's death, *i. e.* on September 4, 1550, the Privy Council wrote to Sir Thomas Cawerden « that the Kinges Majestie ys pleased he shall place oone of his servantes in the rowme of Iohn Bernerd, late comptroller of the Tentes & Pavillions » (*Acts of the Privy Council,* N. S. III. 117), which seems to prove that by that time Barnard's successor was not yet chosen. For biographical data, see note to **19.** 34. In 1547-8, one « Rychard Lees of London mercer » supplied the office with velvet (Loseley MSS. R. 6) ; he probably was the same person who was to become Clerk-Controller a few years later.

7. *Dicletum. Sic* for *dilectum.*

8. *Pauilionum.... necnon.... iocorum revellorum.* Cf. page 6 l.36.

25. *Lewes. Sic* for *Leys.*

30-1. *Solidos...... denarios. (Sic).*

58. 1. *Edward Buggyn.* On 26 April 1559, the Queen appointed Edward Buggyn « clericum & scriptorem litterarum patencium » (Patent Rolls. 1 Eliz. p. 4. m. 3) ; on March 2, 1570-1, he resigned, no doubt on account of his recent appointment to the Clerk-Controllership of the Revels, and the day after another patent was made out, granting Edward Buggyn and Richard Younge... « ac eorum alteri diucius viventi » the said office of « scriptor litterarum patencium » (Patent Rolls. 13 Eliz. p. 3. m. 10).

Buggyn began acting as deputy to Leys a long time before his formal appointment : in an account-book of the Tents, covering the period 30 September 1565 — 30 September 1571, Buggyn's signature appears as early as in 1566, and we should probably find it in the corresponding Revels books, if they had been preserved.

59. 18-23. The last six lines of the document are written in the margin of the original immediately below Buggyn's signature (See page 58 l.9). It has not been possible to preserve this arrangement here.

60. 1. *William Honnyng.* See note to **48.** 14.

27. *Camere nostre. Sic* for *Camerariorum nostrorum.*

61. 3. *Paviliorum. Sic* for *Pavilionum.*

30. *vltimi. Sic* for *vltimo.*

62. 25-31. See note to **59.** 18-23.

63. 20. *Easden. Sic* for *easdem.*

66. 3. *Thomas Phillips*. See note to 6. 19.

16. *Termimo. Sic* for *Termino.*

29. *Bonan. Sic* for *bonam.*

Conuenientem domum. From the Interrogatory in the Loseley Collection, already referred to, we learn interesting details concerning this house. Thomas Hale, the Groom of the Tents said that Phillips dwelt in a little house, in which one Lawrence Bywater then [1572] lived. According to the same witness, the Clerk had also the use of another house (later on transformed by one William Joyner into a school of fence) in which he stored wood as in a « waste rome ». « About the begynnyng of kinge Edwardes tyme when the same [Blackfriars] was geuen vnto...... Cardyn.. the said Phillips contynued the possessyon of it..... aboute two yeres after Mr Cardens graunte & then the said Carden removed the said Phillyps into another house called the Ankers [*i. e.* the Anchoret's]...... and Mr Carden placed in the said Litle howse where Bywater dwellethe one Mr Blagrave clerk of ye tentes » (Loseley MSS. vol. 243. 103-4). From another document in the same Collection, we learn that the Ankers house was situated « betwene the waie leadinge from Carter Lane towardes bridewell.... one the northe part...., and the tenemente or gaterome and garden..... in the tenure and occupacion of Thomas Vautroly printer & bookebinder one the weste & sovthe partes » (vol. 243. 20-1).

68. 1. *Thomas Blagrave.* In the Interrogatory several times mentioned, I find that, in 1572, Thomas Blagrave « of west bedwyn in the County of Wilteshire » was « ageed 50 yeres or thereaboutes » (Loseley MSS. vol. 243. 105); he therefore was born c. 1522. From the same document we learn that in 38 Henry VIII, *i. e.* 1546, he had already entered Sir Thomas Cawerden's service. He must at the same time have begun to deal, in an indirect manner, in the business of the office which his master superintended (Cf. note to Table I). The first mention, however, that we find of Blagrave's services in the office belongs to the year 1550. In a document preserved among the Loseley MSS., and not yet catalogued, Blagrave himself says he has acted as Clerk in 4, 5, 6, and 7 Edward VI. This statement is confirmed by several other documents. In a ledger covering the expenses for the period beginning on the « vj^t of Iune in the iiij^th yeare of the reigne of kinge Edward the vj^to », and ending on the « xvth of Iune in the fyrste and seconde yeares of the most prosperus reignes of our drad souereigne lord and ladye Philipp and Marye » it is said that, for the said charges « Thomas Philipps and Thomas Blagrave were by the order and discression of the seide Sir Thomas Cawerden Master of the seide offices credited and specially apoynted aswell with the recepte of all soche somes of mony as ffor and towardes the paymente and satisfaccion of the same were by warraunte from the late king Edwarde the syxte and his counsell assygned and delyuered to them by the handes of the treasaurours of his courtes of the augmentacions and wardes...... as by thaccomptes of the seid Thomas Philipps and Thomas Blagrave herafter seuerallye in order foloinge &c....... ensuethe »; in one of the original accounts it is expressly mentioned that a sum of money « wes paid the xxviijth daye of December in the Syext year of the Rayegne of.... Edward the Syext by the hands of Sir Thomas Cawerden Knyeght in the presens of Rychard lee Thomas blackegrave clarkes Iohn hoellt Tayeller at the blacke ffryars ». An examination of the accounts for that period shows, besides, that Blagrave had to

perform much of the practical business of the office. For instance, in 5 Edward VI, he spent xxxvijs. for the « cariage and delyuerie of stuff... and for his bote hier as well by nyght as by daye ffrom the black ffryarse to grenewich & returning for knowledg of the counsaylles pleasure in and abowte thordinaunce & state » of the Lord of Misrule. Yet, from several entries, it is equally clear that Phillipps, and not Blagrave, was still the responsible officer. In 4, 5, 6, 7 Edward VI, for instance, I find that Phillipps « Clerk of the Revelles » received various sums, calculated at the usual rate of xviij pence a day, for his services at the time of the different Court festivities. In the same way, the inventory of 1555 is said to have been made by «Sir Thomas Cawerden knighte Master of that office and by Richard lee Clerke Comptrowler Thomas phillipps Clerke and Iohn Holte yeman of the same » ; but I find no mention of Blagrave's name, though he signed the copy of that inventory which was made in 1560. To sum up, my belief is that Blagrave had but a semi-official position in the Revels; but, being Cawerden's personal servant, he must have been entrusted by his master with the supervision of pecuniary matters, and have been led in that way into helping Thomas Philipps who had also a share in the receipt and disbursement of the office money. At any rate, it is certain that Blagrave held in the household of the Master of the Revels a position of no mean importance; Cawerden appointed him, « my late seruant » as he says, overseer of his will, and bequeathed to him « thre corsellettes, sex Almen Ryfettes sex bowes twelve sheffe of Arrowes and sex blacke bylles two geldynges and a colte » (Loseley MSS. clxx). In December 1559, as overseer of Cawerden's will, he authorised Lady Cawerden and William More, executors of the same, to sell the Blackfriars estate to John Birch and others. On March 28, 1560, after the death of Philipps, he, at last, obtained a formal grant of the Office of Clerk of the Tents and Revels. By a privy seal, dated 19 December 1568, the Queen directed the Exchequer to « paye vnto... Thomas Blagrave Esquiour for the surplusage of his accoumpte made for ceartayne concealede goodes, Chattelles and Debtes of the Late Duke of Sommerset the some of one hunderethe nynetene poundes nyntene shillinges and eight pence » (Harleian MSS. 146. f° 36). After Benger's death, he was a petitioner for the office of Master, as has been seen at page 17 of this volume. And at first his hopes seem to have been encouraged. In the beginning of December 1573, he had entered « into the execucon of the Masters office » (See page 191 l.20), and in the course of the year 1574, he obtained « svndry Letters from the Lorde Chamberlayne » which Blagrave appears to have considered as equivalent to a formal appointment (See page 225 l.4-5). But, of course, the Lord Chamberlain had no authority to grant the Mastership of the Revels, and this appointment was to be but temporary. In fact, the Officers of the Exchequer were not so sure of Blagrave's right to the title of Master as he himself was. In a Warrant dated 25 December 1574, Blagrave is styled « Clerke of thoffice of our Revels » (Record Office. Warrants for Issues. Parcel 120). In another Warrant dated 12 December 1575, he is this time called « Master of thoffice of our Revels » (Warrants for Issues. Parcel 120). But this is corrected in the next Warrant (5 August 1576), as well as in that of 24 December 1576, wherein he reappears as « Clerke of our sayd Revells » (Warrants for Issues. Parc. 120 & 121). In the Imprest Certificate Books, the same incertitude is remarkable : in most of them he is called « Clericus Revellorum ». In 1575 and 1576, however, he is styled « magister sive clericus Revellorum » (Record Office. Imprest Cert. Books. Pells. vol. 2. ff. 17 *v*. & 29 *r*.). In 1577, he is again denominated « Clericus Revellorum » (Imprest Cert. Books. Pells. vol. 2 f°. 35 *r*.). In 1578, he is given as « Capitalis officiarius Revellorum » (See page 280), which, no doubt, was the true function he exercised.

But if it is possible that Blagrave should have been able to show some letter from the Lord Chamberlain entrusting him with the indefinite functions of Chief Officer, it is an error to say with Collier (I. 229) and Mr E. K. Chambers *(Tudor Revels*, 52) that Blagrave received any appointment by privy seal. The foundation of this assertion is a misinterpretation of a Brief Declaration, preserved among the Lansdowne MSS. (27. N° 86), a duplicate of which is in the Record Office (Decl. Acc. Audit. Office. Bdle 2045. R. 5). The passage from which Collier and Mr E. K. Chambers conclude that Blagrave had been appointed by privy seal is as follows : « There hath bene receued out of the Receipte of Thexchequier by Thomas Blagrave then cheif Officer of the said Revelles by vertue of a previe Seale dated xxx^mo^ Decembris anno xxj^mo^ Regine predicte aswell in full satisfaccion of the debtes due within the foresaid Office betwene the xxjth of ffebruarie 1576 & the xiiijth of ffebruarie 1577 ccxliiij^li^ ix^s^ j^d^ ob. as also impreste towardes the payinge & defrayinge her graces chardges & expences in the said Office in anno 1578 cc^li^. In all as by Certificatt therof subscribed with thand of Roberte Petre may appeare..............ccccxliiij^li^ ix^s^ j^d^ ob. ». Now, any one comparing this passage with similar ones in the two Declared Accounts printed in this volume (See Tables II & III) will see at a glance that the clause « then cheif Officer » is a mere parenthesis, and that the sense is « There has been received by vertue of a privy seal the sum of 244 pounds &c., which sum has been delivered into the hands of Thomas Blagrave, then chief officer ». Besides, this is proved by the Imprest Certificate I have printed at page 280, which makes it clear that the said privy seal was a Warrant for Issue.

On 24 July 1579, Tyllney, who had much influence at Court, was appointed Master, whilst poor Blagrave returned to the inferior situation of Clerk, and as we have seen (note to **17**. 31), he did not accept his disappointment without some fits of sullenness. He was soon, however, to obtain substantial compensations from the Queen. On 5 January 1584, a lease was made by « the Comisioners... to Thomas Blagrave esq. of the personage of Longuey and of the Scite and hedhowse of the manour of Longuey in the Countie of Glocester for xxj yeres paiyng yerely xx*l*. vj*s*. viij*d*. » (Signet Office. Docquets. Jan. 1584), a profitable bargain, no doubt, as all such transactions with the Crown were. In 1586 (10 November 28 Eliz.), he was granted the reversion of the Office of « Surveyor of the Workes aswell within the Tower of London as of hir Maiesties howses of accesse, &c. » (Patent Rolls. 28 Eliz. p. 3. m. 4). This was a lucky stroke, for Graves, as has already been said (note to **47**. Document IV), died a few months after, so that Blagrave had not long to wait for the reversion. There exists in the Record Office among the Court of Requests Proceedings (Bdle 35. N° 15) a law-suit between Thomas Blagrave and Joan his wife, on the one part, and John Ketcher, on the other, about lands in South Minims, Middlesex. Blagrave must have had lands in Bedwin, too, for we learn from the Revels Accounts that he sometimes lived there (See pp. 266 l.35 ; 277 l.24 ; 297 l.30 ; 301 l.19). He died in 1603, since, on 30 May 1603, William Honings was appointed clerk « on the death of Thos. Blagrave » (State Papers. Dom. Add. vol. ix. Nº 58).

70. 3. *Iohn Holte.* See note to **5.** 12.

26. *Iohn Bridges is contentid &c.* In spite of Brewer's authority, Mr E. K. Chambers asserts (*Tudor Revels*, 11) that Bridges had resigned the post of Yeoman of the Revels by April 1, 1547. The terms of Holte's patent make it beyond doubt that the resignation did not take place before 1550, thus corroborating the facts supplied by Brewer. Holte had been acting all the time only as a deputy (Cf. note to **5.** 12).

71. 20. *Breui.* I have extended the abbreviated word « *bri̅* » of the original into br*eui*; but the scribe may have meant bri*ue*.

72. 1. *Iohn Arnolde.* All we know concerning Arnolde, is that he died before 29 January 1573-4 (See page 73 l.30), having therefore occupied the post for two years only, and perhaps less.

14. *Iustices. Sic* for *Iustes.*

73. 1. *Walter Fyshe.* I ought to have printed Fysshe, which is the proper spelling of his name (See his signatures). Fysshe's patent has already been printed by Chalmers (*Supplemental Apology*, p. 149 *e*). The latter rightly gives Fysshe as the successor to Arnolde, who, he candidly says, « was the earliest keeper of such apparell, from what I have been able to trace ». As most of his predecessors, Fysshe was the Queen's tailor : in Add. MSS. Brit. Mus. 5751. ff. 73, 95, 300, mentions are found of « stuff delivered to Walter Fishe for the Queen's use ».

74. Kirkham's patent has been printed by Halliwell (*Documents respecting the Office of Master of the Revels.* p. 3-4). See note to **48.** 2.

77 &c. *From Christmas 1558 to 30 September 1559.* This very interesting book of expenses contains mentions of several masques hitherto unknown to the historians of the drama. It has been extracted from the ledger preserved in the Loseley Collection and, for the present, catalogued as Nº XIII. It follows the Accounts for Philip & Mary, beginning at fº 25*r.* and ending at fº 42*v.*, fº 43 containing the « Summa Totalis » for the whole book; ff. 28*r.*, 28*v.*, 32*r.*, 32*v.*, & 36*v.* are blank.

This is the first time we have precise details on the Revels held during the first year of the reign of Queen Elizabeth. It is true that Collier (I. 169) had already referred to a document in the Lansdowne Collection, from which, he said, it appeared that « John Fortesque the Keeper of the Great Wardrobe, issued from thence in that year for the purpose of « setting forth the Revels », velvets, silks, cloth of gold &c. to the amount of 106*l.* 13*s.* 4*d.* ». But I am sorry to say that this is one of those « perversions of the truth » which are not uncommon in Collier. The heading of the MS. referred to (Lansdowne MSS. 5. Nº 40 [1]) is as follows : « By a warraunte yeven at Westminster the xxiiijth Daye of October Anno primo Regine Elizᵗ ffor Iohn ffortescue Esquire Mʳ of the qwenes Maᵗᵉˢ great Warderobe, viz...». Then follows an enumeration of stuffs with their prices, and amounting to the sum given by Collier. But the words « setting forth the revels » are of Collier's invention, and it is not doubtful that this document is a wardrobe one.

80. 24. *In yᵉ hole.* i. e. *In the whole.*

81. 1 & 3. *Richarde Bosum ; George Bosom.* They probably belonged to the family of John Bossam « worthy to have been serjeant-painter to any king or emperor » (See Walpole's *Anecdotes of*

Painting, p. 77, ed. 1871). A « Thomas boosame payenter » is mentioned as occupying a « howes in Watter lane » in a rent roll of Blackfriars, *temp.* Sir Thomas Cawerden (Loseley MSS. 244. N° 35).

5. *Edmond Busshe.* He may have been the same person as the « Busshe the goldesmythe » mentioned in the *Privy Purse Expenses of the Princess Mary*, p. 100; for, at that period, painting and working in gold were two crafts closely allied. For instance, Nicholas Hilliard was appointed in 41 Elizabeth « goldsmith and Lymner » to the Queen (See Patent Books. Pells. vol. 2).

10-7. Were some of these properties for a pastoral?

12. *Crogerstaves.* These crosiers were no doubt supplied for the four Cardinals mentioned at page 80 l. 14.

14. *Byrdes.* i. e. *beards.*

82. 13. *And and. Sic* for *and.*

84. 3. *Othe. Sic* for *other.*

86. 4. *Came.* Though I have been unable to discover any trace of a dot, the name might be *Caine.*

89. 17. *The occupyed. Sic* for *there occupyed.*

20-1. In the Summa totalis « vij^{s} » is written over another sum, now indecipherable; the scribe had also added « ix »; he afterwards crossed this sum out and wrote « iij^{d} » instead.

92. 2. *Peter Borrayne alias dorranger.* He lived in Blackfriars, and his name appears several times on William More's lists of tenants, variously spelt Dorangia and Borangia (Loseley MSS. vol. 243).

93. 21. *Tuskinges. Sic* for *tuftinges.*

94. 15. *Iohn Horse.* He was also called Iohn de Horse (See page 100 l. 8). A John de Horse was among William More's tenants in Blackfriars (Loseley MSS. vol. 243).

28. *Fysshermen &c.* Cf. page 28 l. 15.

97. 4. *Astrononers. Sic* for *Astronomers.*

6. *Of of. Sic* for *of.*

99. 5. *viij^{lb}. Sic* for *viij^{li}.*

100. 1. *ij lb ij lb.* (*Sic*).

103. 19. *Supradictum.* (*Sic*).

105. 1. *Auguste &c.* Sir Thomas Cawerden died on August 29, 1559; part of the work in the last pages of the ledger was not, therefore, superintended by him. After his death, William More, the executor of the testament of the late Master of the Revels, « yelded for the said late M^{r} of the said offices of the tentes... and Revelles... an accompte before our Auditors of our prestes, aswell of all suche sommes of money as the same late Master receaved either of our treasour or of our late sisters treasour... as also the employment and issuynge out of the same in the said offices from the fyvetene day of Iune in the first and seconde yeres of the late kynge Philipp and our said sister vnto the feast of sainct Michaell tharchangell in the first yere of our reigne. Vpon whiche accompte it apperethe, that our said servant [*i. e.* More] remayneth in surplusage for money due to the said late master.... the somme of seaven hundred fourty poundes thirtene shillinges tenne pence and one half peny ». This sum was paid by a Warrant dated December 28, 1560, the same from which the preceding quotation has been made (Record Office. Exche-

quer of Receipt. Warrants for Issues. Parcel 114. See also my Collection of Payments, p. 419).

Another document preserved in the Record Office among the State Papers (Dom. Eliz. vol. IV. N° 47) is an « Estymate of the deptes owing in the offices of the Revells and tentes dew from myhellmas in the second and third yeres of King Phillipp & Quene Mary the Accompt of bothe the same then Inclosid yeldyd vpp and Endyd vntill myhellmas last past before the date hereof amountith to ccxlvj[li] and ffrom myhellmas last vntill mydsomer now comyng is and wilbe dew ccccxxx[li] x[s] besides the ordynary fees paide to the patentees half yerely in the Receipt and in thexchequer — DClxxvj[li] x[s]

off whiche summe there hathe byn Recevid but only at Sir Richard Sackfild his handes — ccxx[li]

The vijth of Iune An° 1559. »

5. *Supradictie.* (*Sic*).

Gowinge. In the MS. the «w» is overwritten between «o» and «i». Perhaps the scribe meant to abbreviate the « r » as is usual with overwritten vowels. At any rate the meaning is *growing.*

18. *Robert Reyuer.* Of course, the name might be *Reyner.*

109. *From Christmas 1559 &c.* It is somewhat difficult to determine exactly the period covered by each of the books enumerated in this summing up. All I can make out is this :

1° The « ffiveth booke » (amounting to 438*l.* 10*d.*) is evidently the same as the book mentioned at page 118 l.8, and belonging to « anno ix » *i. e.* Christmas 1566 and Shrovetide 1566-7.

2° The « second booke » must have covered a period ending at Michaelmas 1561 (probably Christmas 1560 and Shrovetide 1560-1) for its 'summa totalis' corresponds to that given at page 113 as covering the expenses of « anno tertio », if we add the 200*l.* received in prest during the Michaelmas term of 1560 (See Collection of Payments, p. 419).

3° If so, the « ffirste booke » must have related to the expenses for Christmas 1559 and Shrovetide 1559-60.

4° Of « third » and « ffourthe » books we can only say that they must have covered the period Michaelmas 1561 — ? Michaelmas 1566.

5° The Progress took place in 8 Elizabeth (See page 118 l.7).

29. *And so Remayneth &c.* This sum was paid by the Warrant printed at page 118.

33. *xl[li].* These forty pounds were paid in the Michaelmas term of 1566 (See Collection of Payments, p. 420) ; they must be added to the 843*l.* 11*s.* 2*d.* 1/4 of line 29 to make up the 883*l.* 11*s.* 2*d.* of the Warrant dated 25 June 1567 (See page 118 l.14, and Collection of Payments, p. 420).

110. *Christmas 1559 &c.* Of this document Collier says : « It is not signed by Sir Thomas Cawerden, but it bears internal evidence that it came from him » (I. 171). The fact is that Cawerden had been dead nearly a year when this estimate was drawn up. Mr E. K. Chambers has rightly assigned it to Benger (*Tudor Revels*, 19-20).

111. 5. *Survey the state of the... office.* See p. 18, Document III & note to the same.

7. *Fees of cast garmentes.* Cf. pp. 25 l.42 ; 27 ll.11, 14, and 24.

13. *Sir Rooland Hill.* He was a mercer ; Lord Mayor in 1550 (See *Dict. Nat. Biog.* XXVI. 410).

14. *Robotham.* Probably the same person with the Robert Robotham who was Yeoman of the

« Garderobe of Robes » to Edward VI (Patent Books. Auditors. vol. 9 & Patent Rolls. 13 Eliz. p. 6), and who is mentioned in Nichols's *Progresses of Q. Elizabeth*, I. 118.

112. 18. I have omitted here three lines and a half enumerating stuffs that were to be delivered to « Katerin Asteley, cheif gentilwoman of the privy chamber », for the Queen's use.

24. *George Bredyman.* He had been appointed Keeper of the Palace of Westminster by Mary (Lansdowne MSS. 156. f° 96*b*.). He was also Keeper of the Wardrobe at Whitehall (See p. 313). He died before 14 May 1594, for in a privy seal of that date, granted to Edmund Bredyman, his son, he is said to be « defunctus » (Record Office. Privy Seals. May. 36 Eliz.). The same statement is again made in a privy seal of 12 January 1597-8 (Privy Seals. Jan. 40 Eliz.).

113. *1560 & 1561.* Collier (I. 172-3) and Mr E. K. Chambers (*Tudor Revels*, 21) quote a so-called « Revels Book » (Lansdowne MSS. 5. N° 1), including payments from April to September 1561, according to which the expenses of the office during the progress of 1561 alone amounted to the sum of 3209*l.* 10*s.* 8*d.* Now the fact that the expenses should have been so exorbitant is contradicted both by the document printed at page 109 and the one printed at page 113. I think that the book thus taken for one belonging to the office of the Revels, is simply a summary of expenses incurred in the Office of the Works ; with the Revels proper I feel pretty sure it has nothing to do. At any rate, Collier's assertion that the document « includes items for Court amusements » is totally unfounded.

10. *Her highnes pryvie Seale.* Cf. Collection of Payments, p. 419.

114. 27. I have omitted nine lines enumerating stuffs delivered for the Queen's use, and that of one of her gentlewomen.

30. *Iohn Fortescue.* See *Dict. of National Biography*. xx. 45.

115. 12. *The some of* 677^{li} 9^{s} 11^{d} *1/2.* Cf. Collection of Payments, p. 419.

20. *Solutio &c.* See Collection of Payments, p. 419.

116. This document has already been printed by Chalmers in his *Apology for the Believers* &c. p. 354-7; but he has made several mistakes, especially in the reading of the marginal notes which are in Cecil's well-known handwriting. For instance, he reads « Mons. Gonvi », instead of « Mos^{r} Gonnor », and « Edwd Hayedy », instead of « Edw*ardes* tragedy ». Collier has analysed the document in his *History of English Dram. Poetry*, I. 182-3.

25. *Mos^{r} Gonnor.* i.e. Artus de Cossé, Seigneur de Gonnor, who, on February 10, 1563, had been appointed « surintendant des finances ». Interesting details on his visit to the Archbishop of Canterbury are to be found in Parker's *Correspondence* (Parker Society Pub.), pp. 212 & 214. On the occasion of this embassy a Warrant was made out on July 1, 1564, commanding the Treasurer « to paye or cause to be paid vnto our welbeloved Servaunt Lewes Stocket Surveiour of our workes the Some of one hundreth Twenty three powndes xj^{s} vij^{d} to paye for the charges of suche workes as were made against the comminge hither and in the time of the beinge here of Monsr Gonnort of late Ambasador owte of ffraunce » (Record Office. Exchequer of Receipt. Warrants for Issues. Parc. 115).

35. *Cristmas.* According to the *Acts of the Privy Council* (New Ser. VII. 187), the players during the Christmas of 1564 were the Earl of Warwick's servants (2 plays) and the Children of Paul's. The latter played also on Candlemas day (*Acts of the Privy Council*. VII. 204).

36. *Edwardes Tragedy.* « Possibly his *Damon & Pythias* » (Collier, I. 183). This is very likely, as the play was licensed for the press in 1566 (though not printed before 1571). As to Richard Edwards's biography, see *Dict. of National Biography.* xvii. 125. It may be of use to know that a copy of his appointment to the Mastership of the Chapel Children is in the Patent Books (Auditors), vol. 9. Oct. 27, 3 Eliz., and that a commission in his name, authorizing him to take up « well singinge children » for his chapel, is among the Record Office Privy Seals (Dec. 4 Eliz.).

117. 1. *Playes by the Gramar skolle of Westmynster.* From a document in the Westminster archives we learn that the plays were « Heautontimoroumenos Terentii and Miles gloriosus Plauti », and that the plays were rehearsed « befôre Sir Thomas Benger » (*Athenæum* 1903, i.220).

6. *Sir Percyvall Harte.* He had been one of the Sewers of the Chamber to Henry VIII. In May 1531, « iij*l.* vj*s.* viij*d.* » were given by the King for « the Cristenyng ot percyvall hartes Childe » (Nicolas, *Privy Purse Expenses of Henry VIII*, p. 136).

11. *Before them &c.* After the word « &c » is another word in a different handwriting, which seems to be « peram » (?) ; but the ink is very pale, and one cannot be sure.

27. The second endorsement is in Burghley's handwriting.

118. *1565-6 & 1566-7.* This document is in a very bad state having been damaged by fire.

6. *The some of viij^{c} &c.* Cf. page 109 l.29.

8. *ciiij^{xx}. vij^{li}. viij^{s}. xj^{d}. ob.* Cf. page 109 l.13.

ccccxxxviij... Cf. page 109 l.11.

9. *By ord......* Add : « re the sum of xl^{li} ». Cf. page 109 l.33.

14. *And t......* Add : « hree pounds eleven shillings ». Cf. page 118 l.6.

18. *xxvth day of Iune.* Add : « 1567 ». See Collection of Payments, Easter Term, 1567, p. 420.

23. *Pattent.* William Patten, the historian, who was also one of the Tellers of the Exchequer.

119. *From 14 July 1567 &c.* The original is in the Record Office (Warrants for Issues. Parcel 116). I have printed from a contemporary transcript preserved among the Harleian MSS. as more accessible. I have ascertained that the two documents contain no other differences but unimportant variations in the spelling.

13. *Seven playes.* The actors during the Christmas festivities were : the Children of Westminster, Lord Rich's (2 plays), & Paul's (2 plays) ; during the Shrovetide festivities : the Children of Windsor & the Children of the Chapel (See Mr E. K. Chambers's most interesting discoveries in *Modern Language Review*, Oct. 1906, p. 3).

14. *Paynfull Plillgrimage.* Can this be *Everyman*? Everyman's journey is several times compared to a hard pilgrimage in the course of the play, and the phrase « paynful pylgrymage » is even pronounced :

Go thou to euery man
And shewe hym in my name
A pylgrymage he must on hym take
Which he in no wyse may escape

ll. 66-9 (ed. Greg in *Materialien*)

Commaunded I am to go a iournaye
A longe waye harde and daungerous
ll. 242-3

a hye kynges chefe offycer
He bad me go a pylgrymage to my payne
ll. 330-1

So must you or thou scape that *paynful pylgrymage*
l. 565

And though this pylgrymage be neuer so stronge
l. 784

15. *Witte and will.* Of the *Marriage of Wit & Science* (lic. 1569-70) Mr Fleay says (*Biog. Chron.* II. 284) that « in his opinion » it is « the same as *Wit & Will* acted at Court 1567-8 » (Cf. p. 288 where he says that *Wit and Will* is « probably the *Marriage of Wit and Science* »). The identity of the two plays is most probable, for Wit and his companion Will are the two principal *dramatis personæ* in the play which has been transmitted to us.

16. *Prodigallitie.* Collier (I. 187) suggests that this « may possibly have been the original of *The Contention between Liberality and Prodigality* » printed 1602. Mr Fleay, on the other hand, asserts that it is « not *Liberality and Prodigality* of 1602 » (*Biog. Chron.* II. 288).

16. *Orestes. A Newe Enterlude of Vice Conteyninge the Historye of Horestes with the cruell reuengment of his Fathers death, vpon his one naturtll* [sic] *Mother* was printed in 1567. Mr Fleay says it must « surely have been the same play as the *Orestes* played at Court ». But I quite agree with Collier (II. 412), who thinks that such a crude production could « never have been performed before any audience but one of the lowest description ».

17. *The kinge of Scottes.* Mrs C. C. Stopes says in *The Athenæum*, 1900, i. 410 : « This early tragedy may have been based on the death of Darnley in 1566; but it is more likely to have been the story of some earlier king, perhaps even the first rendering of the death of Duncan and the succession of Macbeth ». It is difficult to say; it might also have been based upon a romantic story such as that of Juan de Flores's « History of Aurelio and of Isabel daughter of the king of Scots » a translation of which, printed at Antwerp, had been circulated in England since 1556 (Cf. also St. Reg. Aug. 8. 1586, and 20 Nov. 1588).

18. *Gobbyns.* Collier prints « Dobbyns » (I. 188); but there can be no doubt that the first letter is a « G ». I have read « Gobbyns », but of course it might be « Gobbyus ».

32. *Kerry.* The original Warrant has : « Th Kery ».

120. *From 19 February &c.* I have a pretty strong suspicion that this *Liber* belongs to the Office of the Works, and not to the Revels. I print it all the same, as it affords an idea of the tremendous work that was sometimes necessary to prepare the Queen's Revels. Besides, if this is really a book of the Works, it is interesting to know in what way this office collaborated with the Revels.

14. *Dore.* The margin of the original has been cut off by the binder, and this word being at the end of the line, it is impossible to see now whether it was singular or plural.

15. *Iohn Colbrande.* Probably not the same as the John Colebrande who was appointed «Master Carpenter» on 8 February 7 Eliz. (Patent Books. Auditors. vol. 9. Cf. also page 47 l.6).

17. *Nightes.* In the original this word is always written with the old letter ȝ, which I have represented by a « *gh* » italics.

122. 8. *Nicholas Lyzarde.* He was serjeant-painter to Elizabeth, and had also been in the service of Henry VIII and Edward. In 1556 he had been granted « officium servientis Pictoris » with the fee of ten pounds per annum (Patent Rolls. 2 & 3 Ph. & Mary). He died in 1570. There existed several other Lizards who were painters (See for instance, page 134); they probably belonged to the same family.

123. 13. *Storeyard in Scotlande.* i. e. the old House where the Kings of Scotland were formerly received when they came up to London (Stowe, *Survey*, edit. Thoms, p. 168). In Queen Elizabeth's time it was used as a storeyard for the Office of the Works (See Imprest Certificate Books. Pells. Vol. II. f° 88 *v.*).

124. *Christmas 1568 &c.* A duplicate of this document is among the Warrants for Issues (Parcel 117). See my note to **119**.

125. *Christmas 1569 &c.* A duplicate of this document is among the Warrants for Issues, Parcel 117 (wrongly classed among the Warrants for Issues belonging to the year xiii° Eliz.), and another is in Lansdowne MSS. (12. N° 55). The latter bears the following note : « This warrant was subscribed by the late L. Tresorer of England before it cam to her Ma[tes] signature as apperith by the same, passid at the signet ». Cf. also Egerton MSS. 2723. f° 15*b.*, and State Papers. Dom. Add. vol. xviii. N° 13.

126. *From Shrovetide 1569-70 &c.* A duplicate of this document is among the Warrants for Issues (Parcel 117). I have printed from the Imprest Certificate Books as more accessible.

127. *Revels N° 1.* This book consists of sixteen folio leaves 11 2/8 × 17 inches; f° 1*r.* & *v.*, f° 3*v.*, f° 10*v.*, f° 13*r.* & *v.*, f° 14*r.* & *v.*, f° 15*r.* & *v.*, f° 16*r.* & *v.*, are blank.

129. 20. *Repayrng. Sic* for *Repayring.*

130. 5. *Iohn Drawater.* He was Blagrave's servant (See note to **285**).

27. *William Bowll.* Cf. page 131 l.1 and 139 l.1. When Holte died, Bowll petitioned for the office of Yeoman — and not for the Mastership as Collier has it, I. 230 *n.*—, as may be seen at page 408. From the same petition, we learn that Bowll had « longe tyme served as Deputie for the saide Iohn Holte ». On 27 June 1582, he was appointed Groom of the Tents and Pavilions, succeeding John Browne « defunctus » (Patent Books. Auditors. vol. 10). This office he surrendered in February 1593 to his son Robert (Signet Office. Docquets. Feb. 1593). He was also «one of thordonary yeomen » of the Queen's Chamber (See page 416 l.6 & Privy Seals. Jan. 40 Eliz.). From several entries in the Issue Books (Pells), I infer that Bowll died in the beginning of 1598.

133. 11. *Walter Cock.* The MS. has « W[r] cock ». I have extended into « Walter cock »; but I am conscious that the scribe may have meant « Worcock » or something like.

26. *Fugall.* One Thomas Fugal was chaplain to and executor of the will of Sir Thomas Benger.

134. 14 & 17. *Nicholas Sutton*; *Romyn.* In these two names the letter « n » is surmounted by a small ornament which may be a sign of abbreviation. As at page 231 l.22, the name Sutton occurs again but without any sign, I have taken no notice of the ornament.

137. 15. *John Browne.* He may have been the same person with the John Browne mentioned at page 167 l.22, who himself was probably the Groom of the Tents (Cf. note to **130.** 27). But, of course, in a case of John Brown, it is difficult to be affirmative.

138. 20. *Oving.* Probably a mistake for wooving (See Glossarial Index).

141. 14. *Thoms. Sic* for *Thomas.*

142. 18. *Bryan Dodmer.* At page 413 l.9 he is given as Blagrave's servant (Cf. note to **413.**9). He is mentioned in Sir Thomas Cawerden's will : « Also I gyue and bequeth vnto Bryan Dodmer last sonne vnto Thomas Dodmer gentylman one Annuite or yerly rente of twenty marckes by the yere » (Loseley MSS. clxx). He probably died before 1580, for in that year his name no longer stands on the list of Cawerden's legatees to whom William More paid annuities (See Loseley MSS. vol. ccxliii).

145. 3. *Effiginia.* « Translation from Euripides » (Fleay. *Biog. Chron.* II. 287). I know not on what fact this statement is based.

7. *Narcisses.* The scribe has used the abbreviation sign for « es » or « is ». Hence my reading « Narcisses » ; but he may have meant « Narcissus ». « A play with this name is mentioned by Heywood in his *Apologie* : « Art thou proud our scene presents thee with the fall of Phaeton; Narcissus pining in the love of his shadow, &c » (Cunningham).

11. *Paris and vienna.* «The History of the noble and ryght valyaunt & worthy knyght Parys. and of the fayr Vyen̄e the daulphyns doughter of vyennoys, the whyche suffred many adversytees by cause of their true love or they coude enioye the effect therof of eche other, In the tyme of kynge Charles of Fraunce, the yere of our Lorde MCCLXXI » is one of the translations from the French published by Caxton, and probably was the source of the play. The romance was reprinted in 1869, in the *Roxburghe Library*, ed. W. C. Hazlitt.

1-12. For these six playes, cf. the payments recorded in the *Acts of the Privy Council* (VIII. 61-2 & 71), and the Declared Accounts of the Treasurer of the Chamber in the *Modern Language Review*, Oct. 1906, p. 4.

148. 15. *Summa Totalis &c.* The xxvj^{li} iij^{s} ij^{d} added to the MDlviij^{li} xvij^{s} v^{d} ob of page 144 make the sum of 1585^{li} 7^{d} paid by the Warrant of 7 June 1573 (See Collection of Payments, page 420, & page 152 l.16). I had left London when I saw that Mr E. K. Chambers notices that Collier (I. 197) gives the total cost of the Revels for this period as 3905^{li} 0^{s} 7^{d}, instead of 1585^{li} 0^{s} 7^{d} (*Tudor Revels*, 23). I was very much surprised, for two years ago, when I examined the document quoted by Collier in support of this statement, which is a Brief Declaration preserved among the Lansdowne MSS. (9. N° 57), I did not notice any such difference. And, indeed, Dr Furnivall, who has been kind enough to examine the document for me, writes that the total is M$\overset{c\ xx}{viiij}$v^{li}.vij^{d} ; so that the discrepancy pointed out by Mr E. K. Chambers is only due to Collier's carelessness. Mr E. K. Chambers's supposition that « perhaps this includes expenses charged to the Wardrobe » is inadmissible ; for the Wardrobe expenses, amounting to 3066^{li}. 4^{s}. 10^{d} 1/4, were paid that year by another Warrant, dated 11 July 1573 (See Books of Payments by Royal Warrant. vol. 10. f° 9 *r.*).

22. *Signatures.* It is noticeable that Sir Thomas Benger has not signed this book; but we should not find therein « evidence of some disorganization in the Revels at this time » (Chambers. *Tudor Revels*, 25). I have already said that in June 1572, Benger, «sick in body», was making his will, and this is, I suppose, a sufficient reason to explain why he could not sign the books of the Revels. But, moreover, this is the only complete Revels Book we possess relating to Benger's time, and it may have been Benger's habit never to sign the books as it had been his predecessor's. In all the mass of the Loseley MSS., so far as I can remember, I have found Cawerden's signature but once or twice. Shall we say that Cawerden was an unbusinesslike Master?

To have done with that question of an imaginary disorganization in the Office, it is necessary to refute another of Mr E. K. Chambers's arguments. The author of the *Tudor Revels* observes that a sum of 50 pounds was paid on May 4, 1572, to Lewes Stocket, Surveyor of the Works, for what he had done towards the plays of the previous Christmas; that an imprest of 200 pounds was made to him on the occasion of Montmorency's visit to London. And though Mr E. K. Chambers admits that « these payments may of course be explained as relating to expenses normally incurred in the departments of the officers themselves in connection with the festivities », he goes on to say that « they are not observed in other years, and leave a suspicion that certain deficiencies in the Master of the Revels were being supplied by the energy of his colleagues » (*Tudor Revels*, 25-6). Now this is not exact. Similar payments exist for several years before and after Benger's death; *e. g.* in 1563-6 (Warrants for Issues. Parcel 116); in 1567-70 (Audit Office. Declared Accounts. Bd. 2411. N° 2); in 1575-6 (Imprest Certificate Books. Pells. vol. 2. f° 28 *v.*). I have already quoted (note to **116**. 25) a payment to Lewes Stocket for « charges made against the comminge of Mons[r] Gonnort ». Another extract from one of the documents last mentioned will make it clear that it was part of the task of the Works to help the Revels in the preparation of the Court festivities. The Declared Account for 1567-70 mentions the « newe making and setting vp of Scaffoldes, particions and dores and other necessaries for the Maundayes, Playes, Tragedyes, Maskes, Revelles, and Tryvmphes at diuers and sondry tymes ».

149. *Revels N° 2.* This book consists of nineteen folio leaves besides two others forming the cover. The folios were numbered, but some of the numbers have disappeared most of the corners being worn off; 5, 7, 8, 9, 11, 12, 13, 14, 15, 16 are still visible. The two leaves of the cover were unnumbered; f° 1 *v.*, f° 6 *v.*, f° 12 *v.*, f° 19 *v.*, are blank.

151. 6. *The Warderobe stuf.* The Brief Declaration for that year has : « besides certen parcelles of silke and other stuff receyued out of the greate Wardrobe estimated to the Some of $vij^{c}\,iiij^{xx}$j[li] » (Declared Accounts. Audit Office. Bdle 2045. R. 1).

152. The original from which this Certificate was copied is preserved in the Record Office (Imprest Certificate Books. Pells. vol. 1. f° 42 *v.*).

7. *Magno. Sic* for *magne.*

11. *ccc[li]*. These three hundred pounds, received by Fortescue, were never accounted for satisfactorily; for in another Imprest Certificate (Imprest Certificate Books. Pells. vol. 2. f° 17 *v*),

I find the following hopeless remark made by one of the Auditors : « And whether the saide Mr ffortescue haue accompted for the saide somes or noe I knowe not ».

12. *Per breve.* The Warrant here alluded to is to be found among the Warrants for Issues (Parcel 118).

19. *A Privay Seale dated &c.* The greater part of this Warrant has been quoted in my note to **6.** 23.

153. 7. *Duke Mommerancie Embassador.* « About the 9. of Iune, Francis duke of Memorencie chiefe « Marshall of France gouernor and lieutenant of the Isle of France, generall vnto Charles the « ninth king of Fraunce, and Paul de Foix of the priuie counsell to the sayde king, and Bertrande « de Saligners, lord de la Mothefenalon, knights of the order of Saynt Michaell, ambassadors « for the same king, arryued at Douer, and were brought to London.

« The 15. day being sunday, the said ambassadors repaired to the White hall, where they « were honorably receiued of the Queenes maiestie, with her nobilitie, and there in her graces « chappell, about one of the clocke in the afternoone, the articles of treatie, league, or confedera- « cie & sure friendship (concluded at Blois the 19. of Aprill) as is aforeshewed, betwixt the « Queenes maiestie, and the French King, being read, the same was by her maiestie and his « ambassadors confirmed, to be obserued and kept, without innouation or violation, &c. The rest of « that day with great part of the night following was spent in great triumph, with sumptuous ban- « quets.... The twentie-eyght day of June, the aforenamed Ambassadors departed from London « towards France » (Stowe, *Chron.*, p. 672, ed. 1615). From the Warrant for Issue dated 17 June 1572, we learn the very interesting fact (hitherto unknown, I believe) that these festivities were superintended by Sussex and Leicester : the three hundred pounds directed to be paid to John Fortescue « for dyvers thinges to be provided and done aswell within the office of our said great Warderobe, as also in the office of our Revells » were to be « bestowed according to suche direction as shalbe therein gevin by our cosyns the Erle of Sussex and the Erle of Leycester, or either of them » (Warrants for Issues. Parcel 118).

10. *Warderobe stuf.* See note to **151.** 6.

154. 2-5. In the right margin, the original has the following note, written by one of the Auditors : « Probantur perticule summarum sequencium ».

157. 6. *A Castell for Lady Peace.* We may form an idea of what the masque must have been, from the description of the Devices which were to be shown on a similar occasion before Queen Elizabeth and Mary Queen of Scots (Lansdowne MSS. 5. N° 38, printed in Collier, I. 178). Several of the personages and properties were the same in both masques : Lady Peace, Discord, Argus ; a waggon, castle of peace, collar for Discord &c.

158. 12. *Upholster.* Under this word, the Auditor has written : « Nota pro content. ».

22. *Thomas Greene the Cofer maker.* Evidently the same with the Thomas Grene mentioned in Nichols's *Progresses of Q. Elizabeth*, I. 271, and whom Madden supposes (*Privy Purse Expenses of the Pr. Mary*, p. 235) to have been the son of John Grene, of London, coffer-maker, several times mentioned in the aforesaid expenses. Another William Grene was coffer-maker to Henry VIII (Nicolas, *Privy Purse Expenses of H. VIII*, p. 311).

159. 10. *Allphonse.* Probably Alfonso Ferrabosco, an Italian musician, who received a pension of one hundred pounds in 1567 (Patent Books. Auditors. vol. 9).

160. 9. *Petrucio.* « That is, I presume, Petruccio Ubaldino, a Florentine, who was in the receipt of a yearly fee from Queen Elizabeth of forty marks, as I learn from the accounts of the Treasurer of the Chamber » (Cunningham). He was an illuminator on vellum and a scholar. See *Dict. of Nat. Biogr.* lviii. 1 ; cf. also page 301 l.10 of this volume.

22. In the left margin, the Auditor has written : « Nota pro [?] Row ».

162. 2. *Black ffryars brydge.* An account of the charges « towardes the ereccion and buyldynge..... of twoo bridges thone at the blackfreers and thother at the Temple » (18 June 4 Edward VI), is in the Record Office, among the Declared Accounts (Pipe Office. R. 3328).

163. 19. In the left margin, the Auditor has written : « nota pro billa uide ».

20. In the left margin, the Auditor has added : « Bothier & Rewardes ».

165. 1. *William Hunnys.* « This is not the poet, I believe, but another William Hunnys, who was supervizor and Keper of the greate gardens and orchardes at Greenwich » (Cunningham). But, indeed, the poet and the Keeper of the gardens were one and the same person : the terms of the patent appointing Hunnys to the latter post make it clear beyond all doubt (Patent Books. Auditors. vol. 9. 20 June 4 Eliz.).

13. *Skotland.* See note to **123.** 13.

23. *Saint Iones.* Cunningham has read « Saint James » ; of course, there can be no doubt about the word.

172. 17. *Clement.* (*Sic*). Cf. page 195 l.12 ; 215 l.9 & 231 l.21.

173. 17. *Yomen. (Sic).*

174. 15. *Children of Eaten.* According to the Declared Accounts of the Treasurer of the Chamber, the Children of Eton played on Twelfth day. The payee on that occasion was William Elderton (See *Modern Lang. Review*, Oct. 1906, p. 5).

20. *Fardngales. Sic* for *fardingales.*

22. *Munkesters playe.* Richard Munkester or Mulcaster was Master of the Merchant Taylors' School. His Children acted on Shrove Tuesday (*Mod. Lang. Review*, Oct. 1906, p. 5).

24. *Children of Wynsor.* They acted on New Year's day (*Mod. Lang. Review*, Oct. 1906, p. 5).

175. 4. *Cariclia.* Theagenes is mentioned at line 13. The play was probably drawn from Heliodorus.

5. *The Duttons playe.* From the Declared Accounts of the Treasurer of the Chamber (*Mod. Lang. Review*, Oct. 1906, p. 5), it appears that in that year (1572), Lawrence Dutton was in the Earl of Lincoln's company. In the preceding year, « Laurence Dutton and his felowes » were « servauntes to Sir Robert Lane » (*Acts of the Privy Council.* N. S. VIII. 61).

30. *Maske of Ianvs.* Was this the masque shown on New Year's day (See page 180 l.29) ?

34. *Arnolde the paynter.* Walpole, quoting Meres, gives a list of famous English artists amongst whom is Arnolde (*Anecdotes of Painting*, p. 102, ed. 1871).

35. *Picture of Andromadas.* I think it would be a somewhat hasty inference to suppose that a play on the subject of Perseus and Andromeda was performed in that year. This picture of Andromeda may have been a mere stage property, or may as well have been used for ornamental

purposes. Besides, it should not be forgotten that a *Perseus and Andromeda* was played in the ensuing year, and that it is not likely that the Master should have accepted plays on the same subject in two consecutive years, one of the aims of the Revels being certainly to secure as much variety as possible (See page 14 ll.34-6).

176. 2. *Duttons play.* See note to **175.** 5.

4. *Playe of fortune.* Mr Fleay suggests (*Biographical Chronicle*, II. 289) that this is « the *Play of Fortune to know each one their conditions*, &c., entered S. R. 1566-7, revived ». It may be.

177. 7. *Fysshers.* The scribe had written first « Marryners »; he then crossed out the word, and interlineated « ffysshers ».

23. *Iohn Owgle.* The scribe had written « William Owgle » ; « William » was afterwards altered to « Iohn ».

178. 2. The Auditor wrote in the left margin « nota pro quantitate », and, afterwards, crossed out these words.

6. The Auditor has written in the left margin : « nota ut supra ».

8. The Auditor has written in the left margin : « nota pro quantitate ».

12. The Auditor has written in the left margin : « nota ut supra ».

14. *xxij^d ob.* After this sum, the MS. has : « Buttons & Tassells at ij^s the oz. — lxxv^s vj^d » which line has been crossed out.

18. *A greate hanging lock with a keye to it.* This must have been a property — it was supplied by the silk-weaver -- with some emblematical meaning, such as the lock described in the « Devices » to be exhibited before Mary Queen of Scots : « Prudentia shall delyver a locke whereuppon shalbe wrytten *In Eternum.* Then Temperantia shall likewise delyver unto Argus a key whose name shalbe *Nunquam*, signifyinge that when False Report and Discorde are committed to the pryson of Extreme Oblyvion, and locked there everlastinglie, he should put in the key to lett them out *Nunquam* » (Collier. I. 179). It may have been used in the Masque of Janus (Cf. page 175 l.12).

21. *Wylliam Lyzarde.* This name has been written over another, the last letters of which were « arne ». The other letters are not legible.

27. *Assedew.* Cunningham, mistaking the long « s » for an « f », has printed « A Fedew ».

179. 24. The Auditor has written in the left margin : « nota pro quantitate ».

33. This line has been added in different ink.

180. 4. *Farrantes playe.* Farrant was Master of the Children of Windsor (Cf. note to **174.** 24).

15. *The second play of my Lord of Leicesters men.* According to the payments of the Treasurer of the Chamber (*Mod. Lang. Review,* Oct. 1906, p. 5), Leicester's men acted three plays during the Christmas festivities.

39. *Eldertons playe.* i. e. the play acted by the Children of Eton (Cf. note to **174.** 15).

182. 1. *Progresse into Kent.* See Holinshed, iii. 1493. col. 2.

184. 3. *A nother. Sic* for *Another.*

185. 9. *Saving.*? Sawing.

186. 1. *New presses.* Cf. page 411 l.5. The presses remained long in that decayed state; for in 1575, 1578, 1579, 1580, the Clerk still complains of the want of convenient presses (See pp. 254 l.9;

285 l.10; 312 l.8; 329 l.13). In 1581-2, cviij[s] vj[d] were spent in reparations of the Office (See Table II. l. 67), and in April 1581, the allusion to the presses disappears from the Books, never to occur again (See page 341), from which fact we may infer that the presses had at last been mended. (Cf. also a Warrant for payment to the Officers of the Works, dated 29 May 22 Eliz. in Warrants for Issues, Parcel 122).

9. *Not allowid &c.* Two copies of the Declared Account for that year are preserved in the Record Office (Audit Office. Bdle 2045. R. I & II). In both the fifty pounds have been deducted from the « Summa totalis ».

10. *Said presseis.* Cunningham has printed « same »; but there can be no doubt about the « said ».

187. I have extracted from this document only what concerns the Revels. Another document enumerating the same quantities of stuffs, with their prices, is among the Lansdowne MSS. 9 (N° 59). It is endorsed : « Touching S[r] Thomas Benger K: late m[r] of the maskes, Revelles, & Tryvmphes of certen Stuffe Receaved owte of the greate warderobe. — A declaracion of Stuffe delyuerd furth of the great warderobe vnto S[r] Thomas Benger knight for thofice of Revells ».

This document Collier has hopelessly misdescribed. He says (I. 198) that it is written « in the French language », whilst it is in Latin. He styles Sir Thomas Benger « Maitre de lez Maskes, Revelles et Triumphes » whilst the MS. has : « M*agist*ro de lez Maskes &c ». He gives the value of the stuffs as amounting to 3757*l.* 8*s*, whilst the total is 1757*l.* 8*s.* 1 1/2. Besides, he says the account « is dated 12th July 1572 »; but this date is that of the Warrant, and not that of the document which was evidently a certificate made after Benger's death (See the « late master » of the endorsement), probably on the occasion of the Inventory which was taken when Blagrave entered « into the execucon of the Masters office ». Mr E. K. Chambers, who in the last three points follows Collier, adds (*Tudor Revels*, p. 26) that the stuffs were furnished by Fortescue « presumably in part for the reception of Montmorency and in part for the revels of the previous Christmas ». This is impossible, since the Warrant uses the words « We will and commaunde that Immediatlie vppon the sighte herof ye deliuer &c. », which words could hardly have applied to stufis employed at least one month earlier.

189. *Revels N° 3.* This book at first consisted of 22 folio leaves; it now wants ff. 1, 2 and 3; the second of the folios left is numbered 5 and the last 22. The pagination of ff. 7, 8, 13, 15 has disappeared. The book has suffered from damp, and ff. 4, 21 and 22 are loose; f° 5*v.*, f° 6*r.* & *v.*, f° 8*v.*, f° 13*v.*, f° 17*v.* & f° 18*v.* are blank. One of the missing pages must have been the title-page.

191. Cunningham prints here a whole page which does not now exist in the Book. I do not think that we should suspect Cunningham's honesty : the book is in a very bad state, and a folio or more may very well have disappeared since the publication of his *Extracts from the Accounts of the Revels.* Besides, all the facts stated in the said page are supported by other passages in the book (see, for instance, in my Collection of Payments, the privy seal mentioned at the end of the passage), and none of them is interesting enough to have tempted a man into a forgery. I give the page as it is printed in Cunningham :

ffrom the Last of Oct. 1573, xv^{to} untill the ffyrst of March, 1573 xvj^{to}

The Booke of all the Charges growen within Thoffice of her Maties Revells aforesaide within the same Tyme being iiij Monethes including Christmas, Twelftyde Candellmas & Shrovetyde. During all which tyme Thomas Blagrave esquier, served therin as Master, according to her Ma^{tes} pleasure signefyed by the right honorable L. Chamberlaine. Towardes thexecution wherof the saide Blagrave herein also Chargeth him self with all suche her Ma^{tes} Monye as to the use of the same Office hath cum to his handes.

videlicet

Monye Received by the saide Blagrave owte of her Ma^{tes} Exchequer at the handes of Tayler one of the Tellers there by vertue of a prive seale dated the xxiijth of December in the saide xvjth yeare of her Ma^{tes} Reaigne. — cc^{li}.

14. *Inventory*. This inventory I have tried — but in vain — to discover.

19. *The entraunce of the saide Blagrave into the execucon of the Masters office*. See note to **68.** 1

193. 12. *Predor:*. In the MS. the name Predor is followed by a colon; but as it was difficult to decide what was the value given to this sign of abbreviation, I have thought it best to let the sign stand. Perhaps the scribe meant « Predorus ».

15. *Alkmeon*. « Euripides restored » (Fleay, *Biog. Chronicle*, II. 287); — a somewhat bold assertion.

17. *Mamillia*. Was this a play on the same subject as Greene's novel?

25. *Quintus ffabius*. Cunningham prints « Quint ffabi » ; the sign of abbreviation for « us » is perfectly visible.

195. 16. *Iohn Streter*. He may have been the father or the grandfather of the Robert Streater who was appointed serjeant-painter at the Restoration, and who was, as we know, the son of a painter. See Walpole, *Anecdotes of Painting*, p. 221, ed. 1871.

196. 9. *Brokson*. In the MS., this name is interlineated.

199. 5. *Mask of Wyldemen*. These probably were the torchbearers to the Masque of Foresters. Cf. the « attyred in Mosse & Ivye » of page 193 l.34.

29. *Ottett*. Can this be a mistake for « marquesotted » (cf. page 218 l.28)?

201. 1. *Disbrced*. *Sic* for *disburced*.

202. 1. *Pecelles*. *Sic* for *Percelles*.

203. 24. *Foormes ij & stooles*. Probably for the « senat howse » mentioned at line 12.

204. 18. *By the speciall appointment of Mr Iohn Forteskue*. This entry seems to imply that, though Blagrave had entered « into the execucon of the Masters office », Fortescue still had the oversight of the Office as in the preceding year.

22. *Suyng owte the privie seale*. The Warrant is dated 23 December 1573 (See Collection of Payments, page 420).

206. 5. *Munkesters Children*. i. e. the Merchant Taylors'.

21. *Moorecroft*. (*Sic*). But this is a mistake for Moorecrost. Cf. page 214 l.12 & 230 l.21.

211. 18. *Chages*. *Sic* for *Charges*.

213. 13. *Percius & Anthomiris*. Malone conjectured that « Anthomiris » was a blunder of the man who made out the accounts for « Andromeda ». This is most probable.

16. *Torchebearers.* The scribe had written first « Hawncee » ; he afterwards crossed the word out, and wrote over it « Torchebearers ».

216. 15. *A Whissell.* No doubt for the ship-master in the masque of Warriors (cf. page 213 l.15).

223. *Revels Nº 4.* This book consists of sixteen folio leaves, unnumbered ; fº 1*r.* & *v.*, fº 4*v.*, fº 14*v.*, fº 15*r.* & *v.* and fº 16*r.* are blank.

225. 4. *Blagrave esquier being appoynted Master of the same.* See note to **68.** 1 & cf. page 191 l.20.

12. *Progresse to Reading.* The Queen was at Reading in July 1574. Cf. page 227 l.35.

29. In the right margin, the Auditor has written : « kno the begynninge & thendinge of the said dayes ».

227. 6. *Mistris Dane &c.* Cf. page 221 l.11.

37. *Shepherdes hookes &c.* These « sheperdes hookes », together with the « Lamskynnes for Shepperds, Horstayles for the wylde mannes garment, arrowes for Nymphes, shepperdes staves, garlandes, a syth for Saturn », evidently were properties provided for a pastoral (either a masque or a play). This is very important, especially if we remember that Tasso's *Aminta* was performed at Ferrara on July 31, 1573, and that the pastoral before the Queen was shown by Italian players.

228. 23. In the left margin, the Auditor has written : « The quantitie to be expressed ».

27. In the left margin, the Auditor has written : « to expresse the cause ».

31. In the left margin, the Auditor has written : « ut supra ».

34. *Italian prayers. Sic* for *Italian players.*

230. 30. *For clatterbooke.* These words are interlineated in the MS.

236. 3. The Auditor has written in the right margin : « nota pro quantitate ».

7. *Orengeculler. (Sic).*

9 & 13. The Auditor has written in the right margin : « ut supra ».

25. *The horses.* i. e. the hobby horses mentioned at page 237 l.24.

29. In the right margin, the Auditor has written : « kno whither and for what purpose ».

31. In the right margin, the Auditor has written : « nota ut supra ».

32. In the right margin, the Auditor has written : « to whome ».

33. In the right margin, the Auditor has written : « to expresse the quantite ».

238. 7. *Farrantes playe.* According to the Accounts of the Treasurer of the Chamber (in Cunningham, xxxi), the Children of Windsor performed on Twelfth Night.

11. *Lord Chamberlayne.* Thomas Radcliffe, Earl of Sussex, became Lord Chamberlain in July 1572.

12. *Mr Knevett.* Thomas Knyvet has been made famous by his quarrel with the Earl of Oxford. He was a Gentleman of the Privy Chamber, and became later on Keeper of the Store of Westminster Palace (Declared Accounts. Audit Office. Bdle 2045. R. 6), and also of the Store at Whitehall (See Table II. l.97).

21. *The History of Phedrastus & Phigon and Lucia together &c.* Collier (I. 226) thinks that the Chamberlain's servants performed two plays : *The History of Phedrastus* and *Phigon and Lucia.* Mr Fleay, if I understand him rightly, sees three plays in the same (*Biog. Chron.* II. 290). But it seems to me that this may just as well be the title of one single play. For the meaning of the

sentence is, not that two or three plays were shown together, but that « the charges and expenses together amounteth... », a phrase often met with in the accounts, and synonymous with « in all amounteth ».

Of the so-called play *Phigon & Lucia*, Collier says : « This is most likely the same piece that in the Account of the Revels of the preceding year, we have seen named *P[r]edor and Lucia :* perhaps neither was the correct title ». It is much more probable that the two plays were different; for if *Phigon and Lucia* had been played in the preceding year it certainly would not have been submitted again to perusal.

The Books of the Treasurer of the Chamber contain no payment to the Chamberlain's company; possibly they did not perform before the Queen, for we should not forget that the mention in the Accounts concerns a rehearsal and not a performance.

28. *Leicesters menne*. The Books of the Treasurer of the Chamber contain two payments to the Earl of Leicester's players, for two plays performed on St Stephen's day and New Year's day (Cunningham, xxx).

42-7. *Lord Clyntons players*. From the Books of the Treasurer of the Chamber we gather that Lord Clinton's players performed on St John's day and on the Sunday being the second of January (Cunningham, xxx). One of their three plays must therefore have been refused.

44. *Pretestus*. This word has been added in a slightly different handwriting; the ink is the same.

46. *The*. *Sic* for *they*, i. e. Lord Clinton's players.

239. 3. *My Lord of Lesters boyes*. To be distinguished from « My Lord of Leicester's men ». In the Books of the Treasurer of the Chamber, both companies are called « Leicesters players » (See note to **238**. 28).

20. In the right margin, the Auditor has written : « antea ut supputatum ».

25. *Leycesters mennes playe*. From the date of this entry, it is clear that Leicester's *men* played on January 1; therefore the *boys* played on St Stephen's day (See note to **238**. 28).

29. *Vlrick Netsley*. « In consideration of the great knowledge and skill which we have founde to be in our welbeloved Subiectes Vlrick Nestley and Rowlande Behyne straungers borne in the Cunninge makinge of certen new devised Ordinaunce of Iron &c., we doe geve and graunte a certen Pention of three shillinges by the daye» (Patent Books. Auditors. vol. 10. 8 Aug. 29 Eliz.).

241. 26. *Sabastian*. i. e. Sebastian Westcott, Master of the Children of Paul's. From the Accounts of the Treasurer of the Chamber, it appears that they played on Candlemas day (Cunningham, xxxi).

From the following passage in Spenser, we may form an idea of what Vanity's dress must have been like :

> The first was Fansy, like a lovely Boy
> Of rare aspect, and beauty without peare;
> . . . .
> His garment nether was of silke nor say,
> But paynted plumes in goodly order dight,
> Like as the sunburnt Indians do aray
> Their tawney bodies in their proudest plight:
> As those same plumes so seemd he vaine and light.
>
> Masque of Cupid. F. Q. III. C. 12.

34. *Mr Hunyes his playe.* The Books of the Treasurer of the Chamber contain a payment to « Hunys Master of the Children of her Maiesties Chapple for a playe upon Shrovesondaye » (Cunningham, xxxi).

242. 18. In the left margin, the Auditor has written : « to know the parties name ».

244. 11. *The Duttons.* We have seen (note to **175.** 5) that at Christmas 1572, the Duttons were in Edward Clinton, Earl of Lincoln's company. In December 1575, they had passed into the service of the Earl of Warwick (*Mod. Lang. Review*, Oct. 1906, p. 5). But when they played in the Christmas of 1574, they must needs have been still among the Lord Clinton's servants, for in that year the Earl of Warwick's played only during the ensuing Shrovetide (Cunningham, xxx-i).

20. *The playe on Twelfe Nighte.* i. e. the play by the Children of Windsor. Cf. p. 238 l.7 and note.

35. *Hornes... Collers... Leashes... dogghookes.* These properties must have been used in a hunting scene. Cf. a similar scene in *Narcissus*, played also by the Children of the Chapel (p. 141 l.17).

246. 8. *Mirrors.* Cf. p. 238 l.34.

247. 16. *Dodmer.... petition.* Cf. p. 413 l. 6, and note to **412.** 1.

24. *Coserving. Sic* for *Conserving.*

29. *Srovetyde. Sic* for *Shrovetyde.*

248. Under the «Summa Totalis», the Auditor has written the following note : «Memorandum the marcers percelles was mystakyn in the nombre of Elles for xxx was entred for xxxix wheorpon the booke was corrected and afterwardes the Bill was shewed wherin it appered it should haue bene xxxix and so reduced as it was at the first ». This explains several corrections made in the total sum. The clerk wrote first ccclxviij^{li} iij^{s} x^{d} for the Emptions, which sum was afterwards crossed out, and ccclxv^{li} xviij^{s} x^{d} substituted : this latter sum was in its turn scored through, and the first written again. It was the same with the general total, which was first corrected into Dclxvj^{li} xvij^{s} iiij^{d}, then this sum was crossed out, and the word « stet » written over the first sum.

250. 5. *William Dodington.* The Letters Patent appointing him Auditor of the Imprest are transcribed in the Patent Books (Auditors), vol. 9. 28 March 12 Eliz.

251. *Revels N° 5.* This book consists of 14 folio leaves, besides a title-page. The back of the title page is blank and so are f° 13*v*. & f° 14*r*.

255. 9. *Buggin.* Note here and at some of the following pages that Buggyn signs his name with an « i » instead of a « y ».

256. 15. *Toolie.* Query a play on Tully, something like Greene's novel, *Ciceronis Amor* ?

17. *The historie of the Collyer.* The hero of this play may have been the Collier of Croydon, a favourite character in the older drama.

19. *Historie of Error.* Query a play from Plautus' *Menæchmi* ?

22. *Windsore and the Chappell.* Farrant was at that time acting as a kind of substitute to Hunnis, and this probably explains why we find the two companies united on that occasion.

23. *Cenofalles.* i. e. Cenocephali (See Pliny, and Maundeville, ch. xxi. p. 97, ed. Warner).

257. 26. *Robert Peake.* Was this the Robert Peake who was to be serjeant-painter to James I and who has been extolled by Peacham ?

258. 10. *Thomas Stronge.* He was Blagrave's servant (See note to **258**).

266. 15. *Their plaie was deferred vntill the Sundaie folowing.* This evidently applies to Leicester's men, and not to Warwick's men who played on St Stephen's day (cf. p. 256 l.17 & l.13). I suppose that the scribe forgot the preceding entry concerning Warwick's men (ll. 11-3) and that, on becoming aware of his omission, he inserted the said entry after the one he had just been writing, without noticing that he was thus spoiling the sense of the following entry.

22. *That shold have served in the Maske.* The Masque was deferred till the following Shrove Tuesday (See p. 270 l.20).

267. 8. *About the warrant &c.* The Warrant is dated 24 December 1576 (See Collection of Payments, p. 420).

269. 1. *The Duttons plaie.* i. e. *The Paynters Daughter.* The Duttons had been in the Earl of Warwick's company since Christmas 1575 at the latest (See *Mod. Lang. Review*, Oct. 1906, p. 5).

270. 16. *Irisshe Knyght.* One Mariano d'Irlanda (together with his father the King of Ireland) plays a part in chaps. 48-52 of the « Historia del Nobile & Valoroso Cavaliero Felice Magno ». He may have been the hero of the play.

18. *Historye of Titus & Gisippus.* See Boccacio, *Decam.*, Giorn. Decima, Nov. viii. The story had already been told by Sir Thomas Elyot in Bk. II, ch. 12, of his *Governour.* In 1562, Edwarde Lewicke brought out a translation in verse, the title of which was : « The most wonderful and pleasaunt History of Titus and Gisippus, whereby is fully declared the figure of perfect frendshyp drawen into English metre by Edwarde Lewicke. Anno 1562 ». Wynkyn de Worde had also printed another metrical version entitled « The History of Tytus and Gesyppus, translated out of Latyn into englyshe by Willyam Walter ». A play founded on this tale is stated by Bale to have existed amongst those seen by him in the library of their author, Ralph Radcliffe (Warton, III. 308).

22. *Prepared for Twelf Night.* Cf. p. 266 l.22; 267 l.34; 268 ll.20-5.

275. 2. [ ]es. This part of the margin is torn off. The missing word is probably « Nayles ».

17. *Senatours Cappes &c.* for the play of *Titus and Gisippus.* Cf. p. 276 l.19.

24. *Solytarye Knyght.* The title is written in a different hand.

276. 1. *Collyer.* This name was added in a different hand.

277. 12. *The play of Cutwell.* Collier (I.228) seems to think this is another play besides the nine already mentioned for that year (See pp. 256 & 270). Mr Fleay (*Biog. Chron.* II. 289) identifies it with the *Irish Knight.* It is difficult to decide. I incline, however, towards Collier's opinion, as the entry mentions the carriage of the well to St John's, and this seems to point to a rehearsal of a play which was finally not accepted.

26. The total is missing.

281. *Revels N° 6.* This book consists of seventeen folio leaves unnumbered, besides a title-page. Title page *v.*, f° 1*v.*, f° 10*v.*, f° 16*r.* & *v.*, f° 17*r.* & *v.* are blank.

285. This page has been abundantly annotated by the Auditor :

l. 14, after Clatterbooke, he has added « no mans man ».
l. 15, » Wrighte, » « Mr fyshe his man ».
l. 16, » Tyldesley, » « Mr Buggens man ».

l. 17, after Stronge, he has added « Mr Blagraves man ».
l. 18, » Drawater, » « Mr Blagraves man ».
l. 19, » Davyes, » « no mans man ».
l. 20, » Dawncey, » « the porter ».

l. 39, under the total, the Auditor has written : « in computo de anno proximo precedente xxj^{li} $xiiij^{s}$ $iiij^{d}$ ».

286. 16. *St Johns daie.* The Declared Accounts of the Treasurer of the Chamber, as printed by Mr E. K. Chambers in *Modern Lang. Review*, Oct. 1906, p. 7, do not record any play on St John's day, but, on the contrary, give two plays on Twelfth day, the one by the Lord Chamberlain's servants, and the other by the Children of the Chapel. I think that in this case the Account Book is right; firstly, because the fact that two companies performed on the same night is in itself suspicious; secondly, because the date of St John's day for a performance of the Children of the Chapel is supported by the following entry : « The 27th of December...... The same daie for cariage of the stuffe that served the plaie for the children of the chappell to the courte and back agayne » (p. 298 l.21-4).

22. *Marryage of Mynde and Measure.* Mr Fleay suggests at p. 287 (Vol. II) of his *Bibliographical Chronicle*, that this may be « a mistake for *The Marriage of Wit and Wisdom* », and at page 294, his supposition acquiring strength, he says that the two plays « were probably identical ». But is it not more natural to admit that we have here another specimen of « marriage » moralities, which seem to have been favourites with the public?

23. *Sondaie next after Newe yeares daie.* In the Declared Accounts of the Treasurer of the Chamber (*Mod. Lang. Review*, Oct. 1906, p. 7), the Paul's boys are given as performing on January 1. And this is no doubt the true date, since we see at page 298 l.30, that a « frame for master Sabastian » was carried to the Court on January 1. The mistake can be explained easily : the scribe was probably transcribing from a rough copy, and his eye was attracted by the « sondaie next after Newe yeares daie » of line 26, a kind of error well known to paleographers.

28. *Rape of the second Helene.* This was probably founded on an episode of *Florisel de Niquea* by D. Feliciano de Silva. When Florisel reached Apolonia, he found his mistress, whose name was Helena, on the point of marrying the prince of Gaul. Florisel carried off the bride. In the novel, the hero's mistress is termed the « second Helen » (Cf. Dunlop, *Hist. of Fiction*, I. 371).

29. *Twelf daie &c.* The actors were the Lord Chamberlain's servants (See p. 299 l.4-5, and *Modern Lang. Review*, Oct. 1906, p. 7).

287. 4. *The ffrench Imbassadour.* The resident French Ambassador was then M. de Mauvissière. But I think the person here meant was Simier, Alençon's envoy, who arrived early in January to negotiate his master's marriage with Queen Elizabeth.

26. *In her maiesties presence.* It is very difficult to say whether the MS. has « presence » or « absence », for these two words have been written the one over the other. I have finally decided to consider « presence » as the last word written by the scribe, for whilst the letters « ab » of « absence » are in the ordinary handwriting, the « p » with the usual sign of abbreviation for « pre » is rather clumsy, and therefore looks like a correction. Cunningham read « absence ».

288. 16-7. *xxx^{li} iiij^{s} viij^{d}.* Under this sum, the Auditor has written : « in computo de anno proximo precedente nisi xxj^{li} ix^{s} ».

289. 18-20. *xix^{li}.* Under this sum, the Auditor has written : « in computo precedente nisi xviij^{li} ».

23. *Twelftyde.* The scribe had written first « Shrovetyde », but then corrected it into « Twelftyde ».

290. 17. In the right margin, the Auditor has written : « Summa — xxxvij^{li} xvj^{s} in computo precedente nisi xiij^{li} viij^{s} verte ».

293. 34. In the right margin, the Auditor has written : « Summa — xviij^{li} x^{s} vj^{d} in computo precedente nisi xiij^{s} x^{d} ».

294. 34. In the right margin, the Auditor has written under the total : « Summa — xiij^{li} iiij^{s} ij^{d} in computo precedente nisi vij^{li} iiij^{s} xj^{d} ».

38. In the right margin, the Auditor has written under the total : « in computo precedente xliiij^{s} xj^{d} ».

40. In the left margin, the Auditor has written : « nota ».

296. 19. *Doble Maske.* i. e. the Masque of Amazons and Knights. See page 286.

20. In the left margin, the Auditor has written : « nota ».

22. In the right margin, the Auditor has written : « Summa — vj^{li} ij^{s} j^{d} in computo precedente viij^{li} xij^{s} ».

298. 25. *For his boate hier.* After « hier » the scribe wrote : « with others from Powles wharfe », and afterwards crossed these last words out.

29. *At Mr Brydemans.* i. e. at the Wardrobe at Whitehall. See pp. 298 l.10; 299 l.8; 301 l.1.

299. 6. In the right margin, under the total, the Auditor has written : « in computo precedente x^{li} x^{s} vj^{d} ».

14. *Mastes.* Probably a mistake for « Maskes ». Cf. same page, l.16.

300. 8. In the right margin, the Auditor has written : « Summa — cxj^{s} iij^{d} in computo precedente nisi lxiij^{s} viij^{d} ».

17. In the right margin, under the total, the Auditor has written : « in computo precedente viij^{li} xix^{s} x^{d} ».

27. *Mr Nichasius.* i. e. Nicasius Yetsweirt, one of the Clerks of the Signet (See Warrants for Issues. Parcel 112, and Privy Seal Books. Auditors. vol 1^{b} f° 232 *v.*). He was sometime secretary for the French tongue to Queen Elizabeth, and was buried with Mary his wife (daughter to James Bowser) in the church of Sunbury (See Norden, *Spec. Britanniæ*, p. 40, ed. 1723). He is mentioned in the Loseley MSS. vol. 243, p. 92.

301. 25. *Lizardes Lizardes. (Sic).*

310. 7. In the right margin, and over the total, the Auditor has written « 10^{d} ».

17. *Lettres patentes dated the of Iulie.* See page 55.

21. *vj^{li} xiij^{s} iiij^{d}.* Under this sum, the Auditor has written : « Respectuatur ».

24. *Driven to hire an other.* In the Brief Declaration corresponding to this book (Lansdowne MSS. 27. N° 86), I find : « Item Edmond Tylney esquier now Master of the said Office demaundeth to be allowed for the rent [of] a howse for himself accordinge vnto the Quenes maies-

ties graunte made vnto him for that thowse belonginge vnto his Office is otherwise appoynted (as he affirmeth) and for that I fynd no precedent for the like allowaunce I refarre the same vnto your honors consideracions ».

26. *Vntill Mydsomer.* This allowance was continued much longer, for in 1582, Tyllney was paid « house rent » for « iij^{e} yeares di. during which tyme the Master of Thoffice had no house assigned him » (See Table II. l. 69).

31. In the right margin, under the total, the Auditor has written : « in computo precedente viij^{li} x^{s} ».

312. 16. *Sherborne.* This name has been added in a different handwriting.

35. *Summa totalis.* The Brief Declaration corresponding to this book is preserved among the Lansdowne MSS. (27. N° 86) ; it amounts to cccxlj^{li} xj^{s} x^{d} (the vj^{li} xiij^{s} iiij^{d} for Tyllney's house rent being deducted since that sum had not yet been approved of by the Treasurer).

Collier (I. 231) gives the amount of this Declaration as 444 *l.* 9 *s.* 1 1/2 *d.*, and wonders at the difference between the Declaration and the Account Book : « We can only account », he says, « for the difference by supposing that the « Brief Declaration » included items of charge not embraced by the account in the office of the Auditors of the Imprest ». The truth is, that Collier has mistaken the total of the sums « receued out of the Receipte of Thexchequier » since the making out of the « previe Seale dated xxx° Decembris anno xxj° » till the date of the Declaration (cf. Collection of Payments, p. 420, M. T. 1578), which, as usual, are summed up at the end of the Declared Account.

313. 4. *Duringe the tyme of this declaracion.* i. e. from 14 February 1577-8 to 1 November 1579.

7-13. *Crymsyn cloth &c.* A receipt of the stuff delivered by Bredyman, signed by Edwarde Buggyn and Walter Fyshe, and countersigned by Sussex, is preserved among the MSS. of the Rev. Francis Hopkinson (See Historical MSS. Commission, 3rd Report. Appendix, p. 263). It does not contain any new fact or item. Cf. the Correspondence published at page 314 of this volume.

314. 7. *Cloth of Gold &c.* Cf. p. 313 l.7-13.

18. *Yetsweirt.* See note to **300.** 27.

19 &c. This letter, as appears from the preceding document, is by the Lord Chamberlain, the Earl of Sussex, and is in his own handwriting, as I have ascertained by a comparison with another autograph letter of his in the Lansdowne MSS. 846. Somebody has interlined a transcript of the document, which, in my opinion, does not much credit to the paleographical acquirements of the decipherer, whoever he may have been. It should be said, however, that the Lord Chamberlain's handwriting is of the worst kind of XVIth Century cursive writing, and that I do not pretend that my own copy is free from errors.

317. *Revels N° 7.* This book consists of seven folio leaves besides a title-page. The folios are numbered as follows : f° 1*r.* = 1 ; f° 1*v.* = 2 ; f° 2*r.* = 3 ; f° 2*v.* = 4 ; f° 3*r.* = 5 ; f° 3*v.* = 6 &c. ; f° 7*v.* is blank and unnumbered.

320. 25. *Alucius.* This title has been added in a different handwriting.

321. 1. *Cipio Africanus.* Written in a different hand.

18. *Soldan.* The final « n » is surmounted by a stroke of the pen which I have considered as a flourish ; but it may be a sign of abbreviation.

19. *Earle of Derby.* Henry Stanley succeeded to the title in 1572, being fourth Earl of the name.

32. *William Tildeslay.* Buggin's servant. See note to **285**.

322. Between each kind of workmen there is a total indicated according to the Exchequer habit of reckoning with counters (in the MS. represented by dots) ; I have taken no notice of these dots in my transcript.

325. 1. After the word « courte », and over xvij[s] vj[d], the MS. has : « of sondry » ; but as these two words have been scored through, I have not transcribed them, though they are necessary to the sense : it is in fact difficult to understand why the scribe crossed them out.

329. 13. *Requier.* A mistake for « requisite ». Cf. p. 254 l.10 ; 285 l.10 &c.

330. 5. *Suynge on.* The usual phrase is to « sue out » ; perhaps I ought to have printed « ou[t] ».

15. *To viewe and devide the Store &c.* In the Declared Account for 1577/8-1579 (Lansdowne MSS. 27. N° 86), I find : « It is to be remembered (for asmoche as a master of the said Office of the Revelles is newly appoynted by her Maiesties lettres patentes) that not onely there be a perfecte remayne taken in the foresaid Office, for the full chardginge of Theofficers of the same hencefurth, but also a Reere Accompte to be made by Theofficers there of the ymployment of the Stuff bought and delyuered into the foresaid Office, from the death of Sir Thomas Benger knight hitherunto, and so to be contynewed yerelie ».

331. 17 & 18. Between these two lines had been written the following item : « ffor the Ingrossinge of three payre of Indented Inventoryes — xl[s] » ; then this line was crossed out and written a little lower down (See l. 32).

19. *Fewer. Sic* for *fewel.*

33. *Summa totalis &c.* Note that this total is not the same as the one given at p. 332 l.15. I cannot account for the difference.

332. All the totals in this page have been corrected, the original ones not being always decipherable. The definitive totals, however, are clear.

333. *Revels N° 8.* This book consists of five folio leaves unnumbered, besides a title-page ; f° 4*v*. and f° 5*v*. are blank.

336. 7. *Iournig. Sic* for *Iourneying.*

9. *A Comodie called delighte.* Mr Fleay identifies this comedy with the *Play of Plays* (*Biog. Chronicle*, I. 249 & II. 289). His argument is not quite convincing.

17. *Storie of Pompey.* A « Life of Pompeie » is mentioned in the *Third Blast of Retrait from Plaies and Theaters.* 1580 (p. 145, ed. Hazlitt), among the « histories that are knowen », and which are given « a newe face », and turned out « like counterfeites to showe themselves on the stage » ; and Gosson in his *Plays Confuted* alludes to a play of *Pompey* (p. 188, ed. Hazlitt).

337. 3. In the right margin, the Auditor has written : « this wold be entered emongest The officers ».

6. In the left margin, the Auditor has written : « the begyninge and endinge wold be expressed »; and in the right margin : « no suche allounce in the presidente ».

7. *xxj^{s}*. The Auditor has added « viij^{d} », and written in the left margin : « xxj^{s} viij^{d} ».

9. *xxviij^{s}*. The Auditor first crossed out this sum, and substituted « xx^{s} » ; he afterwards crossed out « xx^{s} » and wrote over « xxviij^{s} » the word « stet ».

20. In the left margin, the Auditor has written : « doubptfull that the attendance should be daly Ther hath not any suche allounce beyn gevyn vnto the porter and the master his men », and below these lines : « in anno precedente nisi x^{li} ».

21. In the right margin, the Auditor has written : « Summa — xliiij^{li} », and in the left, under the word « wierdrawers » : « nota ».

24. In the left margin, over the word « Carpenters », the MS. has : « nota ».

29. The total has been scored through by the Auditor, who has written : « lxv^{li} xvij^{s} iiij^{d} ».

338. 3. In the left margin, under the word « Paynters », the Auditor has written : « The parties names wold be expressed ».

15. In the right margin, the MS. has : « ut supra ».

23. In the right margin, the Auditor has written : « ut supra ».

26-8. In the right margin, these three lines are united by a bracket with the sum iiij^{li} ix^{s} scored through, and « xlj^{s} Smyth » substituted in a different handwriting.

29. Under the name Smyth, the word « paynter » has been added in the same handwriting as « Smyth ».

339. 10. After the word « lightes », the Auditor has written : « nota ».

11. Under the word « lightes », the Auditor has written : « nota pro price ».

14. In the left margin, the Auditor has written : « nota pro price ».

28. In the left margin, the Auditor has written the following notes :

« in anno precedente [nisi xlix^{s}, crossed out] lxvj^{s} viij^{d} ».

« anno precedente per spacium xij Septimanarum allocatur nisi c^{s} ».

« non allocatur in anno precedente ».

each note corresponding respectively to one of the three items included in the « ordinary allowaunce ».

35. The Auditor has written in the left margin : « memorandum the parteis names wold be particularly mencioned ».

340. 3. *For the Receaving of the ffrench Comissioners &c.* See Stowe, *Chron.*, pp. 688-9, ed. 1615 ; Holinshed, *Chron.*, IV. 434 ; Goldwel (H.), *A Briefe Declaration of the Shows, Devices &c...1581.*

30. In the left margin, the Auditor has written : « Tymber lentt ».

32. In the left margin, the Auditor has written : « Copper lace », and over these words : « nota pro billa de parcellis sub manu dicti Iohannis ». Under the total, and in the right margin, he has added : « prout per billam datam xxviij die nouembris anno xxiiij^{to} [two words illegible] xv^{li} xvij^{s} iij^{d} ».

34. In the left margin, the Auditor has written : « Cullors ».

36. In the left margin, the Auditor has written : « Patrons ».

38. In the left margin, the Auditor has written : « Billett & other necessaries ».

341. 4. In the left margin, the Auditor has written : « Wages of the Master & his men ».

6. In the lett margin, the Auditor has written : « Bote hyre ».

10. Opposite the bracket, the Auditor has added : « necessaries ».

342. 24. The total was at first « ccxxxij^{li} xiij^{s} iiij^{d} » ; it was afterwards altered to « ccxxx^{li} xv^{s} viij^{d} », and finally to « ccxxxj^{li} iiij^{s} ».

33. At the end of the page, the Auditor has made up the following summing up :

vadia	Officiariorum	xliiij^{li} iiij^{s}	cj^{li} xiij^{s} iiij^{d}
	artificiariorum	lvij^{li} ix^{s} iiij^{d}	

TABLE II. At the back of this roll there is an endorsement, but it is now nearly illegible. All I have been able to decipher is this :

Office of Revelles
The Declaracon of the....
of Edmund
Tilney M^{r} for one hole
yere ended the Last of
October Anno xxiiij^{to}
Mr Dodington

Me............. not declarid
nor subscribed by.....

3-8. Supply the missing words as follows :

l. 3, A breife......
l. 4, and provided for....
l. 5, settinge furthe of....
l. 6, stuffe belonginge.....
l. 7, beginninge........
l. 8, 1582......

11. *ij°*. i. e. ij with the « o » of « two » overwritten.

29. *Sik. Sic* for *silk.*

64. *A Mount &c.* This probably was the same mount which had been prepared in April 1581 (the description is to be found at pp. 345 and 346 of this volume), and which was not used (See p. 340 l.30).

69. *House rent for iij^{e} yeares di.* This contradicts Mr E. K. Chambers's suppositlon (*Tudor Revels,* 70) that Tyllney « moved to St John's in the course of 1579, as the allowance was not repeated ».

79. *Priuye seale &c.* Cf. Collection of Payments (p. 421).

81. This line explains why, in that year, we find only money impressed and no full settlement. Cf. Collection of Payments (p. 421).

346. *A brief note &c.* This document was printed by Collier (I. 235-6), who describes it as « sub-

scribed by Ed. Tyllney as Master, by Edward Buggin as Yeoman [*sic*], and by Edward Kirkham, as Clerk [*sic*] of the Revels ».

5. *Iohn Rose*. Collier reads : « Iohn Boles ».

347. *Revels N° 9*. This document consists of 8 folio leaves unnumbered; f° 1 *r*. & *v*., f° 8 *r*. & *v*. are blank.

At the top of f° 1*r*., and in the left corner, the Auditor has written : « Recepi xxx^mo Octobris ».

349. 1. *Betwene the daie &c*. i. e. « Betwene the first daie of November 1582 Anno xxiv^mo » Cf. l. 11.

11. *From the first &c*. The line was added by the Auditor to fill up the gap of ll. 1 & 2.

12. *A Game of the Cardes*. Mr Fleay thinks that this was probably the show called *Terminus et non Terminus* in which Nash had had a hand (*Biog. Chron*. II. 124). *A Play of Cards* is mentioned by Harrington in his *Brief Apologie of Poetrie* : « Then for comedies, to speake of a London comedie, how much good matter, yea and matter of state, is there in that Comedie cald the play of the Cards ? in which it is showed, how foure Parasiticall knaues robbe the foure principall vocations of the Realme, *videl*. the vocation of Souldiers, Schollers, Marchants, and Husbandmen. Of which Comedie I cannot forget the saying of a notable wise counsellor that is now dead (Sir Fraunces Walsinghame), who when some (to sing *Placebo*) aduised that it should be forbidden, because it was somewhat too plaine, and indeed as the old saying is (sooth boord is no boord), yet he would haue it allowed, adding it was fit that they which doe that they should not, should heare that they would not » (Quoted by Cunningham).

Mr Fleay thinks also that some offence given by the Children of the Chapel in the *Game of Cardes* was the cause of their inhibition (*Biog. Chron*. II. 370).

18. *A Comodie of Bewtie and Huswyfery*. Mr Fleay seems to identify it with *Calisto and Melibœa* (See *Biog. Chron*. II, Index & p. 290).

19. *Lord of Hundesdons servauntes*. i. e. Henry Carey, Lord Hunsdon's. He became Lord Chamberlain of the household in June 1583, from which date down to July 22, 1596, his company was known as the Lord Chamberlain's servants.

23. *A Historie of Loue and ffortune*. « This is the *Rare Triumphs of Love and Fortune*, published by Ed. White in 1589 » (Fleay. *Biog. Chron*. II. 26).

30. *Matachins*. This word has been added in a different handwriting. A matachin was a sort of dance in which the performers were armed. The following passage from Sidney's *Arcadia* gives an idea of what this dance was like : « Which presently was revenged, not onely by the black, but the ill apparelled knight, who disdained another should enter into his quarrel, so as, who ever saw a matachin dance to imitate fighting, this was a fight that did imitate the matachin : for they being but three that fought, every one had two adversaries striking him who strook the third, & revenging perhaps that of him which he had received of the other » (*Arcadia*, Lib. I. p. 62, ed. 1633). See also Douce, *Illustrations of Shakespeare*, II. 435.

34. *Cipres*. There is much indecision touching the exact meaning of this word (See S. W. Beck, *Draper's Dictionary*, 94). Here the sense of « lawn » is evident.

350. 1. *Historie of fferrar.* «Probably the same piece as the History of Error, mentioned under date of 1576-7. Boswell (*Shakespeare,* III. p. 406) not very happily conjectured that this was a play written by the celebrated George Ferrers. It is, no doubt, a mere mistake in the title by the clerk who made out the account, and who wrote by his ear, and not by his copy » (Collier. I. 240). Collier is right in refuting Boswell's supposition ; but he is somewhat bold in affirming that his own conjecture is not doubtful. The man who wrote the books, though he sometimes does make mistakes, was certainly not an unintelligent man (his spelling is consistent and not extravagant) ; and, from several errors already noticed (see note to **266.** 15 and **286.** 23), it is, on the contrary, most probable that he wrote by his copy and not by his ear. It is more simple and more natural to suppose that « Ferrar » may have been one of the principal *dramatis personæ.* Mr Fleay says : « Query Ferrara or written by Ferrars ? » (*Biog. Chron.* II. 290).

6. *Telomo.* « The *Ptolemy* mentioned in Gosson's *School of Abuse* as performed at the Bull » (Fleay. *Biog. Chron.* II. 289). It may be.

11. *Ariodante and Geneuora.* From Ariosto, *Orlando Furioso,* v. This episode had already been translated by Peter Beverley in 1566. The possible indebtedness of Shakespeare to this courtly play was pointed out long ago.

353. 7. In the right margin, under the total, the Auditor has written : « nimis per xij^{d} ».

356. 14. *Mr Cardell.* Evidently the same person with the Mr Cardewell, the schoolmaster, mentioned in the Accounts of Th. Screvin : « Item, geuen to Mr Cardewell the schoolemaster for dauncinge, for Newyeare's giftes, iij^{li} ; to his boy, x^{s}. (« For the Lady Elizabeth Manners, 1599 ». MSS. of the Duke of Rutland, vol. IV. p. 414. Hist. MSS. Commission. 1905).

30. Under the number « xl^{s} », the Auditor has written : « for the Master ».

358. 5. *A longe paire.* Cunningham has read : « large ».

16. Under the total, the MS. has : « nimis per xij^{d} ».

359. 14. *A Companie of players for her Maiestie.* i. e. the company known as the Queen's men, or the Queen's Majesty's players. Stowe says that this company was formed in 1583. Cf. also Walsingham's letter to the Lord Mayor (dated December 1, 1583) explaining the intentions of the Lords of the Council in granting a licence to the Queen's players, and a letter from the Lords of the Council to the Lord Mayor respecting the grant of a licence to the Queen's players (November 26, 1583) in the City Archives (See *Athenæum,* 23 Jan. 1869). They performed at Court for the first time on December 26, 1593. (Thanks are due for this discovery to Mr E. K. Chambers. See *Modern Lang. Review,* Oct. 1906, p. 7).

Speaking of this company, Collier makes two errors : 1° he severely takes Chalmers to task in the following terms : « Chalmers (*Apology,* p. 389) says that the Queen's company was formed in 1581, but this is decidedly a mistake » (I. 247). Now, Chalmers had said nothing of the kind ; he, on the contrary, had prudently refused to accept that date as not being certain enough. Here are his own words : « In 1585, the Queen had certainly a company of players, which is said, without sufficient authority, to have been formed, by the advice of Walsingham, in 1581 ». 2° to remove all doubt on the subject, he quotes the commission dated 24 December 1581 (printed at p. 51-2 of this volume), which has nothing to do with the Queen's company.

TABLE III. This is the « old account » alluded to by Cunningham in his Introduction to the *Extr. from the Acc. of the Revels at Court*, p. xlviii.

87. *Previe Seale*. Cf. Collection of Payments, p. 421.

90. *There hathe also beyn imprested &c.* Cf. Collection of Payments, p. 421.

95. *There hathe not ben any kinde of silkes &c... deliuered*. In the Declared Account for the year 1 Nov. 1584 -- 31 Oct. 1585, I find the following entry which contradicts this statement : « There hath bene deliuered... out of her maiesties greate Wardrobe anno xxv[to] Regine predicte 1583 xviij yeardes of Cloth of golde and siluer braunched, as by the Certificatt of Anthonye Walker Clarke of the saide Wardrobe may appeare » (Rec. Office. Declared Accounts. Audit Office. Bdle 2045. R. 9).

361. *Revels N° 10*. This book consists of 4 folio leaves. Another folio, which was probably the title-page has been cut off, about an inch of it still remaining. F° 4*v*. is blank. The bottoms of the leaves have much suffered from damp and wear ; but with the exception of the right corner of f° 3*v*., which has been completely worn off, no part of the writing has disappeared.

A duplicate of this book, numbered by the Record Office N° 11, is in the same Bundle. It contains no essential difference, having only a few totals which were left blank in the other. N° 10, on the other hand, has been annotated by the Auditor, and receipted by some of the creditors ; it contains also an interesting note in Tyllney's handwriting. This is the reason why I have printed it instead of N° 11, the one followed, I believe, by Cunningham.

363. *Title-page*. The title has been supplied from N° 11.

365. 12. *Choryn*. The « n » is surmounted by a stroke of the pen, which I believe to be a sign of abbreviation ; but as it is difficult to decide the exact value of this sign I have been obliged not to extend it.

14. *Ymployed....... yardes*. Book N° 11 has : « xxxviij yardes ».

19. *Of of*. *Sic* for *of*.

Oxenford his boyes. We owe to Mr E. K. Chambers the discovery of the interesting fact that John Lyly, the dramatist, was at the head of the Earl of Oxford's servants, *i. e.* probably the Oxford's boys here mentioned, for the Earl had also a company of men. Mr E. K. Chambers is a little puzzled by the fact that Lyly's *Campaspe* and *Sapho and Phao*, both printed in 1584, were played before the Queen on New Year's Day and Shrove Tuesday respectively, *i. e.* on the very days on which Lyly, according to the Declared Accounts of the Treasurer of the Chamber, brought Oxford's company to Court in 1584. And as Lyly's plays were performed by the Children of the Chapel and Paul's he seems inclined to entertain the rather startling conjecture that Oxford's boys can « possibly have been, not from Oxford's own Chapel but selected from the royal Chapel and Paul's » (*Mod. Lang. Rev.*, Oct. 1906, p. 8). Mr E. K. Chambers has complicated things which are simple enough. He considers as « natural » that the « New Year's Day » and « Shrove Tuesday » of the title-pages of Lyly's two plays « refer to the year of publication », and he takes for granted that every time Oxford's boys performed at Court they acted Lyly's productions. Now everybody knows that the date of publication of a play is by no means that of its performance (Lyly himself supplies us with abundant proofs of this fact), and that dramatic productions rarely appeared in print before they had exhausted their popularity on the stage (*Campaspe* and *Sapho and Phao*, we must remember, were played also at the Blackfriars). Besides, the Earl of Oxford was himself a famous dramatist, was indeed considered as the best of his time for comedy, and therefore it is most natural to suppose that the Oxford's boys, both in January, Shrovetide 1584, and on St John's day following, acted plays written by their own patron. I firmly believe that *Agamemnon and Ulysses*, (though I agree it might have been a « probable subject for Lyly », as indeed it might have been for any other dramatist of that time), is one of Oxford's lost comedies.

22. *Symons & his fellowes*. An entry in the Declared Accounts of the Treasurer of the Chamber mentions a payment to « Iohn Symonds and Mr Standleyes Boyes.... for Tumblinge and shewinge other feates of Activitie » (Jan. 9, 1586), upon which entry Mr E. K. Chambers remarks : « I suppose these to be the Lord Strange's tumblers of January 15, 1580 *(Modern Lang. Review*, Oct. 1906, p. 8). I agree with him.

24. *Spoyled...... yardes*. Book N° 11 has : « xxiiij^{or} yardes ».

26. *Felix & philiomena*. From an episode in Montemayor's *Diana*. The Spanish pastoral romance had been translated by Bartholomew Yong in 1582 or 1583 (though the translation was not published till 1598). Shakespeare may have used this old play for his *Two Gentlemen of Verona*. Cf. Halliwell, *Illustrations of the Life of Shakespeare*, Pt. I. p. 46, ed. 1874.

30-5. *Fiue playes in one.... three playes in one*. The practice of presenting several plays « in one » seems to have been frequent. Later examples are Yarington's *Two Lamentable Tragedies*, and Beaumont & Fletcher's *Four plays in One*, printed 1647. See also Henslowe's *Diary*. Fleay supposes that the plays performed at Court in 1584-5 are Tarlton's *Seven Deadly Sins* (*Hist. of the Stage*, p. 67, and *Biog. Chron.*, II. 259).

366. 17. Between line 17 and line 18, Book N° 11 has : « xlv^{li} iij^{s} viij^{d} ».

24. Between line 24 and line 25, Book N° 11 has : « xiiij^{li} iiij^{s} ».

38. Book N° 11 has : « cj^{s} iiij^{d} ».

367. 4. Between line 4 and line 5, Book N° 11 has : « cv^{s} iiij^{d} ».

7. Between line 7 and line 8, Book N° 11 has « xl^{s} ».

9. Between line 9 and line 10, Book N° 11 has : « xvj^{s} ».

13. Book N° 11 has : « xix^{li} x^{s} », and under this total, in the middle of the line : « pagina — iiij^{xx} xix^{li} vij^{s} x^{d} ».

369. 45. *Willyam*. This name was added afterwards.

370. 41. *Goate*. Cunningham has read « greate ».

372. 38. *j c^{li} towardes the chardgis off y^{r} yere*. It is most probable that these hundred pounds were sufficient to cover all the expenses for the year 1585-6, for it appears from the Imprest Certificate Books (Pells, II. 139, III. 7, 22 & 73) that no other sum was paid out of the Receipt of the Exchequer from 30 Sept. 1585 to 30 Sept. 1589 (cf. my Collection of Payments, p. 421). As the next Warrant covers the period 31 Oct. 1586 — 31 Oct. 1589, we are pretty sure that there is no gap in the payments; and if so, the Memorandum written by Tyllney may have been a summing up of all the expenses for that year.

374. 7. *The some of vj^c &c.* Cf. Collection of Payments, p. 421, and Docquet Books (Signet Office), April 1590.

375. *Revels N° 12.* This book consists of six leaves of about 8 × 11 1/2 inches with a cover which has been used as title-page; f° 4, f° 5 and f° 6 are blank.

378. 14. In the left margin, the Auditor has written this very sensible note: « the names of the plays wold be expressed ».

14-6. The Declared Accounts of the Treasurer of the Chamber record the following payments, which supply us with the dates of performances:

1587	Dec. 26	Queen's
	Dec. 28	John Simons and his company
1587-8	Jan. 1	Paul's
	Jan. 6	Queen's
	Feb. 2	Paul's
	Feb. 18 (Shrove Sunday)	Queen's

(*Modern Lang. Review*, Oct. 1906, p. 9)

There was, of course, no payment to the Gentlemen of Gray's Inn; their play was the *Misfortunes of Arthur,* shown on Feb. 28.

379. 15. *Attendanttes. Sic* for *attendance.*

380. 1. *Wierdrawer.* Under this word, the Auditor has written: «the parcelles wold be mencioned particulerly» and « xvij^li was awarded xx December 1586 by the Master of the Revelles ».

381. 9-12. In the left margin, the Auditor has written: « the names of the parties and the parcelles wold appere more particulerly ».

13. *l^s.* The scribe wrote iiij^li which was afterwards altered by the Auditor to « l^s ». The Auditor added also the following note, in the left margin: «William Cooke the Masters man was with me the xiiij of December 1586 & told me that the iiij^li was to be maid but l^s». Under this note the name « William Cooke » is written.

19. In the left margin, the Auditor has written: « ut supra ».

383. 9. Under the signatures, the Auditor has written: « Memorandum the parcelles wer wonnt to be more particulerly expressed ».

388. 26-7. The following are the dates of performances according to the Declared Accounts of the Treasurer of the Chamber *(Mod. Lang. Review*, Oct. 1906, p. 9) supplemented by the *Acts of the Privy Council* (N. S. vol. xvii):

1588	Dec. 26	Queen's
	Dec. 27	Paul's
	Dec. 29	Admiral's
1588-9	Jan. 1	Paul's
	Jan. 12	Paul's
	Shrove Sunday	Queen's
	Shrove Tuesday	Admiral's

29. *Feates of Actyvity.* They were shown by the Lord Admiral's men *(Mod. Lang. Review*, Oct. 1906, p. 9).

30. *Matichives. (Sic).*

389. 33. *For 121.* i. e. for 121 days ; this last word may have been cut off by the binder.

392. Collier has printed the description of this masque (from the beginning to line 27) in his *History of Dram. Literature*, I. 263-4.

396. 7. *The some of three hundred &c.* Cf. Collection of Payments, p. 421 ; State Papers, Docquets, 30 May 1594 ; and Docquet Books, Signet Office, May 1594.

397. 8. *The some of twoo hundred &c.* Cf. Collection of Payments, p. 421.

14. *Reformacion and composicion.* I have tried, but in vain, to find the papers relating to this composition ; they would certainly have contained most interesting facts on the state of the Revels at that period. Cf. note to **418.** 16.

17. *The some of three score &c.* Cf. Collection of Payments, p. 421.

21. *January in the fortith yeare.* Another Warrant for the same sum had been made out on January 25, 1596-7 (State Papers, Docquets, 1597, and Signet Office, Docquets, Jan. 1596). The document in the Signet Office has several interesting notes. In the left margin, we read : « Staid by the L. Threasurer », and under the name Tyllney : « Vacat ». In the right margin : « Remanet. neuer passed the seales ». Mr E. K. Chambers says touching this delay : « Edward Buggin, in his Memorandum of 1573, had considered a possible reform of the administration of the Revels Office on lines very similar to those now adopted, and had decided that it was impracticable. Doubtless the same view was held by the officers of 1597, and after the manner of permanent officials they took steps to ensure that it should be impracticable » *(Tudor Revels*, p. 64). There is probably much truth in this. Cf. the allusion to the officers' opposition to Burghley's orders, p. 417 l.17 of this volume.

399. 1. *1598 (?).* I cannot explain this payment, since there is no gap between the payment at p. 398 and that at p. 400. It is noticeable that the year for which the payment was made is not indicated.

400. 10. *1599. Sic* for *1597.*

407. *A Petition of Richard Leys.* This document was written before 30 December 1570, at which date Leys was dead (see p. 58 l.17), and later than 30 September 1559, when he signed the 1559 Book (see p. 108). In 1561 (see p. 113), Leys does not sign the Brief Certificate made out by Benger, Blagrave and Holt. In April 1567, we find his signature again (see p. 109). I suppose therefore that the period of five years during which he refused to sign the books must be placed between 30 September 1559 and April 1567, and that the document was written between 30 September 1564 and April 1567. It may be that the summing up printed at p. 109, was drawn up in answer to Leys's petition.

408. 1. *Bowll.* See note to **130.** 27.

2. *Between 1 and 10 December 1571.* This petition was evidently written after 1 December (since Holte received his wages as Yeoman till 30 November, see p. 130 l. 26), and before 10 December, at which date Arnold was appointed. Collier (I. 230 *n.*) has printed this petition, but oddly enough he thinks that Bowll was making a suit for the Mastership.

6. *Ye lorde treasorer.* i. e. William Paulet, Marquis of Winchester.

17. *To make payment to the workmen.* Cf. pp. 131 & 139.

409. 1. *Thomas Gylles.* As appears from the end of the document, he was a lender of apparel for public and private entertainments. On several occasions, he provided the office with vizards (see pp. 141 l.14; 158 l.19; 184 l.23; 268 l.36). In the Account Books, he is sometimes styled « haberdasher ». Collier (I. 191-2) has given long extracts from this document.

2. *C. December 1572.* This date is given by p. 410 l. 2 and l. 27.

5. *The Yeman.* i. e. John Arnold, who had been appointed 11 December 1571. But he was not the first who had committed such an abuse. In the Loseley MSS. there are many letters from persons asking Sir Thomas Cawerden for the loan of masquing garments.

21. *Takynge the garmentes asonder.* i. e. he asks that the garments may be taken from the Yeoman and kept under lock till they be used again, and not that the garments may be « taken to pieces », as Collier interprets the phrase (I. 191, *n.* 2). Such a proposition would have made the Officers stare with astonishment !

410. 23. *Bodgrowe.* Collier suggests « Budgerow ».

411. *A note of things &c.* This document was written by the Yeoman, this officer alone being entrusted with the custody of the stuff (cf. l. 9, same page). As to the date, the allusion to the presses and the obligation « to laye the garmentes vppon the grounde », enables us to bring the upward limit to October 1573, at which date we hear for the first time of an urgent need of presses (see p. 186). On the other hand, we have seen that the presses were probably mended in 1581-2 (note to **186.** 1), and this supplies us with a downward limit. The allusion to the « two whole yeares charges behinde vnpayde », allows us to narrow the extreme limits. I refer to my Collection of Payments (p. 420), where one can see that between 1573 and 1581-2, there is but one period during which the accounts remained unsettled for two « whole years », and that is from March 1, 1573-4, to March 11, 1575-6. I believe, therefore, the document belongs to some date between 11 March 1575-6 and 5 August 1576, when the officers obtained the Privy Seal (see Collection of Payments, p. 420). If so, the writer was Fysshe, appointed Yeoman on Jan. 29, 1573-4.

Mr E. K. Chambers supposes (*Tudor Revels*, 30 & 50) that this note belongs to the plan of reform of 1573. If the date I assign to the document is the right one, this hypothesis is impossible. And in fact, it is difficult to conceive that the Yeoman's urgent appeal for reparations and payment of debts was calculated to meet the Lord Treasurer's enquiries touching a reorganization of the office and a reduction of its expenses.

412. 1. *A Petition of the Creditors of the Revels.* The date of this document is given by Bryan Dodmer's Supplication, printed at p. 413, where he says (ll. 6-7) that he made suit to the Queen in the xvijth year of her Reign, that is to say, between 17 November 1574 and 16 November 1575. On the other hand, we know that Dodmer and the Creditors obtained satisfaction and were paid their debts by a Warrant dated 25 December 1574 (see Collection of Payments, p. 420). This document can therefore be safely dated November or December 1574.

413. 7. *Privay seale &c.* Cf. p. 247 ll. 11-8 ; p. 412 ; note to **412.** 1, and Collection of Payments, p. 420.

9. *As deputy or servant vnto..... Thomas Blagrave.* This explains why we so often find Dodmer's name in the Accounts. See Index of Proper Names.

11. *Saving ccc*[li] *&c.* Cf. page 152 l.7 & Collection of Payments, p. 420, E. T. 1572.

14. *The Bookes of that office &c.* See the Book printed at p. 149 and sqq.

416. *A Petition of William Bowll.* Collier (I. 290) mentions this petition, and ascribes it to the year 1597, being misled by a note written in pencil by some unknown person and assigning the document to July 1597. (It should be said that none of the present librarians of the British Museum is responsible for this error, which is at least a century old). Collier wrongly gives the sum due to Bowll as 136 pounds (instead of 236), and does not see that this William Bowll is the same person with the Bowll who petitioned for the post of Yeoman, and of whom he says (230 *n.* 1) : « We hear of him nowhere else ».

Mr E. K. Chambers has reprinted the petition in his *Tudor Revels* (pp. 28-29). He thinks that the « two years and three quarters of Bowll's undated letter may perhaps be taken as being the same period [*i. e.* the period of one year nine months covered by Books of the Revels N° 2 and N° 3], with the addition of the year 1571-2, for which we know that he had himself made advances to the other creditors ». But the latter Account-Book, alluded to by Mr E. K. Chambers, as may be seen at p. 127, contains the expenses for one year and three months ; and this period added to the abovesaid one year and nine months makes up three years, and not two and three quarters. Besides, I have added together all the sums due to Bowll during that period, and they amount to 316 *l.* 88 *s.* 10 *d.* I have tried also all the combinations that could be made with the books we possess, but I have failed to find any total corresponding more or less to 236 pounds. Perhaps Bowll meant the period :

Feb. 1576-7 to Feb. 1577-8............ 1 year } 2 years 8 1/2 months
Feb. 1577-8 to 1 November 1579.... 1 year 8 1/2 months }

But the accounts for 1576/7-1577/8 are missing.

417. *A Petition of the Creditors &c.* This document is written in several hands : 1° the petition, probably by one of the Creditors (ll. 4-20) ; 2° the autograph note by Tyllney (ll. 21-7) ; 3° the endorsement, probably by Burghley's secretary (p. 418 ll. 1-10) ; 4° the two notes by Burghley himself (ll. 11-3 and 30-1) ; 5° the report by the Auditors of the Imprest (ll. 14-29).

9. *Five yeares behinde.* Since May 1594, when the Accounts were settled for the sums due, till 1 November 1592, no money had been issued out of the exchequer, with the exception of one hundred pounds in prest, which Tyllney surely did not distribute among the Creditors. See Collection of Payments, p. 421.

418. 16. *It is agreed &c.* All this arrangement will be somewhat mysterious so long as the terms of the composition remain unknown. Deep changes seem to have been introduced into the Office. It is somewhat strange not to find any allowance to the Clerk. Yet the post had not been suppressed, since, at Blagrave's death, it was granted to Hunning. Perhaps Blagrave being old, had practically ceased to attend in the Office, and this may also explain why the old post of Groom of the Revels was reestablished. At the time of Queen Elizabeth's death, the Groom was Thomas Cornewalles, as appears from the following extract from the Account of the Expenses of the Funeral of Queen Elizabeth (Great Wardrobe) : « To the M[r] of the Revells himselfe, ix yardes and his servantes vj ya : — xv yardes. Edmond Pakenham Clarke Comptroller himselfe ix yards and his servauntes iiij ya: — xiij yardes. To Thomas Cornewalles Groome porter at the same rates — xiij yardes. To Edward Kirkeham yeoman of the Revells Edmonde Monday yeoman of the Tents and Toyles Bowles groome every of them iiij ya: a peece — xij yardes » (Record Office. Declared Accounts. Audit Office. Bdle 2344. Nº 30 *a*). From the same passage it is clear that the Groom was also the Porter of the Office; maybe the two posts had been united since 1597.

30. *Better satisficed*. Burghley was no doubt « better satisficed », since he signed the order for the Warrant made out on 11 January 1597-8. See p. 397.

INDEXES.

GLOSSARIAL INDEX

This Index is not exhaustive : only obsolete words or peculiar spellings have been included. Besides, in the case of certain words which occur hundreds of times references are given only to the first pages where such words are to be found.

177. 24 means page 177, line 24 ; **19**. 13 ; 20 means page 19, lines 13 and 20.

LATTYN, latten, **176**. 37; 38
LETTRES PATENTES, letters-patent, **5**. 19; **70**. 25; 27; 30
LEZ, the (plural), **68**. 9
LIDGEARDE, ledger, **T** I. 57
LIGEARDE, V. LIDGEARDE, **14**. 29; 35
LONGING, belonging, **17**. 35
LOOMEWOORKE, **41**. 19; 22; **137**. 13
LUKES, a kind of velvet made at Liège, **24**. 11
LYER, tape, **167**. 19 ; **205**. 5
LYHABLE, **17**. 4
LYTMOSE, litmus, **94**. 11; **100**. 13
MALE, mail, i. e. spot, mole, **217**. 32
MALED, marked with males, or spots, **392**. 14
MARQUESOTTED, **218**. 28 & *n*
MARQUEX, **47**. 13; **49**. 33
MARSHALLINGE, *sb*. **50**. 4; 15; 31
MARSHELLED, **50**. 33
MASTE, **87**. 13; 14; 15; 16
MASTICOTE, massicot, **201**. 8; **210**. 7
MIGHELMAS, **T** I. 50
MILLIONER, milliner, **161**. 15
MITTONS, mittens, **31**. 27
MOWLDEMAN, maker of moulds, **265**. 20
MURRE, MURREY, MURRYE, a dark reddish brown colour, **35**. 5; **39**. 3; 7; 11; 24; **146**. 19
NAYELLS, nails, **157**. 16
NOSSES, **121**. 1
OCCUPIED, used, **14**. 4
OKER DE ROOCE, OKER DE ROWSE, **178**. 25; **201**. 23
OLLYFF, olive, **158**. 7
ORDINARY, *sb*. **7**. 17
ORTEYERDE, orchard, **47**. 36
OVING. (? the same as woovinge silke), **138**. 20
PANCES, pansies, **156**. 39
PANE, a piece of cloth inserted in another and for ornament, **22**. 27 ; 31 ; **25**. 36 ; **26**. 3 ; 21 ; 28
PANE, PAYNE, *v*. **19**. 15 ; **26**. 19
PANED, **20**. 23 ; **21**. 16 ; **25**. 11 ; **39**. 2; **40**. 19 ; **42**. 11 ; **45**. 7 ; 20
PANINGE, **24**. 15 ; 16 ; **25**. 4 ; 39 ; **26**. 6
PARCEMANE LACE, a kind of lace, braid, or cord the core of which was parchment (Mrs Palliser). According to Cotgrave, the word is derived from the Fr. passement, **38**. 10
PARCHEMENT LACE, V. PARCEMANE LACE, **156**. 27
PARIS SYLKE, filoselle, **38**. 15 ; 26 ; **39**. 5 ; 25
PARTELETTES, usually defined : « a kind of woman's ruff » ; but such a description is evidently inexact, for we often find mentions of partlets with sleeves, **43**. 17 ; **44**. 7 ; **88**. 3
PARTIE FLAMED, **40**. 2
PARTIE PANED, **20**. 23 ; **21**. 16 ; **42**. 11
PARTLETE, V. PARTELETTES, **392**. 16
PECINGE THREEDE, **83**. 13 ; **95**. 11 ; **100**. 19
PENNERS, pen-cases, **237**. 26
PERFITED, perfected, **10**. 37
PERFITINGE, **14**. 20
PERFITT, *v*. **6**. 16 ; **9**. 14
PERON, **T** II. 34
PERTY GOWLDE, **94**. 4
PERVITING, perforating, **358**. 17
PERWICKES, periwigs, **263**. 7
PINDUST, **265**. 29
PINKED, **22**. 32
PIPES (for a head dress), **39**. 19
PLACE, office, **5**. 25
PLACKERDE, seems to have been synonymous with stomacher (see Nicolas, *Pr. Purse Exp. of Eliz. of York*, 257), **19**. 22 ; **23**. 9
PLATTE, plot, plan, **8**. 21 ; **11**. 25 ; **T** I. 73 ; **17**. 1
PLATTE FORME, plan, scheme, **9**. 25
PLAUNCHEBOURDE, PLENCH BOORDE, **122**. 19 ; 21 ; 23 ; **262**. 14
PLITES, plaits, **27**. 28
POLL, pole, **358**. 15
POSYE, motto, **39**. 17
POYNTES, tags affixed to the end of a ribbon & used for tying dresses, **83**. 15
POYNTING RIBBON, **156**. 24
POYNTYNG, **162**. 19
POZ , poising, weighing, **94**. 23
PRESIDENT, precedent, **6**. 6 ; **T** I. 74 ; **50**. 14
PREST, advance, loan, **11**. 21 ; **12**. 19 ; **T** I. 20; 51 ; 59 ; **37**. 26
PROCEEDE, *v*. **50**. 33
PROCEEDINGE, procession, **50**. 17 ; 31
PROCURE, obtain, **5**. 29
PROOFE, **176**. 2
PROPERTIEMAKER, **51**. 13 ; **81**. 10; **110**. 8 ; **116**. 15 ; **117**. 19
PROPERTIES, **14**, 7 ; **T** I. 95 ; **105**. 3 ; **129**. 14 ; 22 ; **132**. 9 ; **134**. 6 ; **135**. 2
PROPRIETIES, properties, **T** I. 78 ; 92
PULLED OUT, **22**. 7 ; 26 ; **38**. 3 ; **41**. 5 ; **44**. 14 ; **45**. 8 ; 19
PULLINGE OUT, **23**. 27 ; **24**. 2 ; **28**. 23 ; **31**. 25 ; **84**. 20 ; 23
PUNCHIONS, punchins, **357**. 19
PURLED LACE, a species of lace of gold or silver, used for the edging of ruffs &c. (*Draper's Dict.*), **161**. 13 ; CROWNE PURLE, **139**. 15
PYNCKINGE, **86**. 17
QUARTERBOURDE, **122**. 25
QUELLS, quills, **83**. 21 ; **95**. 16
QUINTEN, a wooden figure at which to tilt, **308**. 25
RASED, RAYSED, *a)* having the pile cut close (obs.). *b)* modern sense. In the present instances it is somewhat difficult to distinguish between the two meanings, **19**. 23 ; **21**. 4 ; **31**. 15 ; **40**. 22 ; **41**. 9
RAYLE, **180**. 39
REALM, ream, **265**. 30
REPUGNE, *v*. to oppose, **10**. 25
REVELLES, REVELS, OFFICE OF THE, **5**. 5 ; 8 ; 12 ; 13 ; 15 ; 21 &c.
REWED, garnished with rows of gold, silver &c., **21**. 12 ; **22**. 32 ; **82**. 17
RIALL, royal, **216**. 13
ROCHETTES, **28**. 27
RONE, **177**. 19 ; 20
ROOME, station, office, **5**. 25
ROSET, a red colour, **274**. 4
ROVE, *v*. **17**. 46
ROWLES, rolls, **38**. 10 ; **41**. 8 ; **82**. 21

TUKES, a kind of buckram, **136**. 37
TUNBBORDE, **99**. 16
TURNEIS, **70**. 12 ; **71**. 3 ; 7 ; **72**. 10
TYENGES, tyings, **28**. 24 ; 29 ; 32 ; **29**. 7 ; **34**. 31 ; 39
TYRINGES, attirings, **23**. 29 ; 36 : **24**. 3
TYSSHEWED, V. TISSUED, **114**. 8
TYSSHIEW, V. TISSEWE, **114**. 8
TYTING, making tight, **177**. 4
UNDER GARMENTES, **38**. 4 ; **42**. 6
UNDER SKIRTED, **38**. 6
UNDER SLEVES, **19**. 29 ; 31 ; **20**. 28 ; **21**. 7 ; 15 ; **22**. 30
UNDERSTANDE, past participle of understand, **10**. 3
UPHOLSTER, upholsterer, **138**. 3 ; **174**. 3 ; **209**. 5
UPPER BODIES, **22**. 21 ; **35**. 23 ; **41**. 9 ; **44**. 13 ; **45**. 1 ; 15
UPPER GARMENTES, **22**. 3 ; **43**. 2 ; 3
VANDELAS, « or Vittry canvas » (*Draper's Dict.* 51), **137**. 31 ; **156**. 38 ; **167**. 1
VELLAT, velvet, **110**. 27 ; **112**. 16
VENETIANS, a kind of breeches imported from Italy : « And the Venetian-hosen, they reach beneath the knee to the gartering place to the Leg, where they are tyed finely with silk points, or some such like, and laied on also with rewes of lace, or gardes » (Stubbes, *Anat. of Abuses*, p. 56, ed. Furnivall), **350**. 21 ; 25 ; 27
VENIS BALLS, Venice balls, **239**. 16
VENIT, *sb.* incoming, entrance, **T** I. 74
VENIYS GOWLD, Venice gold (but veniys may be a mistake for vennys ; see below), **40**. 12
VENNYS GOWLD, Venice gold, **38**. 10 ; **43**. 5
VENYS SYLVER, **234**. 16
VERT, the colour now called green, **178**. 22 ; **201**. 11
VICE CANDELSTICKES, a kind of candlesticks, much used in the XVth century, consisting of a piece of wire rolled into a spiral form and inside which the candle was fixed (Cf. Fr. à vis), **176**. 34 ; **202**. 4 ; **237**. 5
VOYALLES, vials, **275**. 30
WARDEROOPE, WARDEROPPE, WARDROP, **T** I. 66 ; **17**. 11 ; **18**. 9 ; **23**. 2 ; 27 ; **26**. 18 ; **50**. 39 ; **71**. 14
WATCHET, WATTCHETT, generally defined : « blue, pale blue » ; but, from page 34 of this volume, it is evident that the word could be synonymous with « purple », **34**. 17 ; **353**. 5
WEEKE, wick, **158**. 17 ; **179**. 33
WELTING, garnishing with a hem, **23**. 10
WETE, *v.* to know, **70**. 32
WINGES, the projections on the shoulders of a doublet (Fairholt), **19**. 10
WITHIM, with him, **92**. 9
WITT, V. WETE, **51**. 6 ; **72**. 4
WODE, woad, **41**. 10
WOOLVERINGE, wolverene, **236**. 11
WOOVINGE, or WOOVINGE SILKE, **43**. 20 ; **44**. 11
WORKES, embroidered figures, **23**. 18 ; **30**. 3 ; 7 ; 19 ; 23 ; **31**. 4 ; 9
WRETHES, **25**. 32 ; **26**. 14 ; **45**. 7 ; **82**. 21
YMPREST, money advanced (Cf. PREST), **12**. 23

INDEX OF PROPER NAMES

366. 27 means page 366, line 27; numbers preceded by an asterisk refer to signatures.

SUBJECT INDEX

20. 18 means page 20, line 18 ; **32**. 4 ; 14 means page 32, lines 4 and 14 ; **388**. 29 *n* means note to page 388, line 29 ; **193**. 15 & *n* means page 193, line 15, and note to 193. 15

CORRIGENDA.

27.37 } *For* Richard *read* Rychard.
36.20 }

43.26 *For* boltes *read* holtes.

45.28 *For* Richard *read* Rychard.

46.6. *For* T. Blagrave *read* T Blagrave.

47.6 *n*. *For* Russel *read* Russell.

49.43. *For* conccrning *read* concerning.

77.6. *For* 2 May 1558-9 *read* 2 May 1559.

121, *running-title*. *For* 1569-8 *read* 1567-8.

141, *last line*. *For* 30 *read* 25.

167.27. *For* viij *read* viij^{d}.

178, *running-title*. *For* 1672 *read* 1572.

191.33. *For* [x] ji^{d} *read* [x]ij^{d}.

202.1. *For* wyerrawer *read* wyerdrawer.

203.19. *For* nale *read* nayle.

230.9. *For* or *read* for.

» 10. *For* fother *read* other.

236.15. *For* trymme *read* trymme.

238.12 *n*. *For* Table II. l. 97 *read* Table II. l. 86.

240.25. *For* urtyns *read* Curtyns.

244.11. *For* hte Coorte *read* the Coorte.

249, *bottom*. *Add* f° 16 v.

256.23 *n*. *For* Cenocephali *read* Cynocephali.

258.10 *n*. *For* note to **258** *read* note to **285**.

» *bottom*. *Add, in the left margin*, **18**^{s}/.

264.48. *For* 5^{li}/18/^{s} *read* 5^{li}/18^{s}/.

272.5. *For* x [iij^{s}] *read* x [iiij^{s}].

274.12. *For* ef *read* of.

289.18. *For* 19^{li} *read* 19^{li}.

310.27. *For* xxiij^{li} *read* xiij^{li}.

» 42. *For* Tillney *read* Tyllney.

312.41. *For* Tillney *read* Tyllney.

3[illegible]7.4. *For* Socke *read* Stocke.

333, *last line*. *For* Revells *read* Revels.

3[illegible].[illegible]-8. *For* 10 *read* 0.

[illegible]. *For* appeethar *read* appeareth.

[illegible].31. *For* 34.3.2. *read* 54.8.2.